# RESEARCH HANDBOOK ON INTERNATIONAL MARINE ENVIRONMENTAL LAW

## RESEARCH HANDBOOKS IN ENVIRONMENTAL LAW

This highly topical series addresses some of the most important questions and areas of research in Environmental Law. Each volume is designed by a leading expert to appraise the current state of thinking and probe the key questions for future research on a particular topic. The series encompasses some of the most pressing issues in the field, ranging from climate change, biodiversity and the marine environment through to the impacts of trade, regulation, and sustainable development.

Each *Research Handbook* comprises specially-commissioned chapters from leading academics, and sometimes practitioners, as well as those with an emerging reputation and is written with a global readership in mind. Equally useful as reference tools or high-level introductions to specific topics, issues and debates, these *Handbooks* will be used by academic researchers, post-graduate students, practising lawyers and lawyers in policy circles.

Titles in the series include:

Research Handbook on Climate Change Adaptation Law
*Edited by Jonathan Verschuuren*

Research Handbook on Climate Change Mitigation Law
*Edited by Geert Van Calster, Wim Vandenberghe and Leonie Reins*

Handbook of Chinese Environmental Law
*Edited by Qin Tianbao*

Research Handbook on International Marine Environmental Law
*Edited by Rosemary Rayfuse*

# Research Handbook on International Marine Environmental Law

*Edited by*

Rosemary Rayfuse

*Professor, UNSW Australia and Conjoint Professor, Lund University, Sweden*

RESEARCH HANDBOOKS IN ENVIRONMENTAL LAW

**EE** Edward Elgar
PUBLISHING

Cheltenham, UK • Northampton, MA, USA

Published by
Edward Elgar Publishing Limited
The Lypiatts
15 Lansdown Road
Cheltenham
Glos GL50 2JA
UK

Edward Elgar Publishing, Inc.
William Pratt House
9 Dewey Court
Northampton
Massachusetts 01060
USA

A catalogue record for this book
is available from the British Library

Library of Congress Control Number: 2015940681

This book is available electronically in the **Elgar**online
Law subject collection
DOI 10.4337/9781781004777

ISBN 978 1 78100 476 0 (cased)
ISBN 978 1 78100 477 7 (eBook)

Typeset by Columns Design XML Ltd, Reading
Printed and bound in Great Britain by TJ International Ltd, Padstow

# Contents

*v*

# Contributors

**Marie Bourrel**, Deep Sea Minerals Project – Legal Adviser, Geoscience Division, Secretariat of the Pacific Community, Suva, Fiji

**Robin Churchill**, Professor of International Law, School of Law, University of Dundee, UK

**Elisabeth Druel**, Institute for Sustainable Development and International Relations (IDDRI), Paris, France

**James Harrison**, Senior Lecturer in International Law, University of Edinburgh School of Law, UK

**Tore Henriksen**, Professor and Director, K.G. Jebsen Centre for the Law of the Sea, Faculty of Law, University of Tromsø, Norway

**Katherine Houghton**, Research Fellow, Institute for Advanced Sustainability Studies, Potsdam, Germany

**Anna-Maria Hubert**, Doctoral Candidate, MARUM and Bremen International Graduate School for Marine Sciences, University of Bremen, Germany; Project Scientist, Institute for Advanced Sustainability Studies (IASS), Potsdam, Germany; Associate Fellow, Institute for Science, Innovation and Society (InSIS), University of Oxford, Oxford, UK

**Nengye Liu**, Senior Lecturer, School of Law, University of New England, Australia

**Michael Lodge**, Deputy to the Secretary-General and Legal Counsel, International Seabed Authority, Kingston, Jamaica

**Joanna Mossop**, Senior Lecturer, Victoria University of Wellington, New Zealand

**Nilufer Oral**, Professor, Law Faculty, Istanbul Bilgi University, Turkey; Distinguished Fellow, Law of the Sea Institute, University of California, Berkeley, USA

**David Osborn**, Director, IAEA Environment Laboratories, Department of Nuclear Sciences and Applications, International Atomic Energy Agency, Principality of Monaco

**Alexander Proelss**, Professor, Faculty of Law, Trier University, Germany

**Henrik Ringbom,** Professor II, Scandinavian Institute of Maritime Law, Faculty of Law, University of Oslo; Adjunct Professor (Docent) Department of Law, Åbo Akademi University, Turku/Åbo, Finland

**Julien Rochette**, Institute for Sustainable Development and International Relations (IDDRI), Paris, France

**Karen N. Scott**, Professor, School of Law, University of Canterbury, Christchurch, New Zealand

**Tim Stephens**, Professor of International Law, Australian Research Council Future Fellow, Faculty of Law, University of Sydney, Australia

**Yoshifumi Tanaka**, Professor, Faculty of Law, University of Copenhagen, Denmark

**Dire Tladi**, Professor of International Law, University of Pretoria, South Africa; Member, United Nations International Law Commission

**David L. VanderZwaag**, Professor and Canada Research Chair in Ocean Law and Governance, Marine & Environmental Law Institute, Dalhousie University, Canada

**David Vousden**, Professor of Ocean Governance, Rhodes University, Grahamstown South Africa; United Nations Advisor on Ocean and Coastal Management

**Hai Dang Vu**, Institute for East Asian Studies, Faculty of International Law, Diplomatic Academy of Vietnam

**Robin Warner**, Professor, Australian National Centre for Ocean Resources and Security (ANCORS), University of Wollongong, Australia

**Glen Wright**, Institute for Sustainable Development and International Relations (IDDRI), Paris, France

# Foreword

At 3 am in the morning of Saturday 24 January 2015, nine hours after the meeting was scheduled to have ended and while a snowstorm raged outside the UN HQ in New York,[1] an historic document was concluded. The so-called BBNJ Working Group reached consensus on the text of its final recommendations to the UN General Assembly. The process of reaching this consensus has taken nearly a decade; the first meeting of what is properly called the 'United Nations Ad Hoc Open-ended Informal Working Group to study issues relating to the conservation and sustainable use of marine biological diversity beyond areas of national jurisdiction' was held in 2006.

The agreed text recommends that the UN General Assembly 'Decide to develop an international legally-binding instrument under the [Law of the Sea] Convention on the conservation and sustainable use of marine biological diversity of areas beyond national jurisdiction.'[2] This agreement, to start the process of negotiating what is expected to be a third Implementing Agreement to the 1982 UN Law of the Sea Convention, is indeed historic.

Elsewhere I have called the governance of marine areas beyond national jurisdiction the 'final frontier'.[3] These areas are the last great global commons areas on Earth – covering nearly half the surface of the planet. Moreover, it has also been suggested that the current characteristics of the ABNJ regime with regulatory and governance gaps,[4] weak implementation and enforcement of existing rules[5] and widespread illegal, unreported and unregulated fishing[6] are reminiscent of the nineteenth century frontier

---

[1] I am grateful to Kristina Gjerde for the context, and for staying to the end of the meeting.

[2] The text is at http://www.un.org/ga/search/view_doc.asp?symbol=A/69/780 (last accessed 3 June 2015) . The recommendations of the Working Group also envisage the establishment of a preparatory committee, to begin work in 2016 and to report to the UN General Assembly (UNGA) in 2017 with recommendations on a text. These recommendations were adopted by the UNGA on 19 June 2015 in UNGA Resolution A/69/L.65, available at http://daccess-dds-ny.un.org/doc/UNDOC/GEN/N15/138/14/PDF/N1513814.pdf?OpenElement (last accessed 3 July 2015).

[3] David Freestone, 'The Final Frontier: The Law of the Sea Convention and Areas beyond National Jurisdiction' in *Proceedings of the 2012 Law of the Sea Institute Conference on Securing the Ocean for the Next Generation,* vol. 1, (Martinus Nijhoff, 2013) 1–15.

[4] See K. Gjerde, H. Dotinga, S. Hart, E.J. Molenaar, R. Rayfuse and R. Warner, *Regulatory and Governance Gaps in the International Regime for the Conservation and Sustainable Use of Marine Biodiversity in Areas beyond National Jurisdiction* (Gland: IUCN, 2008), available at http://cmsdata.iucn.org/downloads/iucn_marine_paper_1_2.pdf (last accessed 3 June 2015).

[5] See David Freestone, 'Problems of High Seas Governance' in Davor Vidas and Peter Johan Schei, eds, *The World Ocean in Globalisation: Challenges and Responses,* (Martinus Nijhoff, 2011) 99–130. See also R. Warner, *Protecting the Oceans beyond National Jurisdiction: Strengthening the International Law Framework* (Martinus Nijhoff, 2009).

[6] Mary Ann Palma, Martin Tsamenyi and William Edeson, *Promoting Sustainable Fisheries: The International Legal and Policy Framework to Combat Illegal, Unreported and*

areas of the 'wild west' in the USA.[7] The good news is that the recommendation of the BBNJ Working Group to begin a new negotiation presents the opportunity for the international community to provide more effective approaches to many of the issues not specifically addressed by the 1982 Law of the Sea Convention itself.[8]

For generations we have regarded the sea as unpredictable, dangerous and limitless. Four hundred years ago, in *De Mare Liberum*, Hugo Grotius described the sea as 'common to all, because it is so limitless that it cannot become a possession of any one'.[9] The 'Cruel Sea' as he describes it, has traditionally been seen as a realm in which seafarers risk their lives; the primal forces of ocean tides and waves presenting a danger to seafarers as well as coastal dwellers. This traditional perspective has humankind at the mercy of the unpredictable ocean.

In the last half century however we have had to begin to change this long held view. Air travel, scientific advances, including communications technology, has made the world appear smaller and its resources more finite. Now, we discover, we are the dangerous ones; the sea has become the victim.

We still know little about the open ocean. It is said that we know more about the surface of the moon than about the deepest parts of the ocean. However, we do know beyond doubt that we have already had major negative impacts upon oceans everywhere. Anthropogenic pollution has already affected ecosystem functioning in the deep ocean.[10] Plastics and other wastes are accumulating in the great gyres of the Pacific and the Atlantic, contaminating and suffocating pelagic creatures. Our fishing technology has allowed us to increase catches and to push out into deeper and more remote waters, so that fish stocks are failing throughout the world, and deep sea species are being depleted before biologists can determine basic information about them.

High-seas fish stocks are a valuable source of protein for human consumption – but there is evidence of serious depletion in the larger pelagic species, such as tunas and billfishes, resulting in fishing for smaller species, lower down the trophic levels.[11] This gives rise to serious questions about the impact of such fishing on the whole marine

---

*Unregulated Fishing* (Martinus Nijhoff, 2010) xi, who suggest that one-third of all fish harvested are from IUU operations.

[7]    Freestone, above n 3, 15.

[8]    The recommendations of the BBNJ Working Group propose that negotiations will address the topics identified in the package agreed by the Working Group in 2011, namely the conservation and sustainable use of marine biodiversity in areas beyond national jurisdiction, in particular, together and as a whole, marine genetic resources, including questions on the sharing of benefits, measures such as area-based management tools, including marine protected areas, environmental impact assessments and capacity building and the transfer of marine technology.

[9]    Hugo Grotius, *The Freedom of the Seas* (Latin and English version, Magoffin trans.) [1608] James Scot Brown (ed.) available at http://oll.libertyfund.org/titles/552 (last accessed 3 June 2015).

[10]    Through the work of the Census of Marine Life. See, eg, R. Danovaro et al., 'Exponential Decline of Deep-Sea Ecosystem Functioning Linked to Benthic Biodiversity Loss' (2008) 18 *Current Biology* 1.

[11]    See D. Pauly et al., 'Fishing Down Marine Food Webs' (1998) 279 *Science* 860, 862–3.

ecosystem and its long-term sustainability.[12] Economists, as well as biologists, have voiced serious concerns for sustainability, in light of the huge amounts of money spent each year to support fisheries.[13]

At the same time that we discover the important role that the oceans provide as the lungs of the planet, we are also discovering that human industrial emissions are poisoning those lungs. $CO_2$ is increasing the acidity of the oceans. Research had suggested that, at 450 ppm, corals and shellfish, and perhaps even plankton, will have problems in creating and maintaining their carbonate structures[14] but some of these negative impacts are already being felt. Climate change precipitated by emissions of greenhouse gases is also warming the oceans and already causing sea levels to rise.[15]

However, as the BBNJ decision demonstrates, it is not all bad news. And the developments discussed in this book also provide us reason for optimism. Article 192 of the 1982 Law of the Sea Convention provides that 'States have the obligation to protect and preserve the marine environment.' There are few obligations in international law that are so unqualified and unequivocal.

Thirty years ago a book of this kind would have been much shorter – it would doubtless have looked at the work of the International Maritime Organization on vessel source pollution, perhaps also at off-shore oil drilling and the work of the 1972 London Dumping Convention (of course, the last has been so successful in limiting deliberate dumping that it has dropped the word 'dumping' from its name, becoming the London Convention). Such a volume might also have considered the work of the Global Program of Action on Land based Sources of Pollution and the early Regional Seas Agreements. However there would probably have been little consideration of the environmental impacts of seabed mining or of exploitation of the extended continental shelf – although both were contemplated by the 1982 LOSC they still looked technologically unfeasible in the 1980s. Similarly we knew little about seabed vents or cold seeps, and the unique life forms that surround them – or even of the existence of ancient deep cold water corals.

Professor Rayfuse has tasked the authors of the various chapters of the book with documenting critically the progress that has been made under international law in addressing some of the key sectoral activities which pose threats to the marine environment; laying out the positive aspects of these measures as well as their shortcomings. It is a highly topical review of contemporary issues surrounding the regime created by the 1982 Law of the Sea Convention and as a research handbook it surely demonstrates effectively the areas for further work which still exist.

---

[12]   See the suggestion that the high seas be closed to fishing, examined by R. Sumaila et al., 'Winners and losers in a world where the high seas is closed to fishing', *Scientific Reports* 5, Article number: 8481. DOI:10.1038/srep08481.

[13]   See study by the World Bank and FAO, *The Sunken Billions: The Economic Justification for Fisheries Reform* (Washington, DC: The World Bank, 2009), that estimated that USD 1.05 is spent for every USD 1 of fish produced.

[14]   O. Hoegh-Guldberg et al., 'Coral Reefs under Rapid Climate Change and Ocean Acidification,' (2007) 318 *Science* 1737–42.

[15]   See IPCC Assessment Report 5: *Climate Change 2013: The Physical Science Basis*, 1140, available at http://www.climatechange2013.org/images/report/WG1AR5_ALL_FINAL.pdf (last accessed 3 June 2015).

It is a great pleasure for me to have been invited to write this Foreword. I commend the editor and her team of authors and am pleased to recommend this volume as an important, well informed and highly contemporary discussion of this relatively new but important field – marine environmental law.

David Freestone
Executive Secretary, Sargasso Sea Commission
Washington, DC
February 2015

# Preface

In Frank Schatzing's epic science fiction thriller, *The Swarm*, the oceans bite back. From destructive seabed worms to murderous whales, from leaching methane hydrates and underwater land-slides to massive tsunamis that wipe out much of the populated world, from armies of toxic jelly fish and marauding crabs to the mysterious 'yrr', the oceans and their inhabitants wage war against the very humanity that emerged, along with them, from the primordial soup. And who can blame them? Humans have not exactly been kind to the oceans. We have helped ourselves to their resources. We have used them as highways for our unbridled expansion across the earth's surface. We have turned them into dumping grounds, theatres of war, objects of inspiration and wonder and objects of fear, loathing and derision. Through all of this the oceans have stood by us, impressing us with their apparently limitless capacity to provide, inspiring us with their apparently unfathomable depths, and reassuring us with their apparently infinite ability to weather every storm, be it natural or human induced, literal and metaphorical, that comes their way.

Of course, in *The Swarm*, humanity wins – or is at least granted a reprieve from total annihilation. But real life seldom has the happy endings that sell popular fiction and keep movie-goers rapt in an endless suspension of disbelief. In real life bad things happen; and as the chapters in this *Handbook* chronicle, they are happening to the oceans. More than 85 per cent of the world's fish stocks are either fully exploited or over-exploited. Ever increasing numbers of marine species are threatened or endangered as a result of human activities. Destructive fishing practices, ship source pollution, marine debris, noise pollution, construction of artificial islands and pipelines, offshore oil and gas exploration, seabed mining, bioprospecting and marine scientific research all present increasing threats to the health and well-being of the oceans. Add to these the increasingly negative effects of climate change and ocean acidification and the picture becomes bleak indeed.

It is entirely possible for the oceans to exist without humans. However, it is probably not possible for humans to continue to exist on this earth without the food, ecosystem and other services the oceans provide. So it is not only important, but absolutely imperative that we respect, care for and provide for the oceans as they have cared and provided for us. This *Handbook* is in part about the misuse of the oceans. But it is also about giving back to the oceans through contributing to the design and implementation of effective regulation and management of human activities that perturb the marine environment.

The chapters in this *Handbook* are intended to provide a critical survey of the current state of legal research in selected issue areas relating to the legal regime for the protection of the marine environment. The authors were also tasked with going beyond a mere survey of existing law to identify legal lacunae and areas of critical research need for filling those lacunae. Given the potential breadth of the topic and the need to keep the book to a manageable size, hard decisions were necessary as to content and focus. A comprehensive global study of marine environmental law writ large could be expected to fill many volumes. The first decision was thus to restrict consideration to the international legal regime for the protection of the marine environment. Even here, an astute reader might question the comprehensiveness of this volume omitting, as it does, dedicated chapters on important topics such as control of alien invasive species, noise pollution, marine genetic resources, emerging techniques for area based management, protection of vulnerable marine ecosystems, and a number of major regional frameworks. However, the more astute reader will notice that each of these topics is, in fact, addressed in the chapters which are presented under the general rubrics of the legal framework for protection of the marine environment, pollution of the marine environment, seabed activities and the marine environment, protection of marine biodiversity, regional approaches to the protection of the marine environment and climate change and the marine environment. Together, it is hoped that these chapters provide both a representative and extremely thorough, even if not entirely comprehensive, analysis of the critical issues in the spotlight today and that by doing so they will shed some light on the way forward towards ensuring the health and fecundity of the oceans for generations to come.

As with any edited volume, this *Handbook* would not have been possible without the generosity, understanding and hard work of the authors who have persevered with the project even in the face of innumerable delays, or what has elsewhere euphemistically been referred to as a 'lengthy incubation period'. Preparation of the volume has taken place within the law faculties at two institutions, UNSW Australia (formerly known as The University of New South Wales), my home institution, and Lund University, where I am fortunate to enjoy a conjoint visiting professorship. I am indebted to my colleagues at both institutions for their intellectual companionship and the stimulating and interesting environments in which I work. I am grateful to Ms Anisa Kozoei at UNSW Australia for providing general editorial assistance and, finally, I am indebted to Ben Booth and Laura Mann at Edward Elgar for their vision for and support of this project and for their patience in seeing it through to fruition.

Rosemary Rayfuse<br>
Sydney and Lund<br>
February 2015

# PART I

# THE LEGAL FRAMEWORK FOR THE PROTECTION OF THE MARINE ENVIRONMENT

# 1. The LOSC regime for protection of the marine environment – fit for the twenty-first century?
*Robin Churchill*[1]

## 1. INTRODUCTION

The aim of the United Nations Convention on the Law of the Sea (LOSC),[2] according to its preamble, is to establish 'a legal order for the seas and oceans which will', inter alia, 'promote ... the conservation of their living resources, and the study, protection and preservation of the marine environment'.[3] To further these environmental aims, the LOSC dedicates the whole of one of its 13 substantive parts, Part XII, to 'protection and preservation of the marine environment', as well as including numerous provisions elsewhere relating to this issue.

The emphasis on the protection of the marine environment in the LOSC presents a striking contrast to the previous attempt to codify the law of sea, the four Geneva Conventions of 1958. The latter had contained only a handful of rather undeveloped provisions on environmental matters. The main reason for this difference is because 14 years after the adoption of the Geneva Conventions, and one year before the start of the Third UN Conference on the Law of the Sea (UNCLOS III), at which the LOSC was negotiated and eventually adopted, the protection of the environment (including the marine environment) was for the first time placed squarely on the political and legal agenda of the international community with the holding of the UN Conference on the Human Environment at Stockholm in 1972.[4] Thus, the negotiators of the LOSC had before them the Declaration and Action Plan adopted at the Stockholm Conference, as well as the principles adopted in preparation for the Conference by an Inter-governmental Working Group on Marine Pollution.[5] Furthermore, shortly before and

---

[1] I would like to thank my colleagues, Elizabeth Kirk and Nengye Liu, and the editor of this book, Rosemary Rayfuse, for their comments on a previous draft of this chapter. The usual disclaimer applies.

[2] United Nations Convention on the Law of the Sea (adopted and opened for signature 10 December 1982, entered into force 16 November 1994) 1833 UNTS 3. As of 7 January 2015 there were 167 parties to the Convention.

[3] LOSC, Preamble, para. 4.

[4] Provisions on the protection of the marine environment are contained in Principle 7 of the Stockholm Declaration and in Chapter II (Recommendations 70–94) of the Action Plan for the Human Environment, adopted at the Conference, UN Doc. A/CONF.48/14/Rev 1 (1972).

[5] A/CONF.48/IWGMP.II/5 (1971). Recommendation 92 of the Stockholm Action Plan called on States to endorse the principles 'as guiding concepts' for the forthcoming Third UN Conference on the Law of the Sea. See further M.H. Nordquist et al. (eds), *United Nations Convention on the Law of the Sea 1982. A Commentary* (hereafter *Virginia Commentary*), Vol. IV (Martinus Nijhoff 1991) 8–9 and 36–7.

during the early years of UNCLOS III, a number of major treaties relating to the marine environment were adopted. These include the London Dumping Convention, 1972;[6] the International Convention for the Prevention of Pollution from Ships, 1973 (hereafter the MARPOL Convention);[7] a number of regional marine environmental treaties, some concluded pursuant to UNEP's Regional Seas Programme (adopted in 1976);[8] and the first wildlife treaties whose coverage included marine species, such as the Convention on International Trade in Endangered Species (1973) (CITES)[9] and the Convention on Migratory Species (1979) (CMS).[10]

The LOSC is often described as a 'constitution for the oceans'. In accordance with this constitutional nature, the LOSC is perceived politically as being the basic foundation for the whole of the law of the sea and superior to any other treaty concerned with marine matters. Legally, this superiority is reflected in Article 311, which provides that the LOSC prevails over pre-existing treaties inconsistent with it and severely limits the capacity of parties to the LOSC to conclude treaties that modify its provisions inter se. This basic constitutional status of the LOSC probably extends to international marine environmental law,[11] especially as the LOSC remains the only global treaty to address, in however incomplete a fashion, all matters relating to the protection of the marine environment. In this context it is noteworthy that a number of significant treaties relevant to the marine environment provide that they are to be applied consistently with the LOSC.[12] Furthermore, the LOSC itself provides that obligations assumed by States under other marine environmental treaties 'should be carried out in a manner consistent with the general principles and objectives' of the LOSC.[13]

Nevertheless, while the LOSC may have something of a fundamental status in international marine environmental law, it is not in practice the most important treaty

---

[6]   Convention on the Prevention of Marine Pollution by Dumping of Wastes and Other Matter (adopted 29 December 1972, entered into force 30 August 1975) 1046 UNTS 138.

[7]   International Convention for the Prevention of Pollution from Ships (adopted 2 November 1973, entered into force 2 October 1983) 1340 UNTS 62.

[8]   For discussion see Nilufer Oral, 'Forty years of the UNEP Regional Seas Programme: from past to future', Chapter 16 in this volume.

[9]   Convention on International Trade in Endangered Species of Wild Fauna and Flora (adopted 3 March 1973, entered into force 1 July 1975) 993 UNTS 243.

[10]   Convention on the Conservation of Migratory Species of Wild Animals (adopted 23 June 1979, entered into force 1 November 1983) 1651 UNTS 333.

[11]   This position is also taken by M.L. McConnell and E. Gold, 'The Modern Law of the Sea: Framework for the Protection and Preservation of the Marine Environment' (1991) 23 *Case Western Reserve Journal of International Law* 83, 84 and 98.

[12]   See, for example, the London Dumping Convention, Art. XII; the MARPOL Convention, Art. 9(2); the CITES Convention, Art. XIV(6); the CMS Convention, Art. XII(1); and the Convention on Biological Diversity (adopted 5 June 1992, entered into force 29 December 1993) 1760 UNTS 79, Art. 22(2).

[13]   LOSC, Art. 237(2). Note, however, that Art. 237(1) provides that the provisions of Part XII are 'without prejudice to the specific obligations assumed by States under special conventions and agreements concluded previously which relate to the protection and preservation of the marine environment and to agreements which may be concluded in furtherance of the general principles set forth in this Convention'.

for protecting the marine environment, as will become evident in later chapters in this book. That is because much of the LOSC dealing with the protection of the marine environment, like a good deal of the rest of the LOSC, is of a framework nature and contains few detailed norms of environmental protection. There are a number of reasons why this is so. First, because the LOSC aims to settle '*all* issues relating to the law of the sea',[14] it could not provide detailed provisions on every issue without becoming excessively long and unwieldy. Second, if the LOSC had provided detailed provisions on all questions relating to the protection of the marine environment, many of them (especially those concerning the prevention of pollution) would have become rapidly out of date as the need for higher standards of protection became apparent[15] and the desirability of measures to address newly perceived environmental problems became evident.[16] Third, it was in any case not necessary to have detailed provisions on some matters (such as dumping and pollution from ships) because, as noted above, detailed treaties addressing those matters already existed.

The aim of this chapter is not to provide a systematic and detailed analysis of the provisions of the LOSC relating to the protection of the marine environment. That has been done before by others,[17] and in any case lack of space would preclude such an exercise here. Instead, this chapter will try to assess the value of the LOSC today, more than 30 years after its adoption in 1982, and for the years ahead. It does so in two ways. First, it asks how the LOSC would compare with an ideal general treaty on protection of the marine environment that might be drawn up now. Second, the chapter tries to determine the effect and influence that the marine environmental provisions of the LOSC have had on the practice of States and international organizations since its adoption. Some might object that the first of these aims involves an unreasonable and unfair comparison because international environmental law has developed so much since 1982: one cannot expect the LOSC to have anticipated future developments. That, of course, is true; and might therefore lead to the conclusion that the LOSC had become outdated as far as protection of the marine environment was concerned. However, such a conclusion would be premature. The framework nature of the LOSC means that it does not contain a detailed set of norms frozen in time. Furthermore, it has evolved to a degree since its entry into force in 1994. While it lacks a mechanism

---

[14]  Preamble of the LOSC, para. 1 (emphasis added).

[15]  Cf. the way in which MARPOL and the London Dumping Convention have been frequently amended and updated: see further Henrik Ringbom, 'Vessel-source pollution', Chapter 5 in this volume, and David L. VanderZwaag, 'The international control of ocean dumping: navigating from permissive to precautionary shores', Chapter 6 in this volume.

[16]  Examples of such problems include global climate change and its consequences for the marine environment (on which see section 6 of this chapter below), and the existence and significance of deep sea environments, such as seamounts, cold-water coral reefs and hydro-thermal vents, together with their associated ecosystems and biodiversity.

[17]  See, for example, the *Virginia Commentary*, above n 5, especially Vol. IV; K. Hakapää, *Marine Pollution in International Law* (Suomalainen Tiedeakatemia 1981); D.M. Johnson (ed.), *The Environmental Law of the Sea* (IUCN 1981); and Y. Tanaka, *The International Law of the Sea* (2nd edn, Cambridge University Press 2015) chapters 7–9.

resembling the conference or meeting of the parties that many multilateral environmental agreements have in order to drive those agreements normatively forward,[18] it
does have various means of development.[19] These include, inter alia, the conclusion of
implementation agreements (two have so far been concluded, and there is now the
possibility of a third, as explained below); the adoption by the ISA of regulations for
mining in the Area (i.e. the seabed beyond the limits of national jurisdiction); the
adoption of resolutions by the UN General Assembly in response to the UN Secretary-
General's reporting functions under Article 319(2)(a) of the LOSC; and the interpretation of the LOSC by international courts and tribunals.[20] Examples of the use of all of
these means will be given below.

The structure of this chapter is to look in turn at each of those matters with which, it
is suggested, an ideal contemporary general marine environmental treaty would deal,
and to consider how, if at all, the LOSC addresses them. Insofar as it does address
them, some comment will be made about the adequacy and practical effect of the
LOSC provisions in question. The issues to be considered are: (1) principles for marine
environmental policy-making and legislation; (2) the conservation of species; (3) the
protection of habitats (which together with (2) broadly equates to the conservation of
marine biodiversity); (4) the prevention of marine pollution; and (5) climate change.

## 2.  PRINCIPLES FOR MARINE ENVIRONMENTAL
## POLICY-MAKING AND LEGISLATION[21]

Many of the more recent regional agreements for the protection of the marine
environment contain a range of principles to guide States and international organizations when engaged in making policy and legislating to protect the marine

---

18   The LOSC parties do meet annually, but their role is limited to overseeing the three
institutions created by the LOSC (the Commission on the Limits on the Continental Shelf, the
International Tribunal for the Law of the Sea (ITLOS) and the International Seabed Authority
(ISA)). There has been resistance to giving those meetings any greater role. See further T.
Treves, 'The General Assembly and the Meeting of States Parties in the Implementation of the
LOS Convention' in A.G. Oude Elferink (ed.), *Stability and Change in the Law of the Sea: The
Role of the LOS Convention* (Martinus Nijhoff 2005) 55. On the role of conferences/ meetings of
the parties of multilateral environmental agreements, see, inter alia, J. Brunée, 'COPing with
consent: Law-Making under Multilateral Environmental Agreements' (2002) 15 *Leiden Journal
of International Law* 1; and R. Churchill and G. Ulfstein, 'Autonomous Institutional Arrangements in Multilateral Environmental Agreements: A Little Noticed Phenomenon in International
Law' (2000) 94 *American Journal of International Law* 623.

19   See further A.E. Boyle, 'Further Development of the 1982 Law of the Sea Convention:
Mechanisms for Change' (2005) 54 *International and Comparative Law Quarterly* 563.

20   One could add the amendment procedures of the LOSC to this list, but they are widely
considered too cumbersome to be useful: see, for example, D. Freestone and A.G. Oude
Elferink, 'Flexibility and Innovation in the Law of the Sea: Will the LOS Convention
Amendment Procedures ever be used?' in Oude Elferink, above n 18, 180–3.

21   See further Yoshifumi Tanaka, 'Principles of international marine environmental law',
Chapter 2 in this volume.

environment.[22] One would expect the ideal contemporary marine environmental treaty posited above to do the same. As far as the LOSC is concerned, it does contain some such principles but they are somewhat limited, for reasons that will be explained. The principles that one might expect an ideal treaty to contain would include the following.[23]

## 2.1 Prevention of Environmental Harm Principle

A version of this principle is found in Article 194(2) of the LOSC. It requires States to 'take all measures necessary to ensure that activities under their jurisdiction or control are so conducted as not to cause damage by pollution to other States and their environment, and that pollution arising from incidents or activities under their jurisdiction or control does not spread beyond the areas where they exercise sovereign rights in accordance with this Convention.' Article 194(2) is similar to Principle 21 of the 1972 Stockholm Declaration,[24] which has been described as a 'statement of contemporary international law',[25] but is more limited because it covers only 'damage by pollution' whereas Principle 21 refers to damage without qualification as to the type of damage. It is not clear what practical impact Article 194(2) has had on the practice of States.

## 2.2 Environmental Impact Assessment

Although the phrase 'environmental impact assessment' is found nowhere in the LOSC, Article 206 provides for such assessment in all but name. It requires States that 'have reasonable grounds for believing that planned activities under their jurisdiction or control may cause substantial pollution of or significant and harmful changes to the marine environment' to assess, 'as far as practicable, ... the potential effects of such activities on the marine environment' and either to publish the results of such assessments or provide reports to 'the competent international organizations', which should make such reports available to all States. Article 206 is more limited than some other treaties requiring environmental impact assessment as it requires an assessment

---

[22]   See R.R. Churchill and A.V. Lowe, *The Law of the Sea* (3rd edn, Manchester University Press 1999) 335–7. See also the references in Tanaka, Chapter 2 in this volume.

[23]   The list of principles discussed here, which is longer than that in Chapter 2, is based on P. Sands and J. Peel, *Principles of International Environmental Law* (3rd edn, CUP 2012), Chapter 6. The authors of texts on international environmental law differ in the principles they enumerate. Thus, the list of principles discussed here is neither necessarily complete nor one that would command universal support. Other principles that might have been considered are the principle of public participation and transparency and the principle of common but differentiated responsibility. The former is less relevant to a framework treaty like the LOSC than environmental treaties that provide for concrete norms to be revised and developed by an international organization or conference/meeting of the parties. The principle of common but differentiated responsibility is considered briefly below (see text at notes 104 and 105) and is also discussed in Tanaka, Chapter 2 in this volume.

[24]   See above n 4.

[25]   P. Birnie, A. Boyle and C. Redgwell, *International Law and the Environment* (3rd edn, OUP 2009) 145.

only 'as far as practicable'. On the other hand, unlike some other treaties, it is not limited to planned activities that would have only a transboundary impact. It is not evident that Article 206 has had a great deal of impact in practice. It was relied on by Ireland in its claim against the United Kingdom in the *MOX Plant* arbitration,[26] but never considered by the arbitral tribunal as Ireland withdrew its claim for jurisdictional reasons before the tribunal could consider the merits of the case. Article 206 was also invoked by Malaysia in its notification and statement of claim instituting arbitral proceedings against Singapore in respect of the latter's land reclamation activities in the Straits of Johor, Malaysia claiming that Singapore had made no assessment of the impact of its activities on waters under the jurisdiction of Malaysia. As in the *MOX Plant* case, the arbitral tribunal never considered the merits of this claim as the parties reached a negotiated settlement of their dispute. However, the question of an environmental impact assessment was considered by the ITLOS in its order of provisional measures in the case. Noting that no assessment of the effects of its land reclamation activities had been undertaken by Singapore and that 'it cannot be excluded that, in the particular circumstances of this case, the land reclamation works may have adverse effects on the marine environment', the ITLOS ordered Malaysia and Singapore to establish promptly a group of independent experts to determine 'the effects of Singapore's land reclamation and to propose, as appropriate, measures to deal with any adverse effects of such land reclamation'.[27] The ITLOS did not refer explicitly to Article 206, and its language actually suggests a lower threshold for when an assessment is required than Article 206 itself. Apart from these two cases, other instances of challenges to the adequacy of an environmental impact assessment of a marine project that have become public suggest that the States concerned have relied on instruments that provided more detail of what is required of an assessment than the rather sketchy provisions of the LOSC. Thus, in the case of the Nord Stream pipeline project in the Baltic, the States concerned about the project invoked not the LOSC but the Espoo Convention.[28]

In addition to Article 206, specific provisions have been developed for environmental impact assessments to be carried out in relation to activities in the Area. Thus, the 1994 Implementation Agreement requires an application for approval by the ISA of a plan of work for the exploration of minerals in the Area to be accompanied by 'an assessment

---

[26]   Memorial of Ireland, Chapter 7, available at <http://www.pca-cpa.org/showpage.asp?pag_id=1148> (last accessed 6 May 2015).

[27]   *Case concerning Land Reclamation by Singapore in and around the Straits of Johor (Malaysia v Singapore)*, Provisional Measures, Order of 8 October 2003, paras 96 and 106(1), respectively, available at <http://www.itlos.org/fileadmin/itlos/documents/cases/case_no_12/12_order_081003_en.pdf> (last accessed 18 May 2015).

[28]   Espoo Convention on Environmental Impact Assessment in a Transboundary Context (adopted 25 February 1991, entered into force 10 September 1997) (1991) 30 *International Legal Materials* 802. See further S. Vinogradov, 'Challenges of Nord Stream: Streamlining International Frameworks and Regimes for Submarine Pipelines' (2009) 52 *German Yearbook of International Law* 241.

of the potential environmental impacts of the proposed activities'.[29] The three sets of mining regulations so far adopted by the ISA give further effect to this obligation. Thus, they require a contractor to attach to a plan of work for exploration a preliminary assessment of the possible impact of the proposed exploration activities on the marine environment and a description of a programme for oceanographic and environmental baseline studies that would enable an assessment of the potential environmental impact including, but not restricted to, the impact on biodiversity of the proposed exploration activities. In addition, before commencing exploration activities, a contractor must submit to the ISA an impact assessment of the potential effects on the marine environment of the proposed activities; a proposal for a monitoring programme to determine the potential effect on the marine environment of the proposed activities; and data that could be used to establish an environmental baseline against which to assess the effect of the proposed activities.[30] These provisions have been applied in practice in the 22 contracts for exploration that the ISA has so far concluded.[31]

## 2.3 Precautionary Principle

Definitions of the precautionary principle differ, but broadly the principle means that where there is a threat of serious damage to the environment, lack of full scientific certainty as to whether such damage will occur or as to its causes is not to be used as a reason to postpone (cost-effective) measures to prevent such damage.[32] The first international instruments referring to this principle did not appear until after the adoption of the LOSC, in the mid-1980s,[33] so it is not surprising that that there is no reference to the principle in the LOSC. Nevertheless, there is arguably an embryonic use of the principle in the definition of marine pollution in the LOSC. Article 1(1)(4) defines 'pollution of the marine environment' as including the introduction of substances or energy into the marine environment that not only results in deleterious effects but also that 'is likely to result' in such effects. The latter can be argued to have a precautionary element.[34] Be that as it may, the precautionary principle/approach is explicitly referred to in some of the subsequent development of the LOSC. Thus, the

---

[29]   Agreement relating to the Implementation of Part XI of the United Nations Convention on the Law of the Sea of 10 December 1982 (adopted 28 July 1994, entered into force 28 July 1996) 1836 UNTS 42, Annex, section 1, para. 7.

[30]   Regulations on Prospecting and Exploration for Metallic Nodules in the Area (2000, as amended in 2013), reg. 31(6), annex II, section IV, para. 24 and annex IV, section 5, para. 5.2; Regulations on Prospecting and Exploration for Polymetallic Sulphides in the Area (2010), reg. 33(6), annex 2, section IV, para. 24 and annex 4, section 5, para. 5.2; and Regulations on Prospecting and Exploration for Cobalt-Rich Ferromanganese Crusts in the Area (2012), reg. 33(6), annex II, section IV, para. 24 and annex IV, section 5, para. 5.2. The texts of the Regulations are available at <https://www.isa.org.jm/mining-code/Regulations> (last accessed 18 May 2015). See further Michael Lodge, 'Protecting the marine environment of the deep seabed', Chapter 7 in this volume.

[31]   For details, see <https://www.isa.org.jm/deep-seabed-minerals-contractors> (last accessed 18 May 2015).

[32]   See further Birnie, Boyle and Redgwell, above n 25, 152–64.

[33]   S. Marr, *The Precautionary Principle in the Law of the Sea* (Martinus Nijhoff 2003) 5–7.

[34]   See further ibid., 52–3.

three sets of mining regulations so far adopted by the ISA all refer to the precautionary approach,[35] the importance of which was emphasized in the 2011 Advisory Opinion of the Sea-Bed Disputes Chamber;[36] while the UN Fish Stocks Agreement[37] calls on States and regional fisheries management organizations to employ a precautionary approach in the management of straddling fish stocks and highly migratory species. The ITLOS has been urged by the applicants in three provisional measures cases to apply the precautionary principle. While not explicitly endorsing the principle, the ITLOS in each case held that 'prudence and caution' required the parties to co-operate in taking certain actions and prescribed provisional measures reflecting that approach.[38]

## 2.4 Polluter Pays Principle

The polluter pays principle means broadly that the costs of pollution are to be borne by the person causing the pollution and not by its victims or society generally. Although the principle was endorsed by the OECD in a series of recommendations from the early 1970s onwards, it was not until the 1992 UN Conference on Environment and Development that the principle 'for the first time secured international support as an environmental policy'.[39] It is therefore not surprising that there is no trace of the principle in the handful of provisions of the LOSC dealing with liability and compensation for damage caused by pollution.[40]

## 2.5 Sustainable Development

The first use of the term 'sustainable development' occurs in the report of the World Commission on Environment and Development (popularly known as the Brundtland Report), which defines it as 'development that meets the needs of the present without

---

[35]   See the Nodule Regulations, above n 30, Regs 31(2) and (5), and annex IV, section 5.1; Sulphides Regulations, above n 30, Regs 33(2) and (5), and annex 4, section 5.1; and Crusts Regulations, above n 30, Regs 33(2)and (5), and annex IV, section 5.1.

[36]   *Advisory Opinion on the Responsibilities and Obligations of States sponsoring Persons and Entities with respect to Activities in the Area*, paras 131–5, available at <https://www.itlos.org/cases/list-of-cases/case-no-17/> (last accessed 18 May 2015).

[37]   Agreement for the Implementation of the Provisions of the United Nations Convention on the Law of the Sea of 10 December 1982 relating to the Conservation and Management of Straddling Fish Stocks and Highly Migratory Fish Stocks (adopted 4 August 1995, entered into force 11 December 2001) 2167 UNTS 3, Art. 6 and Annex II.

[38]   *Southern Bluefin Tuna Cases (New Zealand v Japan; Australia v Japan)*, Provisional Measures, Order of 27 August 1999, paras 77, 79 and 80 (1999) 38 *International Legal Materials* 1624; *MOX Plant Case (Ireland v United Kingdom)*, Provisional Measures, Order of 3 December 2001, para. 84, available at <https://www.itlos.org/cases/list-of-cases/case-no-10/> (last accessed 18 May 2015); and *Land Reclamation* case, above n 27, para. 99.

[39]   Birnie, Boyle and Redgwell, above n 25, 322.

[40]   LOSC, Arts 139(2), 235 and 304 and Annex III, Art. 22. The last of these comes closest to the principle by stipulating, although without further elaboration, that a contractor undertaking activities in the Area 'shall have responsibility or liability for any damage arising out of wrongful acts in the conduct of its operation' and that the International Seabed Authority has responsibility or liability for damage arising out of its unlawful acts.

compromising the ability of future generations to meet their own needs'.[41] The report was published five years after the adoption of the LOSC, so it is not surprising that the LOSC contains no reference to sustainable development. Nevertheless, ideas of sustainability are to be found in the LOSC. Most obviously they occur in its provisions concerning fisheries. Thus, the LOSC requires a State managing the fisheries of its exclusive economic zone (EEZ) and States co-operating in the management of high seas fisheries to take measures that are 'designed to maintain or restore populations of harvested species at levels which can produce the maximum sustainable yield'.[42] Elsewhere the LOSC provides that 'the Area and its resources are the common heritage of mankind' and that the exploration and exploitation of the mineral resources of the Area are to be 'carried out for the benefit of mankind as a whole'.[43] Arguably these provisions mean that the mining of the mineral resources of the Area should be not only for the benefit of the present generation of humankind but also for the benefit of future generations. Such intra-generational and inter-generational equity is an important element of sustainable development.[44]

## 2.6   Ecosystem Approach

The desirability of an ecosystem approach, under which an ecosystem should be managed as a whole rather than its individual components being managed separately and in isolation from one another, has been developed on the global plane by the Conference of the Parties to the Convention on Biological Diversity (CBD)[45] in general terms[46] and by the Food and Agriculture Organization (FAO) specifically for fisheries.[47] This development considerably post-dates the LOSC,[48] so it is not surprising that the term 'ecosystem approach' is nowhere used in the LOSC. Nevertheless, rudimentary instances of such an approach can be found in its provisions on the

---

[41]   World Commission on Environment and Development, *Our Common Future* (OUP 1987) 43. This definition has subsequently been refined in a variety of international instruments. There is a vast literature on what is involved in sustainable development.

[42]   LOSC, Arts 61(3) and 119(1)(a). See further the following section of this chapter, especially the text at notes 61 and 62.

[43]   LOSC, Arts 136 and 140.

[44]   Birnie, Boyle and Redgwell, above n 25, 119–23.

[45]   Above n 12.

[46]   Conference of the Parties to the Convention on Biological Diversity, Decision V/6 (2000) available at <http://www.cbd.int/decision/cop/default.shtml?id=7148> (last accessed 30 April 2015).

[47]   See, in particular, the Reykjavik Declaration on Responsible Fisheries in the Marine Ecosystem, 2001 available at <ftp://ftp.fao.org/fi/DOCUMENT/reykjavik/y2198t00_dec.pdf> (last accessed 30 April 2015). See further FAO, *Putting into Practice the Ecosystem Approach to Fisheries* (2005) available at <http://www.fao.org/docrep/009/a0191e/a0191e00.htm#TOC> (last accessed 30 April 2005).

[48]   The first international instrument providing for an ecosystem approach actually predates the adoption of the LOSC, although not the substantive negotiation of its environmental provisions: see Convention on the Conservation of Antarctic Marine Living Resources (adopted 20 May 1980, entered in force 7 April 1982) 1329 UNTS 47, Arts II(3) and IX.

conservation of species associated with or dependent on harvested fish stocks (discussed in more detail in the next section) and in relation to activities in the Area, where the ISA is required to adopt regulations to prevent pollution, other hazards to the marine environment and 'interference with the ecological balance of the marine environment', as well as to protect and conserve the natural resources of the Area and prevent damage to the fauna and flora of the marine environment.[49]

## 2.7   Co-operation

The principle of co-operation is deeply embedded in the LOSC, indeed one could say that co-operation is its *leitmotiv*, so frequently do its provisions call for co-operation between its parties in relation to a host of diverse matters. Part XII of the LOSC (on the protection and preservation of the marine environment) contains not only numerous calls for co-operation in relation to specific matters, notably in relation to the development of international rules and standards to prevent marine pollution (discussed further below), but also a general provision on co-operation in Article 197, which requires States to 'co-operate on a global basis and, as appropriate, on a regional basis, directly or through competent international organizations, in formulating and elaborating international rules, standards and recommended practices and procedures consistent with this Convention, for the protection and preservation of the marine environment, taking into account characteristic regional features.' For its part the ITLOS, in the *Mox Plant* case, after noting that 'the duty to cooperate is a fundamental principle in the prevention of pollution of the marine environment under Part XII of the Convention and general international law and that rights arise therefrom which the Tribunal may consider appropriate to preserve under Article 290 of the Convention [on provisional measures],' held that 'prudence and caution' required Ireland and the United Kingdom to cooperate in various ways.[50]

## 3.   CONSERVATION OF SPECIES[51]

One would expect the conservation of marine species to be a major concern of the ideal contemporary marine environmental treaty posited in the introduction to this chapter. In contrast, the LOSC gives the impression that its drafters did not consider the conservation of species to be a significant marine environmental issue. Part XII of the LOSC, although headed 'protection and preservation of the marine environment', contains only a handful of brief, general and rather peripheral obligations relating to the conservation of species. Furthermore, the provisions of the LOSC relating to the

---

49   LOSC, Art. 145.

50   *MOX Plant* case, above n 38, paras 82 and 84. This passage was quoted with approval in the subsequent *Land Reclamation* case, above n 27, para. 92. In that case the ITLOS also prescribed specific co-operative action that the parties should take: see para. 106(1).

51   See also Alexander Proelss and Katherine Houghton, 'Protecting marine species', Chapter 11 in this volume and Dire Tladi, 'Conservation and sustainable use of marine biodiversity in areas beyond national jurisdiction: towards an implementing agreement', Chapter 12 in this volume.

settlement of disputes create something of a dichotomy between protection of the environment and the conservation of living resources.[52] Article 297 excludes from compulsory settlement disputes concerning a coastal State's obligations in the EEZ relating to the conservation of 'living resources', whereas disputes concerning 'the protection and preservation of the marine environment' are not so excluded. The tribunal in the Chagos Marine Protected Area arbitration between Mauritius and the United Kingdom had to consider where the boundary between those two matters lay.[53] Mauritius argued that the marine protected area established by the United Kingdom in the whole of the 200-nautical-mile zone around the Chagos Islands, which included a complete prohibition on fishing, was an environmental matter, whereas the United Kingdom contended that it concerned the conservation of living resources and so was excluded from the tribunal's jurisdiction. The tribunal found that when establishing the marine protected area, the United Kingdom had characterized the measure as primarily an environmental one and could not go back on that characterization in the arbitration proceedings.[54] The ITLOS has struck a blow against the dichotomy between protection of the marine environment and the conservation of living resources, albeit within the limited context of provisional measures. Article 290 of the LOSC provides that where a dispute is before a court or tribunal, provisional measures may be prescribed if it is considered appropriate, inter alia, to 'prevent serious harm to the marine environment'. In the *Southern Bluefin Tuna* cases, the ITLOS, in considering whether there was a threat of such harm, observed that 'the conservation of the living resources of the sea is an element in the protection and preservation of the marine environment'.[55]

Most of the provisions of the LOSC addressing the conservation of species are found, not in Part XII, but in Parts V and VII (on the exclusive economic zone (EEZ) and high seas, respectively). These parts contain conservation obligations relating to 'living resources', 'harvested species' and 'species associated with or dependent upon harvested species'. None of these phrases is defined in the LOSC. The second and third of these three categories are clearly distinct from each other. Given that the LOSC imposes quite different conservation obligations for 'living resources' compared with 'species associated with or dependent upon harvested species' (as will be seen), those two categories would also seem to be quite distinct. Nor would 'living resources' seem to include marine species that are neither 'harvested species' nor 'species associated with or dependent upon harvested species', otherwise such species would be subject to

---

[52] A similar differentiation may also be seen in LOSC Art 21 (on the coastal State's legislative jurisdiction in the territorial sea) and Annex VIII (on special arbitration), although in those cases no practical drawbacks follow from the differentiation.

[53] *Chagos Marine Protected Area Arbitration (Mauritius v United Kingdom)*, Award of 18 March 2015, available at <www.pca-cpa.org/showpage.asp?pag_id=1429> (last accessed 18 May 2015).

[54] Award, paras 283–91.

[55] *Southern Bluefin Tuna Cases*, above n 38, para. 70. This dictum was repeated with approval by the ITLOS in its *Advisory Opinion on the Request submitted by the Sub-Regional Fisheries Commission* (of 2 April 2015), paras 120 and 216, available at <https://www.itlos.org/fileadmin/itlos/documents/cases/case_no.21/advisory_opinion/C21_AdvOp_02.04.pdf> (last accessed 18 May 2015).

more onerous conservation obligations than 'associated or dependent' species, which would appear to go against the scheme of conservation in Parts V and VII of the LOSC. In the absence of a definition of 'living resources', it is reasonable to assume that the word 'resources' has its ordinary dictionary meaning of 'money or means of raising money'[56] or 'a stock or supply of materials or assets'.[57] Thus, 'living resources' would seem to refer to marine species, whether fauna or flora, that either are commercially exploited (equating to 'harvested species') or that have the potential to be commercially exploited.[58] Species 'dependent upon harvested species' would seem to refer primarily to species that are the predators of harvested species. Species 'associated with' harvested species would seem to include species that may be caught incidentally when fishing, species that are the prey of harvested species, or species having some other form of biological association with harvested species. The first of these include not only species of fish caught as by-catch, but also smaller marine mammals (particularly dolphins and porpoises) and amphibians (such as turtles), which are caught in various kinds of net and consequently drown,[59] as well as some sea birds (notably albatrosses), which are attracted to the bait used in long-line fishing and are then caught on the hooks and die.[60] The prey of harvested species includes smaller fish as well as plankton and a variety of other lower life forms. Thus, 'species associated with or dependent upon harvested species' include a wide variety of marine species ranging from mammals and birds to plankton and other lower life forms. However, they and harvested species are unlikely to include all marine species. For those species that are not so included, the LOSC provides no conservation obligations at all. Even if the populations and well-being of such non-included species are not threatened by fishing, they may be adversely affected by other human activities, such as the exploitation of seabed resources and the laying of cables and pipelines. Insofar as such species are adversely affected by pollution, their conservation is obliquely provided for through the LOSC's provisions on the prevention of pollution (discussed below) since the definition of pollution in Article 1(1)(4) of the LOSC includes 'harm to ... marine life'.

In relation to the conservation of 'living resources', Articles 61(2) and (3) of the LOSC require a coastal State within its EEZ 'to ensure through proper conservation and management measures that the maintenance of' such resources 'is not endangered by over-exploitation', taking into account the best scientific evidence available to it. Such measures must be 'designed to maintain or restore populations of harvested

---

[56]   *Chambers English Dictionary* (7th edn, Chambers 1988) 1251.

[57]   *Concise Oxford Dictionary* (10th edn, OUP 1999) 1219.

[58]   See further D. Owen, 'The Application of the Wild Birds Directive beyond the Territorial Sea of European Community Member States' (2001) 13 *Journal of Environmental Law* 39, 49–56.

[59]   See further B. Miller, 'Combating Driftnet Fishing in the Pacific' in J. Crawford and D.R. Rothwell (eds), *The Law of the Sea in the Asian-Pacific Region* (Martinus Nijhoff 1995) 155; and K. Mulvaney and B. McKay, 'Small Cetaceans: Status, Threats and Management' in W.C.G. Burns and A. Gillespie (eds), *The Future of Cetaceans in a Changing World* (Transnational Publishers 2003) 189 at 195–7.

[60]   See further E. Dunn, 'Reducing Seabird Bycatch: From Identifying Problems to Implementing Policy' in D. Vidas and P.J. Schei (eds), *The World Ocean in Globalisation* (Martinus Nijhoff 2011) 247.

species at levels that can produce the maximum sustainable yield, as qualified by relevant environmental and economic factors', taking into account any generally recommended international minimum standards. On the high seas, Articles 117 and 118 require States whose nationals fish there to take, or to co-operate with other States in taking 'measures necessary for the conservation' of living resources. Article 119(1)(a) requires such measures to be designed to maintain or restore populations of harvested species at levels that can produce the maximum sustainable yield (MSY), as qualified by relevant environmental and economic factors. It is immediately evident that the provisions for both the EEZ and high seas are limited, weak and lack precision. In the case of the high seas, unlike the EEZ, there is no obligation to ensure that living resources are not endangered by over-exploitation. The main goal of conservation and management measures, both in the EEZ and on the high seas, is to achieve MSY. However, that is a goal that is heavily qualified. The reference to 'economic factors' suggests that catch limits could be set for economic reasons, such as protecting employment in the fishing industry, at a level that would delay or prevent the restoration or maintenance of stocks to the level of MSY, although not to the extent of endangering the maintenance of living resources.[61] Furthermore, and more fundamentally, the reliance of the LOSC on MSY as the principal policy tool of fisheries management has been criticized because it is difficult to calculate the MSY for a particular stock, it is impossible to apply MSY completely in a multi-species fishery, and MSY is only concerned with limiting catches and does not deal with the need to restrict effort.[62]

Turning to the conservation of 'species associated with or dependent upon harvested species', Article 61(4) of the LOSC requires a coastal State, in adopting conservation and management measures for the living resources of its EEZ, 'to take into consideration' the effect of such measures on associated or dependent species 'with a view to maintaining or restoring populations of such... species above levels at which their reproduction may become seriously threatened'. Article 119(1)(b) lays down a similar obligation on States fishing on the high seas. Those provisions are particularly weak. The obligation on States is merely to 'take into consideration' the effect of their measures on associated and dependent species with a view to maintaining or restoring populations of such species 'above levels at which their reproduction may become

[61]   W.T. Burke, *The New International Law of Fisheries* (Clarendon Press 1994) 54–5; and D.R. Christie, 'The Conservation and Management of Stocks located solely within the Exclusive Economic Zone' in E. Hey (ed.), *Developments in International Fisheries Law* (Kluwer 1999) 395, 402–3.

[62]   See, eg, R. Barnes, 'The Convention on the Law of the Sea: An Effective Framework for Domestic Fisheries Conservation?' in D. Freestone, R. Barnes and D. Ong (eds), *The Law of the Sea: Progress and Prospects* (OUP 2006) 233, 243–4; Burke, above n 61, 52–5; Christie, above n 61, 402–4; E. Hey, 'The Persistence of a Concept: Maximum Sustainable Yield' (2012) 27 *International Journal of Marine and Coastal Law* 763; and M. Markowski, 'The International Legal Standard for Sustainable EEZ Fisheries Management' in G. Winter (ed.), *Towards Sustainable Fisheries Law: A Comparative Analysis* (IUCN 2009) 3, 29.

seriously threatened', not to ensure that their measures maintain or restore populations of associated or dependent species at or to a sustainable level.[63]

The obligations of coastal States to conserve a stock of living resources that is shared with one or more other States, a matter dealt with by Article 63(1) of the LOSC, was the subject of one of the questions on which the ITLOS was asked to give an advisory opinion by the Sub-Regional Fisheries Commission in a request made in March 2013. In its opinion the ITLOS contributed to developing the LOSC by spelling out the rather vague obligation of co-operation in Article 63(1) in ways that strengthen that obligation.[64] However, there have been two cases where the ITLOS has not taken the possible opportunity to strengthen the fisheries provisions of the LOSC through a dynamic interpretation. In the *Volga* case, the ITLOS rejected Australia's argument that Article 73 of the LOSC should be read so as to allow a coastal State, when releasing an arrested fishing vessel on the payment of a bond, to require the released vessel to carry a vessel monitoring system (VMS) and to disclose details of its ultimate beneficial owners.[65] Had the ITLOS accepted Australia's argument, it would have strengthened the capacity of coastal States more effectively to control the activities of foreign fishing vessels in their EEZs. Such illegal fishing is one of the reasons why the world's fish stocks are in a crisis state (see further below). Second, in the *Virginia G* case the ITLOS was asked to interpret the requirement in the LOSC that there be a 'genuine link' between a ship and the State conferring its nationality upon it. An interpretation giving this requirement some content and teeth would strike a blow at flag of convenience fishing vessels, which, as will be pointed out below, are one of the causes of the current crisis in world fisheries. Unfortunately, the ITLOS failed to do so. It held that there were no prerequisites or conditions that had to be satisfied before a State granted its nationality to a ship: it was immaterial if the owner and crew of a vessel were not nationals of the flag State. It was sufficient for a genuine link if the flag State exercised effective jurisdiction and control over a vessel at the relevant time.[66] However, the ITLOS did strike a modest blow for coastal States trying to control the activities of foreign vessels fishing in their EEZs by holding that the bunkering of (i.e. supplying fuel oil to) foreign vessels within the EEZ fell within the jurisdiction of the

---

[63]   For more detailed critiques of the provisions of the LOSC relating to the conservation of living resources and associated and dependent species, see, inter alia, Barnes, above n 62, Burke, above n 61, and Christie, above n 61.

[64]   *Advisory Opinion*, above n 55, paras 182–218. The ITLOS also clarified, and thereby strengthened, the obligations of the flag States of foreign vessels fishing in the EEZ of a coastal State: see paras 109–40. The Advisory Opinion came too late in the production of this chapter to allow proper discussion of its content.

[65]   *The Volga Case (Russian Federation v Australia)*, Judgment of 23 December 2002, available at <http://www.itlos.org/fileadmin/itlos/documents/cases/case_no_11/Judgment.Volga. E.pdf> (last accessed 30 April 2015).

[66]   *The Virginia G (St. Vincent v Guinea)*, Judgment of 14 April 2014, paras 110 and 322–5, available at <http://www.itlos.org/index.php?id=171> (last accessed 30 April 2015). For detailed discussion, and criticism, of the approach of the ITLOS on this issue, see T. Scovazzi, 'ITLOS and Jurisdiction over Ships' in H. Ringbom (ed.), *Jurisdiction over Ships: Post-UNCLOS Developments in the Law of the Sea* (Brill, in press).

coastal State, something that had not been clear in the LOSC.[67] Thus, a coastal State may exercise some control over foreign fishing vessels by prohibiting bunkering in its EEZ, so reducing the amount of time they may spend fishing there, or it may require them to refuel at its ports, thus obtaining some tax revenues from the sale of the fuel.

The conservation obligations outlined above apply only to the EEZ and high seas. In relation to other maritime zones, the provisions of the LOSC relevant to the conservation of species are even weaker. In the case of internal waters and the territorial sea, apart from the general provisions of Part XII outlined below, the LOSC imposes no conservation obligations at all. The same is true of the continental shelf. Even though the continental shelf within 200 miles overlaps with the EEZ, the conservation obligations relating to the latter do not apply to those species that are considered to be part of the natural resources of the continental shelf, namely sedentary species.[68] Such species are defined as 'organisms which at the harvestable stage, either are immobile on or under the seabed or are unable to move except in constant physical contact with the seabed or the subsoil':[69] they include abalone, clams, mussels, various species of crustacean, sponges, coral and some of the organisms found around hydrothermal vents.[70] Only in the case of the Area, i.e. the seabed and subsoil beyond the limits of national jurisdiction, are there some specific conservation provisions. Article 145 stipulates that '[n]ecessary measures shall be taken ... with respect to activities in the Area to ensure effective protection for the marine environment from harmful effects which may arise from such activities.' To that end, the International Seabed Authority shall adopt appropriate regulations for, inter alia, 'the prevention, reduction and control of ... interference with the ecological balance of the marine environment ... and the protection and conservation of the natural resources of the Area and the prevention of damage to the flora and fauna of the marine environment.' The three sets of mining regulations adopted so far by the Authority contain only fairly general provisions aimed at protecting the marine environment and do not refer explicitly to the conservation of species.[71]

As mentioned earlier, Part XII of the LOSC, although headed 'protection and preservation of the marine environment', contains few provisions relating to the conservation of species. Taking the relevant articles in numerical order, Article 192 sets out a basic obligation on States parties to 'protect and preserve the marine environment'. Article 193 goes on to provide that States parties 'have the sovereign right to exploit their natural resources [which obviously include marine living resources] pursuant to their environmental policies and in accordance with their duty to protect and preserve the marine environment'. Even reading those provisions in the light of the

---

[67]   Ibid., paras 217–23.

[68]   LOSC, Art. 68.

[69]   LOSC, Art. 77(4).

[70]   See further J. Mossop, 'Protecting Marine Biodiversity on the Continental Shelf beyond 200 Miles' (2007) 38 *Ocean Development and International Law* 283, 291–2 and the literature referred to there. See also Joanna Mossop, 'Reconciling activities on the extended continental shelf with protection of the marine environment', Chapter 8 in this volume.

[71]   See further the regulations above n 30 and Michael Lodge, 'Protecting the marine environment of the deep seabed', Chapter 7 in this volume.

ITLOS dictum in the *Southern Bluefin Tuna* cases quoted earlier,[72] they are far too abstract and general to impose any meaningful obligations on States to conserve marine species. Perhaps only by causing serious harm to marine species could a State be said to be in breach of its obligations under those Articles.

The next provision in Part XII is Article 194(5), which stipulates that '[t]he measures taken in accordance with this Part [i.e. Part XII] shall include those necessary to protect and preserve rare and fragile ecosystems as well as the habitat of depleted, threatened or endangered species'. Article 194(5) does not protect marine species as such, but only insofar as they are part of 'rare and fragile ecosystems'. Even then, the scope of the obligation of States parties to protect and preserve such ecosystems is not clear. On one view the obligation relates only to the protection of such ecosystems from pollution since Article 194 is headed 'Measures to prevent, control and reduce *pollution* of the marine environment' (emphasis added) and the first four paragraphs of the article are explicitly concerned only with pollution. A broader view is that since Article 194(5) does not mention pollution at all, and refers to measures 'taken in accordance with this Part' (which include any taken pursuant to Articles 192 and 193) rather than 'in accordance with this Article', it requires the protection of rare and fragile ecosystems from any form of interference. In the *Chagos Marine Protected Area* arbitration, the tribunal, without discussing the matter in any detail, favoured the latter view.[73]

The final provision in Part XII that has some relevance to the conservation of species is Article 196(1). It provides that:

> States shall take all measures necessary to prevent, reduce and control pollution of the marine environment resulting from the use of technologies under their jurisdiction or control, or the intentional or accidental introduction of species, alien or new, to a particular part of the marine environment, which may cause significant and harmful changes thereto.

Among such harmful changes would be adverse effects on the health and populations of native species. It is not clear from the text of Article 196(1) whether the reference to the introduction of alien or new species is linked to 'resulting from', and therefore the obligation not to introduce such species applies only as a measure to prevent pollution, or whether such introduction relates to 'prevent, reduce and control', in which case there is an obligation to prevent, reduce and control the introduction of new and alien species unconnected to the prevention of pollution. While grammatically the former reading seems more plausible, the drafting history of Article 196(1) indicates that it is the latter interpretation that represents the true intention of the parties.[74] In some parts of the world, the introduction of alien and new species has had a significant impact on native marine species.[75] Such introduction has occurred in many cases after the LOSC

---

72    See text at n 55. See also *Advisory Opinion*, above n 55, para. 120.

73    Award, above n 53, para. 538. For further discussion of the scope of Art. 194(5), see Y. Takei, *Filling Regulatory Gaps in High Seas Fisheries* (Martinus Nijhoff 2013), 76–7 and literature cited there.

74    *Virginia Commentary*, above n 5, 73–6.

75    R. Balkin, 'Ballast Water Management: Regulatory Challenges and Opportunities' in R. Caddell and R. Thomas (eds), *Shipping, Law and the Marine Environment in the 21st Century* (Lawtext Publishing 2013) 137, 138–40.

entered into force. One of the main ways that alien species enter a marine environment is through the discharge of ballast water. It is therefore a matter of regret, and in the case of some shipping States arguably a breach of Article 196(1), that so few States parties to the LOSC have ratified the Ballast Water Convention,[76] which is designed to prevent the introduction of alien species through ballast water – indeed, the number of ratifications is not yet sufficient to bring the Convention into force.[77]

What has been the practical impact of the provisions of the LOSC relating to the conservation of species? As far as 'living resources' are concerned, it is no exaggeration to say that world fisheries are in serious crisis. According to the biennial reports on the State of World Fisheries and Aquaculture published by the FAO, for the past decade or more nearly 30 per cent of fish stocks have been over-exploited (a percentage that has trebled since the mid-1970s) and nearly 60 per cent of stocks have been fully exploited and therefore are at risk of over-exploitation without effective management.[78] Fishing has also had a serious impact on species other than fish, including smaller marine mammals, turtles and sea birds. Over 550 species of marine fish and invertebrates are listed as threatened in the IUCN Red List.[79] It would be simplistic to blame only the weak conservation provisions of the LOSC for this state of affairs – there are many other causes, including the over-capacity of many fishing fleets (fuelled by heavy subsidies), the use of flags of convenience, developments in technology, the use of non-selective fishing gear, short-termism in fisheries management because of pressure from the fishing industry, and lack of enforcement capability.[80] Nevertheless, while it would be impossible to show cause and effect, it is likely that the shortcomings of the LOSC are also a factor. Certainly, there has been widespread recognition that its conservation provisions are inadequate (even allowing for the framework nature of the LOSC), as shown by the subsequent adoption of a wide range of hard and soft-law measures to remedy those shortcomings.[81] Such measures have been adopted in a wide

---

[76] International Convention on the Control and Management of Ships' Ballast Water and Sediments (adopted 13 February 2004, not yet in force) (2004) 19 *International Journal of Marine and Coastal Law* 446.

[77] As at 5 June 2015, 44 States, representing 32.86 per cent of world shipping tonnage, had ratified the Convention, whereas for its entry into force the Convention requires ratification by 30 States, whose ships account for 35 per cent of world shipping tonnage (art. 18(1)). See IMO, Summary of Status of Conventions, available at <http://www.imo.org/About/Conventions/StatusOfConventions/Pages/Default.aspx> (last accessed 7 July 2015).

[78] See FAO, *The State of World Fisheries and Aquaculture 2014*, 7 and 37–41, available at <http://www.fao.org/3/a-i3720e/index.html> (last accessed 6 May 2015). See also T.J. Pitcher and W.W.L. Cheung, 'Fisheries: Hope or Despair?' (2013) 74 *Marine Pollution Bulletin* 506. They state that 70 per cent of all world fish populations are 'unsustainably overexploited (defined as fish biomass less than half of the biomass at MSY)' (508).

[79] Pitcher and Cheung, ibid, 510.

[80] See further, inter alia, C. Clover, *The End of the Line* (University of California Press 2006); C.-C. Schmidt, 'Economic Drivers of Illegal, Unreported and Unregulated (IUU) Fishing' (2005) 20 *International Journal of Marine and Coastal Law* 479; and WWF, *Poorly Managed Fishing* (available at <http://wwf.panda.org/about_our_earth/blue_planet/problems/problems_fishing/> (last accessed 6 May 2015).

[81] For reasons of space, no details of those measures can be given here. For a recent overview, see R. Churchill, 'Fisheries and Their Impact on the Marine Environment: UNCLOS

range of fora, including the FAO, CITES, CMS, UNEP's Regional Seas Programme and regional fisheries management organizations (RFMOs). One set of measures, the UN Fish Stocks Agreement, may be considered as having been developed within the framework of the LOSC.[82] While a self-standing treaty, the Agreement states that it is designed to implement effectively the provisions of the LOSC concerning the conservation and management of straddling fish stocks (i.e. stocks of fish that are found both in the EEZ and on the high seas or that migrate between the two) and highly migratory species (i.e. those species, such as tuna, that are listed in Annex I of the LOSC).[83] The Agreement is also to be 'interpreted and applied in the context of and in a manner consistent with' the LOSC.[84] The Agreement sets significantly stricter conservation obligations for the species with which it is concerned than the LOSC, including the use of the precautionary approach.[85]

In the past 15 to 20 years the international community has become increasingly concerned about threats to biodiversity beyond the limits of national jurisdiction. In 2004 the General Assembly, within the framework of its annual review of the LOSC and ocean affairs, set up an Ad Hoc Open-ended Informal Working Group on the conservation and sustainable use of marine biodiversity in areas beyond national jurisdiction.[86] One of the options being considered arising out of the work of the Working Group, and for which there appears to be considerable support from States, is the adoption of what would be a third implementation agreement.[87] The conservation of species would be a central element of such an agreement.

## 4.   PROTECTION OF HABITATS

Many marine activities have the potential to cause significant damage to marine habitats, with consequential adverse effects for marine life dependent on those habitats. Such activities include bottom and beam trawling; fishing by using explosives, often leading to the severe damage to or destruction of coral reefs; the exploitation of seabed mineral resources (including hydrocarbons, manganese nodules, polymetallic sulphides and ferro-manganese crusts); and the laying of cables and pipelines. One would therefore expect that the protection of habitats would be a significant concern of the ideal contemporary marine environmental treaty posited in the introduction to this

---

and Beyond' in M. Chantal Ribeiro (ed.), *30 Years after the Signature of the UN Convention on the Law of the Sea: the Protection of the Environment and the Future of the Law of the Sea* (Coimbra Editora 2014) 23, 34–47.

[82]   Above n 37.

[83]   Fish Stocks Agreement, Art. 2.

[84]   Fish Stocks Agreement, Art. 4.

[85]   Fish Stocks Agreement, Arts 5 and 6 and Annex II. See also text, above n 37.

[86]   UN General Assembly Resolution 59/24 (2004), para. 73.

[87]   UN General Assembly Resolution 68/70 (2013), paras 196–201. See further E. Druel, R. Billé and J. Rochette, *Getting to Yes? Discussions towards an Implementing Agreement to UNCLOS on Biodiversity in ABNJ* (2013), available at <www.iddri.org> (last accessed 6 May 2015); and G. Wright et al., *The Scores at Half-Time* IDDRI Brief No. 02/14, available at <www.iddri.org> (last accessed 6 May 2015).

chapter. In the case of the LOSC, however, its provisions dealing with the protection of habitats are very limited, there being only two provisions explicitly concerned with this matter. The first is Article 194(5), which stipulates that '[t]he measures taken in accordance with this Part [i.e. Part XII] shall include those necessary to protect and preserve rare and fragile ecosystems as well as the habitat of depleted, threatened or endangered species'. As discussed above, the arbitral tribunal in the *Chagos Marine Protected Area* arbitration found that this provision requires the protection of the habitats described from any form of interference, not simply from pollution. Nevertheless, the types of habitat to be protected are fairly limited.

The second way in which the LOSC addresses the protection of habitats is through provisions relating to the Area. Article 145 requires the ISA to adopt regulations to prevent interference by seabed mining with 'the ecological balance of the marine environment' and for the 'protection and conservation of the natural resources of the Area and the prevention of damage to the flora and fauna of the marine environment'. This terminology appears broad enough to include the habitats of the Area. In addition, Article 162(2)(w) and (x) authorizes the Council of the ISA to issue emergency orders to suspend mining operations in the Area in order to prevent serious harm to the marine environment and to disapprove areas for exploitation 'where substantial evidence indicates the risk of serious harm to the marine environment'. Such harm would appear to include damage to habitats. In implementation of its powers under Article 145, the ISA has adopted mining regulations that provide some protection for habitats in the Area from prospecting or exploration.[88]

Within the framework of its annual review of the LOSC and ocean affairs, the UN General Assembly has adopted, from 2004 onwards, a number of resolutions that call on States and regional fisheries management organizations to prohibit bottom fishing around vulnerable marine ecosystems (such as seamounts, hydrothermal vents and cold-water coral reefs) beyond the limits of national jurisdiction, unless conservation and management measures have been established to prevent significant adverse impacts on such ecosystems.[89] It is possible that in due course those resolutions will generate new customary international law in the same way as the General Assembly resolutions calling for a prohibition on high seas driftnet fishing, which were adopted before the entry into force of the LOSC and therefore outside its framework, are said to have done,[90] or will be regarded as an agreed interpretation of Article 194(5) of the LOSC. Further protection for habitats in areas beyond national jurisdiction will also be provided if the possible implementing agreement on the conservation of biodiversity beyond areas of national jurisdiction, referred to above, is adopted.

The very broad obligations in Articles 192 and 193 to 'protect and preserve the marine environment', discussed in the previous section, can be read to include the protection of habitats, although the obligations seem too general to be used in practice to restrain damage to habitats except in the most serious cases. Otherwise, the reality is

---

[88]   See further the regulations above n 30 above and M. Lodge, Chapter 7 in this volume.

[89]   UN General Assembly Resolutions 59/25 (2004), paras 66–7; 61/105 (2006), paras 80 and 83–7; 64/72 (2009), paras 113–17 and 119–27; and 66/68 (2011), paras 121–37.

[90]   See G.J. Hewison, 'The Legally Binding Nature of the Moratorium on Large-Scale High Seas Drift Net Fishing' (1994) 25 *Journal of Maritime Law and Commerce* 557.

that within the limits of national jurisdiction the LOSC provides no meaningful protection for habitats except in the case of 'rare and fragile ecosystems' and the habitats of 'depleted, threatened or endangered species'. Instead, most international law relating to the protection of habitats is provided by the CBD, the CMS and agreements concluded thereunder, and regional marine environmental treaties and commissions.

## 5.  PREVENTION OF MARINE POLLUTION

One would expect the ideal marine environmental treaty posited in the introduction to this chapter to deal with pollution of the marine environment, and that is indeed a major concern of the LOSC. There are, in fact, far more provisions in Part XII and elsewhere in the LOSC dealing with marine pollution than with any other marine environmental issue. In essence those provisions define pollution of the marine environment; identify six sources of such pollution; call on States parties to the LOSC to develop international rules and standards to 'prevent, reduce and control pollution' from each of those six sources; require States to legislate to implement such rules and standards and enforce that legislation; set the jurisdictional parameters for individual States to regulate marine pollution going beyond international rules and standards; and briefly address questions of liability and compensation. Those are all the issues with which one would expect the ideal marine environmental treaty to deal, and each is considered in turn below.

Turning first to the definition, 'pollution of the marine environment' is defined in Article 1(1)(4) of the LOSC as follows:

> the introduction by man, directly or indirectly, of substances or energy into the marine environment, including estuaries, which results or is likely to result in such deleterious effects as harm to living resources and marine life, hazards to human health, hindrance to marine activities, including fishing and other legitimate uses of the sea, impairment of quality for use of sea water and reduction of amenities.

This definition is based on one developed by two scientific bodies, the Inter-governmental Oceanographic Commission of UNESCO and the UN's Group of Experts on the Scientific Aspects of Marine Pollution.[91] At the time that the LOSC was drafted, there was no discussion as to whether the definition included noise, now recognized as potentially harmful to the marine environment, particularly to the well-being of cetaceans. It has been cogently argued that noise is a form of energy and is therefore covered by the definition.[92] Compared with what one would expect in a contemporary marine environmental treaty, the definition is deficient and outdated by containing no explicit precautionary element. That omission is understandable given the time at which

---

[91]   *Virginia Commentary*, above n 5, 753–4.

[92]   See H.M. Dotinga and A.G. Oude Elferink, 'Acoustic Pollution in the Oceans: The Search for Legal Standards' (2001) 31 *Ocean Development and International Law* 151; and K.N. Scott, 'International Regulation of Underwater Noise' (2004) 53 *International and Comparative Law Quarterly* 287.

the LOSC was negotiated and adopted.[93] Nevertheless, the phrase 'likely to result in … deleterious effects' can be interpreted to introduce some element of the need for precaution into the definition.

The LOSC identifies six sources of marine pollution and contains separate provisions dealing with each. Those sources are, in the order in which they are dealt with in the LOSC, land-based sources;[94] seabed activities subject to national jurisdiction;[95] activities in the Area, i.e. the seabed and subsoil beyond the limits of national jurisdiction;[96] dumping;[97] vessels;[98] and the atmosphere. In relation to each source, the LOSC requires States to 'prevent, reduce and control' pollution. This phrase is nowhere defined, and the scope of an obligation to 'prevent, reduce and control' pollution is on its face neither very clear nor helpful as the three terms are potentially conflicting: for example, it is possible to control pollution without reducing it; and 'prevent' may imply that there should be no discharges of pollutants at all, rather than controlled or reduced discharges. In using an identical phrase in its draft articles on the non-navigational uses of international watercourses and on transboundary aquifers, the International Law Commission, referring to the use of the phrase in the LOSC, explained that the obligation to 'prevent' relates to new pollution, whereas the obligations to 'reduce' and 'control' relate to existing pollution. The latter obligations reflect the fact that States are willing to tolerate significant pollution, provided that the State causing the pollution is making its best efforts to reduce the pollution to a mutually acceptable level. A requirement that existing pollution be abated immediately could, in some cases, result in undue hardship. On the other hand, failure of a State to exercise due diligence to reduce pollution to acceptable levels would be a breach of its obligations.[99] Given that the ILC refers specifically to the LOSC, it would seem reasonable to give the phrase 'prevent, reduce and control' pollution in the LOSC the same meaning and scope as the ILC does in its draft articles.

Turning next to the adoption of international rules and standards to prevent, reduce and control pollution, the LOSC requires such rules in respect of activities in the Area to be adopted by the International Seabed Authority.[100] The Authority has so far done so in relation to the prospecting for and exploration of seabed minerals, but not for commercial production, which has yet to begin.[101] In relation to the other sources of marine pollution, the LOSC calls on States to act through competent international

---

[93]   See further the section on principles above, text at n 33.

[94]   See further David Osborn, 'Land-based pollution and the marine environment', Chapter 4 in this volume.

[95]   See further J. Mossop, Chapter 8 in this volume.

[96]   See further M. Lodge, Chapter 7 in this volume.

[97]   See further D. VanderZwaag, Chapter 6 in this volume.

[98]   See further H. Ringbom, Chapter 5 in this volume.

[99]   International Law Commission, Draft Articles on the Law of Non-Navigational Uses of International Watercourses, Commentary on Draft Article 21, *Yearbook of the International Law Commission* 1994 vol II(2), 122; and Draft Articles on the Law of Transboundary Aquifers, Commentary on Draft Article 12, *Report of the International Law Commission on the Work of its 60th Session*, UN Doc. A/63/10 (2008), 38.

[100]   LOSC, Arts 209(1) and 145.

[101]   See further the regulations, above n 30 and M. Lodge, Chapter 7 in this volume.

organizations or diplomatic conferences. The nature of this obligation varies, depending on the source. The weaker obligation is in relation to land-based sources, dumping and the atmosphere, where the LOSC stipulates merely that States parties '*shall endeavour to establish* global and regional rules, standards and recommended practices and procedures' (emphasis added).[102] In the case of pollution from seabed activities within national jurisdiction and shipping, the obligation is stronger: here States '*shall establish*' international rules and standards (emphasis added).[103] In the case of pollution from land-based sources, any international rules and standards adopted shall take 'into account characteristic regional features, the economic capacity of developing States and their need for economic development'.[104] This is an early formulation of what has become known as the principle of common but differentiated responsibility,[105] and is its only appearance in the marine environmental provisions of the LOSC, with the exception of Article 194(1), which stipulates that States are to take all necessary measures to control pollution 'in accordance with their capabilities'.

The provisions of the LOSC calling for the adoption of international rules and standards have had little direct practical impact, apart from the Area. In relation to land-based sources, dumping and shipping, a wealth of global and/or regional rules had been adopted by the time the LOSC entered into force in 1994 and have continued to be developed since, but there is no evidence that the various international organizations and treaty regimes under which such development has taken place have been influenced by the provisions of the LOSC referred to above. For atmospheric pollution and seabed activities within national jurisdiction, some global and/or regional rules and standards have been adopted since the LOSC came into force, but again there is no explicit evidence that in doing so the States concerned were influenced by obligations in the LOSC.

The LOSC not only calls on States collectively to adopt international rules and standards to prevent, reduce and control pollution from each source, it also requires them individually to implement such rules and standards through their national legal systems, regardless of whether or not they are parties to the treaties or soft-law measures containing such rules and standards. Again the nature of the obligation varies, depending on the source of marine pollution. The strongest obligation is in relation to pollution from shipping. Here flag States 'shall adopt laws and regulations' to control pollution from their ships that 'shall at least have the same effect as that of generally accepted international rules and standards established through the competent international organization or general diplomatic conference'.[106] Almost as strong are the obligations relating to seabed activities within national jurisdiction, the Area and

---

[102] LOSC, Arts 207(4), 210(4) and 212(3).

[103] LOSC, Arts 208(5) and 211(1).

[104] LOSC, Art. 207(4).

[105] See further Y. Tanaka, Chapter 2 in this volume.

[106] LOSC, Art. 211(2). As to the meaning of the phrase following 'same effect', see International Law Association, 'Final Report of the Committee on Coastal State Jurisdiction relating to Marine Pollution' in *Report of the Sixty-Ninth Conference* (International Law Association 2000) 443. Note that coastal States may, but are not required to, adopt national legislation applicable to foreign ships that gives effect to international rules: see LOSC, Arts 211(4) and (5).

dumping, where States 'shall adopt laws and regulations' to control pollution from those sources that 'shall be no less effective than international rules, standards and recommended practices and procedures'.[107] Far weaker are the obligations that relate to land-based sources and atmospheric pollution, where the national laws and regulations that States must adopt need do no more than 'tak[e] into account' international rules and standards.[108] It is not known how far States have given effect to this set of legislative obligations in practice, and it would be a massive undertaking to try to discover the answer.

States are required to enforce the laws and regulations that they adopt further to the above obligations. The jurisdictional framework for such enforcement is largely in accordance with existing customary international law. Thus, in relation to activities taking place within national jurisdiction with the consent of the territorial State, which covers land-based sources, seabed activities within national jurisdiction and some forms of atmospheric pollution, enforcement is solely by the territorial State. The LOSC requires enforcement, but does not otherwise limit that State's discretion.[109] In the case of dumping, enforcement must be undertaken by flag States in respect of their ships, by coastal States in respect of dumping in their maritime zones, and by port States in respect of ships loading waste in their ports for the purpose of dumping.[110] Clearly there is the potential for overlaps of jurisdiction here. Article 216(2) addresses this issue by providing that no State 'shall be obliged … to institute proceedings when another State has already instituted proceedings'. In the case of national legislation relating to the Area, the LOSC is not wholly clear. It appears to imply that States may enforce their legislation,[111] while the Authority also has the power to enforce its own rules on which national legislation is based.[112]

With shipping the position becomes more complex and departs from customary international law in some significant respects. The traditional position continues to apply to flag States. They shall enforce their laws and regulations in respect of their ships, but may not arrest them in the ports and territorial seas of other States.[113] However, the LOSC develops customary law as far as coastal and port States are concerned. Coastal States' powers depend on the maritime zone in which suspected polluting foreign ships are found. In the territorial sea, a coastal State may undertake physical inspection of a foreign ship in innocent passage that is alleged to have violated that State's laws or applicable international rules and, where the evidence so warrants, arrest it and institute legal proceedings.[114] A coastal State has unrestricted enforcement jurisdiction where a foreign ship has engaged in 'wilful and serious pollution' because that renders the ship's passage non-innocent.[115] However, in those parts of the territorial sea, if any, that constitute straits subject to a right of transit passage, a coastal

[107]   LOSC, Arts 208(1) and (3); 209(2) and 214; and 210(1) and (6).
[108]   LOSC, Arts 207(1) and 212(1).
[109]   LOSC, Arts 213, 214 and 222.
[110]   LOSC, Art. 216(1).
[111]   LOSC, Arts 215 and 139.
[112]   LOSC, Arts 153, 162(2) and 165(2)(c).
[113]   LOSC, Art. 217.
[114]   LOSC, Arts 220(2) and 27.
[115]   LOSC, Art. 19.

State's enforcement jurisdiction is greatly constrained, and it may arrest a polluting ship only if the suspected illegal pollution causes or threatens 'major damage to the marine environment of the straits'.[116] Finally, in its EEZ a coastal State has a graduated enforcement competence, depending on the severity of the alleged illegal pollution committed by a foreign ship. At a minimum the coastal State may request certain information from the alleged offending ship. However, where the alleged violation of national legislation implementing 'applicable international rules' has resulted 'in a substantial discharge causing or threatening significant pollution of the marine environment', a coastal State may undertake physical inspection of the ship in the EEZ or territorial sea if the ship has refused to give, when requested, certain specified information or has given manifestly incorrect information. Only where the alleged violation has resulted 'in a discharge causing major damage or threat of major damage to the coastline or related interests of the coastal State, or to any resources of its territorial sea or exclusive economic zone' may the coastal State, if the evidence so warrants, arrest and prosecute the ship.[117]

The most radical innovation made to enforcement jurisdiction in respect of pollution from ships concerns port States. While Article 220(1) follows customary international law – although supplementing it as a result of the introduction of the EEZ – by providing that a State may arrest and prosecute a foreign ship in one of its ports which is alleged to have violated applicable international rules in that State's territorial sea or EEZ, Article 218 is truly innovative because it provides that a port State may also take legal proceedings against a ship in one of its ports that is alleged to have discharged polluting matter *outside* that State's territorial sea or EEZ 'in violation of applicable international rules'. The port State must not take legal proceedings where the discharge occurred in the internal waters, territorial sea or EEZ of another State unless that State or the flag State so requests. In practice, few port States appear to have enacted the necessary legislation to endow themselves with this radical new enforcement competence; and in the case of those that have, there appear to be no reports of such powers yet having been exercised.[118]

The LOSC not only deals with the adoption and implementation of international rules and standards, it also sets the jurisdictional parameters for individual States parties to regulate marine pollution by national law going beyond international rules and standards. The LOSC contains no restrictions on the legislative or enforcement jurisdiction of States in relation to measures to control pollution going beyond international rules and standards in respect of land-based sources, seabed activities within national jurisdiction, the Area or atmospheric sources. This is scarcely surprising given that the first and second of those sources, and to some extent the fourth, all relate to activities within national jurisdiction that cannot take place without the consent of

---

[116]   LOSC, Art. 233.

[117]   LOSC, Art. 220(3), (5), (6) and (8).

[118]   The USA has prosecuted a foreign ship for alleged pollution committed outside the maritime zones of the USA, but that was not on the basis of the LOSC as the USA is not a party and the prosecution took place before the LOSC entered into force: see S. Gehan, '*United States v. Royal Caribbean Cruises, Ltd.:* Use of Federal "False Statements Act" to extend Jurisdiction over Polluting Incidents into Territorial Seas of Foreign States' (2001) 7 *Ocean and Coastal Law Journal* 167.

the territorial State. The position in relation to dumping is almost the same, the only restriction imposed on a coastal State's freedom of action being that its power to 'permit, regulate and control' dumping in its maritime zones shall not be exercised until after it has engaged in 'due consideration of the matter with other States which by reason of their geographical situation may be adversely affected thereby'.[119]

The only source of marine pollution where there are significant constraints on States' freedom of action to enact legislation going beyond international rules is shipping. The existence of such constraints, which apply largely only to coastal States, reflects the international nature of the shipping industry. In the territorial sea the coastal State may prescribe pollution control measures for foreign ships in innocent passage going beyond international rules, provided that such measures do not 'apply to the design, construction, manning or equipment of foreign ships'.[120] Such measures must be publicized and must be non-discriminatory.[121] However, where the territorial sea consists of straits subject to the regime of transit passage, the coastal State is prohibited from adopting legislation going beyond international rules.[122] Within its EEZ, according to Article 211(6), a coastal State may adopt legislation going beyond international rules only where the latter are considered inadequate to provide sufficient ecological protection for areas of its EEZ that require special measures to prevent pollution for 'recognized technical reasons in relation to [their] oceanographic and ecological conditions as well as … the protection of [their] resources and the character of [their] traffic'. The exercise of this legislative power is subject to certain conditions. The coastal State must not impose design, construction, manning or equipment standards on foreign ships other than generally accepted international rules and standards; it must consult the International Maritime Organization (IMO) and obtain the latter's approval for its proposed measures; and it must not apply its legislation to foreign ships until 15 months after having first approached the IMO.[123] Within areas of the EEZ that are ice-covered where 'particularly severe climatic conditions and the presence of ice covering such areas for most of the year create obstructions or exceptional hazards to navigation' and pollution from ships could cause 'major harm to or irreversible disturbance of the ecological balance', Article 234 provides that a coastal State may unilaterally adopt legislation with significantly fewer constraints. The only conditions are that coastal State measures must be non-discriminatory and have 'due regard to navigation'.[124] There appear to be no instances yet of any State having made any use of the powers given by Article 211(6). However, there have been some instances of unilateral EEZ measures that do not conform to the conditions of Article 211(6). For example, following the *Prestige* disaster in 2002, when an elderly leaking oil tanker caused massive oil pollution after having being sunk by the Spanish authorities, France, Portugal and Spain all adopted laws, without any consultation with the IMO or having given foreign ships the requisite notice, banning from their EEZs single hull tankers

---

119   LOSC, Art. 210(5).
120   LOSC, Arts 21(1)(f) and (2), and 211(4).
121   LOSC, Arts 21(3) and 24(1)(b).
122   LOSC, Art. 42(1)(b).
123   LOSC, Art. 211(6).
124   LOSC, Art. 234.

carrying heavy fuel oil that were more than 15 years old; and Morocco made the entry of such ships into its EEZ subject to prior notification.[125]

The final significant matter concerning marine pollution with which the LOSC deals is the question of liability and compensation. Article 235 provides that States are liable for breaches of their international obligations concerning the prevention, reduction and control of marine pollution and calls on them to ensure that 'recourse is available' under their national legal systems for 'prompt and adequate compensation' in respect of pollution damage caused by those under their jurisdiction. Article 235 goes on to require States to co-operate to implement and develop international law regarding liability and compensation schemes. Before the entry into force of the LOSC, there was already in existence an effective and widely used international regime governing liability and compensation for damage caused by oil pollution from ships.[126] A similar scheme was subsequently adopted for damage caused by hazardous and noxious substances carried by ship, although it is yet to enter into force.[127] However, no international liability and compensation schemes have been adopted for other sources of pollution, nor does the writer know to what extent national schemes have been developed, as called for by Article 235.

Finally, to sum up briefly the significance of the LOSC for the prevention, reduction and control of marine pollution: the LOSC appears to have had little or no impact on the development of international rules and standards to prevent, reduce and control marine pollution, except in relation to activities in the Area, or on the establishment of international schemes dealing with liability and compensation for damage caused by marine pollution. It is not known, and it would be very difficult to discover, what influence the LOSC has had on the adoption of national legislation to control marine pollution. Undoubtedly, the most important contribution of the LOSC has been to establish a clear framework for the exercise of legislative and enforcement jurisdiction by States to prevent, reduce and control marine pollution.

## 6. CLIMATE CHANGE

Increased emissions of greenhouse gases over past decades have had and are continuing to have a number of adverse consequences for the marine environment, including

---

[125]   *Oceans and Law of the Sea: Report of the Secretary-General*, UN Doc. A/58/65 (3 March 2003), 21.

[126]   See International Convention on Civil Liability for Oil Pollution Damage (adopted 27 November 1992, entered into force 30 May 1996) 1956 UNTS 255, replacing an earlier Convention with the same title of 1969; and International Convention on the Establishment of an International Fund for Compensation for Oil Pollution Damage (adopted 27 November 1992, entered into force 30 May 1996) 1953 UNTS 330, replacing an earlier Convention with the same title of 1971.

[127]   See International Convention on Liability and Compensation for Damage in connection with the Carriage of Hazardous and Noxious Substances by Sea (adopted 3 May 1996, not in force) (1996) 35 *International Legal Materials* 1415.

greater acidification of sea water, higher water temperatures and rises in sea levels.[128] One would expect a contemporary marine environmental treaty to say something about climate change, even if only to acknowledge its existence and effects. The LOSC, however, makes no mention of climate change. That is scarcely surprising. While the greenhouse effect had been known about for a long time, climate change was not put on to the international political and legal agenda until the late 1980s, well after the adoption of the LOSC. Greenhouse gas emissions fall within the LOSC's definition of marine pollution and on that basis could be addressed through the provisions of the LOSC, including Article 194(1), which calls on States to take measures to 'prevent, reduce and control pollution of the marine environment from any source'; Article 222 on atmospheric pollution (discussed in the previous section); and the general obligation on all States to 'protect and preserve the marine environment' set out in Article 192 (also discussed earlier). However, in practice the control of greenhouse gas emissions and the adoption of possible measures to mitigate their effects are not being addressed within the framework of the LOSC at all, but in other fora. Thus, international efforts to control emissions are centred on the Conference of the Parties to the United Nations Framework Convention on Climate Change[129] and the International Maritime Organization (IMO) in the case of emissions from ships (a not insignificant source of greenhouse gas emissions); while mitigation measures, such as carbon sequestration and storage and ocean fertilization, are being addressed through the London Convention and some regional dumping regimes and the CBD.[130]

## 7. CONCLUSIONS

The LOSC was adopted at a time when international environmental law was less well developed than today and a number of significant principles as guides to the taking of action to protect the environment, including the precautionary approach/principle, sustainable development and the ecosystem approach, had yet to emerge. It was also a time when there was less awareness and knowledge of environmental matters, particularly global climate change and its consequences for the marine environment, and the existence and significance of deep sea environments such as seamounts, cold-water coral reefs and hydrothermal vents and their associated ecosystems and biodiversity. Nevertheless, even taking those factors into account, it is hard to resist the conclusion that the LOSC has serious deficiencies, especially when compared with the ideal contemporary marine environmental treaty posited at the beginning of this chapter. Above all, it has various normative weaknesses. It either contains no substantive norms of its own (for example, as regards marine pollution), mainly because of the prior existence of a variety of relevant treaties, or, where it does contain substantive norms, they are too imprecise, qualified or ambiguous to be effective (for

---

[128]   On ocean acidification, see further Tim Stephens, 'Ocean acidification', Chapter 20 in this volume.

[129]   Opened for signature 9 May 1992, entered into force 21 March 1994. 1771 UNTS 165.

[130]   On geoengineering, see further Karen N. Scott, 'Geoengineering and the marine environment', Chapter 21 in this volume.

example, as regards the conservation of species and the protection of marine habitats). A few of these normative deficiencies have to some extent been made good through the second implementing agreement, the Fish Stocks Agreement, concerning straddling and highly migratory fish stocks, and could be further made good if a third implementing agreement, on the conservation of marine biodiversity beyond the limits of national jurisdiction, were eventually adopted. The ITLOS (and other courts and tribunals) also have the potential to strengthen the environmental provisions of the LOSC through interpretation. Overall, however, it is a weakness of the LOSC that it does not provide more straightforwardly for its normative development. In this respect it compares unfavourably with many multilateral environmental treaties which have provided the conferences/meetings of their parties with the powers to drive those agreements normatively forward.

The LOSC calls for the development of international rules to prevent, reduce and control marine pollution and to provide for liability and compensation schemes where damage from pollution occurs. Although many such rules now exist, there is little evidence that the LOSC has had much influence on their adoption. The exception is in relation to mining in the Area, where the LOSC has established the International Seabed Authority and endowed it with the responsibility and powers to adopt and enforce rules to protect the marine environment from harm caused by deep sea mining, powers that the Authority has already exercised to a considerable degree. The LOSC also requires national laws to be adopted to implement international rules. What impact that aspect of the LOSC has had is not known and is a question that would benefit from further research.

The most significant contribution of the LOSC to the protection of the marine environment has been to establish a clear jurisdictional framework for the adoption and enforcement of national measures to protect the marine environment. Before the conclusion of the LOSC, this was a matter where there had been much uncertainty and conflict. It is probably also the case that the negotiation and existence of the LOSC have helped to raise awareness of marine environmental issues. That is also a significant contribution. How much influence the LOSC has had on the practice of States, both in concluding treaties relating to protection of the marine environment and in adopting national legislation, is uncertain, and a matter where further research would be desirable. Such research would contribute to our generally rather limited knowledge of the influence of treaties on the behaviour of States.

# 2. Principles of international marine environmental law

*Yoshifumi Tanaka**

## 1. INTRODUCTION

'The dark oceans were the womb of life: from the protecting oceans life emerged'.[1] As can be seen in the words of Arvid Pardo, the former Maltese Ambassador to the United Nations, a healthy marine environment provides a foundation for all life. Thus protection of the marine environment is of vital importance for mankind as a whole. As the International Tribunal for the Law of the Sea (ITLOS) stated in the *Southern Bluefin Tuna* cases, 'the conservation of the living resources of the sea is an element in the protection and preservation of the marine environment'.[2] By the same token, it can be considered that the concept of the marine environment also covers marine biological diversity.[3] Hence one can argue that the concept of marine environment covers not only the environment per se but also marine living resources and biological diversity.

In this regard, it is important to note that, like international law in general, international law governing marine environmental protection is not merely a mosaic of specific rules; rather it must be considered as a *system* governing international relations among States and other entities in respect of their activities both on and in relation to the oceans.[4] In order to properly understand the systemic aspects of the international law of marine environmental protection, it is important to examine the cardinal principles of the international legal system in this field. Thus, this chapter aims to explore principles of international law relevant to the protection of the marine environment.

As a preliminary consideration, some mention must be made of the role of 'principles' in the international law of marine environmental protection. Unlike rules, because of their open-textured and general character, the contents and legal status of principles remains less clear. As a consequence, the invocation of principles does not lead to a particular decision.[5] However, this does not mean that principles are less

---

\* I would like to thank Rosemary Rayfuse, the editor of this book, and the anonymous reviewer for their useful comments and suggestions on a previous draft of this chapter.

[1] United Nations General Assembly 22nd Session, First Committee, 1515th Meeting, A/C.1/PV.1515, 1 November 1967, 2, para. 7.

[2] The *Southern Bluefin Tuna* cases (New Zealand v. Japan) (Australia v. Japan), ITLOS Case Nos. 3 and 4, 27 August 1999, (1999) 38 *International Legal Materials* 1624, 1634, para. 70.

[3] See Article 194(5) of the UN Convention on the Law of the Sea.

[4] Cf. James Crawford, *Brownlie's Principles of Public International Law* (8th edn OUP, 2012) xviii.

[5] Cf. Ronald Dworkin, *Taking Rights Seriously* (Bloomsbury, 1997) 24 and 26.

important in the international law of marine environmental protection. Three functions of principles in particular merit highlighting. First, principles have a valuable role to play in setting out normative frameworks for integrating various legal, economic, social and political considerations into specific fields of international law. Second, principles provide guidance of the interpretation and application of relevant rules in situations of conflicting interpretation. Faced with competing norms, for instance, international courts and tribunals may make a judicial choice to lead to the preferred outcome in light of principles. Third, principles provide predictable parameters for environmental protection and, in appropriate circumstances, provide the orientation for the development of law.[6] In summary, principles characterize the essential nature of a legal system and systematize relevant rules within that legal system, while rules further elaborate principles and set out specific measures concerning the rights and obligations of States.

There is no generally agreed catalogue of principles governing marine environmental protection. Concerning environmental protection in general, for instance, Sands and Peel identify the following principles:

(1)   States have sovereignty over their natural resources and the responsibility not to cause transboundary environmental damage;
(2)   the principle of preventive action;
(3)   the principle of cooperation;
(4)   the principle of sustainable development;
(5)   the precautionary principle;
(6)   the polluter pays principle; and
(7)   the principle of common but differentiated responsibility.[7]

Paradell-Trius further adds the principles of non-discrimination, equitable use and concerted management of natural shared resources, intergenerational equity, and integration of environmental considerations into economic and development project.[8] IUCN's '10 Principles for High Sea Governance' refer to the principles of:

(1)   conditional freedom of activity on the high seas;
(2)   protection and preservation of the marine environment;
(3)   international cooperation;
(4)   science-based approach to management;
(5)   public availability of information;
(6)   transparent and open decision-making processes;
(7)   precautionary approach;

---

    [6]   Cf. Lluís Paradell-Trius, 'Principles of International Environmental Law: An Overview' (2000) 9 *Review of European Community and International Environmental Law (RECIEL)* 93, 95–7; Laurence Boisson de Chazournes, 'Features and Trends in International Environmental Law' in Yann Kerbrat and Sandrine Maljean-Dubois, *The Transformation of International Environmental Law* (Pedone and Hart, 2011) 11; Yoshiro Matsui, *International Law of the Environment: Its Fundamental Principles* (in Japanese) (Tokyo, 2010), 58 et seq.
    [7]   Philippe Sands and Jacqueline Peel, with Adriana Fabra and Ruth MacKenzie, *Principles of International Environmental Law* (3rd edn CUP, 2012) 187 et seq.
    [8]   Paradell-Trius, above n 6, 97–99.

(8)  ecosystem approach;

(9)  sustainable and equitable use; and

(10)  responsibility of States as stewards of the global marine environment.[9]

Whilst, in broad terms, the principles enumerated above may all be relevant to marine environmental protection, their legal status varies. Whilst some principles can be considered as a rule of customary international law or an emerging rule of the law, other principles seems to perform as policy guidelines.

It is beyond serious argument that the principle of *sic utere tuo ut alienum non laedas* (the no harm principle) reflects customary international law.[10] The same can be said of the principle of cooperation. Even though the customary law character of the precautionary principle remains a matter for discussion,[11] the Seabed Disputes Chamber of the International Tribunal for the Law of the Sea, in its advisory opinion, recognized that the precautionary approach 'has initiated a trend towards making this approach part of customary international law'.[12] Thus these three principles deserve serious consideration as part of customary international law or an emerging part of the law. Moreover, as will be discussed in part 5 of this chapter, the concept of sustainable development is increasingly enshrined in treaties concerning the protection of the marine environment and the conservation of marine living resources. Whilst the legal

---

⁹   This instrument is available at: <https://cmsdata.iucn.org/downloads/10_principles_for_ high_seas_governance___final.pdf> (last accessed 18 May 2015).

¹⁰   Patricia Birnie, Alan Boyle and Catherine Redgwell, *International Law and the Environment* (3rd edn OUP, 2008) 137; Sands and Peel, above n 7, 199.

¹¹   Although the tone of the arguments differs, some support the customary international law nature of the precautionary principle. See for instance James Cameron and Juli Abouchar, 'The Status of the Precautionary Principle in International Law' in David Freestone and Ellen Hey (eds), *The Precautionary Principle and International Law: The Challenge of Implementation* (Kluwer, 1996) 29, 29–52; Arie Trouwborst, *Evolution and Status of the Precautionary Principle in International Law* (Kluwer, 2002) 286; Philippe Sands, *Principles of International Environmental Law* (2nd edn CUP, 2003) 279; Owen McIntyre and Thomas Mosedale, 'The Precautionary Principle as a Norm of Customary International Law' (1997) 9 *Journal of Environmental Law*, 221, 235; Sands et al., above n 10, 228. By contrast, other writers are more cautious about accepting the customary law character of the precautionary approach. See for example, Pascale Martin-Bidou, 'Le principe de précaution en droit international de l'environement' (1999) 103 *Revue générale de droit international public (RGDIP)* 631, 658–65; Daniel Bodansky, 'Remarks' (1991) 85 *Proceedings of the American Society of International Law*, 413–17; Yukari Takamura, 'The Precautionary Principle in International Environmental Law: Its Current Status and Functions' (in Japanese), (2005) 104 *The Journal of International Law and Diplomacy*, 233, 250; X. Zhang, 'Issues Concerning Precautionary Principle in Environmental Protection: A Chinese Perspective' (in Japanese), 26 (2007) *Yearbook of World Law*, 62, 69–81; Matsui, above n 6, 135. In light of the uncertainty of the interpretation and application of the precautionary principle, however, as Birnie, Boyle and Redgwell argue, it may be said that: '[T]he position that it is, or that it is not, customary international law is too simplistic'. Birnie, Boyle and Redgwell, above n 10, 160.

¹²   *Responsibilities and Obligations of States Sponsoring Persons and Entities with Respect to Activities in the Area*, List of Cases No. 17, Advisory Opinion, 1 February 2011, 41, para. 135. The advisory opinion is available at: <http://www.itlos.org/> (last accessed 18 May 2015).

nature of the concept remains a matter for debate,[13] it could well be said that sustainable development is regarded as a cardinal concept in environmental protection in general. Given that considerable economic, social and technological differences exist in the international community, however, it is problematic that all States must undertake the same obligations of environmental protection. In this regard, an issue arises as to how it is possible to incorporate the differences of capability between States into relevant rules of international law. Here the concept of common but differentiated responsibility comes into play. All in all, it appears that in particular, these five elements, i.e. the 'no harm' principle, the precautionary principle, the concept of sustainable development, the concept of common but differentiated responsibility and the principle of cooperation, can be considered as pillars of the international law of marine environmental protection. This chapter thus focuses particularly on them.[14]

## 2. LEGAL FRAMEWORK OF THE LOSC CONCERNING MARINE ENVIRONMENTAL PROTECTION

Before turning to the examination of these principles, it is necessary to briefly discuss the legal framework for protecting the marine environment embodied in the United Nations Convention on the Law of the Sea (hereafter the LOSC).[15] The LOSC is the only global treaty which provides a comprehensive framework for marine environmental protection. Part XII of the LOSC is devoted to protection and preservation of the marine environment and rules concerning conservation of marine living resources are provided in other parts of the Convention, in particular, Part V governing the exclusive economic zone and Part VII relating to the high seas. It follows that the LOSC provides two distinct legal regimes governing the protection of the marine environment and conservation of marine living resources.

### 2.1  Principal Features of Part XII of the LOSC

Owing to the wide ratification of the LOSC as well as the degree of acceptance of various treaties on the protection of the marine environment, it could well be said that obligations of the protection of the marine environment embodied in Part XII of the LOSC have become part of customary law.[16] The noteworthy feature of the LOSC framework in Part XII is that it reflects a paradigm shift in international law relating to

---

   [13]   Vaughan Lowe, 'Sustainable Development and Unsustainable Arguments' in Alan Boyle and David Freestone (eds), *International Law and Sustainable Development, Past Achievements and Future Challenges* (OUP, 1999) 19, 23.

   [14]   In this chapter, the term 'principle' refers to a rule of customary international law or an emerging rule of customary international law. In other instances, the term 'concept' is used.

   [15]   Adopted 10 December 1982, entered into force on 16 November 1994. 1833 UNTS 3.

   [16]   Myron Nordquist et al., *United Nations Convention on the Law of the Sea 1982: A Commentary*, Vol. IV (Nijhoff, 1990) 36 et seq; Birnie, Boyle and Redgwell, above n 10, 387. For an overview of Part XII of the LOSC, see also Robin Churchill, 'The LOSC regime for protection of the marine environment – fit for the twenty-first century?', Chapter 1 in this volume.

the marine environment from the freedom to pollute to an obligation to prevent pollution. Traditionally, subject only to the few limitations imposed by customary international law, States had a wide discretion to pollute the oceans; and where environmental damage has been caused in another State's territory, the law of State responsibility came into play. Under the LOSC, however, the primary focus was *not* on obligations of responsibility for damage, but on general and comprehensive regulation to *prevent* marine pollution. In this sense, it can be argued that the cardinal principle of the legal regime for the protection of the marine environment was changed from one involving the discretion of States to the duty of protection by States.

This paradigm shift is reflected in both the generality and the comprehensiveness of the framework under the LOSC. It is general in the sense that the Convention establishes an obligation on all States to prevent marine pollution. To that end, Article 192 places a general obligation upon States to protect and preserve the marine environment. According to its ordinary meaning, the term 'marine environment' includes the ocean as a whole. Thus, the general obligation embodied in Article 192 covers the ocean as a whole, including the high seas and the seabed and subseabed in areas beyond national jurisdiction (the Area) as well as marine living resources. In this regard, it is of particular interest to note that the ITLOS Seabed Disputes Chamber in its advisory opinion of 2011 affirmed the *erga omnes* character of the obligations respecting protection and preservation of the environment of the high seas and the Area.[17] At the same time, the framework established in the LOSC is comprehensive in that it covers all sources of marine pollution. Indeed, LOSC Article 194(1) obliges States to take all measures necessary to prevent, reduce and control pollution of the marine environment from *any source*, using for this purpose the best practicable means at their disposal and in accordance with their capabilities. Likewise LOSC Article 194(3) provides that the measures taken pursuant to Part XII shall deal with *all sources* of pollution of the marine environment. Notably the measures taken in accordance with Part XII are to include those necessary to protect and preserve rare or fragile ecosystems as well as the habitat of endangered species and other forms of marine life under Article 194(5).

Although not an exhaustive list, the LOSC identifies six sources of marine pollution: land-based sources; sea-bed activities subject to national jurisdiction; activities in the Areas; dumping; vessel source pollution; and pollution from or through the atmosphere. Pollution is defined broadly in Article 1(1)(4) to include the release of 'substances or energy into the marine environment' which '[are] likely to result' in deleterious effects.[18] Thus, it is not just the activity or the substance that can be the object of regulation. The reference appears to imply that potential harmful effects on the marine environment can also be the object of regulation.

---

[17]   ITLOS, above n 12, 54, para. 180.

[18]   This provision defines 'marine pollution' as: 'the introduction by man, directly or indirectly, of substances or energy into the marine environment, including estuaries, which results or is likely to result in such deleterious effects as harm to living resources and marine life, hazards to human health, hindrance to marine activities, including fishing and other legitimate uses of the sea, impairment of quality for use of sea water and reduction of amenities'.

## 2.2   Principal Features of the Legal Regime concerning Conservation of Marine Living Resources and Biological Diversity under the LOSC

The legal framework for conservation of marine living resources under the LSOC relies on two basic approaches, namely, the zonal management approach and the species specific approach.[19] Under the zonal management approach, different rules apply to conservation of marine living resources according to each jurisdictional zone. According to the species specific approach, conservation measures are to be determined according to each category of marine species. In this regard, the LOSC specifies rules applicable to conservation of shared fish stocks,[20] straddling fish stocks,[21] highly migratory species,[22] marine mammals,[23] anadromous stocks,[24] catadromous species[25] and sedentary species.[26] However, it is becoming apparent that because of the lack of ecological consideration,[27] the two approaches under the LOSC are inadequate to properly conserve marine living resources. Further, the LOSC contains only two general provisions relating directly to conservation of marine biological diversity.[28] This is not surprising because environmental awareness about the conservation of marine biological diversity remained modest when the LOSC was drafted. As will be discussed in other chapters of this book, however, the conservation of marine biological diversity is becoming a matter of more pressing concern in the international law of the sea.[29]

---

[19]   For these two approaches, see Yoshifumi Tanaka, *The International Law of the Sea* 2nd edn (CUP, 2015) 234 et seq. See also R. Churchill, Chapter 1 in this volume.

[20]   LOSC, Art. 63(1).

[21]   LOSC, Art. 63(2).

[22]   LOSC, Art. 64.

[23]   LOSC, Art. 65.

[24]   LOSC, Art. 66.

[25]   LOSC, Art. 67.

[26]   LOSC, Art. 68.

[27]   Lawrence Juda, 'Considerations in Developing a Functional Approach to the Governance of Large Marine Ecosystems' (1999) 30 *Ocean Development and International Law* 89, 93.

[28]   LOSC, Arts 194(5) and 196(1).

[29]   See the chapters in Part IV of this volume. See also Jeff Ardron, Rosemary Rayfuse, Kristina Gjerde and Robin Warner, 'The Sustainable Use and Conservation of Biodiversity in ABNJ: What can be achieved using existing international agreements?' (2014) 49 *Marine Policy* 98; Rosemary Rayfuse and Robin Warner, 'Securing a Sustainable Future for the Oceans Beyond National Jurisdiction: The Legal Basis for an Integrated Cross-Sectoral Regime for High Seas Governance for the 21st Century' (2008) 23(3) *International Journal of Marine and Coastal Law* 399.

# 3.  THE PRINCIPLE OF *SIC UTERE TUO UT ALIENUM NON LAEDAS*

## 3.1  *Sic Utere Tuo Ut Alienum Non Laedas* as a Fundamental Principle in Environmental Protection

This chapter now turns to an examination, in the context of the protection of the marine environment, of the five specific elements identified at the outset. It is well established that no State has the right to use or permit the use of its territory in such a manner as to cause injury in or to the territory of another State. This is called the principle of *sic utere tuo ut alienum non laedas*, which means 'use your own property so as not to injure that of another' and is commonly referred to as 'the no harm principle'. The principle, first articulated in the *Trail Smelter* arbitration (1938–41),[30] was explicitly reflected in Principle 21 of the 1972 Stockholm Declaration[31] and Principle 2 of the 1992 Rio Declaration.[32] Principle 2 of the Rio Declaration states:

> States have, in accordance with the Charter of the United Nations and the principles of international law, the sovereign right to exploit their own resources pursuant to their own environmental and developmental policies, and the responsibility to ensure that activities within their jurisdiction or control do not cause damage to the environment of other States or of areas beyond the limits of national jurisdiction.

Whereas the older formulation articulated in the *Trail Smelter* arbitration dealt only with transboundary harm to other States, the formulation set out in Principle 2 of the Rio Declaration requires States to protect the environment beyond the limits of national jurisdiction. It seems to follow that the obligation not to cause environmental damage is no longer solely bilateral in nature but relates to the protection of the high seas or the global atmosphere.[33] The formulation of the Rio Declaration was echoed by the International Court of Justice (ICJ) in its *Advisory Opinion concerning the Legality of the Threat or Use of Nuclear Weapons*, stating that '[T]he existence of the general obligation of States to ensure that activities within their jurisdiction and control respect the environment of other States or of areas beyond national control is now part of the corpus of international law relating to the environment'.[34] As noted earlier,[35] the

---

[30]  The Arbitral Tribunal ruled that: '[U]nder the principles of international law, as well as of the law of the United States, no State has the right to use or permit the use of its territory in such a manner as to cause injury by fumes in or to the territory of another or the properties or persons therein, when the case is of serious consequence and the injury is established by clear and convincing evidence'. *Trail Smelter* Case (Canada v. USA), 3 *Reports of International Arbitral Awards* 1905, 1965.

[31]  Stockholm Declaration of the United Nations Conference on the Human Environment, (1972) 11 *International Legal Materials* 1416.

[32]  Declaration of the UN Conference on Environment and Development, UN Doc. A/CONF.151/26, (1992) 31 *International Legal Materials* 874.

[33]  Birnie, Boyle and Redgwell, above n 10, 145.

[34]  *Legality of the Threat or Use of Nuclear Weapons,* Advisory Opinion of 8 July 1996, [1996] ICJ Reports 241–2, para. 29.

[35]  See part 1 of this chapter.

principle is now considered part of customary international law and, as such, applicable to the protection of the marine environment. The principle is also embodied in Article 194(2) of the LOSC.

### 3.2    The Limits of the Principle of *Sic Utere Tuo Ut Alienum Non Laedas*

While the statement of the principle is easy, determining its precise content is less so. It is generally understood that the no harm principle is not absolute, but rather provides an obligation to exercise due diligence to avoid causing transboundary damage.[36] Indeed, the obligation of due diligence lies at the heart of the principle of *sic utere tuo ut alienum non laedas* since a State is not responsible for damage if it has exercised such due diligence.

However, 'due diligence' is an elusive concept and the degree of 'due diligence' may vary depending on the nature of specific activities, technical and economic capabilities of states, and the effectiveness of territorial control etc. In this regard, the view of the ITLOS Seabed Disputes Chamber deserves quoting:

> Among the factors that make such a description difficult is the fact that 'due diligence' is a variable concept. It may change over time as measures considered sufficiently diligent at a certain moment may become not diligent enough in light, for instance, of new scientific or technological knowledge.[37]

In light of its variable nature, it is less easy for an international court or a tribunal to determine the breach of the general obligation of 'due diligence'. Thus there is a need to explore an evolving standard of due diligence which can take account of changes in technology and environmental knowledge over time in order to enhance the effectiveness of the obligation of due diligence.[38]

A possible solution to this difficulty may be to link the obligation of due diligence with the obligation to apply best environmental practices. Indeed, the inter-linkage between these two elements was highlighted by the Seabed Disputes Chamber which stated:

> The adoption of higher standards in the more recent Sulphides Regulations would seem to indicate that, in light of the advancement in scientific knowledge, member States of the Authority have become convinced of the need for sponsoring States to apply 'best environmental practices' in general terms so that they may be seen to have become enshrined in the sponsoring States' obligation of due diligence.[39]

---

[36]    Phoebe Okowa, 'Procedural Obligations in International Environmental Agreements' (1996) 67 *The British Year Book of International Law* 275, 332; Riccardo Pisillo-Mazzeschi, 'The Due Diligence Rule and the Nature of the International Responsibility of States' (1992) 35 *German Yearbook of International Law* 9, 38.

[37]    ITLOS, above n 12, 36, para. 117.

[38]    On this issue, see Yoshifumi Tanaka, 'Reflections on Time Elements in the International Law of the Environment' (2013) 73 *ZaöRV (Heidelberg Journal of International Law)* 140, 161–5.

[39]    ITLOS, above n 12, 42, para. 136.

Admittedly, the Seabed Disputes Chamber did not provide a clear definition of the concept of best environmental practice. However, by way of example, the 1992 Convention for the Protection of the Marine Environment of the North-East Atlantic (hereafter the OSPAR Convention) defines this concept as 'the application of the most appropriate combination of environmental control measures and strategies'.[40] Appendix 1, paragraph 8 of the OSPAR Convention highlights the evolutionary nature of best environmental practices, providing that 'best environmental practice for a particular source *will change with time* in the light of technological advances, economic and social factors, as well as changes in scientific knowledge and understanding'.[41]

As articulated by the OSPAR Convention, the obligation to apply best environmental practices requires States to review the relevance of environmental measures taking into consideration technological, economic and social elements, and to apply the most appropriate measures. Likewise, the obligation to apply best available technologies may also provide an evolutionary standard of due diligence since, as the OSPAR Convention provides, what are 'best available techniques' for a particular process *will change with time* in the light of technological advances, economic and social factors, as well as changes in scientific knowledge and understanding.[42]

In summary, where States are under the obligation to apply best environmental practices and best available techniques, they are required to review and update their technology and practice with regard to environmental protection in the light of technological and scientific advances. If a State whose activities had caused serious environmental damage had failed to fulfil this obligation, it would be difficult to claim that due diligence had been exercised.[43]

However, the identification of best environmental practices and best available techniques may not, itself, be a simple matter. Given differing political, economic, ecological and technical conditions as between States and regions, a standard which represents best environmental practices in one region may not do so in another region.[44] Moreover, as long as technological capacity in developing States remains inadequate, it may be difficult for those States to use best available techniques and best environmental practices which would meet the most demanding regulatory requirements in the world. Thus technical assistance and capacity building to developing countries is increasingly important to properly effectuate the obligation to apply best environmental practices and best available techniques.[45]

---

[40]   Paragraph 6 of Appendix I of the OSPAR Convention (entered into force 25 March 1998), 2354 UNTS 67.

[41]   Emphasis added.

[42]   Emphasis added. Appendix I, paragraph 3.

[43]   Cf. Birnie, Boyle and Redgwell, above n 10, 148.

[44]   André Nollkaemper, 'Balancing the Protection of Marine Ecosystems with Economic Benefits from Land-Based Activities: the Quest for International Legal Barriers' (1996) 27 *Ocean Development and International Law* 153, 159.

[45]   The importance of cooperation in capacity building and transfer of marine technology to developing States was stressed in UN General Assembly Resolution, *Oceans and the Law of the Sea*, A/RES/64/71, adopted on 4 December 2009, seventh preambular paragraph. Rules concerning transfer of marine technology are provided in Part XVII of the LOSC. Generally on this issue, see for instance, David Freestone, 'Capacity Building and the Implementation of the

Further, it must be noted that, in essence, the breach of the obligation of due diligence by a State will only be at issue *after* environmental damage has arisen. However, given that damage to the environment may be irreversible, the traditional State responsibility oriented approach, by which States are only responsible for damage that has already occurred, is of limited value where the environmental protection is concerned. As the ICJ rightly stated in the *Gabčíkovo-Nagymarous Project* case, vigilance and prevention are required in this field.[46] Here the precautionary principle comes into play.

## 4.  THE PRECAUTIONARY PRINCIPLE

### 4.1   The Precautionary Principle in the Context of Marine Environmental Protection

The precautionary principle or approach characterizes a new dimension of international environmental law.[47] Whilst the definition of the precautionary approach varies depending on the instruments, in essence, it seeks to ensure the taking of early action in order to address serious environmental threats which may emerge in cases where there is on-going scientific uncertainty concerning proof of cause and effect. Principle 15 of the 1992 Rio Declaration on Environment and Development formulates this approach as follows:

> In order to protect the environment, the precautionary approach shall be widely applied by states according to their capabilities. Where there are threats of serious or irreversible damage, lack of full scientific certainty shall not be used as a reason for postponing cost-effective measures to prevent environmental degradation.

Although the precautionary principle is not explicitly provided in the LSOC, that principle has been incorporated in a growing number of international instruments dealing with environmental protection and conservation of marine living resources.[48] In the context of marine environmental protection, for instance, Article 2(2)(a) of the

---

Law of the Sea Convention: A View from the World Bank' in Myron H. Nordquist, Ronán Long, Tomas H. Heider, and John Norton Moore (eds), *Law, Science and Ocean Management* (Nijhoff, 2007) 313; Ariel W. González, 'Cutting a Gordian Knot?: Towards a Practical and Realistic Scheme for the Transfer of Marine Technology' in ibid., 345; Vladimir Golitsyn, 'Capacity Building: A View from the United Nations' in ibid., 381.

46   [1997] ICJ Reports 78, para. 140.

47   It appears that the terminology of 'the precautionary approach' or 'the precautionary principle' is not unified. On this issue, see Birnie, Boyle and Redgwell, above n 10, 155. In this chapter, the terms 'the precautionary approach' or 'the precautionary principle' are used interchangeably.

48   Rosemary Rayfuse, 'Precaution and the Protection of Marine Biodiversity in Areas beyond National Jurisdiction' (2012) 27 *International Journal of Marine and Coastal Law* 773, 774. For a survey of international instruments referring to the precautionary principle, see Trouwborst, above n 11, 63 et seq; Nicolas de Sadeleer, 'The Precautionary Principle in International Law' in Yann Kerbrat and Sandrine Maljean-Dubois, above n 6, 73 et seq.

OSPAR Convention places an explicit obligation upon the Contracting Parties to apply the precautionary principle.[49] Likewise Article 3(2) of the 1992 Convention on the Protection of the Marine Environment of the Baltic Sea (the 1992 Helsinki Convention) explicitly obliges the Contracting Parties to apply the precautionary principle as one of the fundamental principles and obligations.[50] In addition, Article 3(1) of the 1996 Protocol to the Convention on the Prevention of Marine Pollution by Dumping of Wastes and Other Matter (1996 London Protocol) places an explicit obligation upon the Contracting Parties to apply 'a precautionary approach to environmental protection from dumping of wastes or other matter [...]'.[51]

In the context of conservation of marine living resources, it is of particular importance to note that the precautionary principle is closely linked to the ecosystem approach which aims to conserve ecosystem structure and functioning within ecologically meaningful boundaries in an integrated manner. In fact, there is a trend that international instruments adopting the ecosystem approach refer to the precautionary principle at the same time.[52] For instance, Article 5(d) the 1995 Fish Stocks Agreement[53] obliges coastal States and States fishing on the high seas to 'assess the impacts of fishing, other human activities and environmental factors on target stocks and species belonging to the same ecosystem or dependent upon or associated with the target stocks'. Under Article 5(e), coastal States and States fishing on the high seas are obliged to adopt, where necessary, conservation and management measures for species belonging to the same ecosystem or dependent on or associated with the target stocks. Article 5(g) places a further obligation upon coastal States and States fishing on the high seas to protect biodiversity in the marine environment. At the same time, Article 6(1) of the Fish Stocks Agreement places a clear obligation upon States to apply the precautionary approach widely to conservation, management, and exploitation of straddling fish stocks and highly migratory fish stocks. In this regard, Annex II of the Agreement provides Guidelines for the Application of Precautionary Reference Points in Conservation and Management of Straddling Fish Stocks and Highly Migratory Fish Stocks.

To take another example, the 1995 FAO Code of Conduct for Responsible Fisheries (hereafter the FAO Code of Conduct) stresses the ecosystem approach as one general principle, by stating that: 'management measures should not only ensure the conservation of target species but also of species belonging to the same ecosystem or associated with or dependent upon the target species'.[54] At the same time, the Code of Conduct

---

49    See also Preamble and Annex V, Article 3(1)(b)(ii) of the OSPAR Convention.

50    Entered into force on 17 January 2000, 1507 UNTS 166.

51    Entered into force 24 March 2006, IMO Doc. LC/SM 1/6 14 November 1996, (1996) 36 *International Legal Materials* 1.

52    Yoshifumi Tanaka, *A Dual Approach to Ocean Governance: The Cases of Zonal and Integrated Management in International Law of the Sea* (Ashgate 2008) 82–7.

53    1995 Agreement for the Implementation of the Provisions of the United Nations Convention on the Law of the Sea of 10 December 1982 Relating to the Conservation and Management of Straddling Fish Stocks and Highly Migratory Fish Stocks (entered into force 11 December 2001), 2167 UNTS 3.

54    Para. 6.2. In addition, the Code of Conduct refers to marine ecosystems in many paragraphs.

clearly states that 'States should apply the precautionary approach widely to conservation, management and exploitation of living aquatic resources in order to protect them and preserve the aquatic environment. The absence of adequate scientific information should not be used as a reason for postponing or failing to take conservation and management measures'.[55] In light of the scientific uncertainty relating to the mechanisms of marine ecosystems, it appears logical that the ecosystem approach should be connected to the precautionary approach.[56]

## 4.2   The Limits of the Precautionary Principle

Despite its articulation in treaties, to date both the ICJ and ITLOS have been wary of applying the precautionary principle in international disputes.[57] In neither the *Nuclear Tests II* case[58] nor the *Gabčíkovo-Nagymaros Project* case,[59] did the ICJ made any explicit mention of the precautionary principle, although the applicability of this principle was at issue before the Court. In the *MOX Plant* case, Ireland argued that the manufacture of MOX fuel at Sellafield involved significant risks for the Irish Sea, since such manufacture would inevitably lead to some discharges of radioactive substances into the marine environment, both via direct discharges and through the atmosphere. According to Ireland, the precautionary principle was applicable as a rule of customary international law. However, ITLOS declined to prescribe the provisional measures requested by Ireland on the ground that there was no urgency of the situation in the short period before the constitution of the Annex VII arbitral tribunal.[60] It is true that ITLOS considered that 'prudence and caution require that Ireland and the United Kingdom co-operate in exchanging information concerning risks or effects of the operation of the MOX Plant and in devising ways to deal with them, as appropriate'.[61] However, no explicit mention was made with respect to the precautionary principle or

---

[55]    Para 7.5.1. See also paras 7.5.2 and 6.5.

[56]    See Stuart M. Kaye, *International Fisheries Management* (Kluwer 2001) 273–274; Lawrence Juda, *International Law and Ocean Use Management: The Evolution of Ocean Governance* (Routledge, 1996) 289; Tanaka, above n 52, 86–7.

[57]    Pierre-Marie Dupuy, 'Le principe de précaution et le droit international de la mer' in 'La mer et son droit' *Mélanges offerts à Laurent Lucchini et Jean Pierre Quéneudec* (Pedone, 2003) 205, 215–20; Nicolaars Schrijver, 'The Status of the Precautionary Principle in International Law and Its Application and Interpretation in International Litigation' in *Liber Amicorum Jean-Pierre Cot: Le procès international* (Bruylant, 2009) 241–53.

[58]    *Request for an Examination of the Situation in Accordance with Paragraph 63 of the Court's Judgment of 20 December 1974 in the Nuclear Tests* (New Zealand *v.* France) Case, [1995] ICJ Reports, 288. For New Zealand's argument on the precautionary principle, see 298, para. 34. See also Written Pleadings by New Zealand, 53–57, paras 105–10.

[59]    *Gabčíkovo-Nagymaros Project* (Hungary *v.* Slovakia), [1997] ICJ Reports, 7. For Hungary's argument on the precautionary principle, see ibid., 62, para. 97.

[60]    *MOX Plant case (Ireland v. United Kingdom)* (Provisional Measures) ITLOS Case No. 10 (3.12.2001), (2002) 41 *International Legal Materials* 405, 415, para. 81.

[61]    Ibid., para. 84.

approach in this case.[62] Again, in the *Land Reclamation* case,[63] ITLOS made no explicit reference to the precautionary approach, while the application of the precautionary principle was discussed by Malaysia.[64]

The customary status of the precautionary principle has similarly been a matter of consternation in the WTO. In the *Beef Hormones* case, for instance, the WTO Appellate Body took the view that: '[w]hether it [the precautionary principle] has been widely accepted by Members as a principle of general or customary international law appears less than clear'.[65] Similarly, the WTO Panel in the *EC-Approval and Marketing of Biotech Products* considered that the 'legal debate over whether the precautionary principle constitutes a recognized principle of general or customary international law is still ongoing. Notably, there has, to date, been no authoritative decision by an international court or tribunal which recognizes the precautionary principle as a principle of general or customary international law.'[66] This judicial reticence is not without reason. In fact, the precautionary principle is not free from difficulty with regard to its practical application at least in three respects.

First, the application of the precautionary principle may entail the risk of restricting economic and industrial activities of States. A difficult question thus arises as to how it is possible to reconcile environmental protection with economic interests. In response, there is a need to consider not only scientific factors but also, inter alia, the cost-effectiveness of proposed measures, their economic and social priorities, and their technical capabilities.[67] As a consequence, the decision-making process involved in the application of the precautionary principle is highly complicated. In essence, this process is a matter of national policy, not law. In light of this political nature, it is less easy for international courts to judge the validity of any national decisions respecting the application of this principle.

Second, the inter-temporality of the precautionary principle must be noted.[68] This principle aims to take preventive measures in order to respond to probable or potential

---

[62]    See also Separate Opinion of Judge Wolfrum, ibid., 428–9; Separate Opinion of Judge Treves, ibid., 431.

[63]    *Case concerning Land Reclamation by Singapore in and around the Straits of Johor* (Malaysia v. Singapore), Provisional Measures, Order of 8 October 2003. Case No. 12.

[64]    Request for Provisional Measures by Malaysia, 4 September 2003, para. 18; Presentation by Professor Schrijver, Verbatim Record, ITLOS/PV.03/02/Corr.1, 25 September 2003, 17. See also 19–20.

[65]    Report of the Appellate Body, *EC Measures Concerning Meat and Meat Products* (Hormones), WT/DS26/AB/R, WT/DS48/AB/R, 16 January 1998, 45–6, para. 123 (original footnotes omitted).

[66]    WTO Panel Report, *European Communities-Measures Affecting the Approval and Marketing of Biotech Products* (EC-Approval and Marketing of Biotech Products), WT/DS291/R, WT/DS292/R, WT/DS293/R, 29 September 2006, para. 7.88.

[67]    Laurent Lucchini, 'Le principe de précaution en droit international de l'environnement: ombres plus que lumières' (1999) 45 *Annuaire française de droit international (AFDI)*, 710, 727–9; Birnie, Boyle and Redgwell, above n 10, 163–4. Principle 15 of the Rio Declaration makes an explicit reference to 'cost-effective measures'.

[68]    Tanaka, above n 38, 165 et seq. The importance of time factor in the application of the precautionary approach is also stressed by Judge Cançado Trindade. Separate Opinion of Judge

risks which cannot be objectively identified through present-day science but which might create environmental damage in the future. However, 'risk' is a complex concept which comprises the probability and scale of harm, the causes and effects of harm on human health, processes in question and their interaction over time.[69] The assessment of potential risks which may trigger the application of the precautionary approach is often difficult to make since such risks may not be well known or it may not be possible to discover them through present-day science.[70] Non-foreseeability of potential risks can be considered an essential element of uncertainty with regard to the implementation of the precautionary approach. Moreover, since scientific knowledge and technology are constantly developing, appropriate preventive measures to respond to potential risks also change over time. The level of environmental risks which is socially acceptable also varies over time. In short, inter-temporality poses an inherent difficulty with the application of the precautionary approach.[71] Hence it seems difficult for international courts and tribunals to judge the breach of the obligation to apply the precautionary approach in a particular case.

Third, the precautionary principle contains no legal guidance about how to control the environmental risks. The application of this principle itself does not automatically specify measures that should be taken. In other words, the precautionary approach can be applied in different ways in different contexts. In light of the differentiated economic and technological capacities between States, not all States can adopt the same measures with regard to the implementation of the precautionary principle.[72] Thus it is less easy for international courts and tribunals to decide whether or not a State breached the obligation to apply the precautionary principle in a particular case.

It is not suggested, however, that the precautionary principle has no normative force. It can be used as an element of interpretation of existing rules of international law.[73] Indeed, in the *Pulp Mills on the River Uruguay* case, the ICJ explicitly stated that 'a precautionary approach may be relevant in the interpretation and application of the provisions of the Statute [of the River Uruguay]'.[74] The *Southern Bluefin Tuna* cases may be the case in point. Although ITLOS did not explicitly refer to 'the precautionary principle', it ruled that: 'the parties should in the circumstances act with prudence and caution to ensure that effective conservation measures are taken to prevent serious harm to the stocks of southern bluefin tuna'.[75] The Tribunal then went to state that although

---

Cançado Trindade in *Whaling in the Antarctic* (Australia *v.* Japan: New Zealand intervening), [2014] ICJ Reports, 21, para. 71.

[69]  Birnie, Boyle and Redgwell, above n 10, 153.

[70]  Pascale Martin-Bidou, above n 11, 647.

[71]  Tanaka, above n 38, 173.

[72]  Fernando Gonsález-Laxe, 'The Precautionary Principle in Fisheries Management' (2005) 29 *Marine Policy* 495, 496.

[73]  Yoshifumi Tanaka, 'Rethinking *Lex Ferenda* in International Adjudication' (2008) 51 *German Yearbook of International Law* 467, 489–93; Alan Boyle, 'Further Development of the Law of the Sea Convention: Mechanisms for Change' (2005) 54 *International and Comparative Law Quarterly* 563, 573–4.

[74]  *Case Concerning Pulp Mills on the River Uruguay (Argentina v. Uruguay)*, [2010] ICJ Reports 51, para. 164.

[75]  The *Southern Bluefin Tuna* cases, above n 2, 1634, para. 77.

it could not 'conclusively assess the scientific evidence presented by the parties', it did consider 'that measures should be taken as a matter of urgency to preserve the rights of the parties and to avert further deterioration of the southern bluefin tuna stock'.[76] In so ruling, ITLOS appeared to take account of the precautionary approach as an element of the interpretation of the requirement of urgency under Article 290 of the LOSC.[77]

The further issue to be considered is how it is possible to enhance the normative force of the precautionary approach. In approaching this issue, particular attention must be paid to the inter-linkage between the precautionary approach and environmental impact assessment (EIA).[78] The 1991 Convention on Environmental Impact Assessment in a Transboundary Context (the Espoo Convention) defines EIA as 'a national procedure for evaluating the likely impact of a proposed activity on the environment'.[79] EIA seeks to detect environmental risks and impacts of a proposed project before authorizing or funding the project, by introducing public scrutiny and elements of independence and impartiality to the decision-making process.[80] It seems difficult to detect potential risks that may trigger the application of the precautionary principle, unless an effective EIA is carried out before a proposed project has begun. Hence there may be some scope for arguing that where an obligation to apply the precautionary principle is provided for in a treaty, a State party whose activities cause serious environmental damage cannot deny the breach of the obligation if it has not conducted EIA effectively.[81] In this sense, EIA can be thought to provide a criterion to determine whether a State has fulfilled the obligation to apply the precautionary principle. By combining the precautionary approach with an obligation of EIA, to a certain extent, the normative force of that approach can be strengthened.[82]

---

[76]   Ibid., para. 80.

[77]   Separate Opinion by Judge Tullio Treves, ibid., 1645, paras 8–9. See also Separate Opinion of Judge Laing, ibid., 1642, para. 19; Separate Opinion of Judge *ad hoc* Shearer, ibid., 1650; Tullio Treves, 'Disputes in International Environmental Law: Judicial Settlement and Alternative Methods' in Yann Kerbrat and Sandrine Maljean-Dubois, above n 6, 290.

[78]   Tanaka, above n 38, 168 et seq.

[79]   (1991) 30 *International Legal Materials* 802, Article 1 para. (vi). For a recent study of the Espoo Convention, see Timo Koivuroiva, 'Could the Espoo Convention become a Global Regime for Environmental Impact Assessment and Strategic Environmental Assessment?' in Robin Warner and Simon Marsden (eds), *Transboundary Environmental Governance: Inland, Coastal and Marine Perspectives* (Ashgate, 2012) 323–42.

[80]   Birnie, Boyle and Redgwell, above n 10, 165. For a detailed study on EIA, see Neil Craik, *The International Law of Environmental Impact Assessment: Process, Substance and Integration* (Cambridge University Press, 2008). See also Robin Warner, 'Environmental assessment in marine areas beyond national jurisdiction', Chapter 14 in this volume.

[81]   *Pulp Mills on the River Uruguay* case, [2010] ICJ Reports, 83, para. 204. See also Tanaka, above n 38, 168 et seq.

[82]   Separate Opinion of Judge Cançado Trindade in the *Pulp Mills on the River Uruguay* case, [2010] ICJ Reports, 171, para. 96. Related to this, it must also be noted that EIA must be complemented by a monitoring system since there is a need to continue monitoring the ongoing environmental risks and impacts after a project has begun, *Pulp Mills on the River Uruguay* judgment, 83–4, para. 205.

## 5.  SUSTAINABLE DEVELOPMENT

### 5.1   The Concept of Sustainable Development in Marine Environmental Protection

The reconciliation between environmental protection and the need for development is a fundamental issue in the international law of the environment and the same applies to international law of marine environmental protection. Sustainable development is a key concept which seeks, in essence, to reconcile the need for development with environmental protection.[83] The basic idea of sustainable development is echoed by the ICJ in the *Gabčíkovo-Nagymaros Project* case, stating that: 'This need to reconcile economic development with protection of the environment is aptly expressed in the concept of sustainable development.'[84]

The basic idea of this concept can already be seen in the 1972 Stockholm Declaration of the UN Conference on the Human Environment, although the term 'sustainable development' was not used.[85] Later, the concept of sustainable development was given currency by the Report of the World Commission on Environment and Development (WCED), 'Our Common Future', in which the WCED defined this concept as 'development that meets the needs of the present without compromising the ability of future generations to meet their own needs'.[86] The reference to 'future generations' suggests that the concept of sustainable development is inter-temporal in nature.[87] It may be said that the concept of sustainable development reflects 'inter-generational equity.'[88]

---

[83]   For a study on the concept of sustainable development, see in particular, Philippe Sands, 'International Law in the Field of Sustainable Development' (1995) 65 *British Yearbook of International Law* 303; Nico Schrijver, *The Evolution of Sustainable Development in International Law: Inception, Meaning and Status* (Nijhoff, 2008); Duncan French, 'Sustainable Development' in Malgosia Fitzmaurice, David M. Ong and Panos Merkouris (eds), *Research Handbook on International Environmental Law* (Edward Elgar, 2010) 51–68. Furthermore, the concept of sustainable development is one of the subjects for discussion in the International Law Association. So far the ILA Committee on the International Law on Sustainable Development has made two reports on this issue, in 2004 and 2006, respectively. These reports are available at the website of ILA <http://www.ila-hq.org/> (last accessed 5 May 2015).

[84]   *Gabčíkovo-Nagymaros Project* (Hungary/Slovakia), [1997] ICJ Reports, 78, para. 140. See also *The Arbitration regarding the Iron Rhine Railway* case (Belgium and the Netherlands), 27 *Reports of International Arbitral Awards (RIAA)* 35, 66–7, para. 59.

[85]   See Stockholm Declaration Principle 13.

[86]   The World Commission on Environment and Development, *Our Common Future* (Oxford University Press, 1987), 43. See also International Law Association, New Delhi Declaration of Principles of International Law Relating to Sustainable Development. This document is available at: <http://www.ila-hq.org/en/committees/index.cfm/cid/25> (last accessed 5 May 2015).

[87]   Schrijver, above n 83, 208–9; Separate Opinion of Judge Cançado Trindade in the *Case Concerning Pulp Mills on the River Uruguay* (Argentina v. Uruguay), [2010] ICJ Reports, 185, para. 133.

[88]   Yoshiro Matsui, 'The Road to Sustainable Development: Evolution of the Concept of Development in the UN' in Konrad Ginther, Erik Denters and Paul J.I.M. de Waart (eds), *Sustainable Development and Good Governance*, (Kluwer, 1995) 53, 69.

Currently the concept of sustainable development or 'sustainable use' is being increasingly incorporated into treaties and non-binding documents relating to the conservation of marine living resources. For instance, the reference to 'sustainable use' can be seen in Articles 2 and 5(h) of the 1995 Fish Stocks Agreement.[89] Likewise the 1992 Convention on Biological Diversity (CBD) – which is applicable to marine biological diversity – also makes clear that one of its objectives is the sustainable use of components of biological diversity.[90] Concerning non-binding documents, the concept of sustainable development or sustainable use can be seen, inter alia, in Chapter 17 of Agenda 21 of 1992,[91] the 1995 FAO Code of Conduct,[92] the 1999 Rome Declaration on the Implementation of the Code of Conduct for Responsible Fisheries,[93] and the 2001 Reykjavik Declaration on Responsible Fisheries in the Marine Ecosystem.[94]

## 5.2　The Limits of the Concept of Sustainable Development

Despite its frequent reference in international instruments, this concept contains some issues which need further consideration with respect to its normativity.[95] A first issue pertains to the uncertainty of the contents of the concept of sustainable development. Whilst some writers attempt to enumerate relevant components of the concept, it appears that there is no uniform understanding on this matter. For example, P.-M. Dupuy considered that the concept of sustainable development would include the following 'principles':

(i)　　Principle of integration between the environment and development;
(ii)　　Precautionary principle;
(iii)　Principle of common concern of humanity;
(iv)　Principle of State sovereignty with State responsibility;
(v)　　Principle of common but differentiated responsibility;
(vi)　Principle of global partnership and cooperation;
(vii)　Polluter-pays principle; and
(viii)　Principle of participatory and informed decision making.[96]

To take another example, Sands and Peel selected four recurring elements of the concept of sustainable development:

(i)　　the need to preserve natural resources for the benefit of future generations (the principle of intergenerational equity);

---

[89]　See also FSA, Art. 5(a).

[90]　CBD, Art. 1. 1760 UNTS 79. Entered into force 29 December 1993.

[91]　Agenda 21, UN Doc. A/CONF.151/26 (Vol. II), 13 August 1992, para. 17.46; para. 17.75.

[92]　Code of Conduct for Responsible Fisheries, (FAO, Rome 1995) Art. 7.2.1.

[93]　Para. 12(n). The text of the Rome Declaration is available at the homepage of the FAO.

[94]　Preamble and para. 2. The text of the Reykjavik Declaration is available at the homepage of the FAO.

[95]　Tanaka, above n 52, 71–5.

[96]　P.-M. Dupuy, 'Où en est le droit international de l'environnement à la fin du siècle' (1997) 101 *Revue General du Droit International Public*, 873, 888–91.

(ii)   the aim of exploiting natural resources in a manner which is 'sustainable,' or 'prudent,' or 'wise' or 'appropriate' (the principle of sustainable use);

(iii)  the 'equitable' use of natural resources, which implies that use by one State must take account of the needs of other States (the principle of equitable use, or intragenerational equity); and

(iv)   the need to ensure that environmental considerations are integrated into economic and other development plans, programmes and projects, and that development needs are taken into account in applying environmental objectives (the principle of integration).[97]

Boyle and Freestone have extrapolated substantive and procedural elements of the concept of sustainable development from the Rio Declaration. The substantive elements are: (i) the sustainable utilization of natural resources; (ii) the integration of environmental protection and economic development; (iii) the right to development; and (iv) the pursuit of equity in the allocation of resources both within the present generation and between present and future generation (intra- and inter-generational equity). The procedural elements include public participation in decision-making and EIA.[98]

Although some common elements may be identified in the opinions of these writers, there remains considerable uncertainty as to the normative content of the concept of sustainable development. The normativity of each component and the inter-relationship between components are also a matter of discussion.[99] The concept of sustainable development seems to be no more than a label for a set of various components of international environmental law at a high level of abstraction. However, the label is itself not law.[100] Hence it seems debatable whether and to what extent this concept can legally constrain the behaviour of States.[101]

A second issue to be considered concerns the justiciability of the concept of sustainable development. In this regard, it is of particular importance to note that the concept of sustainable development ultimately requires a change in the quality and patterns of life. In the words of the WCED, 'In essence, sustainable development is a process of change in which the exploitation of resources, the direction of investments, the orientation of technological development, and institutional change are all in harmony and enhance both current and future potential to meet human needs and aspirations.'[102]

Considering that sustainable development is a matter of national policy of a State, it is hard to a priori determine specific measures to achieve sustainable development in international law. If this is the case, it will be less easy for international courts and tribunals to review the validity of national action by applying the concept of sustainable

---

97   Sands et al., above n 7, 207. See also Sands, above n 83, 338 et seq.

98   Alan Boyle and David Freestone, 'Introduction' in Boyle and Freestone, above n 13, 1, 8–16.

99   Cf. Lowe, above n 13, 26-30.

100   In this regard Lowe argued that: '[T]he concept of sustainable development is inherently incapable of having the status (whether as a result of logical necessity or otherwise) of a rule of law addressed to States […]'. Ibid., 26.

101   Ibid., 23–25.

102   WCED, above n 86, 46. See also Principle 8 of the Rio Declaration.

development.[103] Thus it is open to debate whether the concept of sustainable develop-ment itself can be an independent rule for adjudication. Without authoritative third-party decision-making, it would be hard to elaborate the content of the concept of sustainable development.[104]

It is not suggested, however, that the concept of sustainable development has no legal effect. In the *Gabčíkovo-Nagymaros Project* case, for instance, the ICJ ruled that new norms and standards, including the concept of sustainable development, had to be taken into consideration, and such new standards given proper weight.[105] Thus the Court held that considering the concept of sustainable development, the Parties together should look afresh at the effects on the environment of the operation of the Gabčíkovo power plant.[106] In so stating, the Court regarded this concept as a factor which should be taken into account in the process of decision making by the parties.[107] In conclusion, it may be argued that sustainable development can be considered as a factor orienting the behaviour of States and guiding proper interpretation of relevant rules in the judicial process.[108]

## 6. COMMON BUT DIFFERENTIATED RESPONSIBILITY

According to the concept of common but differentiated responsibility,[109] States take on different obligations depending on their socio-economic situation and their historical contribution to the environmental problem at stake.[110] This principle is clearly embodied in Principle 7 of the Rio Declaration which provides:

> States shall co-operate in a spirit of global partnership to conserve, protect and restore the health and integrity of the Earth's ecosystem. In view of the different contributions to global environmental degradation, States have common but differentiated responsibilities. The

---

[103] Boyle and Freestone, above n 98, 16; Alan Boyle, 'The *Gabčíkovo-Nagymaros* Case: New Law in Old Bottles' (1997) 8 *Yearbook of International Environmental Law* 13, 18.

[104] Günther Handl, 'Environmental Security and Global Change: The Challenge to Inter-national Law' (1990) 1 *Yearbook of International Environmental Law* 3, 25; Peter Malanczuk, 'Sustainable Development: Some Critical Thoughts in the Light of the Rio Conference' in Ginther, Denters and de Waart (eds), above n 88, 23, 50.

[105] [1997] ICJ Reports, 78, para. 140. The Arbitral Tribunal, in the *Iron Rhine Railway* case, echoed this view; above n 84, 29, para. 59.

[106] [1997] ICJ Reports, 78, para. 140.

[107] Boyle, above n 103, 18.

[108] Lowe, above n 13, 31 and pp. 34–5; Tanaka, above n 52, 75.

[109] For a detailed analysis of this concept, see Christopher D. Stone, 'Common but Differentiated Responsibilities in International Law' (2004) 98 *American Journal of Inter-national Law* 276; Duncan French, 'Developing States and International Environmental Law: the Importance of Differentiated Responsibilities' (2000) 49 *International and Comparative Law Quarterly* 35.

[110] Ellen Hey, 'Common but Differentiated Responsibilities' in Rüdiger Wolfrum (ed.), *Max Planck Encyclopedia of Public International Law* (2012) 1. Some argue that the differing capabilities of individual States are already taken into account in the obligation to use due diligence. Birnie, Boyle and Redgwell, above n 10, 136.

developed countries acknowledge the responsibility that they bear in the international pursuit of sustainable development in view of the pressures their societies place on the global environment and of the technologies and financial resources they command.

An early formulation of the concept of common but differentiated responsibility can be found in Article 207(4) of the LOSC which requires States to endeavour to establish global and regional rules and standards to prevent land-based marine pollution, 'taking into account characteristic regional features, the economic capacity of developing States and their need for economic development'. It is also to be noted that under Article 194(1) of the LOSC, States are obliged to take all measures to prevent marine pollution 'in accordance with their capabilities'.[111] In addition, Article 2 of the 1996 London Protocol obliges Contracting Parties to protect and preserve the marine environment from all sources of pollution and take effective measures, 'according to their scientific, technical and economic capabilities'.

In broad terms, the concept of common but differentiated responsibility creates two legal consequences: a 'dual standard' in favour of developing States; and the responsibility of developed States to assist developing States.[112] The notion of a 'dual standard' implies the application of different standards for environmental protection as between developed and developing States. Two types of dual standards exist.[113]

The first type is to provide different substantive obligations between developed and developing States. A striking example on this matter may be the Kyoto Protocol.[114] Under Article 3(1) of the 1997 Kyoto Protocol, only certain Annex I parties to the 1992 Climate Change Convention which are listed in Annex B of the Protocol – developed States and States in transition to a market economy – agreed to reduce their overall emissions of greenhouse gases by at least five per cent below 1990 levels in the commitment period of 2002–12.[115]

The second type is to provide a grace period for developing States. For instance, the 1987 Montreal Protocol allows certain developing country parties to delay their compliance with the control measures set out in Articles 2A to 2E of the Protocol for ten years by virtue of Article 5(1).[116]

Presently it is still open to debate whether the concept of common but differentiated responsibility is considered to have reached the status of customary international law.[117] Accordingly, a dual standard must be explicitly set out in treaties. If not, a dispute may arise with regard to the applicability of the concept of common but differentiated

---

[111]    See also R. Churchill, Chapter 1 in this volume.

[112]    Yoshiro Matsui, 'The Principle of "Common but Differentiated Responsibilities"' in Nico Schrijver and Friedl Weiss (eds), *International Law and Sustainable Development: Principle and Practice* (Nijhoff, 2004) 73, 81.

[113]    Ibid., 81–4.

[114]    Kyoto Protocol to the United Nations Framework Convention on Climate Change. Entered into force 16 February 2005. 2303 UNTS 148.

[115]    See also Ulrich Beyerlin and Thilo Marauhn, *International Environmental Law* (Hart and Beck, 2011) 67.

[116]    Montreal Protocol on Substances that Deplete the Ozone Layer. Entered into force 1 January 1989. 1522 *UNTS* 3.

[117]    Stone, above n 109, 299.

responsibility. In fact, the applicability of this concept was at issue in the Seabed Disputes Chamber's *Advisory Opinion with regard to Responsibilities and Obligations of States Sponsoring Persons and Entities with Respect to Activities in the Area* where the question was whether or not developing sponsoring States enjoyed preferential treatment as compared with that granted to developed sponsoring States under the LOSC and related instruments.[118] None of the general provisions of the LOSC concerning the responsibilities or the liability of the sponsoring State specifically provides for preferential treatment for developing sponsoring States. The Chamber thus concluded that: '[T]he general provisions concerning the responsibilities and liability of the sponsoring State apply equally to all sponsoring States, whether developing or developed'.[119]

However, a close reading of the Advisory Opinion does seem to indicate that the Chamber did not completely ignore the existing differences in capabilities between States. In fact, it held that the above observations did not exclude that rules setting out the direct obligations of the sponsoring State could provide for different treatment for developed and developing sponsoring States; and that the requirements for complying with the obligation to apply the precautionary approach may be stricter for the developed than for the developing sponsoring States.[120] It also stated that, '[w]hat counts in a specific situation is the level of scientific knowledge and technical capability available to a given State in the relevant scientific and technical fields'.[121]

On the one hand, the application of dual or differentiated standards might entail the risk of undermining the effectiveness of international rules respecting environmental protection. On the other hand, the existence of technological and economic gaps between States is an undeniable fact in the international community. Thus, assistance to developing States, which is the second consequence of the principle of common but differentiated responsibilities, is of particular importance. In this respect, the Seabed Disputes Chamber clearly stated that '[d]eveloping States should receive necessary assistance including training'.[122]

---

[118]   ITLOS, above n 12, 46, para. 152. See also Duncan French, 'From the Depths: Rich Pickings of Principles of Sustainable Development and General International Law on the Ocean Floor – the Seabed Disputes Chamber's 2011 Advisory Opinion' (2011) 26 *International Journal of Marine and Coastal Law* 525, 555 et seq; David Freestone, 'Responsibilities and Obligations of States Sponsoring Persons and Entities with Respect to Activities in the Area, Case No. 17. 'Advisory Opinion' (2011) 105 *American Journal of International Law* 755, 758.

[119]   ITLOS, above n 12, 48, para. 158. See also para. 159.

[120]   Ibid., 48, paras 160–61.

[121]   Ibid., 49, para 162. At the same time, the Seabed Disputes Chamber went to add that different treatment does not apply to the obligation to follow best environmental practice set out in regulation 33(2) of the Sulphides Regulations. Ibid., 48, para. 161. In this respect, see Yoshifumi Tanaka, 'Obligations and Liability of Sponsoring States Concerning Activities in the Area: Reflections on the ITLOS Advisory Opinion of 1 February 2011' (2013) 60 *Netherlands International Law Review*, 205, 217–18; French, above n 118, 558 et seq; Rosemary Rayfuse, 'Differentiating the Common? The Responsibilities and Obligations of States Sponsoring Deep Seabed Mining Activities in the Area' (2011) 54 *German Yearbook of International Law* 459, 474 et seq.

[122]   ITLOS, above n 12, 49, para. 163. See also above n 45.

## 7.   INTERNATIONAL COOPERATION

Damage to the marine environment is not necessarily constrained by man-made delimitation lines. Thus, the protection of the marine environment from pollution or over-exploitation of resources can hardly be achieved by a single State. Thus international cooperation is a prerequisite to marine environmental protection. The principle is embodied in many treaties and other international instruments.[123] By way of example, Principle 24 of the Stockholm Declaration states that 'Cooperation through multilateral or bilateral arrangements or other appropriate means is essential to effectively control, prevent, reduce and eliminate adverse environmental effects resulting from activities conducted in all spheres, in such a way that due account is taken of the sovereignty and interests of all States.'[124]

The importance of international cooperation in marine environmental protection was highlighted by the ITLOS in the *MOX Plant* case where the Tribunal confirmed that: '[T]he duty to cooperate is a fundamental principle in the prevention of pollution of the marine environment under Part XII of the Convention and general international law [...]'.[125] This view was echoed by the Tribunal in the *Land Reclamation* case between Malaysia and Singapore.[126] The ICJ, in the *Pulp Mills on the River Uruguay* case, has also stated that: '[I]t is by co-operating that the States concerned can jointly manage the risks of damage to the environment that might be created by the plans initiated by one or other of them, so as to prevent the damage in question [...]'.[127]

Multiple provisions of the LOSC require cooperation with a view to preventing various forms of marine pollution and conservation of marine living resources. For example, under Article 117, all States are under the obligation to cooperate with other States in taking such measures for their respective nationals as may be necessary for the conservation of the living resources of the high seas.[128] Article 197 places a clear obligation upon States to co-operate in formulating and elaborating international rules, standards and recommended practices and procedures consistent with the Convention, for the protection and preservation of the marine environment.[129] Where imminent danger exists, Article 199 requires States in the area affected as well as the competent international organizations to 'co-operate, to the extent possible, in eliminating the effects of pollution and preventing or minimising the damage' and to 'jointly develop and promote contingency plans for responding to pollution incidents in the marine environment'. The obligation to cooperate in the establishment of relevant rules is also indirectly incorporated into the LOSC provisions concerning land-based pollution,[130]

---

[123]   Sands et al., above n 7, 203.

[124]   See also Principle 27 of the Rio Declaration.

[125]   The *MOX Plant* case *(Ireland* v. *United Kingdom)* (Provisional Measures) ITLOS Case No. 10 (3.12.2001), (2002) 41 *International Legal Materials* 405, 415, para. 82.

[126]   The *Land Reclamation* case, above n 63, para. 92.

[127]   *Pulp Mills on the River Uruguay* (Argentina v. Uruguay), [2010] ICJ Reports 14, 49, para. 77.

[128]   See also LOSC, Art. 118.

[129]   The OSPAR Convention states in its preamble that Article 197 reflects customary international law.

[130]   LOSC, Art. 207 (4).

pollution from sea-bed activities subject to national jurisdiction,[131] pollution from dumping,[132] pollution from vessels,[133] pollution from or through the atmosphere,[134] physical investigation of foreign vessels,[135] and responsibility and liability.[136]

Nonetheless, the obligation to cooperate to conserve marine living resources or to prevent marine pollution does not, itself, automatically specify the measures that must be taken. As a consequence, it is hard to determine the breach of the obligation in reality. An essential issue thus arises how it is possible to secure international cooperation in marine environmental protection. In considering this issue, two points in particular merit highlighting.

A first point pertains to the role of international institutions as a mechanism for securing international cooperation in conservation of marine living resources and regulation of marine pollution. In this regard, the role of regional fisheries organs and treaty commissions created by environmental treaties merits particular notice. Whilst the mandates and functions of regional fisheries bodies vary, it is clear that regional fisheries organs facilitate institutionalization of international cooperation in conservation of marine living resources. Thus to be a member of regional fisheries organs can be considered as a fulfilment of the obligation to cooperate in conservation of marine living resources. In this regard, it is of particular interest to note that the Fish Stocks Agreement places an explicit obligation upon the Contracting Parties to be a member of a relevant regional fisheries organ. Article 8(3) of the Fish Stocks Agreement provides:

> Where a subregional or regional fisheries management organization or arrangement has the competence to establish conservation and management measures for particular straddling fish stocks or highly migratory fish stocks, States fishing for the stocks on the high seas and relevant coastal States shall give effect to their duty to cooperate by becoming members of such organization or participants in such arrangement, or by agreeing to apply the conservation and management measures established by such organization or arrangement. States having a real interest in the fisheries concerned may become members of such organization or participants in such arrangement.

However, this provision is binding only upon the Contracting Parties to the Fish Stocks Agreement.[137] It would be going too far to argue that States are obliged to be a member of regional fisheries organs or to accept the regulatory measures adopted by these organs in customary international law.[138]

---

[131]   LOSC, Art. 208 (5).
[132]   LOSC, Art. 210 (4).
[133]   LOSC, Art. 211 (1).
[134]   LOSC, Art. 212 (3).
[135]   LOSC, Art. 226 (2).
[136]   LOSC, Art. 235 (3).
[137]   Cf. Erik Franckx, '*Pacta Tertiis* and the Agreement for the Implementation of the Straddling and Highly Migratory Fish Stocks Provisions of the United Nations Convention on the Law of the Sea' (2000) 8 *Tulane Journal of International and Comparative Law* 49.
[138]   Tore Henriksen, 'Revisiting the Freedom of Fishing and Legal Obligations on States Not Party to Regional Fisheries Management Organisations' (2009) 40 *Ocean Development and International Law* 80, 82 and 91.

Commissions created by environmental treaties can also facilitate the securing of international cooperation between Contracting Parties through international supervision. One may take the OSPAR Commission as an example. The OSPAR Commission is equipped with an advance mechanism for supervision combined with a reporting system.[139] Article 22 of the OSPAR Convention obliges the Contracting Parties to report to the OSPAR Commission at regular intervals on: the legal, regulatory, or other measures taken by them for the implementation of the provisions of the Convention and on decisions and recommendations adopted thereunder; and the effectiveness of, and problems with the measures taken by them. Under Article 23 of the OSPAR Convention, the Commission is empowered to assess their compliance with the Convention and the decisions and recommendations adopted thereunder on the basis of the periodic reports referred to in Article 22 and any other report submitted by the Contracting Parties. Notably it can also decide upon and call for steps to bring about full compliance with the Convention and decisions adopted thereunder, and promote the implementation of recommendations, including measures to assist a Contracting Party to carry out its obligations.[140] The OSPAR Convention seems to represent an advanced model of international supervision for the protection of the marine environment.

A second point concerns the role of international courts and tribunals in securing international cooperation. In this respect, it is noteworthy that ITLOS has taken the opportunity to prescribe specific measures to secure international cooperation between parties to a dispute. In the *MOX Plant* case, in which the specific content of the obligation to cooperate was at issue, ITLOS unanimously ordered Ireland and the United Kingdom to cooperate in order to, inter alia: (a) exchange further information with regard to possible consequences for the Irish Sea arising out of the commission of the MOX plant; and (b) monitor risks or the effects of the operation of the MOX plant for the Irish Seas.[141] Likewise, in the *Land Reclamation* case between Malaysia and Singapore, ITLOS unanimously prescribed provisional measures requiring Malaysia and Singapore to cooperate in order to: (a) establish a group of independent experts to conduct a study on the effects of Singapore's land reclamation and to propose measures to deal with any adverse effects of such land reclamation; (b) exchange information on and assess risks or effects of Singapore's land reclamation works; and (c) implement the commitments noted in this Order.[142] The Parties subsequently established the expert group with the mandate to conduct a study to determine the effects of Singapore's land reclamation and to propose, as appropriate, measures to deal with any adverse effects

---

[139]   Reporting systems provide the foundation for international supervision. Yoshifumi Tanaka, 'Reflections on Reporting Systems in Treaties Concerning the Protection of the Marine Environment' (2009) 40 *Ocean Development and International Law* 146.

[140]   According to a commentator, 'measures to assist' could include administrative or technical or scientific help. Rainer Lagoni, 'Monitoring Compliance and Enforcement of Compliance Through the OSPAR Commission' in Peter Ehlers, Elisabeth Mann-Borgese, Rüdiger Wolfrum (eds), *Marine Issues* (Kluwer, 2002), 155, 161.

[141]   The *MOX Plant* case, above n 125, 416, para. 89.

[142]   The *Land Reclamation* case, above n 63, para. 106.

of such land reclamation.[143] To take another example, in the *Southern Bluefin Tuna* cases, the ITLOS prescribed provisional measures to order that:

(e)  Australia, Japan and New Zealand should resume negotiations without delay with a view to reaching agreement on measures for the conservation and management of southern bluefin tuna;

(f)  Australia, Japan and New Zealand should make further efforts to reach agreement with other States and fishing entities engaged in fishing for southern bluefin tuna, with a view to ensuring conservation and promoting the objective of optimum utilization of the stock.[144]

These provisional measures would contribute to securing cooperation between the disputing parties in the conservation of the southern bluefin tuna stock. Overall it can be argued that the ITLOS provisional measures have a valuable role to play in securing cooperation between disputing parties in the prevention of marine pollution and the conservation of marine living resources.[145]

## 8.  CONCLUDING REMARKS

The five elements discussed in this chapter – the 'no harm' principle, the precautionary principle, the concept of sustainable development, the concept of common but differentiated responsibility and the principle of cooperation – provide a foundation for setting out a normative framework for protecting the marine environment. Principles of the international law of marine environmental protection have great potential value in three respects:

● to integrate legal, economic and technological elements into a legal framework;
● to provide guidance in the interpretation and application of relevant rules; and
● to provide predictable parameters and the orientation for the development of law.

Needless to say, the effectiveness of the international law of marine environmental protection cannot be secured only by principles. In order to enhance the effectiveness of the law, further consideration must be given to two points.

The first point concerns the inter-linkage between principles, specific rules and institutional mechanisms for securing compliance. In order to effectuate principles, it is necessary to combine principles to specific rules. The inter-linkage between the

---

[143]  On 26 April 2005, Malaysia and Singapore signed a settlement agreement to terminate the case upon agreed terms. In the settlement agreement, the Parties agreed that the recommendations of the group of experts provided the basis for an amicable, full and final settlement of the dispute. *Annual Report of the International Tribunal for the Law of the Sea for 2005*, 24 March 2006, SPLOS/136, 10, para. 38; Tullio Treves, 'The International Tribunal for the Law of the Sea (2005)' (2005) 15 *Italian Yearbook of International Law* 255, 261–2.

[144]  The *Southern Bluefin Tuna* cases, above n 2, 1635–6, para. 90.

[145]  Further, see Yoshifumi Tanaka, 'Juridical Insights into the Protection of Community Interests through Provisional Measures: Reflections on the ITLOS Jurisprudence' (2014) 14 *The Global Community Yearbook of International Law and Jurisprudence* (forthcoming).

precautionary principles and EIA is a case in point. Another example is provided by the inter-linkage between the obligation of due diligence and the obligation to apply the best environmental practice and the best available technologies. Further, the effective compliance with relevant principles and rules must be secured by institutional mechanisms, including international supervision through treaty commissions. The interactive process among principles, specific rules and institutional mechanisms is of particular importance in international law governing marine environmental protection.

The second point pertains to the evolving nature of the international law of marine environmental protection. The marine environment, including marine living resources and biological diversity, is dynamic in nature and the situations surrounding the marine environment are constantly changing. Further, environmental knowledge and technology are developing rapidly. Thus an important issue arises how one can take account of change and development in the international law of marine environmental protection. Owing to their flexibility, principles have a valuable role to play in adapting the existing rules of international law in this field to new circumstances. Given that protection and conservation measures taken by States of today may affect the living conditions of future generations, inter-temporal considerations are of particular importance in the interpretation and application of the international law of marine environmental protection.

# 3. Actors and institutions for the protection of the marine environment

*James Harrison*

## 1. INTRODUCTION

States gathering at the 1972 Stockholm Conference on the Human Environment recognized, for one of the first times at the international level, the need to 'take all possible steps to prevent pollution of the seas by substances that are liable to create hazards to human health, to harm living resources and marine life, to damage amenities or to interfere with other legitimate uses of the seas.'[1] The conference sparked an explosion of international law-making. In the intervening 40 years, a large number of international instruments have been concluded to address the protection and preservation of the marine environment. In this period, international institutions have also emerged as significant actors in the negotiation, adoption and implementation of such instruments. The purpose of this chapter is to explore the role of such institutions in the development of the international legal framework for the protection of the marine environment. What types of institutions are involved in this field of law? How do they facilitate the development of the legal framework? How, if at all, do these institutions interact?

It is clear from the framing of these questions that the answers depend upon not only a formal legal analysis of the status and decision-making procedures of these institutions, but also an inquiry into the political dynamics of these processes. This is a topic that falls at the interface of international legal scholarship and international relations theory.[2] Thus, as well as explaining the legal role of such actors, the chapter will also draw upon recent developments in related disciplines in order to provide a deeper understanding of the role of actors and institutions in this field.

---

[1]  Stockholm Declaration on the Human Environment, 16 June 1972, UN Doc A/CONF.48/14/REV.1, Principle 7.

[2]  See generally I. Johnstone, 'Law-Making by International Organizations: Perspectives from IL/IR Theory', in J.L. Dunoff and M.A. Pollack (eds), *Interdisciplinary Perspectives on International Law and International Relations* (CUP 2013) 266. See also M. Hirsche, 'The Sociology of International Law: Invitation to Study International Rules in Their Social Context' (2005) *University of Toronto Law Journal* 891–939.

## 2.  THE MULTIPLICITY OF INTERNATIONAL INSTITUTIONS INVOLVED IN THE PROTECTION OF THE MARINE ENVIRONMENT

There is little doubt that the world's oceans are under significant threat. Given that the oceans and seas form an integrated whole, it is vital that the international community co-operates to protect and preserve the marine environment.[3] This need to co-operate is at the foundation of the international legal framework. As explained by the International Tribunal for the Law of the Sea (ITLOS), 'the duty to cooperate is a fundamental principle in the prevention of pollution of the marine environment under Part XII of the [United Nations Convention on the Law of the Sea (LOSC)] and general international law.'[4]

Today, most inter-state cooperation on the protection of the marine environment takes place through international institutions. Indeed, co-operation through international institutions is explicitly encouraged by the LOSC.[5] Yet, the drafters of the Convention refrained from establishing a single organization that was responsible for all aspects of oceans management. Rather, it was accepted that multiple institutions would be involved in developing the legal framework for the protection of the marine environment. The general reference to 'competent international organizations' throughout Part XII of the LOSC means that states can turn to a range of bodies to address these issues.[6]

When the LOSC was concluded in 1982, there were already a number of international institutions that were active in developing rules for marine environmental protection and the number of 'competent international organizations' has continued to grow. The following sections will give an overview of the range of institutional actors involved in this field, demonstrating the diversity of international institutions, at both global and regional levels. The survey goes beyond those institutions with a clear environmental focus to include a large number of sectoral bodies whose mandates encompass the environmental aspects of a particular activity. For many of these institutions, protection of the marine environment has come to play an increasingly central role in their work, even if it was not anticipated by their founders.

### 2.1  The United Nations

At the centre of the network of institutions involved in the development of the international legal framework for the protection of the marine environment is the United Nations (UN) itself. Although the UN Charter does not explicitly mention

---

³   See The World Commission on Environment and Development, *Our Common Future* (OUP 1987) 264–5.

⁴   *MOX Plant (Ireland v. United Kingdom)* (Provisional Measures, Order of 3 December 2001) ITLOS Reports 2001, 95, para. 82.

⁵   United Nations Convention on the Law of the Sea (adopted 10 December 1982, entered into force 16 November 1994) 1833 UNTS 3 (LOSC), Art. 197. See also Arts 118, 198, 199, 200, 201, 202, 204(1), 205, 207(4), 208(5), 209(1), 210(4), 211(1), 211(6), and 212(3).

⁶   Ibid.

the law of the sea or the protection of the environment, the UN has, since its inception, played a leading role in this field.[7] Based on its overarching competence for the codification and progressive development of international law,[8] the United Nations General Assembly (UNGA) has assumed the role of monitoring developments in this field. The UNGA adopts annual resolutions on the law of the sea and sustainable fisheries, which address a range of environmental issues, from marine pollution to the conservation of marine biodiversity.[9] As will be discussed later in this chapter, these resolutions play an important part in trying to promote cooperation and coordination between other institutions working in this field. Yet, the UNGA is also a key forum for discussing the negotiation of new rules to promote the sustainable development of the oceans. It is the United Nations which provided the institutional framework for negotiating the two implementing agreements on the deep seabed and straddling and highly migratory fish stocks, adopted in 1994[10] and 1995,[11] respectively. Furthermore, at the time of writing, negotiations on the adoption of new rules relating to the protection of biological diversity beyond national jurisdiction are being conducted through an open-ended ad hoc informal working group convened by the UNGA[12] and it is likely that these negotiations will lead to the adoption of another implementing agreement.[13]

It is not only the UNGA that addresses marine environmental protection. The UN sustainable development process, involving a series of global intergovernmental summits and conferences, has also identified oceans and marine resources as priorities for

---

[7]   See eg H. Corell, 'Oversight of the Global Ocean Regime: The Role of the United Nations' in D. Vidas and W. Østreng (eds), *Order of the Oceans at the Turn of the Century* (Kluwer 1999) 337; L. de la Fayette, 'The Role of the United Nations in International Ocean Governance' in D. Freestone, R. Barnes and D. Ong (eds), *The Law of the Sea: Progress and Prospects* (OUP 2006) 63.

[8]   Charter of the United Nations (adopted 26 June 1945, entered into force 24 October 1945) 1 UNTS xvi (UN Charter), Art. 10.

[9]   See eg UNGA Resolution 68/70 (9 December 2013).

[10]   Agreement relating to the Implementation of Part XI of the United Nations Convention on the Law of the Sea of 10 December 1982, (adopted 28 July 1994, entered into force provisionally 16 November 1994 and definitively 28 July 1996) 1836 UNTS 3.

[11]   Agreement for the Implementation of the Provisions of the United Nations Convention on the Law of the Sea of 10 December 1982 relating to the Conservation and Management of Straddling Fish Stocks and Highly Migratory Fish Stocks (adopted 5 August 1995, entered into force 11 December 2001) 2167 UNTS 3 (Fish Stocks Agreement).

[12]   The Ad Hoc Open-ended Informal Working Group on the Conservation and Sustainable Use of Marine Biological Diversity Beyond National Jurisdiction was first established by UNGA Resolution 59/24 (17 November 2004) UN Doc A/RES/59/24, para. 73. The first meeting took place in February 2006 and it has since met seven times, most recently in June 2014.

[13]   See UNGA Resolution 69/292 (19 June 2015) UN Doc A/RES/66/292. For discussion of the possible contents of such an agreement, see E. Druel and K.M. Gjerde, 'Sustaining Marine Life Beyond Boundaries: Options for an implementing agreement for marine biodiversity beyond national jurisdiction under the United Nations Convention on the Law of the Sea' (2014) 49 *Marine Policy* 90–97.

action,[14] leading to the adoption of a series of action plans,[15] which have in turn led to further developments in the legal framework. The process is now overseen by a high-level political forum for sustainable development, which will meet annually under the auspices of the UN Economic and Social Council and the UNGA.[16] Many commentators see the UN sustainable development process as a key catalyst for spurring further international cooperation to address the challenges facing the oceans in the future because of its ability to address a wide range of issues.[17]

There are also a number of other UN organs and bodies which address marine environmental protection issues as part of their broader mandate. One prominent example is the United Nations Environment Programme (UNEP), which was created as a follow-up to the Stockholm Conference on the Human Environment in 1972.[18] Although it is part of the United Nations, UNEP has its own dedicated secretariat, headquartered in Nairobi. UNEP has been described as 'the environmental conscience of the UN system'[19] and it is recognized as a 'major catalytic instrument for global environmental co-operation'.[20] The importance of UNEP is its ability to provide a forum for negotiations on environmental problems that fall outside the mandate of other intergovernmental organizations.[21] UNEP has had its critics in the past,[22] but the institution has recently been reformed to increase its prominence and effectiveness in international environmental affairs.[23] Its work on marine environmental issues has often been considered to be some of its most successful, in particular the role of UNEP in

---

[14]   See S. Lieberman and J. Yang, 'Rio+20 and the Oceans: Past, Present and Future' in A. Chircop, S. Coffen-Smout and M. McConnel (eds), *Ocean Yearbook 27* (Martinus Nijhoff 2013) 84.

[15]   Agenda 21 Action Plan, *Report of the United Nations Conference on Environment and Development* (3–14 June 1992) UN Doc A/CONF.151/26/Rev.l (Vol. I), Res I, Annex II, chapters 21 and 22; Johannesburg Plan of Implementation, *Report of the World Summit on Sustainable Development* (26 August–4 September 2002) UN Doc A/CONF.199/20*, Res 2, Annex, paras 30–36; UNGA Resolution 66/288 (n13) paras 158–77.

[16]   UNGA Resolution 67/290 (9 July 2013).

[17]   K. Toepfer et al., 'Charting Pragmatic Courses for Global Ocean Governance' (2014) 49 *Marine Policy* 85–6; M. Visbeck et al., 'A Sustainable Development Goal for the Ocean and Coasts' (2014) 49 *Marine Policy* 87–9.

[18]   UNGA Resolution 2997(XXVII) (15 December 1972).

[19]   UNEP, 'Information and Outreach' <www.unep.org/newyork/InformationOutreach/tabid/52263/Default.aspx> (last accessed 7 May 2015).

[20]   UNGA Resolution 37/219 (20 December 1982), para. 4.

[21]   See eg C.A. Petsonk, 'The Role of the United Nations Environment Programme (UNEP) in the Development of International Environmental Law' (1990) 5 *American University International Law Review* 351; V.P. Nanda, 'Environment', in C.C. Joyner (ed.), *The United Nations and International Law* (CUP 1997) 296–300.

[22]   M.A. Gray, 'The United Nations Environment Programme: An Assessment' (1990) *Environmental Law* 291–320; J. Hierlmeier, 'UNEP: Retrospect and Prospect – Options for Reforming the Global Environmental Governance Regime' (2001–2002) 14 *Georgetown International Environmental Law Review* 767–806.

[23]   UNGA Resolution 67/213 (21 December 2012) UN Doc A/RES/67/213. The reforms, inter alia, move towards universal membership. The very first meeting of the UN Environmental Assembly (UNEA) took place in April 2014.

promoting the regional seas programme.[24] It is also UNEP which is responsible for the Global Programme of Action for the Protection of Marine Environment from Land-based Activities.[25] Although it is a non-binding instrument, it is overseen by UNEP and its implementation is monitored through a series of ad hoc international meetings and conferences organized by the UNEP Secretariat.[26] UNEP has also been the forum for negotiating treaties dealing with specific sources of land-based sources of marine pollution, such as persistent organic pollutants[27] and mercury.[28]

## 2.2 United Nations Specialized Agencies

UN specialized agencies are established as autonomous institutions with a mandate to promote international cooperation in a specific area of inter-state relations.[29] The work of a number of UN specialized agencies touches upon marine environment protection. In particular, it is worthwhile noting the role of the International Maritime Organization (IMO) and the Food and Agriculture Organization of the United Nations (FAO).

The IMO has provided an important forum for the negotiation of key treaties relating to pollution from ships, such as the 1973/78 International Convention on the Prevention of Pollution from Ships (MARPOL Convention),[30] the 2001 International Convention on Harmful Anti-Fouling Substances,[31] and the 2004 International Convention on Ballast Water Management.[32] These treaties create a legal framework addressing almost all types of vessel-source pollution. The IMO's Marine Environment Protection Committee (MEPC) is charged with overseeing and updating the technical regulations found in the Annexes to the MARPOL Convention,[33] as well as other treaties related to the protection of the marine environment.[34] Often, the binding rules contained in these treaties are complemented by guidance also negotiated through the MEPC. In light of

---

[24]   See P. Hulm, 'The Regional Seas Program: What Fate for UNEP's Crown Jewels?' (1983) 12 *Ambio* 2–13.

[25]   See <http://unep.org/gpa/About/CoordinationOffice.asp> (last accessed 27 May 2015). Land-based sources of marine pollution are addressed in David Osborn, 'Land-based pollution and the marine environment', Chapter 4 in this volume.

[26]   The most recent review took place in 2012; see Report of the Third Session of the Intergovernmental Review Meeting on the Implementation of the Global Programme of Action for the Protection of the Marine Environment from Land-based Activities, Document UNEP/GPA/IGR.3/6 (26 January 2012).

[27]   Stockholm Convention on Persistent Organic Pollutants (adopted 22 May 2001, entered into force 17 May 2004) 2256 UNTS 119.

[28]   Minamata Convention on Mercury, adopted 10 October 2013, text of the treaty available at <https://treaties.un.org/doc/Treaties/2013/10/20131010%2011-16%20AM/CTC-XXVII-17.pdf> (last accessed 7 May 2015).

[29]   See F.L. Kirgis, 'Specialized Law-making' in C.C. Joyner (ed.), *The United Nations and International Law* (CUP 1997) 65–94.

[30]   Convention adopted 2 November 1973, Protocol adopted 17 February 1978, entered into force 2 October 1983, 1340 UNTS 184; 1340 UNTS 61 (also known as MARPOL 73/78).

[31]   Adopted 5 October 2001, entered into force 17 September 2008, 1833 UNTS 397.

[32]   Adopted 13 February 2004. Australian Treaties Library [2005] ATNIF 18.

[33]   MARPOL, above n 30, Art. 16(2).

[34]   See discussion below in section 3.1.

its contribution to shipping regulation, the MEPC has been described as 'one of the unsung heroes of our time' in relation to its work on environmental protection.[35] Indeed, the IMO has moved beyond the regulation of traditional sources of pollution from ships, such as oil or other hazardous substances, to address other marine environmental threats from shipping such as noise pollution.[36]

The FAO has similarly provided a forum for negotiating treaties related to the conservation of marine living resources, including the 1993 Agreement to Promote Compliance with International Conservation and Management by Fishing Vessels on the High Seas[37] and the 2009 Agreement on Port State Measures to Prevent, Deter and Eliminate Illegal, Unreported and Unregulated Fishing.[38] The FAO has also been a catalyst for the creation of regional fisheries treaties, which regulate particular fisheries. The Regional Committee for Fisheries, the General Fisheries Committee for the Mediterranean, the Indian Ocean Tuna Commission, and the Asia-Pacific Fisheries Commission were all established by treaties negotiated under the auspices of the FAO and adopted under Article XIV of the FAO Constitution. In addition, the FAO has used non-binding instruments as a means to address certain challenges in the sustainable use of marine living resources. The Code of Conduct on Responsible Fisheries is a self-standing non-binding instrument, which establishes principles for the elaboration of national and international policies for sustainable fishing.[39] Implementation of the Code is monitored through the Fisheries Committee of the FAO.[40] The Code is also supported by the elaboration of further technical guidance and action plans on key topics, which go beyond the sustainable use of fish stocks to include the wider environmental impact of fishing, such as reducing by-catch.[41]

## 2.3   The International Seabed Authority

The International Seabed Authority (ISA) is established by the LOSC to oversee the seabed mining regime under Part XI of the Convention.[42] The ISA is different from many other international institutions because it has a mandate to adopt rules, regulations and procedures relating to deep seabed resources and to apply them directly to contractors operating in the Area. As part of that mandate, the ISA has a duty to take

---

[35]   L. de la Fayette, 'The Marine Environment Protection Committee: The Conjunction of the Law of the Sea and International Environmental Law' (2001) 16 *International Journal of Marine and Coastal Law* 155–238, 158.

[36]   Guidelines for the Reduction of Underwater Noise from Commercial Shipping to Address Adverse Impacts on Marine Life (7 April 2014) IMO Doc MEPC.1/Circ.833.

[37]   Adopted 24 November 1993, entered into force 24 April 2003, 2221 UNTS 91.

[38]   Adopted in the 36th FAO Conference on 22 November 2009, FAO Doc C 2009/LIM/11 Rev.1.

[39]   Adopted 31 October 1995, FAO Doc. 95/20/Rev/1.

[40]   See G. Moore, 'The Code of Conduct on Responsible Fisheries' in E. Hey (ed.), *Developments in International Fisheries Law* (Kluwer International 1999) 92.

[41]   FAO, *International Guidelines on Bycatch Management and Reduction of Discards* (2011) <http://www.fao.org/docrep/015/ba0022t/ba0022t00.pdf> (last accessed 12 May 2015).

[42]   LOSC, Art. 157.

into account the protection of the seabed environment.[43] Indeed, the ISA has actively promoted key environmental principles in the seabed mining regime, including the precautionary approach[44] and environmental impact assessment.[45] Given our relative lack of knowledge concerning the deep sea environment, the Authority has also sponsored the conduct of scientific research into the deep seabed ecosystems, which led to the adoption of the Clarion-Clipperton Zone Environmental Management Plan (EMP) in 2012.[46] Amongst other things, the EMP calls for the creation of nine protected areas covering a range of deep seabed habitats.

Unusually for an international institution, the ISA also has the power to independently monitor the activities of operators within the Area[47] and to enforce the rules through court proceedings[48] or through emergency orders in order to prevent serious harm to the marine environment.[49]

## 2.4　Regional Fisheries Management Organizations

In the field of fisheries, states often choose to co-operate through regional fisheries management organizations (RFMOS).[50] Indeed the Fish Stocks Agreement mandates states to enter into negotiations to establish such bodies if they do not already exist.[51] Recent practice illustrates that many RFMOs have come to address the wider impacts

---

[43]　LOSC, Art. 145. See generally T. Scovazzi, 'Mining, Protection of the Environment, Scientific Research and Bioprospecting' (2004) 23 *International Journal of Marine and Coastal Law* 383–410; J. Harrison, *Making the Law of the Sea* (CUP 2011) 137–40.

[44]　See Regulations on Prospecting and Exploration for Polymetallic Nodules in the Area (adopted 13 July 2000, as amended July 2013) ISBA/6/A/18 (4 October 2000), Regulations 2(2), 5(1), 31(2), 31(5); Regulations on prospecting and exploration for polymetallic sulphides in the Area (adopted 7 May 2010) ISBA/16/A/12/Rev.1 (15 November 2010), Regulations 2(2), 5(1), 33(2), 33(5); Regulations on Prospecting and Exploration for Cobalt-rich Ferromanganese Crusts in the Area (adopted 27 July 2012) ISBA/18/A/11 (22 October 2012), Regulations 2(2), 5(1), 33(2), 33(5).

[45]　See ibid, Regulations on Prospecting and Exploration for Polymetallic Nodules in the Area (as amended July 2013), Regulations 31(6) 32(1); Regulations on prospecting and exploration for polymetallic sulphides in the Area, Regulations 20(1)(c), 33(6), 34(1); Regulations on Prospecting and Exploration for Cobalt-rich Ferromanganese Crusts in the Area, Regulations 34(1), 33(6).

[46]　Decision of the Council relating to an environmental management plan of the Clarion-Clipperton Zone, (26 July 2012) ISBA/18/C/22. See also Implementation of the environmental management plan for the Clarion-Clipperton Fracture Zone and development of other environmental management plans in the Area (3 March 2015) ISBA/21/LTC/9/Rev.1.

[47]　LOSC, Art. 162(2)(l).

[48]　LOSC, Art. 162(2)(u).

[49]　LOSC, Art. 162(2)(w). See also Regulations on Prospecting and Exploration for Polymetallic Nodules in the Area (n44), Regulation 32(6). Indeed, the Regulations arguably go beyond the Convention and they allow the Secretary-General to take immediate action pending a decision of the Council; Regulations on Prospecting and Exploration for Polymetallic Nodules in the Area, Regulation 32(2).

[50]　The LOSC itself encourages the establishment of RFMOs; see LOSC, Art. 118.

[51]　Fish Stocks Agreement, Art. 8(5).

of fishing on marine biodiversity as part of their regulatory role,[52] in part in response to the provisions of the Fish Stocks Agreement, as well as the Code of Conduct on Responsible Fisheries.

## 2.5   Environmental Treaty Bodies

Many individual treaties on the prevention of pollution of the marine environment also create their own governing bodies, often referred to as a Conference of the Parties (COP), which have powers to oversee the implementation of the treaty commitments. Examples include the Convention on Biological Diversity (CBD),[53] the Convention on International Trade in Endangered Species (CITES),[54] and the Convention on Migratory Species (CMS).[55] These institutions provide a forum for the further development of the treaty regime. COPS are often the source of non-binding instruments designed to assist parties in the implementation of the treaty. For example, the CBD COP is charged with, inter alia, '[considering and undertaking] any additional action that may be required for the achievement of the purposes of this Convention in the light of experience gained in its operation'[56] and it has provided an important source of general guidance for states on the conservation and sustainable use of marine biological diversity, including a programme of work on marine biological diversity[57] and decisions relating to specific aspects of the Convention, such as the identification of

---

[52]   This is explicitly recognized in some of the more modern fisheries treaties, eg, Convention on the Conservation and Management of High Seas Fishery Resources in the South Pacific Ocean (adopted 14 November 2009, entered into force 24 August 2012), Art. 3(1)(a)(ii). The text of the Convention is available at: <https://www.sprfmo.int/basic-documents/> (last accessed 12 May 2015). See further C. Redgwell, 'Protection of Ecosystems under International Law: Lessons from Antarctica' in A.E. Boyle and D. Freestone (eds), *International Law and Sustainable Development* (OUP 1999) 205–24.

[53]   Adopted 5 June 1992, entered into force 29 December 2003. 1760 UNTS 79 (CBD), Art. 23.

[54]   Convention on International Trade in Endangered Species of Wild Fauna and Flora (adopted 3 March 1973, entered into force 1 July 1975) 993 UNTS 243 (CITES), Art. XI.

[55]   Convention on the Conservation of Migratory Species of Wild Animals (adopted 23 June 1976, entered into force 1 November 1983) 1651 UNTS 333 (CMS), Art. VII.

[56]   CBD, Art. 23(4)(i).

[57]   CBD COP 4 Decision IV/5 in Report of the fourth meeting of the Conference of the Parties to the Convention on Biological Diversity, Annex (15 June 1998) Doc UNEP/CBD/COP/4/27; see also CBD COP 5 Decision V/3 in Report of the Fifth Meeting of the Conference of the Parties to the Convention on Biological Diversity, Annex III (22 June 2000) Doc UNEP/CBD/COP/5/23; CBD COP 6 Decision VI/3 in Report of the sixth meeting of the Conference of the Parties to the Convention on Biological Diversity, Annex I (27 May 2002) Doc UNEP/CBD/COP/6/20; CBD COP 7 Decision VII/5 in Report of the seventh meeting of the Conference of the Parties to the Convention on Biological Diversity (13 April 2004) Doc UNEP/CBD/COP/7/21; CBD COP 10 Decision X/29 in Report of the Tenth Meeting of the Conference of the Parties to the Convention on Biological Diversity, Annex (20 January 2011) Doc UNEP/CBD/COP/10/27*.

marine protected areas[58] or biodiversity impact assessment in areas beyond national jurisdiction.[59]

## 2.6 International Economic Organizations

On the face of it, international economic organizations have little to do with the protection of the environment. However, the nature of international economic law means that the rules prescribed by these institutions have the potential to constrain the discretion of states when adopting environmental measures.[60]

The best example is the World Trade Organization (WTO) which oversees the implementation of several multilateral trade agreements disciplining the economic policies of states. These trade rules impact on the ability of states to protect the marine environment by limiting the policy space that is available. This is particularly the case in relation to the conservation and sustainable use of marine living resources, as is demonstrated by a number of disputes on this topic that have come before the dispute settlement organs of the WTO.[61] The regulation of fisheries subsidies is also on the negotiating agenda of the WTO, demonstrating a further link between the conservation of marine living resources and trade.[62]

The need to ensure mutual supportiveness between economic liberalization and environmental protection is often recognized in the decisions of international economic institutions,[63] although achieving this goal is more complicated in practice as it requires cooperation between different organizations, a topic that will be discussed below.

---

[58]   CBD COP 9 Decision IX/20 in Report of the Conference of the Parties to the Convention on Biological Diversity on the Work of its Ninth Meeting (9 October 2008) Doc UNEP/CBD/COP/9/29, Annexes 1 and 2; See also CBD COP 10 Decision X/29, ibid; CBD COP 11 Decision XI/17 in Report of the Eleventh Meeting of the Conference of the Parties to the Convention on Biological Diversity, Annex I (5 December 2012) Doc UNEP/CBD/COP/11/35. For an analysis, see D.C. Dunn et al., 'The Convention on Biological Diversity's Ecologically or Biologically Significant Areas: Origins, Development and Current Status' (2014) 49 *Marine Policy* 137–45.

[59]   CBD COP 10 Decision X/29, above n 57, paras 50 and 51; CBD COP Decision XI/18, ibid.

[60]   See UNCTAD, 'Policy Space: What, for What, and Where?' Discussion Paper No. 191 (October 2008) Doc UNCTAD/OSG/DP/2008/6.

[61]   *United States – Import Prohibition of Certain Shrimp and Shrimp Products*, (12 October 1998) Doc WT/DS58/AB/R; *United States – Measures concerning the Importation, Marketing and Sale of Tuna and Tuna Products*, (13 June 2012) WT/DS381/AB/R. There have been other disputes which have been settled prior to determination by the dispute settlement organs, eg, *Chile – Measures Affecting the Transit and Importing of Swordfish*, Arrangement between the European Communities and Chile (6 April 2001) Doc WT/DS193/3; *European Union – Measures on Atlanto-Scandian Herring*, Joint Communication in Respect of the Faroe Islands and the European Union (21 August 2014) Doc WT/DS469/3.

[62]   Doha Ministerial Declaration, (14 November 2001) Doc WT/MIN(01)/DEC/1 paras 28 and 31.

[63]   See eg WTO, *Decision on Trade and Environment* (14 April 1994) <http://www.wto.org/english/docs_e/legal_e/56-dtenv.pdf> (last accessed 12 May 2015); *Doha Ministerial Declaration* (14 November 2001) Doc WT/Min(01)/DEC/1, para. 31. Negotiations under the Doha mandate have not yet been concluded.

## 3.  FUNCTIONS OF INTERNATIONAL INSTITUTIONS IN RELATION TO THE LEGAL FRAMEWORK FOR MARINE ENVIRONMENTAL PROTECTION

### 3.1   Development of the Normative Framework

One of the principal functions of international institutions has been to provide a forum for the negotiation and adoption of international instruments promoting marine environmental protection. Such instruments may take a number of forms and the choice of instrument will depend upon the powers of an institution, as well as the nature of the issue.

Many institutions have an explicit power to adopt international treaties. In this case, the international institution is merely a forum for negotiation and states are required to formally accept the outcome before any rules can become binding. This need for further ratification makes the development of the legal framework through treaties a slow process and it can take years for some treaties to enter into force. As a result, treaties may not be the ideal form of instrument to address environmental issues, which often require urgent action.[64]

To counteract this problem, some institutions have been given the power to adopt rules that are automatically binding on states without the requirement of further ratification. The ISA is a leading example, as all Member States and contractors must comply with regulations adopted by the Authority.[65] In a similar way, RFMOs are often granted the power to adopt decisions that are binding on their members.[66] However, in this latter context, states are often given the opportunity to opt out of regulations to which they object within a specific period.[67] The tacit amendment procedures that are found in many multilateral environmental agreements, including most IMO treaties on the protection of the marine environment from vessel-source pollution, achieve a very similar result, by introducing a presumption that a state accepts an amendment unless it makes an explicit objection within a specific time period.[68] The opt-out procedures

---

[64]   G. Palmer, 'New Ways to Make International Environmental Law' (1992) 86 *American Journal of International Law* 259–83, 263.

[65]   See eg LOSC, Art. 209.

[66]   Eg, Convention on the Conservation and Management of Highly Migratory Fish Stocks in the Western and Central Pacific Ocean (adopted 5 September 2000), Art. 20(5); International Convention on the Conservation of Atlantic Tuna (adopted 14 May 1966, entered into force 23 March 1969) EU OJ L 162 (18 June 1986) 34 (ICCAT Convention), Art. VIII(2); Convention on the Conservation and Management of High Seas Fishery Resources in the South Pacific Ocean, above n 52, Art. 17(1).

[67]   Eg, Convention on the Conservation and Management of High Seas Fishery Resources in the South Pacific Ocean, above n 52, Art. 6(3); Convention on the Conservation of Anadromous Stocks in the North Pacific Ocean (adopted 11 February 1992, entered into force 16 February 1993), Art. 8(IV).

[68]   See eg MARPOL, above n 30, Art. 16.

have been criticized as a weakness of such tacit amendment procedures[69] and it is sometimes claimed that they are abused.[70] In practice, however, the right to object is used less than one might imagine. When amendments are adopted by consensus, as is the practice in many institutions, there are generally no reasons for states to object.[71] When consensus does not prevail, however, the right to object becomes an important safety valve, thus preserving the consensual character of the international law-making process. For many states, removing this possibility would be a step too far from the current consent-based model of international law-making and it may make any form of agreement unachievable.[72]

Many institutions also use non-binding instruments as a means of developing the normative framework for marine environmental protection. So-called 'soft-law'[73] instruments commonly take the form of decisions, declarations, guidelines, codes of practice, resolutions, or recommendations. The widespread use of these instruments in the field of marine environmental protection can have a number of advantages.

Firstly, it has been noted that decisions of treaty bodies can be crucial in 'ascertaining indeterminate standards under international environmental agreements'.[74] Indeed, if they reflect an agreement of the parties on the interpretation of the treaty, such decisions can be relied upon in legal proceedings as part of the treaty interpretation process.[75]

Secondly, non-binding instruments can be used as a stepping-stone to the negotiation of a treaty. For example, the IMO Assembly first adopted Guidelines on Ship Recycling at its 23rd session in 2003,[76] prior to the negotiation of the Convention for the Safe and Environmentally Sound Recycling of Ships in 2009.[77] This technique has also been used by the FAO Fisheries Committee when it adopted a Model Scheme on Port State

---

[69] M. Bowman, P. Davies and C. Redgwell, *Lyster's International Wildlife Law* (2nd edn, CUP 2010) 516–17; G.G. Stewart, 'Enforcement Problems in the Endangered Species Convention: Reservations Regarding the Reservations Clauses' (1981) 14 *Cornell International Law Journal* 429–56.

[70] R. Reeve, *Policing International Trade in Endangered Species: The CITES Treaty and Compliance* (Earthscan 2002) 35.

[71] R. Churchill and G. Ulfstein, 'Autonomous Institutional Arrangements in Multilateral Environmental Agreements' (2000) 94 *American Journal of International Law* 623–59, 641.

[72] See A. Boyle, 'Saving the World? Implementation and Enforcement of International Law through International Institutions' (1991) 3 *Journal of Environmental Law* 229–45, 241–2; A. Hurrell and B. Kingsbury, 'The International Politics of the Environment: An Introduction' in A. Hurrell and B. Kingsbury (eds), *The International Politics of the Environment* (Clarendon Press 1992) 7–8.

[73] See A. Boyle, 'Soft Law in International Law-Making' in M.D. Evans (ed.), *International Law* (3rd edn: OUP 2010) 122–40.

[74] P.H. Sand, *Transnational Environmental Law: Lessons in Global Change* (Kluwer 1999) 334.

[75] Vienna Convention on the Law of Treaties (adopted 23 May 1969, entered into force 27 January 1980) 1155 UNTS 331, Art. 31(3)(a) and (b).

[76] *Guidelines on Ship Recycling*, IMO Resolution A.962(23) (5 December 2003) IMO Doc A 23/Res.962 (4 March 2004).

[77] The Hong Kong International Convention for the Safe and Environmentally Sound Recycling of Ships (adopted 15 May 2009) IMO Doc SR/CONF/45 (19 May 2009).

Control prior to deciding that a legally binding instrument was necessary and negotiating the 2009 Agreement on Port State Measures to Prevent, Deter and Eliminate Illegal, Unreported and Unregulated Fishing.[78] One advantage of this approach is that it allows legal approaches to be 'tested' before they are incorporated into a formally legally binding instrument.

Finally, non-binding instruments can also be a means of providing an international response to a problem which states would otherwise simply not be willing to address in a formally binding treaty.[79] Despite their non-binding character, the ICJ has on occasion suggested that states must have 'due regard' to such instruments, even if they are not obliged to follow them in every single detail.[80] Indeed, non-binding instruments may even provide evidence of customary international law if they have received widespread and consistent support in state practice and opinio juris.[81]

The use of non-binding instruments continues to grow, particularly in the environmental field. Yet, as noted by Sand, '[the] inherent risk [of non-binding instruments] is precisely that lack of formality that makes them attractive as a short-cut.'[82] There is no guarantee when a non-binding instrument is adopted that it will receive the subsequent support of states. This means that treaties remain an important law-making tool where legal certainty or enforcement may be necessary.

In relation to all of these types of instruments, it is the states that are members of the institution who play the lead role in developing the normative framework. From a formal legal perspective, the international institution simply provides a forum in which instruments can be negotiated. Yet, this conclusion is perhaps too simplistic for at least two reasons. Firstly, the composition and decision-making processes of a particular organization will dictate the dynamics of negotiations. Secondly, as will be seen below, international institutions can influence these negotiations in less formal ways.

### 3.2  Provision of Independent Information and Advice

The development of effective rules for the protection of the marine environment requires a sufficient knowledge and understanding of the problems facing the world's oceans. Article 200 of the LOSC calls on states to 'cooperate, directly or through competent international organizations, for the purpose of promoting studies, undertaking programmes of scientific research and encouraging the exchange of information

---

[78]  2009 Agreement on Port State Measures to Prevent, Deter and Eliminate Illegal, Unreported and Unregulated Fishing <http://www.fao.org/fileadmin/user_upload/legal/docs/1_037t-e.pdf> (last accessed 12 May 2015).

[79]  This point has been made, inter alia, in the fisheries context; W. Edeson, 'Closing the gap: the role of "soft" international instruments to control fishing' (1999) 20 *Australian Yearbook of International Law* 83–104, 103.

[80]  See eg *Whaling in the Antarctic (Australia v Japan: New Zealand Intervening)*, ICJ Judgment of 31 March 2014 (Merits) <http://www.icj-cij.org/docket/files/148/18136.pdf> (last accessed 12 May 2015), para. 83.

[81]  See eg *Legality of the Threat or Use of Nuclear Weapons*, ICJ (Advisory Opinion of 8 July 1996) [1996] ICJ Rep 226, para. 70.

[82]  P.H. Sand, 'Lessons Learned in Global Environmental Governance' (1991) 18 *Boston College Environmental Affairs Law Review* 213–77, 239.

and data acquired about pollution of the marine environment'. The international organizations mentioned in this provision are not only a forum for information exchange. They can also be an independent source of information, which can help to shape the regulatory regime.

In this regard, modern international relations scholarship posits that the establishment of an international institution has significant effects on the dynamics of international law-making by 'influencing how problems are framed and discussed'.[83] Cox and Jacobson have identified a range of possible roles played by the secretariat of an international organization, from the initiation of the negotiation process to having an informal influence over what is actually agreed.[84] The key factor which allows institutions and their staff to play this role is what Alvarez has termed their 'knowledge assets', that is the ability to provide 'relatively unbiased information to all'.[85]

The UNEP Secretariat is often held up as an example of an institution which has played an important role in advancing substantive discussions over the content of several treaties negotiated under its auspices.[86] The Regional Seas Initiative (RSI) provides one illustration of the manner in which international institutions can promote international law-making activities as the programme provides 'a framework that can be transferred successfully from one region to another, while still tailoring environmental activities to the needs and priorities of greatly differing regions.'[87] Originating in the Mediterranean, the RSI now covers 13 regions around the world.[88] These treaties often establish their own treaty bodies which are responsible for developing more detailed plans of action and implementing measures.[89] Haas also uses this example to demonstrate the effectiveness of what he calls 'epistemic communities' of scientists and other officials involved in international institutions to promote new rules for the protection of the marine environment.[90] In this particular example, the institutional framework for the regional seas treaties provides a forum for the exchange of information between experts from government delegations and independent researchers,

---

[83]   E.M. Hafner-Burton, D.G. Victor and Y. Lupu, 'Political Science Research on International Law: The State of the Field' (2012) 106 *American Journal of International Law* 47–97, 57.

[84]   R.W. Cox and H.K. Jacobson, 'The Framework for Inquiry' in R.W. Cox and H.K. Jacobson (eds), *Anatomy of Influence* (Yale University Press, 1973) 12–13.

[85]   J. Alvarez, *International Organizations as Law-Makers* (OUP 2005) 341.

[86]   See S. Bauer, 'The Secretariat of the United Nations Environment Programme: Tangled Up in Blue', in F. Biermann and B. Siebenhuener (eds), *Managers of Global Change: The Influence of International Environmental Bureaucracies* (MIT Press 2009) 186–7.

[87]   P. Hulm, above n 24, 4.

[88]   See UNEP, 'Regional Seas Programme', <http://www.unep.org/regionalseas/> (last accessed 12 May 2015) checked 26 June 2013. Arrangements are in place for the following regions: Black Sea, Wider Caribbean, East Asian Seas, Eastern Africa, South Asian Seas, ROPME Sea Area, Mediterranean, North-East Pacific, North-West Pacific, Red Sea and Gulf of Aden, South-East Pacific, Pacific, and Western Africa.

[89]   Regional agreements are addressed in Nilufer Oral, 'Forty years of the UNEP Regional Seas Programme: from past to future', Chapter 16 in this volume.

[90]   P. Haas, 'Do regimes matter? Epistemic Communities and Mediterranean Pollution Control' (1989) 43 *International Organization* 377–403.

enabling these actors to collectively influence the shape of the regime and its implementation.

International institutions frequently facilitate the provision of independent information during the negotiation process. For example, the IMO Secretariat was requested by Member States to prepare a report on emissions from the international shipping industry[91] and this document provided a substantial contribution to the discussions towards a regulatory regime on energy efficiency for ships.[92] Similarly, the FAO Fisheries Committee often has recourse to independent experts in order to obtain impartial advice on possible regulatory options prior to negotiating codes of conduct or technical guidelines.[93] Such experts do not have the last say but they can, if supported by participating states, introduce new sources of information or ideas into the negotiating process.

### 3.3   Technical and Financial Assistance

In addition to the development of international rules, international institutions can also play an important role in supporting the implementation of those rules. This is particularly important in the field of marine environmental protection, where the ability to implement and enforce treaty commitments will often depend upon the possession of technological or scientific expertise and equipment. To this end, the UNGA has emphasized that:[94]

> capacity-building is essential to ensure that States, especially developing countries, in particular the least developed countries and the small island developing States, as well as coastal African States, are able to fully implement the Convention, benefit from the sustainable development of the oceans and seas and participate fully in global and regional forums on ocean affairs and the law of the sea.

Most international institutions involved in marine environmental protection have some form of capacity-building programme that involves training carried out by secretariat staff or independent experts. For example, the IMO has an Integrated Technical Cooperation Programme 'designed to assist Governments which lack the technical knowledge and resources that are needed to operate a shipping industry safely and efficiently'.[95] The FAO similarly has a capacity development scheme.[96] Such programmes can provide both training for state officials, as well as financial assistance for developing countries.

---

[91]   International Air Pollution Conference 1997, Resolution 8.

[92]   See J. Harrison, 'Recent Developments and Continuing Challenges in the Regulation of Greenhouse Gas Emissions from International Shipping' in A. Chircop, S. Coffen-Smout, M. McConnell (eds), *Ocean Yearbook 27* (Martinus Nijhoff, 2013) 359–84.

[93]   See eg FAO Code of Conduct on Responsible Fisheries, above n 39, Annex, para. 9.

[94]   UNGA Resolution 67/78 (11 December 2012), para. 9.

[95]   See IMO, 'Technical Cooperation' <http://www.imo.org/OurWork/TechnicalCooperation/Pages/Default.aspx> (last accessed 12 May 2015).

[96]   See FAO, 'Capacity Development Portal' <www.fao.org/capacitydevelopment/en/> (last accessed 12 May 2015).

A similar role can be played by international financial institutions supporting marine environmental protection by states.[97] A leading example is provided by the Global Environmental Facility, which, through its International Waters Scheme, provides financial assistance to projects relating to the rebuilding of marine fisheries and the reduction of pollution of coasts and large marine ecosystems, as well as promoting effective management of marine areas beyond national jurisdiction.[98]

One of the challenges for technical and financial assistance programmes is their reliance upon voluntary contributions from governments or other sponsors.[99] International institutions have sought to overcome this obstacle by seeking support not only from governments, but also directly from civil society and corporations.[100] Commentators have noted the increase in partnerships between NGOs on the one hand and international institutions and states on the other hand to promote sustainable development goals.[101] Indeed, the outcome document of the 2012 Rio Conference on Sustainable Development explicitly identifies public-private partnerships as a means of capacity-building.[102] Such initiatives have not been widely pursued in the marine sector, although the UN Oceans Compact, launched by the UN Secretary General in 2012, is aimed in part at generating new partnerships between public and private actors to promote the implementation agreements relating to the protection of the marine environment.[103] This sort of initiative is seen as being necessary to achieve some of the ambitious targets that are necessary if we are to achieve healthy seas once again.

## 4. NON-GOVERNMENTAL ORGANIZATIONS AND THE PROTECTION OF THE MARINE ENVIRONMENT

The institutionalization of international law-making described above has also facilitated the involvement of non-state actors in the development of international rules. The importance of promoting the participation of NGOs in international decision-making is

---

[97]   See eg D. Freestone, 'The Role of the World Bank and the Global Environment Facility in the Implementation of the Regime of the Convention on the Law of the Sea', in D. Freestone, R. Barnes and D. Ong (eds), *The Law of the Sea: Progress and Prospects* (OUP 2006) 308.

[98]   See GEF, 'International Waters Strategy' <http://www.thegef.org/gef/IW_GEF5_strategy> (last accessed 12 May 2015). For examples of case studies, see GEF, *Catalysing Ocean Finance*, volume II (UNDP September 2012).

[99]   J. Rochette et al., 'The Regional Approach to the Conservation and Sustainable Use of Marine Biodiversity in Areas Beyond National Jurisdiction' (2014) 49 *Marine Policy* 109–17, 115–16.

[100]   Eg CITES COP Decision 16.3 <http://www.cites.org/sites/default/files/eng/dec/valid16/E16-Dec.pdf> (last accessed 12 May 2015).

[101]   See eg J.M. Witte, C. Streck and T. Benner (eds), *Progress or Peril? Networks and Partnerships in Global Environmental Governance* (Global Public Policy Institute 2003).

[102]   UNGA Resolution 66/288, above n 13, para. 280.

[103]   UN Secretary-General, The Oceans Compact (UN July 2012) <http://www.un.org/depts/los/ocean_compact/SGs%20OCEAN%20COMPACT%202012-EN-low%20res.pdf> (last accessed 12 May 2015).

increasingly acknowledged, particularly in the sustainable development agenda.[104] Indeed, the constituent instruments of most international institutions recognize the desirability of consultation and cooperation with NGOs.[105]

There are many NGOs which are active in the field of marine environmental protection. Environmental groups such as Greenpeace, Friends of the Earth International, World Wildlife Fund, and IUCN are all concerned with ensuring that states pursue environmental objectives not only at the national level, but also globally. It is not only NGOs with an explicit environmental focus that are involved in this field, however. The NGO community represents a wide range of values, including commercial interests such as the fisheries industry or the shipping sector. Such organizations can become embedded in the epistemic communities that emerge around international institutions and they are themselves an important source of information and advice.

Yet, it must be recognized that NGO participation is a privilege, rather than a right. Access to the proceedings of an institution is usually limited and there will be certain criteria that must be met before an NGO can obtain observer status. The design of these rules is crucial as it dictates which actors have a voice in the decision-making process. For example, consultative status at the IMO was denied to the Green Ship Recycling Association[106] because its members only came from two countries, located in the same geographical region,[107] and it was therefore not sufficiently 'international' in character for the purpose of the IMO Rules. Similarly, there have been threats to remove IMO consultative status from certain environmental groups because their campaigning tactics were considered to be contrary to the core values of the organization by endangering safety of navigation.[108]

One of the principal advantages of observer status is access to documentation and the ability to attend meetings. NGO observers may also have the right to speak at meetings, although this is a privilege that is often strictly controlled. Crucially, as observers, NGOs have no vote in an institution. It follows that the significance of NGO participation in international institutions lies in their ability to influence debate through

---

[104]   See eg Agenda 21, above n 15, para. 27.3; UNGA Resolution 66/288, above n 13, para. 76(h).

[105]   See eg Convention on the International Maritime Organization (as amended) (adopted 6 March 1948, entered into force 17 March 1958) 289 UNTS 3 (IMO Convention), Art. 62; Constitution of the United Nations Food and Agriculture Organization (adopted 16 October 1945) Report of the Conference of FAO, 1st Session, Appendix III(D) (FAO Constitution), Art. XIII(4).

[106]   IMO, *Summary of Decisions at the 102nd Session of the IMO Council*, IMO Doc C102/D (9 July 2009) para. 18(d).2(ii).

[107]   IMO, *Relations with Non-governmental Organizations – Report of the group of Council Members*, IMO Doc C 102/WP.1 (13 July 2009) para. 6.

[108]   IMO, *Summary of Decisions at the 90th Session of the IMO Council*, IMO Doc C90/D (1 July 2003) para. 29(b).2. The IMO Assembly ultimately decided to maintain the consultative status of the NGO, whilst also reminding all NGOs with consultative status of 'the importance of their compliance with their undertakings to the Organization under rule 4 of the Rules Governing Relationship with Non-Governmental International Organizations'; *Relations with Non-Governmental Organizations*, IMO Assembly Resolution A.938(23) (5 December 2003). See also IMO, *Summary of Decisions at the 102nd Session of the IMO Council*, above n 106 para. 18(d).5(iv).

the provision of information and advice which can help to shape debates on the need for rules on the marine environment and their content. To this end, Charnowitz has observed that 'whatever influence [NGOs] have is achieved through the attractiveness of their ideas and values'.[109]

Nevertheless, there is evidence that NGOs have played a significant role in influencing international law-making on the protection of the marine environment. In this context, environmental NGOs can sometimes offer a much-needed voice in support of progressive rules on marine environmental protection and they act as advocates for particular initiatives.[110] For example, NGOs such as Greenpeace played a key role in the regime for ocean dumping at a global and regional level.[111] More recently, Greenpeace has, amongst other NGOs, also been pushing for an implementing agreement on the protection of marine biological diversity beyond national jurisdiction.[112] Some authors have also attributed the success of the protected areas beyond national jurisdiction adopted by the OSPAR Commission to the role of the World Wildlife Fund within this institution.[113] In all of these examples, it must be recognized that the success of NGOs has been linked to the identification of a government which was also willing to 'champion' a particular cause. This conclusion emphasizes that states retain control over international law-making, despite the increased involvement of non-actors in this process.

## 5. POTENTIAL PROBLEMS ARISING FROM THE MULTIPLICITY OF INSTITUTIONS INVOLVED IN THE PROTECTION OF THE MARINE ENVIRONMENT

It has been seen in the previous sections how international law relating to the marine environment has developed in an incremental fashion through a variety of institutional frameworks. Whilst the number of institutions involved in the protection of the marine environment may be seen as an indication of the importance attached to this issue by the international community, this multiplicity can also be a cause for concern because it can lead to potential fragmentation of international law-making. The threat of fragmentation is played down by some commentators such as Prost and Clark who argue that conflicts of competence are unlikely to occur because international institutions are

---

[109]   S. Charnowitz, 'Nongovernmental Organizations and International Law' (2006) *American Journal of International Law* 348–72, 348.

[110]   See M.A. Levy, R.O. Keohane, and P. Haas, 'Improving the Effectiveness of International Environmental Institutions' in M.A. Levy, R.O. Keohane, and P. Haas (eds), *Institutions for the Earth* (MIT Press 1993) 409–10.

[111]   K. Stairs and P. Taylor, 'NGOs and Legal Protection of the Oceans' in A. Hurrel and B. Kingsbury (eds), *The International Politics of the Environment* (OUP 1992) 110–41.

[112]   Greenpeace, 'Suggested Draft High Seas Implementing Agreement' <http://www.greenpeace.org/international/en/publications/reports/Suggested-Draft-High-Seas-Implementing-Agreement/> (last accessed 12 May 2015).

[113]   Rochette et al., above n 99, 111.

designed to deal with specific issues.[114] Yet, overlaps cannot be completely avoided. The LOSC itself recognizes in its preamble that 'the problems of ocean space are closely interrelated'. When overlaps do arise, they are problematic precisely because institutions pursue an issue from their own perspective according to their own set of values and principles.[115] Indeed states can exploit these overlaps by engaging in what is known as 'regime shifting' or 'forum shopping'; that is pursuing a particular issue through an institution in which they know that their own interests will be prioritized.[116]

In the field of marine environmental protection, the Swordfish dispute is a clear illustration of the potential for forum shopping. Following a dispute between the European Communities (EC) and Chile over the conservation and management of swordfish stocks in the South East Pacific, the matter was taken to dispute settlement under the LOSC by Chile.[117] At the same time, the EC commenced litigation at the WTO relating to the decision by Chile to block access to its ports for European fishing vessels.[118] Ultimately, the dispute was settled amicably,[119] although it demonstrates the potential threat of fragmentation.

The de-centralized character of the international legal order poses a challenge for dealing with fragmentation. Yet, such overlaps can be managed through mechanisms that seek to promote cooperation and coordination between the lawmaking activities of international institutions.[120] The need for improved cooperation and coordination between international institutions involved in the law of the sea has been recognized both in the literature[121] and by the international community. The UNGA regularly calls for improved cooperation and coordination at the international level.[122] It is also a theme addressed more broadly by other UN bodies, such as the Commission on

---

[114]    M. Prost and P. Kingsley Clark, 'Unity, Diversity, and Fragmentation of International Law: How Much Does the Multiplication of International Organizations Really Matter?' (2006) 5 *Chicago Journal of International Law* 341–70, 343–4.

[115]    Harrison, above n 43, 240.

[116]    See eg A. Gillespie, 'Forum Shopping in International Environmental Law: the IWC, CITES, and the Management of Cetaceans' (2002) 33 *Ocean Development and International Law* 17–56; K. Raustiala, 'Institutional Proliferation and the International Legal Order' in J.L. Dunoff and M.A. Pollack (eds), *Interdisciplinary Perspectives on International Law and International Relations* (CUP 2013) 293.

[117]    See <http://www.itlos.org/index.php?id=99&L=0> (last accessed 12 May 2015).

[118]    See <http://www.wto.org/english/tratop_e/dispu_e/cases_e/ds193_e.htm> (last accessed 12 May 2015).

[119]    See Arrangement between the European Communities and Chile, above n 61.

[120]    See, however, Koskenniemi who argues that managerialism is not a solution because it 'hides [the] political nature [of the problem]'; M. Koskenniemi, 'Hegemonic Regimes', in M. Young (ed.), *Regime Interaction in Public International Law* (CUP 2012) 324.

[121]    See eg R. Rayfuse and R. Warner, 'Securing a Sustainable Future for the Oceans beyond National Jurisdiction: The Legal Basis for an Integrated Cross-Sectoral Regime for High Seas Governance for the 21st Century' (2008) 23 *International Journal of Marine and Coastal Law* 399–421, 413; G. Ulfstein, 'The Marine Environment and International Environmental Governance' in M.H. Nordquist, J.N. Moore and S. Mahmoudi (eds), *The Stockholm Declaration and the Law of the Marine Environment* (Kluwer International 2003) 104.

[122]    See eg UNGA Res 66/231 (24 December 2011), UN Doc A/RES/66/231 (5 April 2012), para. 235.

Sustainable Development,[123] and its replacement, the High-Level Political Forum on Sustainable Development.[124]

Cooperation often takes place between institutions operating in the same sector. For example, the FAO has sought to coordinate developments in international fisheries management through the convening of joint meetings of RFMOs. The first meeting in 1999 attracted 19 RFMOs and such meetings have continued to be held periodically since that time. In 2005, the title of the initiative was changed to the Regional Fisheries Body Secretariat Network in order to '[emphasize] both network support and ongoing engagement intersessionally between formal meetings'.[125] Similarly, the CBD Secretariat plays a leading role in promoting cooperation amongst the secretariats of conservation treaty bodies by hosting the Biodiversity Liaison Group[126] involving the secretariats of the CBD, CITES, CMS, the Ramsar Convention,[127] the International Treaty on Plant Genetic Resources for Food and Agriculture,[128] and the World Heritage Convention.[129]

Cooperation can also take place across different sectors, such as the links between the North East Atlantic Fisheries Commission and the OSPAR Commission.[130] At present these arrangements are less common. However, if states are to achieve an ecosystems approach to marine management, more of these inter-sectoral forms of cooperation will be necessary.[131]

At a minimum, such arrangements can facilitate exchanges of information, which may help to avoid duplication of effort by institutions. More ambitious models of cooperation include the pursuit of joint work programmes and attempts to positively coordinate policy and legal measures. The CBD Secretariat has been a leader in this regard, agreeing joint work programmes with several other biological diversity related treaty bodies, such as CITES, Ramsar and CMS.[132]

In addition to these arrangements between individual institutions, there have also been attempts to achieve system-wide coordination of international law and policy on

---

[123] Commission on Sustainable Development, *Oceans and Seas*, Decision 7/1 (1999) Doc E/1999/25, Section I. C, para. 37.

[124] UNGA Resolution 67/290, above n 16, para. 19.

[125] See <http://www.fao.org/fishery/rsn/en> (last accessed 12 May 2015).

[126] See Modus Operandi for the Liaison Group of the Biodiversity-related Conventions, available at <http://www.cbd.int/cooperation/doc/blg-modus-operandi-en.pdf> (last accessed 12 May 2015).

[127] Adopted 2 February 1971, entered into force 21 December 1975, 996 UNTS 245.

[128] Adopted 3 November 2001, entered into force 29 June 2004, FAO Conference Resolution 3/2001, FAO Doc CGRFA/MIC-1/02/Inf.1 (September 2002).

[129] Convention Concerning the Protection of the World Cultural and Natural Heritage (adopted 23 November 1972, entered into force 15 December 1975) 1037 UNTS 151.

[130] See Memorandum of Understanding between the North East Atlantic Fisheries Commission (NEAFC) and the OSPAR Commission, available at <http://www.ospar.org/html_documents/ospar/html/mou_neafc_ospar.pdf> (last accessed 12 May 2015).

[131] J.A. Ardron et al., 'The Sustainable Use and Conservation of Biodiversity in ABNJ: What Can Be Achieved Using Existing International Agreements?' (2014) 49 *Marine Policy* 98–108, 104–5.

[132] See CBD, 'Mandates for Cooperation' <http://www.cbd.int/cooperation/related-conventions/mandates.shtml#jwp> (last accessed 12 May 2015).

the protection of the marine environment. In particular, the UNGA has tried to fill this gap through a number of initiatives.

Firstly, the UNGA has sought to promote the widespread dissemination of information concerning ocean-related activities. The UNGA commissions an annual report by the UN Secretary-General on developments in ocean affairs and the law of the sea, on the basis of which it adopts its annual resolution on the subject. The resolution 'notes', 'recalls', or 'welcomes' the work of other international organizations in this field. Moreover, the UNGA has also been known to invite future cooperation on issues where more than one institution is active. There are examples where UNGA resolutions have successfully influenced the agenda of institutions to take coordinated action. A clear example is provided by the UNGA resolutions on driftnet fishing which explicitly called upon RFMOs[133] and UN specialized agencies[134] to study the use of this fishing practice and to take action to prevent unacceptable impacts on the conservation of marine biological diversity. This particular initiative was highly successful in leading to the phasing out of high seas driftnet fishing.[135] Yet, the UNGA has no power to insist upon cooperation and such resolutions rely upon the political will of states to take them forward within other institutions.

Another initiative to promote closer cooperation between institutions involved in ocean affairs is the creation of UN-OCEANS in 2003.[136] This process brings together a wide range of institutions including the Secretariat of the CBD; the FAO; the International Atomic Energy Agency; the International Labour Organization; the IMO; the Inter-governmental Oceanography Commission; UNESCO; the ISA; the UN Department for Economic and Social Affairs; the UN Division for Ocean Affairs and Law of the Sea; the United Nations Development Programme; UNEP; the World Meteorological Organization; the World Bank, the UN Industrial Development Organization; and the World Tourism Organization. The underlying purpose of UN-OCEANS is to strengthen coordination of operational activities related to oceans and coastal areas.[137] Moreover, it is charged with identifying emerging issues, defining joint actions and establishing specific task forces to deal with these.[138]

The protection of the marine environment has been at the heart of much of the activity undertaken by UN-OCEANS to date. Task forces set up under the auspices of UN-OCEANS have addressed Global Marine Assessment, Biodiversity in Marine Areas beyond National Jurisdictions, the Second Intergovernmental Review of the Global

---

[133]    UNGA Resolution 44/225 (22 December 1989), para. 4.

[134]    Ibid, para. 6.

[135]    Some authors even take the view that the moratorium on high seas large-scale pelagic driftnet fishing entered into customary international law; see G.J. Hewison, 'The Legally Binding Nature of the Moratorium on Large-Scale High Seas Driftnet Fishing' (1994) 25 *Journal of Maritime Law and Commerce* 557–79.

[136]    Decision no. 5 of the High Level Committee on Programmes of the Chief Executives Board for Coordination, Doc CEB/2003/7 (8 October 2003). See *Report of the Third Session of the Informal Consultative Process*, UN Doc A/57/80 (2 July 2002) paras 47–8. See also UNGA Resolution 57/141, UN Doc A/RES/57/141 (21 February 2003) para. 63; *Report of the World Summit on Sustainable Development*, UN Doc A/CONF.199/20 (2002) para. 30(c).

[137]    UN-OCEANS <www.unoceans.org> (last accessed 12 May 2015).

[138]    Ibid.

Plan of Action to Combat Land-based Sources of Marine Pollution, and Marine Protected Areas and other Area-based Management Tools.[139] Yet, there are question marks about whether UN-OCEANS has promoted coordination that would not otherwise have happened. It has been pointed out that the coordination on Biodiversity in Marine Areas beyond National Jurisdiction, Global Marine Assessment and the Second Intergovernmental Review of the Global Plan of Action to Combat Land-based Sources of Marine Pollution were largely the result of other intergovernmental processes and it is likely that institutions would have collaborated on these issues anyway.[140] Moreover, the ability of UN–OCEANS to coordinate policy is clearly limited by the fact that it is focused on administrative cooperation. A review of UN-OCEANS carried out at the behest of the UNGA in 2011[141] concluded that 'the UN-OCEANS mechanism has not yet been able to demonstrate its "value added" due to the lack of financial and human resources and of the political will to push the mechanism further.'[142] Indeed, the mechanism was criticized for not really coordinating activities, but rather just information-sharing,[143] an activity that is already facilitated by the preparation of the UNGA resolution on the law of the sea, as discussed above.

These mechanisms are undoubtedly weak, but they reflect the decentralized nature of the international legal system as it currently stands. Suggestions have been made for a more radical approach, including an International Oceans Authority which would 'act as the institutional focal point to provide best practice guidance and global endorsement of decisions and measures adopted by regional or sectoral agreements'.[144] Opponents of such a scheme would argue that the creation of a centralized body is infeasible given the variety of issues that fall under the rubric of marine management.[145] Nevertheless, there is scope to improve cooperation and coordination between existing institutions. This topic is on the agenda of the Ad hoc Open-ended Informal Working Group on Biological Diversity in Areas beyond National Jurisdiction and it has been suggested that this forum could be used to develop a stronger central coordination mechanism, which could be part of a new implementing agreement under the LOSC.[146] It will also be important to ask how such a coordination mechanism will interact with other on-going processes, such as the High-Level Political Forum on Sustainable Development which also has the task of coordinating international policy on sustainable development, including the oceans. Thus, the development of a coordination mechanism remains an important subject of study for legal and international relations scholars.

---

[139]   UN-OCEANS, 'UN-OCEANS Task Forces' <http://www.unoceans.org/task-forces/en/> (last accessed 12 May 2015).
[140]   Joint Inspection Unit, *Evaluation of UN-Oceans*, Doc JIU/REP/2012/3 (2012) para. 58.
[141]   UNGA Resolution 66/231, above n 122, para. 239.
[142]   Joint Inspection Unit, above n 140, para. 62.
[143]   Ibid, para. 59.
[144]   Rayfuse and Warner, above n 121, 420.
[145]   See eg Ulfstein, above n 121, 107. This view was also taken by the International Law Commission when drafting articles on the law of the sea; International Law Commission, 'Regime of the High Seas and Regime of the Territorial Sea' (1956 II) *Yearbook of the International Law Commission* 1–12, paras 9–18.
[146]   E. Druel and K.M. Gjerde, above n 13, 94–6.

## 6.  CONCLUDING REMARKS AND FUTURE RESEARCH

The purpose of this chapter has been to explore the roles played by various actors and institutions in developing the legal and policy framework relating to the protection of the marine environment. It has been seen that most cooperation on this topic takes place through international institutions. Indeed, the mandates of many institutions have evolved to take into account the protection of the environment, demonstrating its centrality and importance on the international agenda.

The institutionalization of international law-making has meant that, whilst states remain the principal actors in international relations, other non-state actors are able to participate and influence the process. Research in international relations theory can be used to complement the legal assessment of international institutions by highlighting some of the informal ways in which these actors can influence the development of the international legal framework. In particular, such actors are able to influence the content of the discussions through the provision of advice and information. The ability to play this role is particularly prominent in relation to the protection of the marine environment, given that this is an area where scientific and technical know-how are vital to successful regulation.

Another feature of the institutional landscape in this field is the fragmentation of law-making activities between a myriad of institutions. However, it is not clear that the answer to this problem is the creation of a single ocean governance organization responsible for all fields of regulation. The number of issues relating to the marine environment would make this an almost impossible task, not to mention the fact that it would require the significant modification of established institutional structures. Thus, the focus of future research may be better directed towards improving existing mechanisms or developing new mechanisms with a view to ensuring effective cooperation and coordination. Indeed, this task must be undertaken with a sense of urgency if we are serious about protecting the marine environment for future generations.

# PART II

# POLLUTION AND THE MARINE ENVIRONMENT

# 4.  Land-based pollution and the marine environment
## David Osborn

> Our challenge is not so much to invent global cooperation as it is to rejuvenate, modernize, and extend it.
>
> Jeffrey Sachs[1]

## 1. INTRODUCTION

Pollution from land-based sources remains one of the most pressing threats to the health, resilience and services of the marine environment. It is simultaneously localized yet global, variable yet ubiquitous. It is heterogeneous to the point that writing about it collectively is scarcely defensible. The solutions are complex, demanding multilateral, collaborative and proactive policy responses, ranging from education and awareness campaigns, to financial and economic incentives, to legislative and regulatory regimes underscored by resolute punitive measures for environmental negligence and industrial laggards. Against these demands, this chapter explores the framework of both hard and soft international law against which both regional and domestic 'policy cocktails'[2] are constructed and contends that the framework requires further elaboration and a rejuvenated, modernized commitment to multilateral cooperation.

## 2. MARINE POLLUTION: MORE THAN A MARINE ISSUE

When addressing the multifarious topic of marine pollution in a text on international marine environmental law, it is important to begin with an appreciation that, for the vast majority of marine pollutants, one must explore a wide-ranging legislative and regulatory array as pertinent to coastal watersheds and atmospheric emissions as to the marine environment. The reason for this is simple. The overwhelming majority of marine pollution is derived not from maritime activities, but from anthropogenic activities linked to land-based urban centres, factories, docklands and farmlands,[3] often

---

[1]   Jeffrey D. Sachs, *Common Wealth: Economics for a Crowded Planet* (Penguin Press, 2008).

[2]   D. Osborn and A. Datta, 'Institutional and policy cocktails for protecting coastal and marine environments from land-based sources of pollution' (2006) 49 *Ocean and Coastal Management* 576; and D. Osborn, 'Policy cocktails for protecting coastal waters from land-based activities' in J. Lundqvist (ed.), *On the Water Front: Selections from the 2010 World Water Week in Stockholm*, (Stockholm International Water Institute (SIWI), 2011) 84.

[3]   Kimball lists the following sources of marine pollution linked to land-based activities: (1) Pollution discharged directly to the sea from point sources like outlets for industrial wastewater,

far removed in both space and time from where the pollution eventually impacts sensitive coastal and marine ecosystems.

At the macro-scale it is estimated that land-based sources contribute about 77 per cent of marine pollution.[4] However, the absolute ratio of land-based to sea-based sources of pollution fluctuates dramatically dependent on physical location, the pollutant concerned, seasonal variability and a suite of other factors. In many cases, 100 per cent of marine pollution is derived from land-based sources.

Among the pollutants that reach and negatively impact the marine environment are heavy metals,[5] persistent organic pollutants,[6] pathogens,[7] radioactive substances,[8] hydrocarbons, petrochemicals, plastics[9] and other forms of solid waste,[10] heat and even noise.[11] Furthermore the quantum of naturally occurring substances, such as reactive nitrogen and carbon dioxide,[12] has been significantly increased due to activities of

---

sewage treatment plants, other pipelines and conveyances, or offshore outfalls carrying, for example, domestic wastewater; (2) Diffuse, non-point sources or run-off washed by rainwater directly into the sea, such as motor oils from urban streets, agricultural chemicals, or untreated sewage; (3) All point and non-point sources that contribute to pollution carried by rivers, estuaries, canals and other watercourses, including underground watercourses, into the sea; (4) Sediments resulting from erosion an land-use practices in upstream and coastal areas; and (5) Airborne pollutants from activities on land. See L.A. Kimball, *International Ocean Governance: Using International Law and Organisations to Manage Marine Resources Sustainably*, (IUCN, 2001) 18.

[4]  Independent World Commission on the Oceans, *The Ocean Our Future: The Report of the Independent World Commission on Oceans*, (Cambridge University Press, 1998) 27.

[5]  T.M. Ansari, I.L. Marr, and N. Tariq, 'Heavy metals in marine pollution perspective–a mini review' (2004) 4(1) *Journal of Applied Science* 1.

[6]  J.W. Farrington and H. Takada, 'Persistent organic pollutants (POPs), polycyclic aromatic hydrocarbons (PAHs), and plastics: Examples of the status, trend, and cycling of organic chemicals of environmental concern in the ocean' (2014) 27(1) *Oceanography* 196.

[7]  Y. Baskin, 'Sea Sickness: the Upsurge in Marine Diseases' (2006) 56(6) *BioScience* 464.

[8]  H.D. Livingston and P.P. Povenic, 'Anthropogenic marine radioactivity' (2000) 43 *Ocean & Coastal Management* 689; also A. Aarkrog, 'Input of anthropogenic radionuclides into the World Ocean' (2003) 50(17–21) *Deep-Sea Research II: Topical Studies in Oceanography* 2597.

[9]  A.A. Koelmans et al., 'Plastics in the marine environment' (2014) 33 (1) *Environmental Toxicology and Chemistry* 5; also J.A. Ivar do Sul and M.F. Costa, 'The present and future of microplastic pollution in the marine environment' (2014) 185 *Environmental Pollution* 352; also M. Gold, 'Plastic pollution: Stemming the tide of plastic marine litter: A global action agenda' (2014) 27 *Tulane Environmental Law Journal* 165; and C. Zarfl et al., 'Microplastics in oceans' (2011) 62(8) *Marine Pollution Bulletin* 1589.

[10]  A. Trouwborst, 'Managing marine litter: Exploring the evolving role of international and European law in confronting a persistent environmental problem' (2011) 27 *Merkourios-Utrecht Journal of International & European Law* 4.

[11]  See UNEP/GPA, *Protecting the Coastal and Marine Environment from Impacts of Land-based Activities: A Guide for National Action* (UNEP/GPA, 2006); also UNEP *Marine Litter: A Global Challenge* (UNEP 2009); and Trouwborst, above n 10.

[12]  Anthropogenic emissions of carbon dioxide impact the marine environment by the increasing presence of hydrogen ions and the decreasing availability of carbonate ions essential for the formation of calcium carbonate – a phenomenon commonly referred to as ocean acidification. Ocean acidification is known to have undesirable and harmful effects on the physiology and growth of a broad range of marine biota, particularly calcifying species. Carbon dioxide can therefore be labelled a marine pollutant under the definition provided by the LOSC

direct benefit to humanity, such as the production of fertilizers[13] and energy.[14] However, for certain marine ecosystems the altered balances of such substances may have a devastating effect. Similarly, land-based activities such as mining, clearing vegetation for agriculture or forestry, and building roads, homes and hotels can destroy critical habitats and fill rivers and estuaries with mud and silt. Development that modifies riparian and littoral zones also limits the capacity of natural systems to filter out increased levels of pollution. In turn, these practices reduce the resilience[15] of coastal and marine ecosystems, making them more susceptible to pressures such as climate change, coastal storms and over harvesting.

Transported to the marine environment on the wind, along rivers, canals, subterranean aquifers, through sewerage outfalls, stormwater channels and industrial discharge pipes, a toxic soup[16] of anthropogenic effluent and jetsam eventually makes its way to the marine environment because of what this author calls the 'Hilltops-2-Oceans', or '$H_2O$' effect.[17] Upon reaching coastal waters this soup feeds algal blooms, generates hypoxic dead-zones, contaminates seafood products, reduces fish stocks, renders swimming and other recreational pursuits unsafe, destroys valuable aesthetics, and produces unpleasant odours. Coastal lagoons, estuaries, harbours, semi-enclosed seas, and even the open ocean with its pollution transporting currents and continental scale gyres, become mirrors of anthropogenic activities on land that pollute the life-giving channels that serve as one-way vectors to the oceans.

Unfortunately, if simply for the convenience of 'out-of-sight, out-of-mind', the absorptive capacity of the oceans is finite and land-based sources of pollution cannot continue unabated. Marine ecosystems and the communities and economic sectors dependent on them have both ecological tipping points[18] and socially determined limits of acceptable change[19] that should not be crossed. Healthy coastal and oceanic systems remove $CO_2$ from the atmosphere, generate oxygen, transport energy and recycle

---

and although it is emerging as the foremost land-based pollutant threatening the marine environment, it is not addressed directly in this chapter. For a comprehensive commentary on ocean acidification see, Tim Stephens, 'Ocean acidification', Chapter 20 in this volume.

[13]   See R.W. Howarth, 'Coastal nitrogen pollution: A review of sources and trends globally and regionally' (2008) 8 *Harmful Algae* 14; also D.W. Schindler and J.R. Vallentyne, *The Algal Bowl: Overfertilization of the World's Freshwaters and Estuaries* (Earthscan, 2008) and J.T.A. Verhoeven et al., 'Regional and global concerns over wetlands and water quality' (2006) 21(2) *TRENDS in Ecology and Evolution* 96–103.

[14]   C. Nellemann, S. Hain and J. Alder (eds), *In Dead Water – Merging of Climate Change with Pollution, Over-harvest, and Infestations in the World's Fishing Grounds* (UNEP, 2008).

[15]   See Simon A. Levin and Jane Lubchenco, 'Resilience, robustness, and marine ecosystem-based management', (2008) 58(1) *BioScience* 27.

[16]   See E. Corcoran et al. (eds), *Sick Water? The Central Role of Wastewater Management in Sustainable Development: A Rapid Response Assessment* (UNEP, 2010).

[17]   D. Osborn, 'Policy cocktails for protecting coastal waters from land-based activities', above n 2.

[18]   See http://oceantippingpoints.org/conceptual-framework (last accessed 13 May 2015).

[19]   See G. Stankey, D. Cole, R. Lucas, M. Petersen and S. Frissell, *The Limits of Acceptable Change (LAC) System for Wilderness Planning*, General Technical Report, Rep. INT-176 (US Department of Agriculture, Forest Service, Intermountain Forest and Range Experiment Station, 1985).

nutrients.[20] They provide cultural backdrops, renewable food supplies, tourism opportunities, transportation highways, biotechnology supermarkets, and many more benefits that must be protected through timely and effective intervention,[21] by governments, industry and civil society. Finally, the broad range of land-based pollutants poses challenges that demand multidisciplinary, cross-sectoral and adaptive approaches.[22]

## 3.   THE LAW OF THE SEA CONVENTION AND LAND-BASED POLLUTION

Contemporary multilateral mechanisms for protecting the marine environment from land-based sources of pollution – whether hard law or soft law – inevitably reflect the rights and principles found in the 1982 United Nations Convention on the Law of the Sea (LOSC).[23] Adopted in Montego Bay, Jamaica, following extensive negotiations over many years, there is almost universal agreement that the LOSC – the 'constitution of the oceans'[24] – sets the legal framework within which all activities in the oceans and seas must be carried out. At Rio+20, the United Nations Conference on Sustainable Development held in Rio de Janeiro, Brazil, in June 2012, States reaffirmed in 'The Future We Want'[25] that oceans, seas and coastal areas form an integrated and essential component of the Earth's ecosystem and are critical to sustaining it, and that international marine law, as found in the LOSC, provides the legal framework for both the conservation and sustainable use of the oceans and their resources. Importantly, the LOSC provides a legally binding and strategic framework for national, regional and global action and cooperation in the marine sector.

---

[20]   Millennium Ecosystem Assessment, *Ecosystems and Human Well-being: Synthesis* (Island Press, 2005); also UNEP-WCMC *Marine and Coastal Ecosystem Services: Valuation Methods and their Application*, Biodiversity Series No. 33 (UNEP-WCMC 2011).

[21]   M. Lockwood, et al. 'Marine biodiversity conservation governance and management: Regime requirements for global environmental change' (2012) 69 *Ocean and Coastal Management* 160.

[22]   See S.B. Olsen, G.G. Page, and E. Ochoa, *The Analysis of Governance Responses to Ecosystem Change: A Handbook for Assembling a Baseline*, LOICZ Reports & Studies No. 34 (GKSS Research Centre, 2009); also J. Soussan, *Making Mainstreaming Work: An Analytical Framework, Guidelines and Checklist for the Mainstreaming of Marine and Coastal Issues into National Planning and Budgetary Processes*, (UNEP, 2007); and C. Folke, 'Social-ecological systems and adaptive governance of the commons', (2007) 22 *Ecological Research* 14.

[23]   United Nations Convention on the Law of the Sea, Montego Bay, 10 December 1982, entered into force 15 November 1994, 1833 UNTS 397.

[24]   Tommy T.B. Koh, 'A Constitution for the Oceans' Remarks made by the President of the Third United Nations Conference on the Law of the Sea, in *Official Text of the United Nations Convention on the Law of the Sea with Annexes and Index* (1983) UN Sales No E.83.V5 at xxxiii. See further, Shirley V. Scott, 'The LOS Convention as a Constitutional Regime for the Oceans' in Alex G. Oude Elferink (ed.), *Stability and Change in the Law of the Sea: The Role of the LOS Convention* (Martinus Nijhoff, 2005) 9. Also Daniel Bodansky, 'Is there an International Environmental Constitution?' (2009) 16(2) *Indiana Journal of Global Legal Studies* 565.

[25]   See http://www.uncsd2012.org/content/documents/727The%20Future%20We%20Want% 2019%20June%201230pm.pdf (last accessed 13 MAY 2015).

Pertinent to the topic of this chapter, and as will be discussed below, the LOSC also provides valuable direction for activities not occurring in or on but relevant to the oceans and seas. In this regard the LOSC is consistent with the relatively youthful discipline of Integrated Coastal Zone Management,[26] which follows the view that economic development and conservation goals at the nexus of land and sea are mutually supportive under the right circumstances.[27]

The relevance of the land to the ocean is addressed in Part XII of the LOSC on the 'Protection and Preservation of the Marine Environment', which uses cascading levels of detail. At the broadest level, the opening article of Part XII, Article 192, declares that 'States have the obligation to protect and preserve the marine environment.'

At first blush this broad statement appears of little real value. However, two key words change this. The first word is 'obligation'. The LOSC goes to great lengths to spell out the inward looking rights and entitlements of coastal states. However, Part XII also speaks of outward looking obligations, implying that states must deliberately and actively address various threats to the marine environment. The second word is one easily over looked by the casual reader. Article 192 speaks of 'the' marine environment, and not 'their' marine environment. This is significant because the LOSC effectively carves up the world's oceans and seas, graduating from the doctrine of *Mare Liberum*[28] to the codification of a system of boundaries, authority and ownership of resources by coastal states. Yet here in the opening article of Part XII, the LOSC advances beyond ownership to a concept of shared resources[29] and stewardship.[30] It reflects the interconnectedness of the oceans and obligates nation states to protect not only their immediate territorial waters or even their more expansive Exclusive Economic Zones (EEZs), but to protect 'the' marine environment, a shared asset, as a whole. It implies collaboration and a mutual obligation to protect – to defend or guard against temporary or persistent threats – and to preserve – to keep the environment in such a condition

---

[26] Integrated Coastal Zone Management is a conceptual governance and management framework that utilizes the capacity of local / sub-national government to work across economic sectors, influence human behaviour and balance competing uses of coastal resources. It seeks to promote the economic development of coastal resources while ensuring their functional integrity is conserved. Refer to T. Chua, *The Dynamics of Integrated Coastal Management: Practical Applications in the Sustainable Coastal Development in East Asia* (GEF/UNDP/IMO/PEMSEA, 2006).

[27] K. Nichols, 'Coming to terms with "Integrated Coastal Management": problems of meaning and method in a new arena of resource regulation' (1999) 51(3) *Professional Geographer* 388.

[28] See R. Rayfuse, 'Moving Beyond the Tragedy of the Global Commons: The Grotian Legacy and the Future of Sustainable Management of Biodiversity of the High Seas', in D. Leary and B. Pisupati (eds), *The Future of International Environmental Law* (United Nations University Press, 2010) 201.

[29] E.M. Borgese, *The Oceanic Circle: Governing the Seas as a Global Resource* (United Nations University Press, 1998).

[30] F. Chapin et al. (eds), *Principles of Ecosystem Stewardship: Resilience-Based Natural Resource Management in a Changing World* (Springer, 2009); National Research Council, *Increasing Capacity for Stewardship of Oceans and Coasts* (The National Academic Press, 2008); K. Mengerink et al., 'A call for deep-ocean stewardship' (2014) 344 *Science* 696.

that future generations might also benefit from the ecosystem services it freely provides.

Sitting under the general obligation to 'protect and preserve the marine environment', Article 194 requires states to take measures to prevent, reduce and control pollution of the marine environment. States are obliged to

> take, individually or jointly as appropriate, all measures consistent with this Convention that are necessary to prevent, reduce and control pollution of the marine environment from any source, using for this purpose the best practicable means at their disposal and in accordance with their capabilities, and they shall endeavour to harmonize their policies in this connection.

They are further obliged to

> take all measures necessary to ensure that activities under their jurisdiction or control are so conducted as not to cause damage by pollution to other States and their environment, and that pollution arising from incidents or activities under their jurisdiction or control does not spread beyond the areas where they exercise sovereign rights in accordance with this Convention.

At the level specifically addressing pollution from land-based sources, Article 207 requires states to adopt laws and regulations to prevent, reduce and control pollution of the marine environment from land-based sources, including rivers, estuaries, pipelines and outfall structures, taking into account internationally agreed rules, standards and recommended practices and procedures, and to take other measures as may be necessary to prevent, reduce and control such pollution. To that end states must endeavour to harmonize their policies in this connection at the appropriate regional level and endeavour to establish global and regional rules, standards and recommended practices and procedures to prevent, reduce and control pollution of the marine environment from land-based sources, taking into account characteristic regional features, the economic capacity of developing states and their need for economic development. These rules, standards and recommended practices and procedures must, in particular, include those designed to minimize, to the fullest extent possible, the release of toxic, harmful or noxious substances, especially those which are persistent, into the marine environment, and are to be re-examined from time to time as necessary.

It could be argued that these respective cascading Articles prematurely stop prior to a level that is prescriptive or that they add nothing to what states already have a right to do by virtue of their sovereignty, with or without the existence of the LOSC. Yet in 2008 in *United States v. Kun Yun Jh*,[31] a case concerning pollution from shipping, the United States Court of Appeals for the Fifth Circuit[32] concluded that the complete marine pollution prevention scheme of the LOSC 'actually broadens the traditional authority given to a port state' to enforce marine pollution laws.[33] Notwithstanding domestic interpretations, the important principle codified by Part XII of the LOSC is,

---

[31]   *United States v. Kun Yun Jh*, 534 F.3d 398 (5th Cir. 2008).

[32]   Note, the US is not a signatory to the LOSC.

[33]   See Michael A. Becker, 'International Law of the Sea' (2009) 43(2) *The International Lawyer* 915; See also A. K.-J. Tan, *Vessel-Source Marine Pollution: The Law and Politics of*

as discussed above, not that states have the *right* to implement the measures outlined in Article 207, but that they have an *obligation* to implement such measures.

Furthermore, the requirement articulated in Article 207 to harmonize policies and establish global and regional rules, standards, practices and procedures, reflects and reaffirms the obligation stated in Article 192 to protect and preserve 'the', and not 'their' marine environment, in other words, to protect and preserve the joined-up, shared asset.

# 4. THE REQUIREMENT OF COOPERATION

## 4.1 The *MOX Plant* Case

The relevance of 'the' versus 'their' marine environment and the need for cooperation was tested and affirmed in 2001 when the Republic of Ireland filed with the International Tribunal for the Law of the Sea (ITLOS) a request for the prescription of provisional measures in a dispute concerning the Sellafield MOX[34] plant in North-West England, international movements of radioactive materials, and the protection of the marine environment of the Irish Sea between Ireland and the United Kingdom.[35] Among other things, Ireland requested the Tribunal to declare that the United Kingdom had breached its obligations under Articles 192 and 193 and/or Article 194 and/or Article 207 and/or Articles 211 and 213 of the LOSC in relation to the authorization of the MOX plant, by failing, inter alia, to take the necessary measures to prevent, reduce and control pollution of the marine environment of the Irish Sea from either intended discharges or accidental releases of radioactive materials and or wastes from the MOX plant.[36]

Ireland contended that the United Kingdom had failed to cooperate in the protection of the marine environment of the Irish Sea by refusing to share information and refusing to carry out a proper environmental assessment of the impacts on the marine environment of the MOX plant and associated activities.[37] Ireland requested, inter alia, that the United Kingdom immediately suspend authorization of the operation of the MOX plant until such time as (1) a proper assessment of the environmental impact of the operation of the MOX plant had been carried out, (2) it was demonstrated that the

---

*International Regulation* (Cambridge University Press, 2005), (especially Chapter 4 – Jurisdiction over Vessel-Source Marine Pollution pp. 176–229). For an Australian perspective on port state control of marine pollution, visit: http://www.icms.polyu.edu.hk/Papers/IFSPA09-Papers/11_M064.pdf (last accessed 13 May 2015).

[34]   Mixed oxide (MOX) fuel is a blend of plutonium and natural uranium or depleted uranium which behaves similarly to the enriched uranium feed for which most nuclear reactors were designed.

[35]   *Request for Provisional Measures and Statement of Case Submitted on Behalf of Ireland* (see https://www.itlos.org/fileadmin/itlos/documents/cases/case_no_10/request_ireland_e.pdf (last accessed 13 May 2015)).

[36]   *MOX Plant* (Ireland v. United Kingdom), Provisional Measures, Order of 3 December 2001, 2001 ITLOS Reports 95, para. 26(1).

[37]   Ibid, para. 26(3).

operation of the MOX plant and related international movements of radioactive materials would result in the deliberate discharge of no radioactive materials, including wastes, directly or indirectly into the marine environment of the Irish Sea, and (3) a comprehensive strategy or plan to prevent, contain and respond to a terrorist attack on the MOX plant and international movements of radioactive waste associated with the plant had been agreed and adopted jointly with Ireland.[38] The United Kingdom countered that Ireland had failed to supply proof that there would be serious harm to the marine environment resulting from the operation of the MOX plant and that, on the facts of this particular case, the precautionary principle had no application.[39]

In ruling on Ireland's request for provisional measures, ITLOS found that the urgency of the situation did not require the prescription of the provisional measures as requested by Ireland,[40] but noted that the duty to cooperate is a fundamental principle in the prevention of pollution of the marine environment under Part XII of the LOSC and general international law. It was the view of the Tribunal that prudence and caution required the two nations to cooperate.[41] The Tribunal unanimously prescribed that Ireland and the United Kingdom must consult and cooperate in: the exchange of further information with regard to possible consequences for the Irish Sea arising out of the commissioning of the MOX plant; the monitoring of risks or the effects of the operation of the MOX plant for the Irish Sea; and the devising, as appropriate, of measures to prevent pollution of the marine environment which might result from the operation of the MOX plant.[42]

### 4.2  Regional Cooperation

The need for cooperation and harmonized approaches is most evident in geographically confined and shared waters, such as the Irish Sea discussed above, or the Mediterranean, Black and Caribbean Seas. However the mobility, persistence and ubiquitous nature of many pollutants make the need for cooperation equally applicable in more open waters, such as the South Pacific or the western Indian Ocean. The obligation to cooperate is made explicit in Article 197 of the LOSC which requires states to cooperate on a global basis and, as appropriate, on a regional basis, directly or through competent international organizations, in formulating and elaborating international rules, standards and recommended practices and procedures for the protection and preservation of the marine environment, taking into account characteristic regional features.

Scovazzi suggests that the

> obligation to cooperate implies a duty to act in good faith in pursuing a common objective and in taking into account the requirements of other interested states. In practice, such an obligation can have several facets (information, consultation, negotiation, joint participation

---

[38]   Ibid, para. 26(5).
[39]   Ibid, paras 72–5.
[40]   Ibid, para. 81.
[41]   Ibid, para. 84.
[42]   Ibid, operative para. 1(a)-(c).

in preparing environmental impact assessments or emergency plans), depending on the circumstances.[43]

The most visible and comprehensive mechanisms for implementing Article 197 are the 18 regional conventions and/or action plans,[44] known collectively as the Regional Seas Arrangements. The Regional Seas Arrangements had their genesis 40 years ago, prior to the adoption of the LOSC, in the Mediterranean Sea, and expanded rapidly to other regions such as the North Atlantic, the Baltic and the Caribbean. The respective Regional Seas Arrangements provide a multilateral platform for neighbouring coastal states to reconcile global conservation priorities with the realities of implementation at the regional level, and to fulfil their responsibilities stemming from other contemporary multilateral mechanisms, such as UNEP Governing Council Decisions, relevant targets of Agenda 21,[45] the Johannesburg Plan of Implementation,[46] the Millennium Development Goals,[47] and the post-MDG Sustainable Development Goals currently being negotiated.[48]

Many of the Regional Seas Arrangements function through action plans, which articulate a comprehensive strategy based on the region's socio-economic and political situation and particular environmental challenges. Fourteen of the Regional Seas have also adopted legally-binding conventions that provide a framework consistent with and complementary to national commitments under the LOSC. Furthermore, many of the regional framework conventions have added legally-binding protocols addressing specific issues such as land-based pollution.

The first regional regimes addressing land-based sources of marine pollution were adopted in 1974 for the Baltic Sea (the Helsinki Convention)[49] and the North-East

---

[43]  T. Scovazzi, 'Implementation of the Environmental Legal Regimes at Regional Level: The Case of the Mediterranean Sea' in D. Leary and B. Pisupati (eds), *The Future of International Environmental Law* (United Nations University, 2010) 79.

[44]  These include the Antarctic, Arctic, Baltic, Black Sea, Caspian, Eastern Africa, East Asian Seas, Mediterranean, North-East Atlantic, North-East Pacific, North-West Pacific, Pacific, Red Sea and Gulf of Aden, ROPME Sea Area, South Asian Seas, South-East Pacific, Western Africa and the Wider Caribbean. See further Nilufer Oral, 'Forty years of the UNEP Regional Seas Programme: from past to future', Chapter 16 in this volume.

[45]  UN GAOR, 46th Sess., Agenda 21, UN Doc A/Conf.151/26 (1992).

[46]  UN General Assembly, World Summit on Sustainable Development: Resolution adopted by the General Assembly, 21 February 2003, A/RES/57/253; See: http://www.un.org/esa/sustdev/documents/WSSD_POI_PD/English/WSSD_PlanImpl.pdf (last accessed 13 May 2015).

[47]  United Nations, *The Millennium Development Goals Report 2013*, available at: http://www.un.org/millenniumgoals/pdf/report-2013/mdg-report-2013-english.pdf (last accessed 13 May 2015).

[48]  See J.D. Sachs, *The Age of Sustainable Development* (Columbia University Press, 2015).

[49]  Convention on the Protection of the Marine Environment of the Baltic Sea (adopted 22 March 1974, entered into force 3 May 1980), as replaced with the Convention for the Protection of the Marine Environment of the Baltic Sea, opened for signature 9 April 1992, entered into force 17 January 2000, 1507 UNTS 167.

Atlantic (the Paris Convention).[50] These were both updated in 1992.[51] Specific protocols concerning land-based sources of marine pollution under Regional Sea Conventions are now in place in the Mediterranean (1980 Athens Protocol),[52] the South East Pacific (1983 Quito Protocol),[53] the Arabian Gulf (1990 Kuwait Protocol),[54] the Black Sea (1992 Bucharest Protocol[55]), the Red Sea and Gulf of Aden (2005 Jeddah Protocol)[56] and the Western Indian Ocean (2010 Nairobi Protocol).[57]

The respective regional conventions and protocols adopt similar definitions of land-based sources of marine pollution but vary in relation to waste disposal to or under the seabed by tunnel or pipeline. Black-listed substances are set out in respective annexes. These frequently include heavy metals such as cadmium and mercury, persistent organic pollutants (POPs), and radioactive substances. The discharge or release of grey-listed substances is subject to authorization by the coastal state. Authorization to release grey-listed pollutants may be influenced by the characteristics and composition of the substance in question, any impacts on the receiving environment, and the availability of alternative disposal methods.

---

[50]   Convention for the Prevention of Marine Pollution from Land-based Sources (adopted 4 June 1974, entered into force 29 September 1989).

[51]   The Paris Convention of 1974 was adopted to supplement the Oslo Convention of 1972 which dealt with dumping at sea. These two convention were unified, updated and extended in 1992 by the merged Convention for the Protection of the Environment of the North-East Atlantic, adopted 22 September, entered into force 25 March 1998, 2354 UNTS 70 (generally referred to as the OPSAR Convention).

[52]   Protocol for the Protection of the Mediterranean Sea against Pollution from Land-Based Sources, adopted 17 May 1980, entered into force 17 June 1983, available at: http://www.ecolex.org/server2.php/libcat/docs/TRE/Full/En/TRE-000544.txt (last accessed 13 May 2015).

[53]   Protocol for the Protection of the South-East Pacific against Pollution form Land-based Sources, adopted 23 July 1983, entered into force 21 September 1986, available at: http://cpps-int.org/cpps-docs/pda/biblioteca/convenios/prot_fuentes_terrestres.pdf (Spanish) (last accessed 13 May 2015), or: http://www.ecolex.org/server2.php/libcat/docs/TRE/Full/En/TRE-000768.txt (English) (last accessed 13 May 2015).

[54]   Protocol to the Kuwait Regional Convention for the Protection of the Marine Environment Against Pollution from Land-Based Sources, adopted 21 February 1990, entered in force 2 January 1993, available at: http://ropme.org/uploads/protocols/land_based_protocol.pdf (last accessed 13 May 2015).

[55]   Protocol on the Protection of the Marine Environment of the Black Sea from Land-Based Sources and Activities, adopted 7 April 2009, entry into force pending, available at: http://www.ecolex.org/server2.php/libcat/docs/TRE/Full/En/TRE-154598.pdf (last accessed 13 May 2015).

[56]   Protocol Concerning the Protection of the Marine Environment from Land-Based Activities in the Red Sea and Gulf of Aden, adopted 25 September 2005, entry into force pending, available at: http://www.persga.org/inner.php?id=62 (last accessed 13 May 2015).

[57]   Protocol for the Protection of the Marine and Coastal Environment of the Western Indian Ocean from Land-Based Sources and Activities, adopted 31 March 2010, entry into force pending, available at: http://www.ecolex.org/server2.php/libcat/docs/TRE/Full/En/TRE-157174.pdf (last accessed 13 May 2015).

## 4.3 European Framework Directives

Like the respective Regional Seas conventions, the European Union's 2000 Water Framework[58] (WFD) and 2008 Marine Strategy Framework[59] (MSFD) Directives are a response to the need for regional collaboration without prescribing specific acts to be undertaken by the participating states. Overlapping spatially (the WFD extends to 1nm from the coastline, the MSFD covers all of the Exclusive Economic Zone from the territorial baseline) and conceptually, they reflect a movement towards integrated catchment to coast, or Hilltops-2-Oceans management.

The MSFD requires the development of marine strategies or measures to achieve 'good environmental status' by the year 2020. Taking into account ecosystem structure and functioning, the MSFD is the first European directive based on an ecosystem-based approach to management. This however is not without its challenges, for 'while we have a good knowledge of the structural aspects of marine systems and the methods for their study, our knowledge of the functioning is much less developed and methods and indices for their study are also more uncertain'.[60] In addition to the challenge of unravelling the bio-physical complexity of European marine waters, implementation of the MSFD is also hampered by Europe's social and political complexity and the need for coordination at numerous levels.[61] At the economic level, the limitations of current environmental valuation methods and their inability to capture the whole total economic value of marine ecosystem services produces substantial deficiencies in the economic cost-benefit analysis of respective improvement measures. In this context, the MSFD allows countries to disregard measures with disproportionately high costs, ie, improvement measures might not be implemented if costs are high and benefits are underestimated. Furthermore, the 'trans-boundary nature of the main European seas adds to the complexity of the valuation task, eg, due to the danger that benefits that occur outside of national territories are neglected'.[62]

## 4.4 A Legal Network of Indirect Influence

The respective conventions, protocols and directives listed above are not legal islands. Indeed, as Scott notes, '[i]n practice … legal instruments rarely function as discrete entities but as part of a network of interrelated treaties'.[63] For example, the WFD and

---

[58]   Directive 2000/60/EC of the European Parliament and of the Council of 23 October 2000 establishing a framework for Community action in the field of water policy.

[59]   Directive 2008/56/EC on establishing a framework for community action in the field of marine environmental policy.

[60]   Scovazzi, above n 43.

[61]   J. Van Leeuwen et al., 'Implementing the Marine Strategy Framework Directive: A policy perspective on regulatory, institutional and stakeholder impediments to effective implementation' (2014) 50 *Marine Policy* 325.

[62]   C. Bertram and K. Rehdanz, 'On the environmental effectiveness of the EU Marine Strategy Framework Directive' (2013) 38 *Marine Policy* 25.

[63]   S.V. Scott, *International Law in World Politics* (Lynne Rienner Publishers, 2004).

MSFD form part of a broader array[64] of environmental management directives, including those for Environmental Impact Assessment[65] (1985/2014), Nitrates control[66] (1991), and Strategic Environmental Assessment[67] (2001).

Examples of multilateral instruments relevant to land-based sources of marine pollution, but not specifically focused on the marine environment, include the 1989 Convention on the Control of Transboundary Movements of Hazardous Wastes and their Disposal (Basel Convention),[68] the 1998 Convention on the Prior Informed Consent Procedure for Certain Hazardous Chemicals and Pesticides in International Trade (Rotterdam Convention),[69] and the 2001 Convention on Persistent Organic Pollutants (Stockholm Convention).[70]

Also relevant to the network of legal instruments affecting land-based sources of marine pollution are multilateral instruments targeting atmospheric pollutants. Examples include the 1979 Convention on Long-range Transboundary Air Pollution (LRTAP)[71] in Europe, initially negotiated in response to concerns regarding acid rain, and the 1992 United Nations Framework Convention on Climate Change (UNFCCC).[72] Negotiators to the UNFCCC were 'aware of the role and importance in terrestrial and marine ecosystems of sinks and reservoirs of greenhouse gases',[73] but perhaps did not fully appreciate at that time the significance of the convention to saving the world's oceans from land-based sources of pollution. Ocean acidification, a direct effect of increased $CO_2$ releases from mostly land-based activities, is emerging as one of the greatest threats to marine biodiversity and trophic integrity. The interplay of these legal instruments is central to the future of the world's oceans. On the one hand, unless urgent action is taken to address atmospheric concentrations of $CO_2$ and curb ocean

---

[64]  See A. Borja et al., 'Marine management – towards an integrated implementation of the European Marine Strategy Framework and the Water Framework Directives' (2010) 60 *Marine Pollution Bulletin* 2175; See also V.N. de Jonge et al., 'Marine monitoring: Its shortcomings and mismatch with the EU Water Framework Directive's objectives' (2006) 53 *Marine Pollution Bulletin* 5.

[65]  Directive 2014/52/EU of the European Parliament and of the Council of 16 April 2014 amending Directive 2011/92/EU on the assessment of the effects of certain public and private projects on the environment.

[66]  Council Directive 91/676/EEC of 12 December 1991 concerning the protection of waters against pollution caused by nitrates from agricultural sources.

[67]  Directive 2001/42/EC of the European Parliament and of the Council of 27 June 2001 on the assessment of the effects of certain plans and programmes on the environment.

[68]  Adopted 22 March 1989, entered into force 5 May 1992 (1989) 28 *International Legal Materials* 657.

[69]  Adopted 11 September 1998, entered into force 24 February 2004 (1999) 38 *International Legal Materials* 1.

[70]  Adopted 22 May 2001, entered into force 17 May 2004 (2001) 40 *International Legal Materials* 532.

[71]  Adopted 13 November 1979, entered into force 16 March 1983 (1979) 18 *International Legal Materials* 1442.

[72]  Adopted 9 May 1992, entered into force 24 March 1994, (1992) 31 *International Legal Materials* 849.

[73]  Ibid, Preamble.

acidification, all other activities to address marine pollution may be of little value.[74] On the other hand, urgent action is needed to reduce marine pollution so that marine ecosystems[75] and coastal communities[76] are more resilient[77] to the threat of increased temperatures, sea level rise, increased storm events and ocean acidification.

The most recent MEA to be thrust upon domestic implementers, which will also contribute to efforts to reduce land-based sources of marine pollution, is the Minamata Convention on Mercury.[78] Opened for signature in October 2013 the objective of the Minamata Convention is to protect human health and the environment from anthropogenic emissions (to the air) and releases (to land and water) of mercury and mercury compounds. Similar to most MEAs, Article 9 of the Minamata Convention calls for parties to 'take measures' to control releases of mercury and suggests the preparation of a 'national plan' setting out the measures to be taken together with expected targets, goals and outcomes. Measures to be taken include, as appropriate, the setting of release limits, the use of best available techniques and best environmental practices to control releases from relevant sources, development of a multi-pollutant control strategy that delivers co-benefits for control of mercury releases and alternative measures to reduce releases from relevant sources.

Not wanting Parties to 'take measures' in isolation, Article 19 calls for cooperation in various areas including, inter alia: the development of inventories of use, consumption, and anthropogenic emissions to air and releases to water and land of mercury and mercury compounds; modelling and geographically representative monitoring of levels of mercury and mercury compounds in vulnerable populations and in environmental media; assessment of the impacts of mercury and mercury compounds on human health and the environment, in addition to social, economic and cultural impacts, particularly in respect of vulnerable populations; the development of harmonized methodologies for the conduct of these activities; and the collection and improvement of information on the environmental cycle, transport, transformation and fate of mercury and mercury compounds in a range of ecosystems, commerce and trade in mercury and mercury compounds and mercury-added products, and on the technical and economic availability of mercury-free products and processes as well as on best available techniques and

---

[74]   See further T. Stephens, Chapter 20 in this volume.

[75]   For a summary of the impacts of climate change on marine ecosystems, refer to: IPCC, 'Summary for Policymakers' in *Climate Change 2013: The Physical Science Basis. Contribution of Working Group I to the Fifth Assessment Report of the Intergovernmental Panel on Climate Change* (Cambridge University Press, 2013).

[76]   For a summary of the impacts and vulnerability of coastal communities to climate change, refer to: IPCC, 'Summary for Policymakers' in *Climate Change 2014: Impacts, Adaptation, and Vulnerability. Part A: Global and Sectoral Aspects. Contribution of Working Group II to the Fifth Assessment Report of the Intergovernmental Panel on Climate Change* (Cambridge University Press, 2014) 1–32.

[77]   See A. Borja, 'Grand challenges in marine ecosystem ecology' (2014) 1 *Frontiers in Marine Ecology* 1; also Levin and Lubchenco, above n 15.

[78]   Adopted 10 October 2013, not yet in force. The text of the convention is available at http://www.mercuryconvention.org/Convention/tabid/3426/Default.aspx (last accessed 13 May 2015).

best environmental practices to reduce and monitor emissions and releases of mercury and mercury compounds.

The underlying rationale for language such as Article 19 of the Minamata Convention is self-evident. Responding effectively and efficiently to the transboundary nature of pollution requires multi-faceted and sustained domestic environmental reforms complemented by targeted bilateral, regional and global cooperation.[79] However, notwithstanding the prudence of multilateral cooperation, it can be extremely complex and expensive. This requirement to cooperate, combined with other complex domestic implementation challenges, such as development and implementation of multi-pollutant control strategies (as suggested in the Minamata Convention), presents a rapidly growing challenge in international environmental law: overlap and confusion. This is an unintended but perhaps inevitable consequence of the complex network of multilateral environmental agreements (MEAs) and other rules of international environmental law having either direct or indirect relevance to marine pollutants.[80] The labyrinth of international law against a backdrop of linguistic and cultural diversity has significant potential, especially for countries with limited capacity for implementation, to generate confusion in terminology, definitional variations or generalities. Moreover, there is a seemingly endless spectrum of possible measures available, leading to endless debate over decision-making processes and decisions, and resulting ultimately, and unhelpfully, in variable interpretation by international tribunals.[81]

## 5.   THE EFFICACY OF THE INTERNATIONAL LEGAL FRAMEWORK ON LAND-BASED SOURCES OF MARINE POLLUTION

Notwithstanding the extensive and increasingly complex labyrinth of multilateral environmental agreements addressing land-based sources of marine pollution, either directly or indirectly, the world's oceans and seas continue to be under the severe threat of pollution. While localized success stories[82] are not entirely absent and much has been learned regarding domestic implementation,[83] the marine environment continues

---

[79]   M. Waldichuk, 'International approach to the marine pollution problem' (1973) 1 *Ocean Management* 211.

[80]   W.B. Chambers, *Interlinkages and the effectiveness of multilateral environmental agreements* (United Nations University Press, 2008).

[81]   See D. Vanderzwaag, 'The Precautionary Principle and marine environmental protection: Slippery shores, rough seas, and rising normative tides' (2002) 33(2) *Ocean Development and International Law* 165.

[82]   See, for example, T. Ko and Y. Chang, 'Integrated marine pollution management: A new model of marine pollution prevention and control in Kaohsiung, Taiwan' (2010) 53 *Ocean and Coastal Management* 624; and P.D. Jones, 'Water quality and fisheries in the Mersey estuary, England: A historical perspective' (2006) 53 *Marine Pollution Bulletin* 144.

[83]   See, for example, S. Tuan Vo, J. Pernetta and C. Paterson, 'Lessons learned in coastal habitat and land-based pollution management in the South China Sea' (2013) 85 *Ocean and Coastal Management* 230; J. Brodie et al., 'Terrestrial pollutant runoff to the Great Barrier Reef: An update of issues, priorities and management responses' (2012) 65 *Marine Pollution Bulletin*

to receive unacceptable levels of pollutants from land-based activities via subterranean, riverine and atmospheric vectors. This rather begs the question as to the relevance and efficacy of the international legal regime in spawning or shaping domestic action relating to land-based sources of pollution.

As Chambers puts it, '[s]ince Grotian times, international law has been grappling with the question of whether it really matters. Since international laws are, for the most part, self-executing rules rather than enforceable rules, the question of whether international law actually has any influence over the behaviour of states has persisted.'[84] He concludes that 'in the end, states comply with treaties because they reflect their interests and because compliance makes economic sense'.[85] One has to assume that the reason a sovereign state becomes a signatory to a treaty is that it is in their interest to do so. However when designing multilateral environmental agreements, this interest is frequently geopolitical rather than economic. Implementing the particular treaty thus becomes an after-thought and often far more difficult than the political machinations of negotiating the treaty in the first place.

As Chinkin observes, '[t]he drawbacks of treaty law and custom have led to the search for new methods of law-making, most notably through so-called 'soft law' techniques, for example General Assembly resolutions, institutional codes, and guidelines.' Soft-law instruments create no formal legally binding obligations. However, they can be instrumental in the development of such binding obligations by providing a flexible and adaptive framework in which principles can be developed and state practice pursued. According to Chinkin, 'the agenda for change contained in many soft-law instruments may harden into binding legal obligation through the generation of sufficient state practice for the creation of a rule of customary law, or by facilitating negotiation of a subsequent treaty.'[86]

For all intents and purposes 'the uncertainty and unpredictability of state compliance with international environmental treaties (as well as other treaties) makes the distinction between "hard" and "soft" instruments more one of degree than form'.[87] Once State representatives return from the rigours of multilateral negotiations to the real world of implementation, the word-smithing of 'shall' and 'may' and 'recommends' and 'notes with concern', pales into relative insignificance amid a complex world of policy, politics, economic vagaries, social infrastructure and competition for resources. While the existence of legally binding obligations to protect the marine environment from land-based sources of pollution, such as those enshrined in the LOSC or the respective Regional Seas conventions, brings the possibility, at least, of holding a state legally responsible for its breach, it is noteworthy that during the last decade of the twentieth century, governments opted for a global soft-law approach – a global

---

81; S.J. Metcalf, 'Identifying key dynamics and ideal governance structures for successful ecological management' (2014) 37 *Environmental Science and Policy* 34.

[84] Chambers, above n 80, 100.

[85] Ibid, 105.

[86] C. Chinkin, 'International Environmental Law in Evolution' in T. Jewell and J. Steele (eds), *Law in Environmental Decision Making: National, European, and International Perspectives* (Clarendon Press, 1998) 245.

[87] Ibid, 236.

programme of action – as the most efficient mechanism to deal with land-based sources of marine pollution.[88]

## 5.1   The Global Programme of Action – a Flexible Approach or Creative Avoidance?

The non-binding 1995 Washington Declaration and Global Programme of Action for the Protection of the Marine Environment from Land-based Activities (GPA)[89] was and remains the primary global instrument recommending practises and procedures for addressing land-based sources of marine pollution in a holistic manner at national and regional scales.[90] Governments recognized that the impact of land-based activities on the marine environment was a local, national and regional problem with global ramifications. In short, governments promised to initiate comprehensive and sustained action, in the form of national programmes of action, and to cooperate at the regional level to prevent the degradation of marine and coastal environments from land-based activities.

The GPA outlines a logical adaptive management framework that encourages governments to assess their respective problems, identify priorities for action, develop strategies, monitor implementation and reassess the effectiveness of management actions based on empirical data from the marine environment. It does not, however, articulate specific strategies for action for each pollutant source category, nor does it provide guidance on appropriate policy combinations and permutations. The flexible nature of the GPA reflects the fact that the type and quantum of pollutants entering the marine environment from land-based activities is a function, not only of the extent of industrial development, urbanization and consumerism, but of the combined policies adopted by governments, industry and civil society. A tangled web of cause-and-effect links these stakeholders in a way that it is extremely difficult, if not impossible, to predict the effect that any one domestic policy, regulation or initiative enacted by any one of the stakeholders will have on the others.

The non-binding and non-prescriptive nature of the GPA seeks to translate the obligation articulated in Article 207 of the LOSC, as well as regional obligations as determined by the respective Regional Seas conventions discussed above, into national frameworks in an entirely flexible way that reflects the reality of domestic environmental regimes. It is consistent with the argument of Robinson[91] 'that environmental policy should dictate the content of environmental law, and not vice versa' and that the 'relative emphasis to place on alternative policy instruments is a controversial matter

---

[88]   T. Mensah, 'The International Legal Regime for the Protection and Preservation of the Marine Environment from Land-based Activities' in A. Boyle and D. Freestone, *International Law and Sustainable Development: Past Achievements and Future Challenges*, (Oxford University Press, 1999) 297.

[89]   UN Doc UNEP(OCA)/LBA/IG2/7, 5 December 1995.

[90]   U. Beyerlin and T. Marauhn, *International Environmental Law* (Hart Publishing, 2011) 129.

[91]   D. Robinson, 'Regulatory Evolution in Pollution Control' in T. Jewell and J. Steele (eds), *Law in Environmental Decision Making: National, European, and International Perspectives* (Clarendon Press, 1998) p. 29.

reflecting [not just law but] political and value judgements'.[92] The GPA's flexibility thus reflects the need for adaptive national approaches that avoid regulatory paradoxes,[93] and respond to 'the nature of and relationships between all components of the system, not just law'.[94] Its non-binding flexible nature allows governments to adopt not only a coercive command-and-control paradigm, but also more exhortatory measures such that polluting firms and consumers can be influenced in their behaviour without taking from them the freedom to make their own decision, or requiring the state to have detailed information on what they are all doing.

Unfortunately, the flexibility of the GPA may also be its undoing.[95] There is no 'leaning' towards preferred approaches that might guide government decision making, for example as to whether to choose industry self-regulation supported by regulatory back-stops (at the regulatory end of the coercion spectrum) or laissez-faire capitalism (at the do-nothing end of the spectrum). While the GPA is sometimes praised for its 'soft law' flexibility,[96] a 'more sceptical view is that once again economic and industrial priorities have prevailed' and that there 'is nothing in the Washington Declaration or its subsequent history to suggest that it has in any way changed international law relating to the pollution of the sea from land-based activities'.[97] After 20 years of limited funding and lacklustre implementation,[98] identifying locations where the GPA has been the driving force of domestic reform is extremely difficult. While it is extremely difficult to anticipate and/or assess the effectiveness of any MEA, hard or soft, in actually changing the behaviour of governments, corporations, and individuals in ways that improve the environment,[99] the broader fleet of binding and more geographically targeted instruments such as the European Marine Strategy Framework Directive and the respective Regional Seas conventions, combined with

---

[92]   Ibid, p. 30.

[93]   Sunstein identifies a number of self-defeating regulatory strategies or 'regulatory paradoxes', produced by a government's failure to understand how the relevant actors, namely the administrators and the regulated entities, will adapt to regulatory programs. Self-defeating regulatory strategies are defined as follows: 'Any statute that fails to produce a net benefit to society can be described as self-defeating if its purpose is described as the improvement of the world. But if the statute's purpose is to benefit a particular group or segment of society, and that purpose is achieved, then the statute is not self-defeating at all.' See C. Sunstein, 'Paradoxes of the regulatory state' (1990) 67 *University of Chicago Law Review* 408.

[94]   Robinson above n 91, p. 30.

[95]   B. Meier-Wehren, 'The global programme of action for the protection of the marine environment from land-based activities' (2013) 17 *New Zealand Journal of Environmental Law* 1. See also, A. Nollkaemper, 'Balancing the protection of marine ecosystems with economic benefits from land-based activities: The quest for international legal barriers' (1996) 27(1) *Ocean Development and International Law* 153.

[96]   See http://www.unep.org/PDF/ourplanet/2007/dec/en/OP-2007-12-en-ARTICLE1.pdf (last accessed 13 May 2015).

[97]   P. Birnie, A. Boyle and C. Redgwell, *International Law and the Environment, Third Edition* (Oxford University Press, 1009) 465.

[98]   D. VanderZwaag and A. Powers, 'The protection of the marine environment from land-based pollution and activities: gauging the tides of global and regional governance' (2008) 23 *The International Journal of Marine and Coastal Law* 423.

[99]   R.B. Mitchell, 'International environmental agreements: A survey of their features, formation, and effects' (2003) 28 *Annual Review of Environment and Resources* 429.

specific pollutant MEAs, such as for POPs and Mercury, probably have more potential in terms of directly facilitating domestic reform than the non-binding GPA.

Being a non-binding mechanism, an inherent weakness of the GPA is that is does not incorporate mandatory reporting, making it too easy for governments to do nothing. The GPA does, however, require periodic intergovernmental reviews. These have occurred in Montreal (2001),[100] Beijing (2005)[101] and most recently Manila (2011).[102] The Manila Declaration[103] again highlights the GPA 'as a flexible and effective tool for the sustainable development of oceans, coasts and islands, and for human health and well-being'. Through the Manila Declaration, governments committed 'to comprehensive, continuing and adaptive action within a framework of integrated coastal management relevant to respective national and regional priorities'.[104]

Reflecting a need to prioritize, governments meeting in Manila chose to focus their activities under the auspices of the GPA. In this regard they decided, amongst other things, to:

> step up ... efforts to develop guidance, strategies or policies on the sustainable use of nutrients so as to improve nutrient use efficiency with attendant economic benefits for all stakeholders, including farmers, and to mitigate negative environmental impacts through the development and implementation of national goals and plans over the period 2012–2016, as necessary.[105]

While none of the pollutant sources categories addressed by the GPA can be ignored, nutrient over-enrichment of marine waters is a problem that rightly demands increased attention due to its accelerating nature.[106] The increased availability of nutrients in the marine environment, such as nitrogen and phosphorus, from point sources (eg, sewage and some industrial practices), non-point or diffuse sources (eg, agricultural fertilizers), and the burning of fossil fuels can cause eutrophication, or increased biological production in sun-lit coastal and near shore waters. As the increased biomass eventually dies, the microbial decomposition process robs the water column of much needed oxygen, generating hypoxic or anoxic 'dead zones' where other forms of marine life

---

[100]   See http://www.unep.org/GC/GCSS-VII/Documents/k0260101.pdf (last accessed 13 May 2015).

[101]   See http://unep.org/gpa/documents/meetings/IGRII/IGRIIBeijingDeclaration.pdf (last accessed 13 May 2015).

[102]   See http://unep.org/gpa/documents/meetings/IGRIII/IGRIIIReportEn.pdf (last accessed 13 May 2015).

[103]   Manila Declaration on Furthering the Implementation of the Global Programme of Action for the Protection of the Marine Environment from Land-based Activities, Ibid, Annex.

[104]   Ibid, Annex, operative para. 2.

[105]   Ibid.

[106]   Human activity has roughly doubled the rate of creation of reactive, biologically available nitrogen on the land masses of Earth, spawning the Green Revolution of the twentieth century. Over 80% of the nitrogen in the protein of the average human on Earth is derived from the Haber-Bosch process of producing reactive nitrogen, first developed in 1909; See Robert W. Howarth, 'Coastal nitrogen pollution: A review of sources and trends globally and regionally' (2008) 8 *Harmful Algae* 14–20.

struggle for survival.[107] It is worth noting, however, that monitoring of nutrient levels where rivers meet the sea is done on a limited scale and there remains considerable uncertainty in estimating spatial and seasonal fluxes, as well as the proportions of natural and anthropogenic inputs from rivers.[108]

Perhaps no other issue of marine pollution highlights the need for a holistic legislative and regulatory framework that goes beyond the limited scope of the marine environment or a single economic sector and adopts a Hilltops-2-Oceans approach. Schindler and Vallentyne observe:

> Simply controlling nutrients from detergents and a few point sources will be insufficient to prevent eutrophication in countries with increasing populations, agriculture, and technology, especially when a warming climate is threatening to reduce water quantity and aggravate problems of water quality. Although it is important to continue to improve nutrient removal, humans must also protect better the catchments that supply their water. Limits must be placed on the amounts of nutrients and other chemicals imported into these catchments, and the location and timing of their use. Wetlands and riparian zones must be protected, restored and maintained to minimize the chance of nutrients getting into surface and ground waters. Unfortunately, catchments typically cross into several political jurisdictions, because the flow of water does not respect interdepartmental, interstate, interprovincial, or international boundaries.[109]

As the GPA celebrates its twentieth anniversary, it is perhaps timely for the international community to question whether the non-binding and flexible GPA is a sufficiently robust multilateral instrument to address the challenge of nutrient over-enrichment in the marine environment, or whether a more prescriptive and holistic legal instrument that links watershed management with estuarine and coastal water quality objectives is required.

## 5.2  Taking it Home – Enforcement and Compliance

As stated above, most MEAs call on parties to take measures at the national or local level. Whether manifest as binding hard law or non-binding soft law, 'in order for an MEA to have impacts on the ground, legislation, administrative measures, and capacity building for implementation and enforcement at the local and national levels are essential'.[110]

With respect to pollution from land-based sources, Article 213 of the LOSC requires all States to 'enforce their laws and regulations' adopted in accordance with article 207, and to adopt laws and regulations and take other measures necessary to implement applicable international rules and standards to prevent, reduce and control pollution of the marine environment from land-based sources. Unfortunately, such an edict is far easier written than implemented. Domestic laws and regulations for managing pollution

---

[107]  See Robert J. Diaz and Rutger Rosenberg, 'Spreading dead zones and consequences for marine ecosystems' (2008) 321 *Science* no. 5891 pp. 926–9.

[108]  Ibid. See also Borgese, above n 29, 37.

[109]  Schindler and Vallentyne, above n 13.

[110]  United Nations Environment Programme, *Manual on Compliance and Enforcement of Multilateral Environment Agreements* (UNEP, 2000) 50.

have a number of inherent weaknesses, especially when they are implemented in isolation of other more exhortatory measures. First, realizing compliance is frequently expensive for both regulators and the respective target industries.[111] As a consequence, fragmented command-and-control systems may result in the transfer of pollutants from one medium to another, ie, pollution shift, not reduction. Industry is very ingenious and when, in the absence of economic benefit, is forced to reduce pollutant loads, industry will identify alternative locations,[112] mediums or systems to discard waste, rather than reduce waste.

Another inherent weakness is that the cost to an enterprise of compliance is distorted by the size of the enterprise. In proportion to total costs, end-of-pipe solutions are more costly to small industry. The same applies to government. Monitoring and policing industrial discharges from small factories can be excessively difficult. The installation of automatic measuring devices or the employment of large numbers of inspectors is expensive.[113] Even at major facilities, where the idea of controlling major pollutants is conceptually simple, refining the system procedurally, adding new substances for control, and extending the controls over facilities not originally caught in the legislation, can result in voluminous and complex laws. The outcome is that even major facilities become difficult to manage from a regulatory perspective and their pollutants contribute to that produced from the small, widespread sources.

Under a purely command-and-control system, there is little or no financial incentive for industry to do better than the law requires. Similarly, under prescriptive systems there is little incentive to develop and experiment with new technology, equipment or management systems that might lead to even greater improvements in environmental performance – pollution will often decline if environmentally friendly technologies become economically attractive. Prescriptive command and control systems also 'assume the existence of an omniscient, ever-present regulatory authority'.[114] Unfortunately this is an assumption that bears little resemblance with reality.

Viewed cynically, the cold realities of regulatory complexity, both internationally and domestically, combined with inadequate enforcement are a win for governments with limited resources. Governments can give the impression they are working hard to prevent profiteering from environmental damage, thus appeasing conservationists by pointing to the existence of the MEA and its domestic manifestation, while keeping polluters on-side by providing quantitatively challenged inspectors with a legal regime that is practically unenforceable or beyond the point of 'feasibility', making regulators reluctant to act.[115] The outcome is a regulatory paradox – over-regulation produces

---

[111]   E.D. Elliot, 'Environmental TQM: anatomy of a pollution control program that works!' (1994) 92 *Michigan Law Review* 1847.

[112]   D.K. Kellenberg, 'An empirical investigation of the pollution haven effect with strategic environment and trade policy' (2009) 78(2) *Journal of International Economics* 242.

[113]   D. Farrier, 'In Search of the Real Criminal Law' in T. Bonyhady (ed.) *Environmental Protection and Legal Change* (Federation Press, 1992) 88.

[114]   Robinson, above n 91, p. 44.

[115]   J.M. Mendeloff, *The Dilemma of Toxic Substance Regulation: How Overregulation Causes Underregulation* (MIT Press, 1988), cited in Sunstein, above n 93.

under-regulation – producing an illogical mosaic of severe controls in some areas and none in others.[116]

Finally, but in no way the least, a major weakness of prescriptive legislative systems for managing pollution is that constitutional frameworks often produce implementation deficits as federal, provincial and local government authorities negotiate and compromise pollution controls.[117]

Nevertheless, notwithstanding the number of real and/or perceived weaknesses of regulatory systems, Gunningham and Grabosky[118] suggests that criticism is overstated, arguing that it focuses on the relatively unrepresentative adversarial approach adopted in the United States. Elsewhere, significant movement towards more flexible and cost-effective forms of regulation, combined with economic incentives or industry-wide voluntary agreements, have succeeded in avoiding the worst excesses of highly prescriptive regulations. Indeed, it would be wrong to regard command-and-control approaches as superseded. Rather, they remain the foundation of many pollution control systems, backstopping less coercive mechanisms. The 'implementation deficit' – the failure of command and control laws to achieve all that they set out to do – is therefore of continuing relevance[119] but must be considered in the context of a cocktail of policy responses.

Irrespective of the legislative system/policy cocktail adopted to translate international obligations into domestic action, the call for precautionary action in the absence of scientific certainty,[120] as articulated in Principle 15 of the Rio Declaration on Environment and Development,[121] is fundamental in combating land-based pollution. Notwithstanding the uncertain status of the precautionary principle as 'a binding principle of customary international law',[122] the precautionary principle requires an urgent 'shift away from the traditional belief in the assimilative capacity of the oceans to absorb wastes and faith in end-of-pipe standards to achieve acceptable environmental

---

[116] Sunstein identifies a number of self-defeating regulatory strategies or 'regulatory paradoxes' produced by government failure to understand how the relevant actors, namely administrators and regulated entities, will adapt to regulatory programs. Self-defeating regulatory strategies are defined as follows: 'Any statute that fails to produce a net benefit to society can be described as self-defeating if its purpose is described as the improvement of the world. But if the statute's purpose is to benefit a particular group or segment of society, and that purpose is achieved, then the statute is not self-defeating at all.' Sunstein, above n 93, p. 412

[117] P. Downing, 'Cross-national comparison in environmental protection: Introduction to the issues' (1983) 11 *Policy Studies Journal* 39–43.

[118] N. Gunningham and P. Grabosky, *Smart Regulation: Designing Environmental Policy* (Oxford University Press, 1998) 5–19.

[119] See Robinson, above n 91.

[120] See further, Yoshifumi Tanaka, 'Principles of international marine environmental law', Chapter 2 in this volume. See also Beyerlin and Marauhn, above n 90, 47.

[121] Report of the United Nations Conference on Environment and Development, Rio de Janeiro 3–14 June 1992, UN Doc A/CONF.151/6/Rev.1, 13 June 1992.

[122] See, for example, *Australia v Japan; New Zealand v Japan* (Provisional Measures, Order of 27 August 1999) ITLOS cases Nos 3 and 4, paras 70 *et seq.*; See also Separate Opinion of Judge Treves, para. 9.

quality standards'.[123] Successfully implementing the precautionary principle at national and sub-national scales requires not only legal reforms that emphasize cleaner production, ie, pollution prevention, but also an array of less extreme or coercive policies and management measures.

### 5.3    A Word about Getting Out the Word: the Role of Information

The effectiveness of international law aimed at protecting the marine environment from land-based pollutants, and subsequent regional or domestic implementation, requires reliable, relevant and timely information that is consumable by policy-makers, local practitioners and the broader public.[124] As Robinson notes 'regulatory, economic, and policy means of controlling pollution are ultimately only as effective as the public wants them to be, and the degree to which information is available and understood is a major influence on public opinion.'[125]

At the nexus of science and policy, information, misinformation and counter-information can be used for a variety of political ends.[126] Key therefore is robust information based on even more robust science. However, science in the marine environment is extremely complex. Anthropogenic pollution from land-based sources is difficult to assess against a variable and uncertain background of natural pollution. Borgese suggests that 'interactions between the sea floor, water column, atmosphere, land and rivers are of unfathomable complexity'.[127] Nevertheless, it is against this 'unfathomable complexity' that sustained research and monitoring of the marine environment are fundamental not only to the international legal framework, but for eradicating poverty, addressing food security, conserving the world's marine environment and resources, helping to understand, predict and respond to natural events, and promoting sustainable development. As Vice-Admiral Lautenbacher, former US Under Secretary of Commerce for Oceans and Atmosphere and NOAA administrator put it: 'We must [also] build new and more effective cooperative and collaborative mechanisms for scientific discovery and for the development of national and global policies in harmony with a sustainable world.'[128]

---

[123]    D. Vander Zwaag, 'Land Based Marine Pollution and the Arctic: Polarities between Principles and Practice' in D. Vidas (ed.) *Protecting the Polar Marine Environment: Law and Policy for Pollution Prevention* (Cambridge University Press, 2000).

[124]    M.J. Nursey-Bray et al., 'Science in policy? Discourse, coastal management and knowledge' (2014) 38 *Environmental Science and Policy* 107.

[125]    Robinson, above n 91, 29.

[126]    P. Spruijt et al., 'Role of scientists as policy advisors on complex issues: A literature review' (2014) 40 *Environmental Science and Policy* 16. See also R.T. Lackey, 'Science, scientists, and policy advocacy' (2007) 21(1) *Conservation Biology* 12; R.V. Pouyat, 'Science and environmental policy – making them compatible' (1999) 49(4) *Bioscience* 281.

[127]    Borgese, above n 29, 37.

[128]    Conrad C. Lautenbacher Jr, 'Ocean and atmosphere – the future' (2009) 59(5) *BioScience* 366.

## 6.  CONCLUSION

Governments meeting at Rio+20 in 2012 once again stressed the importance of ocean resources for sustainable development, including their contribution to poverty eradication, sustained economic growth, food security and the creation of sustainable livelihoods and decent work. Clearly the use and the health of the world's seas and oceans are fundamental to the future of humanity. The question remains, however, whether both can be achieved; whether humanity can have its proverbial cake and eat it too. Part of the answer lies in whether the legislative framework to address land-based sources of marine pollution at both multilateral and domestic scales is adequate. Notwithstanding a labyrinth of national, regional and international instruments devoted to the prevention of marine pollution, the results, in terms of environmental improvement, are mixed. Although successes are not absent in entirety, on a global scale the degradation of coastal and marine ecosystems has continued and in many places has intensified.

As the report of the Blue Ribbon Panel to the Global Partnership for Oceans coordinated by the World Bank notes: 'We are near an ecological and a societal tipping point in terms of the oceans literally being in crisis'.[129] Despite decades of developments in international environmental law, the global environment is still deteriorating and as the world moves into a new geological era, the Anthropocene, it is questionable whether the current fragmented and sectoral system of international environmental law and governance is capable of solving the problem.[130] This is particularly true in the case of the oceans where governance regimes are largely characterized by high levels of sector-specific, uncoordinated institutional fragmentation, often compounded by substantive inadequacy and regulatory ineffectiveness.[131] However, this problem of fragmentation and sectoral unilateralism need not be determinative in the case of the marine environment, where there is not only a natural physical connectivity but also the existence of an overarching legal framework or 'constitution', in the form of Part XII of the LOSC, against which environmental law and practice can be constructed.[132]

Certainly, designing national and international legal regimes to protect the marine environment from the ravages of land-based sources of pollution is no easy task. The options provided to governments and regional organizations by international marine environmental law, both hard and soft, to address land-based sources of pollution range from doing nothing through exhortation to regulation at national and local scales. While in practice it may be difficult to define where one ends and the other begins, the do-nothing option is neither desirable nor palatable. However, varying legal and social frameworks, and the complex linkages between the sources of coastal and marine

---

[129]  *Indispensable Ocean: Aligning ocean health and human well-being*, Guidance from the Blue Ribbon Panel to the Global Partnership for Oceans (2013). Available at: http://www.globalpartnershipforoceans.org/indispensable-ocean (last accessed 13 May 2015).

[130]  R.E. Kim and K. Bosselmann, 'International environmental law in the Anthropocene: Towards a purposive system of multilateral environmental agreements' (2013) 2 *Transnational Environmental Law* 285.

[131]  Lockwood et al., above n 21.

[132]  Borgese, above n 29, 113.

degradation, mean that action by governments to protect a specific coastal/marine system must respond uniquely to the circumstances and priorities of the community in that system. Thus no two 'cocktails' for protecting the marine environment from land-based sources will have quite the same appearance, scope or focus. It is precisely because of these complexities that a rejuvenated effort by a complex and diverse network of landholders, government, industry, community groups and research organizations is urgently needed[133] to give full effect to international marine environmental law and the obligation to protect the marine environment from land-based sources of pollution.

---

[133]   E.L. Miles, 'The concept of ocean governance: Evolution toward the 21st century and the principle of sustainable ocean use' (1999) 27(1) *Coastal Management* 1.

# 5. Vessel-source pollution

*Henrik Ringbom*

## 1. INTRODUCTION

Vessel-source pollution, like shipping more generally, is mostly regulated at the international (global) level. Two very different types of global instruments dominate this field. First, the jurisdictional instruments lay down the general framework for what rules and measures states may and may not adopt to address pollution from ships, differently for each maritime zone. The jurisdictional rules are today authoritatively laid down in the 1982 UN Convention on the Law of the sea (LOSC),[1] frequently referred to as the 'Constitution for the Oceans', which is today widely ratified worldwide and, as far as its provisions on vessel-source pollution are concerned, generally considered to represent customary international law.[2]

Second, technical rules lay down the detailed standards for the ships and their operators, on a variety of matters which affect vessel-source pollution, such as ships' equipment and construction requirements and conditions for discharging substances into the sea. The technical rules are predominantly developed by the International Maritime Organization (IMO), the main treaty on the subject matter being the 1973/78 International Convention on the Prevention of Pollution from Ships (MARPOL).[3] Many of the key technical rules, including MARPOL, are widely ratified and moreover include other forms of innovative (though largely undisputed) mechanisms for ensuring that the required standards are the same for the entire global commercial fleet, irrespective of formal participation in treaties.[4]

In view of this starting point, the regulatory situation for vessel-source pollution could perhaps be characterized as being unusually settled and clearer than ever before. To some extent this is so. There is normally little uncertainty about what standards apply for vessel-source pollution or, in case of doubt, where to look for the answers.

---

[1]   United Nations Convention on the Law of the Sea (adopted and opened for signature 10 December 1982, entered into force 16 November 1994) 1833 UNTS 3 (LOSC).

[2]   As of 29 September 2014, 165 states and the European Union had become parties to the LOSC. The United States is not among these, but has consistently considered that the LOSC provisions discussed here represent customary international law.

[3]   International Convention for the Prevention of Pollution from Ships (adopted 2 November 1973, entered into force 2 October 1983) and its Protocol of 1978 (adopted 17 February 1978, entered into force 1 October 1983) 1340 UNTS 62 (MARPOL).

[4]   See n 95 below on the 'no more favourable treatment' clauses. The precise number of parties to MARPOL and the percentage of the world fleet that these states represent were as follows as at February 2014: Annexes I and II, 152 states representing 99% of the world's tonnage; Annex III: 138 states, 98%; Annex IV: 131 states, 90%, Annex V: 144 states, 98%; and Annex VI: 75 states, 95%.

The relative stability in maritime regulation in this field does not mean, however, that there are no more legal issues to explore. Knowing which rules apply does not do away with the need for interpreting those rules for specific purposes. This task is often challenging, in view of the close inter-relatedness between the technical rules and the jurisdictional rules, the imprecise language which is often employed and the frequent cross-references between the two categories. Nor is, of course, a level playing field in prescription a guarantee for a true harmonization of the standards. Important discrepancies still exist regarding how the rules are implemented in practice, by flag states as well as by coastal and port states or regions.

Apart from that, the tension between the interests at stake has not gone away: the interests of flag states at times still clash with those of coastal and port states. The change of forum of the discussion from a diplomatic conference specifically designing a jurisdictional framework to the largely technical meetings of the IMO has possibly introduced more pragmatism into the debate, but has also at times 'politicized' the discussions at the IMO. Regulatory revolt, or at least a threat of unilateral action by individual states or regions, has become a common feature of the IMO discussions and is in reality a significant force for driving the activities of the organization. Finally, not only the forum, but the legal issues themselves have changed. Post-LOSC state practice has demonstrated that many issues of key importance for the jurisdictional balance as regards vessel-source pollution are not conclusively regulated in the LOSC. Gaps in this area need to be filled and in doing so it seems that general international law has been gaining increased relevance lately.

Section 2 provides a general overview of the jurisdictional provisions of relevance to vessel-source pollution, based on the LOSC, with some comment on subsequent developments where relevant. The next sections review the most important developments within international organizations, in particular the IMO, in the past decades. This review is done, separately for prescriptive standards for preventing pollution of oil, hazardous substances, garbage, air emissions etc. (section 3) and the measures and tools available to implement and enforce those standards (section 4). On this basis, some concluding remarks are made in section 5.

## 2.   THE JURISDICTIONAL SCHEME

### 2.1   General

The rights and obligations of flag states, coastal states and port states are dealt with in considerable detail in several different parts of the LOSC, the provisions on vessel-source pollution being among the most detailed in the entire convention. The interests of flag states in favour of ships' free and unimpeded navigation and the interests of coastal states to regulate and take enforcement measures against foreign ships are balanced differently for each maritime zone, on the basis that coastal state jurisdiction over foreign ships increases with the proximity of the ship to the land territory of the coastal state.

The clear obligations of states to protect and preserve the marine environment in general, which are listed in the beginning of the LOSC Part XII,[5] have to be read together with the more specific provisions for the individual sources of marine pollution which, in the case of vessel-source marine pollution, significantly qualifies the more general environmental obligations.

## 2.2   Flag State Jurisdiction

Flag state jurisdiction represents the traditional cornerstone of regulatory authority over ships. The LOSC establishes that all states have a right to sail ships flying their flag and to fix the conditions for granting nationality to ships.[6] However, the convention also includes a number of detailed and specific duties for flag states. Apart from every state's obligation to 'effectively exercise its jurisdiction and control in administrative, technical and social matters over ships flying its flag',[7] it imposes a number of minimum criteria on flag states' legislation, by reference to the 'generally accepted' international rules and standards.[8] The minimum obligations apply irrespective of whether the flag state has formally signed up to the rules and standards in question.[9]

As regards enforcement, the LOSC similarly imposes obligations on flag states to ensure compliance with the 'applicable international rules and standards' and, in case of non-compliance by ships, to take a variety of enforcement measures, including investigations, institution of proceedings in case of alleged violations, penalties for violations, prohibition from sailing in certain cases and co-operation with other states.[10]

The LOSC, in other words, avoids the need to formulate more precise prescriptive and enforcement obligations by referring to an abstract, and continuously changing, set of international rules to be developed elsewhere. This was a conscious choice by the drafters, the purpose of which was to avoid 'freezing' the requirements at a given technical level or moment in time, while still preserving the international character of the rules in question.[11]

Despite the stringency of flag state duties as set out in the LOSC, the convention is surprisingly silent on the legal consequences of a failure to meet those duties. The only immediate remedy which is provided for any state 'that has clear grounds to believe that proper jurisdiction and control with respect to a ship have not been exercised' is a

---

[5]   Notably LOSC, Arts 192 and 194.

[6]   LOSC, Arts 90 and 91(1).

[7]   LOSC, Art. 94(1).

[8]   LOSC, Arts 94(5) and 211(2).

[9]   See, eg, Conclusion No. 2 of the Final Report of the International Law Association's Committee on Coastal State Jurisdiction relating to Marine Pollution over Vessel-Source Pollution, 2000 ('ILA Report'), available at http://www.ila-hq.org/en/committees/index.cfm/cid/12 (last accessed 14 May 2015).

[10]   LOSC, Art. 217(1) and (2).

[11]   These references, together with a series of other key concepts of the LOSC that are of direct relevance for vessel-source pollution have been subject to significant scholarly attention, not least through the ILA Report, above n 9.

formal factual report, which the flag state has to investigate and act upon as appropriate.[12] A flag state also loses its privilege to take over proceedings from a port state in case of an illegal discharge, if the flag state 'has repeatedly disregarded its obligation to enforce effectively the applicable international rules and standards'.[13]

## 2.3   Coastal and Port State Jurisdiction[14]

### 2.3.1   High seas

Where flag states' jurisdiction over ships applies irrespective of the ship's location, jurisdiction by coastal and port states presumes a certain geographical proximity of the ship to the state in question. The rules are laid down separately for each maritime zone.

The high seas are open to all states and all states have certain freedoms in the high seas, including freedom of navigation.[15] Ships are subject to the exclusive jurisdiction of the flag state in the high seas 'save in exceptional cases expressly provided for in international treaties or in this Convention'.[16] Two such exceptions particularly deal with vessel-source pollution.

First, Article 221 grants specific jurisdiction for coastal states in case of 'maritime casualties' or related acts which may reasonably be expected to result in major harmful consequences for it. Under Article 221 the coastal state may in such cases 'take and enforce measures beyond the territorial sea proportionate to the actual or threatened damage to protect their coastline or related interests, including fishing, from pollution or threat of pollution'. The rule, which represents a maritime application of the doctrine of necessity and is based on the 1969 Intervention Convention,[17] accordingly sets aside the general jurisdictional regime in cases of pollution of a given severity and provides a more extensive jurisdiction by coastal states to protect its interests, including in the EEZ and on the high seas.[18]

Second, an important novel provision of the LOSC was Article 218 permitting port states to take enforcement measures against foreign ships for violations of international discharge standards, even if the discharge took place in the high seas or in the maritime

---

[12]   LOSC, Art. 94(6).

[13]   LOSC, Art. 228(1).

[14]   Due to space constraints, this chapter does not address the regimes of straits used for international navigation or archipelagic waters.

[15]   LOSC, Art. 87(1).

[16]   LOSC, Art. 92(1).

[17]   International Convention Relating to Intervention on the High Seas in Cases of Oil Pollution Damage (adopted 29 November 1969, entered into force 6 May 1975) 970 UNTS 212.

[18]   While the Intervention Convention only referred to the high seas, it seems accepted that Art. 221 of the LOSC also encompasses enforcement measures in the EEZ. See, eg, 'Implications of the United Nations Convention on the Law of the Sea for the International Maritime Organization, Study by the Secretariat of the International Maritime Organization' IMO Doc. LEG/MISC.8 (2014), 70; E.J. Molenaar, *Coastal State Jurisdiction over Vessel-Source Pollution* (Kluwer Law International, 1998) 388. In such cases, Art. 221 presumably overrules Art. 220(6), which lays down a seemingly more restrictive enforcement regime in respect of the same types of incidents. See also A.T. Falkanger, *Maritime Casualties and Intervention, Coastal State Measures when Casualties Pose the Threat of Pollution* (Fagbokforlaget, 2011).

zones of other states. This provision departed from prevailing theories of jurisdiction as it did not condition the enforcement actions to any effect of the pollution to the enforcing (port) state. It has been very sparingly used, but has recently gained renewed prominence through its collective application by the EU Member States through Directive 2005/35.[19]

## 2.3.2   EEZ

The EEZ is a jurisdictional hybrid zone. It does not form part of the coastal state's territory, yet it grants certain 'sovereign rights' for coastal states. With respect to shipping, all states are granted freedom of navigation, while coastal states are granted certain jurisdiction to regulate and enforce shipping-related laws in the zone.[20] The coastal state shall, in exercising its rights and performing its obligations, have 'due regard' to the rights and duties of other states. Those rights and duties include the freedom of navigation of all states in the EEZ, subject to a corresponding duty to have due regard for the rights and duties of the coastal state.[21] The general principle as regards coastal states' jurisdiction to prescribe environmental rules for international shipping in their EEZ is laid down in Article 211(5) of the LOSC, which limits prescriptive jurisdiction to the adoption of 'generally accepted international rules and standards established through the competent international organization'. The same standards which constitute the minimum requirements for flag states, discussed above, accordingly represent the maximum level for coastal state regulation in the EEZ.

Two main exceptions to this rule exist. First, Article 211(6) contains specific provisions for additional measures in special areas of the EEZ. The paragraph is a complex set of essentially procedural requirements for such measures, which place key significance on acceptance by the competent international organization, ie the IMO. It has been of very limited relevance in practice. Second, Article 234 offers the right to prescribe more stringent rules, independent of international rules, for coastal states bordering ice-covered areas. This provision has gained significant relevance again in the past few years with the growing interest in Arctic shipping. Differences of view exist with respect to how various elements of Article 234 should be interpreted, its relationship to other LOSC provisions and hence to what extent it may be relied upon by, in particular, Canada and Russia for regulating shipping in the Arctic.[22]

---

[19]   Directive 2005/35 on ship-source pollution and on the introduction of penalties for infringements, OJ 2005, L255, 11.

[20]   LOSC, Art. 56(1)(b)(iii).

[21]   LOSC, Art. 58(1) and (3). The latter paragraph also provides that States exercising these freedoms 'shall comply with the laws and regulations adopted by the coastal State in accordance with the provisions of this Convention and other rules of international law in so far as they are not incompatible with this Part.'

[22]   See, eg, D. Pharand, 'The Arctic Waters and the Northwest Passage: A Final Revisit', (2007) 78 *Ocean Development and International Law* 3; A. Chircop, 'Regulatory Challenges for International Arctic Navigation and Shipping in an Evolving Governance Environment', paper presented at CMI Conference, Beijing, October 2012, available at www.comitemaritime.org (last accessed 14 May 2015); E.J. Molenaar, 'Status and Reform of International Arctic Shipping Law' in E. Tedsen, S. Cavalieri and R.A. Kraemer (eds), *Arctic Marine Governance: Opportunities for Transatlantic Cooperation* (Springer, 2013) 127–57.

A coastal states' right to take enforcement measures in respect of ship-source pollution in the EEZ is limited to cases where the pollution has already taken place and varies with the severity of the damage caused or likely to be caused.[23] In practice, it seems that the very constrained at-sea enforcement powers have been of limited use by coastal states.[24]

### 2.3.3   Territorial sea

The main rule is that the territorial sea is subject to the territorial sovereignty of the coastal state, subject only to specific exceptions. The main exception is that foreign ships enjoy a right of innocent passage through the territorial sea of other states. The passage shall be 'continuous and expeditious'[25] and must not be 'prejudicial to the peace, good order or security of the coastal state'.[26] Article 19(2) of the LOSC adds a list of activities which render passage non-innocent, which includes 'any act of wilful and serious pollution contrary to this Convention'.[27] Mere non-compliance with the applicable (national or international) pollution rules does therefore not amount to loss of the right of innocent passage under the LOSC. However, in the decades that have passed since the convention was negotiated, a lower threshold for the loss of the right of innocent passage appears to have gained ground, in legal literature as well as in state practice.[28] Moreover, the notion of depriving ships in bad condition which are only *potentially* harmful to the environment of their right of innocent passage has tended to

---

[23]   In the case of a violation of international rules in the EEZ, the coastal state may only require a foreign ship to provide certain basic information about its identity and route (LOSC Art. 220(3)). Where that violation or suspected violation results in a 'substantial discharge causing or threatening significant pollution', the powers of the coastal state extend to undertaking a physical inspection of the ship in respect of matters relating to the violation (LOSC Art. 220(5)). If there is 'clear objective evidence' that the discharge is causing or threatening to cause 'major damage to the coastline or related interests of the coastal State' or to the resources in its coastal zones, the state may, 'if the evidence so warrants', institute proceedings including detention of the ship (LOSC Art. 220(6)).

[24]   See, eg, P. Birnie, A.E. Boyle and C. Redgewell, *International Law & the Environment*, (3rd edn) (Oxford University Press, 2009), 376; ILA Report, above n 9, 463; and E.J. Molenaar, above n 18, 389–99. But see the Swedish Supreme Court cases commented on by S. Mahmoudi in '*Capri Marine Ltd. v. Chief State Prosecutor* – Swedish Supreme Court decision on jurisdiction to impose pollution fees on owners or operators of ships operating in the exclusive economic zone', 99(2) *American Journal of International Law* (2005) 472–8.

[25]   LOSC, Art. 18(2).

[26]   LOSC, Art. 19.

[27]   LOSC, Art. 19(2)(h).

[28]   See K. Hakapää, *Marine Pollution in International Law, Material Obligations and Jurisdiction with Special Reference to the Third United Nations Conference on the Law of the Sea* (Suomalainen Tiedeakatemia, 1981) 197. See also: K. Hakapää and E.J. Molenaar 'Innocent Passage – Past and Present' (1999) 23(2) *Marine Policy* 140–44; ILA Report, above n 9, 493–5; and L.S. Johnson, *Coastal State Regulation of International Shipping* (Oceana Publications, Inc., 2004), 64–6. See also A.K.-J. Tan, *Vessel-Source Marine Pollution, The Law and Politics of International Regulation* (Cambridge University Press, 2006), 208.

gain support.[29] If the ship is *not* in innocent passage, the ship is in principle subject to the full prescriptive and enforcement jurisdiction of the coastal state.

The jurisdiction of coastal states to regulate ships that are in innocent passage is laid down in Article 21 of the LOSC. This includes the right to adopt laws and regulations regarding, inter alia, 'the preservation of the environment of the coastal State and the prevention, reduction and control of pollution thereof'.[30] A very important limitation of this jurisdiction is introduced in paragraph 2, providing that the national laws and regulations 'shall not apply to the design, construction, manning and equipment of foreign ships unless they are giving effect to generally accepted rules or standards'.[31]

With respect to enforcement, the LOSC makes a distinction between rules relating to 'pollution' and other rules. The former is regulated in considerable detail, in Article 220(2), which differentiates the permissible actions on the basis of the degree of suspicion and evidence.[32] Article 230 provides that only monetary penalties shall be imposed, except in the case of an act of wilful and serious pollution in the territorial sea.

### 2.3.4   Ports and internal waters

In contrast to the rigid limitations of coastal state jurisdiction over foreign ships, port states are largely left outside the jurisdictional scheme of the LOSC. Yet it is well-established that internal waters for jurisdictional purposes may be assimilated to the land territory of the state. Ships, through their voluntary presence in the port or internal waters of another state, subject themselves to the territorial jurisdiction of that state. As a starting point, a port state is hence free to impose its national rules on foreign ships and to enforce those rules by (reasonable) means of their choice, at least as far as they do not relate to matters which are completely internal to the ship.[33] It is also widely recognized that ships enjoy no general right of access to foreign ports

---

[29]   Ibid.

[30]   LOSC, Art. 21(1)(f).

[31]   In addition, all laws of the coastal state should be 'in conformity with the provisions of this Convention and other rules of international law' and must not 'hamper' the innocent passage of foreign ships otherwise than in accordance with LOSC Art. 24(1) and Article 211(4). Nor may the coastal state apply discriminatory rules or 'impose requirements on foreign ships which have the practical effect of denying or impairing innocent passage' (LOSC, Art. 24(2)).

[32]   If a coastal state has 'clear grounds for believing' that a ship navigating in the territorial sea has violated the national or international rules on the prevention, reduction and control of pollution, the authorities of the coastal state have the right physically to inspect the ship, which includes the right to stop the vessel and board it, and possibly the right to order it to port. The action must, however, be 'without prejudice to the application of the relevant provisions of [LOSC Part II on innocent passage]'. If the evidence indicates that a violation of the rules has taken place, the ship may be detained and legal proceedings may be instituted: see Molenaar, above n 18, 246; and Johnson, above n 28, 84.

[33]   See, eg, R.R. Churchill and A.V. Lowe, *The Law of the Sea* (Manchester University Press, 1999) 65–9.

under international law.[34] This implies, a fortiori, a right for the port state to make access to its ports conditional on compliance with specific requirements.[35]

In the absence of specific limitations, a port state therefore enjoys a wide discretion to impose access conditions and other requirements on foreign ships entering its ports. This discretion is not without limits, however. Limitations to this a priori unlimited jurisdiction of port states include the restraints that may follow from treaty commitments, whether imposed by bilateral or multilateral, maritime, commercial or other treaties, and from principles of general international law, such as the prohibition of discrimination or of abuse of rights.[36] Proportionality requirements may also place limitations on the enforcement measures which may reasonably be taken against ships that fail to comply with the port State's requirements. This type of limitations, which may be grouped together under the general heading of 'reasonableness criteria', are clearly less specific and more dependent on the circumstances of the individual case than the relatively clear-cut, maximum limits imposed on coastal states for regulating passing ships in their maritime zones.

The extent and limits of port states' jurisdiction to prescribe and enforce rules for foreign ships are therefore not very precise. It is possible that different types of rules need to be distinguished. There are rules relating to 'static' features of ships, such as its design, construction, equipment or manning. These features 'follow' the ship wherever it is; it either complies or not, irrespective of its geographical location. Since a ship operator cannot easily change these features during a voyage, these types of requirements are often considered to be most intrusive with respect to ships' navigational rights. Paradoxically, however, static port state requirements are easier to justify in jurisdictional terms. If a ship fails to comply with a port state's requirement on static features it will be in violation even while within the port or internal waters of the state, where the prescriptive jurisdiction of states is uncontested.

Aside from the odd judgment which has suggested differently,[37] it seems widely accepted that port states may impose these types of requirements on foreign ships.[38]

---

[34]    *Case concerning Military and Paramilitary Activities In and Against Nicaragua* (Nicaragua v. United States of America), 27 June 1986, ICJ Reports 1986, para. 213. See also A.V. Lowe, 'The Right of Entry into Maritime Ports in International Law' (1977) *San Diego Law Review* 597–622; L. de la Fayette, 'Access to Ports in International Law' (1996) 11(1) *International Journal of Marine and Coastal Law* 1. The special case of ships in distress who request permission to go to a port or other place of refuge has been discussed vividly since the beginning of the Millennium. See, eg, A. Chircop, O. Lindén (eds), *Places of Refuge for Ships – Emerging Environmental Concerns of a Maritime Custom* (Martinus Nijhoff Publishers, 2006). Even for such ships, the prevailing view seems to be they do not have a general right of access under customary law, but that each request needs to be assessed separately on its merits.

[35]    See also, to this effect, LOSC, Arts 25(2) and 211(3).

[36]    See also LOSC, Art. 300.

[37]    See notably *Sellers v. Maritime Safety Inspector*, CA 104/98, Judgment of the Court of Appeal in New Zealand, 5 November 1998.

[38]    Generally, see B. Marten, *Port State Jurisdiction and the Regulation of International Merchant Shipping* (Springer, 2014); E.J. Molenaar, 'Port State Jurisdiction: Toward Comprehensive, Mandatory and Global Coverage' (2007) 38(1–2) *Ocean Development and International Law* 225. See also Swedish Case No. M 8471-03, Svea Court of Appeal, Environmental Court of Appeal (Miljööverdomstolen), Judgment of 24 May 2006.

Even where the subject matter in question is subject to (different) international rules, port states appear to retain their right to impose more stringent requirements, as long as the international rules in question do not specifically exclude such complementary standards.[39] The existence of such 'residual' jurisdiction of port states is explicitly recognized in the text of some recent international maritime conventions.[40]

The jurisdictional setting may be different with respect to rules that are not static in the above sense. Here, the scope of port state rules that relate to specific conduct (or other 'operational' requirements) need to be determined in geographical terms, and it cannot be assumed that the violation has necessarily (also) taken place within the port state's own waters. In case the port state seeks to regulate conduct that takes place beyond the areas over which it has explicit prescriptive jurisdiction (in the LOSC), the requirement has clear extra-territorial features, and the jurisdictional foundation for the requirement may be doubted.[41]

However, even for such cases, it is at least theoretically conceivable that the required (prescriptive) jurisdictional basis for port state requirement could be found outside the realm of the LOSC, notably in the principles of extra-territorial jurisdiction under general international law. In addition, it is possible that the jurisdictional acceptability of the port state requirement depends on the enforcement measure taken. Enforcement measures which are unproblematic from a point of view of international law, such as denying the non-complying ship the right to certain services in port, or even access to the port, may be justified even if the prescriptive basis for extra-territoriality is weak,

---

[39] See, eg, Hakapää, above n 28, 172; T.L. McDorman, 'Port State Enforcement: A Comment on Article 218 of the 1982 Law of the Sea Convention' (1997) 28(2) *Journal of Maritime Law and Commerce* 314; E.J. Molenaar, 'Residual Jurisdiction under IMO Regulatory Conventions', in H. Ringbom (ed.), *Competing Norms in the Law of Marine Environmental Protection, Focus on Ship Safety and Pollution Prevention* (Kluwer Law International, 1997) 201; Johnson, above n 28, 40; A.E. Boyle, 'EU Unilateralism and the Law of the Sea' (2006) 21(1) *International Journal of Marine and Coastal Law* 24; H. Ringbom, *The EU Maritime Safety Policy and International Law* (Martinus Nijhoff Publishers, 2008) 337; and Marten, above n 38, 25ff.

[40] See Art. 1(3) of the 2001 International Convention on the Control of Harmful Anti-fouling Systems on Ships (adopted 5 October 2001, entered into force 17 September 2008) IMO Doc. AFS/CONF/26; Art. 2(3) of the 2004 International Convention for the Control and Management of Ships' Ballast Water and Sediments (adopted 13 February 2004, not yet in force) IMO Doc BWM/CONF/36, and MARPOL Regulation I/21(8)(2) (adopted in 2003). See also Art. 4(1)(b) of the 2009 FAO Agreement on Port State Measures to Prevent, Deter and Eliminate Illegal, Unreported and Unregulated Fishing (FAO Doc. C 2009/LIM/11-Rev. 1).

[41] It could also be argued, in particular as far as vessel-source pollution is concerned, that LOSC Article 218 (see above) *a contrario* suggests that there is no such extra-territorial port state jurisdiction. The broad geographical jurisdiction of port states to regulate and enforce violations of discharges under that article suggests that a corresponding extra-territorial jurisdiction does *not* exist with respect to other types of (operational) requirements or to national discharge standards that exceed the international ones. If so, the geographical applicability of operational requirements to foreign ships visiting ports of the state concerned would seem to be limited to the internal waters and territorial sea of these, unless specific approval of the requirement in question can be obtained at international level.

while punitive measures, such as sanctions, may require a firmer prescriptive jurisdictional basis.[42]

With regard to enforcement, any measures taken by port and coastal states are subject to certain important 'safeguards' as listed in section 7 of Chapter XII of the LOSC.[43]

## 3. PRESCRIPTIVE STANDARDS

### 3.1 General

The LOSC regime is neither complete nor static. The convention largely leaves it to international bodies, in particular the IMO, to set the detailed limits of states' prescriptive and enforcement jurisdiction against foreign ships. This section provides a brief review of post-LOSC developments in the IMO and some other international bodies.

Roughly half of the 50 conventions adopted within the IMO specifically relate to environmental protection. They cover a broad range of themes, including accident prevention, rules for ship construction and equipment, operational and management standards, pollution response activities and civil liability rules. The conventions are commonly complemented by more detailed recommendations, guidance documents and other non-binding tools aimed at to harmonizing and facilitating implementation. Here, focus will be on the technical rules which seek to prevent vessel-source pollution (sections 3.2–3.4), but some attention is also given to IMO rules which relate to and possibly affect the jurisdictional regime laid down in the LOSC (section 3.5) and the activities in this field by some other organizations (3.6). It should be noted, however, that many IMO instruments which are primarily devoted to maritime safety also have environmental benefits, as they serve to reduce incidents and accidents at sea.

The main IMO convention specifically dealing with the prevention and reduction of pollution from ships is MARPOL. This convention addresses a whole range of different types of pollutants, both ship and cargo-generated, in its six technical annexes. The five original annexes to MARPOL (Annexes I-V, as amended) are discussed in section 3.2 below. The most recent Annex VI, on air pollution from ships, is discussed separately in section 3.3, while certain environmental topics that have been addressed outside the MARPOL framework, through separate conventions, are briefly introduced in section 3.4.

---

[42]  See in particular E.J. Molenaar, above n 38 and ibid., 'Port State Jurisdiction to Combat IUU Fishing: The Port State Measures Agreement' in D.A. Russell and D.L. VanderZwaag (eds.), *Recasting Transboundary Fisheries Management Arrangements* (Konklijke Brill NV, 2010) 379. See also Marten above n 38.

[43]  In particular, LOSC Arts 226, 228, 230 and 231.

## 3.2 Marine Pollution Prevention and Discharges (MARPOL Annexes I–V)

MARPOL is a comprehensive treaty dealing with a variety of technical aspects of vessel-source pollution, including ship construction standards, monitoring equipment, discharge standards, waste facilities in ports and sanctions for violations. Following repeated adjustments and amendments over the years, the original annexes to MARPOL now follow the same basic structure as far as discharges are concerned. Any discharge of oil, noxious liquid substances, sewage and garbage to the sea is prohibited, unless specific conditions are met with respect to the substance concerned, as regards discharge rate, speed, distance from shore etc. More stringent standards have been agreed for 'special areas'. All annexes also include requirements and standards for certificates, record books as well as requirements for states to provide facilities for receiving waste and residues from ships in ports, with particularly high requirements for ports located within special areas.

The MARPOL standards, like many other key IMO conventions, are regularly updated through the tacit acceptance procedure, which allows the global standards to be updated to reflect technical or policy developments without the need for parties to formally endorse the amendments separately.[44] The most significant recent revisions include the phasing out of single-hull oil tankers (Annex I, 2001 and 2003); the complete revision of the categorization and discharge of noxious liquid substances (Annex II, 2007); the revision of Annex IV to promote its widespread ratification (2004); and the tighter standards for garbage discharges, including bulk cargo residues and wash water (Annex V, 2011).

As a general conclusion, it is probably fair to say that the convention's rules are quite stringent and that operational vessel-source pollution would be a very limited problem if all the Convention's provisions were actually complied with. Despite considerable imperfections in the field of implementation, it is widely acknowledged that the MARPOL has greatly contributed to a significant decrease in pollution from international shipping, accidental as well as deliberate, over the past decades.[45]

## 3.3 Air Emissions

### 3.3.1 General
The discussion on shipping's environmental record increasingly concerns ships' air emissions. A new MARPOL Annex VI was adopted in 1997 to regulate a variety of different types of airborne emissions from ships, ranging from ozone depleting substances and nitrogen and sulphur oxides ($NO_x$) and ($SO_x$) to volatile organic compounds (VOC) and emissions from shipboard incinerators. In an amendment of 2011, certain new requirements with respect to ships' energy efficiency were introduced

---

[44] See eg L. Shi, 'Successful Use of the Tacit Acceptance Procedure to Effectuate Progress in International Maritime Law' *University of San Francisco Maritime Law Journal*, Vol. 11, 1998–1999, 299.

[45] In a review of international ocean management, *The Economist*, 22 February 2014, 48, labels IMO's standards on routine or accidental discharges 'one of the rare success stories of recent decades'.

to the Annex, which represents the first effort to address greenhouse gases (GHGs) from ships.

Two aspects of Annex VI will be discussed in more detail below: the sulphur in fuel requirements (section 3.3.2) and the initiatives to regulate the energy efficiency of ships and thereby reduce their carbon dioxide ($CO_2$) emissions, both the measures already agreed in 2011 (section 3.3.3) and the ones on which the debate is still on-going (section 3.3.4).

### 3.3.2   SOx emissions

Traditionally, marine fuels have been subject to very few regulatory requirements. Benefitting from this, international shipping has largely relied on cheap high sulphur heavy fuel oil. While other users of petroleum-based fuels have gradually been subjected to ever-tighter emission requirements, shipping has increasingly stood out as the main emitter of sulphur oxides and particulate matter, in particular along busy shipping routes.

The first effort to introduce some global limits to the sulphur content in ships' fuels was through Regulation 14 in the 1997 Annex VI to MARPOL, which entered into force in 2005. However, the agreed maximum sulphur content was so high (4.5 per cent sulphur in fuel) that the limitation remained largely devoid of any practical significance.[46]

In 2008 a significant strengthening of the Annex was made. The revised Annex VI, which entered into force in 2010, introduced a progressive reduction of emissions of $SO_x$, $NO_x$ and particulate matter, and further tightening of the standards within emission control areas (ECAs). The global sulphur cap was initially reduced to 3.5 per cent, effective from 1 January 2012, then to 0.5 per cent, effective from 1 January 2020, subject to a feasibility review to be completed no later than 2018. The limits applicable in ECAs for $SO_x$ and particulate matter were reduced to 1.0 per cent, beginning on 1 July 2010; and further to 0.1 per cent, effective from 1 January 2015.

Effectively, the new limits amount to a requirement to use distillate fuel oils (or other than petroleum-based fuels) on board ships in the ECAs. Even world-wide, however, once the global cap of 0.5 per cent enters into force, few heavy fuel oils will be able to meet the standard. The use of exhaust gas cleaning technologies, notably 'scrubbers', together with high-sulphur fuel will still be permitted, which will pose a challenge for the implementation and control of the standards. The new fuel requirements are widely expected to raise fuel costs for shipping and have accordingly given rise to significant unrest, in particular among ship operators and shippers in Northern Europe.

### 3.3.3   Greenhouse gas emissions

International maritime transport contributes to some 3 per cent of the total anthropogenic emissions of $CO_2$, and this share is widely expected to grow.[47] However these emissions do not form part of the global rules which have been adopted to reduce

---

[46]    The main effect of Regulation 14 was the more stringent requirement for special areas (Baltic Sea and North Sea), for which a maximum ceiling of 1.5% was implemented.

[47]    See, *Second IMO GHG Study*, IMO Doc. MEPC 59/INF.10, April 2009, 7 and *Third IMO GHG Study*, IMO Doc. MEPC 67/INF.3, June 2014, 13.

GHGs under the framework of the 1992 United Nations Framework Convention on Climate Change (UNFCCC),[48] and in particular the 1997 Kyoto Protocol.[49] Since the late 1990s, IMO has sought to address the reduction of greenhouse gases from ships, with a particular focus on $CO_2$, which is directly related to the amount of fuel consumed.

In 2011, the first regulatory progress was achieved in this field, when new design requirements for the energy efficiency of new ships were introduced as a new Chapter 4 to MARPOL Annex VI, which entered into force on 1 January 2013.[50] The new rules make mandatory the 'Energy Efficiency Design Index' (EEDI) for new ships. The index is based on a formula dividing the emissions (from main and auxiliary engines, subject to various correction factors) by the benefits for society (capacity and speed of the ship), and establishes index levels which new-built ships (differentiating between different categories of ships) have to comply with before they are entitled to operate. The index requirements will be gradually strengthened, so as to require higher energy efficiency by ships built in the future than of those built today.[51]

The new Chapter 4 also includes a provision which aims at reducing greenhouse gas emissions from ships by means of operational measures. All ships above 400GT are, based on the new Regulation 22, required to have a Ship Energy Efficiency Management Plan (SEEMP). The plan seeks to help ship operators to improve the energy efficiency of a ship by means of operational measures (eg, through improved voyage planning or more frequent hull cleaning, or introduction of technical measures such as waste heat recovery systems or a new propeller). However, the normative effect of the requirement is limited, as it only represents a requirement that such a management plan exists. It does not include any standards on the content of the plan, nor any reduction targets that ships have to meet.[52]

### 3.3.4 Measures under discussion

The IMO's new requirements on energy efficiency measures will reduce the amount of $CO_2$ emissions from international shipping over time. However, in the short run their effect is probably limited (as the reduction requirements concern ships to be built as from 2015), while world trade (and thereby shipping) is widely expected to grow. The IMO therefore continues to seek regulatory solutions for operational and market-based measures, in addition to the design requirements. In these areas, however, progress to date has been very limited.

---

[48] Opened for signature 9 May 1992, entered into force 21 March 1994, 1771 UNTS 165.

[49] Kyoto Protocol to the United Nations Framework Convention on Climate Change (opened for signature 11 December 1997, entered into force 16 February 2005) 2302 UNTS 148. As far as emissions from shipping (and aviation) are concerned, Article 2(2) of the Kyoto Protocol provides that: '[t]he Parties included in Annex I shall pursue limitation or reduction of emissions of greenhouse gases not controlled by the Montreal Protocol from ... marine bunker fuels, working through ... the International Maritime Organization'.

[50] See, IMO Doc. MEPC 62/24/Add.1.

[51] MARPOL Annex VI, Regulation 21, as amended in 2011.

[52] MARPOL Annex VI, Regulation 22. See also IMO Doc. MEPC.1/Circ.684 (Guidelines for voluntary use of the EEOI for new and existing ships). It has been estimated that operational measures could result in up to 50% reduction of $CO_2$ emissions.

The politically most difficult discussion has concerned market-based measures (MBMs), which under a broad definition include taxes, charges, tradable permit schemes and so on. As opposed to direct regulatory measures, MBMs rely on the principle that operators should be free to decide how to achieve the necessary reductions. By raising the price of $CO_2$ emissions they also create an additional incentive to improve fuel efficiency. A variety of MBMs for shipping have been proposed over the years, but the two main proposals are: an emissions trading system; and an international levy imposed on bunker fuel at purchase, established by a given cost level per tonne of fuel bunkered. Both measures have the potential to generate significant funds, which could be used for emission reduction measures where they can be most cost-effectively implemented (including emission reductions outside the realm of shipping).

Overshadowing these negotiations has been the discussion whether any future IMO rules should be based on the 'common but differentiated responsibility'[53] principle, as several developing states insist, or whether the more habitual IMO approach of equal or 'no more favourable' treatment of ships should apply.[54] Given the ease by which ship operators may choose the jurisdiction of their operations (by changing flag), it is feared that linking the obligations to the nationality of the ship will lead to massive evasion and re-flagging of ships to developing countries, without much effect in terms of emission reductions. Industrialized states have instead suggested that favourable treatment of developing states could be achieved in other ways, for example through the allocation of the funds generated by an MBM.

In the absence of global agreement on this issue, other organizations, in particular the EU, have indicated their preparedness to introduce MBMs for ships on a regional level.[55] The absence of global rules in the field would, however, give rise to a number of additional international law challenges, notably relating to how far a port state (or region) may rely on the voluntary presence of ships in its port as a justification for regulating matters which take place beyond its territorial jurisdiction to prescribe rules for foreign ships.[56]

---

[53]   See, eg, Birnie, Boyle and Redgwell, above n 24, 358.

[54]   See at n 95 below.

[55]   See, eg, the third recital of Directive 2009/29 amending Directive 2003/87/EC so as to improve and extend the greenhouse gas emission allowance trading scheme of the Community, OJ 2009 L 140, 63.

[56]   See H. Ringbom, 'Global Problem – Regional Solution? – International Law Reflections on an EU $CO_2$ Emissions Trading Scheme for Ships' (2011) 26 *The International Journal of Marine and Coastal Law* 613–641. See also Case C-366/10, in which the European Court of Justice concluded that the inclusion of foreign airlines in the European emission trading scheme would not be contrary to international law. *Air Transport Association of America and Others v Secretary of State for Energy and Climate Change* 2011 ECR I-13755.

## 3.4   Other IMO Conventions

For the sake of completeness, brief mention should be made of the main environmental rules of the IMO which have not been included in MARPOL, but are regulated in separate conventions.[57]

### 3.4.1   Anti-fouling systems

The 2001 International Convention on the Control of Harmful Anti-fouling Systems on Ships,[58] which entered into force in 2008, prohibits the use of harmful organotins in anti-fouling (underwater hull) paints used on ships and establishes a mechanism to prevent the use of other harmful substances in anti-fouling systems in the future.

### 3.4.2   Ballast water management

Invasive aquatic species present a major threat to marine ecosystems, and shipping is a major pathway for introducing species to new environments, in particular through ships' ballast water. The 2004 Ballast Water Management Convention[59] establishes standards and procedures for the management and control of ships' ballast water and sediments. It is not yet in force, but once it is, all ships in international traffic will need to install on-board ballast water treatment systems, based on a phased-in introduction of the requirements and an interim ballast-water exchange obligation.[60] Ships will also be required to have ship-specific ballast water management plans, certificates and record books on board to ensure that they minimize the ecological risks of their ballast water operations.

The main concern with the Ballast Water Management Convention related for a long time to the absence of available technologies for treating ballast water. This concern has by now largely vanished with ever-more systems being type approved by the IMO. Instead, the imminent entry into force of the convention has given rise to a series of other concerns, such as: the cost of the systems; whether the type approval of treatment technologies is robust enough; how the ballast water samples can be taken in ports in a manner which is both scientifically reliable and meets the needs of ships to proceed with their operations as quickly as possible; or the options for port state control authorities in case the systems prove to be deficient.

---

[57]   The review below does not include the recent Polar Code, which is addressed in detail in T. Henriksen, 'Protecting polar environments: coherency in regulating Arctic shipping', Chapter 17 in this volume.

[58]   See n 40 above.

[59]   See n 40 above.

[60]   In November 2013 IMO adopted a resolution that effectively amended the convention's fixed compliance deadlines by linking the timing of the requirements to the convention's entry into force. In February 2014, 38 states had ratified the convention, which is enough to bring it into force, but those states only represent 30% of the world's tonnage, while the percentage required is 35.

### 3.4.3   Ship recycling

The 2009 Hong Kong International Convention for the Safe and Environmentally Sound Recycling of Ships[61] seeks to ensure that ships, when being dismantled, or 'scrapped', after reaching the end of their operational lives, do not pose any unnecessary risks to human health, safety and to the environment. It deals with environmentally hazardous substances on board the ships, such as asbestos, heavy metals, hydrocarbons and ozone-depleting substances, but also the working and environmental conditions at the ship recycling facilities.[62]

The convention's obligations cover the whole life-span of a ship, including the design, construction, operation and preparation of ships so as to facilitate safe and environmentally sound recycling; the establishment of an appropriate enforcement mechanism for ship recycling, incorporating certification and reporting requirements. Ships will be required to have an initial survey to verify the inventory of hazardous materials, additional surveys during the life of the ship, and a final survey prior to recycling. Recycling yards will be required to provide a 'Ship Recycling Plan', specifying the manner in which each ship will be recycled, depending on its particulars and its inventory. Since much of the convention's focus lies on obligations for recycling facilities, it is crucial for the effectiveness of the convention that those states where ship recycling is actually undertaken will ratify the convention.[63]

At the EU level, a Regulation was adopted in December 2013 to facilitate the ratification and early implementation of the Hong Kong Convention and to complement it where appropriate.[64] The challenge for regional rules in this area is the weak jurisdictional link to the facilities where recycling takes place. The EU regulation seeks to overcome this, inter alia, by establishing and maintaining a European list of ship recycling facilities that meet the EU standards.[65]

---

[61]   1672 UNTS 126.

[62]   One of the reasons underlying the convention was the complex – and to some extent still unresolved – issue of whether sending a ship which includes hazardous material on board for dismantling falls under the scope of the 1989 Basel Convention on the Control of Transboundary Movements of Hazardous Wastes and Their Disposal, 1673 UNTS 57. The extent to which the Hong Kong Convention provides an 'equivalent level of control' to that of the Basel Convention is still not settled. See, eg, www.basel.int/Default.aspx?tabid=2766 (last accessed 14 May 2015).

[63]   The Hong Kong Convention will only enter into force when 15 states, representing 40% of the world's shipping tonnage have become parties. In addition, the convention's Art. 17 includes requirements on the ship recycling capacity of the states parties over the past ten years, which effectively means that several key recycling states need to participate for the convention to enter into force.

[64]   Regulation 1257/2013 on ship recycling and amending Regulation (EC) No 1013/2006 and Directive 2009/16/EC, OJ 2013 L330, 1, Art. 1. The regulation applies from a date which depends on the availability of ship recycling facilities that meet the requirements, but at the latest on 31 December 2018. See also U.D. Engels, *European Ship Recycling Regulation, Entry-Into-Force Implications of the Hong Kong Convention* (Springer, 2013).

[65]   As far as ships are concerned, most of the Regulation applies to ships flying the flag of an EU Member State. However, Art. 12, which deals with the presence of hazardous materials on board ships, extends to any ship calling at a port or anchorage in the Union.

## 3.5 IMO and Jurisdictional Rules

In view of the important role that the LOSC leaves to the IMO in defining the substantive boundaries of states' jurisdiction with respect to vessel-source solution, it is interesting to analyze how the post-LOSC activities of the IMO have effectively impacted the jurisdictional balance. The formal position of the IMO is that its activities are limited to the technical domain and that it therefore refrains from legislating in jurisdictional matters.[66] However, as a few examples of the past decades have illustrated, the distinction between 'technical' and 'jurisdictional' rules is not always clear. Two examples are particularly worth noting, where it comes to the IMO's stance on what environmental measures coastal states may adopt in their coastal zones.

First, certain amendments to Chapter V of the International Convention on Safety of Life at Sea (SOLAS)[67] that have been introduced since 1995 indicate a preparedness by the IMO to address matters which are of direct relevance to states' prescriptive jurisdiction in their coastal waters.[68] Those amendments have, inter alia, clarified that traffic separation schemes and other ships' routeing systems may be more widely used than what a mere reading of the LOSC would suggest, that such systems may include mandatory 'no go' areas within the EEZ of the coastal state, and that they may be adopted for the sole reason of protecting the marine environment. The amendments arguably therefore alter the jurisdictional balance set out in the LOSC, and may be taken as evidence that the organization has recognized the possibility that the law of the sea may be developed through collective international actions and is prepared to make use of this possibility.[69]

This development is not necessarily problematic, however, and its significance should not be exaggerated. A certain development of the jurisdictional balance is even foreseen in the LOSC, within certain limits.[70] In addition, SOLAS is a very widely accepted international convention and amendments thereto, through the tacit acceptance

---

[66] See, eg, IMO Doc. LEG/MISC.8, 18 and A. Blanco-Bazán, 'The Environmental LOSC and the Work of IMO in the Field of Prevention of Pollution from Vessels' in A. Kirchner (ed.), *International Maritime Environmental Law, Institutions, Implementation and Innovations* (Kluwer Law International, 2003). See also C.H. Allen, 'Revisiting the Thames Formula: The Evolving Role of the International Maritime Organization and its Member States in Implementing the 1982 Law of the Sea Convention' (2009) 10(5) *San Diego International Law Journal* 265–333.

[67] Adopted 1 November 1974, entered into force 25 May 1980, 1184 UNTS 278.

[68] See in particular Regulations V/10 on ships' routeing systems, V/11 on ship reporting systems and V/12 on vessel traffic services.

[69] See also G. Plant, 'The Relationship between International Navigation Rights and Environmental Protection: A Legal Analysis of Mandatory Ship Traffic Systems' in H. Ringbom (ed.), *Competing Norms in the Law of Marine Environmental Protection, Focus on Ship Safety and Pollution Prevention* (Kluwer Law International, 1997) 26–7 and the ILA Report, above n 9, 453.

[70] LOSC Arts 311(2) and (3) place limits on *inter se* agreements among LOSC Parties which may affect the object and purpose or 'basic principles' of the Convention or the enjoyment by other states parties of their rights and obligations. See also the somewhat more liberal LOSC Art. 237 which deals specifically with environmental agreements.

procedure,[71] will hence bind a very large number of the states concerned.[72] The development of the jurisdictional balance within the framework of the international organization most directly concerned with the consequences would seem to represent an acceptable way to make allowances for new technical and political developments, and where necessary add a degree of flexibility to the jurisdictional regime, without thereby calling into question the overall legitimacy of the LOSC. Indeed, through an increased recognition by the IMO that the LOSC regime is neither designed nor intended to prohibit any future alterations in the jurisdictional balance, other types of strains on that balance, and on the LOSC as such, can probably be reduced.

The second example is different in that it is not based on a specific convention or other legally binding instrument. The development and implementation of the concept of 'Particularly Sensitive Sea Areas' (PSSAs) is based on a series of guidelines, adopted in the form of IMO Assembly Resolutions, the latest being from 2005.[73] In this case there is no clear legal foundation for the protective measures adopted in the PSSA, in particular for areas designated outside the territorial sea. Despite various attempts within the IMO to clarify the precise role and legal functions of PSSA protective measures, the current PSSA Guidelines still give rise to uncertainty. The available protective measures, as specified in the guidelines, leave open the possibility for the IMO to adopt protective measures which do not have a basis in the existing IMO conventions.[74]

This raises the question whether the IMO's approval of those measures is legally sufficient, or whether measures must be limited to those which have a solid legal basis elsewhere. In the latter case the concept of PSSA adds little to the rights and possibilities that states already have under international law and is, hence, essentially meaningless in jurisdictional terms. On the other hand, the former approach may seem overly liberal, almost like a blank check for the IMO to revise the jurisdictional balance set out in LOSC by means of committee decisions.

The true jurisdictional nature of PSSAs is still unsettled and will eventually have to be established through the practice of the IMO.[75] So far, the protective measures which have eventually been approved for the 14 existing PSSAs have not been overly controversial from this perspective.[76] This, however, does not exclude that the IMO

---

[71]    See at n 44 above.

[72]    As of February 2014, 162 states had ratified or acceded to the 1974 SOLAS, together representing more than 98.8% of the world's tonnage.

[73]    The most recent guidelines are to be found in the Annex to IMO Resolution A.982(24) 'Guidelines for the Identification and Designation of Particularly Sensitive sea Areas', hereinafter 'the PSSA Guidelines'.

[74]    See, in particular, the PSSA Guidelines, para. 7.5.2.3. See also V. Frank, 'Consequences of the *Prestige* Sinking for European and International Law' (2005) 20 *International Journal of Marine and Coastal Law* 29; M. Detjen, 'The Western European PSSA – Testing a Unique International Concept to Protect Imperilled Marine Ecosystems' (2006) 30 *Marine Policy* 449.

[75]    On this question, more generally, see M. Kachel, *Particularly Sensitive Sea Areas – The IMO's Role in Protecting Vulnerable Marine Areas* (Springer, 2008) and Ringbom n 39 above, 457–70 with further references.

[76]    A number of legally controversial proposals have been discussed over the years, however, including notably the measures proposed for the Western European and the Torres Strait PSSAs.

adopts a different approach in the future. Indeed, one of the more ingenious features of the PSSA is that it offers a *possibility* for states to go beyond their regular environmental jurisdiction in exceptional circumstances, without having to rely on more heavyweight procedures such as revisions of the relevant international conventions, including the LOSC. The concept has aptly been described as a 'safety valve' in case of exceptional pressure.[77] In this way, the PSSA has the potential to develop into a (moderate) 'LOSC reviser', exercised through the IMO. This in itself is significant and may serve to explain both the interest in and the controversies still surrounding the concept.

### 3.6 Prescription Outside the IMO

### 3.6.1 Global organizations

While the IMO has clearly been given a key role in the LOSC to regulate matters relating to ship-source pollution, it does not – despite the organization's own contention to that effect[78] – have a regulatory monopoly in this field. First, even if it is widely assumed that the 'competent international organization' (in singular) referred to in the LOSC in most cases refers to the IMO, there may very well be other organizations that are competent within specific regulatory fields. Examples include the International Atomic Energy Agency for nuclear cargoes, the International Labour Organization, for matters relating to seafarers and maritime labour and the framework under the 1989 Basel Convention on the Control of Transboundary Movements of Hazardous Waste and Their Disposal[79] for issues relating to such movements. Moreover, the reference to the competent international organization is usually coupled with the alternative of a 'general diplomatic conference', which opens the door for other international bodies or institutions to develop rules for shipping on an ad hoc basis. So far, however, major institutional clashes have been avoided and where a substantive issue touches upon the responsibility of several international organizations, the matter has usually been resolved by cooperation. A more delicate situation could develop, however, if the global climate change community considers that the IMO's actions to reduce GHGs from ships are insufficient and need to be complemented by measures undertaken within the UN Framework Convention for Climate Change.

---

On these, see J. Roberts, 'Compulsory Pilotage in International Straits: The Torres Strait PSSA Proposal' (2006) *Ocean Development & International Law* 93; and J. Roberts, M. Tsamenyi, T. Workman and L. Johnson, 'The Western European PSSA Proposal: a "Politically Sensitive Sea Area"' (2005) *Marine Policy* 431.

[77] See A. Merialdi, 'Legal Restraints on Navigation in Marine Specially Protected Areas' in Tullio Scovazzi (ed.), *Marine Specially Protected Areas* (Kluwer Law International, 1999), 32, Johnson, above n 28, 110 and L. de La Fayette, 'The Marine Environment Protection Committee: The Conjunction of the Law of the Sea and International Environmental Law' (2001) 16(2) *International Journal of Marine and Coastal Law* 191.

[78] IMO Doc. LEG/MISC.8, 7.

[79] Adopted 22 March 1989, entered into force 5 May 1992, 1673 UNTS 57.

### 3.6.2   Regional organizations

*3.6.2.1   General*   Regional organizations or bodies have not been granted any prominent role in the LOSC for the regulation of shipping. No additional prescriptive jurisdiction for regions is provided in the convention[80] and the very purpose of references like 'the competent international organization' and 'generally accepted international rules and standards' is to exclude the application of requirements that are not widely accepted at global level to foreign ships. Yet, the limitations in the LOSC do not, as illustrated in section 2 above, exclude all complementary regulatory measures for states. For coastal states there is still national jurisdiction as regards, for example, discharge standards, navigational requirements or liability rules in the territorial sea. For port states an even wider discretion exists to impose their own standards for foreign ships. If states decide to implement such requirements in a co-ordinated manner at regional level, the effects of the requirement will intensify and may in practical terms come close to a regional competition with the IMO standards. The potential strength of regional initiatives in the field of ship-source pollution accordingly lies more in the practical effects of co-ordinated action than in additional jurisdictional rights.

Two different types of regional organizations which are involved in the regulation of shipping will be briefly mentioned here: on the one hand, the regional organizations established for the protection and preservation of the environment of particular regional seas; on the other hand the EU, which now comprises 28 member states and whose rules also apply to the three non-member states who participate in the European Economic Area (EEA).

*3.6.2.2   Regional seas organizations*   Since the 1970s, regional bodies have been established to address environmental concerns with respect to particular sea areas. Specific conventions now exist for the Baltic Sea, the North Sea and the 14 regions administered by or associated with the UNEP's Regional Seas Programme worldwide.[81] In general, these regional seas conventions have been cautious to address vessel-source pollution, which has been considered to be the remit of the IMO.[82] To the extent they have included provisions on vessel-source pollution, the efforts have mostly focused on achieving a regionally coordinated implementation of the global rules. Some of the regions, notably the Baltic Sea, have also taken an active role in coordinating initiatives of relevance for the region within the IMO.

In the past decade, however, some of the regional organizations have increased their sphere of activities from only implementing the IMO rules to supplementing them in various ways. Certain instruments have established their own standards, including

---

[80]   Not even Part IX of the LOSC, which deals with enclosed or semi-enclosed seas, provides any additional jurisdiction for coastal states.

[81]   For discussion see, Nilufer Oral, 'Forty years of the UNEP Regional Seas Programme: from past to future', Chapter 16 in this volume.

[82]   For an overview of the activities of the Baltic Sea, North-East Atlantic and the Mediterranean Sea regions in this respect, see V. Frank, The European Community and Marine Environmental Protection in the International Law of the Sea: Implementing Global Obligations at the Regional Level (Martinus Nijhoff Publishers, 2007) 214–25.

requirements concerning foreign ships.[83] However, in jurisdictional terms these activities still remain cautious. Most regional rules for shipping are closely related to the corresponding provisions in the IMO Conventions and where differences have been introduced, they tend to be of a complementary, rather than competing nature. Purely regional standards are usually adopted in the form of recommendations only. The regional instruments sometimes go to considerable pains to emphasize their compatibility with the LOSC regime and some specifically confirm the supreme role of the IMO as the competent international organization to adopt rules for merchant shipping.[84]

*3.6.2.3 The European Union* In the past two decades, the European Union (EU) has developed from a non-actor in shipping regulation to one of the dominant global players, both policy-wise and in terms of substantive regulatory activity. The EU has generally been hesitant to introduce additional requirements for ships flying the flag of its member states only, and has rather focused on developing rules that apply to all ships, mainly for ships that enter ports in the region, but to some extent also for ships in transit through member states' coastal waters. With this starting point, law of the sea restraints will obviously be very relevant for limiting the EU's prescriptive ambitions in this field.[85]

The bulk of the EU's maritime safety and environment legislation implements and builds upon IMO rules. Merely copying rules that exist at international level is not as futile as it may sound, for several reasons. First, the inclusion of the rules into the EU legal order incites implementation of the rule by all member states, irrespective of their formal adherence to the convention in question; second, it brings along the powerful law-enforcement apparatus of the EU; third, EU laws have direct effect or applicability on private individuals; and finally, EU rules affect the division of competence between the EU and its member states for the topic concerned.

Rather than merely copying international rules, EU rules sometimes include elements that are independent of, and go beyond, the IMO standards. A certain development over time may be noticed in this regard, both in terms of prescriptive standards which can be seen to be moving gradually from an earlier implementation of IMO rules or mandatory

---

[83]    An example is the 2002 Malta Protocol Concerning Cooperation in Preventing Pollution from Ships and, in Cases of Emergency, Combating Pollution of the Mediterranean Sea, adopted 25 January 2002, entered into force 17 March 2004, reproduced in A.V. Lowe and S.A.G. Talmon, *The Legal Order of the Oceans: Basic Document on the Law of the Sea* (Hart Publishing, 2009), which includes coastal requirements on issues such as post-accident reporting (Art. 9(2)) or 'measures aimed at reducing the risk of accidents' (Art. 15). See also Regulations 4 and 10–12 to Annex IV of the 1992 Helsinki Convention on the Protection of the Marine Environment of the Baltic Sea Area, adopted 9 April 1992, entered into force 17 January 2000, 2099 UNTS 197, which includes requirements on double-hulled tankers, AIS, PSC, the International Safety Management Code and places of refuge, often with reference to the relevant EU legislation.

[84]    See, eg, Art. 4(2) of Annex V to the 1992 Convention for the Protection of the Marine Environment of the North-East Atlantic (OSPAR Convention), adopted 22 September 1992, entered into force 25 March 1998, reproduced in A.V. Lowe and S.A.G. Talmon, *The Legal Order of the Oceans: Basic Document on the Law of the Sea* (Hart Publishing, 2009) and the preamble and Arts 1(e) and 15 of the 2002 Malta Protocol, above n 83.

[85]    See Ringbom, above n 39 and V. Frank, above n 82.

application of IMO recommendations to rules that complement and possibly even compete with the IMO rules and for the enforcement measures where the possible consequences of non-compliance found through port state control have progressively been tightened and now include the 'banning' of the ship from all EU ports, even permanently; in other cases ships may be refused access to the ports to begin with or, in the case of violation of the MARPOL discharge rules, be subject to criminal sanctions defined by EU law. In some instances, the EU has brought in concepts from its internal legal order that are alien to the law of the sea to deal with specific maritime issues such as the 'host state' concept which is used mainly for regulating passenger ships on regular routes to or from an EU port.[86]

### 3.7 Conclusion on Prescriptive Standards

In conclusion, the IMO has been granted a privileged position in the international law of the sea and has actively contributed to manifest itself as the chief regulator in shipping, including for vessel-source pollution. However, it does not have a regulatory monopoly or a particular 'constitutional' claim to fend off competing regulatory initiatives by others. The risk of competing regulatory action by individual states, regions or other international organizations constantly hangs over the regulatory work of the IMO and maintaining its role as the chief regulator suggests that it cannot leave its more environmentally minded membership unsatisfied. To date, it is widely considered that the IMO has generally responded both quickly and satisfactorily to upcoming challenges in this field, resulting in a notable increase in environmental regulation over the past few decades, even though some of this is yet to enter into force. When it comes to the reduction of GHGs from ships, the Organization's progress is not so impressive and its work has been hampered by an uncharacteristic 'North/South' division among its membership. So far, the IMO's regulatory activities have not significantly altered the jurisdictional balance laid down in the LOSC, but a number of more or less controversial proposals to regulate vessel-source pollution have illustrated that this is a possibility which the Organization is prepared to consider in times of significant political pressure, usually following high-profile pollution incidents.

## 4.  IMPLEMENTATION AND ENFORCEMENT

### 4.1  General

The regulatory overview is not complete without a brief look at how the relevant rules and standards are implemented in practice. In this area the IMO does not have a significant role; the key players are individual states or regions.

---

[86]   See, eg, Directive 1999/35 on a system of mandatory surveys for the safe operation of regular ro-ro ferry and high-speed passenger craft services, OJ 1999 L 138, 1.

## 4.2 Flag States

Generally speaking, the IMO conventions, like the LOSC, place the key obligations on flag states, typically in the form of minimum obligations to which the (flag state) administrations of the states parties are to give effect, irrespective of the ship's trading area.[87]

Despite the unconditional obligations of flag states to implement and enforce a minimum set of international rules and standards for their ships, under the IMO conventions, as well as under the LOSC, there are few remedies available against non-complying flag states. The IMO has traditionally avoided undertaking controls or other follow-up action with respect to poorly performing states. In this area, however, some progress has recently been made through the adoption in December 2013 of the IMO Instruments Implementation Code (III Code).[88] The Code provides a global standard to enable states to meet their obligations as flag, port and/or coastal states, and seeks to make the previously voluntary member state audit scheme mandatory by 2016.[89] As a matter of principle, it is significant that the organization in this way appears to be increasing its control over the performance of its member states, in particular in their capacity as flag states.

In practical terms, much of the technical work of flag states is undertaken by classification societies. These societies have a legally somewhat uncomfortable dual role. On the one hand, they act on behalf of flag states in verifying the ship's compliance with safety and environmental requirements laid down in the international conventions and issue the relevant statutory certificates.[90] On the other hand, classification societies assess the condition of a ship against their own technical standards and issue a 'class certificate' for the ship upon the request of the shipowner. The class certificate as such is not required by any convention, but is a commercial necessity for the ship to operate.[91] Despite their key role in the enforcement system, classification societies are not subject to specific quality criteria or controls by the IMO.[92]

---

[87]   See, eg, the first articles of SOLAS and MARPOL. Annex 2 of IMO Resolution A. 973(24) lists more than 500 specific flag state obligations which follow from the various IMO conventions.

[88]   IMO Resolution A.1070(28) (IMO Instruments Implementation Code (III Code)).

[89]   IMO Resolutions A.1067(28) (Framework and procedures for the IMO Member State audit scheme), and A.1068(28) (Transition from the voluntary IMO Member State audit scheme to the IMO Member State).

[90]   LOSC, Art. 94(4)(a) requires flag States to ensure that 'each ship, before registration and thereafter at appropriate intervals, is surveyed by a qualified surveyor of ships' while Art. 217(3) requires flag States to ensure that their ships carry the necessary certificates and that the ships are 'periodically inspected in order to verify that such certificates are in conformity with the actual condition of the vessels'. The possibility for flag States to entrust inspection and surveys to 'recognized organizations' (ie, classification societies) is acknowledged, inter alia, in SOLAS Regulation I/6 and MARPOL Regulations I/6 and II/8.

[91]   It is required by charterers, insurers and other business partners. See also SOLAS Chapter II-1, Regulation 3-1, which in 1995 added a new requirement that ships are to be 'designed, constructed and maintained in compliance with the structural, mechanical and electrical requirements of a recognised classification society'.

[92]   See IMO Resolution A.739(18) 'Guidelines for the authorization of organizations acting on behalf of the Administration', under which some 50 organizations are recognized. This

### 4.3  Port States

The wide discrepancy in how different flag states choose to implement their international obligations, combined with the ease by which ship operators may change the flag of their ships, has given rise to a secondary layer of ship control, by port states. The principal tool for states to ensure that foreign ships entering their ports meet the international requirements is port state control (PSC), which is specifically provided for in most IMO conventions[93] and partly in the LOSC.[94]

PSC is normally undertaken in a three-step procedure. The initial inspection is limited to a check of the ship's certificates. If the inspector considers that there are 'clear grounds' for believing that the certificates do not accurately describe the condition of the ship, a more detailed inspection may be undertaken. If the more detailed inspection reveals deficiencies which are 'clearly hazardous to safety, health or the environment', the ship will be detained and only released when all such deficiencies have been rectified. It follows that this type of control is normally better suited for technical requirements than for operational issues. Several IMO conventions specifically provide that states shall not differentiate between parties and non-parties to the convention in question.[95]

In practice, there is a growing discrepancy with respect to how port states choose to implement this layer of control. Whereas in some PSC regions, in particular in Europe, PSC has been based on mandatory inspection requirements and sophisticated IT tools for selecting the ships to be inspected, and assessing their risk profile on a daily basis,[96] the more common approach worldwide is still based on an administrative coordination arrangement, which is non-binding and at best includes some targets as to the percentage of ships that should be inspected.[97]

---

contrasts with the more stringent EU-based scheme for monitoring the performance of classification societies recognized by EU member states. Regulation 391/2009 on common rules and standards for ship inspection and survey organizations, OJ 2009 L 131, 11, currently recognizes ten organizations (societies) to work on behalf of EU member states.

[93]    See, eg, SOLAS, Art. I/19; MARPOL Art. 5(2); International Convention on Load Lines, adopted 5 April 1966, entered into force 21 July 1968, Art. 21; International Convention on Standards of Training, Certification and Watchkeeping for Seafarers, adopted 1 December 1978, into force 28 April 1984, Art. X.

[94]    See, eg, LOSC, Arts 219 and 226.

[95]    See, eg, MARPOL, Art. 5(4). The jurisdictional foundation for the 'no more favourable treatment' (NMFT) clause is not in the IMO conventions as such, but is based on the more general right of port states under international law to place obligations on ships entering its ports.

[96]    See, eg, www.parismou.org/ (last accessed 14 May 2015) and http://emsa.europa.eu/psc-main/new-inspection-regime.html (last accessed 14 May 2015).

[97]    For the activities of some of the other regional port state control regimes, see eg www.tokyo-mou.org/, www.iomou.org/, www.medmou.org/, www.caribbeanmou.org/, www.bsmou.org/ and www.riyadhmou.org/ (last accessed 14 May 2015).

## 4.4   Coastal States

Despite the attention given to this matter at the negotiations leading to LOSC, and subsequently in legal literature, coastal states have not played a very important role in the enforcement of rules on vessel-source pollution.[98] This is partly due to the quite limited jurisdiction which is provided to coastal states on this matter, but a more important reason is probably that physical enforcement measures against ships at sea are impractical, difficult and expensive to undertake.

Two strategies seem to have developed for dealing with vessel-source pollution at sea without having to resort to enforcement at sea. One approach has been to 'territorialize' violations, by defining the offence in a way that brings it within the jurisdiction of the port [coastal] state. This can be done by focusing enforcement on 'static' features on board the ship, such as the presence of pipes by-passing the oily-water separator or the absence of proper documentation, instead of the act of pollution as such. Another approach is to focus on secondary violations which occur in the context of the in-port investigation of potential pollution violations, instead of the violation itself. Examples include charging the defendants with making false statements to PSC officials during the investigation, or with offences relating to witness tampering or obstruction of justice. US judicial practice on pollution violations provides several examples of how such techniques have been utilized for dealing with pollution violations at sea.[99]

Another strategy which has been particularly preferred in Europe has been to seek to spot (mainly oil) spills remotely from air planes or, increasingly, by satellites, for subsequent enforcement in port. While a considerable number of likely pollution violations have been detected in this way, the main challenge has been to ensure the cooperation between the different governmental bodies involved in the process between identifying pollution and bringing it to a judicial conclusion (including satellite image operator, maritime surveillance authorities, coast guard authorities, PSC, police

---

[98]   See above n 24. For an unusual example of enforcement measures taken by France and Spain in times of high political pressure, see the incidents referred to by the UN Secretary-General in UN Doc. A/58/65, para 57 ('Oceans and the law of the sea', Report of the Secretary-General, 3 March 2003). On the same subject, see also *Sea Pollution – Report of the Parliamentary Assembly's Committee on the Environment, Agriculture and Local and Regional Affairs*, Council of Europe Report No. 10485, 30 March 2005. It should be noted, however, that coastal states have made significant progress at global as well as regional level to coordinate and regulate the preparedness for and response to shipping accidents. Due to space considerations, these instruments, which normally do not give rise to controversies in international law, are not discussed here.

[99]   For an overview, see R.A. Udell, 'United States Criminal Enforcement of Deliberate Vessel Pollution: A Document-Based Approach to MARPOL' in D. Vidas (ed.) *Law, Technology and Science for Oceans in Globalisation – IUU Fishing, Oil Pollution, Bioprospecting, Outer Continental Shelf* (Martinus Nijhoff Publishers, 2010) 269–90.

authorities, prosecutor, courts).[100] The increased use of satellite images in judicial procedures highlights the need to clarify their status as technical evidence.[101]

More generally, technological advances have allowed coastal states to make increasing use of remote surveillance technologies for monitoring maritime traffic along their coastal waters, for subsequent enforcement actions by flag and/or port states. Some of these tools are based on data from equipment which has been made mandatory for ships to carry,[102] while others are based on other public or commercial initiatives.[103] Such tools allow for a very precise monitoring of the movement of ships, which can be combined with other data, such as (remotely operated) radar or camera images of a given area, or other ship data. Combining ship movement data with information, such as engine particulars or fuel quality, also allows for very accurate estimates of individual ships' air emissions, for example, which could be used for entirely new types of enforcement schemes in the future.

## 5. CONCLUDING REMARKS

The conclusion of the LOSC in 1982 represented a major milestone for the global agreement on a comprehensive jurisdictional framework relating to navigation, including vessel-source pollution. The subsequent widespread acceptance of the convention, and of the IMO instruments to which it commonly refers, has provided stability in maritime regulation in the past decades. The scheme has not escaped criticism, not least by those who feel it is not 'green' enough,[104] but has clearly maintained its authority as the normative standard on the limits of states' prescription and enforcement jurisdiction over shipping over the years. At the same time it has ensured that one of its key objectives, to secure the mainly international nature of the regulation of vessel-source pollution, has been met.

---

[100]   In 2013, the EU-wide CleanSeaNet delivered 2547 satellite images, identifying 2176 possible oil spills. See, eg, *The Pollution Preparedness & Response Activities of the European Maritime Safety Agency, 2013*, Report by the European Maritime Safety Agency, 30 January 2014, 40–44.

[101]   Ibid., 44–6.

[102]   Apart from the introduction of mandatory voyage data recorders (VDRs) in 2005 (SOLAS Reg. V/20), all ships need to be fitted with an automatic ship identification system (AIS) (SOLAS Reg. V/19). This is a VHF-based transmission to other nearby (some 100 NM) ships ground stations which includes very detailed information on ships' particulars, movement and voyage data (including ship identification data and information of current speed, course and the port of destination). Finally, SOLAS Reg. V/19-1 also requires that ships are fitted with 'long-range identification and tracking' (LRIT) senders. This is a satellite based system which allows less frequent and less detailed information, but operates on a global scale (between latitudes 70°N and S).

[103]   Satellite-based AIS, which currently exists only as a commercial service, combines the benefits of the terrestrial AIS and the LRIT systems and hence allows very detailed information of ship particulars and movement to be transmitted through satellites on a world-wide basis, including the polar regions.

[104]   See, eg, D. Bodansky, 'Protecting the Marine Environment from Vessel-Source Pollution: LOSC III and Beyond' (1991) *Ecology Law Quarterly* 719–77.

The success of the LOSC in this regard lies partly in the flexibility which is inherent in its provisions, which tolerates subsequent developments – even in the field of the jurisdictional balance which it seeks to settle itself – without calling into question the overall authority of the convention. In addition, the relative absence of revolt against the LOSC is in large part due to the very proactive role taken by the IMO in responding to new regulatory challenges in the environmental field. Up until now, most environmental challenges have been responded to reasonably swiftly and in a manner which satisfies its demanding and diverse membership.

A third explanation for the authority of the jurisdictional scheme for vessel-source pollution today could be that the convention does not regulate the most critical issues. Whereas the LOSC's main focus is on the balance of interests between flag states and coastal states, subsequent developments in practice have shifted the legal attention elsewhere. Hence, relatively few of the regulatory developments discussed here call for a need to interpret the LOSC-IMO scheme in detail.[105] Rather the attention has shifted to issues which are only superficially dealt with in the convention or not at all. Answers to questions that are not regulated in the LOSC have to be found in general international law.[106]

Such questions include the extent of port states' (territorial) jurisdiction over ships, the relationship between the essentially territorial jurisdictional regime of the LOSC and the bases for extra-territorial jurisdiction under general international law and the responsibility of states for failing to meet their international maritime obligations, or for individuals who fail to do so. Since the legal answers to these type of questions are rarely as precise as – and usually more contested than – individual provisions of the LOSC or IMO conventions, it seems that vessel-source pollution will provide fertile ground for interesting legal research in the future.

---

[105] The main exception being Directive 2005/35, referred to above n 19. The compatibility of this directive with the LOSC/MARPOL scheme was challenged by shipping industry associations before the European Court of Justice. The Court did not conclude on that particular point, however, but upheld the validity of the directive. Case C-308/06 *Intertanko and others*, ECR 2008 I-4057.

[106] This is acknowledged also in LOSC itself. The eighth paragraph of its preamble affirms that 'matters not regulated by this Convention continue to be governed by the rules and principles of general international law'.

# 6.   The international control of ocean dumping: navigating from permissive to precautionary shores
*David L. VanderZwaag*

## 1.   INTRODUCTION

The international legal framework for controlling ocean dumping might be described as having two main shores. On the one hand, the Convention on the Prevention of Marine Pollution by Dumping of Wastes and Other Matter,[1] adopted in 1972 and often referred to as the London Convention (LC), stands out for its entrenching a permissive approach to ocean dumping. With the exception of wastes listed on a prohibited list, often referred to as a black list, almost anything can be dumped at sea as long as a permit is obtained from a Contracting Party.[2] On the other hand, the 1996 Protocol to the London Convention (LP)[3] has grounded a precautionary approach to ocean dumping. Only wastes listed on a global 'accepted list' may be disposed of at sea and only after a detailed waste assessment which considers reuse and recycling options has been undertaken.[4]

The present regulatory picture for ocean dumping might be described as complicated. For Contracting Parties to both the LC and LP, the Protocol supersedes the Convention.[5] Some countries are only party to the London Convention,[6] while others are not party to either agreement.[7] Such non-parties may still be bound to follow at least the LC ocean disposal standards in light of Article 210(6) of the UN Law of the Sea Convention[8] which requires national laws and measures to be no less effective in

---

[1]   29 December 1972, 1046 UNTS 138 (hereinafter LC).

[2]   For an overview of the Convention, see Phillippe Sands et al., *Principles of International Environmental Law* (3rd edn, Cambridge University Press, 2012) 366–8.

[3]   1996 Protocol to the Convention on the Prevention of Marine Pollution by Dumping of Wastes and Other Matter, 7 November 1996, 36 *International Legal Materials* 1 (1997) (hereinafter LP).

[4]   For a further review of the reverse listing approach and associated waste assessment guidance, see Alan Sielen, 'The New International Rules on Ocean Dumping: Promise and Performance (Part 1)' (2009) 21 *Georgetown International Environmental Law Review* 295, 321–4.

[5]   LP, above n 3, Art. 23.

[6]   For example, as of 30 September 2014, Brazil, Panama, the Russian Federation and the United States were just party to the London Convention. For a complete listing of parties, see IMO, Status of Conventions http://www.imo.org/About/Conventions/StatusofConventions/Pages/Default.aspx (last accessed 16 May 2015).

[7]   For example, in the East Asian region, North Korea, Malaysia, Myanmar, Singapore, Thailand and Viet Nam. Ibid.

[8]   10 December 1982, 1833 UNTS 3.

controlling pollution by dumping than the global rules and standards.[9] Doubts continue over whether the London Convention or the Protocol represents the applicable global rules and standards.[10]

The use of the oceans as a dumping ground has certainly been decreasing over the decades but is still substantial. For example, in 2011, a total of 1325 ocean dumping permits were issued by 26 countries with the largest number of permits issued by China (389), Hong Kong, China (154), United Kingdom (104), Philippines (97), Denmark (87), Canada (85), France (61), Sweden (50), and the United States (50).[11] While dredged materials remain the largest quantity of dumped materials, other categories of ocean disposal include fish wastes, sewage sludge, vessels, platforms, organic materials of natural origin, inert inorganic geological materials and spoilt cargoes.[12]

The volumes of dredged materials disposed at sea continue to be massive and of particular concern. For example, in 2011 Egypt reported the dumping of close to 23.5 million tonnes in the Mediterranean and Red Seas; the UK reported disposing of over 13 million tonnes in the North Sea, English Channel, Irish Sea and Malin Sea regions; China licensed disposals close to 144 million tonnes in the East China Sea, about 40 million tonnes in the Bohai and Yellow Seas, and over 30 million tonnes in the South China Sea.[13] Key concerns include possible contamination of dredged wastes with toxic substances and heavy metals and the potential adverse impacts on other uses of the sea including fishing.[14]

This chapter provides an overview of the overall shift from a permissive to a precautionary approach to international waste disposals at sea through a five-part 'cruise.' Part 2 briefly describes the traditional assimilative capacity approach of the London Convention with the assumption that the oceans could absorb considerable types and amounts of wastes with very limited exceptions.[15] Part 3 summarizes the major shifts towards a precautionary approach introduced by the 1996 London Protocol. Part 4 highlights the 'sea of challenges' still being faced in ocean dumping control practice. Various interpretive uncertainties continue to abound, such as what are wastes from normal operations of ships that are excluded from permitting requirements and what precisely are prohibited industrial wastes? Other implementation challenges include: addressing ocean fertilization and geo-engineering activities; strengthening

---

[9]   See David L. VanderZwaag and Anne Daniel, 'International Law and Ocean Dumping: Steering a Precautionary Course Aboard the 1996 London Protocol, but Still an Unfinished Voyage' in Aldo Chircop, Ted L. McDorman and Susan J. Rolston (eds), *The Future of Regime Building: Essays in Tribute to Douglas M. Johnston* (Martinus Nijhoff 2009) 515, 519.

[10]   Canada, Development of a Strategic Plan for the London Convention and Protocol, LC 36/31 (29 August 2014) 2.

[11]   Reporting information should be viewed as incomplete as 55 Contracting Parties did not report for permits issued in 2011. See IMO, Final Report on Permits Issued in 2011, IMO Doc. LC-LP.1/Circ. 68 (2 February 2015) Annex, Table 1.

[12]   Ibid., Annex, 2–4.

[13]   Ibid.

[14]   IMO, Report of the Thirty-Fifth Consultative Meeting and the Eighth Meeting of Contracting Parties, IMO Doc LC 35/15 (21 October 2013), Annex 2 Revised Specific Guidelines for Assessment of Dredged Material.

[15]   David L. VanderZwaag, *Canada and Marine Environmental Protection: Charting a Legal Course Towards Sustainable Development* (Kluwer Law International, 1995) 146.

compliance with reporting and monitoring obligations; securing adequate technical and capacity development assistance; dealing with ocean disposals in internal waters; addressing liability and compensation issues; and achieving wide acceptance of the London Convention and Protocol. Part 5 concludes with an overall assessment of international efforts to control ocean dumping to date and suggests future governance directions, in particular the need for a comprehensive and visionary strategic action plan.

## 2. THE PERMISSIVE SHORES OF THE LONDON CONVENTION

The London Convention is largely permissive in its regulatory approach. With the exception of wastes listed in Annex I where dumping is prohibited,[16] most types of wastes may be disposed of at sea subject to permitting requirements. Annex II lists wastes that require a special permit before ocean disposal with particular care to be exercised, for example, possibly requiring capping of dumped materials.[17] Dumping of other wastes or matter requires a general permit, and Annex III sets out various factors to be considered by authorities in deciding whether to issue a permit. Those factors include toxicity, persistence, tainting and bioaccumulation potentials, possible conflicts with other uses of the sea, and the availability of alternative land-based methods of treatment or disposal.

Even prohibited wastes listed on Annex I might be dumped in some circumstances. Such dumping may be justified if necessary to secure the safety of life, vessels or platforms, for example in cases of *force majeure*[18] and also in emergency situations posing unacceptable risk relating to human health and admitting to no other feasible solution.[19] Dumping of dredged materials and sewage sludge containing trace amounts of some of the prohibited substances may also be allowed.[20]

The focus of the Convention is to control deliberate disposals at sea[21] of wastes or other matter from vessels, aircraft, platforms and other human-made structures[22] and

---

[16]   Those wastes include organohalogen compounds, mercury and mercury compounds, cadmium and its compounds, persistent plastics, various oils, radioactive wastes, biological and chemical warfare materials, and industrial waste. Incineration at sea of industrial waste and sewage sludge is further prohibited. LC, above n 1, Annex I, 10(a).

[17]   Annex II includes wastes containing significant amounts of listed substances, such as heavy metals like lead and nickel, and bulky wastes which may present a serious obstacle to fishing or navigation.

[18]   Such dumping must be the only way of averting the threat and based on a probability assessment that the damage consequent upon such dumping would be less than would otherwise occur. LC, above n 1, Art. V(1).

[19]   LC, Art. V(2).

[20]   Matter allowed in trace amounts include the first five categories of wastes listed, namely, organohalogen compounds, mercury, cadmium, persistent plastics and various oils. LC, Annex I (9).

[21]   Sea is defined broadly to include all marine waters but does not include internal waters of States. LC, Art. III (3).

[22]   LC, Art. III (1)(a)(i).

the deliberate disposal at sea of vessels, aircraft, platforms and other structures.[23] Dumping does not include wastes incidental to the normal operations of vessels, aircraft, platforms or other human-made structures[24] nor disposal of wastes directly arising from seabed mineral operations.[25] Placement of matter other than the mere disposal thereof is also not considered dumping provided the placement is not contrary to the aims of the Convention.[26]

The Convention does pay some attention to pollution prevention but with permissive twists. Article I calls upon Contracting Parties to take all practicable steps to prevent pollution by ocean dumping that is liable to create hazards to human health, to harm living marine resources, to damage amenities or to interfere with other legitimate uses of the sea. Article II requires Parties to take a preventive approach as provided in the following Articles and according to their scientific, technical and economic capabilities. Parties are allowed to prohibit dumping of wastes not mentioned in Annex I.[27]

## 3. TOWARDS PRECAUTION, THE 1996 LONDON PROTOCOL

The precautionary approach, a central norm of international environmental law but with considerable interpretive confusion,[28] has been embraced in the London Protocol in three major ways. First, the Protocol explicitly adopts as one of the general obligations for Parties the application of a precautionary approach to ocean dumping. Appropriate preventative measures are to be taken when there is reason to believe that wastes or other matter introduced into the marine environment are likely to cause harm even when there is no conclusive cause-effect evidence.[29]

A second precautionary shift is the adoption of a 'reverse listing' approach to ocean dumping. Only wastes or other matter listed on Annex 1 may be considered for dumping. Those wastes include: dredged material; sewage sludge; fish waste; vessels and platforms or other man-made structures at sea; inert, inorganic geological material; organic material of natural origin; and bulky items primarily comprising iron, steel, concrete or similarly unharmful materials for which the concern is physical impact.[30] In

---

[23] LC, Art. III (1)(a)(ii).
[24] LC, Art. III (1)(b)(i).
[25] LC, Art. III (1)(c).
[26] LC, Art. III (1)(b)(ii).
[27] LC, Art. IV (3).
[28] See, eg, N. deSadeleer (ed.), *Implementing the Precautionary Principle: Approaches for the Nordic Countries, EU and USA* (Earthscan, 2007) and A. Trouwborst, *Precautionary Rights and Duties of States* (Martinus Nijhoff, 2006).
[29] LP, above n 3, Art. 3-1.
[30] The dumping of bulky items is to be limited to those circumstances where such wastes are generated in locations, such as small islands with isolated communities, having no practicable access to disposal options other than dumping. LP, Annex 1, s. 1.7.

November 2006, Annex 1 was amended to further allow carbon dioxide sequestration in geological formations under the seabed.[31]

A third route towards a precautionary approach is a requirement that any dumping of wastes on Annex I must be subject to a permit, and in issuing permits Parties must follow the detailed waste assessment responsibilities set out in Annex 2 of the Protocol.[32] Parties are urged to subject ocean dumping proposals to waste prevention audits. If an audit reveals opportunities to prevent waste at source, the applicant is expected to formulate and implement a waste prevention strategy.[33] A dumping permit must be refused if the permitting authority determines that appropriate opportunities exist to re-use, recycle or treat the waste without undue risks to human health or the environment or disproportionate costs.[34] A permit is also to be refused if a waste is so poorly characterized that a proper assessment cannot be made of its potential impacts on human health and the environment.[35]

Annex 2 also encourages environmental assessments of potential effects of sea or land disposals. If an assessment reveals adequate information is not available to determine the likely effects of the proposed disposal option, then that option should not be considered further.[36] If a comparative assessment between land and sea dumping shows the ocean dumping option to be less preferable, a permit for ocean dumping should not be granted.[37]

Additional guidance documents have been developed to flesh out the steps and considerations that Parties should follow in undertaking waste assessments. Besides a set of general waste assessment guidelines applicable to all proposed ocean dumping activities allowed under the London Convention or London Protocol,[38] nine separate guidelines for specific waste categories have also been issued which set out particular assessment factors needing to be considered.[39] Those guidelines include:

- Specific Guidelines for Assessment of Dredged Material;
- Specific Guidelines for Assessment of Sewage Sludge;
- Specific Guidelines for Assessment of Fish Waste;
- Specific Guidelines for Assessment of Vessels;
- Specific Guidelines for the Assessment of Platforms or Other Man-Made Structures at Sea;
- Specific Guidelines for the Assessment of Inert, Inorganic Geological Material;

---

[31]   IMO, Report of the Twenty-Eighth Consultative Meeting and First Meeting of Contracting Parties, IMO Doc LC 28/15 (6 December 2006) Annex 6. Article 5 of the LP further prohibits the incineration of sea of wastes and other matter.

[32]   LP, Art. 4.1.2.

[33]   LP, Annex 2, s. 2.

[34]   LP, s. 6.

[35]   LP, s. 7.

[36]   LP, s. 12.

[37]   LP, s. 14.

[38]   Guidelines for the Assessment of Wastes or Other Matter That May Be Considered for Dumping (Generic Guidelines), available at http://www.imo.org/OurWork/Environment/LCLP/Publications/wag/Pages/default.aspx (last accessed 27 May 2015).

[39]   The specific guidelines are available at ibid.

- Specific Guidelines for Assessment of Organic Material of Natural Origin;
- Specific Guidelines for the Assessment of Bulky Items Primarily Comprising Iron, Steel, Concrete, Etc.;
- Specific Guidelines for Assessment of $CO_2$ Streams.

The nine Specific Guidelines are quite similar in their formats with detailed advice provided on various fronts including potential sources of pollution and waste management options.[40] For example, the Specific Guidelines for the Assessment of Platforms highlight the many potential substances of concern, such as hydrocarbons, drilling muds, corrosion inhibitors, biocides and lubricants[41] and suggest various waste disposal options. They include re-use at sea, or on-shore recycling, and final disposal on land or at sea.[42] The Guidelines note that the topsides of platforms containing production, processing and accommodation facilities are generally taken ashore for recycling or re-use.[43]

Additional guidance documents have been issued for setting levels of acceptable contaminants in dredged material[44] and fish wastes.[45] Parties are encouraged to develop action lists setting out constituents of concern because of their potential adverse human health and marine environmental effects and to establish action levels for the constituents. Establishing acceptable (lower benchmark) and unacceptable (upper benchmark) levels for constituents of concern is suggested.

The allowance of sub-seabed disposal of $CO_2$ streams has been controversial and was further expanded in 2009. Concerns continue over the possibility of $CO_2$ leakages into the marine environment which would contribute to further ocean acidification.[46] Through Resolution LP. 3(4) in October 2009, the governing bodies adopted an amendment to the Protocol which would allow the export of $CO_2$ streams, provided that an agreement or arrangement has been entered into by the countries concerned.[47]

---

[40]   For a listing of the common elements, see IMO, *The London Protocol: What It Is and How to Implement It* (IMO, 2013) 34.

[41]   Specific Guidelines for the Assessment of Platforms or Other Man-Made Structures at Sea, above n 39, para. 4.5.

[42]   Ibid., para. 3.1.

[43]   Ibid. Whether offshore installations should be totally removed has been controversial. See Ton Ijlstra, 'Removal and Disposal of Offshore Installations' (1989) 1 *Marine Policy* 269.

[44]   Guidance for Development of Action Lists and Action Levels for Dredged Material (2009) http://www.gc.noaa.gov/documents/gcil_imo_dmaction.pdf (last accessed 27 May 2015).

[45]   2012 Guidelines for the Development of Action Lists and Action Levels for Fish Waste, IMO 2013.

[46]   See Secretariat of the Convention on Biological Diversity, *Geo-engineering in Relation to the Convention on Biological Diversity: Technical and Regulatory Matters*, Technical Series No. 66(2012) 56; and Tim Dixon et al., 'International Marine Regulation of $CO_2$ Geological Storage: Developments and Implications of London and OSPAR' (2009) 1 *Energy Proceedings* 4503.

[47]   Further guidance on how export of $CO_2$ streams should be managed was agreed to by the governing bodies in October 2013. See, Guidance on the Implementation of Article 6.2 on the Export of $CO_2$ Streams for Disposal in Sub-Seabed Geological Formations for the Purpose of Sequestration, Report of the Thirty-Fifth Consultative Meeting and the Eighth Meeting of Contracting Parties, above n 14, Annex 6.

## 4.  SEA OF CHALLENGES

While varying implementation challenges have confronted Parties to the LC and LP, seven challenging issues stand out and are reviewed below. Implementation challenges beyond the scope of this chapter include the harmonization of procedures under the global regime with regional ocean dumping agreements and provisions, such as those for the Mediterranean and Northeast Atlantic,[48] and the establishment of a radiological assessment procedure for determining what level of ionizing radiation in wastes, such as dredged materials, should be permitted so as to ensure the protection of not just human health but marine flora and fauna.[49]

### 4.1  Sorting Out Interpretations

The texts of the London Convention and Protocol raise many questions of interpretation but two of the most controversial issues surround the meaning of key ocean dumping exceptions. Both texts provide that dumping does not include disposal of wastes 'incidental to or derived from the normal operations of vessels'.[50] Also exempted is 'placement of matter for a purpose other than the mere disposal thereof, provided that such placement is not contrary to the aims of [the LC/LP]'.[51]

Whether spoilt cargoes and animal carcasses, arising from mortalities of livestock carried aboard ships, were subject to the normal operations of ship exception was a particularly difficult interpretive issue to resolve and has now been partially clarified. Through 2011 amendments to Annex V of the International Convention for the Prevention of Pollution from Ships (MARPOL),[52] discharge of all garbage not specifically allowed in the regulations under Annex V is now prohibited.[53] Since spoilt cargo is not regulated as garbage under MARPOL Annex V, spoilt cargo may be subject to the London Convention and Protocol if ocean dumping is being considered. The governing bodies of the LC/LP and the IMO's Marine Environment Protection Committee (MEPC) have published a joint circular on Revised Guidance on the Management of Spoilt Cargoes[54] which seeks to minimize the dumping of spoilt cargoes at sea and offers advice on how to meet the LC/LP requirements if the ocean dumping option is chosen. The guidance document emphasizes that the ideal way to manage spoiled cargoes during a voyage would be to offload on land for appropriate

---

[48]   For a summary of the regional conventions and agreements that include regulation of sea dumping, see IMO, above n 40, Annex 10.

[49]   While Guidelines for the Application of the *De Minimis* Concept under the London Convention 1972 (1999, amended in 2003) have been adopted that address assessment of radiological impacts to human health, a methodology for assessing doses to flora and fauna is still under discussion within the scientific groups. See IMO, Report of the Thirty-Seventh Meeting of the Scientific Group of the London Convention and the Eighth Meeting of the Scientific Group of the London Protocol, LC/SG 37/16 (12 June 2014) 31–2.

[50]   LC Art. III (1)(b)(i) and LP Art. 1.4.2.1.

[51]   LC Art. III (1)(b)(ii) and LP Art. 1.4.2.2).

[52]   IMO Marine Environment Protection Committee, Res MEPC. 201(62) (15 July 2011).

[53]   Ibid., para. 2.

[54]   LC-LP 1/Circ. 58 (3 July 2013) and MEPC. 1/Circ. 809 (28 June 2013).

management.[55] Ocean disposal should only be considered where there is a marked degree of urgency, facilities on land are unavailable, and the disposal will not cause harm to the environment or human health.[56] If ocean dumping of a spoilt cargo appears to be appropriate, the permitting requirements of the London Convention or London Protocol will have to be met.[57]

For animal carcasses the applicability of the LC/LP regime is less clear. The 2011 amendments to MARPOL Annex V permit the discharge into the sea of animal carcasses generated during the normal operation of a ship but only if the ship is en route, outside a special area, as far as possible from the nearest land and in accordance with guidelines developed by the IMO.[58] Subsequent Guidelines for Implementation of MARPOL Annex V, issued in 2012,[59] recommend that the discharge into the sea should take place greater than 100 nautical miles from the nearest land and in the maximum water depth possible.[60] The Guidelines draw a rather hazy line between limited and expected animal mortalities during a voyage where MARPOL Annex V applies[61] and mortalities in excess of those generated during the normal operation of a ship where the London Convention and Protocol may apply. The Guidelines provide examples of circumstances that may result in mortalities exceeding those generated during normal ship operation, specifically:

- Weather events such as heat waves or storm systems;
- Infectious disease outbreaks;
- Refusal of cargo offloads by authorities at destination, leading to the need to euthanize some or all of the live animal cargo.[62]

The LC/LP exception for the 'placement of matter for a purpose other than the mere disposal thereof' has also raised interpretation issues with the placement of artificial reefs being a particular concern. The IMO and the United Nations Environment Programme (UNEP) have quite creatively addressed the potential grey area surrounding the application of the LC/LP by issuing Guidelines for the Placement of Artificial Reefs in 2009.[63] The Guidelines emphasize that artificial reef placements should not be used as an excuse for disposal at sea of waste materials, and placements should not be contrary to the aims of the Convention.[64] If materials used in placement activities fall under one of the categories of allowed wastes under the London Protocol, such as

---

[55]   Ibid., para. 2.

[56]   Ibid.

[57]   A regular permit or emergency permit may be issued. Ibid., paras 19 and 20.

[58]   Regulation 4.1.4 of MARPOL Annex V, above n 52.

[59]   Res MEPC. 219(63) (2 March 2012).

[60]   Ibid., para. 2.12.5.

[61]   Paragraph 2.12.2 of the Guidelines provides only general guidance with animal deaths from common causes and low numbers being considered mortalities generated during the normal operation of a ship. Ibid.

[62]   Ibid., para. 2.12.14.

[63]   IMO/UNEP, London Convention and Protocol/UNEP Guidelines for the Placement of Artificial Reefs (2009).

[64]   Ibid., 13.

vessels or platforms, assessments should be carried out in accordance with the relevant Specific Waste Assessment Guidelines.[65]

Other interpretation issues have also arisen in LC and LP implementation practice. What constitutes industrial wastes prohibited from ocean dumping on the one hand, and, on the other, inert, inorganic, geological materials which are allowed, has been the subject of some controversy. Concerns have been raised over Japan's dumping of bauxite residues, sometimes referred to as 'red mud', with many Parties considering such disposal as industrial waste being ineligible for dumping.[66] When the Cook Islands allowed the scuttling of a ship reportedly filled with 300 tonnes of cement containing asbestos and took the position that such disposal met the geological material exception, various Parties questioned that conclusion.[67]

A question of interpretation also hovers over the dumping of platforms and vessels. The London Protocol allows such ocean dumping provided that material capable of creating floating debris or otherwise contributing to pollution of the marine environment has been removed 'to the maximum extent'. Such language leaves some uncertainty as to the extent to which all potentially toxic substances, for example, PCBs contained in solid materials such as electrical cables and gaskets might have to be removed.[68]

### 4.2   Addressing Ocean Fertilization and Geo-engineering Activities

Since geo-engineering is the topic of Chapter 21 in this volume, only a brief summary of efforts under the LC/LP to address ocean fertilization and other geo-engineering activities is provided here.[69] Through a resolution in October 2008, the governing bodies agreed that given the present state of knowledge, ocean fertilization activities other than legitimate scientific research should not be allowed and such other activities

---

[65]   Ibid., 14.

[66]   VanderZwaag and Daniel, above n 9 at 526. Japan has committed to ceasing such dumping by 2015. See IMO, Report of the Thirty-Fourth Meeting of the Scientific Group of the London Convention and the Fifth Meeting of the Scientific Group of the London Protocol, LC/SG 34/15 (24 May 2011) para. 7.2.3.

[67]   VanderZwaag and Daniel, above n 9 at 526.

[68]   An example of this type of issue was raised when Greenpeace International questioned the placement of a former US naval ship as an artificial reef off the coast of Florida with the grounds for the challenge being the insufficient cleaning of PCBs. See VanderZwaag and Daniel, ibid., 523.

[69]   For further discussions of the efforts, see Randall S. Abate and Andrew D. Greelee, 'Sowing Seeds Uncertain: Ocean Iron Fertilization, Climate Change, and the International Environmental Law Framework' (2010) *Pace Environmental Law Review* 555; David L. VanderZwaag, 'Ocean Dumping and Fertilization in the Antarctic: Tangled Legal Currents, Sea of Challenges' in Paul A. Berkman, Michael A. Lang, David W.H. Walton and Oran R. Young (eds), *Science-Diplomacy: Antarctica. Science, and the Governance of International Species* (Smithsonian Institution Scholarly Press, 2011) 245–52; and Rosemary Rayfuse and Robin Warner, 'Climate Change Mitigation Activities in the Ocean: Regulatory Frameworks and Implications' in M. Tsamenyi, C. Schoffield and R. Warner (eds) *Climate Change and the Oceans: Gauging the Legal and Policy Currents in the Asia Pacific Region* (Edward Elgar Publishing, 2012).

should be considered contrary to the aims of the Convention and Protocol.[70] The governing bodies also agreed that until specific assessment guidance was developed, Parties should use utmost caution and best available guidance to evaluate scientific research proposals to ensure marine environmental protection consistent with the LC/LP.[71]

In October 2010, the governing bodies through a further resolution adopted an assessment framework for determining what legitimate scientific research proposals would be acceptable.[72] The resolution also called for the development of a 'global, transparent and effective control and regulatory mechanism for ocean fertilization activities and other activities that fall within the scope of the London Convention and Protocol and have the potential to cause harm to the marine environment …'.[73]

In October 2013, Contracting Parties adopted amendments to the London Protocol to regulate the placement of matter for ocean fertilization and other marine geo-engineering activities.[74] The amendments include a definition of marine geo-engineering; provide for listing geo-engineering activities that may be permitted with the list initially including only ocean fertilization for legitimate scientific research; and adopt through a separate annex an assessment framework for determining whether listed marine geo-engineering activities should be allowed.[75]

## 4.3   Strengthening Compliance

The 1996 Protocol to the London Convention in Article 11 called for the development of compliance procedures within two years after entry into force of the Protocol. The Protocol entered into force in 2006, and in 2007 the Meeting of Contracting Parties established the called for compliance procedures and mechanisms.[76] A Compliance Group of 15 members is the main mechanism for encouraging compliance with three ways in which individual situations of non-compliance might be raised. A Party may report its own lack of compliance.[77] A Party may challenge the non-compliance of

---

[70]   Resolution LC-LP.1 (2008) on the Regulation of Ocean Fertilization (31 October 2008), para. 8.

[71]   Ibid., para. 6.

[72]   Resolution LC-LP.2 (2010) on the Assessment Framework for Scientific Research Involving Ocean Fertilization (14 October 2010). For a detailed review of the framework, see Melissa Eick, 'A Navigational System for Uncharted Waters: The London Convention and London Protocol's Assessment Framework on Ocean Iron Fertilization' (2010) 46 *Tulsa Law Review* 351.

[73]   Res LC-LP.2, para. 5.

[74]   IMO, Report of the Thirty-Fifth Consultative Meeting and the Eighth Meeting of Contracting Parties, above n 14, Annex 4, Res. LP.4(8).

[75]   Through a new Annex 5. Ibid. For a further review of the amendments, see Philomène Verlaan, 'New Regulation of Marine Geo-engineering and Ocean Fertilization' (2013) 28 *International Journal of Marine and Coastal Law* 729.

[76]   Report of the Twenty-Ninth Consultative Meeting and the Second Meeting of Contracting Parties, LC 29/17, Annex 7, Compliance Procedures and Mechanisms Pursuant to LP Article 11, (14 December 2007).

[77]   Ibid., para. 4.1.2.

another Party.[78] The Meeting of Contracting Parties may also raise issues of non-compliance.[79]

Sanctioning powers in response to non-compliance are very limited. The Compliance Group may recommend to the Meeting of Contracting Parties that one or more measures be taken, specifically: the provision of advice and recommendations; the facilitation of cooperation and assistance; the elaboration of compliance action plans including targets and timelines; and the issuing of a formal statement of concern.[80] The Protocol limits the compliance role of the Meeting of Contracting Parties to offering advice, assistance or co-operation to Contracting Parties and non-Contracting Parties.[81]

While pursuant to both the London Convention and Protocol, Parties are required to report on the number and nature of ocean dumping permits issued and on monitoring activities relating to ocean disposal sites,[82] non-compliance has been a continuing problem. Fifty-five Parties did not report on dumping permits issued in 2011.[83] Only 37 Parties provided reports on their dumping activities during that year.[84] Many Parties have not reported on their dumping activities for over five years with 38 Parties not submitting reports for 2008–2012 compared with 32 non-reporting Parties recorded for the period 2007–2011.[85] At the Meetings of Parties on October 2012, the reality that no compliance monitoring reports have been submitted in recent years was noted, and Parties were invited to submit reports on compliance monitoring to the next session of the governing bodies.[86] However, with no monitoring reports submitted to the October 2013 session, Parties were again invited to submit reports to the next session of the governing bodies.[87]

The Compliance Group, not receiving individual complaints, has struggled to address the systemic non-reporting issues. Its future work programme continues to place a priority on identifying and reviewing the factors contributing to non-reporting by

---

[78]   Ibid., para. 4.1.3.

[79]   Ibid., para. 4.1.1.

[80]   Ibid., para. 5.1.

[81]   LP, Art. 11. For a comparison of the compliance provisions under the LP with other international compliance mechanisms, see IMO, Report from the 10th meeting of the Committee Administering the Mechanism for Promoting the Implementation and Compliance of the Basel Convention and the session 'Dialogue with other compliance mechanism', LP-CG 7/10, 11 September 2014.

[82]   Article 9.4 of the Protocol requires annual reports while Article VI(4) of the London Convention calls for submission of ocean dumping and monitoring reports following the procedure to be agreed to by the Parties.

[83]   Final Report on Permits Issued in 2011, above n 11.

[84]   Ibid., 1.

[85]   Status of Compliance with the Notification and Reporting Requirements under Article VI(4) of the London Convention 1972 and Article 9.4 of the London Protocol, LC 36/7/2 (10 September 2014).

[86]   Report of the Thirty-Fourth Consultative Meeting of the Seventh Meeting of Contracting Parties, LC 34/15 (20 November 2012), para. 6.3.2.

[87]   Report of the Thirty-Fifth Consultative Meeting and the Eighth Meeting of Contracting Parties, above n 14, para. 6.27.

Parties to the LP.[88] The Compliance Group has also established a priority to reach out to Parties in order to ensure that a national focal point is designated for each Party.[89]

The governing bodies of the LC and LP continue to follow an encouragement role. At their October 2013 meeting, they urged all Parties, if they have not done so, to provide the Secretariat with their annual reports, including no-dumping reports, as soon as possible.[90] They also encouraged States to continue to reach out to neighbouring countries who are not reporting and offer assistance in preparing their reports on dumping activities.[91]

## 4.4 Securing Adequate Technical and Capacity Development Assistance

The London Convention and the 1996 Protocol contain provisions calling for scientific and technical assistance to be given to the Parties that request it, but neither agreement includes a guaranteed funding commitment or mechanism. The LC directs assistance responsibility to Contracting Parties[92] while the LP also imposes obligations on both Contracting Parties and the International Maritime Organization (IMO) to facilitate technical cooperation and assistance.[93] The LP explicitly states that the IMO's technical assistance functions are subject to the availability of adequate resources.[94]

To strengthen the capacities for countries to implement their treaty obligations under the LC and LP, and to promote membership in the London Protocol, Contracting Parties have followed two main routes. A Long-term Strategy for Technical Co-operation and Assistance under the London Convention and Protocol, first adopted in 2001 and revised in 2006,[95] sets out overall objectives and priorities for technical assistance activities. Helping countries comply within their reporting and monitoring responsibilities and in implementing waste assessments have been identified as issues of particular concern.[96] Since 2007, a 'Barriers to Compliance' (B2C) project has served as a main implementing mechanism for the Strategy.[97] The B2C project has largely focused on offering national and regional training workshops[98] and the project assisted with finalizing a manual on how to implement the London Protocol.[99]

---

[88] Report of the 6th Meeting of the Compliance Group under the London Protocol, *ibid.* at Annex 7, para. 10.1.5.

[89] Ibid., para. 10.1.4.

[90] Ibid., para. 6.24.1.

[91] Ibid., para. 6.24.2

[92] LC, Art. IX.

[93] LP, above n 3, Art. 13.2.

[94] Ibid., Art. 13.2.3.

[95] IMO, Report of the Twenty-Eighth Consultative Meeting and the First Meeting of Contracting Parties, LC 28/15 (6 December 2006), Annex 10.

[96] Ibid.

[97] For a further discussion, see Alan Sielen, 'The New International Rules on Ocean Dumping: Promise and Performance Part 2' (2009) 21 *Georgetown International Environmental Law Review* 495, 503.

[98] From 1998 to 2013, 29 barriers to compliance workshops were held. IMO, above n 40 at 32.

[99] Ibid.

While determining the exact amount of funding available for technical and capacity development assistance is difficult because of the multiple sources of financing, both bilateral and multilateral, ensuring adequate and reliable financial resources has been a challenge.[100] The London Convention / Protocol Technical Cooperation Fund (TCTF) was established by the IMO in December 2009 as a voluntary financial mechanism to support countries in implementing the LC and LP.[101] However, funding contributions to TCTF have been limited. For the period 1 January 2010 to 31 December 2011, total income in US dollars was reported as $131,523 and for the period 1 January 2012 to 31 August 2012,[102] revenue was reported to be $163,561.[103]

### 4.5   Dealing with Ocean Disposals in Internal Waters

The applicability of the LC and LP to dumping within internal waters is very limited.[104] The London Convention explicitly excludes coverage of ocean dumping in internal waters.[105] The London Protocol gives Parties considerable discretion as to whether to apply the Protocol's provisions to internal waters or to adopt other effective permitting and regulatory measures to control the deliberate disposal of wastes or other matter in marine internal waters.[106] Contracting Parties to the Protocol are encouraged to provide the IMO with information on legislation and implementation efforts to control dumping in internal waters and to provide, on a voluntary basis, summary reports on the type and nature of materials dumped in marine internal waters.[107]

A further major internal waters coverage limitation is the exclusion of land-based ocean disposals. The LC and LP only cover deliberate disposals into the sea from vessels, aircraft, platforms or other human-made structures at sea.[108] Thus, various land-based discharges, such as radioactive waste discharge by Japan from the Fukushima Daiichi nuclear plant[109] and disposal of mine tailings via coastal outfalls, are technically outside the Convention and Protocol.

Nevertheless, Parties to the LC and LP continue to study and discuss various coastal management issues. The Scientific Group under the LC and LP have co-operated with UNEP's Global Programme of Action for the Protection of the Marine Environment from Land-based Activities (GPA) in preparing a report on riverine and sub-sea

---

[100]   Sielen, above n 98 at 504.

[101]   Ibid., 31.

[102]   IMO, Report on the LC-LP Trust Fund, LC 34/12 (7 September 2012) Annex at 1. The majority of the funds have been expended on workshops with lesser amounts supporting participation at LC/LP meetings.

[103]   Ibid., 3.

[104]   Internal waters are those waters landward of the territorial sea baselines.

[105]   LC, Art. III (3).

[106]   LP, Art. 7.2.

[107]   LP, Art. 7.3.

[108]   LP, Art. 1.4.1.1 and LC, Art. III(1)(i).

[109]   For a detailed discussion, see Darian Ghorbi, 'There's Something in the Water: The Inadequacy of International Anti-Dumping Laws as Applied to the Fukushima Daiichi Radioactive Water Discharge' (2012) 27 *American University Law Review* 473.

disposals of tailings and associated wastes.[110] The Scientific Groups have agreed that it remains an open question as to which international organization would be the appropriate body or bodies to develop international guidance or codes of conduct.[111] The disposal of hull scraping wastes outside a controllable dockyard environment is an ongoing concern since anti-fouling paint flakes and fouling organisms could interfere with dredged material disposal operations.[112] The governing bodies in October 2013 invited the scientific groups to consider whether an update is required[113] of a previous guidance document on the removal of anti-fouling coatings.[114]

## 4.6   Addressing Liability and Compensation Issues

Both the London Convention[115] and the London Protocol contain similar provisions regarding a commitment by Parties to develop liability procedures relating to ocean dumping. Article 15 of the Protocol states:

> In accordance with the principles of international law regarding State responsibility for damage to the environment of other States or to any other area of the environment, the Contracting Parties undertake to develop a procedure regarding liability arising from the dumping or incineration at sea of wastes or other matter.

However, the issue of liability has not been a high priority and little progress on developing a liability regime has been achieved to date.[116] While the liability issue arose for substantial discussion in 2006 when Parties to the London Protocol were considering an amendment to add $CO_2$ to the reverse list in order to allow sequestration in the seabed, the governing bodies in 2007 agreed not to embark on the development of liability procedures. Rather Parties were requested to report on a voluntary basis to the Secretariat on national regulations applicable to environment-related liability and redress. Such reporting is listed as an ongoing activity.[117]

---

[110]   See International Assessment of Marine and Riverine Disposal of Mine Tailings (30 November 2012) http://www.imo.org/blast/blastData.asp?doc_id=14538&filename=Mine%20 Tailings%20Marine%20and20%20Riverine%20Disposal%20Final%20Report%20November%20 30.pdf (last accessed 16 May 2015).

[111]   IMO, Report of the Thirty-Sixth Meeting of the Scientific Group of the London Convention and the Seventh Meeting of the Scientific Group of the London Protocol, LC/SG 36/16 (1 July 2013) para. 8.27.

[112]   Report of the Thirty-Fifth Consultative Meeting and the Eighth Meeting of Contracting Parties, above n 14, para. 8.3.

[113]   Ibid., para. 8.4.

[114]   Guidance on Best Management Practices for Removal of Anti-fouling Coatings for Ships, including TBT Hull Paints (LC-LP.1/Circ. 31) was published in 2009.

[115]   LC, above n 1, Art. X.

[116]   For a more detailed discussion, see VanderZwaag and Daniel, above n 9, 538–539.

[117]   IMO, Joint Long-Term Programme for the London Convention and Protocol (2013– 2015), LC-LP.1/Circ. 54 (24 January 2013) Annex, 13.

### 4.7   Achieving Wide Acceptance of the Protocol

Getting countries to become Parties to the London Protocol has been a substantial challenge with a modest ratification record to date and acceptances in some regions particularly meagre. As of 30 September 2014, there were 45 Contracting Parties to the Protocol representing 36.6 per cent of the world vessel tonnage.[118] Only four States from East Asia had become Parties to the Protocol: China, Japan, Philippines and the Republic of Korea.[119] Mexico was the only Latin American State to join the Protocol while Suriname, Chile and Uruguay were the only South American Parties.[120] African States have not widely embraced the Protocol with only six African States being Parties: Egypt, Ghana, Kenya, Nigeria, Sierra Leone and South Africa.[121]

## 5.  CONCLUSION

The 1996 Protocol to the London Convention has certainly set a precautionary course for the future of ocean dumping. The Protocol's reverse listing approach of only allowing a globally accepted group of wastes to be disposed of at sea, and the Protocol's further imposition of stringent waste assessment and permitting requirements promise to reduce ocean dumping to a minimum. However, considerable disposals may still be allowed for listed wastes that are considered acceptable, including sub-seabed $CO_2$ sequestration and dredged materials.

As discussed above, the London Convention and Protocol are not without their implementation challenges. One of the greatest difficulties has been ascertaining the meanings and boundaries of key textual terms. Two of the main interpretive issues have been the exceptions to treaty coverage – disposals associated with the 'normal operations of vessels' and placement of matter for a purpose other than the mere disposal thereof, provided that such placement is not contrary to the aims of the Convention/Protocol.

While the London Convention and Protocol have been quite adaptive in responding to new ocean disposal and placement challenges, such as $CO_2$ sequestration in the seabed and ocean fertilization, the agreements certainly do not represent a panacea for addressing international ocean disposals at sea. Land-based discharges to the marine environment remain beyond the scope of LC and LP coverage.[122] The LC and LP exclusions of waste disposals arising from exploration, exploitation and associated off-shore processing of seabed marine resources,[123] is likely to become a growing

---

[118]   IMO, Summary of Status of Conventions http://www.imo.org/About/Conventions/StatusofConventions/Pages/Default.aspx (last accessed 27 May 2015).

[119]   IMO, Status of Conventions, above n 6.

[120]   Ibid.

[121]   Ibid.

[122]   See David Osborn, 'Land-based pollution and the marine environment', Chapter 4 in this volume.

[123]   LC, Art. III(1)(c) and LP, Art. 1.4.2.3.

concern in light of the growing commercial reality of seabed mining.[124] The historical dumping of chemical weapons at sea,[125] before the LC and LP where adopted, has yet to be fully addressed[126] and the role, if any, in addressing the issues of the governing bodies of the LC and LP has yet to be determined.[127]

A key future direction may be the development of an overall Strategic Plan for the London Convention and Protocol. In 2013, Canada submitted a paper to the governing bodies of the LC and LP emphasizing the lack of a single document setting out the Parties' collective strategic directions and priorities and criticizing the failure to keep up with best practices in other multilateral environmental agreements where strategic plans have been adopted, such as under the Convention on Biological Diversity and the Basel Convention on the Control of Transboundary Movement of Hazardous Wastes and Their Disposal.[128] A correspondence group process has been established to draft a Strategic Plan which may include targets for reducing tonnage of materials disposed of at sea and for increasing the number of Parties to the Protocol.[129] The Strategy is proposed for completion in 2015.[130]

Whatever future directions are charted for the Protocol, one reality remains certain. The Protocol will continue to serve as a beacon of light on how a precautionary approach may be put into practice. Those lessons have yet to be fully translated into other areas of international environmental law, such as the control of land-based marine pollution and management of toxic chemicals.[131] Whether the world can wait much longer for the lessons to be transferred remains to be seen.

---

[124] See Greenpeace International, 'Seabed Mining as a Growing Commercial Reality: How Can We Ensure Protection of the Marine Environment?', LC/SG 36/41 (26 April 23).

[125] Some 300,000 tonnes of chemical and biological warfare agents are estimated to have been disposed of by the major military powers into the world's oceans from 1946 until 1965. George M. Morris, 'Truth in Chemical Weapons Disposal: A Call for an International Convention on the Full Disclosure of Chemical Weapons Disposal of at Sea and Pollution Preparedness, Response and Co-Operation' (2005) 12 *University of Baltimore Journal of Environmental Law* 165.

[126] See Report of the Secretary-General, Cooperative Measures to Assess and Increase the Awareness of Environmental Effects Related to Waste Originating from Chemical Munitions Dumped at Sea, A/68/258 (24 July 2013).

[127] Ibid., para. 75.

[128] Canada, Consideration of the Need for a Strategic Plan, LC 35/3/3 (9 August 2013).

[129] Report of the Thirty-Fifth Consultative Meeting and the Eighth Meeting of Contracting Parties, above note 14, Annex 3, Terms of Reference for the Intersessional Correspondence Group to Develop a Strategic Plan for the London Convention and Protocol.

[130] IMO, Report of the Correspondence Group on the Development of a Strategic Plan for the London Convention and Protocol LC/36/3 (1 August 2014) para. 6.5.

[131] VanderZwaag and Daniel, above n 9, 549–50.

# PART III

# SEABED ACTIVITIES AND THE MARINE ENVIRONMENT

# 7. Protecting the marine environment of the deep seabed

*Michael Lodge*

## 1. INTRODUCTION AND SCOPE

This chapter discusses the legal aspects of the protection of the marine environment of the deep seabed, specifically its protection from the potential adverse effects caused by seabed mining. The focus of the discussion is on the environmental regulation of deep seabed mining beyond the outer limits of the continental shelf as defined in Article 76 of the 1982 United Nations Convention on the Law of the Sea (LOSC),[1] although some of the discussion will be equally relevant to seabed mining within national jurisdiction.

The deep seabed beyond the outer limits of the continental shelf is referred to as 'the Area'.[2] The mineral resources of the Area are the 'common heritage of mankind'.[3] LOSC establishes the International Seabed Authority (ISA) as the organization through which States Parties to LOSC are to organize and control exploration for, and exploitation of, the mineral resources of the Area.[4] All rights in the resources of the Area are vested in mankind as a whole, on whose behalf the ISA is required to act.[5]

The legal framework for the protection of the marine environment from activities in the Area is contained in the LOSC, the 1994 Agreement Relating to the Implementation of Part XI of the United Nations Convention on the Law of the Sea,[6] and the rules, regulations and procedures adopted by the ISA. Some of these provisions specifically address protection of the environment, while others are more general but are also relevant to environmental protection. Within the LOSC, important rights and duties are to be found not only in Part XI and the associated Annexes, but also in Part XII.

---

[1]    United Nations Convention on the Law of the Sea (adopted and opened for signature 10 December 1982, entered into force 16 November 1994) 1833 UNTS 3.

[2]    LOSC, Art. 1(1).

[3]    LOSC, Arts 1, para. 1(1), 133 lit.(a) and 136.

[4]    LOSC Art. 1, para. 1(3), uses the term of art 'activities in the Area' to refer to 'all activities of exploration for, and exploitation of, the resources of the Area'.

[5]    LOSC, Art. 137, para. 2.

[6]    Agreement relating to the Implementation of Part XI of the United Nations Convention on the Law of the Sea of 10 December 1982, adopted 28 July 1994, A/RES/48/263, annex, entered into force 28 July 1996, 1836 UNTS 42. The Part XI Agreement was provisionally applied from 16 November 1994 (the date of entry into force of LOSC) and entered into force itself on 28 July 1996. As provided in the General Assembly resolution by which the Agreement was adopted and in the Agreement itself (Art. 2), the provisions of the Agreement and Part XI of LOSC are to be interpreted and applied together as a single instrument: in the event of any inconsistency between the Agreement and Part XI, the provisions of the Agreement prevail.

Rules for the protection of the marine environment are adopted by the ISA and implemented by the ISA itself, States sponsoring activities in the Area, and contractors carrying out such activities. The system is based on the application of the precautionary approach and is evolutionary in nature. Within the context of the overall legal framework, each actor has different responsibilities with respect to the application of the precautionary approach. The responsibility of ISA is to regulate, taking into account the best scientific information, and to monitor all activities in the Area. The responsibility of contractors is to fully implement the regulations, as well as to comply with their contractual commitments. Sponsoring States are required to cooperate with the ISA in the implementation of the regime, to establish a satisfactory national legal regime, and to ensure that entities sponsored by them meet their contractual obligations.

In 2011, the first Advisory Opinion to be issued by the Seabed Disputes Chamber of the International Tribunal for the Law of the Sea,[7] provided important clarification on a number of issues associated with the regulatory framework established by ISA. In particular, the Chamber held that the obligation to apply the precautionary approach is an integral part of the 'due diligence' obligations on sponsoring States. The Chamber also emphasized the importance of applying 'best environmental practices' in the context of activities in the Area and recognized that the obligation to conduct an environmental impact assessment is also 'a general obligation under customary law'.

This chapter will describe the basic legal framework for environmental regulation of activities in the Area and the rules, regulations and procedures issued by ISA to give effect to that framework. The chapter will then discuss the way in which the regulatory system is implemented and continues to evolve through the development and application of best environmental practices as well as a focus on environmental management at regional scale. Finally, note is made of some of the issues that will require further development in the future. First, however, it is necessary to briefly review the potential environmental impacts of deep seabed mining.

## 2.   ENVIRONMENTAL IMPACTS FROM SEABED MINING

Seabed mining has not yet commenced on a commercial scale, although in recent years there has been greatly accelerated interest in the potential for marine minerals both within and beyond national jurisdiction. This interest extends to different types of

---

[7]   *Responsibilities and Obligations of States Sponsoring Persons and Entities with Respect to Activities in the Area (Advisory Opinion),* Seabed Disputes Chamber of the International Tribunal for the Law of the Sea, Case No 17, 1 February 2011. See also D. Freestone, 'Advisory Opinion of the Seabed Disputes Chamber of the International Tribunal for the Law of the Sea' (2011) 15 *ASIL Insights* 7; and R. Rayfuse, 'Differentiating the Common? The Responsibilities and Obligations of States Sponsoring Deep Seabed Mining Activities in the Area' (2011) 54 *German Yearbook of International Law* 459.

mineral deposits, including polymetallic nodules, polymetallic sulphides and cobalt-rich crusts,[8] in all major ocean basins. Each mineral type is associated with different habitats, including hydrothermal vents, seamounts and mid-ocean ridges. Activities carried out during the early stages of prospecting and exploration for minerals are generally recognized to have little, if any, potential for adverse impact on the marine environment, being confined primarily to remote sensing and standardized sampling techniques of the sort commonly deployed during marine scientific research. Once commercial-scale recovery of minerals begins, however, there is the potential for significant and lasting damage to the marine environment, not only from activities at the seafloor, but also as a result of pollution from discharges at the surface and disposal of tailings. For this reason, it is clear that ISA has a central role to play in ensuring protection of the marine environment from the adverse effects of activities in the Area. Nevertheless, because scientific knowledge of the deep sea environment is limited, the regulatory framework for protection of the Area is still evolving.

The potential environmental impacts of deep seabed mining may be summarized as follows.[9] The mining collector at the seafloor will cause localized damage to the

---

[8]   Polymetallic (manganese) nodules have been known since the 1860s and were first described by the *HMS Challenger* expedition from 1872 to 1876. They are small objects about the size of a potato and can be found lying on the seafloor in the abyssal plans, often partially buried in fine grain sediments. They form over millions of years from the accumulation of metallic particles from seawater and sediment pore water, metals that are ultimately supplied to seawater from continental run-off and volcanic, hydrothermal and atmospheric sources. Nodules contain a wide variety of metals, including manganese, iron, copper, nickel, cobalt, lead and zinc, with important but minor traces of molybdenum, lithium, titanium and niobium, among others. By far the richest nodules in copper and nickel, and the most studied area of commercial interest, is the Clarion Clipperton Zone (CCZ) in the eastern Pacific, at water depths of 3500 to 5500 metres. It is estimated that the CCZ contains a potential (inferred) resource of 62 billion tonnes of nodules. Other areas of potential interest are the Central Indian Ocean basin and the EEZs of Cook Islands, Kiribati and French Polynesia. Polymetallic sulphides (also known as Seafloor Massive Sulphides or SMS) are rich in copper, iron, zinc, silver and gold. Deposits are found at tectonic plate boundaries along the mid-ocean ridges, back-arc ridges, and active volcanic arcs typically at water depths of around 2000 metres for mid-ocean ridges. These deposits formed over thousands of years through hydrothermal activity whereby metals precipitate out of water discharged from the earth's crust through hot springs at temperatures of up to 400 degrees Celsius. Cobalt crusts accumulate at water depths of between 400 and 7000 metres on the flanks and tops of seamounts, ridges, and plateaus (underwater mountains). They are formed through precipitation of minerals from seawater and contain iron, manganese, nickel, cobalt, copper and various rare metals, including rare earth elements. Globally, it is estimated that there may be as many as 100,000 seamounts, although relatively few of these will be prospective for cobalt crust extraction. The most prospective area for cobalt crusts is in the Pacific Ocean east of Japan and the Mariana islands, called the Magellan seamounts.

[9]   See generally in relation to this paragraph: Hjalmar Thiel, 'Evaluation of the environmental consequences of polymetallic nodule mining based on the results of the TUSCH Research Association', *Deep Sea Research II* (2001) 3433; Craig R. Smith and Paul Snelgrove, 'Disturbance and Recolonization Processes' in *Proceedings of the International Seabed Authority Workshop Prospects for International Collaboration in Marine Environmental Research to Enhance Understanding of the Deep Sea Environment* (ISA, Kingston, 2002); C. Van Dover

seafloor, including crushing living organisms, removal of substrate habitat and disturbance of sediment. The consequences of this may be significant. For manganese nodules, sediment disturbance will create a sediment plume of as yet unknown size that could bury seafloor organisms or clog the siphons of filter feeding organisms. There is then the possibility of ancillary damage through malfunctions in the riser and transportation system, hydraulic leaks, noise pollution and light. Once ore is brought to the surface in the form of a slurry, there is the problem of discharge of waste processing water. If discharged, deliberately or accidentally, in the near surface water column, this could impact plankton and fish stocks. On the other hand, discharging near the seabed may also create additional sediment plumes as well as geochemical changes due to the composition of tailings.

Much remains unknown, particularly with regard to species composition and distributions, although it is now well known that the biodiversity of the deep seabed is greater than had hitherto been thought.[10] It is nevertheless reasonable to assume that recovery periods are likely to be decadal and that, at least in localized areas, community structures may never recover. Impacts on endemic species may be more profound, especially on seamounts, and there may be irreversible change in the case of species with limited geographical range and small populations.

## 3.   THE BASIC LEGAL FRAMEWORK OF LOSC AND THE 1994 AGREEMENT

The provisions on the protection of the marine environment contained in Part XII of the LOSC, which were developed in the light of the outcomes of the 1972 Stockholm Conference on the Human Environment, constitute the basic framework for the legal regime that establishes the obligations, powers and responsibilities of States with respect to the marine environment. Article 192 of the LOSC establishes the overarching obligation of all States to protect and preserve the marine environment. Part XII also describes the specific measures to be taken by States to prevent, reduce and control marine pollution as well as to ensure that activities under their jurisdiction or control do not cause pollution damage to other States and their environment, and that pollution does not spread beyond the areas where they exercise sovereign rights under the LOSC. In relation to the Area, Article 209 states that '[i]nternational rules, regulations and procedures shall be established in accordance with Part XI to prevent, reduce and control pollution of the marine environment from activities in the Area.'

---

et al., 'Environmental Management of Deep Sea Chemosynthetic Ecosystems: Justification of and Considerations for a Spatially-Based Approach' ISA Technical Study No. 9 (ISA, Kingston, 2011).

   [10]   See Craig H. Allen, 'Protecting the Oceanic Gardens of Eden: International Law Issues in Deep-Sea Vent Resource Conservation and Management' (2001) 13(3) *Georgetown International Environmental Law Review* 563; Lyle Glowka, 'The Deepest of Ironies: Genetic Resources, Marine Scientific Research and the Area' (1996) 12 *Ocean Yearbook* 171; Cyrill de Klemm, 'Fisheries and Marine Biological Diversity' in E. Hey (ed.) *Developments in International Fisheries Law* 423 (Kluwer, 1999).

Under Article 145 of the LOSC, the ISA is required to take necessary measures 'to ensure effective protection for the marine environment from harmful effects which may arise' from activities in the Area. To this end, the ISA is required to adopt appropriate rules, regulations and procedures for, inter alia:

(a)  the prevention, reduction and control of pollution and other hazards to the marine environment, including the coastline, and of interference with the ecological balance of the marine environment, particular attention being paid to the need for protection from harmful effects of such activities as drilling, dredging, excavation, disposal of waste, construction and operation or maintenance of installations, pipelines and other devices related to such activities;

(b)  the protection and conservation of the natural resources of the Area and the prevention of damage to the flora and fauna of the marine environment.

Article 145 provides for the protection of the marine environment as a whole from the harmful effects of mining activities.[11] It juxtaposes Article 192, which sets out the overarching obligation of States parties to protect and preserve the marine environment as further detailed in Articles 194, 204, 206, and 209. The obligation under Article 145 includes taking measures to protect the flora and fauna of the marine environment regardless of whether or not they form part of the Area and whether or not such flora and fauna were known to exist at the time of negotiating the LOSC.

Law-making power in the ISA is vested in the Council of the ISA[12] which, pursuant to Article 162, para. 2(o)(ii), shall adopt the 'rules regulations and procedures' relating to activities of prospecting, exploration and exploitation in the Area. Such activities may be carried out only by qualified entities on the basis of a formal written plan of work approved by the Council.[13] A fundamental feature of the regime is that such a plan of work shall be in the form of a contract between the ISA and the relevant entity.[14] That the rules, regulations and procedures adopted by the Council should include environmental regulations is explicit from the language of Annex III of the LOSC (entitled 'Basic conditions of prospecting, exploration and exploitation'), which requires the ISA, inter alia, to adopt rules, regulations and procedures on 'mining

---

[11]  Scovazzi argues that Art. 145 is not limited to minimizing the effects of mining activities but grants the Authority general competences for marine environmental protection. Tullio Scovazzi, 'Mining, Protection of the Environment, Scientific Research and Bioprospecting: Some Considerations on the Role of the International Sea-Bed Authority' (2004) 19(4) *The International Journal of Marine and Coastal Law* 383, 393.

[12]  The Council is composed of 36 members, divided into five Groups (A, B, C, D and E) and for decision-making four Chambers (A, B, C and the developing countries in Groups D and E). For an overview of the structure and decision-making process within the Council see Michael C. Wood, 'International Seabed Authority: The First Four Years' (1999) 3 *Max Planck Yearbook of United Nations Law* 173.

[13]  LOSC, Art. 153, para. 3. The entities that may be qualified to carry out activities in the Area are the Enterprise, States Parties, state enterprises, natural or juridical persons who possess the nationality of States Parties or are effectively controlled by them or their nationals, when sponsored by such States, or any combination of the foregoing.

[14]  LOSC, Art. 153, para. 3 and Part XI Agreement, annex, sect. 2, para. 4. Exploration contracts have a maximum duration of 15 years.

standards and practices ... including those relating to ... protection of the marine environment'.[15] The 1994 Agreement further emphasizes that 'the adoption of rules, regulations and procedures incorporating applicable standards for the protection and preservation of the marine environment' is one of the matters to be given priority consideration by the ISA between the entry into force of the LOSC and the approval of the first plan of work for exploitation.[16]

Although law-making power is vested in the Council, the Council does not act alone in formulating environmental regulations for the Area. The other organ of the ISA with particular responsibility for the protection of the marine environmental is the Legal and Technical Commission, which is established as an organ of the Council under Article 163. The functions of the Commission are specified in Article 165. The Commission is required to formulate and submit to the Council environmental rules, regulations, and procedures and keep them under review.[17] It is required to make recommendations to the Council both on the implementation of such regulations and on 'the protection of the marine environment, taking into account the views of recognized experts in that field'.[18] Furthermore, the Commission also has to prepare environmental impact assessments of activities in the Area,[19] make recommendations to the Council concerning a monitoring programme to observe, measure, evaluate, and analyze the risks and effects of pollution caused by such activities, ensure that existing regulations are adequate and complied with, and coordinate the implementation of the monitoring programme.[20]

Pursuant to the overarching legal provisions described above, the ISA has adopted three sets of Regulations dealing with prospecting and exploration for mineral resources in the Area. The first set of Regulations was adopted in 2000 and dealt with prospecting and exploration for polymetallic nodules.[21] Regulations on prospecting and exploration for polymetallic sulphides were adopted in 2010[22] and for cobalt-rich crusts in 2012.[23] In 2013, the Regulations on prospecting and exploration for polymetallic

---

[15]   LOSC, Annex III, Art. 17, para. 1(b)(xii).

[16]   Part XI Agreement, annex, sect. 1, para. 5(g).

[17]   LOSC, Art. 165(2)(f)–(g).

[18]   LOSC, Art. 165(2)(e).

[19]   LOSC, Art. 165(2)(d).

[20]   LOSC, Art. 165(2)(h).

[21]   Regulations on Prospecting and Exploration for Polymetallic Nodules in the Area, 13 July 2000. The official text of the Regulations was published as document ISBA/6/A/18, annex (13 July 2000). Reproduced in *The Law of the Sea: Compendium of Basic Documents* (International Seabed Authority/The Caribbean Law Publishing Company 2001) 226. For a general account of the process of negotiating the Regulations and their content, see M.W. Lodge, 'International Seabed Authority's Regulations on Prospecting and Exploration for Polymetallic Nodules in the Area' (2002) 20(3) *Journal of Energy and Natural Resources Law* 270.

[22]   Regulations on prospecting and exploration for polymetallic sulphides in the Area, ISBA/16/A/12/Rev.1, 7 May 2010, available at http://www.isa.org.jm/files/documents/EN/Regs/PolymetallicSulphides.pdf (last accessed 18 May 2015).

[23]   Regulations on Prospecting and Exploration for Cobalt-rich Ferromanganese Crusts in the Area, ISBA/18/A/11, 27 July 2012, available at http://www.isa.org.jm/files/documents/EN/18Sess/Assembly/ISBA-18A-11.pdf (last accessed 18 May 2015).

nodules were revised and updated to be consistent with the 2010 and 2012 regulations.[24] The three sets of regulations are broadly similar in format, scope and content, with differences primarily to reflect the different spatial and geological characteristics of the mineral resources they deal with. Ultimately, it is intended that the Regulations will form part of a Mining Code, regulating all aspects of activities in the Area from prospecting through to exploitation. At present there are no regulations relating to the exploitation of any mineral resources under the administration of the ISA, although the need for such regulations has been identified by the Council as the most urgent task for the Authority in the period up to 2016. For ease of reference, the 2010, 2012 and 2013 Regulations will be referred to and discussed collectively in this chapter as the 'ISA Regulations', with references to specific provisions highlighted where necessary.[25]

## 4. ISA REGULATIONS ON PROSPECTING AND EXPLORATION FOR POLYMETALLIC NODULES, POLYMETALLIC SULPHIDES AND COBALT-RICH CRUSTS

The ISA Regulations are designed to implement the broad provisions of Part XI and Annex III of LOSC and the Part XI Agreement. They thus cover all aspects of the prospecting and exploration phases of mineral development, including the process of applying for approval of a plan of work, the procedure for consideration of applications by the Legal and Technical Commission and the Council, and the form and content of the contract for exploration.

Prospecting is defined in the Regulations as the 'search for deposits [of minerals] including estimation of the sizes and distributions of [mineral] deposits and their economic values, without any exclusive rights'. This broad definition of prospecting refers to general searches for seabed mineral deposits rather than detailed pre-production surveys and is difficult to distinguish from marine scientific research.[26] Nevertheless, the Regulations require a precautionary approach to be taken to prospecting and require that prospecting is not to be undertaken if 'substantial evidence indicates the risk of serious harm' to the marine environment.[27]

---

[24]   Regulations on Prospecting and Exploration for Polymetallic Nodules in the Area, ISBA/19/C/17, 22 July 2013, available at http://www.isa.org.jm/files/documents/EN/19Sess/Council/ISBA-19C-17.pdf (last accessed 18 May 2015).

[25]   Although this chapter will deal only with the latest version of the Regulations, it should be noted that earlier versions of the Regulations may still be applicable to contracts entered into prior to the entry into force of the revised Regulations in 2013. Although contract terms may be revised to 'facilitate the application of any rules, regulations and procedures adopted by the Authority subsequent to the entry into force of the contract' (Regs Annex 4, sect. 24.2), such modifications require the written consent of the contractor and ISA as evidenced by an appropriate instrument in writing.

[26]   See M.W. Lodge (2002) above n 21.

[27]   Reg. 2(3). Implementation of this provision would require a definition of what constitutes 'substantial evidence' indicating a 'risk' of serious harm. Gwenaëlle Le Gurun, 'EIA and the International Seabed Authority' in K. Bastmeier and T. Koivurova, *Theory and Practice of Transboundary Environmental Impact Assessment* (Martinus Nijhoff, 2008) 2211.

Exploration, for the purposes of the Regulations, is defined broadly as 'Searching for deposits of [minerals] in the Area with exclusive rights, the analysis of such deposits, the use and testing of recovery systems, and the carrying out of studies of the environmental, technical, economic, commercial and other appropriate factors that must be taken into account in exploitation.'[28] Annex 4 to each set of Regulations contains standard clauses for exploration contracts which are automatically incorporated into each contract issued by the ISA.

As far as the protection of the marine environment is concerned, the ISA Regulations attempt to strike a balance between a precautionary approach to activities in the Area and an incremental approach to regulation, with an emphasis on gathering sufficient data during the early phase of exploration in order to determine the range of potential environmental impacts.[29] This is a logical approach to take because the various activities encompassed in the broad definition of exploration do not have the same detrimental effect on the marine environment.[30] The Regulations define the marine environment in the broadest possible terms as 'The physical, chemical, geological and biological components, conditions and factors which interact and determine the productivity, state, condition and quality of the marine ecosystem, the waters of the seas and oceans, and the airspace above those waters, as well as the seabed and ocean floor and subsoil thereof.'[31]

The scheme set out in the ISA Regulations places obligations and responsibilities on three main actors or groups of actors – the ISA itself, sponsoring States, and exploration contractors – and is broadly as follows.

First, the Regulations restate the requirement under Article 145 of the LOSC for the ISA to 'establish and keep under review environmental rules, regulations and procedures to ensure effective protection for the marine environment from harmful effects which may arise from activities in the Area.'[32] To this end, it is provided that the Regulations may be supplemented by further rules, regulations and procedures, in particular on the protection and preservation of the marine environment.[33]

Second, both the ISA and sponsoring States are required to apply a precautionary approach, as reflected in Principle 15 of the Rio Declaration on Environment and

---

[28]    Nodules, Sulphides & Crusts, Reg. 1(3)(b).

[29]    The system may be compared to a process of 'scoping' and 'tiering' as used by the United States Council on Environmental Policy, where tiering allows for phasing of the resolution of environmental issues to be compatible with the schedule of activities contemplated in the proposed action. See M.W. Lodge, 'Environmental Regulation of Deep Seabed Mining' in A. Kirchner (ed.) *International Marine Environmental Law: Institutions, Implementation and Innovations* (Kluwer Law International, 2003) 49.

[30]    Le Gurun (2008) above n 27.

[31]    Reg. 1(3)(c). It is noteworthy that there is no definition of the marine environment in LOSC. The definition in the Regulations is comprehensive. It appears to include all constituent elements of the marine environment including, for example, living and non-living resources, the water column above the seafloor and the airspace. It also recognizes the importance of the marine ecosystem as a whole.

[32]    Nodules, Reg. 31(1); Sulphides & Crusts, Reg. 33(1). See also LOSC, Art. 165, paras 2(e), (f) and (h), Annex III, Art. 17, para. 1(b)(xii) and 17, para. 2(f); Part XI Agreement, annex, sect. 1, para. 5(g).

[33]    Nodules, Sulphides & Crusts, Reg. 1(5).

Development, to activities in the Area.[34] The Legal and Technical Commission is to make recommendations to the Council on the implementation of this requirement.[35] The Commission is also required to:

> develop and implement procedures for determining, on the basis of the best available scientific evidence, whether proposed exploration activities would have serious harmful effects on vulnerable marine ecosystems and to ensure that, if it is determined that certain proposed activities would have such effects, those activities are managed to prevent such effects or not authorized to proceed.[36]

Third, the Regulations impose a duty on each contractor to 'take necessary measures to prevent, reduce and control pollution and other hazards to the marine environment arising from its activities in the Area as far as reasonably possible, applying a precautionary approach and best environmental practices'.[37] To give effect to this general duty, the exploration contract requires the contractor, prior to commencing its activities, to submit an impact assessment of the potential effects on the marine environment of the proposed activities.[38] Thereafter the contractor is required to gather environmental baseline data as exploration activities progress and to establish environmental baselines against which to assess the likely effects of its programme of activities under the plan of work for exploration on the marine environment.[39] Contractors are also required to establish and carry out a programme to monitor and report on such effects on the marine environment and to cooperate with the Authority and the sponsoring State or States in the establishment and implementation of such monitoring programmes.[40] In practice this means that contractors are required to submit an annual report on the implementation and results of their environmental monitoring programmes, including relevant data and information. These reports are then forwarded to

---

[34]   Principle 15 of the Rio Declaration on Environment and Development states as follows: 'In order to protect the environment, the precautionary approach shall be widely applied by States according to their capabilities. Where there are threats of serious or irreversible damage, lack of full scientific certainty shall not be used as a reason for postponing cost-effective measures to prevent environmental degradation'. UN Doc. A/CONF/151/26 (Vol.1), located at http://www.un.org/documents/ga/conf151/aconf15126-1annex1.htm (last accessed 25 May 2015).

[35]   Nodules, Reg. 31(3); Sulphides & Crusts, Reg. 33(3).

[36]   Nodules, Reg. 31(4); Sulphides & Crusts, Reg. 33(4). Again, no such recommendations have been made to date. This language was inserted to track the language of General Assembly Resolution 61/105.

[37]   Nodules, Reg. 31(5); Sulphides & Crusts, Reg. 33(5). This duty is said to exist pursuant to Art. 145 of LOSC and para. 2 of the same regulation, i.e. the obligation to apply a precautionary approach.

[38]   Regs. Annex 4, sect. 5.2.

[39]   Nodules, Reg. 32 and Annex 4, sect. 5.2; Sulphides & Crusts, Reg. 34 and Annex 4, sect. 5.2. Note that under the Part XI Agreement, annex, sect. 1, para. 7, each applicant for approval of a plan of work for exploration is required to submit a description of the programme for environmental baseline studies as part of its application.

[40]   Ibid.

the Legal and Technical Commission for its consideration pursuant to Article 165.[41] The Commission reviews and considers these reports each year and makes such comments and recommendations as may be necessary to the Secretary-General, who then draws any relevant issues to the attention of contractors.

## 5. COMPLIANCE AND ENFORCEMENT

A system of environmental regulation is only as effective as its enforcement mechanism. The LOSC equips the ISA with broad powers to ensure compliance and enforcement. Article 153(4) states that the ISA 'shall exercise such control over activities in the Area as is necessary for the purpose of securing compliance' with the LOSC, the Regulations, and approved plans of work for exploration. Moreover, the ISA has

> the right to take at any time any measures provided for under [Part XI] to ensure compliance with its provisions and the exercise of the functions of control and regulation assigned to it thereunder or under any contract. The Authority shall have the right to inspect all installations in the Area used in connection with activities in the Area.[42]

Although this provision is potentially very broad, the sort of compliance measures that have been taken so far have been limited to decisions and resolutions of the Council urging contractors to make better efforts to comply with contractual requirements regarding, for example, the submission of environmental data.

In addition to these general powers, the Council has the mandate to 'exercise control over activities in the Area' in accordance with the general powers listed in Article 153(4), including inspecting activities in the Area through a staff of inspectors.[43] The Legal and Technical Commission has a corresponding mandate to make recommendations to the Council regarding the direction and supervision of such inspections.[44] The exploration contract contains provisions requiring contractors to allow access to inspectors, assist them in the performance of their duty and cooperate with them in carrying out their duties.[45]

---

[41]    Nodules, Reg. 32(2) and Annex 4, sect. 5.5; Sulphides & Crusts, Reg. 34(2) and Annex 4, sect. 5(5). The reference to Art. 165 is interesting because it implies that the Legal and Technical Commission may use the information obtained from contractors' reports not only for the purpose of monitoring compliance with the terms and conditions of the contract, but also for the broader purposes set out in Art. 165 of, inter alia, making broad recommendations on the protection of the marine environment (LOSC, Art. 165, para. 2(e)) and formulating and keeping under review rules, regulations and procedures referred to in Art. 162, para. 2(o) (Art. 165, paras 2(f) and (g)).

[42]    LOSC, Art. 153, para. 5.

[43]    LOSC, Art. 162, para. 2(z). No inspectorate had been established at the time of writing.

[44]    LOSC, Art. 165, para. 2(m).

[45]    Regs. Annex 4, sect. 14.

## 6.  ENVIRONMENTAL EMERGENCIES AND CONTINGENCY PLANS

The LOSC confers upon the Council, acting on the recommendation of the Legal and Technical Commission, a general power (which it has not been necessary to invoke so far) to issue emergency orders to prevent serious harm to the marine environment.[46] Such orders may include orders to suspend or adjust operations.[47] Again, these broad provisions are broken down in the Regulations. Contractors are required to notify the Secretary-General of the ISA of any incidents that 'have caused, are causing, or pose a threat of, serious harm to the marine environment'.[48] Pending any action by the Council in relation to such incident, the Secretary-General is required to take 'such immediate measures of a temporary nature as are reasonable and practical in the circumstances to prevent, contain and minimize serious harm or the threat of serious harm'.[49] Such temporary measures may remain in effect for up to 90 days or until such time as the Council, acting on the recommendation of the Commission, has determined whether to issue an emergency order to prevent, contain and minimize serious harm or the threat of serious harm to the marine environment.[50]

Under the terms of the exploration contract, contractors are bound to comply with emergency orders issued by the Council and with temporary measures determined by the Secretary-General. In the event of non-compliance, the Council may take 'such reasonable measures as are necessary', at the contractor's expense, to prevent, contain and minimize serious harm or the threat of serious harm to the marine environment, and may also impose monetary penalties in accordance with the terms of the contract and the Regulations.[51] It should be noted that contractors are required in any event to submit a contingency plan to respond to environmental emergencies prior to commencing any activities at sea.[52] Depending on the circumstances, it may be that implementation of the approved contingency plan would, in most cases, be an appropriate response to an emergency and would not require further intervention by the Secretary-General or

---

[46]   Serious harm is defined in the Regulations as 'any effect from activities in the Area which represents a significant adverse change in the marine environment determined according to the rules, regulations and procedures adopted by the Authority on the basis of internationally recognized standards and practices'. This definition raises a number of issues common to other environmental treaties, including what constitutes a 'significant adverse change', what 'internationally recognized standards and practices' may be relevant and the question of the threshold at which environmental damage triggers liability. Space does not permit a complete analysis here, but for a general discussion of these issues and a useful comparison of definitions used in other treaties see Philippe Sands and Judith Peel, *Principles of International Environmental Law*, (3rd edn, Cambridge University Press, 2012) 706–9.

[47]   LOSC, Art. 162, para. 2(w) and Art. 165, para. 2(k).

[48]   Nodules, Reg. 33(1); Sulphides & Crusts, Reg. 35(1).

[49]   Nodules, Reg. 33(3); Sulphides & Crusts, Reg. 35(3).

[50]   Ibid.

[51]   Regs Annex 4, sect. 6. No guidance has been developed on the level of such penalties.

[52]   Ibid.

the Council. This view would seem to be supported by the Seabed Disputes Chamber in its *Advisory Opinion on Responsibilities and Obligations in the Area.*[53]

## 7. RESPONSIBILITY AND LIABILITY

The Regulations generally track the provisions of Annex III of the LOSC in providing that the contractor shall be liable for the actual amount of any damage, including damage to the marine environment, arising out of its wrongful acts or omissions. The Regulations provide no guidance as to how these principles might be applied in practice, although useful guidance as to the nature and extent of liability on sponsoring States and contractors was provided by the Seabed Disputes Chamber in its *Advisory Opinion on Responsibilities and Obligations in the Area.*[54] It is likely that there will be the need for the development of guidelines on such matters as acceptable heads of claim regarding damage to the marine environment for which liability may potentially arise,[55] as well as guidelines on levels of monetary penalties that may be imposed by the Council on contractors for damage to the marine environment.[56]

Another matter referred to by the Seabed Disputes Chamber was the possibility that, in the absence of a regime of residual liability for environmental damage, there may be cases of uncompensated damage. To deal with such eventuality, the Chamber suggested that the ISA may wish to give consideration to the establishment of a 'trust fund to compensate for the damage not covered'. The Chamber also reminded States of Article 304 of the LOSC, which not only provides that the rules of the LOSC regarding responsibility and liability are without prejudice to the application of existing rules, but also appears to allow for further development of rules of international law in relation to responsibility and liability.

Although the question of a global trust fund has not yet been taken up by the Authority, the Regulations do envisage the possibility that contractors would be required to provide the Council with a financial guarantee of its capacity to comply with an emergency order issued by the Council in the event of an incident causing serious harm to the marine environment. This requirement would arise at the point when the contractor moves to the stage of testing of collecting systems and processing operations.[57] It remains to be seen how this provision will be implemented in practice and in particular the impact on contractors' business operations of providing such potentially open-ended guarantees. In light of the statements of the Seabed Disputes

---

[53]   In particular, the Chamber rejected a strict liability approach in favour of a due diligence approach defined by 'obligations of conduct'. See also decision of the International Court of Justice in *Pulp Mills on the River Uruguay (Argentina v Uruguay)(Judgment)* General List No 135, 20 April 2010, para. 187.

[54]   Unfortunately space does not allow for a discussion of this topic. Interested readers should see Duncan French, 'From the Depths: Rich pickings of principles of sustainable development and general international law on the Ocean Floor – the Seabed Disputes Chamber's 2011 Advisory Opinion' (2011) 26(4) *International Journal of Marine and Coastal Law* 525.

[55]   LOSC, Annex III, Art. 22; Reg. 30; Annex 4, sect. 16.1.

[56]   LOSC, Annex III, Art. 18, para. 2; Regulations, Annex 4, sect. 21.5.

[57]   Nodules, Reg. 33(8); Sulphides & Crusts, Reg. 35(8).

Chamber, it may go some way towards closing a potential liability gap in that a sponsoring State could assert that it has fulfilled its obligation of due diligence by ensuring that its sponsored entity has provided such a guarantee.

# 8. RECOMMENDATIONS FOR THE GUIDANCE OF CONTRACTORS

To give practical effect to the scheme set out above, the Regulations contain an important provision which enables the Legal and Technical Commission to issue from time to time recommendations of a technical or administrative nature for the guidance of contractors to assist them in the implementation of the rules, regulations and procedures.[58] Contractors are required to observe such recommendations as far as reasonably practicable.[59] As will be seen below, the recommendations relating to environmental matters are intended to reflect 'best environmental practice'. In light of the *Advisory Opinion on Responsibilities and Obligations in the Area*, the contractual commitment to observe the recommendations becomes an important element of the due diligence obligations of contractors.

The first set of recommendations was issued in 2001, one year after the adoption of the first set of Regulations, and dealt with the assessment of possible environmental impacts arising from exploration for polymetallic nodules.[60] The recommendations described the procedures to be followed in the acquisition of baseline data, and the monitoring to be performed during and after any activities in the exploration area with potential to cause serious harm to the environment. They were largely based on the recommendations of an international workshop convened by the ISA in 1998 which had recognized the need for clear and common methods of environmental character-ization based on scientific principles and taking into account oceanographic constraints.

The 2001 recommendations were revised in 2010 in the light of increased under-standing.[61] Following the adoption in 2010 of the Sulphides Regulations and in 2012 of the Cobalt-rich Crusts Regulations, the Commission decided that there was a need to

---

[58]   Nodules, Reg. 39; Sulphides & Crusts, Reg. 41. Unlike the 'rules, regulations and procedures' referred to in Art. 162(2)(o), recommendations for guidance may be issued by the Legal and Technical Commission without further approval by the Council. Recommendations should be 'technical or administrative' in nature. The text of such recommendations must be reported to the Council which, if it finds that a recommendation is 'inconsistent with the intent and purpose of these Regulations', may request the Commission to modify or withdraw the recommendation.

[59]   Regulations, Annex 4, sect. 13.2(e). According to the first Secretary-General of the ISA, the recommendations 'form the basis of an acceptable code of conduct for contractors'. See Satya N. Nandan, 'Administering the Mineral Resources of the Deep Seabed' in D. Freestone, R. Barnes and D.M. Ong (eds), *The Law of the Sea: Progress and Prospects* (Oxford University Press, 2006) 88.

[60]   Recommendations for the guidance of the contractors for the assessment of possible environmental impacts arising from exploration for polymetallic nodules in the Area, ISBA/7/LTC/1/Rev.1**.

[61]   ISBA/16/LTC/7.

create a comprehensive set of environmental guidelines that dealt with all three types of marine minerals. This was achieved in 2013.[62] The revised and updated recommendations take into account new knowledge, including the outcomes of workshops convened by the ISA, and set out the detailed observations and measurements that need to be made while performing specific activities and recommended data collection, reporting and archiving protocols. The recommendations are accompanied by a glossary of key terms and an explanatory commentary.

The recommendations also elaborate on and clarify the obligation on contractors to undertake environmental impact assessments (EIA) by listing the activities that do and do not require prior environmental impact assessment. The threshold where EIA is required is generally around the point at which the contractor begins at-sea testing of collecting and processing systems. Activities which are considered to have no potential for provoking serious harm to the marine environment, and thus do not require EIA, include: gravity and magnetometric observations and measurements; bottom and sub-bottom acoustic or electromagnetic profiling; water, biotic, sediment and rock sampling for environmental baseline study; meteorological observations and measurements; oceanographic observations and measurements; video and still photographic observations; placement of positioning systems; towed plume-sensor measurements; DNA screening of biological samples; and shipboard mineral assaying and analysis.[63]

The recommendations also contain a list of activities which require both prior EIA and monitoring during and after the specific activity. These activities include sampling above specified quantities for each mineral resource; artificial disturbance of the sea floor; testing of collection systems and equipment; drilling; rock sampling; and sampling with epibenthic sledges, dredges and trawls. In each case, a prior EIA and a monitoring programme is to be submitted to the ISA at least one year before the activity takes place. The recommendations include a template for the EIA, as well as details of the observations and measurements to be made during and after the activity in question. It is noted in the Recommendations that the 'baseline, monitoring and impact assessment studies are likely to be the primary inputs to the environmental impact assessment for commercial mining'.[64]

---

[62]   Recommendations for the guidance of the contractors for the assessment of possible environmental impacts arising from exploration for marine minerals in the Area, ISBA/19/LTC/8.

[63]   The standard terms of exploration contract (Regs Annex 4, sect. 5.2) as currently applicable require every contractor to submit an environmental impact assessment 'prior to the commencement of exploration activities'. In the earlier (2000) edition of the Nodules Regulations (ISBA/6/A/18), the requirement for an impact assessment did not arise until the stage of testing of collecting and processing systems, which seems to be more consistent with the guidance issued by the Legal and Technical Commission. It is not completely clear how the requirement under sect. 5.2 is to be interpreted if the activities to be carried out during exploration consist only of those determined by the Legal and Technical Commission not to require prior EIA. One possibility is for the contractor to submit a 'nil impact' assessment until such time as it proceeds to at sea testing.

[64]   ISBA/19/LTC/8, para. 19. In 2011, a first step was taken towards formulating a draft template for EIA prior to mining. See 'Environmental Management Needs for Exploration and Exploitation of Deep Sea Minerals', *Report of a workshop held by the International Seabed Authority in collaboration with the Government of Fiji and the SOPAC Division of the*

## 9. ENVIRONMENTAL MANAGEMENT

So far, the discussion has focused on the environmental regulation of activities in the Area (as defined in the LOSC) and on the responsibilities and obligations of contractors, sponsoring States and the ISA in relation to those activities. The LOSC, however, allows great flexibility to the ISA in adopting measures aimed at the protection of the marine environment from the harmful effects of such activities. Under Article 165, para. 2(d), for example, the Legal and Technical Commission is required to 'prepare assessments of the environmental implications of activities in the Area' whilst under para. 2(e) it shall 'make recommendations to the Council on the protection of the marine environment, taking into account the views of recognized experts in the field'. This is perhaps logical as the Legal and Technical Commission is the only competent expert body within the ISA regulatory system that receives, through the annual reports submitted by contractors, a complete overview of activities in the Area, including ongoing environmental work.

Pursuant to these provisions, the Commission proposed to the Council in 2011 the first regional scale environmental management plan for the deep seabed.[65] The plan covers an area of the seabed located in the Eastern Central Pacific Ocean and known as the Clarion-Clipperton Zone. This area of the seabed, which is some thirteen and a half million square kilometres in size, at depths of four to six thousand metres, is considered to be a prime location for commercially viable deposits of polymetallic nodules and has been the subject of scientific investigation, mineral prospecting and exploration since the 1960s. It is the location of most of the exploration contracts issued by the ISA for polymetallic nodules.

The environmental management plan was approved by the Council in July 2012 in a decision[66] which not only recalled the provisions of Articles 145, 162 and 165 of LOSC, but also placed the environmental responsibilities of the ISA in the context of ongoing discussions at the United Nations General Assembly in relation to the conservation and sustainable use of marine biological diversity beyond areas of national jurisdiction.[67] In particular, the decision recalled General Assembly resolution 63/111, of 12 February 2009, in which the Assembly reaffirmed:

---

*Secretariat of the Pacific Community, Nadi, Fiji, 2011.* ISA Technical Study No. 10 (ISA, Kingston 2012).

[65] The genesis of the plan was a 2007 proposal by a group of scientists to establish a representative network of protected areas in order to protect biodiversity structure and ecosystem functioning of the CCZ from the potential impact of human activities. For background and a description of the process leading to the recommendation by the Commission see M.W. Lodge, 'Some Legal and Policy Considerations Relating to the Establishment of a Representative Network of Protected Areas in the Clarion-Clipperton Zone' (2011) 26(3) *The International Journal of Marine and Coastal Law* 463.

[66] ISBA/18/C/22.

[67] On these discussions see Dire Tladi, 'Conservation and sustainable use of marine biodiversity in areas beyond national jurisdiction: towards an implementing agreement', Chapter 12 in this volume.

the need for States, individually or through competent international organizations, to urgently consider ways to integrate and improve, based on the best available scientific information and the precautionary approach and in accordance with the Convention and related agreements and instruments, the management of risks to the marine biodiversity of seamounts, cold water corals, hydrothermal vents and certain other underwater features.[68]

Space does not permit more than a brief review of the salient points of the environmental management plan. The introduction to the plan, however, makes clear the broad context in which the Legal and Technical Commission viewed the plan.

At the outset, under the heading 'legal framework', the plan recalls the provisions of Articles 143, 145, 192, 194, 204 and 206 of the LOSC, before asserting that '[i]n the … Area, those responsibilities [to protect and preserve the marine environment] are shared between all States parties to the Convention as the Area and its resources are the common heritage of mankind'.[69] The plan then recalls the relevant provisions of the 1994 Agreement and the Regulations, as well as noting the context of various resolutions of the United Nations General Assembly relating to oceans and the law of the sea in which the Assembly had noted the importance of the responsibilities entrusted to the ISA in relation to marine scientific research and the protection of the marine environment.[70] It notes that at 'every stage of their activities … prospectors and contractors have substantial responsibilities to assess and monitor the effects of their activities on the marine environment'.[71] This section of the plan concludes by stating that the plan as a whole is consistent with the above 'obligations, responsibilities, rules, regulations and procedures'.[72]

The guiding principles on which the plan is based are stated as: (a) the common heritage of mankind, (b) the precautionary approach, (c) protection and preservation of the marine environment, (d) prior environmental impact assessment, (e) conservation and sustainable use of biodiversity, and (f) transparency.[73] It notes that, whilst the Clarion-Clipperton Zone is the focus of intense exploration activity, best-practice management of damaging human activities in the marine environment generally involves the use of spatial management tools, including the protection of areas thought to be representative of the full range of habitats, biodiversity and ecosystem structure and functions within the management area.[74] Perhaps the most significant feature of the plan is that it then identifies a network of nine areas which are designated as 'areas of particular environmental interest'. These nine areas, each of which is approximately

---

[68]   A/RES/63/111, para. 132.

[69]   ISBA/17/LTC/7, para. 1.

[70]   Specifically resolutions 64/71, paras 33 and 34; resolution 63/111, paras 33 and 34; resolution 62/215, paras 33 and 34; and resolution 61/222, paras 28–30.

[71]   ISBA/17/LTC/7, para. 9.

[72]   Ibid., para. 11.

[73]   Ibid., Part I, sect. C.

[74]   Ibid., paras 21 and 22. In this regard also, the recommendations for guidance of contractors provide for the use of environmental baseline data for 'regional environmental management', including the need to address molecular taxonomic standardization, whilst the management plan calls for cooperative scientific efforts. A first step towards these aims was taken by convening a taxonomy exchange workshop in Wilhelmshaven, Germany, from 10–16 June 2013.

160,000 square kilometres in size, are located so as to include a wide range of the different habitat types present in the Clarion-Clipperton Zone.[75]

In its decision of 26 July 2012 approving the environmental management plan,[76] the Council noted that the designation of the areas of particular environmental interest gave effect to the precautionary approach as called for by the Regulations and decided that, for a period of at least five years, no application for exploration rights should be granted in such areas. Noting the need for flexibility in its application and further development in the light of improved scientific knowledge, the Council also encouraged further dialogue with stakeholders and requested the Legal and Technical Commission to report on implementation of the plan.

In line with this request, an interim report was provided by the Legal and Technical Commission to the Council in 2014 in which the Commission strongly endorsed the ongoing validity of the plan but also highlighted the need for more data to be collected before any meaningful changes to the plan could be considered. The Council encouraged the Commission to continue its work on the implementation of the plan up to and beyond 2015 and also encouraged the Commission to consider developing environmental management plans in other regions, in particular those where there are currently exploration contracts, notably the Indian Ocean and Atlantic Ocean. The latter suggestion was in line with a similar suggestion made by the United Nations General Assembly in 2013.[77]

The environmental management plan is not only a good example of ecosystem-based management at a regional scale, but also reflects the dynamic and flexible nature of the environmental regime established by the LOSC, the Part XI Agreement and the Regulations. Both the Legal and Technical Commission and the Council have shown themselves to be willing to go beyond a strict and limited interpretation of their powers and functions and to take a broad, purposive approach to the application of the precautionary approach and the principles of integrated, ecosystem-based management of marine space. This approach appears to be consistent with the general approach taken by the Seabed Disputes Chamber in its *Advisory Opinion on Responsibilities and Obligations in the Area*, although the latter is not specifically referenced in the plan or in the decision of the Council adopting the plan. Furthermore, by making explicit linkages with commitments expressed in soft-law instruments such as the Johannesburg

---

[75] The plan makes an explicit link between the establishment of the areas of particular environmental interest and the achievement of the goals and targets set forth in the Plan of Implementation of the 2002 Johannesburg World Summit on Sustainable Development including halting biodiversity; establishing ecosystem approaches to management and developing marine protected areas, in accordance with international law and based on the best scientific information available, including representative networks by 2012. See also A/RES/63/111, para. 134. For a complete description of the process leading to the establishment of the environmental management plan and the designation of the nine areas of particular environmental interest, see M. Lodge et al., 'Seabed Mining: International Seabed Authority environmental management plan for the Clarion-Clipperton Zone. A partnership approach' (2014) 49 *Marine Policy* 66.

[76] ISBA/18/C/22.

[77] See ISBA/20/C/31. The relevant General Assembly resolution is para. 51 of resolution 68/70.

Plan of Implementation[78] and the resolutions of the General Assembly, the plan demonstrates that the regime for the Area is not divorced from the broader environmental governance regime for the oceans as a whole.

## 10.   UNANSWERED QUESTIONS AND FUTURE DEVELOPMENTS

It is to be hoped that this chapter has demonstrated that ISA has made commendable progress in developing environmental standards for prospecting and exploration for deep seabed minerals. Both the Regulations adopted by the Council and the detailed recommendations for guidance issued by the Legal and Technical Commission further contribute to the effective implementation of the broad environmental principles embodied in the modern law of the sea, including by specifying the details of the obligation to conduct prior environmental impact assessments. In addition, the Authority has taken a noteworthy first step towards regional scale, ecosystem-based management of activities in the Clarion-Clipperton Zone.

Nonetheless, there remain many unanswered questions and many provisions contained in Part XI, the 1994 Agreement, and the Regulations that will require further elaboration if they are to become operative in the future. The inherently evolutionary design of Part XI should allow the ISA to further develop its environmental regulations in line with new scientific knowledge and in the light of new evidence relating to the impact of mining activities. Suggested areas for further development include the following:

(a)   Criteria for identification of areas which the Council disapproves for exploitation in cases where 'substantial evidence indicates the risk of serious harm to the marine environment'.[79]
(b)   Recommendations on the application of the precautionary approach, measures for the protection of 'vulnerable marine ecosystems' and 'best environmental practices' as required by the Regulations.[80]

---

[78]   Although agreed after the environmental management plan was adopted, the plan is also consistent with target 11 of the Aichi biodiversity targets adopted by the Parties to the Convention on Biological Diversity at its COP10 in Nagoya, Japan, in 2010. This calls for 10 per cent of coastal and marine areas, 'especially areas of particular importance for biodiversity and ecosystem services, to be conserved through effectively and equitably managed, ecologically representative and well-connected systems of protected areas and other effective area-based conservation measures, and integrated into the wider landscapes and seascapes.' The areas protected from mining under the environmental management plan for the Clarion-Clipperton Zone cover approximately 12 per cent of the Zone and thus meet or exceed this target at the regional scale.

[79]   LOSC, Art. 162, para. 2(x) and Art. 165, para. 2(l).

[80]   Nodules, Reg. 31(4) and 33(3); Sulphides & Crusts, Regs 33(4) and 35(3). It is notable that the Seabed Disputes Chamber placed a strong emphasis on 'best environmental practices' as imposing a higher standard of due diligence than other commonly used formulae such as 'best available technology'.

(c) Criteria for determination of whether an effect from an activity in the Area represents, or is likely to represent, a significant adverse change in the marine environment.[81]

(d) Development of rules and procedures for environment impact assessment at the stages of test mining and commercial scale exploitation.

(e) Development of a mechanism for environmental guarantees, guidelines on monetary penalties that may be imposed by the Council for damage to the marine environment and the development of a liability fund for uncompensated damage to the marine environment.

(f) Guidelines on decommissioning.

(g) Implementation of an inspection regime.

There is also significant potential for the ISA to advance its efforts towards ecosystem-based management of deep ocean resources through taking a more strategic, long-term, approach towards the development of rational resource allocation strategies for the deep seabed. Ideally, this would include spatial and temporal strategies for allocation to ensure that non-living, non-renewable resources are apportioned in a manner consistent with their status as the common heritage of mankind while at the same time ensuring the conservation and sustainable management of associated renewable living resources. It would also include enhanced use of tools and strategies that preserve biodiversity and ecosystem structure and function, mitigate harm, and facilitate recovery from deep sea disturbances, including use of environmental management plans and systematically planned protected areas in relation to all types of seabed mineral deposits. Such strategies would also benefit from benefit-cost analysis to ensure that unpriced external costs, such as seafloor damage and ecosystem degradation, are considered when calculating the net benefits of resource use.

---

[81] In order to bring some clarity to the definition of 'serious harm to the marine environment' in the Regulations.

# 8. Reconciling activities on the extended continental shelf with protection of the marine environment

*Joanna Mossop*[1]

## 1. INTRODUCTION

Approximately 80 states may be entitled to claim sovereign rights over the resources of their continental shelf beyond 200 nautical miles from their coast, known as the 'extended continental shelf' or 'ECS'.[2] Already some activities take place that impact on the extended continental shelf, including marine scientific research, fishing on seamounts, and even oil and gas exploration. As technology improves to allow activities in deep water, states will continue to authorize exploitation of ECS resources. Coastal states expect that an ECS will provide significant economic benefits. However, coastal states must consider their responsibilities to protect the marine environment of both their extended continental shelf and of the water column of the high seas above.

As in all maritime zones, rights and obligations in relation to the ECS are balanced between the coastal state and flag states. Flag states have legislative jurisdiction over their vessels and therefore can require them to comply with environmental standards. The coastal state has sovereign rights over the resources of the continental shelf and can expect other states to respect those rights. However, when considering the ECS, vessels operating above it are actually on the high seas, and therefore the coastal state must ensure that any attempts to protect the environment of the shelf are consistent with high seas freedoms established in the 1982 United Nations Convention on the Law of the Sea (LOSC).[3]

This chapter examines the legal issues that coastal states will confront in attempting to reconcile their rights and obligations in respect of the ECS with other states' rights and obligations in areas beyond national jurisdiction. It begins with a discussion of the risks to the marine environment of the ECS and why the seabed environment may need protection. Next, the chapter provides an overview of the LOSC provisions establishing coastal state rights to the ECS. It is notable that ECS rights and obligations exist even before a state has received the recommendations from the Commission on the Limits of the Continental Shelf (CLCS) on the outer limits of its shelf. These obligations include

[1]   The author gratefully acknowledges the support of the New Zealand Law Foundation in funding research that contributed to this chapter.
[2]   At the time of writing, 66 countries have filed one or more submissions with the Commission on the Limits of the Continental Shelf, and a further 14 countries have filed preliminary information with the Commission. See www.un.org/Depts/los (last accessed 19 May 2015).
[3]   Opened for signature 10 December 1982, entered into force 16 November 1994, 1833 UNTS 397.

a range of requirements to protect the marine environment on and above the ECS including a duty to ensure that environmental impact assessments are concluded in many situations. Finally, the chapter will consider the legal issues facing coastal states wanting to establish marine protected areas on the extended continental shelf.

## 2. RISKS TO THE MARINE ENVIRONMENT FROM ACTIVITIES ON THE EXTENDED CONTINENTAL SHELF

According to Article 76(1) of the LOSC the juridical continental shelf of a coastal state

> comprises the seabed and subsoil of the submarine areas that extend beyond its territorial sea throughout the natural prolongation of its land territory to the outer edge of the continental margin, or to a distance of 200 nautical miles from the baseline where the outer edge of the continental margin does not extend up to that distance.

The continental margin is defined as comprising 'the seabed and subsoil of the shelf, the slope and the rise'.[4] Although a continental shelf in general is the continuance of the land mass until it reaches the deep sea, it will rarely yield a uniform geological and biological profile.[5] In reality the continental shelf can extend to depths of 3500 metres.[6] It can host a variety of geomorphological features including submarine ridges, seamounts, and hydrothermal vents.

The period following the negotiation of the LOSC saw a plethora of new discoveries about the living and non-living resources of the seafloor, including those located on continental shelves. It is now understood that diverse ecosystems can be found on continental shelves in areas previously thought to be barren. For example, scientists have discovered cold water corals, sponges and molluscs living on seamounts thousands of metres below the sea surface.[7] Such deep water species are typically characterized by slow growth, low fecundity and late maturity.[8] It is estimated that 9 to 35 per cent of species discovered on individual seamounts may not be found elsewhere in the ocean.[9] In addition, many seamounts support a wide diversity of fish species,

---

[4]  Art. 76(3). References to the continental shelf or ECS in this paper refer to the area covered by the legal definition.

[5]  P. Symonds et al., 'Characteristics of Continental Margins' in P.J. Cook and C.M. Carleton (eds), *Continental Shelf Limits: The Scientific and Legal Interface* (Oxford University Press, 2000) 29.

[6]  Ibid.

[7]  E. Ramirez-Llodra et al., 'Deep, Diverse and Definitely Different: Unique Attributes of the World's Largest Ecosystem' (2010) 7 *Biogeosciences* 2851, 2863; T. Koslow, *The Silent Deep: The Discovery, Ecology and Conservation of the Deep Sea* (UNSW Press, 2007) 125.

[8]  Malcolm Clark, 'Deep-sea Seamount Fisheries: A Review of Global Status and Future Prospects' (2009) 37(3) *Latin American Journal of Aquatic Research* 501, 507.

[9]  Gregory Stone et al., 'Seamount Biodiversity, Exploitation and Conservation' in L.K. Glover and S.A. Earle (eds), *Defying Ocean's End: An Agenda for Action* (Island Press, 2004) 50.

making them targets for the fishing industry.[10] It is also apparent that continental shelf ecosystems vary between different climatic zones and ocean basins.[11]

Another surprise was the discovery of hydrothermal vents where hot water laced with chemicals is forced from the sea floor at high pressure. Here, chemosynthesis produces ecosystems considered to be amongst the most productive on Earth.[12] Biologists are interested in creatures known as 'extremophiles' found at hydrothermal vents because of their ability to survive in superheated, oxygen deprived, locations. Cold seeps are found where slow releases of gases and chemicals emerge from the seafloor. These seeps attract concentrations of species including bivalves, tubeworms and crustaceans.[13]

The activities that can take place on the extended continental shelf pose varying risks to the marine environment. With the exception of low impact marine scientific research, most human activities on the shelf can create a potential for harm that must be considered by the coastal state. Unique ecosystems can be found at any point on the continental shelf, and not just beyond 200 nm of the coastline. However, much less is known about marine ecosystems on the ECS or in deeper waters, increasing the problem of scientific uncertainty.

Although oil and gas companies prefer to exploit resources closer to shore, in the future the extended continental shelf will be the target for greater levels of exploitation. It is accepted that hydrocarbon deposits may be found on continental slopes,[14] some of which extend beyond 200 nm from the coastline. It is not uncommon for companies to access oil and gas reserves at depths of 2000 to 3000 metres, making the more distant ECS feasible for exploitation.[15] At least three countries have already begun exploration activities on their continental shelves beyond 200 nm. The Canada-Newfoundland and Labrador Offshore Petroleum Board has issued seven current exploration licences in respect of its ECS in the Grand Banks region. These licences have resulted in two validation wells in the area to date.[16] Two significant discovery licences have also been issued for that area.[17] In the United States, exploration leases have been issued in respect of approximately 92,000 acres in the northern part of the Western Gap, an area of the ECS that was the subject of a boundary agreement with Mexico.[18] Finally,

---

[10]   Clark, above n 8.

[11]   Koslow, above n 7, 69.

[12]   Ramirez-Llodra et al., 'Deep, Diverse and Definitely Different', above n 7.

[13]   Ibid, 2862.

[14]   V. Prescott, 'Resources of the Continental Margin and International Law' in P.J. Cook and C.M. Carleton (eds), *Continental Shelf Limits: The Scientific and Legal Interface* (Oxford University Press, 2000) 76.

[15]   E. Ramirez-Llodra, P. Tyler et al., 'Man and the Last Great Wilderness: Human Impact on the Deep Sea' (2011) 6(7) PLoS ONE e22588. DOI:10.1371/journal.pone.0022588, at 12.

[16]   Canada-Newfoundland and Labrador Offshore Petroleum Board, 'Current Exploration Licences', 13 August 2014, at www.cnlopb.ca/pdfs/elgbr.pdf (last accessed 19 May 2015).

[17]   Canada-Newfoundland and Labrador Offshore Petroleum Board, 'Current Significant Discovery Licences', 30 September 2013, at www.cnlopb.ca/pdfs/sdlgbr.pdf (last accessed 19 May 2015).

[18]   Personal communication, Bureau of Ocean Energy Management. See Treaty with Mexico on Delimitation of Continental Shelf, 9 June 2000.

Norway has issued exploration licences in respect of three relatively small areas that either straddle or are beyond the 200 nm EEZ limit.[19]

Major pollution incidents such as the explosion at the Deepwater Horizon oil rig in the Gulf of Mexico in 2010 have drawn attention to the dangers of deep water drilling.[20] Such activity also poses lower scale risks such as day-to-day accidents or discharges. There is also the issue of decommissioning the platform once the resource is exhausted.[21]

Mineral deposits are also a possible resource for coastal states. Some seamounts form manganese crusts that are rich in cobalt, and there is interest in mining these by removing the crust from the underlying rock.[22] Chimneys and large deposits containing metals and sulphides are created around hydrothermal vents.[23] These deposits can contain large amounts of zinc, copper, cobalt, silver and gold and are potentially exploitable.[24] Marine phosphates can be found far off-shore and may attract the attention of mining interests in the future.[25] At present, mining for such resources is still in early stages as the expense of extracting the mineral makes land-based sources more economically feasible.[26] One example of deep sea mining is a project undertaken in Papua New Guinea by Nautilus Minerals. Solwara 1 is a mineral deposit site located in the Bismarck Sea, approximately 50 km north of Rabaul. The project aims to extract seafloor massive sulfides (SMS) from the sea floor to recover gold and copper.[27] The exploration phase has concluded and the company is developing the technology for exploitation. Although this project is within 200 nm of the coast, it is an example of the emerging interest in mining in deep waters.

---

[19] Harald Brekke, 'Licensing System in Norway', presentation to ISA Workshop, 26–30 November 2012. See www.isa.org.jm/sites/default/files/workshop/presenters-2012.pdf (last accessed 19 May 2015).

[20] Bruce C. Glavovic, 'Disasters and the Continental Shelf: Exploring New Frontiers of Risk' in Myron Nordquist et al. (eds), *The Regulation of Continental Shelf Development: Rethinking International Standards* (Martinus Nijhoff, Leiden, 2013) 225. See also Nengye Liu, 'Protection of the marine environment from offshore oil and gas activities', Chapter 9 in this volume.

[21] Robert Beckman, 'Global Legal Regime on the Decommissioning of Offshore Installations and Structures' in Myron H. Nordquist et al. (eds), *The Regulation of Continental Shelf Development: Rethinking International Standards* (Martinus Nihoff, Leiden, 2013).

[22] Koslow, above n 7, 170.

[23] Peter A. Rona, 'Resources of the Seafloor' (2003) 299 *Science*, 673.

[24] Mark Hannington et al., 'The Abundance of Seafloor Massive Sulphide Deposits' (2011) 39(12) *Geology*, 1155; Koslow, above n 7, 171.

[25] Prescott, above n 14, 77.

[26] Hannington et al., above n 24, 1158; Rona, above n 23, 674.

[27] http://www.nautilusminerals.com/s/Projects-Solwara.asp (last accessed 19 May 2015). See also P. Hoagland et al., 'Deep-sea Mining of Seafloor Massive Sulfides' (2010) 34 *Marine Policy* 728, 731; Marie Bourrel, 'Protection and preservation of the marine environment from seabed mining activities on the continental shelf: perspectives from the Pacific Islands region', Chapter 10 in this volume and Michael Lodge, 'Protecting the marine environment of the deep seabed', Chapter 7 in this volume.

Mineral exploitation of a commercial scale will have an impact on ecosystems in the surrounding area. Some predicted effects include the destruction of the sites themselves, sediment disturbance that will impact on surrounding areas, pollution from waste water and potential chemical pollution.[28] Koslow has suggested that the impact of mining inactive hydrothermal vent cites would be less problematic, but cautions that not enough is known about ecosystems associated with inactive vents.[29] Mining of gas hydrates poses some risks due to sudden gas releases and triggering underwater landslides.[30]

Fishing activities also pose a risk to the benthic marine environment. For the coastal state, the issue is two-fold. First, the coastal state has exclusive jurisdiction over sedentary species and may regulate access to those resources.[31] Second, the seabed environment (including sedentary species) can be impacted by fishing that is targeting non-sedentary species. A variety of fishing methods can be used to target species located close to the sea floor, however bottom trawling, in which large and heavy nets are dragged along the ocean floor, is considered to be the most destructive for seafloor environments.[32] Studies have shown that bottom trawling tends to result in high levels of sedentary species such as coral being caught as bycatch. For example, in the first year of trawling for orange roughy on the South Taman Rise (1997–98), vessels landed 1.6 tonnes of corals per hour and in total took over 1100 tonnes.[33] It is possible for bottom trawling to remove approximately 90 per cent of the native corals and sponges, usually within the early stages of an area being targeted by fishers.[34] In terms of the water column, bottom fishing risks following a 'boom and bust' pattern, whereby the majority of the biomass is harvested in the first few years of exploitation following which the population falls to drastically low levels.[35] Often the population does not recover even once fishing has stopped.[36] Bottom fishing can result in the environment of the seafloor and the surrounding waters being irreparably altered.[37]

The concern about the impact of destructive fishing methods on the seabed environment is reflected in General Assembly calls for states and regional fisheries

---

[28]   Ramirez-Llodra et al., above n 15, 12.

[29]   Koslow, above n 7, 172.

[30]   Koslow, above n 7, 174.

[31]   Sedentary species are 'organisms which, at the harvestable stage, either are immobile on or under the seabed or are unable to move except in constant physical contact with the seabed or subsoil.' LOSC, Art. 77(4).

[32]   Koslow, above n 7, 220. See also Glen Wright, Julien Rochette and Elisabeth Druel, 'Marine protected areas in areas beyond national jurisdiction', Chapter 13 in this volume.

[33]   Elliott A. Norse et al., 'Sustainability of Deep-Sea Fisheries' (2012) 36 *Marine Policy* 301, 315.

[34]   Norse et al., above n 33.

[35]   D.M. Bailey et al., 'Long-term Changes in Deep-water Fish Populations in the Northeast Atlantic: a Deeper Reaching Effect of Fisheries?' (2009) 276 *Proceedings of the Royal Society of Britain* 1965, 1968; M. Clark et al., 'The Ecology of Seamounts: Structure, Function and Human Impacts' (2010) 2 *Annual Review of Marine Science* 253, 263.

[36]   Clark et al., above n 35, 266.

[37]   The detrimental impact on species from bottom trawling may extend as far as 70 kilometres from the fishing area. D.M. Bailey et al., above n 35, 1968.

management organizations (RFMOs) to protect vulnerable marine ecosystems.[38] These resolutions primarily relate to areas beyond national jurisdiction and are without prejudice to state rights over the ECS,[39] however the request that states identify and protect benthic habitats from the impacts of fishing indicates a high level of concern for the potential impacts of fishing wherever the ecosystem is located.

A final activity that could have a negative impact on the marine environment is marine scientific research. Depending on the nature of the research project, it is possible that ecological niches may be disturbed simply by studying them.[40] One example that has been given is that researchers investigating the mineral content of chimneys formed by hydrothermal vents may remove them, which can impact on the surrounding organisms.[41]

## 3. THE LAW OF THE EXTENDED CONTINENTAL SHELF

The LOSC establishes the right for states with continental shelves that physically extend beyond 200 nm to exercise sovereign rights to the edge of the continental margin.[42] Article 76 contains detailed provisions governing how a coastal state should determine the limit of their ECS beyond 200 nm from the coast. Because states may dispute how those provisions are interpreted and applied, the Commission on the Limits of the Continental Shelf (CLCS) was established to consider submissions about the appropriate extent of states' ECS. If a state establishes the limits of its ECS in accordance with the recommendations of the CLCS, those limits are considered to be final and binding.[43] The CLCS has received 75 full or partial submissions[44] as well as several indications from other states of their intention to submit a claim in the future. Some states have made several separate submissions in relation to different parts of their ECS. A number of states have received their recommendations and are able to set their final and binding extended limits.[45]

---

[38] For example, see General Assembly Resolution 59/25 (17 November 2004), paras 66–8; General Assembly Resolution 61/105 (6 March 2007), para. 83; and General Assembly Resolution 64/72 (19 March 2010), paras 119–24.

[39] General Assembly Resolution 64/72 (19 March 2010), para. 115.

[40] Philomène A. Verlaan, 'Experimental Activities that Intentionally Perturb the Marine Environment: Implications for the Marine Environmental Protection and Marine Scientific Research Provisions of the 1982 Convention on the Law of the Sea' (2007) 31 *Marine Policy* 210. See also, Anna-Maria Hubert, 'Marine scientific research and the protection of the seas and oceans', Chapter 15 in this volume.

[41] L. Glowka, 'Putting Marine Scientific Research on a Sustainable Footing at Hydrothermal Vents' (2003) 27 *Marine Policy* 303, 304.

[42] LOSC, Art. 76.

[43] LOSC, Art. 76(8).

[44] As at 8 December 2014.

[45] Two of the first countries to set outer continental shelf limits following CLCS recommendations were Ireland (in respect of the Porcupine Abyssal Plain, (2010) 71 *Law of the Sea Bulletin* 34) and Australia *Seas and Submerged Lands (Limits of Continental Shelf) Proclamation 2012 (Australia)*.

A coastal state has sovereign rights over the continental shelf for the purpose of exploring and exploiting its natural resources – both living and non-living.[46] Nonliving resources include mineral resources while living resources include sedentary species. Sedentary species are organisms 'which, at the harvestable stage, either are immobile on or under the seabed or are unable to move except in constant physical contact with the seabed or the subsoil'.[47] Sedentary species can include corals, sponges, oysters, scallops and lobsters and all other benthic organisms.[48] Although it cannot be ruled out that commercial sedentary fish species may be found on the ECS, states are more likely to be interested in organisms found on seamounts and around hydrothermal vents and cold seeps, which may have value for bioprospecting.

An important question is whether coastal states must wait until the CLCS has issued its recommendations before they exercise their sovereign rights over the ECS. One argument is that this is not possible for fear of inadvertently exercising jurisdiction over an area rightly considered to be the deep seabed and managed by the International Seabed Authority (ISA). This view is in part supported by a decision of the International Court of Justice that it could not delimit a boundary between Nicaragua and Honduras beyond 200 nm because 'any claim of continental shelf rights beyond 200 miles must be in accordance with Article 76 of UNCLOS and reviewed by the [CLCS]…'[49] The difficulty with this view is that it leads to the possible outcome that coastal states may lose their ability to exercise authority for the purposes of protecting their interests in the resources of the ECS or the health of its marine environment until the CLCS process is completed.

A better view is that the coastal state is entitled to exercise jurisdiction over the resources of the ECS even before the CLCS issues its recommendations.[50] According to the traditional doctrine of the continental shelf, a coastal state has jurisdiction over the resources of the continental shelf without the need to declare or proclaim that jurisdiction.[51] According to the 1958 Geneva Convention on the Continental Shelf, the indeterminacy of the extended limit did not prevent states from exercising jurisdiction over the continental shelf.[52] The LOSC did not alter this presumption, despite the

---

[46]   LOSC, Art. 77(1).

[47]   LOSC, Art. 77(4).

[48]   J. Mossop, 'Protecting Marine Biodiversity on the Continental Shelf Beyond 200 Nautical Miles' (2007) 38 *Ocean Development and International Law* 283, 291.

[49]   *Territorial and Maritime Dispute between Nicaragua and Honduras in the Caribbean Sea* (Judgment, ICJ Reports 2007) 659, para. 319. See Bjørn Kunoy, 'The Admissibility of a Plea to an International Adjudicative Forum to Delimit the Outer Continental Shelf Prior to the Adoption of Final Recommendations by the Commission on the Limits of the Continental Shelf' (2010) 25 *International Journal of Marine and Coastal Law* 237.

[50]   See Bjarni Már Magnússon, 'Is There a Temporal Relationship between the Delineation and the Delimitation of the Continental Shelf beyond 200 Nautical Miles?' (2013) 28 *International Journal of Marine and Coastal Law* 465.

[51]   See LOSC, Art. 77(2).

[52]   Article 1 of the Geneva Convention, adopted 29 April 1958, entered into force 10 June 1964, states that the continental shelf is the seabed and subsoil of the shelf 'to a depth of 200 metres or, beyond that limit, to where the depth of the superjacent waters admits of the exploitation of the natural resources of the said areas'.

creation of the CLCS.[53] Therefore, states are entitled to their rights to the ECS as a consequence of their sovereignty over territory adjacent to the shelf. Moreover, it is and always has been the coastal state that determines the outer limit of its continental shelf.[54] The advantage for a coastal state in setting the outer limits according to the CLCS's recommendations is that the limits of the shelf are then considered 'final and binding' and must be accepted by other states.[55] However, a coastal state is not precluded under the LOSC from setting limits unilaterally.

More recently, the International Tribunal for the Law of the Sea has confirmed that a coastal state may exercise jurisdiction over the extended continental shelf despite the lack of a final delineation of its limits. In the *Bangladesh v Myanmar* case, the Tribunal considered an argument that it could not delimit the boundaries between the two extended shelves without the final recommendations of the CLCS. It held that there was no juridical distinction between the parts of the continental shelf within or outside the 200 nm limit and so no reason why the extended shelf should be treated differently from the shelf within 200 nm.[56] The Tribunal also emphasized that there is a difference between entitlement to an extended shelf and the determination of the extended shelf limits.[57] Making reference to Article 77 of the LOSC, it stated that '[a] coastal State's entitlement to the continental shelf exists by the sole fact that the basis of entitlement, namely, sovereignty over the land territory, is present. It does not require the establishment of the extended limits.'[58]

The difference between entitlement to sovereign rights and the determination of the extended limits means that states have the right to exercise jurisdiction over the resources of the ECS prior to any recommendations on the limits of the shelf issued by the CLCS. This jurisdiction includes rights and obligations such as those relating to the protection of the marine environment. There is a practical concern for states that, in exercising rights close to the potential outer limit of the continental shelf, the coastal state may mistakenly exercise rights over an area that ultimately is determined to belong to the deep seabed. This would engage international responsibility for breaching Part XI of the LOSC. Another possibility is that coastal states might exploit an area that is appropriately considered a transboundary resource.[59] Coastal states would therefore be wise to act cautiously in such areas and in consultation with the ISA.

---

[53]   LOSC, Art. 77(3).

[54]   *Dispute Concerning Delimitation of the Maritime Boundary between Bangladesh and Myanmar in the Bay of Bengal (Bangladesh/Myanmar)* International Tribunal for the Law of the Sea, Case No.16, Judgment 14 March 2012, para. 407; Ted L. McDorman, 'The Continental Shelf beyond 200 NM: A First Look at the Bay of Bengal (Bangladesh/Myanmar) Case' in Myron H. Nordquist et al. (eds), *The Regulation of Continental Shelf Development: Rethinking International Standards* (Martinus Nijhoff, Leiden, 2013) 93.

[55]   LOSC, Art. 78(8). See also Ted L. McDorman, above n 54, 99.

[56]   *Bangladesh/Myanmar*, para. 361.

[57]   *Bangladesh/Myanmar*, para. 406.

[58]   *Bangladesh/Myanmar*, para. 409.

[59]   Aldo Chircop, 'Managing Adjacency: Some Legal Aspects of the Relationship between the Extended Continental Shelf and the International Seabed Area' (2011) 42 *Ocean Development and International Law* 307, 312.

## 4.  COASTAL STATE OBLIGATIONS TO PROTECT THE MARINE ENVIRONMENT ON THE EXTENDED SHELF

As in other maritime zones, coastal states have treaty and customary obligations to protect the marine environment of the extended continental shelf. One significant consideration with the ECS is that the seabed area under the coastal state's jurisdiction lies underneath the high seas. This makes obligations not to cause harm to areas beyond national jurisdiction all the more pertinent.

A fundamental international environmental obligation is not to allow a state's jurisdiction to be used in a way that causes harm to the environment of another state.[60] It is reflected in Principle 2 of the Rio Declaration, which provides:

> States have ... the sovereign right to exploit their own resources pursuant to their own environmental and developmental policies, and the responsibility to ensure that activities within their jurisdiction or control do not cause damage to the environment of other States or of areas beyond the limits of national jurisdiction.[61]

Although this declaration is non-binding in itself, the principle is generally accepted as a rule of customary international law.[62]

This principle is reflected in the LOSC, which provides that coastal states must prevent, reduce and control pollution of the marine environment and ensure that activities under their jurisdiction do not cause pollution damage that spreads 'beyond the areas where they exercise sovereign rights in accordance with' the LOSC.[63] The protection must also be afforded to rare or fragile ecosystems and the habitat of depleted, threatened, or endangered species.[64] States must monitor the risks or effects of pollution of the marine environment[65] and, where they have reasonable grounds for believing that planned activities under their jurisdiction or control may cause 'significant and harmful changes to the marine environment', they must undertake assessment of the potential effects of the marine environment.[66]

Closely associated with this principle is the obligation on a state to exercise due diligence in meeting its environmental protection goals. This does not impose an obligation to avoid all harm, but a state must take measures within its legal system that are 'reasonably appropriate' to fulfil its obligations.[67] In the *Pulp Mills* case, the International Court of Justice (ICJ) stated 'It is an obligation which entails not only the

---

[60]   *Trail Smelter Arbitration (United States v Canada)* 3 RIAA 1907 (1941).

[61]   UN Doc. A/CONF.151/26, (1992) 311 *International Legal Materials* 874.

[62]   *Legality of the Threat or Use of Nuclear Weapons* [1996] ICJ Reports 266 at para. 29; Philippe Sands and Jacqueline Peel, *Principles of International Environmental Law* (3rd edn, Cambridge University Press, 2012) 196.

[63]   LOSC, Art. 194.

[64]   LOSC, Art. 194(5).

[65]   LOSC, Art. 204.

[66]   See Robin Warner, 'Environmental assessment in marine areas beyond national jurisdiction', Chapter 14 in this volume.

[67]   *Responsibilities and Obligations of States Sponsoring Persons and Entities with Respect to Activities in the Area* (Advisory Opinion) (ITLOS Case No 17, 1 February 2011), para. 120.

adoption of appropriate rules and measures, but also a certain level of vigilance in their enforcement and the exercise of administrative control applicable to public and private operators, such as the monitoring of activities undertaken by such operators'.[68]

There is also a customary international law obligation on a coastal state to conduct environmental impact assessments prior to authorizing activities. This was enunciated by the ICJ in *Pulp Mills* in relation to risks of significant adverse transboundary harm[69] and the International Tribunal for the Law of the Sea held that the principle also applies to harm to areas beyond national jurisdiction.[70] A failure to conduct an environmental impact assessment would mean that the state concerned had failed to exercise due diligence.[71] The precise content of the environmental impact assessment is a matter for domestic law, although states are expected to have regard to international guidelines. The assessment must be conducted prior to the implementation of a project and there should be continuous monitoring of the project's effect on the environment.[72]

In light of the treaty and customary law obligations, it is arguable that a state must conduct an environmental impact assessment when there is a risk of significant adverse impact on the environment beyond their national jurisdiction from a project focusing on the resources of the ECS. The harm could include substantial pollution or significant and harmful changes to the marine environment.[73] This could be triggered by potential harm to another state's jurisdiction, the high seas environment or the deep seabed ('the Area').

These obligations are particularly relevant to the area on the extended continental shelf. Ecosystems on the continental shelf are likely to be subject to two jurisdictional regimes: the high seas in the case of non-sedentary species and the continental shelf in the case of sedentary species. This makes the need for such prior assessment more acute as the harm to the surrounding environment could include the global commons and not simply another area under the same state's jurisdiction. Therefore, the obligations outlined above are most likely to be particularly acute for any significant operations on the extended continental shelf. States must exercise due diligence to avoid or mitigate harm to the marine environment which will include taking steps to implement effective decision making processes. Therefore, states will be obliged to have regulatory mechanisms for evaluating the environmental impact of activities on the extended continental shelf.

A range of other international and regional treaties impose obligations on coastal states that may be relevant to the ECS. These include the Convention on Biological Diversity (CBD),[74] which requires states to develop national plans for the conservation and sustainable use of biological diversity,[75] and to take measures to protect biological diversity in situ where possible.[76] The CBD contains an obligation to conduct prior

---

68   *Pulp Mills*, para. 197.
69   *Pulp Mills*, para. 204.
70   *Advisory Opinion on the Responsibility of States*, para. 148.
71   *Pulp Mills*, para. 204.
72   *Pulp Mills*, paras 120, 205.
73   LOSC, Art. 206.
74   Opened for signature 5 June 1992, entered into force 29 December 1993, 1760 UNTS 79.
75   CBD, Art. 6(1).
76   CBD, Art. 8.

environmental assessment of proposed projects that are likely to have significant adverse effects on biological diversity.[77] The CBD applies to areas within national jurisdiction[78] and its principles therefore have application to the extended shelf. It is important to note that the CBD must be implemented in a manner consistent with the LOSC,[79] and so could not be used, for example, to justify interference with innocent passage or the freedoms of navigation.[80]

Although the majority of obligations to protect the marine environment on the ECS are owed by coastal states, it should not be forgotten that other states are also under treaty and customary obligations as well. States whose vessels operate in the vicinity of the continental shelf will be obliged to ensure that their vessels comply with international standards such as that contained in International Maritime Organization (IMO) conventions, as well as more general obligations contained in the LOSC and applicable coastal state laws.

## 5. MARINE PROTECTED AREAS ON THE EXTENDED CONTINENTAL SHELF

Recent attention has turned to the value of marine protected areas as a tool for protecting marine habitats and biodiversity. The term 'marine protected area' (or MPA) covers a range of different types of protected areas: from no-take zones to areas where certain activities are managed. The key commonality is that it involves 'a clearly defined geographical space, recognized, dedicated and managed ... to achieve the long-term conservation of nature with associated ecosystem services and cultural values'.[81] The international community has set a number of goals for the creation of MPAs in all parts of the ocean. For example, in 2002 state participants in the World Summit on Sustainable Development (WSSD) called for the establishment of networks of MPAs by 2012.[82] The parties to the CBD have also set targets for MPAs. In 2006 the parties confirmed the WSSD target and agreed that 10 per cent of the world's ecological regions should be effectively conserved and that areas of particular importance to biological diversity should be protected.[83] In 2010 the parties agreed to seek to protect 10 per cent of coastal and marine areas through networks of MPAs and other effective measures by 2020.[84]

---

[77]   CBD, Art. 14(1)(a).

[78]   CBD, Art. 4.

[79]   CBD, Art. 22.

[80]   Donald K. Anton, 'Law for the Sea's Biological Diversity' (1998) 36 *Columbia Journal of Transnational Law* 341, 358.

[81]   IUCN World Commission on Protected Areas (IUCN-WCPA) *Establishing Marine Protected Area Networks – Making it Happen* (2008, Washington, DC) 3.

[82]   *Plan of Implementation of the World Summit on Sustainable Development* (2002), para. 32(c).

[83]   Mark D. Spalding et al., 'Protecting Marine Spaces: Global Targets and Changing Approaches' (2013) 27 *Ocean Yearbook* 213, 218.

[84]   Ibid.

It is therefore probable that coastal states will, consistent with these global targets, seek to put in place MPAs on the ECS where the conservation and ecosystem values mean it is important to protect the benthic environment. As indicated above, continental shelves are highly geologically diverse and therefore support a range of types of habitat.[85] Therefore, it can be expected that the extended continental shelf will contain important ecological areas worthy of protection from human activities. For example, a reasonable proportion of species discovered on seamounts, a feature of some continental shelves, may not be found elsewhere in the ocean.[86] Many cold seeps and hydrothermal vent ecosystems are of very high scientific value, and calls have been made for their protection under national legislation.[87] The differences in depth and geomorphology across the entire continental shelf leads to high diversity among the species found there. In a recent study, scientists compared the genetic make-up of two species found across a range of benthic habitats and found that there were significant genetic differences within one of the species found on seamounts and on continental slopes.[88] The authors concluded that the design of MPAs on the continental shelf should reflect the likelihood of differences in benthic communities in different depths and habitats.[89] More than one MPA will be needed on the continental shelf to protect representative areas of the marine environment, and a network should arguably include areas on the extended continental shelf.

## 5.1 Unilateral Coastal State Measures and Preventing Unjustifiable Interference with High Seas Rights

For extractive hydrocarbon and mineral activities on the ECS, the coastal state has undoubted rights to determine which activities should occur, where and when.[90] This allows the coastal state to prevent such activities from occurring in MPAs. Similarly, the coastal state may prohibit fishing for sedentary species on the continental shelf with little controversy.

More challenging is the problem posed by activities on the high seas which may have an impact on the benthic environment. One primary example of this, mentioned above, is where fishing vessels use bottom trawls to catch fish that swim close to the sea floor. These trawl nets cause considerable destruction to the habitat and species on the sea floor, many of which will be classed as sedentary species and therefore under the exclusive jurisdiction of the coastal state. The coastal state, in order to protect the species of a sea-floor MPA, may wish to prohibit bottom trawling or other destructive

---

[85]  Ramirez-Llodra et al., 'Deep, Diverse and Definitely Different' above n 7, 2857.

[86]  Gregory Stone et al., above n 9, 50. However, some authors question the robustness of such findings, emphasizing the enormous variation between seamount ecosystems and limited sampling. See Clark et al., above n 35, 255.

[87]  C.L. Van Dover et al., 'Designating Networks of Chemosynthetic Ecosystem Reserves in the Deep Sea' (2012) 36 *Marine Policy* 378.

[88]  E.K. Bors et al., 'Patterns of Deep-Sea Genetic Connectivity in the New Zealand Region: Implications for Management of Benthic Ecosystems' (2012) *PLoS ONE* 7(11): e 49474. DOI:10.1371/journal.pone.0049474.

[89]  Ibid., 14.

[90]  The rights to the resources of the continental shelf are exclusive: see LOSC, Art. 77(2).

fishing practices in the area. There is no doubt that it can prevent its own ships from undertaking bottom trawling over the ECS MPA. The question is whether it unilaterally can prevent vessels flagged to other states from doing so when they are not targeting sedentary species.

A second problem may arise in relation to regulating marine scientific research (MSR) on or above the extended shelf MPA. Although the coastal state has jurisdiction over MSR on the continental shelf, MSR in the water of the high seas is a high seas freedom.[91] The coastal state may be concerned that MSR targeting high seas resources may impact on the species of the shelf through the nature of research. Alternatively, the coastal state may also want to ensure that the researchers do not (possibly inadvertently) target sedentary species without permission. The question is whether the coastal state has any jurisdiction over MSR activities that may have an incidental impact on ECS resources.

For both of these scenarios it is important to remember that the rights of the coastal state to the continental shelf resources do not affect the rights of other states in the adjacent water column.[92] In addition, Article 78(2) of the LOSC states that the rights of the coastal state must not 'infringe or result in any unjustifiable interference' with freedoms under the LOSC.

Arguably, the requirement not to infringe or unjustifiably interfere with high seas freedoms does not prevent a coastal state from taking justifiable steps to protect its interests in the continental shelf.[93] For example, it is unarguable that if a coastal state wishes to exploit the resources of the seabed that other states would not be able to insist on their rights to navigation in the place where the mining or extraction is taking place. It is consistent with the provisions of Part VI that where a high seas activity directly destroys continental shelf resources, the coastal state would be justified in prohibiting that activity in a marine protected area. In the context of the 1958 Geneva Convention, Young argued that a coastal state could prohibit trawling over oyster beds.[94] During the drafting of the 1958 Geneva Convention, the International Law Commission stated that the term 'sovereign rights' covered 'all rights necessary for and connected with the exploration and exploitation of the natural resources of the continental shelf. Such rights include jurisdiction in connexion with the prevention and punishment of violations of the law'.[95] Therefore, the coastal state has the rights to protect its interests in the shelf against other users. However, the presumption in Article 77(2) is clearly that the freedoms of the high seas are expected to be mostly unimpeded and that the coastal state should only interfere where the continental shelf resources are of great importance to the coastal state.[96]

---

[91]   See LOSC, Arts 87 and 246(1).

[92]   LOSC, Art. 78(1).

[93]   J. Mossop, 'Regulating Uses of Marine Biodiversity on the Outer Continental Shelf' in Davor Vidas (ed.), *Law, Technology and Science for Oceans in Globalisation* (Brill, 2010).

[94]   Richard Young, 'Sedentary Fisheries and the Convention on the Continental Shelf' (1961) 55 *American Journal of International Law* 359, 372.

[95]   Myron H. Nordquist (ed.), *United Nations Convention on the Law of the Seas 1982: A Commentary,* Vol. II (Martinus Nijhoff, 1993) 896.

[96]   Myers S. McDougal and William T. Burke, *The Public Order of the Oceans: A Contemporary International Law of the Sea* (New Haven Press, 1987) 721.

It is useful to remember that high seas freedoms have a number of limitations imposed by custom and the LOSC. For example, users of the oceans are expected to give due, or reasonable, regard to other states' rights.[97] The possibility that high seas freedoms may occasionally conflict is recognized in Article 87(2), where freedoms must be exercised with 'due regard' for the interests and rights of other states in the high seas and the Area.[98] The practice of closing areas of the high seas for the purposes of weapons tests, although controversial in some cases, has been largely accepted despite the interference with the freedom of navigation.[99]

If one accepts the possibility that coastal states may, in domestic regulation, establish laws in relation to activities by other states affecting the continental shelf, it must be considered what would be a 'justifiable' interference with high seas freedoms. This author has suggested elsewhere that in determining whether domestic coastal state laws would violate Article 78(2), several factors can be considered.[100] The strong presumption must be in favour of protecting high seas freedoms.

First, what is the evidence that the regulated activity is interfering, or could interfere, with the coastal state's rights over ECS resources? There should be a real possibility that a particular activity could impact on the resource before a coastal state would have a right to restrict such an activity. This should not require evidence of *actual* harm, rather a real likelihood that if the activity takes place there will be harm to the resources. This is consistent with a precautionary approach to environmental management.

Second, what is the nature and level of harm or interference that would result for the shelf resources as a result of the activity to be regulated? Is the potential or actual damage trivial, or more serious? This may require consideration not just of the amount of physical harm, but the impact on the coastal state's interest in the resource. This could be affected by the level of the conservation value of the benthic ecosystem.

Third, the coastal state must balance the relative importance of the interests potentially affected, and how many actors will be affected by the regulation.[101] This may require a comparison of the relative economic values and conservation values. Therefore, if there is an area that a coastal state considers to have high biodiversity value because it contains endemic species, this should be factored into the decision making.

---

[97]   Anderson argues that this is a customary law principle. David Anderson, *Modern Law of the Sea: Selected Essays* (Martinus Nijhoff, 2008) 234. See also LOSC Arts 56(2), 58(3) and 87(1). See also *Fisheries Jurisdiction Case (UK v Ireland)* Merits, Judgment, ICJ Reports 1974, 3, paras 50, 62 and 79.

[98]   A similar requirement is found in Art. 58(3) in respect of the exclusive economic zone: states must have 'due regard' to the rights of the coastal state.

[99]   Natalie Klein, *Maritime Security and the Law of the Sea* (Oxford University Press, 2011) 56.

[100]   These factors have been explored in J. Mossop, 'Beyond Delimitation: Interaction between the Outer Continental Shelf and High Seas Regimes' in C. Schofield, S. Lee and M.S. Kwon (eds), *The Limits of Maritime Jurisdiction* (Martinus Nijhoff, Leiden, 2014); and above n 93.

[101]   See McDougal and Burke, above n 96 at 721; David Attard, *The Exclusive Economic Zone in International Law* (Oxford: Clarendon Press, 1987) 144.

The fourth point to be considered is whether the proposed interference with the high seas rights is as minimal as possible to achieve the coastal state's objectives, or whether the state can use a less restrictive option. Is the restriction procedural in nature (for example a requirement for conducting environmental impact assessments or reporting on activities) or is it a substantive restriction (for example a prohibition on activities covered by the freedoms of the high seas)? If there is a less restrictive method of achieving the coastal state's goals it is arguable that the more restrictive approach will be unjustifiable. For example, a coastal state wishing to protect seabed ecosystems that prohibits all bottom fishing above its outer continental shelf may be found to be unjustifiably interfering with the freedom of fishing, but a state that only restricts bottom fisheries in the vicinity of MPAs established to protect vulnerable marine ecosystems may not be.

The weighing of these factors in different contexts is likely to lead to different outcomes. So, some forms of substantial interference with high seas freedoms may be justifiable. Other forms of interference may be insignificant but yet unjustifiable.[102] It must be recognized that the reasonableness of any significant decision to adopt unilateral measures that infringe on high seas freedoms is likely to be contested by other states. Therefore, where possible, coastal states are strongly advised to seek to establish MPAs in cooperation with other states and relevant international organizations.

## 5.2  International Cooperation to Establish a Marine Protected Area

So far, the chapter has examined the situation in which a coastal state creates an MPA unilaterally. As discussed above, such action, although of potentially limited application and difficult to monitor and enforce, is within the rights of a coastal state. However, it would be more beneficial for a coastal state to cooperate with relevant international organizations who can then assist the coastal state to reinforce its conservation goals through the imposition of rules adopted by those organizations with which other states will be obliged to comply.

There are a number of possible partners for coastal states. These include regional seas arrangements which often focus on cooperation relating to pollution and other activities. In addition, the International Maritime Organization (IMO) can establish rules for navigation and pollution in particularly sensitive sea areas.[103] Finally, regional fisheries management organizations (RFMOs) may have authority to put in place conservation measures that would limit destructive fishing practices on or close to the ECS of states.

---

[102]   David Attard, above n 102, 144.

[103]   See, for example, Tullio Scovazzi, 'Marine Protected Areas in Waters Beyond National Jurisdiction' in Marta Chantal Ribeiro (ed.), *30 Years after the Signature of the United Nations Convention on the Law of the Sea: the Protection of the Environment and the Future of the Law of the Sea* (Combira Editora, 2014) 209, 218; Markus J. Kachel, *Particularly Sensitive Sea Areas: The IMO's Role in Protecting Vulnerable Marine Areas* (Springer, 2008); Hélène Lefebvre-Chalain, 'Fifteen Years of Particularly Sensitive Sea Areas: A Concept in Development' (2007) 13 *Ocean and Coastal Law Journal* 47; Henrik Ringbom, 'Vessel-source pollution', Chapter 5 in this volume.

One of the first examples of a network of MPAs in areas beyond national jurisdiction involved cooperation between a coastal state wishing to protect areas of its ECS and international organizations. Portugal is a member of the OPSAR Commission[104] and has identified a number of areas on its ECS as suitable for inclusion in a network of marine protected areas. These include a hydrothermal vent field and seamounts.[105] The parties to the OSPAR Commission have established, at Portugal's request, MPAs in respect of the high seas above these sensitive areas of the ECS. Non-binding recommendations to OSPAR members include ensuring that activities are carefully planned to avoid harm to the area and conducting environmental impact assessments before authorizing activities in the areas.[106] At the same time, Portugal has implemented domestic legislation creating MPAs in respect of the seabed and subsoil of these areas.[107]

However, OSPAR's competency is limited to environmental protection and does not extend to sectoral activities such as fishing or shipping. Fishing in the OSPAR areas that are beyond national jurisdiction is managed through the North East Atlantic Fisheries Commission (NEAFC).[108] NEAFC has worked on plans to protect vulnerable marine ecosystems since 2004, and following discussions with the OSPAR Commission, a number of areas were subsequently closed to bottom fishing. Kvalvik notes that that the areas closed by NEAFC only partially overlap with the OSPAR MPAs, and further cooperation will be needed to streamline the protection of these areas.[109]

The work of Portugal, OSPAR and NEAFC provides a possible model for future development of MPAs on and above the ECS of coastal states. There are some limitations, however. Portugal has recently identified potential areas for protection on the ECS that are located south of the OSPAR and NEAFC area, where the opportunities

---

[104] Established by the Convention for the Protection of the Marine Environment of the North-East Atlantic, opened for signature 22 September 1992, entered into force 25 March 1998, 32 *International Legal Materials* 1069. The OSPAR Convention is intended to provide environmental protection for an area of the North East Atlantic ocean. It has 15 state parties. See www.ospar.org (last accessed 20 May 2015). Unusually for a regional seas convention, the OSPAR Convention area covers areas beyond national jurisdiction as well as areas within national jurisdiction. E.J. Molenaar and A.G. Oude Elferink, 'Marine Protected Areas in Areas Beyond National Jurisdiction: The Pioneering Efforts under the OSPAR Convention' (2009) 5 *Utrecht Law Review* 5, 13.

[105] OSPAR Commission, *2012 Status Report on the OSPAR Network of Marine Protected Areas,* 26. See also Marta Chantal Ribeiro, 'The "Rainbow": The First National Marine Protected Area Proposed under the High Seas' (2010) 25 *International Journal of Marine and Coastal Law* 183.

[106] See, eg, OSPAR Recommendation 2010/15 Management of the Antialtair Seamount High Seas Marine Protected Area, OSPAR 10/23/1-E, Annex 41.

[107] Marta Chantal Ribiero, 'Marine Protected Areas: The Case of the Extended Continental Shelf' in Marta Chantal Ribeiro (ed.), *30 Years after the Signature of the United Nations Convention on the Law of the Sea: the Protection of the Environment and the Future of the Law of the Sea* (Combira Editora, Coimbra, 2014) 179, 195.

[108] There is significant overlap between the members and geographical coverage of the NEAFC Commission and the OSPAR Commission. See Ingrid Kvalvik, 'Managing Institutional Overlap in the Protection of Marine Ecosystems on the High Seas: The Case of the North East Atlantic' (2012) 56 *Ocean and Coastal Management* 35.

[109] Kvalvik, ibid, 37.

for international cooperation are hindered by the lack of competent international organizations. In other areas of the world, there may be less agreement on the goals of environmental protection among the relevant institutions, which will make the aim of achieving protection more difficult.

A second possible model for cooperation is presented by the bilateral approach that Mauritius and the Seychelles have taken to their ECS. In 2011 the CLCS issued a recommendation that confirmed that the two countries were entitled to an ECS. Mauritius and the Seychelles subsequently entered into a treaty declaring that they would 'exercise sovereign rights jointly' in a 'joint zone'.[110] They have also established a co-management institution which will manage the development of the joint zone.[111] The states have agreed to cooperate to protect natural resources, apply the precautionary principle, control destructive fishing practices and prevent and minimize pollution affecting the joint zone.[112] It is clear that this treaty would allow Mauritius and the Seychelles to implement MPAs in the ECS area. This approach has potential to minimize disputes over activities in areas where the primary actors in the region are party to the treaty. However, the treaty will not bind third party states and so a more regional or international approach may also be necessary.

International cooperation is the best way to deal with the limitations facing coastal states seeking to protect the marine environment on the ECS. The disadvantages to relying on international coordination include the need to achieve consensus on the need for protective measures, and the existence of competent organizations in the relevant geographical areas.

### 5.3    Limitations on a Coastal State's Right to Refuse Consent for Marine Scientific Research on the ECS

It is important to note that there is a limitation on coastal state jurisdiction over marine scientific research (MSR) on the ECS which coastal states will need to consider when establishing regulations for MPAs beyond 200 nm. A situation may arise, for example, where a coastal state establishes MPAs on the ECS and wishes to prohibit MSR in that area because it may have direct significance for the exploitation of living resources.

A coastal state may withhold consent for a MSR project on the continental shelf[113] or in the EEZ, under Article 246(5) of the LOSC, for four reasons: a) if the research is of direct significance for the exploration and exploitation of living or non-living

---

[110]    Treaty Concerning the Joint Exercise of Sovereign Rights Over the Continental Shelf in the Mascarene Plateau Region between the Government of the Republic of Mauritius and the Government of the Republic of the Seychelles, entry into force 18 June 2012. See (2012) 79 *Law of the Sea Bulletin* 25.

[111]    Treaty Concerning the Joint Management of the Continental Shelf in the Mascarene Plateau Region between the Government of the Republic of Mauritius and the Government of the Republic of the Seychelles, entry into force 18 June 2012. See (2012) 79 *Law of the Sea Bulletin* 41.

[112]    Ibid, Art.12.

[113]    Soons argues that these provisions apply to MSR conducted in respect of the continental shelf, whether it is conducted in the water column or on the seabed. Alfred A Soons, *Marine Scientific Research and the Law of the Sea* (Kluwer, The Hague, 1982) 216.

resources; b) if the project involves drilling into the shelf, use of marine explosives or the introduction of harmful substances into the marine environment; c) if the project uses artificial islands, installations or structures; or d) inaccurate information is provided or other obligations have not been met. The last three reasons are available for MSR concerning all parts of the continental shelf.

Beyond 200 nm, special rules apply in relation to coastal state discretion to refuse consent in relation to research that is of direct significance for the exploration and exploitation of resources. Paragraph 6 of Article 246 provides:

> Notwithstanding the provisions of paragraph 5, coastal States may not exercise their discretion to withhold consent under subparagraph (a) of that paragraph in respect of marine scientific research projects to be undertaken in accordance with the provisions of this Part on the continental shelf, beyond 200 nautical miles ... outside those specific areas which coastal States may at any time publicly designate as areas in which exploitation or detailed exploratory operations focused on those areas are occurring or will occur within a reasonable period of time. ...

Therefore, unless the coastal state has declared an area to be one in which exploratory operations or exploration will take place, the coastal state must not refuse consent for MSR on the basis that the research has significance for resources. This paragraph was a compromise in recognition of the extension of coastal state rights beyond 200 nm. It grants researchers greater freedoms while still protecting the rights of the coastal state to undertake exploration and exploitation. Clearly, the paragraph reflects the focus of the negotiators on mineral resources.[114] The question is whether paragraph 6 prevents states from setting aside areas of the extended continental shelf for conservation, rather than for exploration and exploitation, while also controlling the types of marine scientific research undertaken there.

There are several reasons why paragraph 6 should not prevent states taking steps to prevent marine scientific research that targets living resources within an MPA on the extended shelf. First, there are obligations on states to protect and preserve the marine environment found in the LOSC and other treaties. In addition, the coastal state (as well as the flag state) has a customary law obligation to undertake due diligence to assess and minimize significant adverse harm to the environment outside the state's jurisdiction from activities within their jurisdiction. The coastal state's sovereign rights are to be exercised in conformity with these obligations, making environmental protection a legitimate goal for the state.

Second, Article 246(7) provides that the provisions of paragraph 6 'are without prejudice to the rights of coastal States over the continental shelf as established in Article 77'. Therefore, if a coastal state can demonstrate that its interests – including environmental protection – in the resources of the shelf are negatively affected by the marine scientific research in an MPA, it may argue that it can still refuse consent for a project concerning the continental shelf. The fact that there is no intention to undertake exploration or exploitation in the MPA should not be fatal to this argument.

---

[114] Myron H. Nordquist (ed), *United Nations Convention on the Law of the Sea 1982: A Commentary* (Volume IV, Martinus Nijhoff, Dordrecht, 1991) 502.

It is difficult for another state to challenge a coastal state's refusal of consent for MSR projects. The LOSC excludes the exercise of coastal state rights or discretion under Article 246 from Section 2 of Part XV, which requires states to submit to compulsory dispute settlement. A dispute may be submitted to a conciliation commission 'provided that the conciliation commission shall not call in question the exercise by the coastal State of its discretion to designate specific areas as referred to in Article 246, paragraph 6, or of its discretion to withhold consent in accordance with Article 246, paragraph 5'.[115] Therefore there is a practical limitation on other states' ability to contest a decision to refuse consent for research projects on the extended continental shelf. The dispute is likely to be diplomatic in nature.

## 6.   CONCLUSION

Although many environmental issues were not known at the time of the negotiation of the LOSC, coastal states have obligations to protect the marine environment that apply to activities on the ECS. These treaty and customary international law obligations require states to consider the impact of activities on the marine environment when authorizing an activity, as well as monitoring the ongoing consequences for the environment. This obligation is not limited to concerns about the environmental impact on the resources of the continental shelf, but also on the resources of the water column. In fact, because the obligation of due diligence particularly arises in the context of possible harm to transboundary or commons resources, this obligation is acute when considering activities on the continental shelf beyond 200 nm. This is because continental shelf resources and high seas resources exist in very close proximity to each other.

Although this chapter has focused on the rights and obligations of coastal states, it must not be forgotten that flag states also have obligations to protect the marine environment, including the resources of the ECS. These obligations are found in customary law (eg, the obligation of due diligence), the LOSC and other multilateral treaties.

One tool that coastal states should consider as part of their obligation to protect the marine environment of the ECS is the establishment of marine protected areas where vulnerable ecosystems are known to occur. These could be ecologically diverse seamounts or hydrothermal vent areas. These types of ecosystems are often locations with potential for valuable commercial activities such as fishing and mining, which do have negative impacts on the marine environment. Therefore, coastal states may choose to protect a representative sample of such ecosystems in order to give effect to their obligations to protect the marine ecosystem and biodiversity in situ. This chapter has established that this is possible under the law of the sea, despite some problematic provisions in the LOSC. Unilateral restrictions by coastal states on activities that impact on the continental shelf will be controversial, due to the requirement in Article 78(2) not to infringe or unjustifiably interfere with navigation and other rights and freedoms in the water column. Therefore, states should explore the possibilities of

---

[115]   LOSC, Art. 297(b).

working through international organizations, such as the IMO and RFMOs, to achieve broader legal protections in relation to activities in the water column above the ECS.

As states begin to expand their activities on the extended continental shelf, and consider environmental protection, it is likely that clashes between coastal state rights and high seas freedoms will become evident. State practice in response to these disputes will be very important in clarifying the interpretation of some of the more ambiguous aspects of the LOSC in relation to the rights of coastal states on the extended continental shelf.

# 9. Protection of the marine environment from offshore oil and gas activities

*Nengye Liu*

## 1. INTRODUCTION

Global energy consumption has doubled since the early 1970s. According to the International Energy Agency, this is likely to increase by 2035 by more than one-third, due to world population growth and development in the major emerging economies of China and India.[1] As a consequence, the oceans are attracting growing attention as a resource reservoir.[2] One-third of the oil and one-quarter of the natural gas consumed in the world today come from underwater areas[3] and oil and gas exploration and exploitation are moving further and deeper offshore. A number of companies are already pursuing exploration projects in remote areas, such as the Arctic. Examples include Shell's operations in the Chukchi and Beaufort Seas; Cairn Energy's operations in offshore Greenland; Rosneft/ExxonMobil's operations in the Kara Sea; and Rosneft/ENI operations in the Russian Barents Sea.[4] Meanwhile, the latest world record offshore drilling depth was established in January 2013 off the coast of India at a depth of 3165 metres.[5] Worldwide, there are around 900 large-scale oil and gas platforms.[6] The most important current offshore production regions include the North Sea, the Persian Gulf, Western and Central Africa, the Gulf of Mexico, the Mediterranean, the Caspian Sea and Southeast Asia.[7]

It is well known that pollution from offshore oil and gas activities can cause serious damage to marine ecosystems. Pollution may be either operational or accidental. Operational pollution may occur as a result of the oil contained in drilling muds and cuttings, production water and displacement water, chemicals used in drilling, oil from drainage systems on platforms, and the disposal of sewage, garbage and other wastes

---

[1]   International Energy Agency, *World Energy Outlook*, 2012 (OECD/IEA 2012).

[2]   *World Ocean Review volume 3, Marine Resources – Opportunities and Risks* (maribus gGmbh 2014) 10.

[3]   Offshore oil extraction currently accounts for 37 per cent of global production. At present, 28 per cent of global gas production takes place offshore and this is increasing. Ibid, 17.

[4]   Michal Luszczuk, Debra Justus, Jennie Thomas, Chris Klok and Federica Gerber, 'Developing Oil and Gas Resources in Arctic Waters', in Adam Stepein, Timo Koivurova and Paula Kankaanpaa (eds), *Strategic Assessment of Development of the Arctic* (Arctic Centre, University of Lapland, 2014) 71, 76.

[5]   Global Ocean Commission, *From Decline to Recovery: A Rescue Package for the Global Ocean*, (GOC 2014) 65.

[6]   *World Ocean Review 3*, above n 2.

[7]   Ibid.

from installations.[8] Accidental pollution can result from a blow-out, rupture of a pipeline, a collision between a ship and an installation, an accident while a tanker is being loaded from an installation, or destruction of a suspended well-head or sub-sea completion system.[9] In addition, there are other significant risks associated with offshore oil and gas activities in the marine ecosystem, including the disturbance of fish stocks and marine mammals during seismic surveys, carbon dioxide and methane emissions through gas flaring and venting and pollution of the marine environment through the discharge of various substances.[10]

On 20 April 2010, the Deepwater Horizon oil rig exploded in the Gulf of Mexico. Estimates are that the Macondo well spilled close to five million barrels of oil into the Gulf of Mexico during 87 days between the blowout and when the well was successfully capped on 15 July 2010.[11] Globally, the Deepwater Horizon disaster is not alone in recent years. In 2009, the Montara oil spill occurred in the Timor Sea, off the northern coast of Western Australia. In total, approximately 64,000 litres of oil leaked from the well each day from 21 August 2009 to 3 November 2009. This cumulated in 6.7 million litres of oil leaked from the well over 106 days.[12] In 2011, China experienced the worst oil spill disaster from offshore oil exploitation platforms in its history. In the Bohai Bay oil spill disaster, ConocoPhillips China (the managing company of the oil exploitation platforms), a subsidiary of the U.S.-based oil company ConocoPhillips, reported that oil and mud leaking from two of the company's platforms in the Penglai 19-3 oilfield totalled 2500 barrels.[13] The disaster caused serious pollution in almost 7 per cent of China's Bohai Bay.

The number of recent serious oil spill incidents demonstrates certain deficiencies in the way that petroleum companies conduct offshore operations and the manner in which national authorities control them.[14] Ironically, disasters often act as a catalyst for legal development. The Deepwater Horizon disaster has provided a boost to the development and further strengthening of accidental pollution regimes worldwide. For example, the Mediterranean (Madrid) Offshore Protocol[15] was finally ratified and

---

[8]   R.R. Churchill and A.V. Lowe, *The Law of the Sea* (3rd edn, Manchester University Press 1999) 371.

[9]   Ibid.

[10]   Julien Rochette, Matthieu Wemaere, Lucien Chabason and Sarah Callet, 'Seeing beyond the Horizon for Deepwater Oil and Gas: Strengthening the International Regulation of Offshore Exploration and Exploitation', IDDRI, *Working Paper* N01/14, 8.

[11]   The Bureau of Ocean Energy Management, Regulation and Enforcement, *Report Regarding the Causes of the April 20, 2010 Macondo Well Blowout*, (BOEMRE 2011) 24.

[12]   Tina Hunter, 'The Montara Oil Spill and the National Marine Oil Spill Contingency Plan: Disaster Response or Just a Disaster?' (2010) 24 *Australia and New Zealand Maritime Law Journal* 47.

[13]   'Oil spill in China's Bohai Sea rises to 2500 barrels' (Xinhua, 12 August 2011) http://news.xinhuanet.com/english2010/china/2011-08/12/c_131045663.htm (last accessed 20 May 2015).

[14]   Sergei Vinogradov, 'The Impact of the Deepwater Horizon: the Evolving International Legal Regime for Offshore Accidental Pollution Prevention, Preparedness, and Response', (2013) 44 *Ocean Development and International Law* 350.

[15]   Protocol for the Protection of the Mediterranean Sea against Pollution Resulting from Exploration and Exploitation of the Continental Shelf and the Seabed and its Subsoil, adopted 14

entered into force in March 2011, 17 years after its adoption.[16] While the international legal framework for offshore energy activities is anchored in the United Nations Convention on the Law of the Sea (LOSC),[17] it is complemented by an array of relevant instruments and measures at the global, regional and national levels.[18] This chapter examines the current international and regional legal regime for the protection of marine environment from offshore oil and gas activities, including the regimes relating to prevention, reduction and control of operational and accidental pollution as well as liability and compensation regimes. In particular, the chapter focuses on recent legal developments at the regional level (eg, the European Union, the Arctic) since the Deepwater Horizon disaster.

## 2.  THE INTERNATIONAL LEGAL FRAMEWORK

### 2.1   The LOSC

It must be emphasized that international law relating to offshore oil and gas activities is not as advanced as the legal regimes relating to other sources of marine pollution such as shipping. Over the past few decades, particularly since the *Torrey Canyon* oil spill disaster in 1967, the international community has made a concerted effort to establish a complex international legal regime for the prevention of vessel-source pollution.[19] In contrast, no international convention specifically sets construction, design, equipment and manning standards (CDEM standards) determining the conditions under which states should issue offshore drilling permits and no international agreement provides specific rules on liability and compensation for damage from seabed activities subject to national jurisdiction.[20] This is to a certain extent understandable. The LOSC provides that coastal states shall adopt laws and regulations to prevent, reduce and control pollution of the marine environment arising from or in connection with seabed activities subject to their jurisdiction and from artificial islands, installations and structures under their jurisdiction.[21] Indeed, most offshore oil and gas activities currently occur in waters under national jurisdiction. For example, in the *Arctic Ocean Review* published by the Arctic Council Working Group on the Protection of the Arctic Marine Environment (PAME) in 2013, the Arctic 8 (U.S, Russia, Canada, Norway, Denmark, Finland, Iceland and Sweden) note that:

---

October 1994, entered into force 17 March 2011, UNEP *Register of International Treaties and Other Agreements in the Field of the Environment* (UNEP 2005) 569.

[16]   For discussion, see Vinogradov, above n 14, 349.

[17]   United Nations Convention on the Law of the Sea (adopted 10 December 1982, entered into force 16 November 1994) 1833 UNTS 3 (LOSC).

[18]   Catherine Redgwell, 'Mind the Gap in the GAIRS: The Role of Other Instruments in LOSC Regime Implementation in the Offshore Energy Sector' (2014) 29 *International Journal of Marine and Coastal Law* 600.

[19]   Nengye Liu, 'International Legal Framework on the Prevention of Vessel-Source Pollution' (2010) 12 *China Oceans Law Review* 238.

[20]   See Rochette, above n 10, 9.

[21]   LOSC, Art. 208(1).

Unlike shipping, which operates in a global market, offshore petroleum activity is under the jurisdiction of the coastal state. Individual coastal states regulate and control industrial activity in their offshore areas, taking into consideration individual characteristics such as judicial traditions and the distribution of responsibility between industry and authorities. As a consequence, there are differences in the national regulatory frameworks.[22]

However, this does not mean there is no need to enhance the current international regime. According to Article 208(5) of the LOSC, states, acting especially through competent international organizations or diplomatic conference, shall establish global and regional rules, standards and recommended practices and procedures to prevent, reduce and control pollution of the marine environment arising from or in connection with seabed activities.[23] Moreover, although the LOSC does not contain any specific provision on liability for damage from offshore oil and gas activities, Article 235(3) provides that states shall cooperate in the implementation of existing international law and the further development of international law relating to responsibility and liability for the assessment of and compensation for damage and the settlement of related disputes, as well as, where appropriate, development of criteria and procedures for payment of adequate compensation, such as compulsory insurance or compensation funds.[24]

## 2.2 The Convention on Biological Diversity

International law relating to the protection of the marine environment lies in an area of overlap between the law of the sea and international environmental law, containing elements of each and belonging to both.[25] As mentioned above, pollution from offshore oil and gas activities can cause serious damage to marine ecosystems. The Convention on Biological Diversity (CBD)[26] is therefore the most relevant international legal instrument for protection of marine biodiversity from offshore oil and gas activities. The CBD reflects an integrated approach concerning the protection of biodiversity in providing for the conservation of biological resources, the protection of ecosystems, and by obliging states parties to adopt and implement the principle of sustainability in the use of biological resources.[27] The provisions of the CBD extend to both terrestrial and marine biodiversity. The CBD mandates each state party to develop national

---

[22] PAME, *The Arctic Ocean Review Project, Final Report,* (Phase II 2011–2013), Kiruna May 2013 (Protection of the Arctic Marine Environment (PAME) Secretariat, Akureyri 2013), 56 (*Arctic Ocean Review*).

[23] LOSC, Art. 208(5).

[24] LOSC, Art. 235(3).

[25] Louis De La Fayette, 'The Marine Environment Protection Committee: The Conjunction of the Law of the Sea and International Environmental Law' (2001) 16 *International Journal of Marine and Coastal Law* 158.

[26] Convention on Biological Diversity, adopted 5 June 1992, entered into force 29 December 1993, (1992) 31 (4) *International Legal Materials* 818 (CBD).

[27] Rudiger Wolfrum and Nele Matz, 'The Interplay of the United Nations Convention on the Law of the Sea and the Convention on Biological Diversity' (2000) 4 *Max Planck Yearbook of United Nations Law* 459.

strategies, plans or programmes or to adapt existing strategies, plans or programmes to ensure that loss of biodiversity is prevented.[28]

As a framework convention, the CBD has faced criticism since its adoption. For example, the CBD does not place binding obligations on state parties; rather, in code-like fashion it merely spells out standards that state parties are to follow, making it easy for states to justify compliance.[29] Moreover, there are no proper measures initiated through the CBD to prevent or reduce the negative impacts of oil and gas activities on species, habitats and ecosystems resulting from oil and gas operations and production.[30]

### 2.3    The International Maritime Organization

The main purposes of the International Maritime Organization (IMO) are to provide a platform for co-operation among governments in the field of governmental regulation and practices relating to technical matters of all kinds affecting shipping engaged in international trade; and to encourage and facilitate the general adoption of the highest practicable standards in matters concerning maritime safety, efficiency of navigation and prevention and control of marine pollution from ships.[31] In 2012, however, the IMO Legal Committee declined to extend to offshore installations the coverage of IMO Strategic Direction 7.2, under which the IMO focuses on mitigating and responding to environmental impacts of shipping incidents and operational pollution from ships.[32] Nevertheless, a series of international conventions and guidelines adopted under the auspices of the IMO are relevant to the protection of the marine environment from offshore oil and gas activities.

#### 2.3.1    MARPOL
MARPOL is a combination of a convention adopted in 1973 and a protocol adopted in 1978 and updated by amendments over the years.[33] While the LOSC provides the general framework, MARPOL provides the substance and regulatory teeth for the prevention of pollution from ships through a standard-setting approach and a compliance system.[34] MARPOL and its amendments cover technical aspects to prevent and

---

[28]    CBD, Art. 6.

[29]    Sylvester Oscar Nliam, 'International Oil and Gas Environmental Legal Framework and the Precautionary Principle: The Implications for the Nigeria Delta' (2014) 22 *African Journal of International and Comparative Law* 31.

[30]    Ibid, 32.

[31]    Convention on the International Maritime Organization, adopted 6 March 1948, entered into force 17 March 1958, 289 UNTS, Art. 1(a).

[32]    *Arctic Ocean Review*, above n 22, 58.

[33]    International Convention for the Prevention of Pollution from Ships, adopted 2 November 1973, as amended by the Protocol, adopted 1 June 1978, entered into force 2 October 1983, 1340 UNTS 61 (MARPOL).

[34]    Aldo Chircop, 'The Designation of Particularly Sensitive Sea Areas: A New Layer in the Regime for Marine Environmental Protection from International Shipping' in Aldo Chircop, Ted McDorman and Susan Rolston (eds), *The Future of Ocean-Regime Building, Essays in Tribute to Douglas M. Johnston* (Martinus Nijhoff Publishers 2009) 578.

reduce pollution from ships. It has six Annexes that contain regulations for the prevention of various forms of pollution: Annex I (discharges of oil and oily mixtures); Annex II (noxious liquid chemicals); Annex III (pollution by hazardous substances in packed form); Annex IV (sewage); Annex V (garbage); and Annex VI (air pollution). According to Article 2 of the MARPOL Convention, 'Discharge' does not include (i) dumping within the meaning of the Convention on the Prevention of Marine Pollution by Dumping of Wastes and Other Matter, done at London on 13 November 1972 or (ii) release of harmful substances directly arising from the exploration, exploitation and associated offshore processing of sea-bed mineral resources.[35] Nevertheless, this exclusion did not prevent the Arctic Council's Arctic Offshore Oil and Gas Guidelines (AOOGG)[36] from recommending, for example, that with respect to production waste discharges from the operation of offshore industrial facilities, operators should apply certain MARPOL 73/78 requirements, or their equivalent.[37] Furthermore, MARPOL Annex V also contains provisions[38] on the discharge of garbage from fixed or floating platforms, to the extent such discharge does not fall under MAPROL's exclusion of discharges arising directly from certain seabed mineral activities.[39]

### 2.3.2 The London Dumping Convention

The 1972 Convention on the Prevention of Marine Pollution by Dumping of Wastes and Other Matter (London Convention)[40] defines 'dumping' as (i) any deliberate disposal at sea of wastes or other matter from vessels, aircraft, platforms or other man-made structures at sea; (ii) any deliberate disposal at sea of vessels, aircraft, platforms or other man-made structures at sea.[41] The London Convention does not cover the disposal of wastes or other matter directly arising from, or related to the exploration, exploitation or associated offshore processing of sea-bed mineral resources.[42] However, in the 1996 Protocol to the Dumping Convention (London Protocol, as amended in 2006), the definition of dumping was expanded to 'any abandonment or toppling at site of platforms or other man-made structures at sea, for

---

[35] MARPOL Art. 2(3)(b).

[36] Arctic Council Protection of the Arctic Marine Environment Working Group, *Arctic Offshore Oil and Gas Guidelines*, 2009.

[37] *Arctic Ocean Review*, above n 22, 59.

[38] See, eg, MARPOL Annex V, Regulation 4, Special requirements for disposal of garbage: (1) Subject to the provisions of para.(2) of this regulation, the disposal of any materials regulated by this Annex is prohibited from fixed or floating platforms engaged in the exploration, exploitation and associated offshore processing of sea-bed mineral resources, and from all other ships when alongside or within 500 metres of such platforms; (2) The disposal into the sea of food wastes may be permitted when they have been passed through a comminuter or grinder from such fixed or floating platforms located more than 12 nautical miles from land and all other ships when alongside or within 500 metres of such platforms. Such comminuted or ground food wastes shall be capable of passing through a screen with openings no greater than 25 millimetres.

[39] *Arctic Ocean Review*, above n 22, 59.

[40] Adopted 15 February 1972, entered into force 7 April 1974, 1975 UKTS 119 (LC).

[41] LC, Art. 3(1)(a).

[42] LC, Art. 3(1)(c).

the sole purpose of deliberate disposal'.[43] Therefore, the London Convention extends its jurisdiction to the particular activities of decommissioning and abandonment of petroleum installations and structures at sea, either totally or partially.[44]

### 2.3.3   Oil pollution preparedness, response and cooperation

The International Convention on Oil Pollution Preparedness, Response and Cooperation[45] (OPRC) was adopted in 1990 and entered into force in 1995. As of 6 January 2015, the OPRC had in total 107 contracting parties.[46] The OPRC provides that Parties undertake, individually or jointly, to take all appropriate measures in accordance with the provisions of this Convention and the Annex thereto to prepare for and respond to an oil pollution incident.[47] The objective of the OPRC is to provide for international cooperation in responding to pollution emergencies and to enhance existing national, regional and global capacities.[48] OPRC applies to 'offshore units', which means any fixed or floating offshore installation or structure engaged in gas or oil exploration, exploitation or production activities, or loading or unloading of oil.[49] It covers a range of issues regarding oil pollution response, including emergency plans (Article 3), reporting procedures (Article 4), action on receiving an oil pollution report (Article 5), national and regional systems for preparedness and response (Article 6), international co-operation (Article 7), research and development (Article 8), technical co-operation (Article 9) as well as promotion of bilateral and multilateral co-operation in preparedness and response (Article 10).

### 2.3.4   Non-binding codes and guidelines

The IMO regularly adopts non-binding codes, recommendations and guidelines, which serve as interpretive tools, and supplement and provide guidance for the effective implementation of binding provisions.[50] When it comes to offshore oil and gas activities, there are two instruments that are particularly relevant. The first is the Guidelines and Standards for the Removal of Offshore Installations and Structures on the Continental Shelf and in the Exclusive Economic Zone which were adopted in 1989

---

[43]   Protocol to the Convention on the Prevention of Marine Pollution by Dumping of Wastes and Other Matter, adopted 7 November 1996, entered into force 24 March 2006 (1997) 36 *International Legal Materials* 1 (LP), Art. 1.4.1.4.

[44]   Zhiguo Gao, 'Environmental Regulation of Oil and Gas in the Twentieth Century and Beyond: An Introduction and Overview' in Zhiguo Gao (ed.), *Environmental Regulation of Oil and Gas* (Kluwer Law International 1998) 15.

[45]   International Convention on Oil Pollution Preparedness, Response and Co-operation, 1990, and Final Act of the Conference (1991) 30 *International Legal Materials* 733 (OPRC).

[46]   Status of Multilateral Conventions and Instruments in respect of which the International Maritime Organization or its Secretary-General Performs Depositary or Other Functions, as at 6 January 2015, 464, http://www.imo.org/About/Conventions/StatusOfConventions/Documents/Status%20-%202015.pdf (last accessed 21 May 2015).

[47]   OPRC, Art. 1(1).

[48]   See Vinogradov, above n 14, 342.

[49]   OPRC, Art. 2(4).

[50]   Angelica Bonfanti and Francesca Romanin Jacur, 'Energy from the Sea and the Protection of the Marine Environment: Treaty-Based Regimes and Ocean Corporate Social Responsibility' (2014) 29 *International Journal of Marine and Coastal Law* 627.

(1989 IMO Guidelines and Standards).[51] The second is the Code for the Construction and Equipment of Mobile Offshore Drilling Units (MODU Code) which was first adopted in 1979[52] and subsequently updated in 1989[53] and 2009.[54]

Although some believe that the 1989 IMO Guidelines and Standards were called for in the text of Article 60 (3) LOSC,[55] which refers to generally accepted international standards established in this regard by the competent international organization (IMO),[56] the role of the non-binding Guidelines and Standards for the protection of marine environment from offshore oil and gas activities should not be overestimated. Indeed, there is abundant discussion on the legal interpretation of 'general acceptance'. The International Law Association (ILA)'s Committee on Coastal State Jurisdiction Relating to Marine Pollution concludes in its final report (London 2000 Conference Report) that: 'the application of generally accepted international rules and standards (GAIRSs) to the environmental sphere in the LOSC is believed to make compulsory for all states certain rules which had not taken the form of an international convention in force for the states concerned, but which were nevertheless respected by most states. GAIRSs cannot be equated with customary law, nor with legal instruments in force for the states concerned. GAIRSs are primarily based on state practice, attaching only secondary importance to the nature and status of the instrument containing the respective rules or standards.'[57] By way of example, China only recognizes IMO conventions and subsequent amendments that China has ratified. Therefore, non-binding IMO resolutions and guidelines in general are not applicable in maritime areas under China's jurisdiction.[58]

---

51 IMO Resolution A. 672(16), 19 October 1989.

52 1979 MODU Code, IMO Resolution A.414 (XI), 15 November 1979.

53 1989 MODU Code, IMO Resolution A.649 (16), 19 October 1989.

54 2009 MODU Code, IMO Resolution A. 1023 (26), 2 December 2009.

55 LOSC Art. 60(3) reads: 'Due notice must be given of the construction of such artificial islands, installations or structures, and permanent means for giving warning of their presence must be maintained. Any installations or structures which are abandoned or disused shall be removed to ensure safety of navigation, taking into account any generally accepted international standards established in this regard by the competent international organization. Such removal shall also have due regard to fishing, the protection of the marine environment and the rights and duties of other States. Appropriate publicity shall be given to the depth, position and dimensions of any installations or structures not entirely removed.'

56 Youna Lyons, 'The New Offshore Oil and Gas Installation Abandonment Wave and the International Rules on Removal and Dumping' (2014) 29 *International Journal of Marine and Coastal Law* 491.

57 International Law Association London Conference (2000), 'Committee on Coastal State Jurisdiction relating to Marine Pollution, Final Report' in Erik Franckx (ed.), *Vessel-Source Pollution and Coastal State Jurisdiction: The Work of the ILA Committee on Coastal State Jurisdiction Relating to Marine Pollution (1999–2000)* (Kluwer Law International 2001) 107. There are however different opinions about the meaning of the GAIRSs (such as customary international law). For a recent example, see James Harrison, *Making the Law of the Sea: A Study in the Development of International Law* (Cambridge University Press 2011) 165–78.

58 Nengye Liu, *Prevention of Vessel-Source Pollution, a Comparative Study between European and Chinese Law* (PhD dissertation Ghent University 2012) 135.

## 3.   REGIONAL LEVEL

### 3.1   Regional Sea Programmes

As mentioned above, the international legal framework for offshore energy activities is complemented by an array of relevant instruments and measures at the global, regional and national levels. After its establishment by the United Nations Conference on the Human Environment in 1972, the United Nations Environment Programme (UNEP) launched its Regional Seas Programme (RSP) in 1974. The RSP aims to address the accelerating degradation of the world's oceans and coastal areas through the sustainable management and use of the marine and coastal environment, by engaging neighbouring countries in comprehensive and specific actions to protect their shared marine environment.[59] The RSP covers several of the most important current offshore production regions, including the Persian Gulf, Western Africa, the Wider Caribbean (the Gulf of Mexico), the Mediterranean, and South-East Asia. Partner programmes of the RSP also exist for the Caspian Sea, the North-East Atlantic and the Arctic. The Regional Sea Programmes function through action plans.[60] Relevant articles may vary from one region to another, however most RSP conventions and action plans include general provisions dealing with pollution from activities relating to exploration and exploitation of the seabed.[61] Specific instruments can then be developed based on general provisions. Given that the UNEP RSP is canvassed more fully in Chapter 16 in this volume, the sections below focus on two particularly active partner regions: the North-East Atlantic and the Arctic. In addition, legal developments within the European Union (EU),[62] a unique regional economic integration organization, are discussed.

### 3.1.1   The North-East Atlantic
The Convention for the Protection of the Marine Environment of the North-East Atlantic (OSPAR)[63] brings together the 15 states of the western coasts and catchments of Europe, together with the European Union, to cooperate in the protection of the marine environment of the North-East Atlantic. The OSPAR Convention is concerned both with the prevention and elimination of pollutants as well as ensuring sustainable use of the ocean.[64] Prevention and elimination of pollution from offshore sources are dealt with in Annex III to the Convention. The major offshore oil and gas developments

---

[59]   Regional Seas Programme, United Nations Environment Programme http://www.unep.org/regionalseas/about/default.asp (last accessed 21 May 2015). For fuller discussion see, Nilufer Oral, 'Forty years of the UNEP Regional Seas Programme: from past to future', Chapter 16 in this volume.

[60]   Ibid.

[61]   See Rochette, above n 10, 11.

[62]   The EU is a unique economic and political partnership between 28 European countries that together cover much of the continent of Europe. http://europa.eu/about-eu/index_en.htm (last accessed 21 May 2015).

[63]   Convention for the Protection of the Marine Environment of the North-East Atlantic (1993) 32 *International Legal Materials* 1069 (OSPAR Convention).

[64]   K.I. Johnsen, B. Alfthan, L. Hislop, J. Skaalvik (eds), *Protecting Arctic Biodiversity* (United Nations Environment Programme, GRID-Arendal 2010), 26.

within the OSPAR area are in the North Sea and Norwegian Sea. While oil and gas are produced in the northern areas of both seas, production in the southern North Sea focuses primarily on gas.[65] The North Sea, which is characterized by large-scale oil and gas exploration and production,[66] has been a core area subject to collaboration on the protection of the North-East Atlantic marine environment since the early 1970s.[67]

In 2010, the OSPAR Commission adopted the North-East Atlantic Environment Strategy for 2010–2020,[68] which includes a section on offshore oil and gas industry. The Strategy provides that:

> the Offshore Oil and Gas Industry Strategy will be implemented progressively, through appropriate actions and measures, with the target: 1) to achieve, by 2020, a reduction of oil in produced water discharged into the sea to a level which will adequately ensure that each of those discharges will present no harm to the marine environment; 2) to have phased out, by 1 January 2017, the discharge of offshore chemicals that are, or which contain substances, identified as candidates for substitution, except for those chemicals where, despite considerable efforts, it can be demonstrated that this is not feasible due to technical or safety reasons.[69]

It is noted that programmes and measures in relation to offshore oil and gas activities will be guided by general principles such as the precautionary and polluter pays principles, the application of best available techniques and best environmental practices, as well as the ecosystem approach.[70] In particular, protection of marine environment from offshore oil and gas activities is not treated from a sectoral perspective, but rather as part of implementing an ecosystem approach.

In addition to the North-East Atlantic Environment Strategy for 2010–2020, in 2010 the OSPAR Commission also adopted Recommendation 2010/18 on the Prevention of Significant Acute Oil Pollution from Offshore Drilling Activities.[71] This can be seen as a direct response from the OSPAR Commission to the Deepwater Horizon disaster.[72]

---

[65] OSPAR Commission, 'Offshore Oil and Gas Industry', *Quality Status Report 2010*, http://qsr2010.ospar.org/en/ch07_01.html (last accessed 21 May 2015).

[66] Hannah Katharina Müller and Martha M. Roggenkamp, 'Regulating Offshore Energy Sources in the North Sea – Reinventing the Wheel or a Need for More Coordination' (2014) 29 *International Journal of Marine and Coastal Law* 717.

[67] Jon Birger Skjærseth, 'Protecting the North-East Atlantic: One Problem, Three Institutions' in Sebastian Oberthür, Thomas Gehring and Oran Young (eds), *Institutional Interaction in Global Environmental Governance: Synergy and Conflict among International and EU Policies* (MIT Press 2006) 103.

[68] OSPAR, Strategy of the OSPAR Commission for the Protection of the Marine Environment of the North-East Atlantic 2010–2020, (North-East Atlantic Environmental Strategy) available at www.ospar.org (last accessed 21 May 2015).

[69] OSPAR, North-East Atlantic Environment Strategy, ibid, 19, para. 1.3.

[70] OSPAR, 'Guiding Principles, Part I: Implementing the Ecosystem Approach', North-East Atlantic Environment Strategy, ibid, 5.

[71] OSPAR Recommendation 2010/18 on the Prevention of Significant Acute Oil Pollution from Offshore Drilling Activities, OSPAR 10/23/1-E, Annex 46.

[72] Preamble, OSPAR Recommendation 2010/18: 'DEEPLY CONCERNED by the accident on the Deepwater Horizon drilling rig in the Gulf of Mexico in April 2010.'

According to the Recommendation 2010/18, OSPAR Contracting Parties should: 1) as a precaution continue or, as a matter of urgency, start reviewing existing frameworks, including the permitting of drilling activities in extreme conditions; 2) take extra care to apply all relevant learning from the Deepwater Horizon accident.[73]

### 3.1.2   The Arctic[74]

Summer temperatures in the Arctic in recent decades have been warmer than any time in the past 2000 years and the region is warming twice as fast as the rest of the planet.[75] Arctic summer sea ice cover – and particularly the amount of multi-year ice – is decreasing at an accelerating rate.[76] The Arctic contains vast oil and natural gas reserves; the US Geological Survey estimates that the Arctic could contain 1670 trillion cubic feet (tcf) of natural gas and 90 billion barrels of oil, or 30 per cent of the world's undiscovered gas and 13 per cent of oil.[77] Climate change is gradually making access to the Arctic marine area easier, and as such, offshore hydrocarbon exploitation is anticipated to be a major future economic activity in the Arctic.[78]

The Arctic Council is currently the most important forum for international cooperation in the region. The Arctic Council was established in 1996 as a high-level forum by the Declaration on the Establishment of the Arctic Council (Ottawa Declaration) adopted by the Arctic states (US, Russia, Canada, Norway, Denmark, Finland, Sweden and Iceland). By welcoming China, India, Italy, Japan, Republic of Korea and Singapore as new Observer states in the Eighth Ministerial Meeting in 2013,[79] it is anticipated that the Arctic Council will play a more important role in future Arctic governance.[80]

There are two regional instruments that have been adopted under the auspices of the Arctic Council that specifically address offshore oil and gas extraction in the Arctic. First, the Arctic Offshore Oil and Gas Guidelines (AOOGC) proposes a non-binding set of suggested best practices for oil and gas extraction designed to advise industry officials and government regulators.[81] Second, the Agreement on Cooperation on

---

[73]   OSPAR Recommendation 2010/18, Art. 3.1.

[74]   For a comprehensive study on regulation of offshore oil and gas activities in the Arctic, see, for example, Rachael Lorna Johnstone, *Offshore Oil and Gas Development in the Arctic Under International Law Risk and Responsibility* (Martinus Nijhoff 2014).

[75]   Conservation of Arctic Flora and Fauna (CAFF). Arctic Biodiversity Assessment: Report for Policy Makers (CAFF 2013) 9.

[76]   Ibid.

[77]   United States Geological Survey (USGS), 'Circum-Arctic Resource Appraisal: Estimates of Undiscovered Oil and Gas North of the Arctic Circle, Fact Sheet 2008-3049' (USGS 2008).

[78]   Kamrul Hossain, Timo Koivurova and Gerald Zojer, 'Understanding Risks Associated with Offshore Hydrocarbon Development' in Elizabeth Tedsen, Sandra Cavalieri and R. Andreas Kraemer (eds), *Arctic Marine Governance, Opportunities for Transatlantic Cooperation* (Springer 2014) 160.

[79]   See, Kiruna Declaration Report of the Eighth Ministerial Meeting, MM08-15 May 2013, Kiruna, Sweden, 6.

[80]   Nengye Liu, 'The European Union's Potential Contribution to Enhanced Governance of Arctic Shipping' (2013) 73 *Zeitschrift für ausländisches öffentliches Recht und Völkerrecht* 716.

[81]   Emily Hildreth, 'Holes in the Ice: Why a Comprehensive Treaty will not Succeed in the Arctic and How to Implement an Alternative Approach' (2011) 3 *Yearbook of Polar Law* 556.

Marine Oil Pollution, Preparedness and Response in the Arctic[82] was adopted in 2013, but has yet to enter into force. It must be pointed out that OSPAR also covers part of the Arctic Ocean.[83] The AOOGC therefore reference OSPAR practices as providing potential Arctic-wide standards for environmental monitoring of oil and gas activities, testing acute toxicity, decommissioning structures, and requiring best available technology and best environment practice.[84]

### 3.1.3 The European Union

The Deepwater Horizon disaster played a major role in the EU's realization that the risk of a major offshore oil or gas accident occurring in Union waters was significant and that the existing fragmented legislation and diverse regulatory and industry practices did not enable all achievable reduction in the risks throughout the Union.[85] One of the clearest changes brought by the Treaty of Lisbon was that energy is now explicitly included in the list of EU competences, one mainly shared between the EU and Member States.[86] EU competences for environmental policy are furthermore linked with the shared competence in energy. This is evident in Article 194 of the Treaty on the Functioning of the European Union (TFEU), which states that EU energy policy is to be set in 'the context of the establishment and functioning of the internal market and with regard for the need to preserve and improve the environment'.[87] A direct output of this was the adoption, in 2013, of Directive 2013/30/EU[88] which aims at establishing minimum requirements for preventing major accidents in offshore oil and gas operations and limiting the consequences of such accidents.[89]

Directive 2013/30/EU however pays most attention to accidental pollution from offshore oil and gas activities, rather than operational pollution. As described by the

---

[82] Agreement on Cooperation on Marine Oil Pollution, Preparedness and Response in the Arctic (adopted Kiruna, 15 May 2013, not yet in force).

[83] See OSPAR Convention Art. 1, definition of 'maritime area'. For graphic representation see Region I – Arctic Waters www.ospar.org/content/content.asp?menu=00420211000000_000000_000000 (last accessed 21 May 2015).

[84] *Arctic Ocean Review*, above n 22, 61.

[85] Proposal for a Regulation of the European Parliament and of the Council on Safety of Offshore Oil and Gas Prospections, Exploration and Production Activities, COM (2011) 688 of 27 October 2011, 2.

[86] Consolidated Versions of the Treaty on the Functioning of the European Union (TFEU) [2010] OJ C83/47, Art. 4(2): Shared competence between the Union and the Member States applies in the following principal areas: (a) internal market; (b) social policy, for the aspects defined in this Treaty; (c) economic, social and territorial cohesion; (d) agriculture and fisheries, excluding the conservation of marine biological resources; (e) environment; (f) consumer protection; (g) transport; (h) trans-European networks; (i) energy; (j) area of freedom, security and (k) common safety concerns in public health matters, for the aspects defined in this Treaty. 26.10.2012 Official EN Journal of the European Union C 326/51.

[87] TFEU, Art. 194.

[88] Directive 2013/30/EU on safety of offshore oil and gas operations and amending Directive 2004/35/EC (Text with EEA relevance) [2013] OJ L178/66.

[89] Directive 2013/30/EU, Art. 1(1).

European Commission, a set of rules has been established in Directive 2013/30/EU to prevent accidents:

> 1) before exploration or production begins, companies must prepare a Major Hazard Report for their offshore installation. This report must contain a risk assessment and an emergency response plan; 2) companies must keep resources at hand in order to put them into operation when necessary; 3) when granting licenses, EU countries must ensure that companies are well financed and have the necessary technical expertise; 4) technical solutions which are critical for the safety of operators' installations must be independently verified. This must be done prior to the installation going into operation; 5) national authorities must verify safety provisions, environmental protection measures, and the emergency preparedness of rigs and platforms. If companies do not respect the minimum standards, EU countries can impose sanctions, including halting production; 6) information on how companies and EU countries keep installations safe must be made available for citizens; 7) companies will be fully liable for environmental damages caused to protected marine species and natural habitats. For damage to marine habitats, the geographical zone will cover all EU marine waters including exclusive economic zones and continental shelves.[90]

Directive 2013/30/EU could even possibly have an impact outside EU waters. First, Article 20 of Directive 2013/30/EU provides that 'Member States shall require companies registered in their territory and conducting, themselves or through subsidiaries, offshore oil and gas operations outside the Union as licence holders or operators to report to them, on request, the circumstances of any major accident in which they have been involved.'[91] Therefore, oil giants like British Petroleum (BP) and Shell, whose headquarters are based in EU Member States (London and The Hague) are required to follow Directive 2013/30/EU and to report their major accidents even where they occur outside the EU.[92] Second, it is noted that the Directive 2013/30/EU has identified itself as 'EEA relevant'. This means that it is applicable in the European Economic Area.[93] However, this position has been challenged by Norway.[94]

## 4.   TOWARDS AN INTERNATIONAL CONVENTION?

With perhaps the exception of the provisions in the LOSC, there is no general multilateral convention dealing specifically with environmental control of petroleum

---

[90]   DG Energy, European Commission, 'Offshore Oil and Gas Safety', available at http://ec.europa.eu/energy/en/topics/oil-gas-and-coal/offshore-oil-and-gas-safety (last accessed 21 May 2015).

[91]   Directive 2013/30/EU, Art. 20(1).

[92]   Nengye Liu, 'The European Union's Potential Contribution to Enhanced Governance of Offshore Oil and Gas Operations in the Arctic' (2015) 24 *Review of European, Comparative and International Environmental Law* (DOI: 10.1111/reel.12111).

[93]   The European Economic Area (EEA) unites the EU Member States and the three European Free Trade Association (EFTA) States (Iceland, Liechtenstein, and Norway) into an Internal Market governed by the same basic rules. For information see http://www.efta.int/eea (last accessed 21 May 2015).

[94]   See Luszczuk, above n 4, 83.

operations.[95] Thus Gao suggests that the international community may wish to consider the need and possibility of adopting a new international legal instrument devoted entirely to the offshore industry.[96] He argues that an international convention would be able to consolidate and complement all the existing provisions in various treaties and at different levels; it could serve to coordinate the regulatory functions currently exercised by a variety of organizations; it could rectify the present piecemeal approach to environmental regulation of oil and gas activities; and it would fill the gap of lack of international law.[97] Gao is not alone in expressing these thoughts. Recommendations for a specific international convention regarding offshore oil and gas activities have been made by numerous scholars, organizations and national governments for many years.

Within academia, for example, Rares believes that there is an imperative need for an international convention to regulate the risks and consequences of existing and future offshore drilling activities.[98] In 2013, the European Commission published a Report prepared by Maastricht University entitled 'Civil Liability and Financial Security for Offshore Oil and Gas Activities'.[99] This Report recommends that the EU should take the initiative in establishing an international agreement dealing with the problem of spills from offshore activities though it recognizes that there is no real prospect of such an agreement coming into existence in the foreseeable future as there appears to be an absence of the necessary political will.[100]

As early as 1977, the Comité Maritime International (CMI) published a draft Convention on Offshore Mobile Craft (Rio Draft). The Rio Draft was forwarded to the Legal Committee of the IMO without any further consideration until 1990.[101] The Rio Draft was then amended by the CMI at its Sydney meeting in 2004, and renamed the Sydney Draft. In 2014, the Global Ocean Commission,[102] in its 'Rescue Package for the Global Ocean', proposes to adopt and improve international safety and environmental standards for offshore drilling on the continental shelf, including regional

---

[95] See Gao, above n 44.

[96] Ibid, 31.

[97] Ibid.

[98] Steven Rares, 'An International Convention on Offshore Hydrocarbon Leaks?' (2012) 26 *Australian and New Zealand Maritime Law Journal* 10.

[99] Kristel De Smedt, Michael Faure, Jing Liu, Niels Philipsen and Hui Wang, *Civil Liability and Financial Security for Offshore Oil and Gas Activities, Final Report* (Maastricht European Institute for Transnational Legal Research, Faculty of Law, Maastricht University).

[100] Report of the IWG on Offshore Activities, Comité Maritime International, available at http://www.comitemaritime.org/Uploads/1.Report%20of%20the%20IWG%20on%20Offshore%20Activities%203.pdf (last accessed 21 May 2015).

[101] Baris Soyer, 'Compensation for Pollution Damage Resulting from Exploration for and Exploitation of Seabed Mineral Resources' in Baris Soyer and Andrew Tettenborn (eds), *Pollution at Sea Law and Liability* (Informa Law 2012) 73.

[102] The Global Ocean Commission (GOC) is a recently established NGO, originated as an initiative of The Pew Charitable Trusts, in partnership with Somerville College at the University of Oxford, the Adessium Foundation and Oceans 5. For information see www.globaloceancommission.org (last accessed 21 May 2015).

protocols to establish and implement such standards, with provisions for response-preparedness and capacity building in developing countries.[103]

States have voiced similar concerns. In 2010, Russian President Medvedev used a speech on World Environment Day to highlight the need to put in place a modern framework of international law, perhaps in the form of a convention or several agreements to address issues of the kind arising from disasters such as that in the Gulf of Mexico.[104] Indonesia, whose waters were damaged by pollution from the 2009 Montara oil spill, submitted a proposal regarding development of an international regime for liability and compensation for oil pollution damage resulting from offshore oil exploration and exploitation activities to the Legal Committee of the IMO in 2010.[105] However, in 2012 the IMO Legal Committee finally rejected the Indonesian proposal, considering that the issue should be addressed at regional level.[106]

Fortunately, developing common standards and a liability regime for offshore oil and gas activities at the regional level does appear to be a realistic option for the foreseeable future. In the EU, for example, Directive 2013/30/EU has established a set of rules to prevent accidental pollution. Uniform standards on construction, design, equipment and manning standards (CDEM standards) to prevent operational pollution from offshore installations in European waters, if achieved, could not only improve safety levels of offshore oil and gas operations from the North Sea to the Mediterranean, but could potentially also establish a good example for industry performance in neighbouring waters.[107] An international convention must accommodate interests from around the world. On the one hand, it might not be able to pay special attention to sensitive and vulnerable areas (eg, the Arctic). On the other hand, counties with advanced regulatory regimes for offshore oil and gas activities, such as the UK and Norway, might benefit from the adoption of an international convention that would effectively export their standards to other developing countries. It also must be recognized that even a country like China, whose level of development, economic influence and capacity to implement exceeds that of many other developing states, might still lack the capacity to implement high safety standards set up in the convention. This is underlined by the fact that, despite China's extensive efforts to catch up with developments of international law on the prevention of marine pollution from shipping over the last few years, it still evidences shortcomings in some areas.[108]

---

[103]   See *Global Ocean Commission*, above n 5 , 64.

[104]   See   http://www.unep.org/wed/2010/english/PDF/PresidentMedvedev_WED.pdf   (last accessed 27 May 2015).

[105]   IMO, Report of the Legal Committee on its ninety-seventh session, LEG 97/15, 1 December 2010.

[106]   See Rochette, above n 10, 26.

[107]   Liu, above n 92.

[108]   Liu, above n 58, 179.

## 5.  CONCLUDING REMARKS

This chapter has surveyed the international and regional legal regime for the protection of the marine environment from offshore oil and gas activities. Unlike shipping, international law on the regulation of offshore oil and gas activities is not well advanced. Although the LOSC, the CBD and several IMO conventions and guidelines all touch the issues, no specific international convention addressing the issue is likely in the foreseeable future. It, however, needs to be researched to what extent and how the adoption of an international convention is feasible. In particular, an international convention on the compensation and liability regime for pollution from offshore oil and gas activities might still be attractive, especially for those developing countries who lack a domestic liability regime.

By contrast, regulation of offshore oil and gas activities at the regional level seems more feasible. In response to the Deepwater Horizon disaster, developments have occurred in many regions, such as the North-East Atlantic and the Arctic. In particular, the EU established a set of mandatory rules for the prevention of accidental pollution from offshore oil and gas operations, which are applied in the EU waters, from the North Sea to the Mediterranean. It will be interesting to see whether in the foreseeable future the EU can further develop common CDEM standards for offshore oil and gas operations in the whole EU waters.

# 10. Protection and preservation of the marine environment from seabed mining activities on the continental shelf: perspectives from the Pacific Islands region

*Marie Bourrel**

More than an ocean, the Pacific was like a universe, and a chart of it looked like a portrait of the night sky. This enormous ocean was like the whole of heaven, an inversion of earth and air, so that the Pacific seemed like outer space, an immensity of emptiness, dotted with misshapen islands that twinkled like stars, archipelagos like star clusters (...)

Paul Theroux, *The Happy Isles of Oceania*

## 1. INTRODUCTION

Over the last half-century metal grades in terrestrial mineral deposits have been decreasing steadily. Due to the progressive increase in metal prices, triggered by growing international demand,[1] which has been accompanied by improved efficiency in mining technologies, extraction of massive low-grade deposits is now becoming economical.[2] These factors have also turned the attention of investors and developers to alternative sources of metals, including the deep sea,[3] as marine deposits often have significantly higher grades.[4] The existence of minerals on the seabed[5] has been known

&ast;   We thank Jenny Hyatt and Alison Swaddling for the review of this chapter. The views and opinions expressed in this chapter are those of the authors and do not necessarily reflect the official policy or position of the Secretariat of the Pacific Community or the European Union.

[1]   Notably from rapidly expanding economies (i.e., China, India, Brazil, Indonesia). See C. Roche and J. Feeman, 'Drivers for the development of deep sea minerals in the Pacific' in Elaine Baker and Yannick Beaudoin (eds), *Deep Sea Minerals: Deep Sea Minerals and the Green Economy*, vol. 2 (Secretariat of the Pacific Community, 2013) 28.

[2]   P.A. Rona, 'The changing vision of marine minerals' (2008) 33 *Ore Geology Reviews* 618–66.

[3]   Secretariat of the Pacific Community, *Deep Sea Minerals: Summary Highlights*, (SPC, 2013), 3.

[4]   J. Hein, K. Mizell, A. Koschinsky and T.A. Conrad, 'Deep Ocean mineral deposits as a source of critical metals for high- and green-technology applications: comparison with land-based resources' (2013) 51 *Ore Geology Reviews* 1, 9.

[5]   Marine minerals encompass minerals that occur on shallow and deep sea ocean environment including near shore and continental shelf areas as well as deeper ocean seamounts, mid-ocean ridges and ocean basins. Marine minerals that occur in the deeper parts of the ocean are referred to as 'deep sea minerals'; SPC-EU DSM Project, Information brochure No. 3, *Marine Minerals*, (Secretariat of the Pacific Community, 2012).

for many years and there have been numerous research cruises in the Pacific region aimed at understanding and documenting these potentially rich deposits.[6] In fact, more mineral deposits have been discovered in the Pacific Ocean than in any other ocean, and it appears that some of the world's most promising and abundant marine mineral resources are to be found in the Pacific.[7]

Three main classes of deep sea minerals have been identified as of economic interest in the Pacific region, namely: sea-floor massive sulphides, manganese nodules, and ferromanganese cobalt-rich crusts.[8] These seabed mineral deposits are composed predominantly of metals such as copper, gold, silver, zinc, lead, cobalt and platinum. Bearing in mind that deep ocean mineral deposits will not replace land-based mining for many countries, recovering such deposits could offer an additional source of raw materials to meet the increasing demand.[9] It is nevertheless worth mentioning that in comparison to land-based mining, seabed mining is relatively new and as a result, raises some concerns with regards to its potential environmental and social impacts. However, this new industry is technically very innovative[10] and should therefore be fully capable of providing adequate technologies that will ensure that appropriate management and mitigation measures are applied.

Regardless of technological developments, however, some general environmental impacts are expected to occur, though their extent and severity will be site specific, depending on local conditions and the methodology of mineral extraction.[11] The impact of mining will also differ among the three types of deposits.[12] Pollution from seabed

---

[6]   D. Cronan, R. Hodkinson, S. Miller and L. Hong, 'Part 1: An evaluation of manganese nodules and cobalt-rich crusts in south Pacific exclusive economic zones – nodules and crusts in and adjacent to the EEZ of the Cook Islands (the Aitutaki-Jarvis transect)' (1991) 10(4) *Marine Mining* 1; J.R. Hein, M.S. Schulz and L.M. Gein, 'Central Pacific cobalt-rich ferromanganese crusts: Historical perspective and regional variability' in Barbara H. Keating, Barrie R. Bolton (eds), *Geology and Offshore Mineral Resources of the Central Pacific Basin* (Springer, 1992) 261–283; D. Cronan and R. Hodkinson, 'An evaluation of manganese nodules and cobalt-rich crusts in south Pacific exclusive economic zones. Part iii. Nodules and crusts in the EEZ of Tuvalu (Ellice Islands)' (1993) 11(2) *Marine Georesources & Geotechnology* 153; J. Hein et al., 'Critical metals in manganese nodules from the Cook Islands EEZ, abundances and distributions' (2015) 68 *Ore Geology Reviews*, 97–116; J. Hein and A. Koschinsky, 'Deep-ocean ferromanganese crusts and nodules' in H. Holland and K. Turekian (eds), *Treatise on Geochemistry*, (2nd), vol 13 (Elsevier, 2014) 273, 275.

[7]   A. Tawake and H. Lily, 'Towards Pacific Island responsible development of marine mineral resources' in Elaine Baker and Yannick Beaudoin (eds), *Deep Sea Minerals: Deep Sea Minerals and the Green Economy*, 2013, vol 2 (Secretariat of the Pacific Community, 2013) 9.

[8]   Sea-floor massive sulphides deposits are found in water depths ranging from 1500 to 5000 metres while nodules are predominantly found in ocean basins at 4000 to 6000 metres deep. Cobalt-rich crusts generally occur on seamounts and around flanks of volcanic islands at about 400 to 4000 metres deep; SPC-EU DSM Project, Information brochure No. 3, Marine Minerals, Secretariat of the Pacific Community, 2012.

[9]   Hein, et al., above n 4; Hein et al., above n 6.

[10]   Hein and Koschinsky, above n 6, 286.

[11]   A. Swaddling, 'Environmental management considerations for deep seabed mining', (2015) *Global Island News*, 34–5.

[12]   A large body of literature on potential environmental impacts of deep seabed mining activities exists. See for example and discussion: A. Littleboy and N. Boughen, 'Exploring the

activities may be caused by the release of harmful substances arising directly from the exploration, exploitation and processing of seabed minerals. Potential environmental risks include introduction of new materials (processing wastes, tailing and discharges) or energy (in the form of heat, light or seismic and acoustic waves) into the marine environment, and highly turbid, potentially toxic, sediment plumes resulting from seabed mining activities which will likely impact benthic communities. Destruction and modification of the deep seabed ecosystem will be unavoidable in deep sea mining. Accordingly, it is of critical importance to ensure appropriate environmental management and mitigation measures are imposed, so that the environmental impact of such activities can be assessed, monitored, minimized or avoided. Moreover, similar requirements should also apply to the preliminary phases of mining and especially to exploration activities.

Appropriate environmental management is possible if two main conditions are respected. First, risk assessments, including in situ experiments where practicable, need to be conducted.[13] Second, responsible management based on best internationally agreed standards should be both required by relevant legislation and be properly monitored and enforced. To this end, states under whose jurisdiction or control seabed activities are conducted need to adopt the necessary measures to protect and preserve the marine environment from pollution and safeguard other important activities such as the safety of navigation and fisheries. Such obligations are clearly stated in the United Nations Convention on the Law of the Sea (LOSC)[14] and in particular in Article 192 which imposes a general obligation on States to protect and preserve the marine environment both within and outside areas of national jurisdiction. This fundamental obligation is commonly considered as having become a norm of customary international law.[15] Several other legally binding, globally and regionally applicable treaties

---

social dimensions of an expansion to the seafloor exploration and mining industry in Australia: Synthesis Report', Report P2007/917 (CSIRO, 2007); D.V. Ellis, 'A review of some environmental issues affecting marine mining' (2001) 19 *Marine Georesources & Geotechnology* 51; P. Hoagland et al., 'Deep-sea mining of seafloor massive sulphides' (2010) 34 *Marine Policy* 728; A. Ahnert and C. Borowski, 'Environmental risk assessment of anthropogenic activity in the deep sea' (2000) 7 *Journal of Aquatic Ecosystem Stress and Recovery* 299; J.M. Markussen, 'Deep seabed mining and the environment: consequences, perceptions, and regulations' in H.O. Bergeseen and G. Parmann (eds), *Green Globe Yearbook of International Co-operation on Environment and Development* (Oxford University Press, 1994) 31; Continental Shelf Associates Inc., 'Synthesis and Analysis of Existing Information regarding Environmental Effects of Marine Mining: Executive Summary' (U.S. Department of Interior, Minerals Management Service, Office of International Activities and Marine Minerals, 1993).

13   Hein, et al., above n 4, 12.
14   Adopted 10 December 1982, entered into force 16 November 1994, 1833 UNTS 3.
15   This key principle has its roots in the *Trail Smelter* Case (US v. Canada), 3 *Reports of International Arbitral Awards* 1905, 1949; Principle 21 of the Stockholm Declaration (The United Nations Conference on the Human Environment, Stockholm, 1972), (1972) 11 *International Legal Materials* 1416; the International Law Commission Draft Articles on Prevention of Transboundary Harm from Hazardous Activities, GA.Res.62/68, Annex, UN Doc.A/RES/62/68, 6 December 2007; and, more recently, in the decision of the International Court of Justice in the *Pulp Mills on the River Uruguay* Case (Argentina v. Uruguay), Merits, 2010 ICJ Reports. See M. Bourrel, 'Pollution du fait d'un navire dans une aire marine protégée en haute mer: quel

complement, enhance and implement the overarching obligation imposed by the LOSC including the relevant conventions adopted by the International Maritime Organization (IMO)[16] and other environment related conventions.[17] This legal framework is complemented by a large range of global and regional non-binding instruments which address, both directly and indirectly, activities that raise environmental concerns with regards to seabed mining which may occur on the continental shelf of Pacific Island States.[18]

More than ever, mining companies are now preparing to explore and extract minerals from the seabed of the Pacific Ocean. The first commercial sea-floor massive sulphide mining venture[19] should start in Papua New Guinea (PNG) in 2017. Several more deep sea mineral (DSM) exploration licences have been granted by other Pacific Island States (PIS)[20] and some other PIS are actively seeking foreign investment in this new industry. As of January 2013, exploration contracts have been signed, or are pending signature, for about 1,843,350 km² of the global seabed, half of which have been signed by coastal states relating to operations in their respective exclusive economic zones (EEZs) or on their continental shelves.[21] Most of these states are PIS. For many PIS with limited economic onshore mineral resources, the potential to engage with the DSM industry is seen as an opportunity to support their economic growth and limit

---

rôle pour le Tribunal international du droit de la mer?' in 2012 (XVII) *Annuaire du Droit de la Mer*, 197; J.P. Beurier, *Droit international de l'environnement* (4th) (Pedone, 2010) 141; J.M. Van Dyke, 'Giving teeth to the environmental obligations in the LOS convention' in A. Oude, Elferink, D.R. Rothwell (eds), *Oceans Management in the 21st Century: Institutional Frameworks and Responses* (Brill Publishers, 2004) 164.

[16]  Eg, the Convention for the Prevention of Pollution from Ships (MARPOL) 1973/1978, (1973) 12 *International Legal Materials* 1319 and (1978) 17 *International Legal Materials* 546; the 1972 Convention on the Prevention of Marine Pollution by Dumping of Wastes and Other Matter (LDC), (1972) 11 *International Legal Materials* 1294 and its 1996 Protocol, (1997) 36 *International Legal Materials* 1; the 1990 International Convention on Oil Pollution Preparedness, Response and Cooperation (OPRC) (1990) 30 *International Legal Materials* 735.

[17]  Eg, the 1998 Convention on Access to Information, Public Participation in Decision Making and Access to Justice in Environmental Matters (Arhus Convention) (1999) 38 *International Legal Materials* 517; the 1991 Convention on Environmental Impact Assessment in a Transboundary Context (Espoo Convention) (1991) 30 *International Legal Materials* 802.

[18]  Eg, Agenda 21, 'Programme of Action for Sustainable Development', Chapter 17 (1992) in Annex II to the Report of the UN Conference on Environment and Development, UN Doc. A/CONF.151/26 Vol. I-III, and more particularly for the Pacific Islands region, the Palau Declaration, '"The Ocean: Life & Future", Chartering a Course to Sustainability', endorsed by all Pacific Leaders at the 45th Pacific Islands Forum, Koror (Palau), in July 2014, available at http://www.forumsec.org/resources/uploads/attachments/documents/AnnexB_Palau_Declaration_on_The_Ocean_Life_and_Future.pdf (last accessed 21 May 2015).

[19]  This joint venture has been concluded by the Government of Papua New Guinea and Nautilus Minerals Inc. for the Solwara 1 Project located in the Bismarck Sea in PNG's EEZ. It is anticipated that copper, gold and silver will be extracted. See, eg, http://www.nautilus minerals.com/s/Home.asp (last accessed 21 May 2015).

[20]  For the purpose of this chapter, the term 'Pacific Islands States' means all the States within the Secretariat of the Pacific Community's region but does not include Australia, France, New Zealand or the United States of America.

[21]  Hein, et al., above n 4, 13.

their dependence on foreign development aid.[22] In this context, PIS have remained firm in their commitment to ensuring that this new industry will contribute to the long-term economic sustainability and social development of the people of the Pacific. This early commitment led, in 1999, to the organization of a regional workshop in PNG to highlight the opportunities related to offshore minerals as well as the potential environmental, social and cultural impacts that may be caused by the development of DSM activities within the Pacific region. As a result, the Mandang Guidelines were adopted with the aim at assisting states in formulating effective policy and legislation for offshore mineral development.[23] In 2011, the PIS decided to strengthen their cooperation and undertook to work collectively through the Secretariat of the Pacific Community (SPC)[24] to develop a regional legislative and regulatory framework for DSM activities. This framework, also called the Pacific Islands Legislative and Regulatory Framework (RLRF),[25] has been developed in close collaboration with all PIS as well as key stakeholders including mining companies, non-government organizations and academics. The main objective of the RLRF is to provide PIS with the tools and guidelines for the formulation of a comprehensive national policy, legal framework, and institutional capacity to efficiently regulate and monitor deep sea mining activities, regardless of whether these activities occur within areas under national jurisdiction or in areas beyond national jurisdiction. This regional framework is used by all PIS which have decided to engage with DSM activities.

As interest in deep sea minerals has recently increased worldwide, but particularly in the Pacific Islands region, this chapter will focus on the national responses adopted by PIS, in term of rules and regulations, to protect and preserve the marine environment from seabed mining activities conducted on their continental shelves.[26] Laws and

---

[22]    Roche and Feeman, above n 1, 34.

[23]    SOPAC, 'The Madang Guidelines: Principles for the development of national offshore mineral policies' (South Pacific Applied Geoscience Commission, Secretariat of the Pacific Community, 1999) available at http://ict.sopac.org/VirLib/MR0362.pdf (last accessed 21 May 2015).

[24]    SPC is an international development organization owned and governed by its 26 Pacific Community members – all 22 Pacific Island countries and territories, plus Australia, France, New Zealand and the United States of America. Founded in 1947, the SPC draws upon skills and capabilities from around the world to empower the people of the Pacific, providing a range of important scientific and technical support, including in the fields of public health, fisheries, energy, agricultural development, disaster risk reduction, geoscience, transportation services and statistics. In 2011, the SPC and the European Union (EU) established a four year project to provide support and assistance to 15 Pacific State members of the EU's grouping for African-Caribbean-Pacific (ACP) countries in respect of deep sea mining within their national jurisdiction (the Cook Islands, Federated States of Micronesia, Fiji, Kiribati, the Republic of the Marshall Islands, Nauru, Niue, Palau, Papua New Guinea, Samoa, Solomon Islands, Timor Leste, Tonga, Tuvalu and Vanuatu).

[25]    SPC, 'Pacific ACP States regional legislative and regulatory framework for deep sea minerals exploration and exploitation' (RLRF), SPC-EU DSM Project, July 2012 available at <http://www.sopac.org/dsm/public/files/2014/RLRF2014.pdf> (last accessed 21 May 2015).

[26]    The continental shelf, as defined by the LOSC, is the seafloor that extends up to 200 nautical miles from the territorial sea baselines or beyond that to outer edge of the continental margin; LOSC, Art. 76.

regulations adopted by PIS to regulate and manage activities undertaken in the international seabed area (the Area) by companies they sponsor are excluded from the scope of this analysis, although some comments addressing DSM activities conducted in areas beyond national jurisdiction will also be of relevance.[27] Specific initiatives taken by PIS to establish specialized agencies to ensure compliance and enforcement of relevant national laws will also be examined. Brief comments outlining the benefits that may be derived from strengthening the regional approach with the view of preventing, reducing and controlling pollution from the marine environment, as recommended by LOSC, will follow.

## 2. INTERNATIONAL AND REGIONAL LEGAL OBLIGATIONS PERTAINING TO SEABED MINING ACTIVITIES UNDERTAKEN ON THE CONTINENTAL SHELF

Although it is true to say that the international legal regime for the prevention of pollution from seabed activities is underdeveloped,[28] the LOSC establishes a basic framework of general obligations which have been progressively supplemented by specific obligations set out in regional treaties, by various international courts and tribunals, and voluntary industry instruments.

For DSM activities that may be conducted within areas under national jurisdiction, Article 208 of LOSC requires coastal states to 'prevent, reduce and control pollution of the marine environment arising from or in connection with seabed activities subject to their jurisdiction and from artificial islands, installations and structures under their jurisdiction'. States are also required to endeavour to harmonize their policies at the appropriate regional level.[29]

As the LOSC has been ratified by all PIS, it is their responsibility to ensure that they adhere to the obligations set out therein when regulating DSM activities. In doing so, and as expressly recalled by the International Tribunal for the Law of the Sea (ITLOS) in its Advisory Opinion on the *Responsibilities and Obligations of States Sponsoring Persons and Entities with Respect to Activities in the Area*, the laws and regulations adopted by these states must be 'no less effective than international rules, regulations and procedures',[30] such as the ones adopted by the International Seabed Authority

---

[27]  See Michael Lodge, 'Protecting the marine environment of the deep seabed', Chapter 7 in this volume.

[28]  See, P. Sands and J. Peel, *Principles of International Environmental Law* (3rd edn) (Cambridge University Press, 2012) 926, 387.

[29]  LOSC, Art. 208(4).

[30]  *Responsibilities and Obligations of States with Respect to Activities in the Area*, Seabed Disputed Chamber of the International Tribunal for the Law of the Sea, Advisory Opinion, 1 February 2011, (2011) ITLOS Reports 78. This key principle has been expressly enshrined in the LOSC as a result of discussions during the Third United Nations Conference on the Law of the Sea. See J.L. Vallarta, 'Protection and preservation of the marine environment and marine scientific research at the Third United Nations Conference on the Law of the Sea' (1983) 46(2) *Law and Contemporary Problems* 147, 148. It is worth noting however that the formulation used by the ITLOS is not exactly the same as the one found in Art. 208(3) of the LOSC which refers

(ISA), collectively referred to as its 'Mining Code'.[31] Additionally, no preferential consideration is granted to developing states in complying with the general obligations of international law in regulating DSM activities.

It is worth noting that several other international conventions that most PIS have ratified or acceded to are relevant to ensuring protection of the marine environment from seabed mining activities. For example, the Convention for the Protection of Natural Resources and the Environment of the South Pacific Region[32] (the Noumea Convention) aims at ensuring that resource development in the Pacific is done in harmony with the maintenance of the unique environmental quality of the region and the evolving principles of sustained resource management.[33] In accordance with Article 8 of the Noumea Convention, states are required to take all appropriate measures to prevent, reduce and control pollution in the Convention area 'resulting directly or indirectly from exploration and exploitation of the seabed and its subsoil'. The Noumea Convention also contains an Environmental Impact Assessment (EIA) requirement, which must include provision of an opportunity for public comment and consultation with other states who may be affected. A similar requirement is a key principle found in the Convention on Biological Diversity[34] (CBD) which has been ratified by all PIS and thus, requires them to protect in situ ecosystems and habitats within areas under national jurisdiction. Parties to CBD also have duties to identify and monitor impacts,[35] establish a system of marine protected areas[36] and, promote consultation regarding processes and activities that may adversely affect biodiversity.[37] As DSM activities are mainly conducted through the use of vessels, PIS will have to ensure that such vessels

---

to 'international rules, standards and recommended practices and procedures'. For further commentary see R. Rayfuse, 'Differentiating the common? The responsibilities and obligations of States sponsoring deep seabed mining activities in the area' (2012) 54 *German Yearbook of International Law* 459; T. Poisel, 'Deep seabed mining: implications of Seabed Disputes Chamber's Advisory opinion' (2012) 19 *Australian International Law Journal* 213; D. Freestone, 'Responsibilities and obligations of States sponsoring persons and entities with respect to activities in the Area' (2011) 105 *American Journal of International Law* 755; D. Anton, R. Makgill and C. Payne, 'Seabed mining – Advisory opinion on responsibility and liability' (2011) 41 *Environmental Policy and Law* 60; and D. French, 'From the depth: rich pickings of principles of sustainable development and general international law on the ocean floor – the Seabed Disputes Chamber's 2011 Advisory opinion' (2011) 26 *International Journal of Marine and Coastal Law* 525.

31    For discussion, see M. Lodge, Chapter 7 in this volume.

32    Adopted 25 November 1986, entered into force 22 August 1990, (1987) 26 *International Legal Materials* 38. As of January 2015, Contracting parties to the Noumea Convention include: Australia, Cook Islands, Federated States of Micronesia, Fiji, France, Nauru, New Zealand, Papua New Guinea, Republic of the Marshall Islands, Samoa, the Solomon Islands and the United States of America.

33    It is worth noting that the Noumea Convention applies to contracting Parties' EEZs and also to areas of the high seas beyond national jurisdiction that are completely enclosed by these EEZs; See, RLRF, above n 25, 11.

34    Adopted 5 June 1992, entered into force 29 December 1993, (1992) 31 *International Legal Materials 822*, Art. 14(a).

35    CBD, Art. 7.

36    CBD, Art. 8.

37    CBD, Art. 14(c).

comply with international obligations set out by IMO conventions. A critical aspect of this will be for PIS to ensure that flag states take all necessary measures for ensuring safety at sea, in accordance with Article 94 of the LOSC, and conform to 'generally accepted international regulations, procedures and practices'.[38]

Relevant provisions and recommendations can also be found in a range of voluntary industry codes of practice such as the code of conduct developed by Interridge to promote 'Responsible Research Practices'[39] and, the International Marine Minerals Society Code for Environmental Management of Marine Mining (IMMS Code), as revised in 2011.[40] The IMMS Code is of particular interest as it provides a very comprehensive framework for the development and implementation of an environmental programme for marine minerals exploration and exploitation by marine mining companies. It also provides benchmarks for stakeholders to assess proposals and the application of best environmental practices at marine mining sites.[41] Moreover, key provisions contribute to meeting the marine mining industry's requirements for regulatory predictabilities and minimization of risks, including environmental regulatory risks.

## 3. PROTECTING THE MARINE ENVIRONMENT THROUGH THE DEVELOPMENT OF STRONG AND EFFECTIVE NATIONAL LEGISLATIVE AND REGULATORY FRAMEWORKS

Establishing strong and effective national regulatory frameworks is a prerequisite to ensuring that the prospecting, exploration and exploitation of seabed minerals that are found on the continental shelf are conducted in conformity with international obligations set out in LOSC and other relevant international conventions and internationally agreed standards such as the precautionary approach,[42] best environmental

---

[38] LOSC, Art. 194(5).

[39] For information see, Interridge Code of Conduct on Responsible Research Practices at Deep-Sea Hydrothermal Vent Sites, http://www.interridge.org/node/16907 (last accessed 22 May 2015).

[40] International Marine Minerals Society, Code for the Environmental Management of Marine Mining, 2011, available at http://www.immsoc.org/IMMS_downloads/2011_SEPT_16_IMMS_Code.pdf (last accessed 22 May 2015).

[41] International Seabed Authority, 'The International Marine Minerals Society's Code for Environmental Management of Marine Mining, Note by the Secretariat' ISBA/16/LTC/2, 11 February 2010.

[42] With regard to deep seabed mining, as stated by the Seabed Disputes Chamber of the ITLOS, States are required to apply a precautionary approach to protect the marine environment and 'where there are threats of serious or irreversible damage, lack of full scientific certainty shall not be used to prevent environmental degradation'. The Chamber further determined that 'the reference to "capabilities" is only a broad and imprecise reference to the differences in developed and developing States. What counts in a specific situation is the level of scientific knowledge and technical capability available to a given State in the relevant scientific and technical fields'. Advisory Opinion, above n 30, paras 126 and 161.

practice,[43] and EIA.[44] To this end, and since DSM activities (exploration or exploit-ation of the seabed and its subsoil) in areas under national jurisdiction take place on the continental shelf, including on the seabed of the territorial sea or internal waters, the recognition of national jurisdiction of states to legislate and enforce their laws is of critical importance. Additionally, unless maritime boundaries are certain, states and investors cannot know which mineral deposits lie within a state's jurisdiction and which lie outside it, within a neighbouring state's continental shelf or within the Area under international waters. In the Pacific Islands region, this constitutes a key challenge as most PIS have either not finalized their national maritime boundaries or are awaiting the determination of submissions claiming extended continental shelves submitted to the Commission on the Limits of the Continental Shelf. In a few cases, PIS have shown reluctance to engage in discussions with neighbouring countries on delimitation matters.[45]

Currently, legislative instruments that govern the territorial sea, EEZ and continental shelf of individual PIS are largely limited to a declaration of sovereign rights and ownerships of the non-living resources of the seabed.[46] Most existing legislation in PIS concerning minerals and mining only applies to on-land exploration and exploitation, with little or no mention of offshore mineral resources.[47] To address the concerns raised regionally and internationally regarding the absence or inaccuracy of national legal and regulatory frameworks, many PIS – with the assistance of the SPC, through the SPC-EU DSM Project – have engaged in the development of tailored national policies and legislation that apply specifically to DSM activities.

---

[43]   As confirmed by the Seabed Disputes Chamber in its Advisory Opinion and as provided for in the ISA Mining Code, States involved in DSM activities are required to ensure the employment of best environmental practices which generally refers to widely accepted norms or customs of environmental and risk management. The concept originally focussed upon technical and physical aspects (also known as 'best available technology') but has since evolved to take into account a wider remit of concerns for social, community and gender issues. See, RLRF, above n 25, 39.

[44]   In its Advisory Opinion, the Seabed Disputes Chamber, referring to the ICJ's *Pulp Mills* judgment, stressed that conducting an EIA is 'a direct obligation under the Convention and a general obligation under customary international law'. Advisory Opinion, above n 30, para. 145.

[45]   For further discussion see, V. Becker-Weinberg, 'Seabed activities and the protection and preservation of the marine environment in disputed maritime areas of the Asia-Pacific region', in *Securing the Ocean for the Next Generation*, LOSI Conference Papers 2012 (Law of the Sea Institute, UC Berkeley-Korea Institute of Ocean Science and Technology Conference, 2012), available at http://www.law.berkeley.edu/files/Becker-Weinberg-final.pdf (last accessed 24 May 2015).

[46]   See Cook Islands Territorial Sea and Exclusive Economic Zone Act 1977, Preamble; Fiji Continental Shelf Act 1970, s. 3(1); Kiribati Marine Zones (Declaration) Act 1983, s. 8(2); Niue Continental Shelf Act 1964, s. 3; Papua New Guinea National Seas Act 1977, Preamble; Samoa Maritime Zones Act 1999, s. 20(1); Tonga Maritime Zones Act 2009, s. 16(1); Tuvalu Marine Zones Act 1983, s. 10(2); and Vanuatu Maritime Zones Act 198, s. 10(a) and (b).

[47]   See for instance the PNG Mining Act 1992; the Solomon Islands Mines and Minerals Act 1996; and the Vanuatu Mines and Minerals Act 1988. See also M. Tsamenyi, S. Kaye and K. Mfodwo, 'Exploring the social dimensions of an expansion to the seafloor exploration and mining industry in Australia: A desktop study of international and selected country experiences' in S. Johns and N. Boughen (eds), (CSIRO-ANCORS, 2007).

## 3.1 Development of National DSM Policy

At time of writing, Cook Islands has adopted its national DSM policy[48] and Fiji is conducting a review of its own policy.[49] The Republic of the Marshall Islands submitted their policy to Cabinet for adoption in January 2015, and Kiribati, Tuvalu and Vanuatu are conducting national consultations on their draft national DSM policies. PNG is ready to submit a draft of its national DSM Policy as is Solomon Islands and Niue. Generally, such national policies follow the same structure (policy context, national goals and objectives, national strategies and implementation) although each government's specific priorities and challenges are clearly identified and addressed. All national DSM policies developed so far take into consideration the existing regulatory, economic, social and cultural contexts of the country. As a result, for the vast majority, multi-criteria analyses have been conducted based on: the state's development priorities and pre-existing revenue portfolio; the DSM occurrence, and mining interest/economic potential within its jurisdiction; and the assessment of impact, risk and available mitigation techniques. As such, the appropriate degree and area of interest in DSM activities for each particular state has been assessed and used to support informed debate amongst relevant stakeholders and the communities. In some cases, for example in Palau and Timor Leste, this has led to a policy decision to delay development of DSM activities until better data on the various economical, ecological and governance impacts are attained, through observing the efforts of other pioneering countries. Alternatively, some PIS have chosen to impose production limits on the DSM minerals of their continental shelves so that these finite mineral deposits are not necessarily developed as fast as technically possible. For example, the Government of the Cook Islands expressly recognizes the opportunity, in order to mitigate the risks of early DSM exploitation, to develop, if necessary, 'a strategy for the release of seabed areas that reserves some high-potential SBM [seabed mineral] resources for later exploitation'.[50] Additionally, national DSM policies that have been developed by PIS expressly recognize key principles including: the importance of the non-renewable nature of DSM resources and the importance of their management in the nation's best interests in the short and long term; the importance of the ocean to the States' citizens' well-being and livelihoods; the necessity to conserve and protect the marine and coastal environment; public ownership of the resources as generally stated in national constitutions;[51] the importance of public participation in the planning, decision-making,

---

48    Cook Islands National Seabed Minerals Policy, 2014, available at http://www.seabed mineralsauthority.gov.ck/index.php/laws-policies-and-regulations/cook-islands-seabed-minerals-policy (last accessed 24 May 2015).

49    The Fiji Offshore Minerals Policy, 2009 is currently under review.

50    Cook Islands National Seabed Minerals Policy, 2014, above n 48, 13.

51    See for instance the Kiribati Constitution, Preamble (3); the Constitution of the Republic of Palau, s. 2; the Constitution of the Independent State of Papua New Guinea, s. 2; and the Constitution of Solomon Islands, Preamble. It is also worth noting that the 2014 Constitution of Fiji states that: 'All minerals in or under any land or water, are owned by the State, provided however, that the owners of any particular land (whether customary or freehold), or of any particular registered customary fishing rights shall be entitled to receive a fair share of royalties

and conduct of DSM activities; and the importance of gathering, analyzing and disseminating scientific and technical data.

Preserving and protecting the marine environment from seabed mining on the continental shelf is at the core of all national DSM policies. As such the Cook Islands' National Seabed Minerals Policy (2014) expressly states that because DSM activities are expected to occur at depths between 4000 m and 5000 m where very little data and scientific research has been conducted, the precautionary approach shall apply to ensure the 'prevention, mitigation, or remedy' of potential environmental impacts.[52] As a result, the Cook Islands' Government is determined to implement a wide range of 'best environmental practice measures' such as the sound and reasonable allocation of sites for DSM activities which will be supported by specific plans for associated control sites, buffer zones and marine protected areas. Moreover, title holders proposing to engage in DSM activities are required to obtain environmental permits which will be issued depending on the potential impacts of the exploration techniques resulting from the EIA. Reporting requirements, impact mitigation measures, application of the precautionary approach by DSM operators and obligation to remedy environmental harm and mine closure are also key elements promoted in the national DSM policy.[53]

## 3.2   Enabling National DSM Policy Implementation Through the Establishment of Strong and Efficient Regulatory Frameworks

The most proactive of the PIS have been the Cook Islands, Fiji, Tonga and Tuvalu which all have enacted dedicated national legislation to ensure that DSM activities, when conducted, will protect and preserve the marine environment.[54] All are at the

---

or other money paid to the State in respect of the grant by the State of rights to extract minerals from that land or the seabed in the area of those fishing rights'. Constitution of the Republic of Fiji, s. 30(1).

[52]   Cook Islands National Seabed Minerals Policy, 2014, above n 48, 7.

[53]   Cook Islands National Seabed Minerals Policy, 2014, above n 48, 8.

[54]   It is worth noting that only the Fiji International Seabed Mineral Management Decree 2013, the Tonga Seabed Minerals Act 2014 and the Tuvalu Seabed Minerals Act 2014 define 'Marine Environment' in the same terms as the ISA, which defines the term as meaning 'the environment of the sea, and includes the physical, chemical, geological and biological and genetic components, conditions and factors which interact and determine the productivity, state, condition and quality of the marine ecosystem, the waters of the seas and oceans and the airspace above those waters, as well as the seabed and ocean floor and subsoil thereof' (ISA's Mining Code, Regulation 1(3)(c): ISBA/16/A/12/Rev.1 (polymetallic sulphides), 2010; ISBA/18/A/11 (cobalt-rich crusts), 2012 ; ISBA/18/C/17 (Polymetallic nodules), 2013); Fiji International Seabed Mineral Management Decree 2013, s. 2(1); Tonga Seabed Minerals Act 2014, s. 2; and Tuvalu Seabed Minerals Act 2014, s. 3. In some other cases, specific definitions have been adopted that show the State's strategic interest in protecting and preserving the marine environment from seabed activities. For instance, the Cook Islands Seabed Minerals Act 2009 refers to the definition given by the Cook Islands Environment Act 2003, which provides that '"Environment" (a) Means the ecosystems and the equality of those ecosystems as well as the physical, biological, cultural, spiritual, social and historic processes and resources in those ecosystems; and (b) Includes (i) land, water, air, animals, plants and other features of human habitat; and (ii) those natural, physical, cultural, demographic, and social qualities and

forefront of legislative development worldwide, with Cook Islands being the first country to enact tailored legislation regulating DSM activities within national juris-diction[55] while Fiji was the first to adopt a decree dedicated to regulating seabed mineral activities carried out in the Area under its sponsorship.[56] More recently, Tonga became the first country in the world to put in place a law that manages seabed mineral activities both within its jurisdiction and under its sponsorship in the Area.[57] Tuvalu followed Tonga in adopting the Seabed Minerals Act 2014, but went further and became the first country in the world to impose a requirement for consultation with coastal communities on matters concerning the regulation and management of seabed minerals that are to be found in the Area, and that are conducted under the sponsorship of Tuvalu.[58] In PNG, where the first commercial deep sea mining project worldwide is planned to commence in 2017, the applicable regulatory regime is based on two separate pieces of legislation originally developed to cover exclusively on-land minerals exploration and exploitation, namely: the Mining Act 1992 and the Environment Act 2000.[59] As of January 2015, only primary DSM legislation has been enacted by PIS as described above, however several are currently engaged in developing secondary legislation (Licensing Regulations and Environmental Regulations) setting out the operational detail of the main legislation that covers DSM activities.[60]

The vast majority of the DSM legislation in place in PIS have been specifically tailored to translate the obligations set out in relevant international instruments into national legal systems with the view of ensuring that any DSM activities carried out within national jurisdictions will be conducted in conformity with states' duties to protect and preserve the marine environment.[61] To this end, contractors are required to adhere to specific provisions set out in DSM legislation or specific national laws

---

characteristics of an area that contribute to people's appreciation of its pleasantness, aesthetic coherence, and cultural and recreational attributes'.

[55]   Cook Islands Seabed Minerals Act 2009.

[56]   Fiji International Seabed Mineral Management Decree 2013 (No 21 of 2013), available at http://faolex.fao.org/docs/pdf/fij136641.pdf (last accessed 24 May 2015).

[57]   Tonga Seabed Minerals Act 2014.

[58]   Tuvalu Seabed Minerals Act 2014.

[59]   Although no specific definition of 'Marine Environment' is given by the PNG Environment Act 2000, the approach adopted by PNG through the definition of the 'Environment' is broad and inclusive enough to encompass all constituent elements of the marine environment. As such the PNG Environment Act 2000 states that '"Environment" includes (a) ecosystems and their constituent parts including people and communities and including human-made or modified structures and areas; and (b) all natural and physical resources; and (c) amenity values; and (d) the qualities and characteristics of locations, places and areas, however large or small, that contribute to their biological diversity and integrity, intrinsic or attributed scientific value or interest, amenity, harmony and sense of community; and (e) the qualities and characteristics of locations, places and areas, however large or small, that contribute to their biological diversity and integrity, intrinsic or attributed scientific value or interest, amenity, harmony and sense of community'; PNG Environment Act 2000, s. 2. See also the Solomon Islands Environment Act 1998, s. 2.

[60]   Specifically, Cook Islands, Fiji and Tonga.

[61]   See, eg, Cook Islands Seabed Minerals Act 2009, s. 3(2)(e); Fiji International Seabed Mineral Management Decree 2013, s. 3(1)(d); Tonga Seabed Minerals Act 2014, s. 5(c) and s. 11(c)(i) and; Tuvalu Seabed Minerals Act 2014, s. 5(c) and s. 11(c)(i).

establishing conditions and processes for protection and preservation of the marine environment including marine pollution prevention. For instance, the Tongan Seabed Minerals Act 2014 requires any title holder (prospecting, exploration, exploitation) engaged in DSM activities within Tonga's national jurisdiction to respect the provisions of the Tonga Marine Pollution Prevention Act 2002, the Environmental Impact Assessment Act 2003, the Tonga Environment Management Act 2010, any regulation made under the Seabed Minerals Act 2014, the terms and conditions of the title permitting the seabed mineral activities, and any environmental conditions arising from the EIA process.[62] Additional requirements complement the duties and responsibilities of DSM contractors, including the obligation to: comply with national laws incorporating international standards developed to ensure maritime safety and security, good working living conditions onboard vessels used for ancillary operations, and the protection of the marine environment;[63] employ best environmental practice;[64] apply the precautionary approach;[65] and take necessary measures to avoid, remedy, or mitigate the adverse effects of DSM activities on the marine environment and prevent, reduce, and control pollution and other negative associated impacts.[66] To this end, the legislation expressly states that no marine reserve or marine protected area covering an area of the Tongan continental shelf can be designated as an area to be released for the purpose of DSM activities.[67] Additionally, any area may be resumed by the regulating Authority for purposes of marine spatial management or environmental protection.[68] In line with this, appropriate insurance policies that provide adequate cover for identified risks and costs of damage that may be caused by DSM activities are also required.[69] The legislation also empowers the regulating Authority to require an environmental

---

[62]   Tonga Seabed Minerals Act 2014, s. 38(1). See also the Tuvalu Seabed Minerals Act 2014, s. 44(1).

[63]   Tonga Seabed Minerals Act 2014, s. 39(1)(a). See also the Tuvalu Seabed Minerals Act 2014, s. 45(l).

[64]   Tonga Seabed Minerals Act 2014, s. 39(1)(b). See also the Tuvalu Seabed Minerals Act 2014, s. 45(a).

[65]   Tonga Seabed Minerals Act 2014, s. 39(1)(c). See also the Tuvalu Seabed Minerals Act 2014, s. 45(a). It is worth noting that the Tonga Seabed Minerals Act 2014 refers to the 'Precautionary Approach' as follows: 'The precautionary approach, in accordance with Principle 15 of the 1992 Rio Declaration on Environment and Development, means that, in order to protect the environment, where there are threats of serious and irreversible damage to the Marine Environment or threats to human health in the Kingdom, a lack of full scientific certainty regarding the extent of adverse effects shall not be used as a reason for postponing cost-effective measures to prevent or minimise environmental degradation arising in any way from a matter or person or activity regulated under this Act'; Tonga Seabed Minerals Act 2014, s. 2. The same definition can be found in the Tuvalu Seabed Minerals Act 2014, s. 3.

[66]   Tonga Seabed Minerals Act 2014, s. 39(1)(d) and (e). See also the Tuvalu Seabed Minerals Act 2014, s. 45(a).

[67]   Tonga Seabed Minerals Act 2014, s. 32(i) and s. 71. Same requirements are set out in the Tuvalu Seabed Minerals Act 2014, s. 38(1) and s. 79; and the Cook Islands Seabed Minerals Act 2009, s. 50(a).

[68]   Tonga Seabed Minerals Act 2014, s. 32(3). See also the Tuvalu Seabed Minerals Act 2014, s. 38(3); and the Cook Islands Seabed Minerals Act 2009, s. 50(b).

[69]   Tonga Seabed Minerals Act 2014, s. 39(1)(f). See also the Tuvalu Seabed Minerals Act 2014, s. 45(k).

bond from the DSM operator(s). Such bond, which will be taken in advance and returned at the end of operations, aims at ensuring the ability of the regulating Authority to address unanticipated environmental damage resulting from the DSM operator's failure. This includes clean-up or compensation costs in respect of any damage caused by pollution or other incident occurring as a result of the DSM activities.[70] Finally, at the end of the exploration licence, mining licence, or upon earlier suspension, revocation or surrender of the title, the DSM operator has the obligation to remove all installations, equipment and materials in the licensed area, and to provide a final report including information on the rehabilitation of the title area.[71]

Although similar requirements are found in some non-DSM specific legislation (eg, on-land legislation), currently in place in other PIS, it must be recognized that gaps and loopholes sometimes exist. For example, while the PNG Environment Act 2000 requires that a precautionary approach be followed when assessing the risk that may be generated to the environment,[72] no definition of the 'precautionary approach' is given.[73] Thus, the concept of the precautionary approach itself lacks substance, which may lead to conflicting interpretations during the implementation and enforcement phases and impede effective and efficient protection and preservation of the marine environment. For all these reasons, several PIS are now committed to developing specific legislation with the aim of addressing the specific particularities and risks of DSM activities. This is the case in the Federated States of Micronesia, Kiribati, the Republic of the Marshall Islands, Nauru, Niue and Solomon Islands.

## 4. ESTABLISHING IMPLEMENTING AGENCIES TO ENSURE COMPLIANCE AND ENFORCEMENT OF RELEVANT NATIONAL LAWS

In addition to enacting legislation, pursuant to Article 214 of the LOSC, coastal states involved in DSM activities carried out on their continental shelves have the duty to take all necessary measures to ensure that national laws enacted to implement international regulations and standards are properly enforced.

### 4.1 Institutional Implementation

Acknowledging the critical importance of implementation and enforcement of the regimes created, the vast majority of PIS which want to engage with DSM activities have established a specialized body with the mandate of regulating DSM operators for DSM activities conducted either within national jurisdiction or in the Area. Until operations commence and proceeds flow, in most cases, PIS have chosen to strengthen the capacity of the existing responsible ministry or department. This has been the

---

[70]   Tonga Seabed Minerals Act 2014, s. 93. See also the Tuvalu Seabed Minerals Act 2014, s. 44(1); and the Cook Islands Seabed Minerals Act 2009, s. 303.

[71]   Tonga Seabed Minerals Act 2014, s. 39(1)(u); Tuvalu Seabed Minerals Act 2014, s. 45(g).

[72]   PNG Environment Act 2000, s. 4(h).

[73]   No definition is given in the PNG Mining Act 1992 or in the PNG Environment Act 2000.

approach taken by Fiji (Ministry for Lands and Mineral Resources), Kiribati (Ministry of Fisheries and Marine Resources), Samoa (Ministry of Natural Resources and Environment), Tonga (Ministry of Lands, Environment, Climate Change and Natural Resources), Tuvalu (Ministry of Natural Resources) and Vanuatu (Ministry of Lands and Natural Resources). In PNG, the statutory agency is the Mineral Resources Authority established in 2006. Although this national agency was initially established to regulate on-land mining activities, its scope of action also embraces DSM resources and activities.

To date, only the Cook Islands has established a dedicated statutory agency responsible for regulating seabed mining activities.[74] The Cook Islands Seabed Minerals Authority is a body corporate with perpetual succession and a common seal, capable of holding real and personal property and of suing or being sued as well as 'doing and suffering all such other acts and things as corporations may lawfully do and suffer'.[75] The Authority is composed of civil servants and is headed by the Seabed Minerals Commissioner. A key aspect of the institutional scheme established by the Cook Islands is the creation of an Advisory Board which aims to operate as the 'official venue for consultation between the Government and the community on matters concerning the regulation and management of the seabed minerals of the Cook Islands'.[76] To this end, the Advisory Board, which is composed of a Chair (as appointed by the Minister of Marine Resources), the Seabed Minerals Commissioner, and at least five members representing the 'island communities of the Cook Islands',[77] is entitled to provide recommendations to the Authority. Such recommendations may be in relation to the management of DSM resources or the grant, renewal, suspension and cancellation of titles as well as to the negotiation and conclusion of seabed minerals agreements.[78]

The Advisory Council established under the Tuvalu Seabed Minerals Act 2014 is very similar to the Cook Islands' Advisory Board with the same functions, responsibilities and composition scheme. However, two main differences may be highlighted. First, the role of the Tuvalu Seabed Minerals Advisory Council is not to support a statutory agency like the one created in the Cook Islands, but rather supports an existing ministry responsible for regulating seabed mining activities. Second, unlike the Cook Islands' Advisory Board whose responsibilities are limited to the activities conducted within the country's national jurisdiction, the Tuvalu Seabed Minerals Advisory Council will be able to effectively consult the coastal communities on matters concerning the regulation and management of seabed activities conducted both within national jurisdiction and in the Area.[79]

Generally, regulating authorities are responsible for: receiving and assessing applications to explore and exploit DSM; setting the terms of permitted activities, by issuing licences; receiving and assessing reporting documents from licenced operators; monitoring compliance with the terms of the licence; taking actions to amend the terms of

---

74    Cook Islands Seabed Minerals Act 2009, s. 17.
75    Cook Islands Seabed Minerals Act 2009, s. 16(2)(d).
76    Cook Islands Seabed Minerals Act 2009, s. 33.
77    Cook Islands Seabed Minerals Act 2009, s. 35(c).
78    Cook Islands Seabed Minerals Act 2009, s. 34(1).
79    Tuvalu Seabed Minerals Act 2014, s. 87(4).

licences or suspend activities if necessary; and enforcing sanctions for non-compliance. It should be noted that in Tonga and Tuvalu, public officials are prohibited from acquiring title rights while they remain as public officials employed by the regulating Authority and are prohibited from acquiring or retaining any share in a private company carrying out DSM activities.[80] Under the Cook Islands Seabed Minerals Act 2009, the Authority is also responsible for developing a 'Seabed Mining Environmental Emergency Contingency Plan' specifying the duties and functions of relevant national agencies to combat, mitigate and remedy the effects of a pollution incident on the environment.[81]

## 4.2 Compliance and Enforcement

All DSM legislation enacted to date in the Pacific region provides for sanctions against non-compliance. In general five different sanctions have been established: three concern the rights of the contractor according to the title (variation, suspension and termination) while the other two are criminal offences. For instance, variation, suspension or revocation of an exploration licence or a mining licence may be decided if the DSM operator ceases to meet the environmental obligations and requirements set out in the national legislation[82] or if the environmental bond is not deposited.[83] An equivalent decision can be taken if the DSM activities constitute an unacceptable risk or are clearly no longer in the interests of the country due to changes in the circumstances pertaining to the activities including changes to best environmental practice, the state of technology utilized, or the capacity of the DSM operator to adapt to the changes in circumstances.[84] In Tonga and Tuvalu, the regulating Authority is also empowered in lieu of variation, suspension or revocation of the licence, to take administrative actions or impose upon the DSM operator monetary penalties which exclude any compensation payable for damage or harm to the environment.[85] Upon termination of a title, the DSM operator shall deliver to the regulating Authority all relevant information in its possession including all environmental and social consultation and related reports, documents, surveys and data prepared in relation to the DSM activities.[86] Any DSM operator who fails to comply with these requirements commits

---

[80] Tonga Seabed Minerals Act, s. 116(1) and (2); Tuvalu Seabed Minerals Act 2014, s. 121(1) and (2).

[81] Cook Islands Seabed Minerals Act 2009, s. 310.

[82] See the Tonga Seabed Minerals Act 2014, s. 73(1)(a); the Tuvalu Seabed Minerals Act 2014, s. 82(1)(a); and the Cook Islands Seabed Minerals Act 2009, ss 210, 214 and 215.

[83] See the Tonga Seabed Minerals Act 2014, s. 73(1)(b); the Tuvalu Seabed Minerals Act 2014, s. 82(1)(b); and the Cook Islands Seabed Minerals Act 2009, ss 210, 214 and 215.

[84] See the Tonga Seabed Minerals Act 2014, s. 73(1)(k); the Tuvalu Seabed Minerals Act 2014, s. 82(1)(k).

[85] See the Tonga Seabed Minerals Act 2014, s. 73(4); the Tuvalu Seabed Minerals Act 2014, s. 82(5).

[86] See the Tonga Seabed Minerals Act 2014, s. 107(2)(c); the Tuvalu Seabed Minerals Act 2014, s. 111(2)(c).

an offence and is liable to a fine not exceeding $100,000.[87] Additionally, in both Tonga and Tuvalu, any title holder will commit an offence punishable upon conviction to a fine not exceeding $250,000 if its performance in conducting marine scientific research interferes with the State's obligation of conservation of the resources of the sea or the seabed.[88] Finally, in these two countries, clear provisions have been made should an offence be committed by a body corporate. Under the respective Seabed Minerals Acts, when a mining company has committed an offence

> with the consent or connivance, or is attributable to the neglect, of any Director or officer of the body corporate, that officer as well as the body corporate is guilty of that offence and, in respect of an offence punishable by a fine only, if the court finds that the offence was committed by that person wilfully, recklessly, corruptly or for the purpose of personal gain, that officer is liable to imprisonment

for a period of two years in Tonga[89] and up to eight years in Tuvalu.[90] Additionally, but more generally, recourse is available within domestic legal systems for prompt and adequate compensation or other relief in respect of damage caused by pollution of the marine environment, any other related economic loss, or any other related injury to other sea users.

In all PIS the established enforcement regimes rely on the involvement of the national implementing agency which is empowered to conduct inspections and is responsible for compiling a report or preparing an action plan on the basis of which official notice and directions will be given to the DSM operator to comply with. In general, this will then be followed by increased monitoring and inspection. However, in practice such actions may be hampered by the lack of human and financial resources faced by most of the PIS. It this therefore of major importance that emphasis be placed on building in-country capacity and improving retention plans. Increasing transparency processes should also be identified as a key priority by all PIS which want to engage with DSM activities as a means to avoid and/or limit corruption.

## 5. SUPPORTING NATIONAL DEVELOPMENT OUTCOMES THROUGH CONSOLIDATED REGIONAL COOPERATION

The Pacific Islands region has an agreed Regional Ocean Policy[91] which promotes regional cooperation as one of its key principles. This has been complemented by a multi-national ocean governance framework adopted by all Pacific Islands countries

---

[87]  See the Tonga Seabed Minerals Act 2014, s. 107(3) and (4); the Tuvalu Seabed Minerals Act 2014, s. 111(3) and (4).

[88]  See the Tonga Seabed Minerals Act 2014, s. 109(2)(a)(v); the Tuvalu Seabed Minerals Act 2014, s. 113(3)(a)(v).

[89]  Tonga Seabed Minerals Act 2014, s. 120.

[90]  Tuvalu Seabed Minerals Act 2014, s. 124.

[91]  Pacific Islands Regional Ocean Policy and Framework for Integrated Strategic Action, Secretariat of the Pacific Community, 2005. Available at http://www.forumsec.org.fj/resources/uploads/attachments/documents/PIROP.pdf (last accessed 25 May 2015).

and territories, known as The Pacific Oceanscape,[92] which emphasizes the importance of a regional approach to the sustainable development, management and conservation of the ocean and its resources. This regional policy is guided by international law which requires states to endeavour to harmonize policies relating to seabed activities at the appropriate regional level[93] as well as to establish detailed international and regional rules, standards and recommended practices.[94]

It is on the basis of such requirements that the PIS have mandated SPC through the SPC-EU DSM Project to develop the RLRF. This regional framework contributes to the establishment of common standards and practices throughout the Pacific region and facilitates a stable and transparent operating environment and a collaborative approach to securing improved knowledge and expertise in the region concerning the regulation of DSM activities. Since 2011, the SPC-EU DSM Project has successfully worked with PIS and has made significant progress by convening regional and national consultation workshops; providing assistance in drafting national seabed mineral policies, legislation and regulations; and coordinating awareness of DSM and information-sharing initiatives mainly through in-country stakeholders' consultation. Support has also been provided to several PIS to assist them to attend the ISA's annual session and participate in the global dialogue on the governance of seabed mining, and to assist them in negotiating contract agreements with DSM operators. Capacity-building initiatives are also underway and include DSM training workshops, establishment of a legal and environmental internship programme, and support for senior officials to participate to international training programmes worldwide, including shipboard training. In addition to this, and building upon the RLRF, a Regional Financial Framework, and a Regional Environmental Management Framework are being developed by the SPC to provide further in depth, and harmonized guidance on these two key aspects of DSM management. A regional marine minerals database is also in the process of being established by SPC to assist in the management of DSM resources.

Further benefits of a regional approach to DSM may be expected as it is commonly agreed that it is key to maximizing the potential benefits that a DSM industry may bring to PIS, and avoiding a 'race to the bottom scenario'.[95] First, it will send a clear message to private sector investors who are interested in engaging in DSM activities in the Pacific region. Second, while the approach ultimately adopted by individual PIS may differ in the detail of their rules, and in the incentives offered to investors (reflecting different levels of mineral prospectivity or commercial development), it is anticipated that a regionally agreed set of standards will strongly contribute to assist PIS to develop regulatory regimes that are comprehensive, efficient, workable, and consistent with international obligations, rules and standards. Moreover, such an approach will be particularly useful to develop harmonized environmental standards and equivalent regulatory requirements in the event of potential trans-boundary effects

---

[92]   Framework for a Pacific Oceanscape: a catalyst for implementation of ocean policy. Available at http://www.forumsec.org/resources/uploads/embeds/file/Oceanscape.pdf (last accessed 25 May 2015).
[93]   LOSC, Art. 208(4).
[94]   LOSC, Art. 208(5).
[95]   SPC, RLRF, above n 25, 46.

between different national jurisdictions, or between areas under and areas beyond national jurisdiction. Indeed, in practice, some aspects of regulation such as expert review of marine scientific research and EIA reports, or independent monitoring of mining sites, may be more efficiently approached at a joint regional level, rather than on a country-by-country basis.[96] This will be more feasible if the respective national legislative regimes of those PIS who want to engage with DSM activities share common features and standards. Third, because many PIS have limited capacity, the potential benefit of strengthening the existing regional approach could lead to improving monitoring and enforcement, mutualizing resources and creating an enabling environment that promotes business activities and entrepreneurships. One may also anticipate that fostered regional cooperation in DSM will strongly contribute to improve governance, transparency and accountability of DSM contractors and coastal States by avoiding the perception of bias, and providing checks and balances against undue influence and conflicts of interest. Last but not least, it is also likely to bring cost benefits, if it allows for consolidation of infrastructure and administrative mechanisms on a regional basis.

The legal basis for strengthening a regional approach in the Pacific Islands region is primarily found in the LOSC which not only urges States to harmonize their policies at the regional level but also requires them to establish, through competent international organizations and diplomatic conferences, standards and recommended practices and procedures to prevent, reduce and control pollution from the marine environment arising from or in connection with seabed activities.[97]

## 6. CONCLUDING REMARKS

Seabed mining is one of the range of activities that may impact the marine environment of PIS and the 'common heritage of mankind'. It is therefore important for States to strengthen the governance in this field which necessarily includes developing strong and comprehensive regulatory frameworks and establishing national structures responsible for their implementation and enforcement. Meaningful consultations with all stakeholders are also a key requirement.

Acknowledging the fact that the long-term economic development of the DSM industry is dependent upon a regulatory regime which fully addresses the environmental, social and cultural aspects of Pacific Islands' societies, all PIS are committed to comply with their international obligations including protecting and preserving the marine environment. More work needs to be done, but the significant achievement of PIS in having enacted or drafted new laws encompassing extensive environmental requirements and establishing implementing agencies responsible for compliance and enforcement, needs to be acknowledged. Pacific Leaders will certainly pursue and strengthen the initiatives adopted so far, paving the way for the benefit of strong and resilient Pacific communities.

---

[96]   Ibid, 47.
[97]   LOSC, Art. 208(4) and (5).

To this end, particular consideration should be given to improve Pacific islanders' expertise in geology, law, environmental, economics of natural resources etc., as a means of consolidating current initiatives and ensuring long-term sustainability and adaptability of inclusive governance mechanisms. Meanwhile, environmental protection and use of natural resources at a sustainable rate should be seen as a key priority for supporting a 'green economy' within Pacific Island countries.

# PART IV

# PROTECTION OF MARINE BIODIVERSITY

# 11. Protecting marine species

*Alexander Proelss and Katherine Houghton*

## 1. DEVELOPMENT OF LEGAL RULES AND RELEVANT ISSUES

The legal regime for the protection of marine species is not based on a single regulatory approach. To this day only very few legal instruments are specifically dedicated to the protection and conservation of marine species. From a historical perspective, the issue of species protection and conservation was first and foremost regarded as a means of resource management. In this respect, the 1946 International Convention for the Regulation of Whaling (ICRW)[1] was only converted by its parties into a de facto protection-oriented treaty by way of adoption of a complete ban on commercial whaling in 1982 when it had become clear that the original intention of the contracting parties, namely to safeguard the stocks of large whales as a natural resource, could no longer be achieved due to serious overexploitation of the stocks concerned.[2] Similarly, while closed fishing areas and seasons may have been adopted within the context of Regional Fisheries Management Organizations (RFMOs), such measures have aimed at safeguarding the future management of the pertinent stocks. Traditionally, marine species protection has merely constituted a side-effect of exploitation-oriented instruments.

The strong management-oriented approach predominant in the legal treatment of marine species has been further reinforced by the zonal nature of the law of the sea. Access to the living resources of the sea has constituted one of the driving factors of regulating marine affairs since ancient times.[3] The historic origins of the concept of the exclusive economic zone (EEZ) are intrinsically tied to the desire of many coastal states to gain control over the fish stocks in marine areas beyond their territorial seas by denying other states access to those stocks. Given that the law of the sea is, as far as the management of living resources in areas beyond national jurisdiction (ABNJ) is concerned, principally based on a 'first come first serve' approach, it is not surprising that the issue of conservation of marine biodiversity of these vast areas is one of the most contentious aspects of the law of the sea.[4] Indeed, the 'constitution for the oceans',[5] the 1982 United Nations Convention on the Law of the Sea

---

[1]   International Convention for the Regulation of Whaling, adopted 2 December 1946, entered into force 10 November 1948. 161 UNTS 72.

[2]   Rule 10(e) of the ICRW Schedule. The moratorium came into force in 1986.

[3]   For an overview see Wolfgang Graf Vitzthum, 'Begriff, Geschichte und Rechtsquellen des Seerechts' in idem. (ed.), *Handbuch des Seerechts* (2006) 1, 9–44.

[4]   See also Dire Tladi, 'Conservation and sustainable use of marine biodiversity in areas beyond national jurisdiction: towards an implementing agreement', Chapter 12 in this volume.

[5]   Statement made by the President of the Third United Nations Conference on the Law of the Sea (UNCLOS III), Tommy T.B. Koh, on the occasion of the adoption of the Convention,

(LOSC),[6] contains only one provision which addresses the protection of endangered marine species irrespective of their commercial potential.[7]

Since the 1970s, the legal regime applicable to the protection of marine species has been strongly influenced by developments outside the scope of the law of the sea. Marine species were included in the annexes of multilateral environmental agreements such as the 1973 Convention on International Trade in Endangered Species of Wild Fauna and Flora (CITES),[8] the Bonn Convention on Migratory Species of Wild Animals (CMS)[9] and the 1971 Convention on Wetlands of International Importance Especially As Waterfowl Habitat (Ramsar Convention).[10] With the entry into force of the 1992 Convention on Biological Diversity (CBD),[11] the endangered species/habitat approach on which these agreements are based was supplemented, or superposed respectively, by the biodiversity concept and the associated ecosystem approach. More recent developments, characterized by their comparatively strong precautionary nature, include the adoption of proactive approaches to the listing of species, attempts to include commercially relevant species into CITES and the CMS, a shift from the adoption of further protection measures to issues of compliance and enforcement, and a reorientation to specific marine issues, in particular in relation to the protection of biodiversity in ABNJ.

From today's perspective, the international legal regime dedicated to the protection of marine species must be regarded as a cross-sectoral and multifaceted regime connecting the law of the sea with international environmental and economic law.[12] There has been considerable evolution in the nature of the legal instruments and strategies at the international level, but this evolution has been governed in a

---

available online: http://www.un.org/Depts/los/convention_agreements/texts/koh_english.pdf (last accessed 25 May 2015).

  [6]   United Nations Convention on the Law of the Sea adopted 10 December 1982, entered into force 16 November 1994, 1833 UNTS 3.

  [7]   Article 194(5) of the LOSC states that '[t]he measures taken in accordance with this Part shall include those necessary to protect and preserve rare or fragile ecosystems as well as the habitat of depleted, threatened or endangered species and other forms of marine life.'

  [8]   Convention on International Trade in Endangered Species of Wild Fauna and Flora, adopted 3 March 1973, entered into force 1 July 1975, 993 UNTS 244.

  [9]   Convention on the Conservation of Migratory Species of Wild Animals, adopted 23 June 1979, entered into force 1 November 1983, 1651 UNTS 333.

  [10]   Convention on Wetlands of International Importance Especially As Waterfowl Habitat, adopted 2 February 1971, entered into force 21 December 1975, 996 UNTS 246.

  [11]   Convention on Biological Diversity, adopted 5 June 1992, entered into force 29 December 1993, 1760 UNTS 79.

  [12]   It is interesting to note that the majority of textbooks on the international law of the sea do not contain separate chapters on marine species protection. Rather, the issue is usually addressed as part of 'marine resource management' or 'fishing', respectively. See, eg, Donald R. Rothwell and Tim Stephens, *The International Law of the Sea* (2010) 285–319; Robin R. Churchill and A. Vaughan Lowe, *The Law of the Sea* (3rd edn) (1999) 279–327; but see Yoshifumi Tanaka, *The International Law of the Sea* (2012), which contains a separate section on 'conservation of marine biological diversity' (312–34). In the majority of cases, the field of 'marine environmental protection' is understood in a purely pollution-oriented manner (see again Rothwell and Stephens, 338–82). A comprehensive approach is taken by A. Proelss, *Meeresschutz im Völker- und Europarecht*, 2004.

de-centralized and fragmented manner, and it has been influenced by a plethora of different actors and interests. Improvements in scientific knowledge as well as societal considerations (economic demand for species, pressure for conservation from civil society) have further increased the complexity of regulation. Different scales and types of protection strategies have emerged, ranging from those addressing individual species and species habitats to those that treat species protection as a component of the broader categories of biodiversity and ecosystem-based management and, finally, to science-driven precautionary measures that proactively regulate potentially adverse impacts on species, habitats, food webs and ecosystems. While the multifaceted nature of marine species protection undoubtedly requires a variety of regulatory strategies, the increasing proliferation of relevant rules and principles at the same time implies the risk of norm collision and may prepare the legal ground for forum shopping.[13] Against this background, attention ought not only to be paid to the individual protection instruments, but also to how they interact and mutually influence each other.

This chapter examines the complex legal regime for the protection of marine species by focusing on the issue from two angles: First, it examines the approaches taken in the law of the sea. It then turns to an examination of the approaches that have been included in several multilateral environmental agreements. The chapter concludes with some brief comments on the interrelationship of these two regimes and the need to ensure their complementary interaction.

## 2. MARINE SPECIES PROTECTION UNDER THE LAW OF THE SEA

### 2.1 The Regime of the LOSC

#### 2.1.1 The constitutional framework

The LOSC is not primarily a conservation or environmental instrument per se but rather establishes a legal framework that regulates the rights and obligations of states in different maritime zones and essentially governs all activities and uses of the ocean. The LOSC does, however, contain specific provisions for the protection of marine species alongside more general provisions for the protection of the marine environment which are vitally important for the systematization of species and habitat protection and their balancing with other legitimate uses of the ocean. Without the system of maritime zones codified and further developed in the LOSC, progress in enforcement, regional cooperation and implementation, as well as coordination between legal instruments on related subject matter might have proven impossible.

The LOSC marks an important turning point in the protection of the oceans. For the first time in history, an international agreement codified rules and principles for the protection and preservation of the marine environment applicable not only to individual maritime zones, but to the entire marine environment as such. In particular, Part XII of

---

[13] Alexander Gillespie, 'Forum Shopping in International Environmental Law: The IWC, CITES, and the Management of Cetaceans' (2002) 33 *Ocean Development and International Law* 17, 25–7 and 31–8.

the LOSC which deals with protection and preservation of the marine environment contains a number of quasi-constitutional principles on environmental protection, which are substantiated in the following sections with regard to individual sources of pollution.[14] For example, by prohibiting the indirect or direct transfer of damage or hazards from one area to another, and the transformation of one type of marine pollution into another, Article 195 codifies the principle of origin.[15] For its part, Article 194 clearly implements the principle of prevention. While Part XII does not contain any express reference to the precautionary approach, it has convincingly been argued that the wording of the definition of pollution codified in Article 1(1)(4), together with the broad framing of the duty to protect and preserve the marine environment (Article 192), and the obligation to undertake an environmental impact assessment whenever States have 'reasonable grounds for believing that planned activities under their jurisdiction or control may cause substantial pollution of or significant and harmful changes to the marine environment' (Article 206), imply that the LOSC 'reflects a precautionary spirit'.[16] This conclusion was implicitly confirmed by the International Tribunal for the Law of the Sea (ITLOS) in the *Southern Bluefin Tuna* cases, when it held that 'the parties should in the circumstances act with prudence and caution to ensure that the effective conservation measures are taken to prevent serious harm to the stock of southern Bluefin tuna'.[17] In his separate opinion, Judge Laing noted that, as far as the impact of the precautionary approach was concerned, the Tribunal's statement was 'pregnant with meaning', and that it could not 'be denied that UNCLOS adopts a precautionary approach'.[18] Judge Shearer supported this view, stating that 'the measures ordered by the Tribunal are rightly based upon considerations deriving from a precautionary approach'.[19]

The order of ITLOS in the *Southern Bluefin Tuna* cases, which addressed the conservation of an endangered living marine resource, suggests that the environmental protection principles codified in Part XII are not only applicable vis-à-vis the issue of pollution, but also to species protection and conservation measures. Indeed, the Tribunal expressly held that 'the conservation of the living resources of the sea is an element in the protection and preservation of the marine environment'.[20] Although specific reference was not made to Article 194(5) which requires measures taken to

---

[14]   David D. Dzidzornu, 'Four Principles in Marine Environmental Protection: A Comparative Analysis' (1998) 29 *Ocean Development and International Law* 91, 97 et seq.

[15]   Proelss, above n 12, 84.

[16]   Simon Marr, *The Precautionary Principle in the Law of the Sea* (2003) 52; see also David Freestone, 'International Fisheries Law Since Rio: The Continued Rise of the Precautionary Principle' in Alan Boyle and David Freestone (eds), *International Law and Sustainable Development* (1999) 135, 238; Bénédicte Sage-Fuller, *The Precautionary Principle in Marine Environmental Law* (2013) 68; Proelss, above n 12, 82 et seq.

[17]   *Southern Bluefin Tuna* (Australia v. Japan; New Zealand v. Japan), Order of 27 August 1999, (1999) ITLOS Reports, 280, 296 (*Southern Bluefin Tuna* cases).

[18]   *Southern Bluefin Tuna* cases, Separate Opinion of Judge Laing, (1999) ITLOS Reports, 305, 310 et seq.

[19]   *Southern Bluefin Tuna* cases, Separate Opinion of Judge Shearer, (1999) ITLOS Reports, 320, 327.

[20]   *Southern Bluefin Tuna* cases, above n 17, 280, 295.

'include those necessary to protect and preserve rare or fragile ecosystems as well as the habitat of depleted, threatened or endangered species and other forms of marine life', the provision can clearly be regarded as the legal basis for that conclusion. While the exact scope and nature of Article 194(5) are subject to ongoing debate,[21] it has convincingly been argued that this provision gives a stamp of nature conservation to the LOSC by extending the scope of the principles and standards contained in Part XII to other parts of the Convention. Admittedly, measures taken in accordance with Article 194(5) must be 'consistent' with the Convention. Nature conservation activities are thus subject to certain legal limitations.[22] However, Part XII in general, and the principles of environmental protection codified in Articles 192 to 196 in particular, must be seen to be applicable also to the protection of species, stocks and habitats.[23]

This conclusion is particularly relevant in the context of the regime of the EEZ. While Article 56(1)(b)(iii) LOSC, as far as protection and preservation of the marine environment is concerned, links the scope of the coastal state's jurisdiction to 'the relevant provisions of this Convention', Articles 61 to 67 which set out the coastal state's rights for the purpose of conserving and managing marine living resources set limits on the measures that can lawfully be taken in accordance with Article 194(5). Arguably, critiques of the LOSC as having created initial fragmentation by disconnecting regulation of protection of the marine environment from regulation of the conservation and management of marine living resources[24] do not sufficiently take into account the Convention's complicated but at the same time well-balanced system of reciprocal references and limitations governing the issue of marine species protection. This is not to deny that the regime established by the LOSC suffers, as far as the preservation of marine biodiversity is concerned, from serious shortcomings. However, taking into account the general framework convention character of the agreement, it is submitted that the LOSC is on the whole more sustainability-oriented than is often thought.

### 2.1.2 Species management and conservation in the EEZ

The origins of the EEZ regime can be traced back to controversies concerning the scope and quality of coastal states' rights in respect of the management of living resources located in areas beyond the outer limits of the territorial sea in relation to the

---

[21] See, eg, Nina Wolff, *Fisheries and the Environment* (2002), 66; Rainer Lagoni, 'Die Errichtung von Schutzgebieten in der ausschließlichen Wirtschaftszone aus völkerrechtlicher Sicht,' (2002) *Natur und Recht* 121, 123 and 128 et seq.

[22] In particular, Article 194(5) of the LOSC cannot be referred to as an autonomous legal basis for establishing closed areas and marine protected areas (MPAs) in the EEZ or on the high seas. In addition, according to Article 211(6)(a) of the LOSC, the closure of a clearly defined area of the EEZ to foreign navigation for reasons related to, inter alia, the ecological conditions of the area concerned and the protection of its resources may only be implemented subject to the consent of the International Maritime Organization (IMO).

[23] Proelss, above n 12, 106.

[24] Philippe Sands and Jacqueline Peel, *Principles of International Environmental Law* (3rd edn) (2012), 448.

freedom of fishing of third States.[25] It is therefore not surprising that the primary focus of Part V of the LOSC, which establishes the legal regime for the EEZ, is on the utilization and conservation of the living resources of the EEZ.[26] In this respect, the general rule is codified in Article 56(1)(a), according to which in the EEZ every coastal State has 'sovereign rights for the purpose of exploring and exploiting, conserving and managing the natural resources, whether living or non-living, of the waters superjacent to the seabed and of the seabed and its subsoil …' This rule is then specified by zonal requirements concerning the utilization and conservation of fish stocks occurring in the EEZ, and by species-specific requirements that are applicable only in relation to particular categories of fish stocks. Article 73 supplements the coastal state's sovereign rights by authorizing it to take the necessary compliance and enforcement measures against ships flying the flag of third states.[27]

As far as the general standards for stock management are concerned, Article 61 obliges the coastal state to determine the allowable catch (total allowable catch – TAC) of the living resources in its EEZ, and to ensure 'through proper conservation and management measures that the maintenance of the living resources in the exclusive economic zone is not endangered by over-exploitation'. What constitutes 'over-exploitation' is neither defined in the LOSC nor in any other international agreement. However, when considered together with the non-exhaustive list of potential measures that may lawfully be taken by the coastal state as provided in Article 62(4), this implies that the coastal state has been allocated a wide margin of discretion as to the suitability of the measures concerned. If the coastal state does not have the capacity to harvest the entire allowable catch, it is obliged by Article 62(2) to give other states access to the surplus, paying particular regard to the interests of land-locked and geographically disadvantaged states.

A particular limitation of the coastal state's relative freedom to prescribe management measures derives from Article 61(3), according to which fisheries management measures adopted by the coastal state 'shall also be designed to maintain or restore populations of harvested species at levels which can produce the maximum sustainable yield, as qualified by relevant environmental and economic factors, including the economic needs of coastal fishing communities and the special requirements of developing States, and taking into account fishing patterns, the interdependence of stocks and any generally recommended international minimum standards, whether subregional, regional or global.' What constitutes 'maximum sustainable yield' (MSY) is open to debate, although the obligation has been reiterated in the (non-binding) Johannesburg Plan of Implementation (JPOI), according to which fish stocks are to be maintained at or restored to 'levels that can produce the maximum sustainable yield with the aim of achieving these goals for depleted stocks on an urgent basis and where

---

[25]   For details see Winston Conrad Extavour, *The Exclusive Economic Zone* (1979), 169 et seq.; Alexander Proelss, 'Ausschließliche Wirtschaftszone (AWZ)' in Wolfgang Graf Vitzthum (ed.), above n 3, 222, 222 et seq.

[26]   For an overview see Ellen Hey, 'The Fisheries Provisions of the LOSC' in ibid. (ed.), *Developments in International Fisheries Law* (1999) 13.

[27]   For an overview of the basis, scope and limits of the coastal state's enforcement jurisdiction see Tanaka, above n 12, 242–50; see also Rosemary G. Rayfuse, *Non-Flag State Enforcement in High Seas Fisheries* (2004).

possible not later than 2015',[28] and in the outcome document of the Rio+20 summit.[29] Notwithstanding its ambiguous content, MSY must thus be seen as the decisive fisheries management parameter agreed upon at the international level. What can be said is that the wording of Article 61(3) implies that the coastal state also enjoys a scope of discretion in fulfilling the obligation to maintain or restore populations of harvested species to MSY-producing levels,[30] and that this can lawfully lead to economic and social objectives being given a higher weighting than environmental objectives depending on the individual circumstances. Individual TACs can therefore differ from the biomass necessary to produce MSY on a continuing basis. Having said that, the scope of discretion of the coastal state cannot be regarded as being unlimited, since low biomass and low catches have negative impacts with regard to environmental, economic, social and political goals in the long term, and the persistent disregard for biomass development and other environmental factors cannot be held to be in accordance with the LOSC.[31] It should also be noted that the reference contained in Article 61(3) to the 'generally recommended international minimum standards, whether subregional, regional or global' can be interpreted as incorporating the relevant soft law of the United Nations Food and Agriculture Organization (FAO), in particular the FAO Code of Conduct for Responsible Fisheries,[32] into the LOSC.[33] There is thus sufficient indication in the text of the LOSC that the regime of the EEZ does indeed require coastal states to substantially consider biodiversity- and species protection-related aspects.

With respect to the legal requirements applicable to particular categories of fish stocks, Part V of the LOSC on the EEZ makes a distinction between (1) shared fish stocks, (2) straddling fish stocks, (3) highly migratory species, (4) marine mammals, (5) anadromous species and (6) catadromous species. Part V does not apply to sedentary species which are, instead, governed by the regime of the continental shelf. Whether or not marine genetic resources, ie, organisms that live at or nearby hydrothermal vent sites and use energy from chemosynthesis rather than photosynthesis to produce organic matter from carbon dioxide and mineral nutrients, can be qualified as living resources in terms of the articles on marine living resources, is not entirely

---

[28] 'Johannesburg Plan of Implementation', Report of the World Summit on Sustainable Development, 6, para 31(a), UN Doc. A/CONF.199/20, available at: http://www.un.org/jsummit/html/documents/summit_docs/131302_wssd_report_reissued.pdf (last accessed 25 May 2015).

[29] 'The Future We Want', UN Doc. A/RES/66/288, 11 September 2012, Annex, para. 168.

[30] William T. Burke, *The New International Law of Fisheries* (1994), 52, et seq.

[31] See German Advisory Council on the Environment, *Marine Environment Protection for the North and Baltic Seas* (2004), 114, available at: http://www.umweltrat.de/SharedDocs/Downloads/EN/02_Special_Reports/2004_Special_Report_Marine_Environment_Protection.pdf?__blob=publicationFile (last accessed 25 May 2015). See also Rainer Froese, Trevor A Branch, Alexander Proelss, Martin Quaas, Keith Sainsbury and Christopher Zimmermann, 'Generic Harvest Control Rules for European Fisheries' (2011) 12 *Fish and Fisheries* 340; Marion Markowski, *The International Law of EEZ Fisheries* (2010) 28.

[32] Code of Conduct for Responsible Fisheries, 31 October 1995, available at: http://www.fao.org/docrep/005/v9878e/v9878e00.HTM (last accessed 25 May 2015).

[33] Proelss, above n 12, 108.

clear. It is submitted that the answer to this question should generally be yes, provided that the organisms concerned ought not to be qualified as sedentary species.[34]

Concerning shared, straddling and highly migratory fish stocks, the LOSC does no more than press the coastal state and states fishing for the same stocks or stocks of associated species on the high seas, or in an adjacent EEZ respectively, to (indirectly or directly) cooperate in the management of the stocks concerned in order to agree upon the necessary management measures.[35] This *pactum de negotiando* implies that states are under an obligation to 'not only ... go through a formal process of negotiations but also to pursue them as far as possible with a view to concluding agreements',[36] but it does not establish an obligation of result in terms of a duty to achieve bi- or multilateral agreements. The duty contained in Article 63(2) only refers to measures necessary for the conservation of these stocks 'in the adjacent area'; it does not directly deal with the management of straddling stocks in the EEZ, which is why it does not seem plausible to argue that it constitutes an exhaustive rule for the management of straddling fish stocks.[37] Given that Article 63(2) does not contain any guideline as to how it is possible to allocate straddling stocks between the coastal state and those states fishing on the high seas,[38] and that it does not give any indication of how straddling stocks shall be conserved in case no cooperation agreement can be reached,[39] it cannot be denied, though, that the soft nature of the obligation contained therein has provided an incentive for overexploitation of the stocks concerned. The practical relevance of this development is particularly serious, as world markets consider straddling fish stocks as the most valuable marine living resource. As discussed further in Section 2.2 below, this is where the 1995 Agreement for the Implementation of the provisions of the United Nations Convention on the Law of the Sea of 10 December 1982 Relating to the Conservation and Management of Straddling Fish Stocks and Highly Migratory Fish Stocks (UNFSA)[40] comes into play.

Articles 66 and 67 of the LOSC address the management of anadromous (ie, species that spawn in fresh water but spend most of their life in the sea, such as salmon and

---

[34]   Alexander Proelss, 'ABS in Relation to Marine GRs' in Evanson C. Kamau and Gerd Winter (eds), *Genetic Resources, Traditional Knowledge and the Law: Solutions for Access and Benefit Sharing* (2009) 57, 60 et seq.; See also idem., 'Marine Genetic Resources under UNCLOS and the CBD' (2008) 51 *German Yearbook of International Law* 417. The issue of marine genetic resources is dealt with in detail in D. Tladi, Chapter 12 in this volume.

[35]   See Moritaka Hayashi, 'The Management of Transboundary Fish Stocks under the LOSC' (1993) 8 *International Journal of Marine and Coastal Law* 245, 249.

[36]   *Railway Traffic between Poland and Lithuania*, Advisory Opinion of 15 October 1931, [1931] *PCIJ*, Ser. A/B, No. 42, 107–123, 116.

[37]   José Luis Meseguer, 'Le régime juridique de l'exploitation de stocks commun de poisons au-delà des 200 milles' (1982) 28 *Annuaire Français de Droit International* 885, 898. See also Jonna Ziemer, *Das gemeinsame Interesse an einer Regelung der Hochseefischerei* (2000) 46 et seq.

[38]   Tanaka, above n 12, 228.

[39]   Proelss, above n 25, 238.

[40]   Agreement for the Implementation of the Provisions of the United Nations Convention on the Law of the Sea of 10 December 1982 Relating to the Conservation and Management of Straddling Fish Stocks and Highly Migratory Fish Stocks, adopted 4 August 1995, entered into force 11 December 2001, 2167 UNTS 3.

sturgeon) and catadromous (ie, species that spawn in the ocean and migrate to fresh water for most of their life) fish stocks. The particular challenge in the conservation of these stocks arises because these species migrate through areas subject to different jurisdictional regimes, ranging from territorial sovereignty to functional jurisdiction to freedom of fishing. It is thus not surprising that both provisions contain limitations on the freedom to fish on the high seas which is codified in Article 87(1)(e) LOSC.[41] Essentially, neither species may be harvested on the high seas. Rather, the coastal state in whose rivers anadromous stocks originate or in whose waters catadromous stocks spend the greater part of their life cycle has the primary management responsibility for these species.

As far as the management of catadromous stocks in the EEZ is concerned, the coastal state is bound to the general obligations such as those relating to the fixing of TACs and the duty to maintain or restore populations at MSY-producing levels. Where catadromous fish migrate through the EEZ of another state, Article 67(3) requires conclusion of a management agreement between the two relevant states. With regard to anadromous stocks, the coastal state of origin is only required to take appropriate regulatory measures for fishing in all waters landward of the outer limits of its EEZ and to cooperate with those states through whose waters located landward of the outer limits of the EEZ an anadromous stock migrates.

With respect to marine mammals, Article 65 provides minimum standards for the protection of marine mammals referencing the rights of coastal states and the competence of international organizations to enact stricter measures.[42] Article 120 extends this regulation to the conservation and management of marine mammals on the high seas. As a matter of principle, Article 65 as well as the list of highly migratory species contained in Annex I, which includes several cetaceans,[43] reveal that the LOSC generally regards marine mammals as harvestable living resources. That said, it has convincingly been argued that marine mammals are exempted from the requirement of optimum utilization laid down in Article 62 LOSC.[44] Article 65 must thus be seen as a *lex specialis*, which permits (albeit not obliges) coastal states to regulate the exploitation of marine mammals in the EEZ more strictly than other marine living resources. In this context, the focus of the LOSC is more on conservation rather than on utilization.

As has been noted elsewhere,[45] the wording of Article 65 gives rise to some ambiguities. It is striking that the first sentence of the provision uses the singular form when referring to 'an international organisation', whereas its second sentence, with

41   Proelss, above n 25, 239.

42   For a discussion on the meaning of the term 'marine mammals' see Patricia Birnie, 'Marine Mammals: Exploiting the Ambiguities of Article 65 of the Convention on the Law of the Sea and Related Provisions' in David Freestone, Richard Barnes and David Ong (eds), *The Law of the Sea: Progress and Prospects* (2006) 261, 264–6.

43   The term 'cetaceans' refers to whales, dolphins, and porpoises, ie, to the oldest, most diverse, and most fully marine-adapted group of marine mammals.

44   Patricia Birnie, Alan Boyle and Catherine Redgwell, *International Law and the Environment* (3rd edn) (2009) 724; Alexander Proelss, 'Marine Mammals' in Rüdiger Wolfrum (ed.), *Max Planck Encyclopaedia of Public International Law*, vol. VI, 1036, 1039.

45   Proelss, ibid.,1039.

regard to cetaceans, speaks of 'the appropriate international organizations' in the plural form. Interpreting Article 65 as meaning that the International Whaling Commission (IWC) is the only appropriate organization therefore does not seem justifiable. Rather, Article 65 allows for a moderate shift of emphasis from preservation to sustainable management of cetaceans, provided that the coastal state or competent international organization (which may be the IWC) has not exercised its competence 'to prohibit, limit or regulate exploitation of marine mammals more strictly'.[46] In addition, the vague phrase 'work through' cannot be taken as specifying the expected manner and/or intensity of cooperation required.[47] In particular, there is no obligation on the coastal state to become a member of the relevant international organization, or to adhere to the regulations adopted by that organization.[48] Nevertheless, as far as existing international law is concerned, no doubt exists that the IWC is one (if not the only) appropriate international organization for the purposes of Article 65.

### 2.1.3   Species management and conservation on the high seas

As far as stock management on the high seas is concerned, Article 116 emphasizes the traditional principle that all States have the right to fish on the high seas. This general rule is then substantiated by requirements addressing the conservation of high seas fish stocks contained in Articles 118 to 120. Both the structure of these provisions and the comparatively soft wording of their conservation-oriented obligations imply that the conservation level established in the high seas context is weaker than that applicable in the EEZ. States have a wider margin of discretion in adopting measures for the conservation of the living marine resources of the high seas. For example, while Article 118 foresees the establishment of RFMOs as a means of cooperation in the conservation and management of fish seas fish stocks, it does not oblige states fishing on the high seas to follow that path, although such obligation is now incorporated in the UNFSA. Similarly, while Article 119(a) requires that fisheries management measures be designed to maintain or restore populations of harvested species at levels which can produce MSY, and that the generally recommended international minimum standards ought to be taken into account, it neither requires the fixing of TACs nor (at least not in express terms) that states shall ensure stocks are not endangered by overexploitation.[49] Moreover, the qualification of the right to fish as being subject to the rights, duties and interests of coastal states provided for, inter alia, in Articles 63(2) and 64 to 67 is poorly drafted and, as a result of the disparate conservation standards as between the high seas and EEZ regimes, has resulted in the serious decline of most commercially relevant high seas stocks. This has ultimately resulted in the acceptance of an

---

[46]   Ted L. McDorman, 'Canada and Whaling: An Analysis of Art. 65 of the Law of the Sea Convention' (1998) 29 *Ocean Development and International Law* 179, 184 et seq. See also Proelss, above n 44, 1039.

[47]   Proelss, above n 44, 1039.

[48]   See also Steinar Andresen, 'The International Whaling Regime: Order at the Turn of the Century?' in Davor Vidas and Willy Østreng (eds), *Order for the Oceans at the Turn of the Century* (1999) 215, 222; Birnie, Boyle and Redgwell, above n 44, 724; Tanaka, above n 12, 229.

[49]   Birnie, Boyle and Redgwell, above n 44, 720 et seq.; Proelss, above n 12, 115.

obligation to adopt compatible measures concerning the EEZ and the high seas in Article 7 UNFSA.

With respect to the conservation of deep seabed species, reference has already been made to the existing controversy addressing the legal status of marine genetic resources. The majority view is that the high seas regime is indeed applicable to other living resources such as hydrothermal vent organisms.[50] The consequence is that states are under an obligation to cooperate in the conservation and management of marine genetic resources and that marine scientific research on hydrothermal vent organisms is, in principle, unrestricted.[51] Nevertheless, in recognition of the vagueness of the high seas regime and the differing opinions on the matter, on 23 January 2015 the *Ad Hoc* Open-ended Informal Working Group to Study Issues Related to the Conservation and Sustainable Use of Marine Biodiversity beyond Areas of National Jurisdiction (BBNJ Working Group)[52] recommended to the UN General Assembly that it develop an internationally binding legal instrument under the LOSC on the conservation and sustainable use of marine biological diversity of areas beyond national jurisdiction.[53] The future agreement will not be limited to seabed species in general or to marine genetic resources in particular.

## 2.2 Impact of the UN Fish Stocks Agreement

The UNFSA was first and foremost concluded in order to ensure the long-term conservation and sustainable use of straddling fish stocks and highly migratory fish stocks. However, it also reflects the consciousness that adverse impacts on the marine environment need to be avoided, that marine biodiversity needs to be preserved and that the integrity of marine ecosystems ought to be maintained, and that the risk of long-term or irreversible effects of fishing operations must be minimized. The terminology used in the preamble and in Article 3(1) of the UNFSA, which speaks of areas beyond national jurisdiction (ABNJ) instead of 'areas beyond the limits of national jurisdiction' as used in the LOSC, reflects the fact that the UNFSA was heavily influenced by the language, approaches and objectives of the CBD. Given that the conference which led to the adoption of the UNFSA was initiated in 1993, just one year after the United Nations Conference on Environment and Development (UNCED)

---

[50] Proelss, above n 34, 422 et seq. See also Churchill and Lowe, above n 12, 239; Gaetan Verhoosel, 'Prospecting for Marine and Coastal Biodiversity: International Law in Deep Water' (1998) 13 *International Journal of Marine and Coastal Law* 91, 98; Richard J. McLaughlin, 'Foreign Access to Shared Marine Genetic Materials: Management Options for a Quasi-Fugacious Resource' (2003) 34 *Ocean Development and International Law* 297, 309; Montserrat Gorina-Ysern and Joseph H. Jones, 'International Law of the Sea, Access and Benefit Sharing Agreements, and the Use of Biotechnology in the Development, Patenting and Commercialization of Marine Natural Products as Therapeutic Agents' (2006) 20 *Ocean Yearbook* 221, 258.

[51] See Anna-Maria Hubert, 'Marine scientific research and the protection of the seas and oceans', Chapter 15 in this volume.

[52] The working group was established by UN General Assembly Resolution 59/24, 4 February 2005, para. 73.

[53] An advance and unedited version of the document is available at: http://www.un.org/depts/los/biodiversityworkinggroup/documents/ahwg-9_report.pdf (last accessed 25 May 2015).

adopted the CBD, the close interrelationship between the two agreements seems only natural. With regard to marine species protection and conservation, the UNFSA may thus be considered a missing link between the law of the sea and international environmental law. This also becomes apparent in the general principles contained in Article 5 UNFSA, which include, inter alia, obligations to apply the precautionary approach, to protect biodiversity in the marine environment, to implement elements of an ecosystem approach, and to minimize impacts on endangered species.

The UNFSA has been extensively analyzed elsewhere,[54] so the following assessment attempts only to highlight its most important features, in particular as far as the further development of the regime established by the LOSC is concerned.

First, when interpreting and applying the provisions of the UNFSA account must be taken of the implementing character of the agreement. While the UNFSA is not automatically binding on parties to the LOSC, Article 2 clarifies that its main objective is to ensure the long-term conservation and sustainable use of straddling fish stocks and highly migratory fish stocks through effective implementation of the relevant provisions of the LOSC. Article 4 further substantiates the relationship between the LOSC and the UNFSA by expressly demanding that the UNFSA ought to be interpreted and applied in the context of and in a manner consistent with the LOSC. Assuming that not all provisions of the UNFSA have developed into norms of customary international law, the rule codified in Article 4 UNFSA leads to problems if and to the extent to which the UNFSA goes beyond the LOSC. Examples of such provisions include the duty of cooperation through RFMOs codified in Article 7(2) of the UNFSA and the far-reaching enforcement powers allocated to port states by Article 23.[55]

Second, the UNFSA introduces new concepts such as the precautionary and the ecosystem approach to the regime of high seas fisheries. According to Article 6(2) UNFSA, the States parties 'shall be more cautious when information is uncertain, unreliable or inadequate. The absence of adequate scientific information shall not be used as a reason for postponing or failing to take conservation and management measures.' Article 6(3) UNFSA then prescribes comparatively specific guidelines as to how the precautionary approach ought to be implemented. The criteria contained in Annex II of the UNFSA concerning the application of precautionary reference points in conservation and management of straddling fish stocks and highly migratory fish stocks not only substantiate the duty to apply the precautionary approach, but also assist in the

---

[54]   See, eg, David Freestone and Zen Makuch, 'The New International Environmental Law of Fisheries: The 1995 United Nations Straddling Stocks Agreement' (1996) 7 *Yearbook of International Environmental Law* 3; Peter G.G. Davies and Catherine Redgwell, 'The International Legal Regulation of Straddling Fish Stocks' (1996) 67 *British Year Book of International Law* 199; Peter Örebech, Ketill Sigurjonsson and Ted L. McDorman, 'The 1995 United Nations Straddling and Highly Migratory Fish Stocks Agreement: Management, Enforcement and Dispute Settlement' (1998) 13 *International Journal of Marine and Coastal Law* 119; Moritaka Hayashi, 'The Straddling and Highly Migratory Fish Stocks Agreement' in Hey, above n 28, 55; Jaye Ellis, 'The Straddling Stocks Agreement and the Precautionary Principle as Interpretive Device and Rule of Law,' (2001) 32 *Ocean Development and International Law* 289.

[55]   Freestone and Makuch, above n 54, 50; see also Proelss, above n 12, 156 et seq., 173 et seq. The issue is discussed by Davies and Redgwell, above n 54, 265 in relation to Articles 8, 17 and 21 UNFSA.

lawful application of the duty to manage stocks at MSY-producing levels in terms of both Article 61(3) of the LOSC and Article 5(b) of the UNFSA. The introduction of the precautionary and ecosystem approaches into the UNFSA is perfectly in line with the precautionary spirit reflected in the LOSC and the careful ecosystem imprinting embodied in Articles 61(4), 119(1)(b), 145 and 194(5).

Third, Article 7(2) of the UNFSA attempts to close the gap left by Article 63(2) of the LOSC by requiring that '[c]onservation and management measures established for the high seas and those adopted for areas under national jurisdiction shall be compatible in order to ensure conservation and management of the straddling fish stocks and highly migratory fish stocks in their entirety'. While it is true that the adoption of compatible measures may be seen as an expression of the duty to cooperate in Article 63(2) of the LOSC, the requirement of compatibility may well go beyond the framework set by the LOSC. For those parties to the UNFSA that are also parties to the LOSC, Article 4 UNFSA thus requires a restrictive application of the obligation prescribed by Article 7(2) UNFSA, which arguably makes it impossible for a coastal state to enforce the compatibility of the pertinent management measures.

Finally, Articles 8 and 17 of the UNFSA address the crucial role allocated by the agreement to RFMOs in the context of cooperation in the management and conservation of high seas fish stocks. Where a RFMO exists and has been allocated the competence to establish conservation and management measures for particular straddling fish stocks or highly migratory fish stocks, Article 8(3) requires that states parties fishing for the stocks concerned in the high seas area for which the organization is responsible either ought to become members of that organization, or must agree to apply the conservation and management measures established by it. It is furthermore prescribed that only states that have a 'real interest' in the fisheries concerned may become members of that organization or participants in such arrangement, and that only these states shall have access to the fishery resources to which those measures apply. Article 17 then addresses the duties of those states who refuse to become a member of a competent RFMO, or a participant in a subregional or regional fisheries management arrangement respectively. Unsurprisingly, the compatibility of these provisions with the principle *pacta tertiis nec nocent nec prosunt* as codified in Article 34 of the 1969 Vienna Convention on the Law of Treaties (VCLT)[56] has been questioned.[57] However, the freedom to fish in Article 116(a) of the LOSC is subject to the treaty obligations of the states parties, which implies that the states parties to the LOSC are generally free to subject themselves to stricter management standards. For states who become party to the UNFSA, Articles 8 and 17 must thus be seen as being freely accepted and thus applicable, even if they have refused to become members to the relevant RFMOs, or arrangements respectively.[58]

---

[56] Vienna Convention on the Law of Treaties, adopted 23 May 1969, entered into force 27 January 1980, 1155 UNTS 331.

[57] See, eg, Davies and Redgwell, above n 54, 265; Ziemer, above n 37, 123, 193; Hayashi, above n 54, 59.

[58] Proelss, above n 12, 165. See also Rosemary Rayfuse, 'The United Nations Agreement on Straddling and Highly Migratory Fish Stocks as an Objective Regime: A Case of Wishful Thinking?' (2000) 20 *Australian Yearbook of International Law* 253.

A more challenging issue, however, relates to the scope of the 'real interest' criterion. The term is not defined in the agreement and opinions differ as to whether the fact of having fished in the past or the intention to do so in the future is sufficient to satisfy the requirement.[59] It is existing members of an RFMO or arrangement who will be responsible for determining whether a state has a real interest in a fishery.[60] However, their decision-making power is not unfettered. Article 8(3) UNFSA prescribes that '[t]he terms of participation in such organization or arrangement shall not preclude such States from membership or participation; nor shall they be applied in a manner which discriminates against any State or group of States having a real interest in the fisheries concerned'. Clearly, the potential exists for controversies over access to regulated high seas fish stocks,[61] although this can be overcome by requiring states wishing to become a member to a RFMO, or to participate in an arrangement respectively, to formally demonstrate a sufficiently close link between its interests and the pertinent fisheries, eg, by submitting evidence of fishing traditions. Nevertheless, the potential impact of the real interest criterion on the traditional doctrine of freedom of fishing on the high seas is potentially significant. On the one hand, the liberal approach on which the international law of the sea was based for centuries is in the process of shifting towards an access control system, while on the other hand, the comparatively strict requirements for participation in high seas fisheries introduced with the UNFSA may cause a significant increase in illegal, unreported and unregulated (IUU) fishing, which is generally considered as a central threat to ocean ecosystems and sustainable fishing.[62]

### 2.3  Protection of Cetaceans

The 1931 Convention on the Regulation of Whaling[63] was the first international treaty concerned with the establishment of a global regime for the management of cetaceans.[64] Concluded within the framework of the League of Nations the 1931 Convention, as well as its successor treaty, the International Agreement for the Regulation of Whaling of 8 June 1937,[65] aimed at maintaining the stocks of large whales at a constant

---

[59]   In the affirmative Erik Jaap Molenaar, 'The Concept of "Real Interest" and Other Aspects of Cooperation through Regional Fisheries Management Mechanisms' (2000) 15 *International Journal of Marine and Coastal Law* 475, 494.

[60]   Örebech, Sigurjonsson and McDorman, above n 54, 122.

[61]   Gordon Munro, Annick Van Houtte and Rolf Willmann, *The Conservation and Management of Shared Fish Stocks: Legal and Economic Aspects* (2004) 40, who refer to disputes that have arisen in the course of negotiations that led to the adoption of the Western and Central Pacific Fisheries Convention.

[62]   Birnie, Boyle and Redgwell, above n 44, 740. For an assessment of the negative impacts of IUU fishing see, eg, Marine Resource Assessment Group, *IUU Fishing on the High Seas: Impacts on Ecosystems and Future Science Needs* (2005), available at http://www.marine megafauna.org/wp-content/uploads/2013/02/IUU-Fishing.pdf (last accessed 25 May 2015).

[63]   Convention on the Regulation of Whaling, adopted 24 September 1931, entered into force 16 January 1935, 155 LNTS 349.

[64]   For an historical overview see Proelss, above n 44, 1037 et seq.

[65]   International Agreement for the Regulation of Whaling, adopted 8 June 1937, entered into force 1 July 1937, 190 LNTS 79.

level in order to secure the prosperity of the whaling industry. Both agreements failed due to a lack of acceptance by and/or compliance with by some major whaling nations.[66]

The ICRW, adopted in 1946, was concluded to manage human pressures on a limited number of commercially exploited whale species and restore population levels to ensure the continuity of the commercial whaling industry. The most prominent example of early post-World War II international legal measures concerning marine species, the ICRW also referred, in its preamble, to 'safeguarding for future generations the great natural resources represented by the whale stocks', indicating a nascent awareness of conservation issues and a trajectory as to how the treaty might eventually develop. Since the ICRW's entry into force, declining demand for whale-derived products and ever-increasing scientific and societal efforts to protect whales as the *leitmotif* of the global conservation movement have entirely changed the context in which the ICRW operates. By enacting increasingly strict catch limits and ultimately enacting a moratorium on commercial whaling in 1982,[67] the ICRW has significantly contributed to the obsolescence of the commercial whaling industry. The moratorium became effective in the 1985/1986 whaling season and is still in force today, virtually shifting the focus from conservation to protection. At the same time, the International Whaling Commission (IWC), the ICRW's governing body, has adopted conservation measures such as the designation of whale sanctuaries in the Indian Ocean (1979) and the Southern Ocean (1994), which have further contributed to the recovery of species.[68]

Since its adoption, the necessary annual decision to renew the moratorium has resulted in fierce debates between opponents and supporters of commercial whaling. While the latter argue that the text of the ICRW only provides for a temporary ban on commercial whaling as long as the relevant whale stocks have not recovered to sustainable numbers, anti-whaling nations as well as many non-governmental organizations take the view that the ICRW has legally developed into a pure preservation agreement.[69] Leaving ethical concerns and the economical questionability of commercial whaling aside, this extreme view seems difficult to defend, particularly given that some of the contracting parties whose interests are particularly affected by the moratorium have refused to support any protection-oriented interpretation and application of the ICRW.[70] Nevertheless, that a more limited form of conservation mindedness has emerged in the IWC, as evidenced by its work on a Revised Management Procedure to apply in the case of resumption of whaling, cannot be doubted.

---

66   For details see Patricia W. Birnie, *International Regulation of Whaling: From Conservation of Whaling to Conservation of Whales and Regulation of Whale-Watching* (1985), vol. I, 128 et seq.

67   The legal basis is Article V(1)(e) ICRW in conjunction with Rule 10[e] of the ICRW Schedule.

68   See Elisa Morgera, 'Whale Sanctuaries: An Evolving Concept within the International Whaling Commission' (2004) 35 *Ocean Development and International Law* 319.

69   See, eg, Anthony D'Amato and Sudhir K. Chopra, 'Whales: Their Emerging Right to Life' (1991) 85 *American Journal of International Law* 21, 45.

70   Maria Clara Maffei, 'The International Convention for the Regulation of Whaling' (1997) 12 *International Journal of Marine and Coastal Law* 287, 301; Proelss, above n 12, 186.

Indeed, even prior to the judgment of the International Court of Justice (ICJ) in the *Whaling in the Antarctic* case[71] it was difficult to see how whaling activities by some parties to the ICRW could be legally justified under the 'scientific whaling' exemption in the Convention. According to Article VIII(1) of the ICRW, a state 'may grant to any of its nationals a special permit authorizing that national to kill, take, and treat whales for purposes of scientific research … , and the killing, taking, and treating of whales in accordance with the provisions of this Article shall be exempt from the operation of this Convention'. In 2010, Australia instituted proceedings against Japan before the ICJ concerning Japan's JARPA II whaling programme and potential breaches of the ICRW and other, including customary, legal obligations concerning the preservation of marine mammals and the marine environment. In its judgment, the ICJ held that 'JARPA II involves activities that can broadly be characterized as scientific research … , but that the evidence does not establish that the programme's design and implementation are reasonable in relation to achieving its stated objectives'.[72] It concluded that 'the special permits granted by Japan for the killing, taking and treating of whales in connection with JARPA II are not "for purposes of scientific research" pursuant to Article VIII, paragraph 1, of the Convention'.[73] Unfortunately, the Court neglected to establish criteria for scientific research which would also have been relevant for other treaties containing scientific exception clauses.[74] It is also questionable whether the standard of review applied by the Court, that of reasonableness,[75] complies with the requirements of Article VIII(1) of the ICRW.[76]

Nevertheless, it has been extensively argued that the IWC is in danger of losing its effectiveness if it insists on maintaining a complete ban on commercial whaling.[77] Developing a mechanism that combines a species-specific approach based on pre-caution and scientific evidence with a strict enforcement and control scheme must surely be an adequate alternative. In this respect, the Revised Management Procedure (RMP) adopted by the IWC in 1994 may be taken into consideration. However, although this tool is widely considered as one of the most rigorous and conservative management schemes for living marine resources ever developed, its implementation and supplementation by the enforcement-oriented Revised Management Scheme (RMS) have not yet been accomplished due to continuous opposition from anti-whaling nations. In the absence of a long-term compromise, the frustration of whaling nations

---

[71]   *Whaling in the Antarctic* (Australia v. Japan, New Zealand Intervening), Judgment of 31 March 2014, available at: http://www.icj-cij.org/docket/files/148/18136.pdf (last accessed 25 May 2015).

[72]   Ibid., para. 227.

[73]   Ibid.

[74]   See the critique by Tobias Hofmann, 'Walfang in der Antarktis' (2014) 12 *Zeitschrift für Europäisches Umwelt- und Planungsrecht* 325, 327. See also Tim Stephens, 'After the Storm: The Whaling in the Antarctic Case and the Australian Whale Sanctuary' (2014) 31 *Environmental and Planning Law Journal* 459; Jeffrey J. Smith, 'Evolving to Conservation?: The International Court's Decision in the Australia/Japan Whaling Case' (2014) 45 *Ocean Development and International Law* 301.

[75]   *Whaling in the Antarctic* case, above n 71, para. 67.

[76]   *Whaling in the Antarctic* case, Dissenting opinion of Judge Owada, para. 39.

[77]   Proelss, above n 12, 189.

with the work of the IWC threatens to result in the establishment of competing regional whaling organizations and thus in a fragmentation of the entire whaling regime.

The conclusion of the Agreement on Cooperation in Research, Conservation and Management of Marine Mammals in the North Atlantic[78] in 1992 may be seen as a first step in such a development, particularly given that all of its members, namely Norway, Iceland, Greenland and the Faroe Islands are, in one way or the other, engaged in whaling activities.[79] The Agreement resulted in the establishment of the North Atlantic Marine Mammal Commission (NAMMCO), an international organization with the objective 'to contribute through regional consultation and cooperation to the conservation, rational management and study of marine mammals in the North Atlantic'. However, to date, no sign exists that the NAMMCO would indeed challenge the IWC's authority as regards the management and conservation of large whales. The Commission is not a regulatory body but a forum for the collection of statistical data on marine mammals. While it has adopted a Joint Scheme for the Hunting of Marine Mammals aimed at monitoring the hunting and inspection activities of its members, this scheme has for the most part been modelled on the terms of the RMS developed in the IWC context.

Three further regional arrangements, all of which are based on a purely protectionist approach, should also be mentioned: The Agreement concerning the Creation of a Marine Mammal Sanctuary in the Mediterranean[80] concluded by France, Italy and Monaco establishes a sanctuary for all marine mammals encompassing an area twice the size of Switzerland. In this area, any deliberate taking or intentional disturbance of the animals concerned is prohibited and the states parties are positively obliged to adopt appropriate measures in order to ensure the favorable conservation status of marine mammals. The Agreement on the Conservation of Cetaceans of the Black Sea, Mediterranean Sea and Contiguous Atlantic Area of 24 November 1996 (ACCOBAMS)[81] and the Agreement on the Conservation of Small Cetaceans of the Baltic and North Seas of 17 March 1992 (ASCOBANS)[82] were both concluded under Article IV(4) of the CMS. The main focus of these agreements is on the conservation of small cetaceans, an issue which has so far not been adequately addressed by the IWC regime. They prescribe comprehensive conservation and management plans obliging the states parties to engage in habitat protection and management, surveys and research, pollution mitigation and public information.

---

[78] Agreement on Cooperation in Research, Conservation and Management of Marine Mammals in the North Atlantic, adopted 9 April 1992 entered into force 8 July 1992, 1945 UNTS 4.

[79] Note that the inhabitants of Greenland and the Faroe Islands benefit from the right to aboriginal subsistence whaling according to Rule 13 of the ICRW Schedule.

[80] Agreement Relative to the Creation of a Mediterranean Sanctuary for Marine Mammals, adopted 25 November 1999, entered into force 21 February 2002. Available at: http://www.cetaceansanctuary.com/santuario/accordoeng.htm (last accessed 25 May 2015).

[81] Agreement on the Conservation of Cetaceans of the Black Sea, Mediterranean Sea and Contiguous Atlantic Area, adopted 24 November 1996, entered into force 1 June 2001, 2183 UNTS 321.

[82] Agreement on the Conservation of Small Cetaceans of the Baltic and North Seas, adopted 13 September 1991, entered into force 29 March 1994, 1772 UNTS 217.

## 3. MARINE SPECIES PROTECTION UNDER MULTILATERAL ENVIRONMENTAL AGREEMENTS

As noted at the outset, the legal regime applicable to the protection of marine species has been strongly influenced by developments beyond the law of the sea context. This section examines the range of approaches that have been adopted in multilateral environmental agreements (MEAs).

### 3.1  Species- and Habitat-specific Approaches

#### 3.1.1  International trade in endangered species
The 1973 Convention on International Trade in Endangered Species of Wild Fauna and Flora (CITES) is one of the most universally accepted MEAs in existence. In contrast to other more broadly framed environmental agreements, CITES focuses on the management of human pressures on terrestrial and marine species by introducing controls on the import, export, re-export and introduction from the sea of listed species in order to ensure that international trade does not threaten their survival. CITES also applies to 'specimens of species' whether living or dead, defined in Article I(b) as including 'any readily recognizable part or derivative thereof' in order to ensure that all types of trade in wildlife and wildlife-derived materials are addressed under the treaty. CITES notably does not include specific provisions for the protection of habitats and ecosystems related to listed species, which might arguably be better addressed through other agreements using different regulatory strategies. Perhaps because of this narrow focus and its strong emphasis on national implementation and enforcement mechanisms, CITES is generally, but not unanimously, considered an effective mechanism for protecting species from over-exploitation due to trade when considered as part of a broader landscape of agreements on related subject matter.[83] The role of CITES in the protection of marine species more specifically, however, raises a number of issues and challenges which will play an increasing role in the evolution of the treaty in years to come.

CITES currently protects more than 35,000 species of plants and animals based on listings in its three appendices according to the degree of threat faced by that species.[84] Appendix I lists 'all species threatened with extinction, which are or may be affected by trade', while Appendix II lists species that 'although not necessarily now threatened with extinction may become so' if trade is not strictly controlled to prevent detrimental impacts on the survival of that species. Finally, Appendix III lists species where individual states have requested assistance from other states in establishing specific controls on trade. After a species is listed in Appendix I or II, export permits can only

---

[83]   Michael Bowman, 'A Tale of Two CITES: Divergent Perspectives upon the Effectiveness of the Wildlife Trade Convention' (2013) 22 *Review of European Comparative & International Environmental Law* 228.

[84]   Although it is not explicitly mentioned in the treaty text, CITES listings reflect to a great degree the IUCN Red List of Threatened Species. See Ana S.L. Rodrigues, John D. Pilgrim, John F. Lamoreux, Michael Hoffmann and Thomas M. Brooks, 'The Value of the IUCN Red List for Conservation' (2006) 21 *Trends in Ecology and Evolution* 71.

be issued following a non-detriment finding by the relevant national scientific authority. Resolution 16.7 of the Conference of the Parties (COP)[85] sets out a framework of non-binding guiding principles to guide scientific authorities in conducting science-based assessments for determining whether trade in a given species would be detrimental to its survival.[86]

Provision is made for amendments to Appendices I and II including an additional duty for the Secretariat in regard to marine species to consult and coordinate with intergovernmental bodies regarding scientific data and the enforcement of conservation measures. COP Resolution 9.24,[87] subsequently revised at COP 16 in 2013, provides criteria for the amendment of Appendices I and II including biological criteria such as population decline, decrease in distribution, and decline in area and quality of habitat as well as precautionary measures in response to anticipated risks to the species. Particular guidelines for the interpretation of decline in abundance, distribution and habitat in regard to commercially exploited aquatic species are also included. Referred to as the 'Fort Lauderdale Criteria', these criteria replaced the original 'Bern Criteria'[88] adopted at COP 1 in 1976 which eventually proved too strict in their application of the precautionary principle regarding the de-listing or down-listing of species to effectively manage the vast number of species listings that had occurred since the treaty's entry into force.[89]

Although the overall number of CITES Appendix listings at first seems vast, closer examination of the appendices shows that marine species are significantly underrepresented in the CITES regime in comparison to terrestrial species. Moreover, the selected species are not necessarily appropriate indicator or umbrella species from which further conclusions could be made about the state of the marine environment. This is a common critique of species-based approaches to conservation in general and underlines the fact that although such species lists are increasingly science-based and methodologically sound, they are nonetheless the product of extensive political, social and economic debate and are often more indicative of the political will of states to conserve a particular, often well-known, species than an objective need from a broader ecological or scientific standpoint.[90] Not surprisingly, the vast majority of the already low overall number of marine species listings under CITES concern mammals (whales, sea otters and manatees) or other iconic species such as sea turtles, seahorses, giant

---

[85] CITES, Non-detriment Findings, COP Resolution 16.7.

[86] Taking into account that marine species distribution and migratory patterns are notably broad, the marine environment poses particular difficulties in making non-detriment findings (which fall within the responsibility of the individual States parties).

[87] CITES Conference of the Parties, Criteria for Amendment of Appendices I and II. Resolution Conf. 9.24 (Rev. CoP16).

[88] CITES, Resolution Conf. 1.1.

[89] Michael Bowman, Peter Davies, Catherine Redgwell, *Lyster's International Wildlife Law* (2nd edn) (2010) 492. See also Peter H. Sand, 'Whither CITES? The Evolution of a Treaty Regime in the Borderland of Trade and Environment' (1997) 8 *European Journal of International Law* 29–45.

[90] Hugh P. Possingham, Sandy J. Andelman, Mark A. Burgman, Rodrigo A. Medellin, Larry L. Master and David A. Keith, 'Limits to the Use of Threatened Species Lists' (2002) 17 *Trends in Ecology and Evolution* 503.

clams and corals, which were historically profoundly over-exploited but where inter-national consensus now exists on their need for protection. In contrast, marine species which are currently commercially relevant – particularly fish stocks – remain neglected under CITES, despite the fact that many such species are considered acutely threatened from a scientific standpoint. Although the overarching explanation for this situation is that the economic interests of the fishing industry and consumer preferences continue to outweigh conservation concerns, there are also a number of legal issues yet to be resolved which currently hinder the protection of commercial species under CITES.

The case of bluefin tuna exemplifies the challenges surrounding the listing of commercially relevant species. Efforts to protect bluefin tuna, which is a highly migratory species in terms of Article 64 LOSC, have been undertaken through various legal instruments with global and regional scope but with few signs of success. As one of the world's most profoundly overfished fish stocks, bluefin tuna clearly satisfies the criteria for inclusion in Appendix I as set out in Article II CITES. In an effort to test the capacity of the regime to protect commercial fish stocks, Monaco presented a draft resolution at the 15th meeting of the CITES COP in 2010 calling for the listing of bluefin tuna in Appendix I. Although this initiative was ultimately unsuccessful, it nonetheless drew attention to the fundamental challenges now faced by CITES in its efforts to remain relevant and effective.

The central argument frequently advanced is that the management and conservation of fish stocks are subject to other treaties, in particular the LOSC, the UNFSA and a multitude of agreements establishing RFMOs. Indeed, the issue of conserving commer-cially relevant fish stocks is located at the junction between biodiversity conservation law, international trade law and the law of the sea, which is why measures taken for the protection of marine species regularly involve considerable cross-regime interactions. The traditional international law answer concerning such treaty overlaps has been to include conflict clauses and to consider hierarchies between the different instruments. In this respect, Article 311(2) of the LOSC establishes priority of the LOSC over all other international agreements, existing or future, including CITES.[91] In contrast, the collision clause contained in Article XIV(4) of CITES, which is applicable specifically to the protection of marine species included in Appendix II, seems to cover treaties already in force before CITES only and furthermore relieves the states parties of the obligations imposed on it under CITES 'with respect to trade in specimens of species included in Appendix II that are taken by ships registered in that State and in accordance with the provisions of such other treaty, convention or international agreement'. As far as the relationship between CITES and the LOSC is concerned, it thus seems that the case is resolved in favor of the law of the sea.[92]

---

[91]   Article 311(2) LOSC states: 'This Convention shall not alter the rights and obligations of States Parties which arise from other agreements compatible with this Convention and which do not affect the enjoyment by other States Parties of their rights or the performance of their obligations under this Convention.'

[92]   For a detailed assessment see Erik Franckx, 'The Protection of Biodiversity and Fisheries Management: Issues Raised by the Relationship between CITES and LOSC' in Freestone, Barnes and Ong, above n 42, 210.

However, it is submitted that such a formalistic approach is not appropriate for biodiversity-related conventions which, taking into account their objects and purposes, must be regarded to be designed to supplement rather than supplant.[93] In order to render forum shopping impossible by those states that have an interest in commercial fisheries, parallel regulation under multiple agreements is indeed desirable, provided that it is based on an intended cooperation between the relevant bodies (initiated, eg, by way of adoption of a memorandum of understanding between the secretariats of the overlapping agreements) and that the pertinent conservation and protection measures are adopted in a coordinated manner. The future role of CITES can thus not be seen to replace other fisheries agreements, but instead to complement and support fisheries management measures adopted by RFMOs.[94]

Despite the failure to include the majority of commercially relevant marine species, some recent progress has been made regarding sharks, rays and sea cucumbers,[95] indicating that the treaty regime is increasingly shifting its focus. One example of this shift is the recent work surrounding the unique CITES term 'introduction from the sea' defined in Article I(e) of CITES as 'transportation into a State of specimens of any species which were taken in the marine environment not under the jurisdiction of any State', which is becoming increasingly relevant for the protection of marine species. COP Resolution 14.6,[96] also revised at COP 16 in 2013, takes into account legal and institutional changes in the law of the sea since the treaty's adoption in 1973, such as the creation of the EEZ, and provides clarification regarding the issuance of introduction from the sea certificates (including non-detriment findings), import/export permits and special procedures for transshipment.

### 3.1.2 Protection of migratory species

Like the ICRW and CITES, the Bonn Convention on Migratory Species of Wild Animals (CMS) uses a species listing approach with Article III(2) and (3) providing for the listing of endangered terrestrial and marine migratory species in Appendix 1 based on the best available scientific evidence as well as criteria for delisting that species should it no longer be endangered and not at risk of becoming re-endangered due to loss of protection.[97] Article III(4) of the CMS sets out the duties of the range states to conserve and restore habitats and address activities which might impede or prevent migration, while Article III(5) prohibits the taking of listed species with only limited exceptions for scientific research, subsistence uses and for purposes of enhancing

---

[93] Richard Caddell, 'The Integration of Multilateral Environmental Agreements: Lessons from the Biodiversity-Related Conventions' (2011) 22 *Yearbook of International Environmental Law* 37, 48.

[94] Amanda C.J. Vincent, Yvonne J. Sadovy de Mitcheson, Sarah L. Fowler and Susan Lieberman, 'The Role of CITES in the Conservation of Marine Fishes Subject to International Trade' (2014) 15 *Fish and Fisheries* 563.

[95] For example the 2014 listing of manta ray species due to increasing patterns of trade even though species are still comparatively abundant.

[96] CITES Resolution Conf. 14.6 (Rev. CoP16) Introduction from the Sea.

[97] For an overview on the CMS see Alexander Proelss, 'Migratory Species, International Protection' in Wolfrum, above n 44, vol. VII (2012) 160, 163.

breeding and survival of the species.[98] Given that Appendix I listed species are also listed in the ICRW Schedules and CITES Appendices, the CMS can be seen as a further reinforcement of species-based approaches to the protection of endangered marine species which builds on and complements the practices established by the other two treaties.

The CMS introduces a new species-based regulatory approach in Article IV where it is set out that migratory species with an unfavorable conservation status which require international agreements for conservation and management and species which would otherwise benefit from international cooperation under an international agreement are to be listed in Appendix II. Range states parties to the CMS shall then endeavor to conclude agreements for the benefit of these species in accordance which are open to all range States irrespective of whether they are parties to the CMS or not. Article V then sets out guidelines for the adoption and content of such agreements including the overarching objective of restoring and maintaining the species in a favorable conservation status. These include provisions for review of conservation status, coordinated conservation and management plans, information exchange, maintenance of habitat networks in relation to migration routes, provision of new favorable habitats, elimination of factors impeding migration as well as measures to control and manage taking of migratory species and suppress illegal taking.

A number of legally binding regional multilateral agreements concerning marine species have already been adopted under the CMS, including the 1991 Wadden Sea Seal Agreement,[99] ASCOBANS and ACCOBAMS. In addition, a number of memoranda of understanding concerning marine species have been adopted concerning turtles, cetaceans, sharks, dugong and aquatic mammals, which although legally non-binding have strongly encouraged intergovernmental cooperation on the development of conservation and management plans and the creation of appropriate institutions to facilitate these activities and may eventually lead to legally binding rules. The CMS can thus be credited with creating a global framework for the protection of endangered migratory species which encourages regional approaches to implementation.

---

[98]    Note that the Scientific Council of the CMS considers that the definition of 'taking' in terms of Article I(1)(i) CMS 'could not be restricted to exclude incidental taking, and that any discrepancy between the provisions of the Convention and unpreventable accidental catches could be avoided by resorting to the possible exceptions to the prohibition of taking given under Article III, paragraph 5 (d)'. Report of the Sixth Meeting of the CMS Scientific Council, Bonn, 1–3 November 1995, 11, available at: http://www.cms.int/sharks/sites/default/files/document/ ScC_report_06_0.pdf (last accessed 29 May 2015). One must thus conclude that the prohibition of taking codified in Article III(5) CMS also covers incidental taking, such as caused by non-intentional by-catch. For an in-depth analysis of this issue see Alexander Proelss, 'Internationaler Arten- und Naturschutz im nationalen Recht: Rechtsprobleme beim Vollzug der Zustimmungsgesetze zur CMS und zur Berner Konvention' in Jost Delbrück, Uschi Heinz, Kerstin Odendahl, Nele Matz-Lück and Andreas von Arnauld (eds) *Aus Kiel in die Welt: Kiel's Contribution to International Law* (2014) 725.

[99]    Agreement on the Conservation of Seals in the Wadden Sea, adopted 16 October 1990, entered into force 1 October 1991, available at: http://www.auswaertiges-amt.de/cae/servlet/ contentblob/607230/publicationFile/158786/VertragstextOriginal.pdf (last accessed 25 May 2015).

Similar to the case of CITES, a particular challenge to the regime established by the CMS results from its overlap with other relevant treaties.[100] Treaties such as the ICRW which are open to all states may not be considered as Appendix II agreements due to the fact that accession to such agreements is restricted to range states. From a formal viewpoint, the relationship between the CMS and other relevant conventions is addressed by Article XII(2) of the CMS which states that '[t]he provisions of this Convention shall in no way affect the rights or obligations of any Party deriving from any existing treaty, convention or Agreement'.[101] Thus, with regard to overlaps between, say, the CMS on the one hand and the ICRW on the other on the field of cetacean protection, the CMS confines itself to a supporting, non-conflicting role. In order to harmonize the obligations arising from the two treaties, their secretariats negotiated a memorandum of understanding, according to which '[t]he UNEP/CMS and IWC Secretariats will to the extent possible, coordinate their programme of activities to ensure that their implementation is complementary and mutually support-ive'.[102] Therefore, the failure to include the majority of large whales in Appendix I of the CMS appears to be a symbol of the ICRW's leadership in the conservation of these species rather than a lack of willingness on behalf of the states parties to the CMS to protect the species concerned.[103] As far as the relationship with the CBD is concerned, its COP 6 explicitly recognized in its decision VI/20 'the Convention on Migratory Species as the lead partner in conserving and sustainably using migratory species over their entire range' and 'that the Convention on Migratory Species provides an international legal framework through which range states can cooperate on migratory species issues'.[104] In June 2007, the CMS COP-8 endorsed a revised CBD-CMS Joint Work Programme aimed at, inter alia, the implementation of joint activities, reviewing the relationship between the CBD's ecosystem approach and the CMS's migratory range approach, and integrating migratory species considerations into environmental impact assessment procedures.[105]

---

[100] Proelss, above n 97, 165.

[101] Note that Article XII (2) CMS is not applicable to conventions concluded after the entry into force of the CMS. In case such conventions do not contain similar conflict clauses which give priority to the then already existing CMS (such as the CBD in its Article 22(1)), all relevant treaties will apply in parallel, subject to deviant principles of treaty interpretation and application.

[102] Memorandum of Understanding between the Secretariat of the International Whaling Commission (IWC Secretariat) and the Secretariat of the Convention on the Conservation of Migratory Species of Wild Animals (CMS) (UNEP/CMS Secretariat). UNEP/CMS/Conf.7.11, 21 August 2002, Annex I.

[103] With regard to the protection of small cetaceans that are not dealt with in the ICRW context, the COP of the CMS has claimed a more active role of the agreement and will do so in respect of the issue of noise pollution; see Draft Resolution on Adverse Anthropogenic Marine/Ocean Noise Impacts on Cetaceans and other Biota, UNEP/CMS/Resolution 9.19, 15 October 2008.

[104] Cooperation with other Organizations, Initiatives and Conventions, UNEP/CBD/COP/6/20, 19 April 2002, Annex I, Decision VI/20. 212–6.

[105] UNEP/CMS/Resolution 8.18, 16 May 2007, Annex III.

## 3.2   Broader Spatial Approaches to the Protection of Marine Species: From Habitat Protection to Global Reach

Although approaches primarily based on species listing such as the ICRW, CITES and CMS have made important contributions, they represent only one potential strategy to the protection of marine species. Each of these treaties has been forced in the course of its evolution to take into account the broader spatial context in which protected species occur, which has prompted measures for the protection of individual habitats as sanctuaries (ICRW) and networks of habitats across migratory routes (CMS), as well as the adoption of procedures to ensure that treaty implementation remains compatible with the maritime zones established under the law of the sea (CITES). A second strand of regulatory activity toward the protection of marine species can be found in legal instruments which systematically address broader spatial considerations relevant for protection and management, whether from the standpoint of habitat protection (Ramsar Convention and World Heritage Convention), or from the standpoint of ecosystem-based management of biodiversity and its components (CBD).

### 3.2.1   Ramsar Convention
The 1971 Convention on Wetlands of International Importance Especially As Waterfowl Habitat (Ramsar Convention) uses a listing approach like the treaties discussed above, however, for the first time in international law, for habitat sites rather than individual species.[106] Although the treaty is designed to protect wetlands, which it defines in Article 1 (1) as 'areas of marsh, fen, peatland or water, whether natural or artificial, permanent or temporary, with water that is static or flowing, fresh, brackish or salt, including areas of marine water the depth of which at low tide does not exceed six metres', it is nonetheless relevant for the protection of marine species given the importance of wetlands as spawning and nursery grounds for fish, seals and sharks, as well as marine turtles which move across environmental media in order to breed. Additional marine sites have been listed as Wetlands of International Importance under the Ramsar Convention due to the presence of vulnerable corals and sea grasses and for providing habitats for sea otters, dugongs and manatees, irrespective of the presence of waterfowl. The Ramsar Convention also introduced the concept of 'wise use of wetlands', which it has consistently reviewed and revised to mean the 'maintenance of their ecological character, achieved through the implementation of ecosystem approaches, within the context of sustainable development'.[107] Although the ecosystem approach as later developed in the context of the CBD was not foreseen at the time the Ramsar Convention was drafted and sustainable development had only just begun to emerge, 'wise use' nonetheless represents a conceptual development in habitat protection with relevance for a number of marine species.

---

[106]   Bowman, Davies and Redgwell, above n 89, 449. Many species mentioned in the annotated descriptions of Ramsar-protected sites are listed in CITES Appendices and the IUCN Red List, indicating the integral relationship between species and habitat.

[107]   Ramsar Convention Secretariat, *Handbook 1: Wise Use of Wetlands* (4th) (2010) 16.

## 3.2.2 World Heritage Convention

The 1972 World Heritage Convention (WHC) provides a legal basis for the protection of 'natural heritage' which it defines in Article 2 as:

> natural features consisting of physical and biological formations or groups of such form-ations, which are of outstanding universal value from the aesthetic or scientific point of view; geological and physiographical formations and precisely delineated areas which constitute the habitat of threatened species of animals and plants of outstanding universal value from the point of view of science or conservation; natural sites or precisely delineated natural areas of outstanding universal value from the point of view of science, conservation or natural beauty.[108]

Article 3 of the WHC then sets out an obligation for each State party to identify and delineate such properties 'situated on its territory'.

Although Article 2 WHC specifically provides for the protection of habitats of threatened species, which would logically include marine areas and species, these were not explicitly mentioned in the treaty which led to some initial uncertainty about the WHC's scope of application. This has since been resolved through the practice of the parties and the frequently revised Operational Guidelines for the implementation of the WHC.[109] Over time, considerable overlaps have also emerged between natural heritage sites protected under the WHC and brackish/marine wetland areas protected under the Ramsar Convention, and many of the threatened marine species named to justify the designation of their habitats as having outstanding universal value for conservation purposes under the WHC are also listed in CITES and the CMS, as well as the IUCN Red List of Endangered Species. This can be seen as demonstrating the important role of interactions between these instruments in mutually reinforcing and enhancing the protection of species and habitats.

Particular questions have arisen with regard to the relationship between the WHC and the LOSC. Article 3 of the WHC might, for example, be narrowly interpreted to restrict the Convention's scope of application to marine areas under the sovereignty of coastal states in line with the law of the sea valid at the time of adoption to the WHC rather than extending into coastal states' EEZs. With the entry into force of the LOSC, however, the coastal state enjoys sovereign rights for the purpose of managing living natural resources, as well as jurisdiction with regard to the protection and preservation of the marine environment in its EEZ on the basis of Article 56(1) LOSC. The exercise of these rights by the coastal state for the protection of natural heritage in its EEZ is compatible with the object and purpose of both the WHC and the LOSC, provided that the sites are designated and maintained with due regard for the rights and duties of other states in the EEZ as required under the international law of the sea. The WHC makes no explicit provision for the protection of natural heritage located on the high seas, although the conservation of wildlife and habitats in areas beyond the limits of

---

[108] Convention for the Protection of the World Cultural and Natural Heritage, adopted 16 November 1972, entered into force 17 December 1975, 1037 UNTS 152.

[109] Bowman, Davies and Redgwell, above n 89, 457.

national jurisdiction has recently been identified by expert groups as areas of future action for the WHC.[110]

### 3.2.3   Convention on Biological Diversity

In contrast to the ICRW, CITES and the CMS which only apply to listed species, and to the limited geographic scope of habitat protection under the Ramsar Convention and the WHC, the CBD, like the LOSC, is global in scope and addresses all forms of genetic, species and ecosystem biodiversity at all scales. In the early stages of drafting it was agreed that the CBD would not take a species-listing approach as previous treaties had done but would instead take a broader view toward biodiversity,[111] emphasizing instead diversity 'within species, between species and of ecosystems' (Article 2). While previous treaties have only addressed issues of habitat protection in direct relation to specifically listed species, the CBD has expanded the available catalogue of conservation measures to include a system of protected areas designed to protect ecosystems and their interactions as 'dynamic complexes', thereby placing particular emphasis on ecological interstices and interdependencies – a highly complex regulatory task which had not been attempted before – which is essential for species survival. This emergent 'ecosystem approach' to conservation, developed legally largely by the CBD,[112] has proven to be a significant regulatory innovation whose influence clearly informs the implementation of other biodiversity-related treaties.[113] Some have even gone so far as to describe the ecosystem approach as one of the CBD's 'greatest collaborative achievements'.[114]

Despite its ecologically comprehensive perspective and the near-universal participation it enjoys, the CBD was not intended to serve as a framework treaty to overarch the other biodiversity-related treaties or consolidate their content. This has given rise to a number of questions concerning its broader implementation in relation to other legal instruments. The CBD, although it performs a *de facto* central role in biodiversity protection, is nonetheless a treaty *inter pares* which increasingly interacts with other treaties on overlapping subject matter. These emergent linkages are sometimes functional in instances where the respective treaties employ the same legal approaches to otherwise divergent subject matter, or are found more fundamentally in the shared object and purpose of the treaties and their respective institutional arrangements. In the

---

[110]   Dan Laffoley and Josephine Langley (eds), *Bahrain Action Plan for Marine World Heritage. Identifying Priorities and Enhancing the Role of the World Heritage Convention in the IUCN WCPA Marine Global Plan of Action for MPAs in our Oceans and Sea* (2010) 14–15.

[111]   The CBD does not completely depart from the species-listing approach, however, but instead shifts the obligation to engage in species listing to the individual parties on the basis of Article 7(a) which sets out an obligation for parties to identify components of biodiversity important for conservation and sustainable use on their own based on criteria contained in Annex I. These criteria address ecosystems, habitats, species, communities and clearly reflect the listing practices under other biodiversity-related treaties.

[112]   Convention on Biological Diversity, Conference of the Parties, Decision V/6, Ecosystem Approach.

[113]   Bowman, Davies and Redgwell, above n 89, 579.

[114]   Bernd Siebenhühner, 'Administrator of Global Biodiversity: The Secretariat of the Convention on Biological Diversity' (2007) 16 *Biodiversity Conservation* 259, 267.

case of the CBD and the other biodiversity-related treaties, these interactions have necessitated the development of a variety of inter-treaty cooperation mechanisms, both formal and informal, which underline that the treaties are intended to supplement rather than compete with each other.[115] To date, the CBD Secretariat has concluded formal memoranda of cooperation with the Secretariats of a number of multilateral agreements including the Ramsar Convention, the CMS, the WHC and CITES on the basis of Article 23(4)(h) CBD, which, although currently more administrative than implementation-oriented and of unclear legal status, nonetheless provide a starting point for future cooperative activities within the family of biodiversity-related treaties.

The potential ambit of the CBD reaches beyond the biodiversity-related treaties, however, particularly in regard to marine issues. With its two-pronged approach to biodiversity protection involving both conservation and sustainable use, the CBD also seeks to bring about a paradigm shift in other treaties' approaches to the protection of living organisms distinct from their conservation status. The CBD's unique formulation of the precautionary principle in its preamble gives expression to this ambition, which is then further substantiated in Article 22(1) of the CBD, which, when read in its converse implication, provides a legal basis upon which the CBD shall expressly affect the rights and obligations of parties under existing international agreements when a threat to biological diversity is found to exist. Article 22(2) relativizes this mandate for action in relation to the marine environment, however, by setting out a compatibility imperative in relation to the law of the sea, which mirrors the content of Article 311(2) of the LOSC. While most authors interpret this provision as establishing a general superiority of the LOSC over the CBD in relation to the marine environment, it has at the same time been observed that this formulation neglects a broader category of legal elements – namely approaches and principles – which do not constitute rights and obligations in terms of the treaty per se.[116] The ecosystem approach and the precautionary principle – the CBD's methods for addressing conservation and sustainable use, respectively – fall precisely into this grey area of treaty interaction with the LOSC when applied to the marine environment and species, and potentially stipulate higher protection standards.

With regard to marine conservation in situ – a key operational domain for the ecosystem approach – the CBD sets out a general obligation for parties to establish marine protected areas (MPAs) as a key conservation tool, defined in COP Decision VII/5 as:

> any defined area within or adjacent to the marine environment, together with its overlying waters and associated flora, fauna and historical and cultural features, which has been reserved by legislation or other effective means, including custom, with the effect that its marine and/or coastal biodiversity enjoys a higher level of protection than its surroundings.[117]

---

[115] Caddell, above n 93, 49.

[116] Rüdiger Wolfrum and Nele Matz, *Conflicts in International Environmental Law* (2003) 125.

[117] Convention on Biological Diversity, Conference of the Parties, Decision VII/5, Marine and Coastal Biological Diversity.

The overarching goals and modalities of MPA establishment and management have been continually refined in subsequent CBD work programs and given further emphasis in non-binding instruments such as the relevant sections of Agenda 21,[118] the Johannesburg Plan of Implementation[119] and the CBD's own Aichi Targets.[120] It should be noted, however, that MPAs are intended to manage conflicting uses of the marine environment and species rather than eliminate human uses entirely for purposes of conservation, and therefore exist in a variety of different forms. As a consequence of this variety, the establishment of a protected area does not necessarily resolve conflicts between the objectives of different regimes.[121] The majority of existing MPAs continue to be found in areas within the limits of national jurisdiction, although MPAs are increasingly being established by multiple states and further away from shore in order to improve ecological coherence between sites and proactively address emergent threats – precisely what the CBD's formulations of the ecosystem approach and the precautionary principle would appear to call for. Adding to this complexity, the ecosystem approach has also been widely incorporated into various regional seas conventions such as the OSPAR Convention,[122] where it has been increasingly used in partnership with the precautionary principle as a rationale for the establishment of MPA networks and other area-based management measures, which span multiple maritime zones and progressively extend into high seas areas.[123] This dynamic 'push and pull' between various legal instruments at the regional and international levels and between the often conflicting objectives and philosophies of the CBD and the law of the sea demonstrates the challenges associated with achieving legally consistent and effective strategies for protecting marine species using spatial approaches.

One of the most challenging current interactions between the CBD and the LOSC revolves around the CBD's scope of application in Article 4(b) in regard to processes and activities carried out in 'areas beyond the limits of national jurisdiction', the general duty of cooperation in regard to 'areas beyond national jurisdiction' contained in Article 5, and their compatibility with the provisions of the LOSC. While the latter does use the term 'areas beyond the limits of national jurisdiction' in reference to the

---

118   United Nations Conference on Environment and Development, Agenda 21: Programme of Action for Sustainable Development. UN Doc. A/Conf.151/26, 12 August 1992.

119   See above n 28.

120   Convention on Biological Diversity, Conference of the Parties, Decision X/2, Strategic Plan for Biodiversity 2011–2020. Target 11 reads as follows: 'By 2020, at least 17 percent of terrestrial and inland water areas, and 10 percent of coastal and marine areas, especially areas of particular importance for biodiversity and ecosystem services, are conserved through effectively and equitably managed, ecologically representative and well connected systems of protected areas and other effective area-based conservation measures, and integrated into the wider landscapes and seascapes.'

121   Rüdiger Wolfrum and Nele Matz, 'The Interplay of UNCLOS and CBD' (2000) 4 *Max Planck Yearbook of United Nations Law* 445, 468.

122   Convention for the Protection of the Marine Environment of the North-East Atlantic, adopted 22 September 1992, entered into force 25 March 1998, 2354 UNTS 67.

123   Julien Rochette, Sebastian Unger, Dorothee Herr, David Johnson, Takehiro Nakamura, Tim Packeiser, Alexander Proelss, Martin Visbeck, Andrea Wright and Daniel Cebrian, 'The Regional Approach to the Conservation and Sustainable Use of Marine Biodiversity in Areas Beyond National Jurisdiction' (2014) 49 *Marine Policy* 109.

Area and refers to ocean space 'beyond the exclusive economic zone' in relation to certain species, it is currently unresolved whether the CBD's concept of 'areas beyond national jurisdiction' (ABNJ) is consistent with the maritime zone of the high seas as defined in Article 86 of the LOSC.[124] The recent decision taken by the BBNJ Working Group[125] to recommend to the UN General Assembly to decide to develop an internationally binding legal instrument under the LOSC on the conservation and sustainable use of marine biological diversity in ABNJ will test the extent to which states wish to bend the framework established under the LOSC in order to accommodate key features of the CBD. Given that central proponents of a new legal instrument such as the European Union have already underlined that they do not support the inclusion of fisheries issues in the negotiations, it will remain to be seen whether this new agreement – should it eventually come into being – will accomplish a truly teleological linkage between the CBD and the LOSC regarding the protection of marine biodiversity which supplants the exploitation of marine living resources or will merely establish functional linkages between the two instruments in regard to specific legal tools and methodologies.

## 4. CONCLUSION

The issue of protecting marine species is a matter that falls within the interface of the international law of the sea and international environmental law. As far as the international law of the sea is concerned, the issue is first and foremost addressed from a resource-oriented angle. In contrast, focus of the pertinent MEAs is on species protection sensu stricto, even though the approaches on which these agreements are based (species-based, spatially-based and precautionary-based) differ significantly. The law of marine species protection is thus characterized by the concurrence and overlap of different legal traditions and underlying interests. It is neither productive nor adequate to approach the issue exclusively from either one or the other side. The fact that past decades have witnessed a significant increase in the number of relevant treaties and concepts makes it rather essential to focus on the question of how the existing interactions between the different instruments and categories may best be tackled.

As far as the protection of commercially relevant marine species is concerned, the UNFSA attempts to tie together the legal traditions arising from the international law of the sea and those from international environmental law – a fact that explains the

---

[124] Katherine Houghton, 'Identifying New Pathways for Ocean Governance: The Role of Legal Principles in Areas Beyond National Jurisdiction' (2014) 49 *Marine Policy* 118, 122–3. Boyle argues that consistency in the implementation of the CBD with the provisions of the law of the sea is to be judged more generally in relation to the overarching principles and objectives of the LOSC rather than against each individual provision, thereby better accommodating evolving concepts; see Alan Boyle, 'Further Development of the Law of the Sea Convention: Mechanisms for Change' (2005) 54 *International and Comparative Law Quarterly* 563, 569, 579.

[125] See above n 53.

significant difficulties in effectively implementing and enforcing the rules and principles contained therein. The experiences gained in the context of attempting to establish an effective management regime for straddling and highly migratory fish stocks should guide the negotiations of the planned implementation agreement concerning protection and sustainable use of biodiversity in ABNJ. It can be expected that this agreement will only become a legal reality if the requirements and traditions of both the international law of the sea and international environmental law described above are considered in the negotiating process.

# 12. Conservation and sustainable use of marine biodiversity in areas beyond national jurisdiction: towards an implementing agreement

*Dire Tladi*

## 1. INTRODUCTION

Perhaps no other aspect of the law of the sea has been as contentious as the conservation and sustainable use of marine biodiversity, in particular marine genetic resources, in areas beyond national jurisdiction. While the 1982 UN Convention on the Law of the Sea[1] (hereinafter the 'Convention' or the 'LOSC') regulates all aspects of oceans governance, the content of the rules established by the Convention in relation to the conservation and sustainable use of marine biological diversity remain contested. In particular, there exists a divergence of views of a legal, political and ideological nature.

The contested terrain in relation to marine resources in areas beyond national jurisdiction concerns two separate but related issues. The first, and legally the most contentious, concerns the legal regime applicable to marine genetic resources on the deep seabed.[2] The nature of the legal contestation with respect to the marine genetic resources question concerns not only what the law should be, but also what the law is. The second issue concerns the adoption of measures for the preservation and conservation of the marine environment, including through the establishment of marine protected areas.[3] While, with respect to the adoption of preservation and conservation

---

1    United Nations Convention on the Law of the Sea, adopted 10 December 1982, entered into force 16 November 1994, 1833 UNTS 3 (LOSC).
2    See for detailed discussion of the marine genetic resources debate Fernanda Millicay, 'A Legal Regime for the Biodiversity of the Area' in Myron H. Nordquist, Thomas H. Heidar and John N. Moore (eds), *Law, Science and Ocean Management* (Martinus Nijhoff, 2007); Dire Tladi, 'Marine Genetic Resources on the Deep Seabed: The Continuing Search for a Legally Sound Interpretation of UNCLOS' 2008 *International Environmental Law and Diplomacy Review* 65; Dire Tladi, 'Genetic Resources, Benefit Sharing and the Law of the Sea: The Need for Clarity' (2007) 13 *Journal of International Maritime Law* 183. For a recent exposition of the arguments and counter-argument, see Petra Drankier, Alex G. Oude Elferink, Bert Visser and Tamara Takács, 'Marine Genetic Resources in Areas beyond National Jurisdiction: Access and Benefit Sharing' (2012) 27 *International Journal of Marine and Coastal Law* 375, especially 399 et seq. A study of the role of state practice in the creation, interpretation and re-interpretation of the principles relevant to marine biodiversity in areas beyond national jurisdiction is presented in Dire Tladi, 'State Practice and the Making and (Re)Making of International Law: The Case of the Legal Rules Relating to Marine Biodiversity in Areas Beyond National Jurisdiction' (2013) 1 *State Practice and International Law Journal* 97.
3    For other discussions see Kristina M. Gjerde and Anna Rulska-Domino, 'Marine Protected Areas beyond National Jurisdiction: Some Practical Perspectives for Moving Ahead' (2012) 27

measures, the law is relatively clear, governance gaps have been identified, leading some to call for the strengthening of the law. Moreover, even where the law is clear, the practice of states and other entities indicates a concerted effort to push the boundaries of the law using existing rules.

The contestation has taken place in various forums of the United Nations, most notably the General Assembly. At times, however, the contestation has spilled over into other forums as states and other entities jockey for position. The engagements of parties in these areas have been geared both to the creation of new rules and to the interpretation (and re-interpretation) of existing rules. The purpose of this chapter is to examine how this contestation has taken place and, in particular, how different role players have tried to interpret existing rules while shaping possible new rules to govern the conservation and sustainable use of marine biodiversity in areas beyond national jurisdiction. In the next section the contestation relating to the legal regime applicable to marine genetic resources is described. An overview of the contestation surrounding conservation measures under the LOSC is then provided. I then describe recent developments within the United Nations and other forums, focusing on attempts by different role players to interpret and re-interpret existing rules, while also seeking to shape new rules relative to the conservation and sustainable use of marine biological diversity in areas beyond national jurisdiction. A few concluding remarks are then offered. Because both aspects of the debate have been covered in great detail elsewhere, there is no attempt to reproduce all of these discussions in any comprehensive manner in this chapter. The chapter will only attempt to show how various stakeholders have used forums available to them to advance particular positions and, in this way, provide an overview of recent developments in this highly contested area of the law of the sea.

## 2. THE LEGAL REGIME APPLICABLE TO MARINE GENETIC RESOURCES

The term 'marine genetic resources' refers to genetic material of plants, animals and micro-organisms in the oceans and which have become increasingly important in the pharmaceutical industry. The contestation over which legal regime applies to marine genetic resources arises mainly from an ambiguity in the LOSC. The deep seabed beyond national jurisdiction, referred to as the 'Area' in the Convention, is governed by Part XI of the Convention which establishes the deep seabed as the common heritage of

---

*International Journal of Marine and Coastal Law* 351, 352. See also Richard A. Barnes, 'Consolidating Governance Principles for Areas beyond National Jurisdiction' (2012) 27 *International Law Journal of Marine and Coastal Law* 261, 273. Richard Barnes, 'The Convention on the Law of the Sea: An Effective Framework for Domestic Fisheries Conservation?' in David Freestone, Richard Barnes and David Ong (eds), *The Law of the Sea: Progress and Prospects* (Oxford University Press 2006), 233. Kristina Gjerde, 'High Seas Fisheries Management under the Convention on the Law of the Sea' in David Freestone, Richard Barnes and David Ong (eds), *The Law of the Sea: Progress and Prospects* (Oxford University Press 2006), 281. Pierre Jacquet, Rajendra K. Pachauri and Laurence Tubiana (eds), *Oceans: The New Frontier* (The Energy and Resources Institute, 2011).

mankind.[4] In a nutshell Part XI establishes a regime, complete with an international organization, the International Seabed Authority, to ensure that the benefits from the exploitation of the resources on the deep seabed are shared by all humanity.[5]

Article 133 unambiguously provides that for 'the purposes' of Part XI, the word 'resources' means 'all solid, liquid or gaseous mineral resources in situ in the Area at or beneath the seabed, including polymetallic nodules'. This definition is clear and unambiguous and its application would imply that the regime established by Part XI was not applicable to marine genetic resources which, by definition, are biological and can therefore not be said to be 'solid, liquid or gaseous mineral resources'. However, this conclusion is complicated by the presence of another, equally clear and unambiguous provision of the Convention, namely Article 136 which provides that the 'Area *and its resources* are the common heritage of mankind' (emphasis added). Thus, it is not just the resources, as defined in Article 136, which are the common heritage of mankind but also the deep seabed itself.

In the face of this ambiguity, different groups of States have proposed different narratives on the law applicable to marine genetic resources on the deep seabed.[6] On the one side of the divide, there is a group of States – the United States, Russia, Iceland, Norway, Canada and Japan – in whose view marine genetic resources on the deep seabed are governed by Part VII of the Convention. While Part XI promotes the idea of the common heritage of mankind and benefit sharing, Part VII is the antithesis of this and promotes freedom of the seas and a 'first come, first serve' approach.[7] Another group of States, in particular the Group of 77 and China (hereinafter the 'G77'), argue that marine genetic resources are governed by the common heritage of mankind principle.

Those States that adopt the approach that Part VII, and not Part XI, applies to marine genetic resources on the deep seabed point, first and foremost, to the definition of resources in Article 133 which, on its face, excludes marine genetic resources. Additionally, even Article 140, which provides that '[a]ctivities in the Area ... shall be for the benefit of mankind' qualifies this statement by 'as provided for in this Part'.[8] With respect to resources, by virtue of Article 133, Part XI is limited to mineral resources. If Part XI is not applicable to marine genetic resources on the deep seabed, so the argument goes, then Part VII must be applicable. Part VII, which governs the high seas, provides that the high seas are 'open to all States'.[9] Under these provisions

---

[4]  LOSC, Art. 1(1) defines the 'Area' as 'the seabed and ocean floor and subsoil thereof, beyond the limits of national jurisdiction'. See Art. 136 which determines the Area to be the common heritage of mankind. To avoid confusion between 'area' beyond national jurisdiction, marine protected 'areas' and 'Area', I use the 'deep seabed' and not the 'Area' throughout the chapter.

[5]  See especially LOSC, Art. 130.

[6]  See for discussion Valentina Germani and Charlotte Salpin, 'The Status of High Seas Biodiversity in International Policy and Law' in Jacquet, Pachauri and Tubiana, above n 3, 194. See also the literature cited in n 2 above.

[7]  See LOSC, Art. 87.

[8]  LOSC, Art. 140(1).

[9]  LOSC, Art. 87(1).

of Part VII the resources of the high seas are available for exploitation by whoever is able to exploit them.

Compelling though the argument for the freedom of the high seas approach may be, particularly in the light of the clear text of Article 133, the approach does suffer from some flaws. First, Part VII lists a number of activities which are subject to the freedom of the high seas.[10] The exploitation of marine genetic resources is not included in the list.[11] The exploitation of marine genetic resources is qualitatively different from fishing such that it could not be subsumed under fishing. While exploitation of fisheries is concerned with the individual fish harvested from the oceans with the possibility for others to exploit whatever remains in the ocean, the exploitation of marine genetic resources is concerned more with the identification of gene sequencing or information and not so much the exploitation of the individual resource physically harvested from the ocean.[12] Thus, what is harvested are samples from the sea, from which genetic information is identified and patented with a view to legally precluding later use of similar resources.[13] Similarly, while an argument could be made that exploitation of marine genetic resources amounts to scientific research, the freedom to conduct marine research in Article 87(1) is subject to Part XIII of the Convention which in turn suggests that marine scientific search in the deep seabed is subject, not to Part VII, but to Part XI.[14]

The most serious flaw of the freedom of the high seas argument, however, is that it ignores the fundamental logic of the Convention, namely that the regulation of various resources in the Convention, and the rights and obligations of States Parties in relation to such resources, is dependent on the maritime zone in which the resource is found and not on the nature of the resource. The relevant zones are the territorial waters, the exclusive economic, the continental shelf, the high seas and the deep seabed. The high seas – the water column above the deep seabed – are legally, though not biologically, separate and distinct from the deep seabed. Part VII and the rights contained therein apply only to the high seas and not to the deep seabed.

It is thus safe to say that the differences of views between States on the legal regime applicable to marine genetic resources in areas beyond national jurisdiction cannot be resolved by reference to the text of the Convention. Moreover, the *trauvaux preparatoire* are unlikely to offer any assistance since, at the time of the negotiation of the Convention, it was assumed that the lack of sunlight in the deep seabed made life impossible. As a result the negotiators focused on mineral resources for which the

---

10   Ibid.

11   The list includes freedom of navigation, freedom of overflight, freedom to lay cables and pipelines, freedom to construct artificial islands and other installations, freedom of fishing and freedom of scientific research.

12   See for discussion of the process Salvatore Arico and Charlotte Salpin, *Bioprospecting of Genetic Resources in the Deep Seabed: Scientific, Legal and Policy Aspects* (United Nations University, 2005) especially at 15.

13   See David Leary, 'Marine Genetic resources: The Patentability of Living Organisms and Biodiversity Conservation' in Jacquet, Pachauri and Tubiana, above n 3, 183 especially at 189 et seq.

14   See LOSC, Art. 256 of the Convention. The freedom to conduct marine scientific research in the high seas, not subject to Part XI, is contained in Art. 257.

prospects of exploitation seemed more likely.[15] In this respect there was very little discussion of the definition of resources in the course of the negotiations.[16]

## 3. CONSERVATION MEASURES UNDER THE LAW OF THE SEA CONVENTION

The LOSC creates a general obligation on States Parties 'to protect and preserve the environment'.[17] While it recognizes the right of States Parties to exploit marine resources, this right is made subject to the obligation to preserve and protect the marine environment.[18] Concretely, the Convention requires States to take measures, jointly or individually, to 'prevent, control or reduce' pollution of the marine environment.[19] A central element of the Convention's approach to the protection and preservation of the marine environment is the obligation to cooperate.[20]

Over and above the general provisions on the protection and preservation of the marine environment, specific parts of the LOSC governing specific maritime zones also create obligations to preserve and protect the environment. Article 61, for example, obliges coastal States to 'ensure, through proper conservation and management measures that the maintenance of the living resources in the exclusive economic zone is not endangered by over-exploitation'.[21] With respect to the high seas, the Convention requires States to take measures, individually or collectively, for the conservation of the living resources.[22] Given the freedom of the high seas, any such measures can only be applicable to the nationals of the States taking such measures.[23] With respect to the deep seabed, the Convention requires measures to be taken to 'ensure effective protection for the marine environment' and in particular requires that measures be adopted for 'the prevention, reduction and control of pollution' and the 'protection and conservation of the natural resources ... and the prevention of damage to the flora and fauna of the marine environment'.[24] Moreover, the Convention establishes a duty on States Parties to cooperate in respect of highly migratory species and marine mammals and cetaceans occurring in the various zones.[25]

While the LOSC contains all these provisions on the conservation and preservation of the marine environment, questions have been asked about environmental effectiveness of the Convention.[26] Gjerde and Rulska-Domino, for example, assert that while

---

[15]  See Millicay, above n 2, 739. See also Drankier, Elferink, Visser and Takács, above n 2, 376.
[16]  See Millicay, above n 2, 778 to 779 on the evolution of the definition.
[17]  LOSC, Art. 192.
[18]  LOSC, Art. 193.
[19]  See LOSC, Arts 194, 195, 196, 207, 208, 209, 210, 211 and 212.
[20]  LOSC, Art. 197.
[21]  See LOSC, Art. 61(2).
[22]  See LOSC, Arts 116–19.
[23]  Ibid.
[24]  LOSC, Art. 145.
[25]  LOSC, Arts 64, 65, 118 and 120.
[26]  See for discussion Tladi, above n 2.

the threats to marine biodiversity in areas beyond national jurisdiction – both the high seas and the deep seabed – have grown exponentially, the governance framework, including the Convention 'has not kept pace'.[27] Barnes observes that the Convention has failed to 'spell out sufficiently coherent obligations [on States Parties] to steward resources' of the oceans leading to the near collapse of fisheries.[28] Gjerde attributes the declining high seas fish stocks and rising biodiversity concerns specifically to the inadequacy of the Convention.[29]

At the heart of the environmental problems in oceans governance is the Grotian principle of the freedom of the seas which is not only confirmed but entrenched in the Convention.[30] The freedom of the high seas effectively re-enacts Hardin's 'tragedy of the commons' by allowing States (and vessels under their jurisdiction) to behave with few restrictions.[31] The vague general obligation to protect and preserve the environment as well as the call for self-regulation in Article 117 of the Convention are clearly not sufficient. In this respect, while States or groups of States could take measures for the conservation of the marine environment, as is called for in Article 117, such measures would only be applicable to the nationals of the cooperating States.[32] At the same time a governance system that purports to mandate a State or group of States to legislate for the international community would not only be inconsistent with the general structure of international law but would be unacceptable to most States.

The contestation over the protection and preservation of the marine environment in areas beyond national jurisdiction has been championed mainly by the EU. The EU has sought to highlight the gaps in the governance of marine biodiversity in areas beyond national jurisdiction. To fill these gaps the EU has proposed, as short term measures, greater utilization of existing rules such as the duty to cooperate described above and the duty to perform impact assessments. However, as a long-term measure, the EU has argued for the strengthening of the existing rules, including through the adoption of an implementing agreement to the LOSC. Other states, most notably the US, have baulked at the idea of the adoption of new rules as it was felt that the current rules were sufficient and that the problem was not of governance gaps but rather gaps in implementation.

---

[27]   Gjerde and Rulska-Domino, above n 3, 352.

[28]   Richard Barnes, 'The Convention on the Law of the Sea: An Effective Framework for Domestic Fisheries Conservation?' in David Freestone, Richard Barnes and David Ong (eds), *The Law of the Sea: Progress and Prospects* (Oxford University Press 2006), 233.

[29]   Kristina Gjerde, 'High Seas Fisheries Management under the Convention on the Law of the Sea' in Freestone, Barnes and Ong, above n 3, 281.

[30]   Dire Tladi, 'Oceans Governance: A Fragmented Regulatory Framework?' in Jacquet, Pachauri and Tubiana, above n 3, 103.

[31]   Garrett Hardin, 'The Tragedy of the Commons' (1968) 162 *Science* 1243. Hardin's 'tragedy of the commons' postulates that finite resources in the 'commons' or areas open to all will eventually be depleted if each actor is free to consume the resources without regulation. In other words, short-term interests will dictate overexploitation even though this is not in the interest of anyone's long-term interest.

[32]   P. Dee Boersma and Julia K. Parrish, 'Limiting Abuse: Marine Protected Areas, A Limited Solution' (1999) 31 *Ecological Economics* 287, 289.

## 4.  RECENT DEVELOPMENTS: IDEA OF AN IMPLEMENTING AGREEMENT TAKES HOLD

The contestation over marine biodiversity in areas beyond national jurisdiction has taken place primarily in the General Assembly and its subsidiary bodies, including the UN Open-ended Informal Consultative Process on Oceans and the Law of the Sea (hereinafter the 'Informal Consultative Process') and the UN Ad Hoc Informal Working Group to Study Issues Relating to the Conservation and Sustainable Use of Marine Biological Diversity Beyond Areas of National Jurisdiction (hereinafter the 'Ad Hoc Working Group'). However, the contestation has not been limited to the General Assembly and it has spilled over into other forums including forums of the Convention on Biological Diversity and the Rio+20 World Summit on Sustainable Development.

In the context of the marine genetic resources and the applicable regime, this contestation has mainly taken the form of delegations making arguments to the effect that the Convention and customary international law support their position. The statements of the G77 and China have been fairly consistent in their approach to marine genetic resources in areas beyond national jurisdiction question in the General Assembly, in particular in the Informal Consultative Process and the Ad Hoc Working Group.[33] These statements have also often been supported by interventions of individual delegations of the G77, as a strategy to emphasize the group's solidarity on the issue. Needless to say, the few States supporting the freedom of the high seas as the applicable legal regime have also spoken to ensure that their narrative is reflected in the diplomatic forums. The various reports of the Co-Chairs of the Ad Hoc Working Group, for example, consistently reflect the divergence of views of States.[34]

---

[33]  See, eg, Statement on behalf of the G77 and China by Minister Holger Martisen, Permanent Mission of Argentina, during the Informal Consultative Process on Oceans and the Law of the Sea, 20 June 2011, New York (hereinafter 'G77, ICP, 2011') available at www.g77.org/statement/2011.html (last accessed 26 May 2015); Statement on behalf of the G77 and China by Fernanda Millicay, Counsellor, Permanent Mission of Argentina to the United Nations, on the Fourth Agenda Item during the Ad Hoc Working Group on Marine Biodiversity in Areas Beyond National Jurisdiction, 1 June 2011, New York (hereinafter 'G77, ABNJ2, 2011'); Statement on behalf of the G77 and China by Minister Diego Limeres, Deputy Permanent Representative of the Mission of Argentina, during the Ad Hoc Working Group on Marine Biodiversity in Areas Beyond National Jurisdiction, 31 May 2011, New York (hereinafter 'G77, ABNJ, 2011') available at www.g77.org/statement/2011.html (last accessed 26 May 2015). See also South African Statement on Behalf of the G77 and China during the Informal Consultative Process on Oceans and the Law, 15 June 2006, New York ('G77, ICP, 2006') available at www.g77.org/statement/2006.html (last accessed 26 May 2015).

[34]  See, eg Recommendations of the Ad Hoc Working Group on Marine Biodiversity in Areas Beyond National Jurisdiction to the General Assembly and the Co-Chair's Summary of the Discussions of the Meeting held from 7 to 11 May 2012, UN Doc. A/67/50, para. 14; Recommendations of the Ad Hoc Working Group on Marine Biological Diversity in Areas Beyond National Jurisdiction to the General Assembly and the Co-Chair's Summary of the Discussions of the Meeting held from 31 May to 3 June 2011, UN Doc. A/66/119, para. 15. See also Recommendations of the Ad Hoc Working Group to the General Assembly on Marine Biodiversity in Areas Beyond National Jurisdiction and the Co-Chair's Summary of the Discussions of the Meeting held from 1 to 5 February 2010, UN Doc. A/65/68, paras 71–72;

The G77 and China's consistent raising of the issue in these forums serves several purposes including to spotlight the divergence of views in order to prevent the establishment of a practice that might be construed as establishing the agreement of the parties to the interpretation of the Law of the Sea Convention under Article 31(3)(b) of the Vienna Convention on the Law of Treaties.[35] This practice is so important to the countries of the G77 and China that in 2007 when, during the Informal Consultative Process, the United States refused to accept reference to the divergence of views in the agreed consensual elements[36] the G77, under the chairmanship of Pakistan, refused to negotiate on any other part of the text. In a marathon session ending at midnight of the last day of the Informal Consultative Process, the meeting ended without the adoption of the agreed consensual elements – a rare event up to that date.[37]

Until recently, neither the G77 and China, nor the states supporting freedom of the high seas in respect of marine genetic resources, supported the creation of new rules or the adoption of new instruments. By and large, both sides argued that the law, as it stood, justified their respective positions and the creation of new rules was unnecessary. This is in stark contrast to the long-standing position of the EU, on conservation measures, calling for a new binding instrument to 'further specify and implement' the provisions of the Convention on the Law of the Sea, in particular as it relates to conservation measures.[38]

Over and above the long-term project for an implementing agreement, the EU had also sought to 'push the envelope' in the use of existing rules for the conservation of marine biodiversity in areas beyond national jurisdiction. The precautionary principle provides an illustration of how an existing principle has been used to achieve a more conservation-friendly approach to marine biodiversity in areas beyond national jurisdiction than what is contemplated under the Convention. While the status of the precautionary principle under general international law remains in doubt,[39] it is clear that the LOSC does not make provision for a precautionary approach to conservation.

---

Joint Statement of the Co-Chairpersons of the Ad Hoc Working Group on Marine Biodiversity in Areas Beyond National Jurisdiction, 28 April to 5 May 2008, UN Doc. A/63/79, para. 36. See also Co-Chairperson's Summary of Discussions of the Ad Hoc Working Group on Marine Biodiversity in Areas Beyond National Jurisdiction, 13 to 17 February 2006, UN Doc. A/61/65, paras 39–40.

[35]   Vienna Convention on the Law of Treaties (adopted 23 May 1969, entered into force 27 January 1980) 1155 UNTS 331.

[36]   The 'agreed consensual elements', a set of recommendations to the General Assembly, was the outcome of choice for the Informal Consultative Process. As its name suggests, this outcome document reflects the consensus of states.

[37]   It has since been agreed, in 2009, that the Informal Consultative Process will no longer strive for agreed consensual elements as outcomes.

[38]   See, eg, para. 12 of the EU Presidency intervention during the discussion of agenda item 5 in the Ad Hoc Working Group on 28 April 2008 (on file with the author). See especially the EU Presidency Statement on the role of Area-Based Management Tools during the Ad Hoc Working Group meeting on 29 April 2008 in which the EU argues that there is 'a need for a global regime in this regard'. Available at http://eu-un.europa.eu/articles/en/article_7850_en.htm (last accessed 26 May 2015).

[39]   *Cf. The Case Concerning Pulp Mills on the River Uruguay (Argentina v. Uruguay),* ICJ Judgement of 20 April 2010. See especially the separate opinion Judge Cançado Trindade.

However, it would be hard to deny that, as a result of practice, precaution is part of the fabric of the law of the sea. Precaution is reflected, first and foremost, in the Fish Stocks Agreement – an implementing agreement under the LOSC.[40] While Nolte has opined that the Fish Stocks Agreement is probably not a subsequent agreement (or practice) within the meaning of Article 31(3)(a) of the Convention due to the large number of States Parties to the LOSC that oppose it;[41] the opposition of these States Parties is directed at the provisions of the Fish Stocks Agreement authorizing the boarding of vessels on the high seas.[42] The precautionary principle, as reflected in the Fish Stocks Agreement, is generally accepted by States Parties and indeed non-States Parties as being part of the law of the sea, and the practice of States implementing the Fish Stocks Agreement, invoking the precautionary approach in negotiations and the supporting annual General Assembly resolutions on oceans and the law of the sea which consistently include precaution, amounts to subsequent practice within the meaning of Article 31(3)(b) of the Vienna Convention.[43]

Efforts at advancing the cause of conservation and preservation and, as a consequence, eroding freedom of the high seas have perhaps been most evident in the practice of States relating to marine protected areas.[44] Marine protected areas in areas beyond national jurisdiction are fully consistent with the LOSC and can be seen as joint measures for the protection of the environment under, inter alia, Articles 194 and 197 of the Convention. However, flowing from the freedom of the high seas, the rules arising from the establishment of any marine protected area will only be binding on the States that establish the marine protected area and the vessels flying their flags.[45] Some States, groups of States and other actors have sought to go around the freedom of the high seas by seeking international legitimacy for marine protected areas with a view to creating political pressure, if not a legal obligation, on third States to respect the rules of the relevant marine protected areas.[46]

The principal way in which the marine protected areas agenda has been advanced is through inclusion of language in the General Assembly's annual resolution on oceans

---

[40] See Arts 5 and 6 of the 1995 Agreement for the Implementation of the Provisions of the United Nations Convention on the Law of the Sea of 10 December 1982 Relating to the Conservation and Management of Straddling Fish Stocks and Highly Migratory Fish Stocks, adopted 5 August 1995, entered into force 11 December 2001, 2167 UNTS 3 ('Fish Stocks Agreement' of 'FSA').

[41] Georg Nolte, *Third Report for the ILC Study Group on Treaties over Time: Subsequent Agreements and Subsequent Practice of States Outside of Judicial or Quasi-Judicial Proceedings* at 57 seq. (on file with the author).

[42] See especially FSA Arts 21–22.

[43] See UNGA Resolution on Oceans and the Law of the Sea UN Doc. A/Res/66/231, paras 135, 156 and 173; UNGA Resolution on Oceans and the Law of the Sea UN Doc. A/Res/65/37, paras 151 and 173; and UNGA Resolution on Oceans and the Law of the Sea, UN Doc. A/Res/64/71, paras 133 and 150.

[44] Marine protected areas can be loosely defined as a marine area which has been reserved by law or other means for the purposes of conserving and protecting the environment therein.

[45] See generally P. Dee Boersma and Julia K. Parrish, 'Limiting Abuse: Marine Protected Areas, A Limited Solution' (1999) 31 *Ecological Economics* 287 at 289.

[46] For discussion see, Glen Wright, Julien Rochette and Elisabeth Druel, 'Marine protected areas in areas beyond national jurisdiction', Chapter 13 in this volume.

and the law of the sea. The World Summit on Sustainable Development's Plan of Implementation had, already in 2002, committed States to 'promote the conservation and management of the oceans' including through taking action to develop and 'facilitate the use of diverse approaches and tools, including the ecosystem approach' and 'the establishment of marine protected areas consistent with international law and based on scientific information, including a representative network by 2012'.[47] Moreover, the General Assembly, has consistently called on States to 'strengthen, in a manner consistent with international law, in particular the Convention, the conservation and management of marine biodiversity and ecosystems and national policies in relation to marine protected areas'.[48] Similarly, the General Assembly has been consistent in reaffirming the need for States to 'develop and facilitate the use of diverse approaches and tools for conserving and managing vulnerable marine ecosystems, including through the possible establishment of marine protected areas, consistent with international law as reflected in the Convention'.[49]

The principal driver of these conservation initiatives, the EU, has seen these as short-term measures which, while serving to push the boundaries of what is possible under the current law, are also aimed at establishing legitimacy for the conservation and perseveration measures yet to be put in place. The ultimate objective of these measures would be the conclusion of a legally binding (and implemented) instrument which establishes a global process for the establishment of marine protected areas along with other conservation measures which would, presumably, be universally binding.

While the G77 and China as a bloc was originally lukewarm to the idea of an implementing agreement, some individual members like South Africa openly supported and campaigned for the idea as a means to address the question of the legal regime applicable to marine genetic resources.[50] With the G77 and China insisting that progress on the conservation and preservation issues would depend on the progress on the marine genetic resources question, the discussions appear to be headed for a terminal impasse.

The impasse is reflected in the constant restatement of both debates in the reports of the Ad Hoc Working Group.[51] On the area-based management tools, including marine

---

[47]   2002 Johannesburg Plan of Implementation of the World Summit on Sustainable Development, para. 32(c).

[48]   See, eg, UN Doc. A/Res/66/231, para. 175; UN Doc. A/Res/65/37, para. 176; and UN Doc. A/Res/64/71, para. 152.

[49]   See, UN Doc. A/Res/66/231, para. 176; UN Doc. A/Res/65/37, para. 177; and UN Doc. A/Res/64/71, para. 153. See also UN Doc. A/Res/66/231, para. 177, which recognizes the work of the Biological Diversity Convention to develop criteria for the identification of 'marine areas that require protection' in the light of objectives of the World Summit on Sustainable Development to 'use diverse approaches and tools, such ecosystem approaches and the establishment of marine protected areas'.

[50]   See, statement of South Africa to the UN General Assembly on Oceans and the Law of the Sea, 4 December 2009. See also statement of South Africa during the Ad Hoc Working Group, 2 February 2010 (both on file with the author).

[51]   See especially Recommendations of the Ad Hoc Working Group on Marine Biodiversity in Areas Beyond National Jurisdiction to the General Assembly and Co-Chair's Summary of the Discussions of the Meeting held from 7 to 11 May 2012, UN Doc. A/67/95. The marine genetic resources debate, for example, is reflected in paras 71 and 72 of Recommendations and

protected areas, the report of the 2012 meeting begins by stating that the 'the importance of area-based management tools' was noted and the view was expressed that marine protected areas 'should be established'.[52] The report also refers to the suggestion by some delegations to consider a process for the identification of marine protected areas in areas beyond national jurisdiction.[53] At the same time, however, the report refers to the position of some delegations that there was no multilaterally agreed legal regime for marine protected areas in areas beyond national jurisdiction and that the establishment of marine protected areas unilaterally or by a group of States raises questions of the legitimacy of such marine protected areas.[54] Similarly divergent views on the legal regime applicable to marine genetic resources are reflected in the report.[55] The result of the impasse has been that the General Assembly has been able only to request States to consider the two issues in the context of the mandate of the ad hoc Working Group without providing any guidance on the direction that should be followed.[56]

The dynamics changed in the ad hoc Working Group meeting of 2011, when the G77 and China agreed to support the call for an implementing agreement. The result was a powerful alliance between the EU, the G77 and China and other states such as Australia, Mexico and New Zealand. The alliance was a tenuous one mainly because it was built not on substance but on process – working towards an implementing agreement whose content would be determined through negotiations. However, it did serve the important function of isolating the six States – United States, Russia, Iceland, Norway, Canada and Japan – as the only States not willing to consider the elaboration of a binding instrument to clarify and further develop the governance and legal principles applicable to marine biodiversity in areas beyond national jurisdiction. The result was immediate. In 2011, the Ad Hoc Working Group recommended that

A process be initiated, by the General Assembly, with a view to ensuring that the legal framework for the conservation and sustainable use of marine biodiversity in areas beyond national jurisdiction effectively addresses those issues by identifying gaps and ways forward, including through the implementation of existing instruments and the possible development of a multilateral agreement under the United Nations Convention on the Law of the Sea.[57]

---

Co-Chairs Summary of the ad hoc Working Group meeting of 2010, above n 34; paras 15, 16 and 17 of the Recommendations and Co-Chairs Summary of the Ad Hoc Working Group meeting of 2011, above n 33. The debate over conservation tools is reflected in, for example, paras 64–7 of the Recommendations and Co-Chairs Summary of the Ad Hoc Working Group meeting of 2010, above n 34; paras 26 and 27 of the Recommendations and Co-Chairs Summary of the Working Group meeting of 2008.

[52] Recommendations of the Ad Hoc Working Group, above n 51, para. 19.

[53] Ibid., para. 21.

[54] Ibid.

[55] Ibid., paras 14-16.

[56] See, eg, UN Doc. A/Res/64/71, para. 142, which calls for states to 'further consider' the issue of 'the relevant legal regime on marine genetic resources in areas beyond national jurisdiction'. In para. 148 of UN Doc. A/Res/64/71 the General Assembly invites states 'to further consider' the issue of 'marine protected areas'. See also UN Doc. A/Res/61/222, para. 91.

[57] Recommendations and Co-Chairs Summary of the ad hoc Working Group meeting of 2011, above n 50, para. 1.

The ad hoc Working Group further recommended that the process should address, inter alia, 'marine genetic resources, including the question of sharing benefits, measures such as area-based management tools, including marine protected areas ...'[58] This recommendation was taken up by the General Assembly which decided to initiate the process as recommended by the ad hoc Working Group i.e. a process that could lead to the elaboration of an implementing agreement.[59]

While the G77 and China and the EU had hoped also to pursue the implementing agreement through the Rio+20 process,[60] Venezuela, due to its opposition to the LOSC, blocked a G77 position on the implementing agreement. In response, South Africa organized a group of like-minded countries which, supported by the EU, called for an implementing agreement. In the final text adopted at the Rio+20 conference, world leaders took note of the work of the ad hoc Working Group and committed themselves to 'address, on an urgent basis [and before the end of the 69th session of the General Assembly], the issue of the conservation and sustainable use of marine biological diversity of areas beyond national jurisdiction including by taking a decision on the international instrument under' the LOSC.[61]

This paragraph does not, in and of itself, create a mandate for the elaboration of an instrument. But what it does do is endorse the process initiated by the General Assembly under the Ad Hoc Working Group and, in this way, contributes to the impetus to elaborate an instrument to address gaps in the conservation and sustainable use of marine biodiversity. That it was accomplished in the face of strong opposition from major powers and – due to the Venezuela's position – without G77 and China unity, is testament to the intense pressure brought to bear by the EU and the countries of the G77 and China over a period of several years. The agreement reached in Rio is also particularly important because it highlights the urgency of the process and sets out that a decision on how to proceed should be made at the end of the 69th session – roughly three years from the time of the Rio Summit.

In the interim, the General Assembly has requested the Working Group to make 'recommendations on the scope, parameters and feasibility' of an implementing agreement 'in order to prepare for the decision [on the implementing agreement] to be taken at' its 69th session.[62] During the first two meetings of the Working Group, held in April and June 2014, there seemed to be some softening of attitudes towards an

---

58   Ibid.

59   General Assembly Resolution, UN Doc. A/Res/66/231, para. 167.

60   The first draft of the Rio+20 outcome text included a paragraph, proposed by G77 and China and supported by the EU, going beyond para. 167 of A/Res/66/231 by actually committing to initiating a process 'towards negotiation of an implementing agreement to' the Convention on the Law of the Sea. See para. 80 of the chair's zero draft of the Rio+20 Outcome Document (on file with author).

61   United Nations Conference on Sustainable Development Outcome Document, 'The Future We Want', UN Doc. A/Res/66/288, Annex, para. 162.

62   General Assembly Resolution on Oceans and the Law of the Sea, UN Doc. A/Res/68/70, para. 198.

implementing agreement with some delegations traditionally opposed to an implementing agreement focusing attention on the scope of such an agreement.[63] Iceland, for example, long known to be opposed to both the implementing agreement and the application of the common heritage of mankind, argued during the April and June meetings of the Working Group, that if there is an implementing agreement, it should focus on aspects in which there are real gaps such as the sharing of benefits from the exploitation of marine genetic resources.[64] A final meeting, scheduled for January 2015, is likely to consider what recommendations, if any, to make to the General Assembly. If the meeting is not able to come to some decision, some delegations are preparing to table a resolution, independent of the Working Group process, to initiate negotiations on an implementing agreement.

## 5. CONCLUSION

The contestation over marine biological diversity in areas beyond national jurisdiction, both with respect to the legal regime applicable to marine genetic resources and to the adoption of conservation measures, involves not only a contestation about how the current rules should be understood but also whether new rules are required and what the content of such rules should be. The decisions of the General Assembly and the Rio+20 Summit to initiate a process that could lead to an implementing agreement are significant milestones in the path towards the establishment of a legal regime to more equitably and sustainably govern marine areas beyond national jurisdiction. Whether the process initiated by the General Assembly will lead to the adoption of a new binding instrument remains to be seen. What is clear, however, is that the resolve of States will determine not only whether an implementing agreement will be negotiated and adopted but also the content of such an implementing agreement.

---

[63] For a report of the first two meetings, unfortunately not reflecting individual positions of states, see Co-Chairs' summary of discussions at the Ad Hoc Open-ended Informal Working Group to study issues relating to the conservation and sustainable use of marine biological diversity beyond national jurisdiction, 1–4 April 2014, UN Doc A/69/82 and 16-19 June 2014 (advanced and unedited version), UN Doc A/69/17.

[64] See, eg, ibid., para. 25.

# 13. Marine protected areas in areas beyond national jurisdiction

*Glen Wright, Julien Rochette and Elisabeth Druel*

## 1. INTRODUCTION

Marine areas beyond national jurisdiction (ABNJ) represent approximately half of the planet's surface. Consisting of both the 'high seas',[1] and the 'Area',[2] ABNJ host a significant proportion of the earth's biodiversity.[3] While marine ecosystems in general are poorly understood, the more we learn about them, the more apparent their importance becomes. The world's oceans, both within and beyond national jurisdiction, are critical providers of the ecosystem services on which humanity depends.

The conservation of marine biodiversity is essential to securing these ecosystem services for all, including future generations. Nevertheless, pressure on these ecosystems is mounting due to growing exploitation of living marine resources, climate change, ocean acidification, and pollution. Further pressure is on the horizon as scientific discoveries and technological developments now make it possible to exploit new resources in ABNJ, such as marine generic resources and deep-sea minerals.

Marine protected areas (MPAs) are one of a number of tools aimed at improving the conservation and sustainable use of marine biodiversity in ABNJ. This chapter examines the current status of efforts to designate MPAs in ABNJ. It begins with a brief overview of the concept of MPAs and a discussion of the legal and practical challenges inherent in applying the concept to ABNJ. It then examines the practice in regional bodies and international sectoral frameworks. Finally, it assesses the potential role that a new international agreement on the conservation and sustainable use of marine biodiversity in ABNJ could play in the designation and management of MPAs.

## 2. CONTEXT

Despite the global importance of marine biodiversity, significant regulatory and governance gaps impede its effective conservation and sustainable use in ABNJ. The Law of the Sea Convention (LOSC) provides general obligations relating to the

---

[1]  The high seas consist of the water column beyond the economic exclusive zones of coastal states.

[2]  Defined as 'the seabed and ocean floor and subsoil thereof, beyond the limits of national jurisdiction': United Nations Convention on the Law of the Sea (LOSC), (adopted 10 December 1982, entered into force 16 November 1994) 1833 UNTS 3, Art. 1(1).

[3]  Census of Marine Life (2011), *Scientific results to support the sustainable use and conservation of marine life – A summary of the Census of Marine Life for decision makers.*

protection and preservation of the marine environment, including the obligation to adopt measures 'necessary to protect and preserve rare or fragile ecosystems as well as the habitat of depleted, threatened or endangered species and other forms of marine life'.[4] This obligation is echoed by the Convention on Biological Diversity (CBD),[5] which establishes a duty of cooperation with respect to ABNJ, requiring that contracting parties cooperate, directly or through a competent international organization, in respect of matters relevant to the conservation and sustainable use of marine biodiversity in ABNJ.[6] Nevertheless, no specific methodologies are provided as to how this is to be achieved.

MPAs are widely acknowledged as an important tool for biodiversity conservation,[7] and ecologically connected networks of MPAs are crucial for sustaining high seas ecosystems.[8] Such networks can safeguard larval sources, migration routes, and feeding, nursery and breeding grounds. At a broader level, representative networks of MPAs can be an important component of a precautionary approach, in that they offer protection of not only what we know to be important today, but also what may transpire to be important in the future. MPAs can therefore help to sustain marine life in the face of ever-increasing pressures by building resilience and giving time for ecosystems to adapt.[9] Research shows that the most effective MPAs are longstanding, large, geographically isolated and well-enforced 'no take' areas.[10]

The international community has undertaken, within several fora, to establish a network of MPAs covering a large portion of the oceans. At the World Summit on Sustainable Development in 2002, the creation of this network was discussed. The Johannesburg Plan of Implementation encourages States to develop 'MPAs consistent with international law and based on scientific information including representative networks by 2012'.[11] In 2010 however, the CBD noted that only one percent of the

---

[4]   LOSC, Article 194(5).

[5]   Convention on Biological Diversity (adopted 5 June1992, entered into force 29 December 1993) 1760 UNTS 79 (CBD).

[6]   CBD, Art. 5.

[7]   Graham J. Edgar, Garry R. Russ, and Russ C. Babcock, 'Marine protected areas' in Sean D. Connell and Bronwyn M. Gillanders (eds), *Marine Ecology* (Oxford University Press, 2007) 533–55.

[8]   Ussif Rashid Sumaila, Dirk Zeller, Reg Watson, Jackie Alder, Daniel Pauly, 'Potential costs and benefits of marine reserves in the high seas' (2007) 345 *Marine Ecology Progress Series* 305–10.

[9]   UNEP, *Ecosystems and Biodiversity in Deep Waters and High Seas*, UNEP Regional Sea Reports and Studies No. 178. (UNEP/IUCN, 2006) at www.unep.org/pdf/Ecosystem Biodiversity_DeepWaters_20060616.pdf (last accessed 26 May 2015).

[10]   Graham J. Edgar, Rick D. Stuart-Smith, Trevor J. Willis, Stuart Kininmonth, Susan C. Baker, Stuart Banks, Neville S. Barrett, Mikel A. Becerro, Anthony T.F. Bernard, Just Berkhout, Colin D. Buxton, Stuart J. Campbell, Antonia T. Cooper, Marlene Davey, Sophie C. Edgar, Günter Försterra, David E. Galván, Alejo J. Irigoyen, David J. Kushner, Rodrigo Moura, P. Ed Parnell, Nick T. Shears, German Soler, Elisabeth M.A. Strain, and Russell J. Thomson, 'Global conservation outcomes depend on marine protected areas with five key features' (2014) 506 *Nature* 216–20.

[11]   Johannesburg Plan of Implementation (UN Doc. A/ CONF.199/20, 4 September 2002), Resolution II, Annex, Point 32(c).

oceans were covered by MPAs, and the vast majority of these were located in areas under national jurisdiction.[12]

In this context, the Conference of the Parties (COP) to the CBD, decided to extend the deadline for the establishment of a network of MPAs covering 10 per cent of the oceans from 2012 to 2020. In particular, Target 11 of the so-called 'Aichi targets' adopted by Contracting Parties to the CBD states: 'by 2020, at least … 10 per cent of coastal and marine areas, especially areas of particular importance for biodiversity and ecosystem services, are conserved through effectively and equitably managed, ecologically representative and well-connected systems of protected areas and other effective area-based conservation measures'.

States have also agreed to develop a set of Sustainable Development Goals (SDGs), building upon the previously agreed Millennium Development Goals (MDG).[13] The SDGs will incorporate the MDGs' goal of alleviating poverty, but will also address environmental concerns. In July 2014, the Open Working Group on Sustainable Development Goals forwarded a proposal for the SDGs to the UN General Assembly (UNGA).[14] The proposed goal on oceans, goal 14, is to 'conserve and sustainably use the oceans, seas and marine resources for sustainable development'.

A number of discrete targets are proposed, to be met by 2020, including to: 'sustainably manage and protect marine and coastal ecosystems to avoid significant adverse impacts, including by strengthening their resilience, and take action for their restoration, to achieve healthy and productive oceans'; and 'conserve at least 10 per cent of coastal and marine areas, consistent with national and international law and based on best available scientific information'.

The proposed goal 14 would also call on states to 'ensure the full implementation of international law, as reflected in UNCLOS for states parties to it, including, where applicable, existing regional and international regimes for the conservation and sustainable use of oceans and their resources by their parties'. This implies an increased focus on, and role for, the existing regional arrangements discussed below, as well as better implementation of existing international and sectoral measures.

Despite these encouraging steps towards improved conservation and sustainable use of marine biodiversity in ABNJ, the fact remains that only a tiny proportion of the ocean is currently protected. Most recent estimates suggest that less than 3 per cent has been designated as MPAs.[15] In ABNJ, the percentage is even lower, around 0.14 per cent.[16]

---

[12]   CBD COP 10 Decision X/29 on Marine and Coastal Biodiversity, para. 4: 'despite efforts in the past few years, just over 1 per cent of the ocean surface is designated as protected areas'.

[13]   The MDGs were created in 2000 to set out measurable targets and indicators by which the international community could track the success of its commitments.

[14]   United Nations, Open Working Group proposal for Sustainable Development Goals 2014.

[15]   For up-to-date information, consult the World Database on Protected Areas: http://www.protectplanetocean.org/official_mpa_map (last accessed 4 June 2015).

[16]   United Nations, The Millennium Development Goals Report 2013 (United Nations, 2013).

# 3.  MARINE PROTECTED AREAS

## 3.1  Definition of Marine Protected Areas

There is no universally agreed definition of 'marine protected area', though a number of definitions have been developed by different organizations and institutions.[17]

At the international level, the CBD defines the broader term 'protected area' in its Article 2 as 'a geographically defined area which is designated or regulated and managed to achieve specific conservation objectives'. In Decision VII/5 adopted by the Conference of the Parties in 2004, reference is made to the definition given by the Ad Hoc Technical Expert Group on Marine and Coastal Protected Areas (the Ad-Hoc Group) in its 2003 report[18] which defines an MPA as:

> an area within or adjacent to the marine environment, together with its overlying waters and associated flora, fauna, and historical and cultural features, which has been reserved by legislation or other effective means, including custom, with the effect that its marine and/or coastal biodiversity enjoys a higher level of protection than its surroundings.

The FAO defines MPAs as 'temporally and geographically defined areas that afford natural resources greater protection than is afforded in the rest of an area as defined in relation to fisheries management'.[19] The International Union for Conservation of Nature (IUCN) proposes a definition according to which an MPA is 'any area of intertidal or sub-tidal terrain, together with its overlying water and associated flora, fauna, historical and cultural features, which has been reserved by law or other effective means to protect part or all of the enclosed environment'.[20]

In MPAs, the level of protection may vary depending on the pressures on the area to be protected and on the needs of conservation. Some MPAs may be entirely or partly marine reserves, with no-take zones, while in others only certain activities such as fishing or tourism will be regulated and not necessarily prohibited. As a consequence, in every forum the definition of MPAs is always a broad one. The basic idea, however, remains that MPAs will have 'a special status in comparison with the surrounding area due to their more stringent regulation of one or more human activities ... by one or more measures ... for one or more purposes'.[21]

## 3.2  Marine Protected Areas in ABNJ

There is currently strong interest in the establishment of multi-purpose MPAs in ABNJ, or MPAs which seek to regulate a large variety of human activities with the ultimate

---

[17]   E. Druel, 'Marine protected areas in areas beyond national jurisdiction: The state of play' IDDRI Working Paper 7 (2011).

[18]   See document UNEP/CBD/SBSTTA/8/INF/7.

[19]   FAO website: http://www.fao.org/fishery/topic/4400/en (last accessed 26 May 2015).

[20]   General Assembly Resolution 17.38 of 1988, re-affirmed by Resolution 19.46 of 1994.

[21]   E. Molenaar and A.G. Oude Elferink, 'Marine Protected Areas in areas beyond national jurisdiction: The pioneering efforts under the OSPAR Convention' (2009) 5(1) *Utrecht Law Review* 5–20.

objective to conserve marine biodiversity. However, there is no global mechanism for the establishment of such multi-purpose or multi-sectoral MPAs. Instead, the prevailing approach to conservation and sustainable use at the international level is sectoral.

Several international organizations are already able to establish what can be called 'sectoral MPAs' or 'area-based management tools' in ABNJ. For example:

- The International Maritime Organization (IMO) can designate Particularly Sensitive Sea Areas (PSSA) to protect areas that, for recognized ecological, socio-economic or scientific reasons, may be vulnerable to damage by international maritime activities.[22] No PSSAs have been designated in ABNJ to date.
- The International Seabed Authority (ISA) can designate Areas of Particular Environmental Interest (APEI) and preservation reference zones.[23] The ISA has declared nine APEIs in the Clarion-Clipperton Zone (North Central Pacific).[24]
- Regional Fisheries Management Organizations (RFMO) can designate closures of certain fisheries to protect or restore the stocks they manage, or to protect the vulnerable marine ecosystems (VMEs) located on the seabed (pursuant to relevant UNGA resolutions).[25] Approximately 30 such closures have been made in the North-East Atlantic, the North-West Atlantic, and the South-East Atlantic.[26]

In parallel, a scientific process has been ongoing under the auspices of the CBD to identify ecologically or biologically significant marine areas (EBSAs). In 2008, the CBD adopted scientific criteria for this purpose.[27] These criteria are: uniqueness or rarity; special importance for life-history stages of species; importance for threatened, endangered or declining species and/or habitats; vulnerability, fragility, sensitivity or slow recovery; biological productivity; biological diversity and naturalness. Regional workshops to identify EBSAs are currently organized by the CBD together with relevant international and regional organizations.[28] Identification of an EBSA does not have any immediate legal effect, and the management of these marine areas remains in the hands of the competent authorities.

---

[22]    IMO, Revised guidelines for the identification and designation of Particularly Sensitive Sea Areas (PSSAs), 2005; A.982(24).

[23]    ISA, Decision of the Council of the International Seabed Authority relating to amendments to the Regulations on Prospecting and Exploration for Polymetallic Nodules in the Area and related matters. 2013; ISBA/19/C/17; Section V.31.6.

[24]    ISA, Decision of the Council relating to an environmental management plan for the Clarion-Clipperton Zone. 2012. ISBA/18C/22. https://www.isa.org.jm/files/documents/EN/18Sess/Council/ISBA-18C-22.pdf (last accessed 4 June 2015).

[25]    In particular Resolution 61/105: Sustainable fisheries, including through the 1995 Agreement for the Implementation of the Provisions of the United Nations Convention on the Law of the Sea of 10 December 1982 relating to the Conservation and Management of Straddling Fish Stocks and Highly Migratory Fish Stocks, and related instruments, UN Doc. A/RES/61/105 (2006).

[26]    Glen Wright, Jeff Ardron, Kristina Gjerde, and Julien Rochette, 'Advancing marine biodiversity protection through regional fisheries management: a review of high seas bottom fisheries closures' (2014) IDDRI Working Papers.

[27]    CBD COP 9, Decision IX/20 on Marine and coastal biodiversity, Annex I.

[28]    CBD COP 10, Decision IX/29 on Marine and coastal biodiversity, para. 36.

The need to establish an international framework for the creation and management of multi-sectoral and internationally-recognized MPAs in ABNJ has been considered in detail within the Ad Hoc Open-ended Informal Working Group to study issues relating to the conservation and sustainable use of marine biological diversity beyond national jurisdiction or 'BBNJ Working Group'.[29] Specific issues discussed have included the scientific basis for the establishment of MPAs in ABNJ, the processes to designate these areas, and the processes to adopt and enforce management measures relating to these areas.

## 4. REGIONAL INITIATIVES

Despite the difficulties of establishing MPAs in ABNJ, the practice is gaining momentum at the regional level where a number of initiatives have been taken to date. The regional approach to marine environmental protection provides an appropriate scale for the implementation of an ecosystem approach to conservation and often allows for political consensus among limited numbers of parties that share similar history, culture and interests in the region.[30] It is therefore appropriate that the LOSC has emphasized regional cooperation with regard to the marine environment, stipulating that States 'shall cooperate on a global basis and, as appropriate, on a regional basis' for the protection of the marine environment, 'taking into account regional features'.[31] Regional initiatives include those undertaken in the Mediterranean, the Southern Ocean, the North-East Atlantic, and the Sargasso Sea, although levels of success vary.

### 4.1  The Mediterranean

In 1995, the parties to the Barcelona Convention for the Protection of the Marine Environment and the Coastal Region of the Mediterranean[32] adopted the Protocol concerning Specially Protected Areas and Biological Diversity in the Mediterranean (SPA/BD Protocol),[33] which aims to 'protect, preserve and manage in a sustainable and environmentally sound way areas of particular natural or cultural value, notably by the establishment of specially protected areas'.[34] The Protocol invites states to designate

[29]   Elisabeth Druel, Julien Rochette, Raphaël Billé, and Claudio Chiarolla, A long and winding road: International discussions on the governance of marine biodiversity in areas beyond national jurisdiction (IDDRI Study 7/13. Paris 2013).

[30]   J. Rochette and L. Chabason, 'A regional approach to marine environmental protection: the regional seas experience', in P. Jacquet, R. Pachauri, L. Tubiana (eds), *A Planet for life 2011*, (TERI Press 2011) 111–21.

[31]   LOSC, Art. 197.

[32]   Convention on the Protection of the Mediterranean Sea against Pollution, 1976; amended in 1995 and renamed Convention for the Protection of the Marine Environment and the Coastal Region of the Mediterranean.

[33]   Protocol Concerning Specially Protected Areas and Biological Diversity in the Mediterranean (adopted 10 June 1995, entered into force 12 December 1999).

[34]   SPA/BD Protocol Article 3-1.

Specially Protected Areas of Mediterranean Importance (SPAMI), including in 'zones partly or wholly on the high seas'.[35]

In 1999, France, Monaco and Italy established the Pelagos Sanctuary for Mediterranean Marine Mammals to protect the eight resident cetacean species in the area.[36] The Sanctuary incorporates the territorial waters of these three states, but also ABNJ. In 2001, the Sanctuary was recognized as a SPAMI by the parties to the SPA/BD Protocol;[37] this means that all contracting parties to the Protocol must abide by the regulations adopted for the Sanctuary. A joint management plan was approved in 2004.[38] The Pelagos Sanctuary was therefore a first MPA partly covering high seas established within the framework of a regional sea.

A number of steps have been taken to ensure respect for and adherence to the MPA.[39] In a demonstration of both the need for and the potential of inter-organization cooperation and coordination, the General Fisheries Commission of the Mediterranean (GFCM) has closed the Sanctuary to fishing with towed dredges and bottom trawl-nets.[40] In recognition of its own obligations under the agreement, the Italian Navy has refrained from conducting naval exercises in the area; the Italian Ministry of the Environment discontinued discharge of certain wastes in Sanctuary waters; and a number of shipping companies have agreed to use the real time plotting of cetaceans (REPCET) system to avoid collisions with cetaceans.[41] The founding States have also committed to seeking recognition as a Particularly Sensitive Sea Area, though this has not yet come to fruition.[42]

Nevertheless, despite its ground-breaking nature, there is concern as to the effectiveness of the Pelagos Sanctuary. As noted by Sciara in 2009, 'in the 10 years since its creation, Pelagos has failed to fulfil its main goal of significantly improving the conservation status of the area's marine mammal populations, which are threatened by

---

[35]   SPA/BD Protocol Article 9-1.

[36]   Agreement Concerning the Creation of a Marine Mammal Sanctuary in the Mediterranean (25 November 1999). For information in English, see http://www.sanctuaire-pelagos.org/en (last accessed 26 May 2015).

[37]   UNEP/MAP, Report of the twelfth ordinary meeting of the Contracting Parties to the Convention for the protection of the Mediterranean Sea against pollution and its protocols, Monaco; 14–17 November, 2001, UNEP(DEC)/MED IG.13/8, 30 December 2001, Annex IV.

[38]   See http://www.sanctuaire-pelagos.org/en/about-us/management-plan (last accessed 26 May 2015).

[39]   Sabine Christiansen, 'Background document for the High Seas MPAs: Regional Approaches and Experiences side event at the 12th UNEP Global Meeting of the Regional Seas Conventions and Action Plans, 20th of September 2010' (WWF Germany 2010).

[40]   REC-GFCM/30/2006/3. There are no particular regulations for pelagic fishing.

[41]   REPCET website, http://www.repcet.com/docs/SE_2014_01_03_Pres-REPCET_en.pdf (last accessed 26 May 2015).

[42]   Pascal Mayol, Hélène Labach, Jérôme Couvat, Denis Ody, and Philippe Robert, 'Particularly Sensitive Sea Area (PSSA): An IMO status as an efficient management tool of Pelagos' (2013); Anaï Mangos and Sophie André, 'Analysis of Mediterranean marine environment protection: the case of the Pelagos Sanctuary' (Plan Bleu 2008). A list of declared PSSAs is available on the IMO's website: http://www.imo.org/OurWork/Environment/PSSAs/Pages/Default.aspx (last accessed 4 June 2015).

intense human pressures'.[43] Indeed, the management of the Pelagos Sanctuary has encountered difficulties over the years, mainly due to the absence of a dedicated management body.[44] However, in 2013, management of the Sanctuary was revitalized with the establishment of a permanent secretariat.

## 4.2 The Southern Ocean

The Antarctic continent and surrounding Southern Ocean are governed by the Antarctic Treaty System (ATS). The ATS comprises the Antarctic Treaty[45] (AT) and later agreements and conventions including, importantly, the Convention on the Conservation of Antarctic Marine Living Resources[46] (CAMLR Convention). A number of States had previously made territorial claims in Antarctica, though the AT 'freezes' all such claims.[47] The maritime area covered by the AT and the CAMLR Convention is generally considered to be ABNJ. The AT's governing body, the Antarctic Treaty Consultative Meeting (ATCM) has the competence to adopt measures, decisions and resolutions,[48] including on the 'preservation and conservation of living resources'.[49] In 1964 the parties adopted Agreed Measures for the Conservation of Antarctic Fauna and Flora,[50] which provided for the designation of Specially Protected Areas (SPA) to be protected through, inter alia, a prohibition on collecting native plants and the establishment of a permitting system.[51] These Measures were eventually supplanted by the Protocol on Environmental Protection to the AT (Madrid Protocol),[52] Annex V of which provides for the creation of two types of protected areas: Antarctic Specially Protected

---

[43]   Giuseppe Notarbartolo di Sciara. The Pelagos Sanctuary for the conservation of Mediterranean marine mammals: an iconic High Seas MPA in dire straits. In: 2nd International Conference on Progress in Marine Conservation in Europe. Stralsund, Germany, 2–6 November 2009.

[44]   Julien Rochette, Sebastian Unger, Dorothée Herr, David Johnson, Takehiro Nakamura, Tim Packeiser, Alexander Proelss, Martin Visbeck, Andrew Wright, and Daniel Cebrian, 'The regional approach to the conservation and sustainable use of marine biodiversity in areas beyond national jurisdiction' (2014) 49 *Marine Policy* 109–17.

[45]   Antarctic Treaty (adopted 1 December 1959, entered into force 23 June 1961) 402 UNTS 71 (AT).

[46]   Convention on the Conservation of Antarctic Marine Living Resources (20 May 1980, entered into force 7 April 1982) 1329 UNTS 48 (CAMLR Convention).

[47]   CAMLR Convention, Article IV.

[48]   According to Article IX of the AT, decisions and resolutions are not legally binding for Contracting Parties, whereas measures are legally binding once they have been adopted by all Contracting Parties.

[49]   Article IX(1)(f) of the AT.

[50]   Recommendation ATCM III-VIII, *Agreed Measures for the Conservation of Antarctic Fauna and Flora.*

[51]   Ibid., Article VIII.

[52]   Protocol on Environmental Protection to the Antarctic Treaty (adopted 4 October 1991, entered into force 14 January 1998) (Madrid Protocol).

Areas (ASPA) and Antarctic Specially Managed Areas (ASMA). In such areas, activity is prohibited, restricted or managed in accordance with Management Plans.[53]

The establishment of an ASPA or an ASMA is effected by submission of a proposed management plan through the Committee for Environmental Protection (CEP), to the ATCM.[54] ASPAs and ASMAs can contain a marine component, or be entirely marine-based, in which case their designation must be coordinated with the Commission on the Conservation of Antarctic Marine Living Resources (CCAMLR), established by the CCAMLR Convention. Initially only small coastal zones were protected as part of a wider terrestrial protected area. However, more recently, small protected zones have been created solely for marine areas[55] and in 2009, the CEP agreed to work towards the establishment of effective, representative and coherent spatial protection of marine biodiversity through the designation of ASPAs and ASMAs.[56] This has effectively brought CCAMLR to the forefront of the move to establish MPAs in the Southern Ocean.

Established in 1982, CCAMLR is charged with ensuring the conservation, defined as including 'rational use', of Antarctic marine living resources.[57] Famously known for its express invocation of the 'ecosystem approach'[58] the Commission is tasked, inter alia, with implementing conservation measures[59] which may include the 'opening and closing of areas, regions or sub-regions for purposes of scientific study or conservation, including special areas for protection and scientific study'.[60]

CCAMLR's parties have long agreed, in principle, on the need for and desirability of MPAs. Moving beyond in principle agreement has, however, been hampered, inter alia, by concerns of fishing states regarding restrictions on access to lucrative fishing areas. In 2008 the Report of the CCAMLR Performance Review Panel highlighted the need for CCAMLR to progress MPAs,[61] calling for CCAMLR to propose marine areas as either ASPAs or ASMAs, and to utilize the provisions of CAMLR Convention allowing for the closure of certain areas for conservation purposes.[62] Building on the work of CCAMLR's Scientific Committee, which had been tasked to provide advice on identifying a coherent and representative network of MPAs in the Southern Ocean, eleven priority areas for conservation were adopted by the Commission in 2008.[63]

---

[53]   Madrid Protocol, Annex V. The difference between the two types of protected areas that might be created through Annex V of the Madrid Protocol is the degree of protection granted.

[54]   Madrid Protocol, Annex V, Art. 5(1). While the CEP and the Scientific Committee are also able to submit plans, they are generally submitted by the Contracting Parties.

[55]   Eg, ASPAS No. 144, 145, 146, 152 153, and 161. ASMA No. 7 is a good example of a protected area that covers more marine area than terrestrial. See *List and status of Antarctic Specially Protected Area and Antarctic Specially Managed Area Management Plans*, available on the ATS website: http://www.ats.aq/e/ep_protected.htm (last accessed 26 May 2015).

[56]   Final Report of the Thirty-second Antarctic Treaty Consultative Meeting, Baltimore, United States, 6–17 April 2009,119.

[57]   CAMLR Convention, Art. II.

[58]   CAMLR Convention, Art. II.

[59]   CAMLR Convention, Art. IX(1)(f).

[60]   CAMLR Convention, Art. IX(2)(g).

[61]   CCAMLR, Performance Review Panel (1 September 2008).

[62]   CAMLR Convention, Art. IX(2)(g).

[63]   CCAMLR, Report of the Twenty-seventh meeting of the Commission (2008).

In 2009, CCAMLR endorsed a roadmap established by its Scientific Committee in order to fulfil the international requirements to establish a coherent and representative network of MPAs by 2012. The same year CCAMLR adopted its first MPA on the continental shelf of the South Orkney Islands in which fishing and the dumping or discharge of wastes by fishing vessels was prohibited.[64] To avoid the problems caused by free riders the Secretariat was tasked with the role of informing non-parties of the measure where their nationals or vessels were in the area.

In 2011 a scientific workshop discussed several additional MPA proposals,[65] including a proposal by the UK on the protection of regional sea-ice and ice shelf features subject to climate change; a proposal by Australia and France for an area in East Antarctica and two concurrent proposals by the USA and by New Zealand in the Ross Sea. The Commission also adopted Conservation Measure 91-04 (2011) which sets up a general framework for the establishment of CCAMLR MPAs. However, despite some progress, and the 2009 Road Map commitments, CCAMLR has come to something of a standstill regarding MPAs. At its 2012 meeting, the Commission failed to reach agreement on the designation of new MPAs.[66] Believing agreement was close the Commission took the unusual step of calling for a special meeting to discuss the proposals further, only the second such meeting to have taken place in the history of the Commission. At the Special Meeting of the Commission held in July 2013, there was again no agreement.[67] Indeed, some states began to question the entire MPA creation process, asserting that the CCAMLR may not have the legal authority required to designate MPAs.[68] The proposals are yet to be adopted.

### 4.3   The North-East Atlantic

The OSPAR Convention[69] encompasses both ABNJ and the national waters of the fifteen contracting parties within its area. Annex V on the Protection and Conservation of the Ecosystems and Biological Diversity of the Maritime Area specifically encourages the parties to take measures to protect and conserve marine biodiversity in the Convention area, and to restore adversely impacted areas.[70]

---

[64]   CCAMLR, CM 91-03 (2009), Protection of the South Orkney Islands Southern Shelf, para. 1.

[65]   CCAMLR, WS-MPA-11, Report on the Workshop on Marine Protected Areas, paras 6.5 and 6.6. Work to develop MPAs within the 11 previously identified priority areas was still encouraged.

[66]   CCAMLR, Report of the Thirty-First Meeting of the Commission 2012, paras 7.60–7.109.

[67]   *Ibid.,* paras 7.105–7.109.

[68]   CCAMLR-SM-II/BG/10, On absence of legal ability to organize marine protected areas in the high seas of the World Ocean, including the Antarctic waters, Delegation of Ukraine.

[69]   Convention for the Protection of the Marine Environment of the North-East Atlantic (adopted 22 September 1992, entered into force 25 March 1998) 2354 UNTS 67 (OSPAR Convention).

[70]   OSPAR Convention Annex V on the protection and conservation of the ecosystems and biological diversity of the maritime area (24 July 1998, last updated 18 May 2006).

For several years, the OSPAR Commission has focused attention on the management of human activities in ABNJ. At the 2003 ministerial meeting, the Parties agreed to establish an ecologically coherent network of well-managed MPAs by 2010.[71] As it became clear that this objective would not be met, revised targets were adopted at the 2010 ministerial meeting with the parties agreeing to establish an ecologically coherent network of MPAs by 2012, with the objective that it should be well-managed by 2016.[72] At the same meeting, six decisions and six recommendations were adopted regarding the establishment of six MPAs in ABNJ. The legally binding decisions formally established the MPAs and defined their geographical boundaries,[73] while the non-legally binding recommendations deal with management.[74] A seventh MPA was agreed in 2012.[75] Despite this apparent success however, an assessment of ecological coherence has since been conducted, finding that OSPAR's MPA network is not yet fully coherent, and gaps remain.[76]

To move these processes forward in 2009 the OSPAR Commission initiated the 'Madeira Process' which developed a draft 'Collective Arrangement' setting out the joint principles and specifications for collaborative management of selected aspects of biodiversity protection. The OSPAR Commission endorsed the text in 2011[77] and the Secretariats of the other participating organizations, the North East Atlantic Fisheries Commission (NEAFC) and the International Seabed Authority (ISA), are currently considering their position.[78] In the meantime, OSPAR has moved ahead with the development of Guidelines for the management of its MPAs[79] which may serve as a starting point for the development of a collective management plan for a pilot site.

Despite these promising developments, it is recognized that such processes are 'time- and labour-intensive' particularly where the other organizations involved have 'different levels of technical scrutiny and sometimes complex and mutually incompatible annual

---

[71]    OSPAR Recommendation 2003/3 on a network of Marine Protected Areas.

[72]    OSPAR Recommendation 2010/2 on amending Recommendation 2003/3 on a network of Marine Protected Areas.

[73]    OSPAR Decisions 2010/1-6. See David Freestone, David Johnson, Jeff Ardron, Kate Killerlain Morrison, and Sebastian Unger, 'Can existing institutions protect biodiversity in areas beyond national jurisdiction? Experiences from two on-going processes' (2014) 49 *Marine Policy* 167–75.

[74]    OSPAR Recommendations 2010/12-17.

[75]    OSPAR Commission, 2012 Status Report on the OSPAR Network of Marine Protected Areas (2013), http://www.ospar.org/documents/dbase/publications/p00618/p00618_2012_mpa_status%20report.pdf (last accessed 26 May 2015).

[76]    D. Johnson and others, 'An Assessment of the Ecological Coherence of the OSPAR Network of Marine Protected Areas in 2012' (OSPAR Commission 2013).

[77]    OSPAR Convention for the Protection of the Marine Environment of the North-East Atlantic. Meeting of the OSPAR Commission: London. Summary Record; 2011, Annex 15.

[78]    David Johnson, 'Can Competent Authorities Cooperate for the Common Good: Towards a Collective Arrangement in the North-East Atlantic' in Paul Arthur Berkman and Alexander N. Vylegzhanin (eds), *Environmental Security in the Arctic Ocean* (Springer Netherlands 2013).

[79]    Guidelines for the Management of Marine Protected Areas in the OSPAR Maritime Area (Ref: 2003-18) as amended in 2006 by the OSPAR Biodiversity Committee (BDC) (BDC Summary Record 2006 (0610/1) para. 3.46).

meeting cycles'.[80] This makes agreement on a comprehensive and holistic MPA difficult. Nonetheless, the Collective Arrangement provides an example of how more formal cooperation between competent organizations could be advanced at the international level.

With respect to the seven MPAs already designated in ABNJ, there have been discussions within the OSPAR Commission to consider a proposal for possible IMO protective measures. France was tasked by the OSPAR Commission to undertake a technical study to assess the vulnerability of the MPAs to the impacts of shipping and the possibility to use IMO's spatial tools for environmental protection (such as PSSAs) to protect one or several of these areas. It concluded that:

> apart from the 'spatial tools', Special Areas and Particularly Sensitive Sea Areas, the IMO may develop regulations to address the specific impacts detailed previously ... A way forward to work on the implementation of specific regulations to protect the OSPAR HSMPAs from the impacts of shipping could consist in selecting a pilot case study. ... the Josephine seamount HSMPA could be a relevant candidate.[81]

The study was presented during the OSPAR Commission meeting in June 2012[82] and it was decided that France, with the support of other contracting parties, would undertake the proposed pilot study on the Josephine seamount MPA.[83]

### 4.4 An Initiative for the Governance of the Sargasso Sea

In comparison to other regional marine areas, the institutional landscape in the Sargasso Sea is underdeveloped. There is no regional treaty regime specifically applicable to the marine environment of the Sargasso Sea and the only fisheries regime is that of the International Commission for the Conservation of Atlantic Tunas (ICCAT) which applies to tuna in the area.[84]

However, despite lacking a defined regional governance framework, novel and creative efforts have been made to establish area-based management tools in the area.[85] In 2011, the Sargasso Sea Alliance (SSA) was launched as a partnership among the Government of Bermuda, NGOs, scientists and private donors. The SSA aims to establish a management regime, use existing regimes to secure protection of the

---

[80]  Freestone et al., above n 73.

[81]  OSPAR Document 12/6/7 Rev.1-E, *Progress on a proposal for possible IMO protective measures in the OSPAR HSMPAs*, 25.

[82]  Ibid.

[83]  If agreed by Portugal, as the continental shelf of this area is subject to a submission to the CLCS made by this country. OSPAR Document 12/22/1-E, *Summary Record of the 2012 Meeting of the OSPAR Commission*, 19.

[84]  The International Commission for the Conservation of Atlantic Tunas (ICCAT) is the only competent RFMO in the region: its area of competence covers a much greater area than the Sargasso Sea alone, and it is only responsible for the conservation of tunas and tuna-like species. The Northwest Atlantic Fisheries Organization (NAFO) regulatory area may overlap very slightly with Sargasso Sea, but this is insignificant.

[85]  K.K. Morrison and D. Freestone, 'The Sargasso Sea' (2104) 29 *International Journal of Marine and Coastal Law* 345–62.

Sargasso Sea, and to act as an example what can and cannot be delivered through existing institutions in ABNJ.[86]

Bermuda, with the support of the Alliance, has already submitted information to the CBD regarding the Sargasso Sea for its potential designation as an Ecologically or Biologically Significant Marine Area (EBSA).[87] A range of additional actions for advancing the conservation of this region is currently being considered by the Alliance. These options include: recognition of the Sargasso Sea as a UNESCO World Heritage Site; regulation of tuna fishing activities that may have adverse impacts on the marine environment through ICCAT;[88] regulation of navigation through IMO, possibly through the designation of a PSSA with associated protective measures;[89] coordination and cooperation with ISA with respect to mining activities; and initiation of coordination and cooperation with relevant actors.[90]

In March 2014, the Hamilton Declaration on Collaboration for the Conservation of the Sargasso Sea was adopted.[91] This is a non-binding agreement to collaborate to pursue conservation measures through existing regional and international organizations. It was signed by Bermuda, Azores, Monaco, UK and USA. Five international and regional organizations also participated as observers.[92] The Declaration proposes new institutional arrangements, including regular meetings of the signatories, the establishment of a Secretariat, and the creation of a scientific advisory body, the Sargasso Sea Commission (which was constituted in August 2014). The Declaration also considers funding modalities and establishment of a financial mechanism, including a trust. According to the Declaration, the Commission will develop proposals for submission to competent regional and international bodies.

## 4.5 Regional Initiatives: Challenges and Lessons Learnt

The foregoing discussion has highlighted the role of regional organizations in the conservation of marine biodiversity in ABNJ and identified a number of important challenges that require further consideration.

The first challenge relates to lack of geographic coverage. It will be immediately apparent that only a handful of regional agreements currently exist that have a mandate

---

[86]  Freestone et al., above n 73.

[87]  Decision Adopted by the Conference of the Parties to the Convention on Biological Diversity at its Eleventh Meeting, XI/17. Marine and Coastal Biodiversity: Ecologically or Biologically Significant Marine Areas, UNEP/CBD/COP/DEC/XI/17, 23, item 13.

[88]  The UK is a member of ICCAT.

[89]  Again this would have to be carried out in conjunction with the UK as Bermuda is not a member of IMO.

[90]  Through a collective arrangement or agreement, either based on the OSPAR model or an international declaration or agreement modelled on the 1999 Titanic Agreement (The Agreement Concerning the Shipwrecked Vessel *RMS Titanic* of 1999 was signed by Canada, France, the UK and the USA and concerned the protection of the shipwrecked vessel *RMS Titanic*, which lies in ABNJ in the North East Atlantic Ocean).

[91]  See Morrison and Freestone, above n 85.

[92]  OSPAR; the ISA; the Inter-American Convention for the Conservation of Atlantic Sea Turtles, the CMS; and IUCN.

covering ABNJ and therefore the capacity to establish MPAs in these areas. This represents a critical obstacle for the development of regional initiatives in ABNJ, although there is increasing interest in leveraging other existing agreements, including those adopted under the UNEP Regional Seas Programme, in ABNJ. In the South Pacific, for example, the Permanent Commission for the South Pacific (CPPS) adopted in 2012 the Galapagos Declaration, in which signatories committed to promote a coordinated action 'regarding their interests on living and non-living resources in marine areas beyond national jurisdiction'.[93] More recently, contracting parties to the Abidjan Convention[94] adopted in 2014 Decision CP 11/10 requesting the Secretariat 'to set up a working group to study all aspects of the conservation and sustainable use of marine biological diversity beyond areas of national jurisdiction within the framework of the Abidjan Convention'.

The second challenge is that of ensuring coordination and cooperation among and across sectoral organizations. As has been demonstrated in the OSPAR case, coordination and cooperation is critical for the establishment of MPAs in ABNJ because many activities fall under the mandate of particular sectoral organizations dealing with, for example, whaling, fishing, navigation and seabed mining. The establishment of a number of memoranda of understanding (MoUs) between organizations provides one possibility for cooperation. However, this approach has its limitations given that MoUs only establish bilateral cooperation, their conclusion among and between multiple actors is time consuming, and the existence of multiple MoUs increases the complexity of an already crowded regulatory landscape. The 'Madeira Process' initiated by OSPAR is a promising solution that could improve cooperation, though it too has proved time consuming and difficult to advance in practice.

A third challenge that can be identified relates to leadership and vision. The limited experience to date suggests that, under current regional governance arrangements, successful implementation of MPAs in ABNJ requires a regional 'champion' that has the political will to advance marine biodiversity protection in ABNJ. In this regard, the OSPAR Commission has demonstrated its leadership in establishing the first network of MPAs in ABNJ, while the SSA is showing strong initiative in the absence of an established regulatory framework or precedent.

A fourth challenge is that of ensuring ecological coherence. Regional agreements and organizations must strive to establish ecologically coherent protection. For example, within the OSPAR MPAs, almost 10 per cent of the Greater North Sea is covered by MPAs[95] whereas less than 2 per cent of the Arctic waters are covered.[96] Shared scientific organizations and the ESBA process may have a role to play. For example, OSPAR and NEAFC jointly receive scientific advice from the International Council for the Exploration of the Sea (ICES), which guarantees a certain level of consistency.

---

[93]   Commitment to Galapagos for the XXI Century, Permanent Commission for the South Pacific, VIII Meeting of Ministers of Foreign Affairs, Puerto Ayora, Galápagos, Ecuador, 17 August 2012.

[94]   Convention for the Co-operation in the Protection and Development of the Marine and Coastal Environment of the West and Central African Region (adopted 23 March 1981, entered into force 5 August 1984) 20 *International Legal Materials* 746.

[95]   Including areas within and beyond national jurisdiction.

[96]   OSPAR, 2011 Status Report on the OSPAR Network of Marine Protected Areas, 15.

ESBAs can serve both a scientific and 'promotional' importance, even though designation will not automatically secure additional protection.

Finally, it is crucial to underline that many regional organizations remain weak in terms of human and financial resources. Developing regional activities in ABNJ would therefore necessitate the provision of additional and adequate resources.

## 5. INTERNATIONAL PROVISION FOR MPAs IN ABNJ

While a number of international agreements and institutions have mandates to establish area-based management measures in ABNJ, there is currently no institution with an explicit mandate to establish cross-sectoral MPAs, nor a global procedure to bring together the various organizations in order to achieve this. Given the increasing awareness of the growing threats to marine biodiversity in ABNJ, the international community has increasingly turned its attention to the possibility of negotiating an implementing agreement to the LOSC relating specifically to the conservation and sustainable use of marine biodiversity in ABNJ.

### 5.1   A New International Legally Binding Instrument on Marine Biodiversity in ABNJ

Current discussions on marine biodiversity in ABNJ have their origins in the BBNJ Working Group established by the United Nations General Assembly in 2004. In 2012, the United Nations Conference on Sustainable Development (Rio+20) committed to address, on an urgent basis, the issue of the conservation and sustainable use of marine biological diversity of areas beyond national jurisdiction including by taking a decision on the development of an international instrument under LOSC.[97] Three meetings of the BBNJ Working Group were held in order to discuss whether or not negotiations should commence, culminating in January 2015 with the historic step of agreeing to open negotiations for a new international legally binding instrument under the LOSC.[98]

### 5.2   MPAs under a New LOSC Implementing Agreement

While the precise content of any eventual implementing agreement (IA) remains a matter of speculation, it is clear that it will include provisions on 'measures such as

---

[97]   UN, 'The Future We Want' (2012) para. 162; Glen Wright, Julien Rochette, Sebastian Unger, Kristina Gjerde, and Jeff Ardron, 'The Scores at Half Time: An update on the international discussions on the governance of marine biodiversity in areas beyond national jurisdiction' (IDDRI Issue Brief 2/14. Paris 2014).

[98]   Julien Rochette, Glen Wright, Kristina Gjerde, Thomas Greiber, Sebastian Unger, and Aurélie Spadone, 'A new chapter for the high seas? Historic decision to negotiate an international legally-binding instrument on the conservation and sustainable use of marine biodiversity in areas beyond national jurisdiction' (IDDRI Issue Brief 2/15. Paris, 2015).

area-based management tools, including marine protected areas'.[99] In order to consider what the substantive content of the new LOSC IA may be in relation to MPAs, it is helpful to think of the designation of an MPA as a process requiring a number of steps to be taken. These include: (i) the description of a suitable area according to determined scientific criteria; (ii) the proposal of an MPA; (iii) official designation by a competent authority; and (iv) the adoption of a management plan and management measures aimed at meeting the objectives of the MPA.

A number of sets of scientific criteria for identifying MPAs, or similar areas, have already been developed, such as EBSAs, VMEs, and PSSAs, mentioned above. A new IA could utilize any one of these approaches, establish a new set of criteria inspired by them, or both. There is even the possibility that the criteria could go beyond merely scientific factors so as to include areas of socio-economic, cultural, and educational importance.[100]

As to the manner in which an MPA might be proposed, options include proposal by one or a number of states, by a specific body convened under the auspices of the IA, or by NGOs or organizations with state support. Provision may be needed to ensure that a dedicated scientific body considers proposals and that they are officially designated by a Conference of the Parties or relevant organizational meeting. Rules for decision-making will also be needed, for example provision that MPA designations must be approved by two-thirds (or greater or lesser) majority of the COP or relevant organization.

Given the fragmented nature of international marine governance, there are many potential structures that could be implemented for the adoption of management plans and management measures for meeting the objectives of an MPA. Indeed, adoption of a management plan may not be necessary; the focus being placed instead on the adoption of specific management measures. Alternatively, a proponent may be required to submit a management plan when proposing an MPA, or one could be subsequently developed and adopted by an organ of the IA. In any event, management measures will be an essential part of ensuring the effectiveness of the MPA and mechanisms for their adoption will be needed. Such mechanisms could include proposals along with the MPA, or development by states cooperating directly and through competent international, regional, and sectoral organizations. To this end, regional working groups or advisory bodies could be established to bring together states, competent organizations, scientists, and other stakeholders in order to consider the management of MPAs in a given region.

---

[99] Recommendations of the Ad Hoc Open-ended Informal Working Group to study issues relating to the conservation and sustainable use of marine biological diversity beyond areas of national jurisdiction to the sixty-ninth session of the General Assembly, 23 January 2015, para. 6.

[100] This is already the case for PSSAs. The IMO criteria for identification of PSSAs identifies 'social, cultural, and economic criteria' and 'scientific and educational criteria' as two of the three categories for designation of a PSSA. An area can be designated as a PSSA on the basis of one criterion alone: IMO resolution A.982 (24) of 1 December 2005, s. 44.

### 5.3   Relationship between an LOSC IA and Regional Initiatives

A critical issue to be considered in the development of a new IA will be its relationship with existing regional and sectoral agreements and arrangements. States have already been discussing the relationship between a new agreement and regional initiatives at a general level within the BBNJ Working Group. Indeed, the discussion has already begun with many delegations at the June 2014 BBNJ Working Group meeting,[101] recognizing the need to leverage existing regional mechanisms. However, the specific role of existing regional mechanisms within any future LOSC IA is yet to be determined.

In guiding that determination it seems that an underlying assumption should be that legal instruments and governance approaches at the global and regional levels would complement each other. In other words, while a global agreement will strengthen the legal mandate for regional activities, regional organizations can also facilitate implementation of the overarching global legal framework. Thus, in specific relation to MPAs, the possibility should be considered that existing regional MPAs could either be formally recognized under a new IA, or at least presented as proposals for internationally recognized MPAs, so long as they fulfil the criteria for being adopted. Once an MPA has been adopted, regardless of the process, regional frameworks will likely have a key role to play in implementing the management plan and measures, and potentially a role in oversight and review. Table 13.1 sets out some of the options available for the designation of MPAs under a new LOSC IA.

Despite its future promise, the opening of the negotiations for an international instrument does not diminish the need to advance sectoral and regional initiatives to conserve and sustainably use marine biodiversity in ABNJ. To achieve truly meaningful protection of marine biodiversity in ABNJ these must be strengthened hand in hand with the development of the new agreement. As the outcome of the negotiations and the entering into force of the new agreement remains unpredictable, the development of regionally driven measures should not be postponed.

## 6.   CONCLUSION

As this chapter has demonstrated, the establishment of MPAs in ABNJ is neither easy nor straightforward and their success is not assured. However, as the regional experiences discussed in this chapter illustrate, the protection of biodiversity in ABNJ through the designation of MPAs can be incrementally increased through existing frameworks. Nevertheless, it is also clear that, despite much progress, there are significant limitations to the MPA approach. These efforts may not be able to keep pace with rapidly increasing pressures in ABNJ. At the same time, area-based tools at the international level are fragmented across a range of sectoral institutions and are not currently utilized in a unified manner conducive to the creation of MPAs in ABNJ. To this end, the recent decision of the BBNJ Working Group to recommend the commencement of negotiations for a new international agreement is encouraging.

---

[101]   Wright et al., above n 97.

*Table 13.1 Potential options for the designation of MPAs under a new LOSC IA*

| Scientific basis | Proposal | Designation | Adoption of management measures | Implementation | Review/oversight |
|---|---|---|---|---|---|
| • One or multiple bases<br>• EBSAs<br>• VMEs<br>• Criteria from regional organizations<br>• New set of criteria<br>• Amalgamation of existing sectoral/regional criteria | • UNCLOS IA Scientific Committee<br>• Dedicated MPA body<br>• Regional Organizations<br>• Group of States<br>• International organizations (e.g. UNESCO, CBD, IOC, IMO, FAO, UNEP, etc.)<br>• Continuation/ evolution of the BBNJ WG<br>• Stakeholder/civil society body<br>• INGOs/Groups of NGOs | • UNCLOS COP<br>• UNCLOS COP after Scientific Committee approval<br>• UNGA – annual oceans resolution<br>• CBD<br>• Other international organization(s) nominated by IA. | • Cooperation and coordination between competent organizations in drafting management plan<br>• Either through agreed mechanism, or 'informally', as at present<br>• Elaboration by Scientific Committee/ regional sub-committees | • States<br>• Regional organizations<br>• Relevant international sectoral organizations | • Compliance Committee (potential division between enforcement and facilitation)<br>• COP<br>• Stakeholder Forum<br>• Secretariat<br>• Civil society |

*Source:* Author.

289

Overall, it seems that a two-pronged approach to achieving progress towards the international community's expressed goals for the establishment of MPAs in ABNJ is necessary. First, existing institutions and regional frameworks should be supported, reinforced, and their use expanded. This will strengthen protection of ABNJ in the interim, while also feeding into the ongoing international process. Second, states should approach the negotiations for a new international agreement with a sense of urgency and ambition, cognizant of the challenges that lie ahead,[102] but determined to improve the capacity of oceans governance frameworks to meet the challenges of the future.

---

[102]   Rochette et al., above n 98.

# 14. Environmental assessment in marine areas beyond national jurisdiction

*Robin Warner*

## 1. INTRODUCTION

The range and volume of human activities affecting the marine environment has risen exponentially since the birth of the environmental movement in the 1960s. Conventional uses of the oceans such as navigation and fishing are intensifying while the catalogue of new uses such as hydrocarbon and minerals exploitation, bioprospecting, marine geo-engineering and ocean energy production continues to grow. Knowledge of the threats posed to the oceans by human activity has expanded beyond marine pollution to encompass recognition of the risks posed to vulnerable marine ecosystems by overfishing, destructive fisheries practices and invasive exploitation of living and non-living marine resources. However, with the developing state of marine scientific research into marine ecosystems and the biodiversity of the oceans, the majority of activities at sea continue to take place in a climate of uncertainty as to their long term impacts on the components of marine biodiversity. Our appreciation of the nature and extent of human impacts on the marine environment is still to a large degree bounded by the embryonic state of our knowledge of the marine biodiversity of the oceans.

Assessing the impact of human activities on the marine environment introduces additional challenges to those confronted on land. Many of these differences stem from the three dimensional nature of the marine environment with its great depths, pressure and lack of light beneath the photic zone.[1] Others relate to the slow growth rates of many marine organisms leading to delays in recovery from impacts and the extensive interconnections between marine ecosystems compounding the adverse effects of the initial impact. In addition to these physical challenges, there are practical challenges in assessing the impacts of activities which occur in remote locations far from land with scant logistical support.[2] While governance structures will generally exist to facilitate environmental assessment[3] in marine areas within national jurisdiction closer to the

---

[1]   Report of the Expert Workshop on Scientific and Technical Aspects relevant to Environmental Impact Assessment in Marine Areas beyond National Jurisdiction UNEP/CBD/EW-EIAMA/2, 20 November 2009, http://www.cbd.int/doc?meeting=EWEIAMA-01 (last accessed 26 May 2015).

[2]   Ibid, Annex II, paras 3–6.

[3]   In this chapter, the term 'environmental assessment' is used to refer to all facets of measuring the impact of human activities on the environment. This includes the typical process of prior environmental impact assessment and extends through post-activity monitoring of environmental impacts. Within those processes the term environmental assessment also encompasses the conduct of environmental baseline studies and the measurement of single as well as cumulative impacts on marine environments over time. Cross jurisdictional application of

shore, these structures are still developing for marine areas beyond national jurisdiction (ABNJ).⁴

Notwithstanding these significant challenges, global and regional organizations and national governments have devised some governance structures to underpin the measurement of human impacts on the marine environment. These encompass legally binding instruments at global and regional levels and national legislation supplemented by non-binding guidelines and other policy documents. In addition, customary practices have developed for environmental assessment in different marine sectors. This chapter reviews the existing international law and policy framework for environmental assessment in ABNJ highlighting key gaps in legal and institutional coverage at global, regional and sectoral levels. It explores the complex challenges involved in implementing environmental assessment in ABNJ and the steps that have been taken within particular marine sectors to develop a more comprehensive and robust framework for environmental assessment in these extensive areas of the ocean. It discusses recent global initiatives for developing the international law framework for conservation and sustainable use of marine biodiversity in ABNJ and the rationale for including environmental assessment provisions in a potential international agreement under the LOSC. Finally, it critically analyzes options for incorporating environmental assessment elements in such an agreement.

## 2.  INTERNATIONAL LAW FRAMEWORK FOR ENVIRONMENTAL ASSESSMENT IN ABNJ

Environmental impact assessment is acknowledged as a key element in the suite of tools for biodiversity conservation, and its application to activities affecting the marine environment has been endorsed in many international law instruments, policy statements by governments and international organizations and the decisions of international tribunals.⁵ For ABNJ, however, many of these instruments and decisions posit general

---

Environmental Impact Assessment (EIA) and strategic environmental assessment (SEA) of plans, programmes and policies likely to impact on the marine environment over longer periods and broader geographical areas are also included in the term environmental assessment.

⁴  Marine areas beyond national jurisdiction (ABNJ) include both the high seas water column and the deep seabed beyond national jurisdiction (the Area).

⁵  These instruments include the regional seas conventions, the 1982 United Nations Convention on the Law of the Sea (LOSC); the Protocol on Environmental Protection to the Antarctic Treaty (Madrid Protocol), 4 October 1991, 1998 ATS 6 (entered into force 14 January 1998); 1995 Agreement for the Implementation of the Provisions of the UN Convention on the Law of the Sea of 10 December 1982 relating to the Conservation and Management of Straddling Fish Stocks and Highly Migratory Fish Stocks, New York, 4 August 1995, 2167 UNTS 3 (entered into force 11 December 2001) (UN Fish Stocks Agreement or UNFSA); and the International Seabed Authority's Regulations for exploration contractors, see footnotes 64 and 65 and accompanying text, infra. Cases of international tribunals include *Gabčíkovo-Nagymaros Project* (Hungary/Slovakia) (1997) ICJ Rep 7, para. 141; *Mox Plant* Case (Provisional Measures) ITLOS No 10 (2001) para. 82; *Pulp Mills on the River Uruguay Case* (Argentina/Uruguay) (Provisional Measures) (2006) ICJ Rep, para. 204 and the International

obligations to conduct EIA rather than specific implementing provisions or underpinning institutional infrastructure.

## 2.1 Global Instruments

### 2.1.1 United Nations Convention on the Law of the Sea (LOSC)

The 1982 United Nations Convention on the Law of the Sea (LOSC)[6] imposes a general obligation on States Parties to assess the potential effects of activities under their jurisdiction or control that may cause substantial pollution of, or significant and harmful changes to, the marine environment. Although the general obligation to conduct environmental assessment of activities with the potential for significant and harmful impacts on the marine environment is well established in both customary and conventional international law, implementation of this obligation for marine areas beyond national jurisdiction (ABNJ)[7] is fragmented between different sectors and regions. There is no overarching international agreement which develops in more specific terms the obligation contained in Article 206 of the LOSC to assess the potential effects of planned activities under States' jurisdiction or control in ABNJ. The LOSC obligations are broad in scope extending to all parts of the marine environment but there are no detailed methodological or procedural requirements specified for environmental assessment in marine and coastal areas. States Parties have a duty to publish reports of assessments to 'competent international organizations', but these organizations are not specified and the timescale for provision of reports is not prescribed. Similarly, institutional coverage for ABNJ under the LOSC is far from comprehensive with no global body having overarching responsibility for protection and preservation of the marine environment or conservation of marine biodiversity beyond national jurisdiction.[8] The International Seabed Authority (ISA) has comprehensive environmental protection powers for seabed mining activities affecting the Area,[9] but this advanced environmental governance situation for the deep seabed beyond national jurisdiction is not matched by a global institution with comparable environmental protection powers for the high seas water column. These general obligations to conduct environmental assessment and monitoring under the LOSC must therefore be read in conjunction with the more specific environmental principles and procedural provisions which have been developed in other hard and soft international

---

Tribunal of the Law of the Sea, *Advisory Opinion on Responsibilities and Obligations of States Sponsoring Persons and Entities with Respect to Activities in the Area*, 1 February 2011, http://www.itlos.org/fileadmin/itlos/documents/cases/case_no_17/adv_op_010211.pdf (last accessed 26 May 2015), p. 44, para. 145.

[6] Opened for signature 10 December 1982, entered into force 16 November 1994, 1833 UNTS 3.

[7] Marine areas beyond national jurisdiction (ABNJ) include both the high seas water column and the deep seabed beyond national jurisdiction (the Area).

[8] Dire Tladi, 'Conservation and sustainable use of marine biodiversity in areas beyond national jurisdiction: towards an implementing agreement', Chapter 12 in this volume.

[9] Michael Lodge, 'Protecting the marine environment of the deep seabed', Chapter 7 in this volume.

environmental law instruments such as the UNEP Goals and Principles of EIA and the Convention on Biological Diversity (CBD)[10] and its EIA associated guidelines.

### 2.1.2   UNEP Goals and Principles of EIA (UNEP Principles)

The 1987 UNEP Principles represent one of the earliest global elaborations of the objectives and fundamental procedures encompassed in EIA.[11] They provide an internationally accepted model of the minimum requirements for effective EIA. Principle 1 specifies that an EIA should include a description of the proposed activity, a description of the potentially affected environment, including specific information necessary for identifying and assessing the environmental effects of the proposed activity, a description of the practical alternatives, and an assessment of the likely or potential environmental impacts of the proposed activity and alternatives, including the direct, indirect, cumulative, short-term and long-term effects. The proponent of the activity subject to an EIA should also provide an identification and description of measures available to mitigate adverse environmental impacts of the proposed activity and alternatives, and an assessment of those measures. Finally the proponent should indicate any gaps in knowledge and uncertainties that may be encountered in compiling the required information and whether the environment of any other state or of ABNJ is likely to be affected by the proposed activity or alternatives.

The general obligation to consult with interested stakeholders on an EIA before a decision is made to proceed with an activity is recognized in Principle 7 which provides that '… government agencies, members of the public, experts in relevant disciplines and interested groups should be allowed appropriate opportunity to comment on the EIA'. For activities affecting the marine areas of ABNJ, this immediately raises the question of who qualifies as an interested stakeholder particularly for ABNJ, and which global, regional or national organization is responsible for administering and responding to such consultation. This question is considered further in section 6 of this chapter which discusses the potential EIA elements of any new international agreement to conserve and sustainably use marine biodiversity in ABNJ.

In relation to decisions or actions taken by the proponent following an EIA, the UNEP Principles adopt a due diligence approach requiring the proponent to fully examine the potential environmental impacts of a particular project or activity and give due consideration to the interests of affected parties but not imposing a particular decision path on the proponent. Although the UNEP Principles do not extend the proponent's obligations beyond this due diligence approach, it could be argued that if an EIA concludes that significant harm is likely to marine areas, under the international law duty to prevent transboundary harm set out in Principle 21 of the Stockholm

---

[10]   Convention on Biological Diversity (opened for signature 22 May 1992, entered into force 29 December 1993) 1760 UNTS 79) (CBD).

[11]   UNEP, United Nations Environment Programme Goals and Principles of EIA (UNEP Principles) at http://www.unep.org/Documents.Multilingual/Default.asp?DocumentsID=1008 ArticleID=1658 (28 April 2012) (last accessed 26 May 2015).

Declaration[12] and Principle 2 of the Rio Declaration[13] and confirmed by the International Court of Justice (ICJ) in its *Advisory Opinion on the Legality of the Threat or Use of Nuclear Weapons*,[14] the state conducting such an EIA would be under a positive obligation to mitigate that harm or refrain from the activity.[15]

### 2.1.3 Convention on Biological Diversity (CBD)

The Convention on Biological Diversity establishes a link between the fundamental obligation of Contracting Parties to conserve biodiversity including marine biodiversity and the conduct of environmental assessment and monitoring. Contracting Parties must introduce appropriate procedures requiring EIA of proposed projects that are likely to have significant adverse effects on biodiversity with a view to avoiding or minimizing such effects.[16] Having identified processes and activities which have or are likely to have significant adverse impacts on the conservation and sustainable use of biological diversity, Contracting Parties are also required to monitor their effects through sampling and other techniques (Article 7(c)). These obligations apply to processes and activities carried out under the jurisdiction or control of Contracting Parties in all parts of the marine and terrestrial environment, regardless of where their effects occur (Art. 4(b)) The critical importance of collaboration between States in minimizing adverse impacts to biodiversity in transboundary areas and areas beyond national jurisdiction is emphasized in Article 14(1)(c) which requires Contracting Parties to promote reciprocal notification, exchange of information and consultation on activities under their jurisdiction or control which are likely to significantly affect adversely the biological diversity of other States or areas beyond the limits of national jurisdiction. In the case of imminent or grave danger or damage, originating under their jurisdiction or control, to biodiversity under the jurisdiction of other States or in areas beyond the limits of national jurisdiction, Contracting Parties must notify immediately the potentially affected States as well as initiate action to prevent or minimize such danger or damage.

The obligations in the CBD have been elaborated in Voluntary Guidelines on Biodiversity-Inclusive Impact Assessment (CBD Guidelines) that emphasize the importance of including biodiversity-related criteria in the screening process.[17] The Guidelines reflect a best practice standard for EIAs of activities with the potential to significantly affect all aspects of biodiversity, including those components situated in ABNJ. They depend on a detailed level of knowledge of species, habitats and

---

[12]   Declaration of the United Conference on the Human Environment, Stockholm, 16 June 1972 (1972) 11 *International Legal Materials* 1416.

[13]   Rio Declaration on Environment and Development, Rio de Janeiro, 3 to 14 June 1992, UN Doc A/CONF.151/5/REV.1 (1992) 31 *International Legal Materials* 876.

[14]   International Court of Justice, *Advisory Opinion on Legality of the Threat or Use of Nuclear Weapons*, 8 July 1996, http://www.icj-cij.org/docket/files/95/7495.pdf.PHPSESID= 244d61421d993dcdd51859ee9c657b1b, 241–242, para. 29 (last accessed 26 May 2015).

[15]   Neil Craik, *The International Law of Environmental Impact Assessment* (Cambridge University Press, 2008) 67.

[16]   CBD, Art. 14(1)(a).

[17]   Biodiversity in Impact Assessment. Background Document to Decision VIII/28 of the Convention on Biological Diversity. Voluntary Guidelines on Biodiversity-Inclusive Impact Assessment, https://www.cbd.int/doc/publications/cbd-ts-26-en.pdf (last accessed 1 June 2015).

ecosystems and their interconnections in a particular marine area. A process has also been undertaken in the CBD to define the special considerations to be taken into account in EIAs of activities with the potential to significantly affect biodiversity in marine and coastal areas, including ABNJ. In November 2009 the CBD Secretariat convened an Expert Workshop on Scientific and Technical Aspects relevant to EIA in ABNJ.[18] This highlighted some of the governance and practical challenges related to the implementation of EIA for activities in ABNJ.

The Workshop emphasized the practical difficulties associated with conducting EIAs. These included the fact that the industry proposing the activity and the national flag state jurisdiction are often far from the marine area affected. This would result in EIAs and any management, control, monitoring, surveillance and follow-up activities being more costly and potentially less effective for a given budget. The Workshop also considered that capacity building needs for EIA in ABNJ would be greater as customs of practice are less established, methodologies less mature, and multiple assessment cultures may converge in the same area.[19] It emphasized the complex and fragmentary nature of the law and institutions governing ABNJ including the split legal framework for ABNJ – high seas (LOSC Part VII) and deep seabed beyond national jurisdiction, the Area, (LOSC Part XI and Part XI Implementation Agreement), the diverse institutional framework for ABNJ encompassing States, non-State actors and global and regional organizations, and the need for cooperation between all these actors to conserve biodiversity. It also raised the issue that stakeholders are harder to define for ABNJ, because communities do not have immediate proximity to these areas, and the variability in standards of compliance among states with environmental assessment obligations under international conventions.[20]

The Workshop's Report was considered by the tenth Conference of Parties of the CBD in 2010 which endorsed the development of voluntary guidelines for the consideration of biodiversity in EIAs for marine and coastal areas drawing on the guidance from the Workshop.[21] Guidelines were then developed for all marine and coastal areas, rather than simply for ABNJ, thereby emphasizing the interconnections between ocean ecosystems across jurisdictional boundaries. These guidelines were endorsed by the eleventh COP of the CBD in 2012.[22] This initiative represents an important step in defining the special characteristics of EIA for activities in ABNJ and provides a valuable reference for scientific and technical information on EIA for all sectors operating in ABNJ.

---

[18]    See Report of the Expert Workshop, above n 1.

[19]    Ibid, Annex II, paras 10–14.

[20]    Ibid, Annex II, paras 7–9.

[21]    Decision X/29, para. 50, Report of the Tenth Meeting of the Conference of the Parties to the Convention on Biological Diversity, UNEP/CBD/COP/10/27, 20 January 2011, Annex, http://www.cbd.int/cop10/doc/ (last accessed 26 May 2015).

[22]    Decision XI/18, Report of the Eleventh Meeting of the Conference of the Parties to the Convention on Biological Diversity, UNEP/CBD/COP/11/27, 5 December 2012, Annex, 7, http://www.cbd.int/cop/?11=cop-11 (last accessed 26 May 2015).

### 2.1.4 Convention on the Conservation of Migratory Species of Wild Animals (CMS)

The Convention on the Conservation of Migratory Species of Wild Animals (CMS)[23] is also relevant to the range of species that typically traverse ABNJ. Its objective is to conserve migratory species of wild animals including certain marine species, such as cetaceans and seabirds, which migrate through marine areas within and beyond national jurisdiction. In pursuit of this objective, States Parties have obligations to prevent, remove, compensate for or minimize the adverse effects of activities or obstacles that seriously impede or prevent the migration of the species. In its Resolution 7.2 on Impact Assessment and Migratory Species of 8 September 2002 the Conference of Parties (COP) of the CMS urged States to include in EIAs and SEAs 'as complete a consideration as possible of effects involving impediments to migration, of transboundary effects on migratory species, and of impacts on migratory patterns or migratory ranges'. More detailed obligations to conduct environmental assessment of human activities on migratory species in the marine environment are reflected in some of the subsidiary agreements to the CMS.

The 2001 Agreement for the Conservation of Albatross and Petrels[24] provides in Annex 3 that the Parties shall assess the potential impact on albatrosses and petrels of policies, plans, programmes and projects which they consider likely to affect the conservation of albatrosses and petrels before any decision on whether to adopt such policies, plans, programmes and projects is made and to make the results of these assessments publicly available. The 1996 Agreement on the Conservation of Cetaceans of the Black Sea, Mediterranean Sea and Contiguous Atlantic Area (ACCOBAMS)[25] is more rigorous, requiring Parties to carry out EIAs in order to provide a basis for either allowing or prohibiting the continuation or the future development of activities that may affect cetaceans or their habitat in the Agreement area. These activities include fisheries, offshore exploration and exploitation, nautical sports, tourism, and cetacean watching, as well as establishing the conditions under which such activities may be conducted. In Resolution No 4, Adverse Effects of Sound, Vessels and other Forms of Disturbance on Small Cetaceans of 12 December 2006 adopted by the Parties to the 1992 Agreement on the Conservation of Small Cetaceans of the Baltic, North East Atlantic, Irish and North Seas (ASCOBANS),[26] the Parties called for the development, with military and other relevant authorities, of effective mitigation measures, including EIAs and relevant standing orders, to reduce disturbance and potential physical damage to small cetaceans.

---

[23] Convention on the Conservation of Migratory Species of Wild Animals (opened for signature 23 June 1979, entered into force 1 November 1983) 19 *International Legal Materials* 15 (CMS).

[24] Agreement on the Conservation of Albatrosses and Petrels (opened for signature 19 June 2001, entered into force 17 May 2004) 40 *International Legal Materials* 532 (ACAP).

[25] Agreement on the Conservation of Cetaceans of the Black Sea, Mediterranean Sea and Contiguous Atlantic Area (opened for signature 24 November 1996, entered into force 1 June 2001) 36 *International Legal Materials* 777 (ACCOBAMS).

[26] Agreement on the Conservation of Small Cetaceans of the Baltic, North East Atlantic, Irish and North Seas (opened for signature 17 March 1992, entered into force 29 March 1994) 1772 UNTS 217 (ASCOBANS).

## 2.2   Decisions of International Tribunals

The process of environmental assessment, particularly EIA, is one of the means by which States can implement a range of international environmental law principles. An EIA plays a fundamental role in discharging States' obligations to prevent transboundary harm, adopt a precautionary approach and promote sustainable development.[27] The customary international law status of EIA including its marine components, has been discussed in a number of recent judgements of the ICJ and an advisory opinion of the International Tribunal for the Law of the Sea (ITLOS). In the *Gabčíkovo-Nagymaros* case the ICJ considered assessment, notification and consultation, effectively the elements of an EIA process, to be a necessary step in a State's implementation of the duty to prevent transboundary harm and the concept of sustainable development.[28] In the *Pulp Mills* case, the ICJ found that '… it may now be considered a requirement under general international law to undertake an environmental impact assessment where there is a risk that the proposed industrial activity may have a significant adverse impact in a transboundary context, in particular, on a shared resource.'[29]

In the *Mox Plant* case, ITLOS concluded that the United Kingdom had breached its obligations under Article 206 of the LOSC by failing to carry out an adequate assessment of the potential impacts of a nuclear fuel reprocessing plant in Cumbria on the marine environment of the Irish Sea.[30] The 2011 advisory opinion of the Seabed Disputes Chamber of ITLOS on the *Responsibilities and Obligations of States Sponsoring Persons and Entities with Respect to Activities in the Area*, also acknowledged the customary international law status of the obligation to conduct EIAs for activities with the potential for significant impacts on the marine environment, including for ABNJ, specifically the Area.[31]

---

[27]    Craik, above n 15, 54, 77 and 224.

[28]    *Gabčikovo-Nagymaros Project (Hungary/Slovakia)* (1997) ICJ Rep 7, para. 141; Alan Boyle, 'The Gabčikovo-Nagymaros Case: New Law in Old Bottles' (1997) 8 *Yearbook of International Environmental Law* 18; Craik, above n 15, 114.

[29]    *Pulp Mills on the River Uruguay Case (Argentina/Uruguay) (Provisional Measures)* (2006) ICJ Rep, para. 204.

[30]    *Mox Plant Case (Provisional Measures)* ITLOS No. 10 (2001), para. 82; Alan Boyle, 'Environmental Jurisprudence of the International Tribunal for the Law of the Sea' (2007) 22(3) *International Journal for Marine and Coastal Law* 377; Marie Cordonnier Segger, Marcus Gehring and Andrew Paul Newcombe, *Sustainable Development in World Investment Law* (Kluwer Law International, 2011) 152.

[31]    International Tribunal of the Law of the Sea, *Advisory Opinion on Responsibilities and Obligations of States Sponsoring Persons and Entities with Respect to Activities in the Area*, 1 February 2011, 44, para. 145, http://www.itlos.org/fileadmin/itlos/documents/cases/case_no_17/adv_op_010211.pdf.

# 3. REGIONAL FRAMEWORKS FOR ENVIRONMENTAL ASSESSMENT IN ABNJ

## 3.1 Regional Seas Conventions

There are broad obligations on environmental assessment in most of the UNEP and non-UNEP regional seas agreements but only a few regional seas programs have specific environmental protection responsibilities for ABNJ areas.[32] Parties to the regional seas conventions are typically responsible for developing EIA guidelines, legislation and processes that prevent or minimize harmful effects on the Convention Area with the assistance of competent global, regional and sub-regional organizations. The conventions do not incorporate screening, scoping and content prescriptions for EIA, leaving this responsibility to the more detailed legislative enactments of their member states. Different versions of the duty to notify and consult on EIAs with other parties and the relevant regional seas organization appear in many of the conventions, but most are relatively loose prescriptions urging rather than obligating states to disseminate results of EIAs and consult with affected parties.

The 1995 Convention for the Protection of the Marine Environment and Coastal Region of the Mediterranean (Barcelona Convention)[33] makes specific mention of notification and consultation among Contracting Parties where activities are likely to have a significant adverse effect on ABNJ. Article 4(3)(c) provides that:

> the Contracting Parties shall promote cooperation between and among States in environmental impact assessment procedures related to activities under their jurisdiction or control which are likely to have a significant adverse effect on the marine environment of other States or *areas beyond the limits of national jurisdiction* on the basis of notification, exchange of information and consultation.

This provision recognizes the mandatory responsibility of Contracting Parties to protect and preserve the marine environment beyond national jurisdiction in their region.

The OSPAR Commission established to implement the 1992 *Convention for the Protection of the Marine Environment of the North-east Atlantic* (OSPAR Convention)[34] is moving towards more collaborative arrangements between competent regional

---

[32] The scope of application of the 1986 Convention for the Protection of the Natural Resources and Environment of the South Pacific Region (Noumea Convention), the 1992 Convention for the Protection of the Marine Environment of the North-east Atlantic (OSPAR Convention) and the 1995 Convention for the Protection of the Marine Environment and the Coastal Region of the Mediterranean (Barcelona Convention) extend to ABNJ. See Nilufer Oral, 'Forty years of the UNEP Regional Seas Programme: from past to future', Chapter 16 in this volume.

[33] Convention for the Protection of the Marine Environment and Coastal Region of the Mediterranean (opened for signature 10 June 1995, entered into force 9 July 2004) text at www.unep.ch/regionalseas/regions/med/t_barcel.htm (Barcelona Convention) (last accessed 27 May 2015).

[34] Convention for the Protection of the Marine Environment of the North-East Atlantic (opened for signature 22 September 1992, entered into force 29 December 1993) 32 *International Legal Materials* 1069 (OSPAR Convention).

and global authorities for EIA and SEA of activities, plans, programmes and policies affecting ABNJ marine protected areas (MPAs) within the convention's area of responsibility. The OSPAR Ministerial Meeting in 2010 established six MPAs in ABNJ encompassing four seamounts, an area of the deep seabed beyond national jurisdiction in the southern area of the Charlie Gibbs Fracture Zone and an area to the north of the Azores Islands in the Atlantic.[35] OSPAR is continuing its liaison with global and regional organizations with responsibilities for managing activities such as fisheries, deep seabed mining and ships routeing in these MPAs including the North East Atlantic Fisheries Commission, the International Seabed Authority and the International Maritime Organization. Under this arrangement, joint management plans are in the course of being developed for each of the six MPAs including provisions for cooperation on EIAs and SEAs.[36]

### 3.2    Protocol on Environmental Protection to the Antarctic Treaty (Madrid Protocol)

The test applied for screening activities for EIA under the Madrid Protocol to the Antarctic Treaty[37] is more complex and multi-layered than many other international instruments and clearly applies to ABNJ, although there are significant exceptions to its application to certain activities. The screening process has three levels – the preliminary assessment, initial environmental evaluation and comprehensive environmental evaluation.[38] A preliminary assessment is carried out at the national level for all activities subject to the Protocol with less than a minor or transitory impact. If an activity has no more than a minor or transitory impact, an initial environmental evaluation must be carried out, and if it has more than a minor or transitory impact, a comprehensive environmental evaluation must be carried out. All activities, both governmental and non-governmental, in the Antarctic Treaty area (south of 60° S latitude) are subject to these provisions, except for fishing, sealing, whaling and emergency operations as these are covered by other international instruments.[39]

---

[35]    OSPAR Commission, *OSPAR Network of Marine Protected Areas*, http:www.ospar.org/content/content.asp?menu=00700300100011_000000_000000 (last accessed 27 May 2015).

[36]    'Designation and Management of OSPAR MPAs Beyond National Jurisdiction in the North-East Atlantic', Presentation by Dr. Henning von Nordheim and Tim Packeiser, IUCN/German Federal Agency for Nature Conservation Seminar on the Conservation and Sustainable Use of Marine Biodiversity beyond National Jurisdiction, 3–6 December 2011, Bonn, Germany. See also Joanna Mossop, Reconciling activities on the extended continental shelf with protection of the marine environment', Chapter 8 in this volume.

[37]    Protocol on Environmental Protection to the Antarctic Treaty (opened for signature 4 October 1991, entered into force 14 January 1998) 30 *International Legal Materials* 1455 ('Madrid Protocol').

[38]    Madrid Protocol, Art. 8(1); K. Bastmeijer and R. Roura, 'Environmental Impact Assessment in Antarctica' in K. Bastmeijer and T. Koivurova, *Theory and Practice of Transboundary Environmental Impact Assessment* (Martinus Nijhoff Publishers, 2008), 182.

[39]    Madrid Protocol, Art. 8(2).

# 4. SECTORAL FRAMEWORKS FOR ENVIRONMENTAL ASSESSMENT IN ABNJ

The principal sectors of activity in ABNJ, fishing, shipping and deep seabed mining have prescribed limited environmental assessment measures for some of their activities; however, for some newer activities such as bioprospecting, already taking place in ABNJ, there are no mandatory environmental impact assessment instruments or processes.

## 4.1 Fisheries Sector

Parties to the UN Fish Stocks Agreement[40] must assess the impacts of fishing, other human activities and environmental factors on target stocks and species belonging to the same ecosystem or associated or dependent ecosystems and develop data collection and research programmes to assess the impact of fishing on non-target and associated or dependent species and their environment.[41] This obligation has been further elaborated in the 2009 FAO International Guidelines for the Management of Deep Sea Fisheries in the High Seas (Deep Sea Fisheries Guidelines),[42] which were developed to help states and RFMOs implement a call from the United Nations General Assembly (UNGA) to prevent significant adverse impacts on vulnerable marine ecosystems or not to authorize the bottom fishing activity to proceed.[43] Significant adverse impacts are defined as those that compromise ecosystem integrity (i.e. ecosystem structure or function) in a manner that:

(i)    impairs the ability of affected populations to repair themselves;
(ii)   degrades the long-term natural productivity of habitats; and
(iii)  causes, on more than a temporary basis, significant loss of species richness, habitat or community types.[44]

The Guidelines also specify that impacts should be evaluated individually, in combination and cumulatively.[45] They call for states to adopt measures to prevent significant adverse impacts on vulnerable marine ecosystems (VMEs). This is achieved through identifying VMEs in regional fisheries management organizations (RFMOs) areas of responsibility[46] and implementing measures such as fisheries closures in areas around VMEs and encounter protocols requiring fishing vessels to move a minimum distance from a location where species indicating the presence of a VME are captured by their

---

[40]   Above, n 5.
[41]   UN Fish Stocks Agreement, Arts 5(d) and 6(3)(d).
[42]   FAO, *International Guidelines for the Management of Deep Sea Fisheries in the High Seas*, 2009, http://www.fao.org/docrep/011/i0816t/i0816t00.HTM (last accessed 3 June 2015).
[43]   UNGA Resolution 61/105, paras 80–91.
[44]   Ibid, 4, para. 17.
[45]   Ibid.
[46]   Ibid, paras 42–6.

gear.[47] States, through RFMOs, have also been developing data collection and research programmes to assess the impact of fishing on target and non-target species and their environment.[48] The Guidelines list the characteristics of VMEs that should be subject to assessments and give examples of potentially vulnerable species groups, communities and habitats, as well as features that potentially support them.[49] Although there are still significant problems with implementing the Deep Sea Fisheries Guidelines in a sufficiently precautionary manner, the fact that progress in implementation of the UNGA Resolutions and the Guidelines has been reviewed twice by the UNGA may be a significant factor in prompting many RFMOs to close areas to fishing based on the known presence of vulnerable species.[50]

## 4.2   Shipping Sector

In the shipping sector, only a limited number of activities that ships may engage in beyond national jurisdiction, such as dumping of wastes and ocean fertilization, are subject to risk and environmental assessment processes.[51] For States Parties to the London Convention,[52] dumping of non-prohibited substances is only allowed subject to the requirements of prior environmental impact assessment, permitting and ongoing monitoring set out in Annex III of the Convention.[53] For States Parties to the London Protocol,[54] dumping of all waste and other matter is prohibited, except for five listed categories of substances the dumping of which is nevertheless subject to the stringent assessment, permitting and ongoing monitoring requirements of Annex 2 of the Protocol.[55] Any application for a permit to dump these listed substances must be accompanied by an assessment of the sea disposal options, including information on waste characteristics, conditions at the proposed dump site, fluxes and proposed

---

[47]   Ibid, paras 63 and 67–8.

[48]   Ibid, 9–11.

[49]   Ibid, 4, paras 14–16.

[50]   M. Gianni, D.E.J. Currie, S. Fuller, L. Speer, J. Ardron, B. Webber, M. Gibson, G. Roberts, K. Sack, S. Owen, A. Kavanagh, 'Unfinished business: a review of the implementation of the provisions of UNGA resolutions 61/105 and 64/72 related to the management of bottom fisheries in areas beyond national jurisdiction', Deep Sea Conservation Coalition, September 2011; Peter J. Auster, Kristina Gjerde, Eric Heupel, Les Watling, Anthony Grehan and Alex David Rogers, 'Definition and Detection of Vulnerable Marine Ecosystems on the High Seas: Problems with the 'Move-on' Rule' (2011) 68(2) *ICES Journal of Marine Science*, 255.

[51]   See David VanderZwaag, 'The international control of ocean dumping: navigating from permissive to precautionary shores', Chapter 6 in this volume.

[52]   Convention on the Prevention of Marine Pollution by Dumping of Wastes and Other Matter (opened for signature 29 December 1972, entered into force 30 August 1975) 11 *International Legal Materials* 1294 (London Convention).

[53]   London Convention, Art. IV and Annex III, available online: http://www.imo.org/OurWork/Environment/LCLP/Pages/default.aspx (last accessed 3 June 2015).

[54]   Protocol to the Convention on Prevention of Marine Pollution by Dumping of Wastes and Other Matter (opened for signature 7 November 1996, entered into force 24 March 2006) 36 *International Legal Materials* 1 (London Protocol).

[55]   London Protocol, Art. 4 and Annex 2, available online: http://www.austlii.edu.au/au/other/dfat/treaties/2006/11.html (last accessed 27 May 2015).

disposal techniques and specify the potential effects on human health, living resources, amenities and other legitimate uses of the sea. These assessments can apply to dumping of wastes in marine areas beyond national jurisdiction as well as to areas within national jurisdiction.

A statement adopted by the Scientific Groups of the London Convention and London Protocol in July 2007 'noted with concern the potential for ocean fertilization activities to have negative impacts on the marine environment and human health' and recommended that the parties to the London Convention and London Protocol consider the issue with a view to its regulation.[56] This statement was endorsed by the States Parties during their joint annual meeting in November 2007 where the parties agreed that while it was the prerogative of each state to consider proposals for ocean fertilization projects on a case-by-case basis in accordance with the Convention and/or Protocol, knowledge about the effectiveness and potential environmental impacts of open ocean fertilization was currently insufficient to justify large scale projects. They also agreed that ocean fertilization fell within their regulatory competence and that they would 'further study this issue from scientific and legal perspectives with a view to its regulation.'[57]

An intersessional Technical Working Group on Ocean Fertilization was established to develop an Assessment Framework for Scientific Research Involving Ocean Fertilization to provide a mechanism for assessing, on a case-by-case basis, whether proposals for ocean fertilization activities represent legitimate scientific research.[58] An Assessment Framework was adopted, by consensus, in a non-binding resolution at the October 2010 meeting of the parties to the London Convention and London Protocol.[59] This Framework is described as a 'tool … to determine if the proposed activity constitutes legitimate scientific research that is not contrary to the [LC/LP] aims'. It sets out a two-stage process involving an initial assessment and an environmental assessment. The purpose of the initial assessment is to determine whether the proposed ocean fertilization activity constitutes legitimate scientific research.[60] Proposals that meet these criteria may then proceed to the next stage, the environmental assessment that includes requirements of risk management and monitoring. The environmental assessment stage entails a number of components including the problem formulation, a

---

[56] LC/LP Scientific Groups, 'Statement of Concern Regarding Iron Fertilization of the Ocean to Sequester $CO_2$', Doc. LC-LP.1/Circ.14, 13 July 2007.

[57] International Maritime Organization, *Report of the 29th Consultative Meeting of the Contracting Parties to the Convention on the Prevention of Marine Pollution by Dumping of Wastes and Other Matter, 1972 and 2nd Meeting of the Contracting Parties to the 1996 Protocol thereto*, IMO Doc. LC29/LP2 (2007).

[58] LC.30/16, para. 2.3.

[59] Assessment Framework for Scientific Research Involving Ocean Fertilization, Resolution LC-LP.2 (2010), 32nd Consultative Meeting of Contracting Parties to the Convention on the Prevention of Marine Pollution by Dumping of Wastes and Other Matter, 1972 (London Convention) and 5th Meeting of Contracting Parties to the 1996 Protocol thereto (London Protocol).

[60] Rosemary Rayfuse and Robin Warner, 'Climate change mitigation activities in the ocean: turning up the regulatory heat' in Robin Warner and Clive Schofield (eds), *Climate Change and the Oceans: Gauging the Legal and Policy Currents in the Asia Pacific and Beyond* 253–7 describes the development of the Assessment Framework for ocean fertilization in more detail.

site selection and description, an exposure assessment, an effects assessment, risk characterization and risk management sections.[61] Only after completion of the environmental assessment, is a decision made on whether the proposed activity constitutes legitimate scientific research that is not contrary to the aims of the London Convention and/London Protocol. If so, the activity is permitted to proceed. In October 2013, the Contracting Parties to the London Convention and London Protocol adopted an amendment to the Protocol which, when it enters into force, will make this risk assessment framework mandatory for all specified marine geo-engineering activities.[62] The only marine geo-engineering activity specified at this stage is ocean fertilization.

## 4.3   Deep Seabed Mining Sector

Deep seabed mining activities in ABNJ are subject to a well developed framework of environmental assessment obligations.[63] An exploration contractor must submit an assessment of the potential environmental impacts of proposed activities with an application for approval of a plan of work together with a description of proposed measures for the prevention, reduction, and control of possible impacts on the marine environment to the International Seabed Authority (ISA).[64] The Recommendations for the Guidance of the Contractors for the Assessment of the Possible Environmental Impacts Arising from Exploration for Polymetallic Nodules in the Area, issued by the Authority's Legal and Technical Commission in revised form in 2010 specify the particular activities of exploration contractors that are subject to EIA.[65] The sponsoring

---

[61]   Assessment Framework for Scientific Research Involving Ocean Fertilization, LC 32/15, Annex 6, 5–19, http://www.imo.org/OurWork/Environment/LCLP/EmergingIssues/geo engineering/OceanFertilizationDocumentRepository/AssessmentFramework/Pages/default.aspx (last accessed 3 June 2015).

[62]   Report of the Working Group on the Proposed Amendment to the London Protocol to Regulate Placement of Matter for Ocean Fertilization and other Marine Geo-engineering Activities, LC Doc 35/WP.3, 17 October 2013; Philomene Verlaan, 'Current Legal Developments. London Convention and London Protocol' (2013) 28(4) *International Journal of Marine and Coastal Law* 729–36. See also, Karen Scott, 'Geoengineering and the marine environment', Chapter 21 in this volume.

[63]   Michael Lodge, 'Protecting the marine environment of the deep seabed', Chapter 7 in this volume.

[64]   Agreement Relating to the Implementation of Part XI of the United Nations Convention on the Law of the Sea of 10 December 1982 (opened for signature 28 July 1994, entered into force 28 July 1996) 1836 UNTS 3 ('Part XI Implementation Agreement'), Annex, para. 7; Regulations for Prospecting and Exploration of Polymetallic Nodules (Polymetallic Nodule Regulations), https://www.isa.org.jm/files/documents/EN/Regs/MiningCode.pdf (last accessed 3 June 2015).

[65]   Recommendations for the Guidance of Contractors for the Assessment of the Possible Environmental Impacts Arising from Exploration for Polymetallic Nodules in the Area, http://www.isa.org.jm/files/documents/EN/7Sess/LTC/isba_7ltc_1Rev1.pdf (last accessed 27 May 2015), para. 10.

state for an exploration contractor is under a due diligence obligation to ensure that an exploration contractor fulfils all these obligations.[66]

## 5. CHALLENGES TO IMPLEMENTING ENVIRONMENTAL ASSESSMENT IN ABNJ

The governance structures underpinning environmental assessment in marine areas are directly related to the scheme of maritime jurisdiction and different maritime zones prescribed in the LOSC. The ability of states to fulfil this obligation in ABNJ is largely dependent on individual flag States supplemented by the limited collaborative institutions and mechanisms they have established for environmental assessment in ABNJ. Lack of an integrated system of environmental governance for ABNJ presents considerable problems for implementing comprehensive environmental assessment processes in these vast areas of the ocean. The predominant form of jurisdiction in ABNJ is flag state jurisdiction. For shipping transiting ABNJ, it falls to individual flag States rather than any regional or global body to regulate and enforce the activities of their flag vessels including their impacts on the marine environment. This results in variable levels of compliance with environmental standards, no auditing of individual flag State performance or sanctioning of sub-standard performance. Many of the stages in an environmental impact assessment process require coordinating authorities which are conspicuously lacking in the fragmentary and disjunctive system of governance applicable to most ABNJ activities. These stages include the initial screening process to select which activities are subject to environmental assessment, the scoping process to decide the terms of reference for an environmental assessment, the public notification and consultation process to engage relevant stakeholders, the post EIA decision-making phase and the ongoing monitoring of environmental impacts.

## 6. GLOBAL INITIATIVES TO DEVELOP THE INTERNATIONAL LAW FRAMEWORK FOR ENVIRONMENTAL ASSESSMENT IN ABNJ

In the nine meetings since its inception in 2005, the United Nations General Assembly (UNGA) Ad Hoc Open-ended Informal Working Group, created to study issues related to the conservation and sustainable use of marine biological diversity beyond areas of national jurisdiction (BBNJ Working Group), has consistently identified EIA for activities affecting marine areas beyond national jurisdiction as an important component of its work. In 2011, the Co-Chairpersons recommended to the UNGA that a process be initiated, by the General Assembly, to ensure that the legal framework for the conservation and sustainable use of marine biodiversity in ABNJ effectively addresses relevant issues including EIA by identifying gaps and ways forward. These

---

[66]　ITLOS Advisory Opinion, above n 5, 43–4, paras 141–143; Polymetallic Nodules Regulation 31(6) and Polymetallic Sulphides Regulation 33(6).

issues would be dealt with through the implementation of existing instruments and the possible development of a multilateral agreement under the LOSC. In particular, it was recommended that the process address measures such as EIA.[67] The UNGA in its annual Oceans and Law of the Sea Resolution on 24 December 2011 endorsed the BBNJ Working Group recommendations.[68] A recommendation to support the initiation of a process to develop an implementation agreement under the LOSC which would address the conservation and sustainable use of marine biodiversity in ABNJ including EIA was endorsed by the UN Conference on Sustainable Development (Rio+20) in June 2012. This commitment was recalled by the United Nations General Assembly (UNGA) in its 67th session,[69] and reaffirmed in the recommendations to the UNGA developed at the sixth meeting of the BBNJ Working Group in 2013.[70] The same meeting also agreed to establish a process to make recommendations to the UNGA 'on the scope, parameters and feasibility of an international instrument under the Convention' in order to prepare for the decision to be taken at the 69th session of the UNGA in 2015, whether to start the negotiation of an international instrument on the conservation and sustainable use of biodiversity in areas beyond national jurisdiction (ABNJ).[71] This process has involved three meetings to discuss the scope, parameters and feasibility of an international instrument in April 2014, June 2014 and January 2015. In the meetings of the BBNJ Working Group held in April and June 2014, EIA continued to be discussed by member States as a potential element of any new instrument although the specific structure and provisions of any instrument that may be negotiated in the future were not discussed in detail. This is due to a number of factors including the view of some country delegations to the BBNJ Working Group that discussion of specific provisions of an agreement at this stage would prejudge the decision of the UN General Assembly on whether a new agreement should be negotiated at all. Country delegations have made more general interventions on the current status of EIA in international law, the application and improved implementation of current EIA provisions to ABNJ and the potential value of any new agreement for extending EIA processes to new and emerging activities in ABNJ. Some delegations at the June 2014 meeting of the BBNJ Working Group referred to the potential of EIA provisions in an international instrument on conservation and sustainable use of marine

---

[67]    Letter from the Co-Chairs of the Ad Hoc Open-ended Informal Working Group to the President of the General Assembly, 30 June 2011, http://daccess-dds-ny.un.org/doc/UNDOC/GEN/N11/397/64/PDF/N1139764.pdf (last accessed 27 May 2015), Annex, Section I, paras (a) and (b).

[68]    UNGA Resolution on Oceans and the Law of the Sea, UN Doc. A/RES/66/231, 28 November 2011, para. 167; UN Conference on Sustainable Development – Rio+20, 'The Future We Want – Zero Draft of the Outcome Document', http://www.uncsd2012.org/thefuturewewant.html, para.80 (last accessed 3 June 2015).

[69]    UNGA Resolution on Oceans and the Law of the Sea, UN Doc. A/RES/67/78, 11 December 2012, para. 181.

[70]    Report of the Ad Hoc Open-ended Informal Working Group to study issues relating to the conservation and sustainable use of marine biological diversity beyond areas of national jurisdiction and Co-Chairs' summary of discussions. UN Doc. A/68/399, 23 September 2013, Annex.

[71]    Ibid.

biodiversity in ABNJ to provide uniform and best practice standards for the preparation and review of EIAs and to establish a centralized mechanism for information sharing on EIAs prepared for proposed activities in ABNJ.[72] The UNGA has now decided to develop an international legally binding instrument under the Convention on the conservation and sustainable use of marine biological diversity in areas beyond national jurisdiction and to establish, prior to holding an intergovernmental conference, a preparatory committee to make substantive recommendations to the General Assembly on the elements of a draft text, including elements relating to environmental impacts assessments.[73]

### 6.1 Rationale and Objectives for Including EIA Elements in Potential Implementing Agreement

The BBNJ Working Group has discussed reasons for including EIA as one of the key components in any future Implementing Agreement on the Conservation and Sustainable Use of Marine Biodiversity in Areas beyond National Jurisdiction.[74] A key plank of the rationale for including EIA elements is to capture activities occurring in ABNJ that are not already subject to sectoral EIA processes, in effect, to provide a default EIA system for activities such as bioprospecting and marine geo-engineering. Another reason for including EIA elements is to provide best practice standards for EIA in ABNJ where scientific knowledge of marine biodiversity is still nascent. Developing best practice standards for EIA in ABNJ may well entail the incorporation of new elements into the generally accepted components of the EIA process. Rather than perpetuating a situation where EIA is simply a procedural hurdle for the proponents of a particular activity, a best practice standard could require a process that is biodiversity inclusive, transparent and subject to international scrutiny with associated powers to impose conditions in the interest of mitigating adverse impacts on the marine environment or to disallow the activity where there is the potential for substantial harm to the marine environment.

---

[72]  Co-Chairs Summary of discussions at the Ad Hoc Open-ended Informal Working Group to study issues relating to the conservation and sustainable use of marine biological diversity beyond national jurisdiction, 16–19 June 2014, UN Doc. A/69/177, paras 65–70.

[73]  UNGA Resolution, 'Development of an international legally-binding instrument under the United Nations Convention on the Law of the Sea on the conservation and sustainable use of marine biological diversity in areas beyond national jurisdiction', UN Doc A/69/L.65, 22 June 2015.

[74]  Letter from the Co-Chairs of the Ad Hoc Open-ended Informal Working Group to study issues related to the conservation and sustainable use of marine biodiversity in areas beyond national jurisdiction to the President of the General Assembly, 30 June 2011, UN Doc A/66/119, Annex, Section I, paras (a) and (b).

## 6.2  Options for Incorporating EIA Elements into Implementing Agreement

Typical components of an EIA process include screening, scoping of the terms of reference for an EIA, public notification and consultation, reporting and post report decisions on whether to impose conditions on the activity or to disallow it.[75]

### 6.2.1  Screening

The screening component of an EIA process determines whether particular activities or projects will be subject to an EIA. The threshold of significant effects on the environment as the trigger for subjecting activities to EIA has gained wide acceptance in global and regional instruments as well as national legislation.[76] The Environmental Protocol to the Antarctic Treaty (Madrid Protocol) is a notable exception to this generally accepted threshold with the screening process involving three levels – the preliminary assessment level, the initial environmental evaluation level and the comprehensive environmental evaluation level. A preliminary assessment is carried out at the national level for all activities subject to the Protocol with less than a minor or transitory impact.[77] If an activity will have no more than a minor or transitory impact, an initial environmental evaluation must be carried out at the national level.[78] If it has more than a minor or transitory impact, a comprehensive environmental evaluation must be carried out and submitted to the Committee on Environmental Protection (CEP) of the Madrid Protocol.[79] This is a potential option for screening thresholds in ABNJ, at least for activities intended to occur in sensitive areas of the ABNJ environment such as identified vulnerable marine ecosystems (VMEs) and ecologically and biologically significant areas (EBSAs).

In addition to threshold criteria, many EIA regimes list activities which will automatically be subject to EIAs and criteria to assist in determining which other activities should be subject to EIAs.[80] An indicative list of such activities for ABNJ would include deep sea fishing, aquaculture, dumping of waste, marine geo-engineering, offshore hydrocarbon production, bioprospecting, marine scientific research, laying of submarine cables and pipelines, ballast water exchange, deep sea tourism expeditions and ocean energy operations. Criteria to assist States in determining which other activities should be subject to EIAs could be modelled on the CBD Voluntary Guidelines for Biodiversity-Inclusive EIA[81] particularly as the proposed international agreement will relate to conservation and sustainable use of biodiversity in ABNJ. These might include whether the proposed activity is located in or close to an area of special environmental sensitivity or representative international importance and whether the intended activity would affect the biophysical environment directly or

---

[75]  Craik, above n 15, 132.

[76]  Ibid, 133.

[77]  Madrid Protocol, Annex I, Art1(1).

[78]  Ibid, Annex I, Arts 2(1) and 3(1).

[79]  Ibid, Annex I, Art. 3(2).

[80]  Craik, above n 15, 134–5.

[81]  Voluntary Guidelines on Biodiversity-Inclusive Impact Assessment, *Biodiversity in Impact Assessment. Background Document to Decision VIII/28 of the Convention on Biological Diversity.* https://www.cbd.int/doc/publications/cbd-ts-26-en.pdf (last accessed 3 June 2015).

indirectly in such a manner that it will increase risks of extinction of genotypes, cultivars, varieties, populations of species or increase the chance of loss of habitat or ecosystems. In addition, whether the intended activity would surpass the maximum sustainable yield i.e. the carrying capacity of a habitat/ecosystem or the maximum allowable disturbance level of a resource, population or ecosystem or whether the proposed activity would have particularly complex and potentially adverse effects including those giving rise to serious effects on valued species or organisms or those which threaten the existing or potential use of an affected area.

### 6.2.2 Scoping

Once the need for an EIA has been agreed, a scoping process follows that determines the focus, depth and terms of reference for the EIA.[82] The fundamental objective of the scoping process is to identify those issues arising from the proposed activity which are most likely to have a significant impact on the environment and to describe alternatives that avoid, mitigate, or compensate for adverse impacts on the environment. The content of the EIA report or Environmental Impact Statement (EIS) is derived on the basis of these elements. The scoping stage of EIAs for activities in ABNJ while addressing the same issues could also incorporate examination of impacts and alternatives which take into account the shared interests of the international community such as the long-term sustainability of marine resources, continuing marine scientific research and the stability of global climate.

### 6.2.3 Reporting

The EIS, which is usually prepared by the proponent of the activity, forms the basis for subsequent decisions by the relevant authorities on whether an activity should proceed and whether conditions should be imposed on the activity. The potential elements of an EIS for proposed activities in ABNJ could include a description of the proposed activity including its purpose, location, duration and intensity, the initial environmental reference state and a prediction of the future environmental reference state in the absence of the proposed activity. Other elements of the EIS could be a description of the programme for oceanographic and environmental baseline studies that would enable an assessment of the potential environmental impact including but not restricted to the impact on biodiversity of the proposed activity, the practical alternatives, including the alternative of not proceeding and the consequences of those alternatives and an assessment of the likely or potential environmental impacts of the proposed activity and alternatives, including the direct, indirect, individual and combined, cumulative, short term and long term effects of these in the light of existing and planned activities. An EIS could also encompass a description of the expected biophysical changes resulting from proposed activities, including a description of ecosystems lying within the range of influence of such changes and the spatial and temporal scale of influence of each

---

[82]   Craik, above n 15, 29–30 explains the origins of the scoping component of EIA which is derived from domestic law systems but is now reflected in some international law instruments such as the Madrid Protocol, above n 37 and the Convention on Environmental Impact Assessment in a Transboundary Context (opened for signature 25 February 1991, entered into force 10 September 1997) (1991) 30 International Legal Materials 800 (Espoo Convention).

biophysical change, identifying effects or connectivity between ecosystems, and potential cumulative effects. Whether there will be adverse impacts on biodiversity or ecosystems affected by the expected biophysical changes in terms of composition, structure (spatial and temporal) and key processes highlighting any irreversible impacts and irreplaceable loss. It could also identify, in consultation with the scientific and technical advisory body to the Conference of the Parties (COP) of the Implementing Agreement, the current and potential ecosystem services provided by the affected ecosystems and determine the values these represent for the international community highlighting any irreversible impacts and irreplaceable loss. It would also be beneficial to include in an EIS, as complete a consideration as possible of effects involving impediments to migration, of transboundary effects on migratory species and of impacts on migratory patterns or migratory ranges. The EIS could define possible alternatives to the proposed activity including 'no net biodiversity loss' or 'biodiversity restoration' alternatives and location, scale, siting, lay out and technology alternatives. Further elements which might be considered for the EIS are an assessment, in consultation with the Intergovernmental Panel on Climate Change (IPCC), of the likely impacts on global climate of the proposed activity, whether positive or negative and a description of the methods, data and underlying assumptions used to forecast the impacts of the proposed activity. An identification and description of measures available to prevent or avoid adverse environmental impacts of the proposed activity and alternatives and an assessment of those measures could be incorporated as well as a description of the effects of the proposed activity on the conduct of scientific research and on other existing uses and values. Finally the EIS could identify whether the proposed activity would affect the proponent's compliance with its obligations under customary or conventional international law and any gaps in knowledge and uncertainties encountered in compiling the information required for the EIA report. The EIS should also contain a non-technical summary of the information provided under the previous clauses.

### 6.2.4   Public notification and consultation

The duty to notify and consult with affected parties is an integral component of environmental impact processes in both the national and transboundary arenas.[83] The general obligation to notify and consult, derived from the international law duty to cooperate and found in a variety of hard and soft-law instruments, can be adapted to activities in ABNJ. When information provided as part of an EIA indicates that the environment of ABNJ is likely to be significantly affected by a proposed activity, the proponent of the activity being planned should notify and consult with potentially affected stakeholders and provide them with relevant information. In the ABNJ context, potential stakeholders could include States, members of the public, international and regional organizations, inter-governmental and nongovernmental organizations, industry representatives and corporate entities. Before a decision is made on whether an activity proceeds and on what conditions, these stakeholders should be provided with an opportunity to comment. To assist in this process, States could be encouraged to notify other States and competent international organizations of planned activities under their

---

   [83]   Craik, above n 15, 141.

jurisdiction or control which may have a significant effect on marine biodiversity in ABNJ. There is also the potential for a more enhanced role for the regional seas organizations as dissemination points and consultation hubs on EIAs and as technical advisers on mitigation measures.

### 6.2.5  Post EIS decision-making

Under most EIA regimes, the obligation on the final decision-maker is one of due diligence encompassing a full examination of the potential environmental impacts of a particular project and due consideration of the interests of affected parties.[84] The global commons status of biodiversity in ABNJ calls for a more stringent and inclusive standard of decision making on whether an activity should be allowed to proceed and on what conditions. This could involve developing a further set of criteria related to the permissible levels of impact on marine biodiversity in ABNJ and a decision-making structure which involves a level of international scrutiny over EIAs prepared by proponents of particular activities.

### 6.3  Links between EIA Elements and other Components of the International Agreement

The EIA components of an international agreement should be consistent with the overarching objectives and general principles articulated in the agreement. For example the EIA process prescribed in the agreement should be focused on the conservation and sustainable use of marine biodiversity in ABNJ. The institutional infrastructure required for the EIA process prescribed in the international agreement should utilize as far as possible existing global and regional organizations with the relevant expertise as well as the institutions of the international agreement itself. For example the Conference of the Parties (COP) of the international agreement advised by a Subsidiary Scientific and Technical Body could function as the decision making body for EIAs. Its functions would include setting standards for best practice EIA and reviewing EIAs undertaken by sectoral bodies for activities in ABNJ. It could have powers to impose conditions or disallow activities based on criteria developed around thresholds for adverse impacts on marine biodiversity in ABNJ. The Subsidiary Scientific and Technical Body and the COP could also function as default review and decision-making bodies for EIAs of new and emerging activities in ABNJ not covered by existing sectoral EIA regimes. In addition the EIA screening criteria developed under an international agreement should take into account any network of MPAs designated by the COP of the agreement.

## 7.  CONCLUSIONS

The obligation to identify the environmental impacts of human activities and to mitigate their adverse effects is equally critical to combating these threats to bio-diversity in ABNJ as it is in marine areas under national jurisdiction. While legal and institutional frameworks for environmental assessment are well established in many

---

[84]  Ibid, 150–51.

countries for marine areas under national jurisdiction, collaborative structures and mechanisms to achieve the same objectives in ABNJ are still fragmentary and underdeveloped. Establishing these governance structures in ABNJ is a much more complicated endeavour involving multiple stakeholders including states, global and regional organizations, marine industries and non-governmental organizations focused on protecting the marine environment. The potential negotiation of an international agreement for the conservation and sustainable use of marine biodiversity in ABNJ offers the opportunity to develop best practice standards for biodiversity inclusive EIA for all activities with the potential for adverse impacts on the marine biodiversity of ABNJ. With appropriate elaboration and adaptation from existing EIA regimes, it can provide a process for assessing the impacts of previously unexamined activities in ABNJ and new and emerging activities. An EIA regime for ABNJ also provides an opportunity for the shared interests of the international community in conserving and sustainably using marine biodiversity to be represented in a transparent and inclusive process which takes into account the interests of multiple ocean stakeholders of current and future generations. The development of an EIA regime for ABNJ is a fundamental prerequisite for the conservation and sustainable use of marine biodiversity across the whole spectrum of ABNJ activities.

# 15. Marine scientific research and the protection of the seas and oceans

*Anna-Maria Hubert**

## 1. INTRODUCTION

The preamble of the United Nations Convention on the Law of the Sea[1] (LOSC) declares the intention of its drafters to establish a legal order for the seas and oceans to promote 'the study, protection and preservation of the marine environment'. This pronouncement connotes a seamless order and harmony between the aims of science and marine environmental protection. In practice, the relationship is much more complex, punctuated occasionally by conflict surrounding the implementation and development of the parallel legal regimes for marine scientific research (MSR) and protection of the marine environment found in Part XIII and Part XII of the LOSC, respectively. This chapter aims to examine the progressive development of the legal regime for MSR with a view to understanding its legal and practical implications for progress on the protection and preservation of the marine environment.

It is apt to point out from the start that science and international law have always been in dynamic tension with each other: science 'buffets' international law, whilst 'at the same time, international law is in turn exerting a continuing and deep influence on the advancement of science itself'.[2] On the one hand, law must somehow try to keep up with scientific and technological progress as it marches into unchartered terrain beyond the boundary of existing scientific regulatory and institutional frameworks.[3] On the other hand, societal values and culture, embodied in science legal, policy and institutional frameworks, also exert a strong influence over the scientific system and the

---

\* I would like to express my gratitude to my dissertation advisor, Prof Dr Gerd Winter, for his advice and inspiration, as well as the MARUM and Bremen International Graduate School for Marine Sciences. I would also like to acknowledge the support of Prof Dr Mark Lawrence and the Institute for Advanced Sustainability Studies (IASS). Any errors or omissions remain the responsibility of the author.

[1] United Nations Convention on the Law of the Sea (adopted 10 December 1082, entered into force 16 November 1994) 1833 UNTS 3 (LOSC).

[2] Dennis Livingston, 'An International Law of Science: Orders on Man's Expanding Frontiers' (1968) 24 *Bulletin of the Atomic Scientists* 6, 6.

[3] See, eg, John A. Knauss, 'Development of the Freedom of Scientific Research Issue of the Third Law of the Sea Conference' (1973) 1 *Ocean Development & International Law* 93, 94 observing regarding the negotiations of the LOSC that '[o]ne of the problems facing those attempting to determine ocean policy today is that advancing technology provides little time for contemplation'. Cf Michel Callon, Pierre Lascoumes and Yannick Barthe, *Acting in an Uncertain World: An Essay on Technical Democracy* (MIT Press 2009).

work of individual scientists.[4] Where sites of friction and conflict co-exist, there is potential for evolution and progress on shared objectives.

Tracing this potential through the historical development of the law of the sea, until the mid-twentieth century scientists were basically free to move throughout the oceans without constraint.[5] In the 1950s and 1960s, rapid post-war innovations led to the development of new oceanographic instruments, equipment and data collection methods, opening up greater opportunities for investigating the oceans. Ironically, growth in research also gave rise to restrictions on the mobility and access of scientists to make 'observations when and where they wished'.[6] In particular, states drew the link between obtaining improved knowledge of the oceans and their growing interests in exploiting offshore natural resources and technological advances that might be relevant to naval security.[7] On one hand, this recognition led to the promotion of MSR, further fuelling new discoveries. On the other, it was the main impetus for expanding regulation of MSR under international law.

The most important legal development relating to the conduct of marine scientific research (MSR) was the adoption of the LOSC. The recognition of coastal state sovereign rights and jurisdiction over extended or new maritime zones limited the access of scientists to the marine environment. However, these were not the only interests that contributed to increasing and more complex regulation of MSR. Concerns about the consequences of rapid scientific and technical progress led to the recognition of the need to address 'mankind's collective responsibility for preserving the marine environment and minimizing ocean pollution'.[8] Re-examination the freedom of scientific research and its legal limits culminated in the adoption of Part XIII of the LOSC which now provides the legal framework for the conduct of MSR.

Much has changed since the adoption of the LOSC nearly 30 years ago. In the past, MSR primarily involved short-term research expeditions conducted at sea, taking measurements from research vessels and using fixed installations and platforms. Today, technological innovations have transformed marine environmental research, opening up many more possibilities to explore and better understand the oceans, including observation from space, expeditions traversing the globe from pole-to-pole or journeys in submersibles to the deep sea, all occurring over sustained periods of months to years.[9] However, scientists now face new constraints on access arising from legal and

---

[4]   See Sheila Jasanoff, 'Is Science Socially Constructed – And Can it Still Inform Public Policy?' (1996) 2 *Science and Engineering Ethics* 263.

[5]   Alfred Soons, 'The International Legal Regime for MSR' (1977) 24 *Netherlands International Law Review* 393.

[6]   Soons, above n 5, 394.

[7]   Milner B. Schaefer, 'Freedom of Scientific Research and Exploration in the Sea' (1969) 4 *Stanford Journal of International Studies* 46, 46, noted that this led to what he referred to as a 'paradox' that 'scientific progress necessary for a fuller utilization of ocean resources is being retarded by new regimes which were established because of such enhanced utilization'. See also Fletcher A. Blanchard and Robert W. Corell, 'Man's Adaptation to the Sea: A Key to the Ocean's Resources' (1969) 4 *Stanford Journal of International Studies* 71; Knauss, above n 3, 93.

[8]   Knauss, above n 3, 94.

[9]   See Florian H. Th Wegelein, *MSR: the Operation and Status of Research Vessels and other Platforms in international Law* (Martinus Nijhoff Publishers 2005) ch 3.

geopolitical changes. In addition, the potential for conflicts has increased due to intensified and expanding uses of the oceans, such as renewable energy production, bioprospecting and marine geoengineering. While advances in science and technology have certainly contributed to increased human activities that impact the oceans, human pressures have pushed the global ocean into a state of rapid decline caused by, inter alia, habitat destruction, biodiversity loss, overfishing, pollution, climate change and ocean acidification.[10] In response, science's relationship with society is also changing. While it is recognized that '[s]cientific and technical advances bring unquestioned benefits,... they also generate new uncertainties and failures, with the result that doubt continually undermines knowledge, and unforeseen consequences confound faith in progress'.[11] This growing ambivalence and fundamental questioning of the narrative of scientific progress has contributed to a trend in contemporary democracies leading to calls for responsible governance of science and innovation.[12] Concerns relate not only to the direct physical environmental impacts of experimental and observational activities,[13] but also to the need to ensure that science serves the public good and that knowledge stays within the public domain so that everyone can benefit.[14]

Under pressure from these different forces, issues of MSR and marine environmental protection are increasingly intertwined and complex, further influencing the evolving interpretation and implementation of the relevant provisions in the LOSC. This chapter focuses on several issues in which these two regimes interact with each other and with other parts of the Convention. The chapter begins with an examination of the legal relationship between Part XII on the protection and preservation of the marine environment and Part XIII on MSR. It then turns to an overview of the provisions of Part XIII and current legal developments as they relate to the protection of the marine environment. In particular, this section examines general principles, the implications of the zonal approach for the regulation of MSR under the LOSC, and the provisions on scientific research equipment and installations. Finally, the analysis turns to the issue of legal responsibility for environmental damage from the conduct of MSR and the settlement of disputes. Needless to say, an exhaustive analysis of all of the issues related to the legal relationship between MSR and the protection of the marine environment is beyond the scope of this chapter. Thus, what is presented here is a survey of topical issues intended to stimulate further research and reflection upon the

---

[10]   See GESAMP (IMO/FAO/UNESCO-IOC/WMO/WHO/IAEA/UN/UNEP Joint Group of Experts on the Scientific Aspects of Marine Environmental Protection and Advisory Committee on Protection of the Sea), A Sea of Troubles (Rep. Stud. GESAMP No. 70 2001) unesdoc.unesco.org/images/0012/001229/122986e.pdf (last accessed 27 May 2015).

[11]   Sheila Jasanoff, 'Technologies of Humility: Citizen Participation in Governing Science' (2003) 41 *Minerva* 223, 224.

[12]   For an overview of this issue from a social science perspective see Jack Stilgoe, Richard Owen and Phil Macnaghten, 'Developing a Framework for Responsible Innovation' (2013) 42 *Research Policy* 1568.

[13]   Anna-Maria Hubert, 'The New Paradox in MSR: Regulating the Potential Environmental Impacts of Conducting Ocean Science' (2011) 42 *Ocean Development & International Law* 329.

[14]   Helga Nowotny, 'The Changing Nature of Public Science' in Helga Nowotny and others, *The Public Nature of Science under Assault: Politics, Markets, Science and the Law* (Springer 2005).

ever-changing legal relationship between ocean science and the safeguarding of the marine environment for present and future generations.

## 2. THE RELATIONSHIP BETWEEN PART XII ON THE PROTECTION OF THE MARINE ENVIRONMENT AND PART XIII ON MSR

While not necessarily the case, the conduct of MSR may have adverse effects on the marine environment.[15] In addition, the knowledge gained from MSR activities may be used to promote natural resource exploration and exploitation or may give rise to new technologies or uses that have possible adverse impacts on the marine environment.[16] This latter observation may have relevance to calls for responsible governance of the modern 'techno-sciences' in which there is a blurring of the distinction between science and its potential uses in society.[17] This gives rise to the question of the relationship between Parts XII and XIII of the LOSC.

Part XII is specifically dedicated to the protection and preservation of the marine environment, though provisions on environmental protection are also set out in other parts in the LOSC and other marine environmental agreements.[18] A basic reading of the LOSC might lead to the assumption that there is a 'hierarchical order' between Parts XII and XIII.[19] In particular, according to Article 240(d), MSR 'shall be conducted in compliance with all relevant regulations adopted in conformity with this Convention for the protection and preservation of the marine environment'.[20] However, contextual

---

[15]   See Philomène A. Verlaan, 'Experimental Activities that Intentionally Perturb the Marine Environment: Implications for the Marine Environmental Protection and MSR Provisions of the 1982 United Nations Convention on the Law of the Sea' (2007) 31 *Marine Policy* 210; Hubert, above n 13.

[16]   Silvio Funtowicz and Jerome Ravetz, 'Science for the post-normal age' (1993) 25 *Futures* 739.

[17]   Some marine geoengineering methods may fall within this category of 'post-normal' science which is characterized as involving high uncertainties and high stakes given the societal implications of the knowledge gained from such studies. See generally Rob Bellamy, 'Beyond Climate Control: "Opening up" Propositions for Geoengineering Governance' (Climate Geo-engineering Governance Working Paper Series: 011, 27 May 2014) www.geoengineering-governance-research.org/perch/resources/workingpaper11bellamybeyondclimatecontrol.pdf (last accessed 27 May 2015); Lisa Dilling and Rachel Hauser, 'Governing Geoengineering Research: Why, When and How?' (2013) 121 *Climatic Change* 553. Regarding the lack of a clear distinction between science and application in the case of ocean fertilization research see Aaron L. Strong, John J. Cullen and Sallie W. Chisholm, 'Ocean Fertilization: Science, Policy and Commerce' (2009) 22 *Oceanography* 236.

[18]   See Robin Churchill, 'The LOSC regime for protection of the marine environment – fit for the twenty-first century?', Chapter 1 in this volume.

[19]   See Wegelein, above n 9, 75–6.

[20]   Note, however, that Art. 240(d) qualifies the general principle that: 'MSR shall be conducted in compliance with all relevant regulations *adopted in conformity with this Convention* including those for the protection and preservation of the marine environment' (emphasis added).

interpretation reveals not the 'primacy' of Part XII, but rather that the two Parts must be read in a mutually supportive manner.[21]

The backbone of Part XII is the fundamental duty of states to protect and preserve the marine environment,[22] yet the focus of this part is on the prevention, reduction and control of marine pollution. Article 194(1) requires that states take 'all measures consistent with [the] Convention that are necessary to prevent, reduce and control pollution of the marine environment from any source, using for this purpose the best practicable means at their disposal and in accordance with their capabilities.' Marine pollution is defined as the introduction by man, directly or indirectly, of substances or energy into the marine environment which results or is likely to result in harm to the marine environment.[23] Clearly, this definition may cover some MSR methods; for example, those involving the use of harmful chemical or radioactive tracers, or the use of equipment or autonomous or manned vehicles that introduce light or sound into the marine environment.[24] However, as a due diligence obligation, Article 194(1) may be read as requiring the conduct of on-going scientific research.[25] As confirmed by the Seabed Disputes Chamber of the International Tribunal for the Law of the Sea (ITLOS) in its *Advisory Opinion on the Responsibilities and Obligations of States Sponsoring Persons and Entities with Respect to Activities in the Area,* the content of this obligation of due diligence 'may change over time as measures considered sufficiently diligent at a certain moment may become not diligent enough in light, for instance, of new scientific or technological knowledge'.[26]

The corresponding backbone of Part XIII is Article 238, which provides that all states and competent international organizations have the right to conduct MSR. However, this right is 'subject to the rights and duties of other States as provided for in this Convention'.[27] Hence, the right is qualified by the provisions of Part XII for the protection and preservation of the marine environment. Article 194(4) stipulates that in taking measures to address marine pollution, States 'shall refrain from *unjustifiable interference* with activities carried out by other States in the exercise of their rights and in pursuance of their duties in conformity with this Convention' (emphasis added). Thus, a state can justify certain restrictive measures aimed at preventing pollution of

---

[21]   See Wegelein, above n 9, 76.

[22]   LOSC, Art. 192.

[23]   LOSC, Art. 1(4).

[24]   J. Breslin, D. Nixon, and G. West, 'Code of Conduct for MSR Vessels, International Ship Operators Meeting (ISOM)' (October 17–20, 2007) http://irso.unols.org/wp-content/uploads/International_RV_Code_final.pdf (last accessed 4 June 2015); Cindy Lee Van Dover, 'Impacts of Anthropogenic Disturbances at Deep-Sea Hydrothermal Vent Ecosystems: A Review' (2014) 102 *Marine Environmental Research* 59; Harm M. Dotinga and Alex G. Oude Elferink, 'Acoustic Pollution in the Oceans: The Search for Legal Standards' (2000) 31 *Ocean Development & International Law* 151.

[25]   See Wegelein, above n 9, 76; Alex G. Oude Elferink, 'Governance Principles for Areas Beyond National Jurisdiction' (2012) 27 *International Journal of Marine and Coastal Law* 205, 224.

[26]   *Seabed Mining Advisory Opinion*, paras 111–7.

[27]   LOSC, Art. 238.

the marine environment, even if their actions have the effect of limiting the conduct of MSR, where a reasonable case can be made for taking such measures.

Moreover, even within Part XII are several obligations relating to the promotion, facilitation and international cooperation in scientific and technical matters, the purpose of which are to improve the availability and quality of information about the state of the marine environment and potentially harmful activities. Article 200 requires that states promote and cooperate in scientific research and exchange information relating to marine pollution for the purpose of assessing its nature and extent, as well as pathways, risks and remedies. Article 201 obligates states to cooperate in the establishment of appropriate scientific criteria for the formulation and elaboration of rules, standards and recommended practices and procedures to address marine pollution. This requirement is reflected in other provisions of the LOSC, for example, that conservation and management measures relating to marine living resources and the protection of ice-covered areas should be based on the 'best scientific evidence available'[28] or that monitoring risks or effects of pollution should be carried out using 'recognised scientific methods'.[29] Even if not expressly required, scientific expertise and information are nonetheless necessary to ensure that the provisions of Part XII are effectively implemented.[30]

The precautionary approach tempers the requirement for a high level of scientific evidence where there is scientific uncertainty. However, the precautionary approach, confirmed by the Seabed Disputes Chamber to be 'an integral part of the due diligence obligation',[31] is generally accepted as not rendering scientific data unnecessary.[32] Rather, precautionary measures are subject to review in light of new scientific information.[33] This implies that marine scientific research must be carried out even after precautionary measures are adopted in order 'to elicit or generate the necessary scientific data' to support the regulatory process.[34]

In short, MSR is an information gathering activity that is necessary for effective environmental regulation and resource management. The provisions of Part XII for the protection and preservation of the marine environment should be read as mutually supportive of Part XIII, rather than hierarchical in manner, such that MSR may be regulated for environmental protection purposes as long as that regulation is in

---

[28]    LOSC, Arts 61(2), 119(1)(a) and 234. See also UN Agreement Relating to the Conservation and Management of Straddling Fish Stocks and Migratory Fish Stocks (1995) 34 *International Legal Materials* 1542.

[29]    LOSC, Art. 204.

[30]    Patricia Birnie, 'Law of the Sea and Ocean Resources: Implications for MSR' (1995) 10 *International Journal of Marine and Coastal Law* 229, 245.

[31]    *Responsibilities and Obligations of States Sponsoring Persons and Entities with Respect to Activities in the Area* (Advisory Opinion), [2011] ITLOS Case No. 17, (2011) 50 *International Legal Materials* 458 (*Seabed Mining Advisory Opinion*), para. 113.

[32]    Yoshifumi Tanaka, *A Dual Approach to Ocean Governance: the Cases of Zonal and Integrated Management in International Law of the Sea* (Ashgate Publishing 2008) 227–8.

[33]    European Commission, 'Communication from the Commission on the Precautionary Principle' COM(2000) 1, 3 February 2000, 12.

[34]    Ibid. Cf. 2000 Convention on the Conservation and Management of Highly Migratory Fish Stocks in the Western and Central Pacific Ocean (2001) 40 *International Legal Materials* 277, Art. 6(1).

accordance with an (implicit) mitigating principle of 'not-unreasonable interference with scientific research'.[35]

## 3. LEGAL REGIME FOR MSR IN PART XIII

Turning to the specific legal regime for MSR, the main body of principles and rules is laid down in Part XIII of the LOSC, although given the crosscutting nature of the topic, scientific research is also dealt with in other parts of the Convention.[36] This section examines the interpretation and application of Part XIII in light of a main objective of the LOSC to protect and preserve the marine environment.

### 3.1 Promotion, Facilitation and International Cooperation in MSR

While MSR may be carried out for a variety of purposes, there is a critical and growing need for better information about the profound influence human activities are having as the predominant driver of change in the global ocean system. Research provides the essential knowledge base for promoting understanding of the marine environment and its proper environmental management through the identification of environmental risks, environmental assessment and monitoring, and the establishment of rules, standards, recommended practices and procedures to achieve environmental goals.

Fundamental terms in science's 'social contract' with society are said to be the generation of reliable knowledge by scientists in exchange for relative autonomy, research funding, and other support necessary to carry out their work.[37] Though subject to limitations, these conditions are reflected in various provisions in the LOSC dealing with the promotion, facilitation and international cooperation in scientific research generally.[38] Moreover, as noted above, science is specifically pressed into service to provide the necessary input for the conservation and the proper management of marine ecosystems and resources in Part XII.

---

[35]  Gerald Francis Graham, 'The Freedom of Scientific Research in International Law: Outer Space, the Antarctic and the Oceans' (DPhil Thesis, Université de Genève 1980) 8. See also Hubert, above n 13, 337–8.

[36]  LOSC, Arts 19, 21 and 52 (innocent passage), Art. 40 (transit passage), Art. 54 (archipelagic sea lanes passage, Arts 56 and 62 (EEZ), Art. 87 (high seas), Art. 123 (enclosed or semi-enclosed seas) and Arts 143 and 155 (the Area). Part XII on 'Protection and Preservation of the Marine Environment', Part XIV on 'Development and Transfer of Marine Technology,' Part XV on 'Settlement of Disputes' and Annex VIII 'Special Arbitration'.

[37]  Michael Gibbons, 'Science's New Social Contract with Society' (1999) 402 *Nature* C81; J. Francisco Alvarez and Jesus Zamora-Bonilla, 'The Social Contract of Science' in Christoph Luetge (ed.) *Handbook of the Philosophical Foundations of Business Ethics* (Springer 2013).

[38]  Myron Nordquist and others (eds), *United Nations Convention on the Law of the Sea 1982. A Commentary*, Vol. IV (Martinus Nijhoff 1991) (Virginia Commentary) 437, para. XIII.14.

Part XIII begins by establishing the qualified right in Article 238 of all states and competent international organizations to conduct MSR.[39] This is followed by the recognition of a duty to promote and facilitate the development and conduct of MSR.[40] Stemming from this general duty to promote MSR is the specific obligation in Article 243 that states and international organizations cooperate, first, by concluding international agreements to create favourable conditions for the conduct of MSR, and, second, by integrating the efforts of scientists studying ocean phenomena and processes.[41] The specific content of obligation to create 'favourable conditions' is open to interpretation, though the legislative history of this provision indicates that it may include the 'removal of obstacles' to MSR.[42] To that end, the LOSC espouses the rule of law as the mode for creating favourable research conditions.[43] Article 255 stipulates that states shall 'adopt *reasonable* rules, regulations and procedures to promote and facilitate MSR' (emphasis added) in all areas where they do not have absolute sovereignty.[44] This article also calls upon coastal states to support the logistics of doing research by providing research vessels access to their harbours and to provide assistance where required.[45]

The duty to promote and facilitate marine research is complemented by several provisions on international cooperation. In general, states and international organizations are to promote international cooperation in MSR for peaceful purposes in accordance with the respect for sovereignty and jurisdiction and on the basis of mutual benefit.[46] While the concept of mutual benefit is reflected in other regimes, including the Antarctic and Outer Space treaties and international human rights instruments,[47] its application in the context of scientific research has not yet been studied thoroughly. Although the specifics of the concept are context-dependent, it is derived from the idea of the 'universality' of science in securing the interests of all people in sharing in

---

[39]    See further Paul Gragl, 'MSR' in David J. Attard, Malgosia Fitzmaurice, and Norman A.M. Gutiérrez, *The IMLI Manual on International Maritime Law*, vol. 1 Law of the Sea (Oxford University Press 2014).

[40]    LOSC, Art. 239; see also LOSC, Art. 251.

[41]    LOSC, Art. 243.

[42]    Virginia Commentary, above n 38, 474, para. 243.2.

[43]    For a domestic law comparison regarding the interpretation of the German Basic Law see Eric Barendt, *Academic Freedom and the Law: A Comparative Study* (Hart 2010) 206–7.

[44]    See also Graham, above n 35, 8 citing a 'principle of not-unreasonable interference with scientific research' derived from the body of rules dealing with scientific research in international law.

[45]    LOSC, Art. 255.

[46]    LOSC, Art. 242(2).

[47]    See Antarctic Treaty (1959) 402 UNTS 71, Preamble, Treaty on Principles Governing the Activities of States in the Exploration and Use of Outer Space, Including the Moon and other Celestial Bodies (1967) 6 ILM 386 (Outer Space Treaty), Preamble and Article 1; Universal Declaration of Human Rights (1948) UNGA Res. 217 A(III) (UDHR), Art. 27(1); International Covenant on Economic, Social and Cultural Rights (1966) 999 UNTS 171 (ICCPR), Art. 15(1) and (3). See also Report of the Special Rapporteur in the field of cultural rights, Farida Shaheed: The right to enjoy the benefits of scientific progress and its applications, A/HRC/20/26 (14 May 2012).

scientific advancement and its benefits[48] and 'in bringing about genuine equality'.[49] As it has evolved in the modern law of the sea, the principle of mutual benefit has shifted in emphasis 'from an essentially "negative" one whereby for instance, certain acts deemed harmful to mankind are prohibited, to one which is prescriptive, ie, one which would oblige states to act in a certain way for the benefit of all'.[50]

In fact, both of these applications find expression in the provisions of Part XIII. An obvious implementation of the mutual benefit principle relates to provisions that ensure widespread access to the 'products' of research, namely, by requiring the sharing of information, facilitating the flow and transfer of scientific data, and through the publication and dissemination research results.[51] The drafting history of these provisions suggests that equitable considerations relating to the need to accommodate the special needs and interests of developing countries also lie at the heart of this concept.[52] Against this background, 'mutual benefit' encapsulates the provisions in the LOSC on the transfer of knowledge, strengthening research capabilities, education and training of technical and scientific personnel, and the development and transfer of marine technology.[53] The effective implementation of these provisions, which recognize the differentiated needs of developing states in MSR, inter alia, helps to strengthen their position in the elaboration, application and interpretation of their obligations to protect and preserve the marine environment.[54]

## 3.2 General Principles

Part XIII also lays down general principles for the conduct of MSR, including the requirements that research be conducted for peaceful purposes, with appropriate scientific methods and means, and that it not unjustifiably interfere with other legitimate uses of the oceans.[55] These provisions apply regardless of where the research activity is taking place, including on the high seas where the freedom of scientific research is explicitly recognized.[56]

As noted above, the general principle in Article 240(d) is key to understanding the legal relationship between the regimes for MSR and the protection of the marine environment in the LOSC.[57] It stipulates that MSR be conducted in compliance with all relevant regulations for the protection and preservation of the marine environment.

---

[48]   Graham, above n 35, 42.

[49]   Li Shishi, 'Bilateral investment promotion and protection agreements: practice of the People's Republic of China' in Paul de Waart, Paul Peters and Erik Denters (eds), *International Law and Development* (Martinus Nijhoff 1988) 166.

[50]   Graham, above n 35, 44.

[51]   LOSC, Arts 242(2) and 244(1)–(2).

[52]   Virginia Commentary, above n 38, 468, para. 242.2.

[53]   LOSC, Art. 244(2) and Part XIV.

[54]   See generally Philippe Sands and Jacqueline Peel, *Principles of International Environmental Law* (3rd edn, Cambridge University Press 2012) 233–6.

[55]   LOSC, Art. 240.

[56]   The freedom of scientific research laid down in Art. 87 is subject to Parts XIII and VI of the Convention.

[57]   See above n 15.

Although in general the environmental threat posed by MSR is estimated to be low relative to other ocean uses,[58] it is widely documented that some marine research activities may contribute to environmental damage.[59] Research-specific impacts may be physical, acoustical, and chemical and may be deliberate or accidental in nature.[60] The language of Article 240(d) indicates that the scope of this principle is not limited to the provisions of Part XII. Rather, MSR is to be carried out in accordance with all environmental protection regulations adopted in conformity with the LOSC, including those incorporated in relevant regulations adopted pursuant to other regional and international treaties and in national law.

However, expanding the sphere of marine environmental regulations at all levels increases the potential for conflicts with MSR activities. In addition, implementation of obligations to protect and preserve the marine environment may stifle the conduct of MSR by limiting access and creating overly onerous administrative requirements.[61] This issue is compounded by the fact that some MSR is directly related to the formulation and implementation of environmental policy and law. In short, restrictions on MSR may give rise to 'secondary' or substitute risks by undermining the generating source of the information needed to underpin environmental regulation and rational management.[62] In view of the requirements in the LOSC to cooperate in MSR and to take scientific criteria into account in devising environmental regulations, the application of Article 240(d) and the exercise of jurisdiction to impose restrictions on MSR should be necessary and reasonable in light of the circumstances.[63]

A companion principle enunciated in Article 240(b) requires MSR to be conducted 'using appropriate scientific methods and means compatible with this Convention.' The term 'appropriate' is undefined in the Convention, but on its ordinary meaning can be interpreted as referring to those methods and means that are 'suitable or proper in the circumstances'.[64] Soons observes that this provision was probably included to restrict those methods and means that are 'unnecessarily and unreasonably damaging to the marine environment or to other uses of the sea'.[65] Support for this interpretation can be found within the context of the Convention as a whole, in particular, taking into

---

[58]    See, eg, Angela R. Benn and others, 'Human activities on the deep seafloor in the North East Atlantic: an Assessment of Spatial Extent' (2010) 5 *PLos ONE*: e12730D V http://journals.plos.org/plosone/article?id=10.1371/journal.pone.0012730 (last accessed 29 May 2015).

[59]    For an overview see Hubert, above n 13, 330–31.

[60]    ISOM Code of Conduct for MSR Vessels, above n 24.

[61]    See David Kenneth Leary, *International Law and the Genetic Resources of the Deep Sea* (Martinus Nijhoff 2007) 194.

[62]    See Hans-Heinrich Trute, 'Democratising Science: Expertise and Participation in Administrative Decision-making' in Helga Nowotny and others, *The Public Nature of Science Under Assault: Politics, Markets, Science and the Law* (Springer 2005) 87.

[63]    Elmar Döhler and Carsten Nemitz, 'Wissenschaft und Wissenschaftsfreiheit in internationalen Vereinbarungen' in Helmut Wagner (ed.), *Rechtliche Rahmenbedingungen für Wissenschaft und Forschung. Forschungsfreiheit und Staatliche Regulierung*, vol 1 (Namos 2000). See also Graham above n 35, 8; Hubert, above n 13, 337–8.

[64]    Angus Stevenson (ed.), *Oxford Dictionary of English* (3rd edn, Oxford University Press 2014).

[65]    Alfred H.A. Soons, *MSR and the Law of the Sea* (Kluwer Law 1982) 136.

account the principle that MSR be carried out in compliance with all relevant environmental regulations,[66] and the requirements that states prevent marine pollution from the release of toxic, harmful or noxious substances,[67] installations and devices operating in the marine environment,[68] and from the use of technologies under their jurisdiction or control.[69]

In practice, the use of inappropriate methods and means is unlikely to be a major issue given the high costs and advance planning necessary to carry out marine research expeditions to collect reliable and reproducible scientific data for the peer review publication process.[70] However, an ocean fertilization experiment conducted in 2012 by the Haida Salmon Restoration Corporation (HSRC) just outside the 200 nautical mile limit off the western Canadian coast underscores the contemporary importance of this, albeit very general, principle.[71] With a cost estimated to be on the order of US $2.5 million, the HSRC research project deposited 100 tonnes of iron sulphate into ocean[72] – exceeding the amount used in any of the previous 13 tests by approximately fivefold.[73] The HSRC's declared objective was to induce a large plankton bloom to investigate the possibility of using ocean fertilization to enhance local salmon stocks.[74] The project sparked a global controversy and widespread doubts were expressed from within the scientific community about the scientific rigor of the experimental design and execution of the research,[75] including from internationally recognized scientists within the field who questioned whether the perturbation experiment was carried out in

---

[66]  LOSC, Art. 240(d).

[67]  LOSC, Art. 194(3)(a).

[68]  LOSC, Art. 194(3)(d).

[69]  LOSC, Art. 196(1).

[70]  Soons, above n 65, 135–6.

[71]  See Neil Craik, Jason Blackstock and Anna-Maria Hubert, 'Regulating Geoengineering Research through Domestic Environmental Protection Frameworks: Reflections on the Recent Canadian Ocean Fertilization Case' (2013) 2 *Carbon & Climate Law Review* 117.

[72]  Zoe McKnight, 'B.C. Company at Centre of Iron Dumping Scandal Stands by its Convictions' (Part 1 of a 2-part special Report) *Vancouver Sun*, 4 September 2013, www.vancouversun.com/technology/company+centre+iron+dumping+scandal+stands+convictions/88 60731/story.html (last accessed 29 May 2015).

[73]  For a summary of the amounts and scales of previous ocean fertilization experiments see Secretariat of the CBD, 'Scientific Synthesis of the Impacts of Ocean Fertilization on Marine Biodiversity' (Technical Series No. 45, 2009) www.cbd.int/doc/publications/cbd-ts-45-en.pdf (last accessed 29 May 2015).

[74]  Martin Lukacs, 'World's Biggest Geoengineering Experiment "Violates" UN Rules' *The Guardian*, 15 October 2012, www.theguardian.com/environment/2012/oct/15/pacific-iron-fertilisation-geoengineering (last accessed 29 May 2015). However, regarding the implications of dual-purpose research, the HSRC also made public statements indicating that they planned to generate revenue by attempting to sell carbon credits on international markets for the carbon dioxide they assumed would be sequestered by the project. See 'West Coast Ocean Fertilization Project Defended' *CBC News*, 19 October 2012, www.cbc.ca/news/canada/british-columbia/west-coast-ocean-fertilization-project-defended-1.1226125 (last accessed 29 May 2015); Jeff Tollefson, 'Ocean-fertilisation project off Canada sparks furore' *Nature News*, 23 October 2012, www.nature.com/news/ocean-fertilization-project-off-canada-sparks-furore-1.1163 (last accessed 29 May 2015).

[75]  McKnight, above n 72; Tollefson, above n 74.

the 'best way' given that studying ocean fertilization is 'quite sophisticated science and it would have been good if scientists had carried it out'.[76] Although a key proponent of the project asserted that the work yielded a 'greater density and depth of scientific data than ever before',[77] concerns were also raised about the quality of the scientific information gained from this field test and whether results would be made publically available in a timely manner. The HSRC's website includes information about their data-sharing policy and information on publications related to the project to date.[78] In this regard, the scientific community has an important role to play in scrutinizing the merits and scientific quality of marine scientific research, including through the peer review process.[79]

Apart from the general principles laid down in Article 240, however, the LOSC is silent on the rules for the conduct of environmentally responsible MSR. Indeed, though guidance on the ethical conduct of research on humans and animals is established and longstanding, environmental standards and guidelines for field research is a relatively novel concept that has only recently received attention.[80] This is an area where the conventional regime on MSR is ripe for progressive development.[81] An array of legally binding and non-binding instruments have been introduced over the past decade which address the environmentally responsible conduct of MSR and give shape to the general principles in Article 240 of the LOSC.[82] The most comprehensive and detailed of these is the OSPAR 'Code of Conduct for Responsible Marine Research in the Deep Seas

---

[76]   Tollefson, above n 74.

[77]   Lukacs, above n 74.

[78]   The HSRC has published its scientific data policy on its website www.haidasalmonrestoration.com (last accessed 29 May 2015) stating that researchers, organizations and individuals are free to use their scientific data library for 'legitimate research endeavours' subject to the execution of a memorandum of understanding for access privileges. Their website also states that their first academic publication on the Haida experiment is forthcoming, see, John S. Bird and others, 'Initial Investigation of the North East Pacific Salmon Feeding Waters with Slocum Gliders' (MTS/IEEE Oceans 2013 conference, San Diego 2013). Separate to the HRSC, others have published a peer reviewed publication analyzed satellite measurements taken of the experiment, which did not rely directly on the release of data by the HSRC see Peng Xiu, Andrew C. Thomas and Fei Chai, 'Satellite Bio-optical Alimeter Comparisons of Phytoplankton Blooms Induced by Natural and Artificial Iron Addition in the Gulf of Alaska' (2014) 145 *Remote Sensing of Environment* 38.

[79]   See *Daubert v Merrell Dow Pharmaceuticals, Inc* 509 US 579 (1992) 593. Regarding the requirement of peer review see Resolution LC-LP.2(2010) 'Assessment Framework for Scientific Research Involving Ocean Fertilization', 11–15 October 2010, para. 2.2.3; Resolution LP.4(8) on the amendment to the London Protocol to regulate the placement of matter for ocean fertilization and other marine geoengineering activities, Annex 5, para. 8.

[80]   Helene Marsh and Richard Kenchington, 'The Role of Ethics in Experimental Marine Biology and Ecology' (2004) 300 *Journal of Experimental Marine Biology and Ecology* 5; Elizabeth J. Farnsworth and Judy Rosovsky, 'The Ethics of Ecological Field Experimentation' (1993) 7 *Conservation Biology* 463.

[81]   See generally Hubert, above n 13.

[82]   OSPAR Commission, 'OSPAR Code of Conduct for Responsible Marine Research in the Deep Seas and High Seas of the OSPAR Maritime Area' OSPAR 08.24/1, Annex 6 (2008) www.ospar.org (OSPAR Code of Conduct for Responsible Marine Research) (last accessed 29 May 2015); Deutsche Senatskommission für Ozeanographie der DFG and Konsortium Deutsche

and High Seas of the OSPAR Maritime Area' which sets out good practices and standards for the conduct of MSR.[83] Furthermore, in the case of the HSRC project, discussed above, specific guidance was in fact already in place for ocean fertilization research under a series of joint legally non-binding resolutions[84] adopted by the Parties to the 1972 London Convention[85] and its 1996 London Protocol[86] (LC/LP). In particular, a 2010 resolution established an assessment framework for determining whether a proposed ocean fertilization project has 'proper scientific attributes' and made all proposals subject to a full environmental risk assessment.[87] Though not yet in force, the substance of these resolutions has been incorporated into the 2013 amendment to the London Protocol on marine geoengineering, transforming them into legally binding international law.[88]

### 3.3 Maritime Zone-specific Provisions

Following the general structure of the LOSC, Part XIII adopts a zonal approach to the regulation of MSR such that the rights of the coastal state diminish *vis-à-vis* researching states moving farther seaward from the baseline. Therefore, in principle, the freedom to conduct scientific research is strongest on the high seas.

Nearest to the baseline, coastal states, by virtue of their sovereignty, have the exclusive right to regulate, authorize and conduct MSR in their territorial sea.[89] In this zone, MSR may only be conducted with the express consent and subject to the

---

Meeresforschung (KDM), 'Erklärung zu einer verantwortungsvollen Meeresforschung' (Commitment to Responsible German Marine Research), reproduced in English in the International Council for the Exploration of the Sea (ICES), Report of the ICES NAFO Joint Working Group on Deep Water Ecology (WGDEC) (March 10–14, 2008), ICES CM 2008/ACOM:45, Annex 13.4, 97 www.ices.dk/sites/pub/Publication%20Reports/Expert%20Group%20Report/acom/2013/WGDEC/wgdec_2013.pdf (last accessed 29 May 2015); Irish Department of the Environment, Heritage and Local Government, 'Code of Practice of MSR at Irish Coral Reef Special Areas of Conservation' (September 2006) http://www.marine.ie/Home/sites/default/files/MIFiles/Docs/ResearchVessels/Code%20of%20Practice%20for%20Marine%20Scientific%20Research%20at%20SACs.pdf (last accessed 4 June 2015); Department of Fisheries and Oceans Canada, 'Endeavour Hydrothermal Vents Marine Protected Area Regulations' (SOR/2003-87) and Management Plan www.dfo-mpo.gc.ca/oceans/marineareas-zonesmarines/mpa-zpm/pacific-pacifique/endeavour-eng.htm (last accessed 29 May 2015); InterRidge, 'InterRidge Statement of Commitment to Responsible Research Practices at Deep-Sea Hydrothermal Vents' (2006) www.interridge.org/IRStatement (last accessed 29 May 2015); ISOM Code of Conduct for MSR Vessels, above n 24.

[83]    Ibid. Cf LOSC, Art. 194(5).

[84]    Resolution LC-LP.1(2008), 31 October 2008; Resolution LC-LP.2(2010) 'Assessment Framework for Scientific Research Involving Ocean Fertilization', 11–15 October 2010.

[85]    Convention on the Prevention of Marine Pollution by Dumping of Wastes and Other Matter (1972) 1046 UNTS 120.

[86]    Protocol to the Convention on the Prevention of Marine Pollution by Dumping of Wastes and Other Matter (1996) 36 *International Legal Materials* 1.

[87]    Resolution LC-LP.2(2010).

[88]    Resolution LP.4(8). See Karen N. Scott, 'Geoengineering and the marine environment', Chapter 21 in this volume.

[89]    LOSC, Art. 245.

conditions established by the coastal state, including any restrictive measures imposed for protection of the marine environment. The carrying out of research is furthermore considered prejudicial to the right of innocent passage within the territorial sea.[90]

A major innovation in the development of the LOSC was the establishment of the 200 nautical mile exclusive economic zone (EEZ) in which coastal states enjoy sovereign rights over living and non-living natural resources and jurisdiction over installations and structures, MSR, and the protection and preservation of the marine environment.[91] The logic underlying the creation of this maritime zone was further transposed into the provisions dealing with the conduct of MSR in the EEZ and on the continental shelf. Part XIII contains an elaborate consent regime that aims to balance rights and obligations between coastal and researching states.[92] The coastal state has the right to regulate, authorize, and conduct MSR in its EEZ and on its continental shelf,[93] and its consent is required for other states or competent international organizations to conduct research in these areas.[94]

However, the coastal state's right to authorize research is not absolute. In 'normal circumstances', it is obliged to consent to projects that are 'exclusively for peaceful purposes' and aim to 'increase scientific knowledge of the marine environment for the benefit of all mankind'.[95] As an exception to the general presumption in favour of authorization, the coastal state enjoys a discretionary power to refuse its consent to research projects that touch on certain recognized state interests enumerated in Article 246(5). Subparagraph 5(b) provides 'the most explicit legal basis' for a refusal of consent to MSR having potential environmental impacts where the project involves drilling into the continental shelf, the use of explosives or the introduction of harmful substances into the marine environment.[96] Although this exception captures several potentially dangerous activities, the wording does not capture all environmental risks potentially associated with the conduct of MSR, such as sound and light emissions.[97] Beyond the four exceptions set out in Article 246(5), the DOALOS Revised Guide on the MSR regime refers to other 'exceptional situations' in which the coastal state may refuse its consent to a research project in its EEZ or on it continental shelf.[98] These situations relate to circumstances in which it is clear, based on the information required by Article 248, that a research project is not carried out in accordance with the

---

[90]    LOSC, Art. 19.

[91]    LOSC, Art. 56.

[92]    LOSC, Arts 246 to 255.

[93]    LOSC, Art. 246(1).

[94]    LOSC, Art. 246(2).

[95]    LOSC, Art. 246(3).

[96]    Marta Chantal Ribeiro, 'The "Rainbow": The First National Marine Protected Area Proposed Under the High Seas' (2010) 25 *International Journal of Marine and Coastal Law* 183, 204.

[97]    Hubert, above n 13, 335.

[98]    Division for Ocean Affairs and the Law of the Sea Office of Legal Affairs, 'Law of the Sea: MSR: A Revised Guide to the Implementation of the Relevant Provisions of the United Nations Convention on the Law of the Sea' (New York: United Nations, 2010) (DOALOS Revised Guide) 42.

Convention.[99] Article 248 relates to the duty of the researching state to provide information to the coastal state including the nature and objectives of the project, methods and means used, and precise location of the proposed project. This information is useful in assessing whether and the extent to which a proposed research activity will have adverse effects on the marine environment in advance of it being carried out.[100]

In recognition of the grant of extended jurisdiction and the need to balance the interests of other states, the LOSC also seeks to safeguard access to the EEZ and continental shelf by ensuring consistency, transparency and predictability in the consent process. Coastal states are required to establish rules and procedures for ensuring that consent will be granted within a reasonable time.[101] Consent is implied if the coastal state does not respond after four months of notification of the proposed project.[102]

Moving farther seaward to the high seas, the freedom of scientific research is expressly enumerated as a high seas freedom in Article 87 of the LOSC,[103] and the right of all states to conduct MSR in the water column beyond the limits of the EEZ is confirmed in Article 257. All scientific research[104] carried out on the high seas must be exercised in accordance with the Convention,[105] including Part XII for the protection and preservation of the marine environment.[106] The freedom of scientific research may be further constrained by 'other rules of international law',[107] such as those relating to the carrying out of nuclear tests on the high seas,[108] scientific whaling,[109] research on other protected species[110] and marine geoengineering.[111]

---

[99]  See also LOSC, Art. 246(3) and Art. 240(d).

[100]  Cf Ocean Fertilization Assessment Framework.

[101]  LOSC, Art. 246(3).

[102]  LOSC, Art. 252.

[103]  LOSC, Art. 87.

[104]  There are certain discrepancies in the terminology used in Art. 87 and Art. 257, most notably, that the freedom to conduct 'scientific research' in Art. 87(1)(f) is seemingly broader than just 'marine' scientific research in Art. 257. The DOALOS Revised Guide, above n 98, para. 56 suggests that the more extensive freedom in the regime on the high seas 'also extends to activities such as hydrographic surveys'. However, this interpretation is cast into doubt by the several provisions in the LOSC referring to 'research or survey activities' as distinct objects. See also Ashley Roach, 'Defining Scientific Research: Marine Data Collection' in Myron H. Norquist, Ronan Long, Thomas H. Heidar and John Norton Moore (eds), *Law, Science and Ocean Management* (Martinus Nijhoff 2007).

[105]  According to Art. 87(1)(f) the freedom of scientific research on the high seas is subject to Parts VI and XIII, and Article 257 states that the right to conduct MSR must be carried out 'in conformity with this Convention'.

[106]  Virginia Commentary, above n 38, 611, para. 257.6(a).

[107]  LOSC, Art. 87(1).

[108]  See Gragl, above n 39.

[109]  International Convention for the Regulation of Whaling (1946) 161 UNTS 74. See also *Whaling in the Antarctic Case (Australia v Japan)* [2014] ICJ http://www.icj-cij.org/docket/files/148/18136.pdf (last accessed on 30 May 2015).

[110]  *Southern Bluefin Tuna Cases (New Zealand v. Japan; Australia v. Japan)* (Provisional Measures) (1999) ITLOS Case Nos. 3 & 4; 38 International Legal Materials 1624.

[111]  Resolution LP.4(8).

The right to conduct MSR also extends to research carried out in the Area.[112] This right is to be exercised in conformity with Part XI to the extent that those provisions are applicable. Under Part XI, Article 143 lays down specific principles and conditions for the conduct of MSR that reflect the overall structure and principles of the regime for the Area as the common heritage of mankind.[113] This provision recognizes the competence of the International Seabed Authority (ISA) to carry out MSR and its resources, and its duty to promote the conduct of MSR in the Area and encourage knowledge transfer and dissemination.[114] Article 143(3) requires that states promote international cooperation in MSR in the Area, including by effectively disseminating the results of research and analysis. Part XI also stipulates that necessary measures must be taken in accordance with the LOSC to ensure the protection of the marine environment from adverse effects potentially arising from activities carried out in the Area.[115] However, MSR conducted on the seabed and ocean floor and in the subsoil therefore in areas beyond the limits of national jurisdiction,[116] but which falls outside of the regulatory scope of the legal regime governing the Area, arguably remains within the high seas regime.[117] In other words, MSR which does not relate to mineral resources within the meaning of 'activities in the Area' pursuant to Article 1(3) is governed by the provisions on MSR for the high seas.[118] If MSR moves on to the stage of prospecting and exploring for mineral resources such 'applied research' would fall within the mandate of the ISA.[119] It would have to be determined based on the relevant circumstances whether a given activity constitutes MSR or constitutes prospecting or exploitation.[120]

---

[112]   LOSC, Art. 256. The 'Area' is defined in Art. 1(1) of the LOSC as 'the seabed and ocean floor and subsoil thereof, beyond the limits of national jurisdiction'.

[113]   LOSC, Art. 256. See Jeff Ardron, 'Ocean sustainability through transparency: Deep sea mining and lessons learnt from previous resource booms' (2014 Potsdam Ocean Governance Workshop Background Document 3) www.iddri.org/Evenements/Ateliers/potsdam_annex%203.pdf (last accessed 29 May 2015).

[114]   LOSC, Arts 143(2) and 144(1)(b).

[115]   LOSC, Art. 145.

[116]   LOSC, Art. 1(1).

[117]   Soons, above n 65, 226; Leary, above n 61, 50, stating 'under Article 240(d) the ISA clearly has competence to implement measures to regulate MSR associated with the exploitation of mineral resources in the Area. However, if such applied research did not relate to the mineral resources of the Area, for example, bioprospecting for genetic resources in the Area, it would not be subject to control by the ISA'.

[118]   'Activities in the Area' is defined in Article 1(3) as 'all activities of exploration for, and exploitation of, the resources of the Area.'

[119]   Leary, above n 61, 50.

[120]   The terms 'prospecting' and 'exploration' are both defined in the ISA Regulations. See Regulations on Prospecting and Exploration for Polymetallic Nodules in the Area, 13 July 2000, official text published as document ISBA/6/A/18, annex (13 July 2000); Regulations on prospecting and exploration for polymetallic sulphides in the Area, ISBA/16/A/12/Rev.1 (7 May 2010) http://www.isa.org.jm/files/documents/EN/Regs/PolymetallicSulphides.pdf (last accessed 30 May 2015); Regulations on Prospecting and Exploration for Cobalt-rich Ferromanganese Crusts in the Area, ISBA/18/A/11 (27 July 2012) http://www.isa.org.jm/files/documents/EN/16Sess/Council/ISBA-16C-WP2.pdf (last accessed 30 May 2015); Regulations on Prospecting

In any event, MSR conducted on the high seas or in the Area is subject to the 'due regard'[121] or 'reasonable regard'[122] requirements, respectively, such that the freedom must be exercised by taking into account the interests of other states in the exercise of their freedoms of the high seas and in the Area. Such interests would include, inter alia, the protection and preservation of the marine environment in these marine areas beyond national jurisdiction.[123]

Nevertheless, the zonal approach taken in the LOSC has a downside for both the pursuit of MSR and the achievement of progress on environmental protection. Access to the oceans for taking scientific measurements and samples and making observations is of paramount importance to gaining a more complete understanding of the marine environment and the impact of human activities on it. However, environmental phenomena and processes do not respect artificial legal boundaries. Sometimes there is a direct conflict in which research access is limited or restricted geographically by the designation and adoption of measures for specially protected marine areas.[124] Increasingly, however, there is a need for data collection on the functioning of the ocean system as a whole, particularly as it relates to climate change and ocean acidification. The zonal approach can serve to limit the conduct of ocean-wide MSR and gives rise to jurisdictional questions and legal uncertainties in the interpretation and implementation of the Convention.

By way of example, considerable controversy has surrounded the Argo Floats Programme carried out jointly between IOC-UNESCO and the World Meteorological Organization (WMO). The programme involved the deployment of a global array of more than 3000 free-drifting profiling floats that collect information about temperature and salinity in the upper water column. A critical application of this international ocean-observing programme was to better understand the role of the oceans in the global climate system, and to assess the extent and impacts of climate change on the oceans. States sharply disagreed over whether these activities fell within the ambit of Part XIII of the LOSC as a form of 'MSR' or within a separate category of information

---

and Exploration for Polymetallic Nodules in the Area, ISBA/19/C/17 (22 July 2013) http://www.isa.org.jm/files/documents/EN/Regs/PolymetallicSulphides.pdf (last accessed 30 May 2015).

[121] LOSC, Art. 87(2). According to Tullio Treves, 'MSR' in Rüdiger Wolfrum (ed.), *Max Planck Encyclopedia of Public International Law* (Oxford University Press 2008) the 'due regard' requirement is pertinent regarding a coastal state's sovereign rights over scientific research carried out in the high seas above the extended continental shelf or over the continental shelf where no EEZ has been proclaimed.

[122] LOSC, Art. 147(1).

[123] See further Recommendations of the Ad Hoc Open-ended Informal Working Group to study issues relating to the conservation and sustainable use of marine biological diversity beyond areas of national jurisdiction to the sixty-ninth session of the General Assembly (23 January 2015) www.un.org/depts/los/biodiversityworkinggroup/documents/AHWG_9_recommendations.pdf (last accessed 30 May 2015). See also 'Our Common Future: Report of the World Commission on Environment and Development' UN Doc A/42/427, Annex (4 August 1987), ch 10 'Managing the Commons'; See Global Ocean Commission, 'From Decline to Recovery: A Rescue Package for the Global Ocean' (2014) http://www.globalocean commission.org/wp-content/uploads/GOC_report_2015.pdf (last accessed 4 June 2015).

[124] Leary, above n 61, 151–4.

gathering activities under the umbrella of 'operational oceanography'.[125] On the one hand, although deployed on the high seas, the profiling floats could passively enter into marine areas under national jurisdiction, and some coastal states argued that the information collected could be directly relevant to understanding their natural resources, so that prior consent was required.[126] On the other hand, it was argued that profiling floats were not 'MSR' but 'operational oceanography' and thus constituted an exercise of the freedom of the high seas by the deploying state or organization.[127] In any event, from a policy perspective, the practicalities of requiring consent would severely hamper the implementation of the programme. The matter was brought before the Advisory Body of Experts on the Law of the Sea (IOC/ABE-LOS) which provides advice to the Intergovernmental Oceanographic Commission (IOC) of the United Nations Educational Scientific and Cultural Organization (UNESCO). After several years of deliberation over the legal implications, they adopted a simplified non-binding guideline and compromise agreement requiring prior notification with a provision that coastal states have a right to restrict the release of data if it is directly relevant to exploration or exploitation of living or non-living natural resources.[128] This halfway house solution 'serve[d] as a pragmatic basis for international cooperation within the Argo programme' and 'cannot be applied to the collection of oceanographic data in general'.[129] As a consequence, the debate regarding the extent to which operational oceanography is distinct from MSR remains unsettled.

The discussions in IOC/ABE-LOS largely focused on a narrow characterization of the activity in terms of the zone-specific provisions on MSR in the LOSC. However, the case can also be examined from the broader perspective of the duties in the LOSC and the United Nations Framework Convention on Climate Change (UNFCCC)[130] to promote and facilitate scientific data collection and international cooperation on scientific and technical matters to achieve the protective objectives of those legal instruments.[131]

Access for marine research purposes is also a particular problem due to geopolitical constraints and legal uncertainties relating to the extended continental shelf under the

---

[125]   On this distinction see Wegelein, above n 9, 20; Gragl, above n 39, 403–5. See further Roach, n 104.

[126]   LOSC, Arts 246, 248 and 249.

[127]   See further Roach, above n 104.

[128]   See IOC/EC-XLI/3, Annex II, 41st Sess. of the Executive Council adopted resolution EC-XLI.4: Guidelines for the implementation of Resolution XX-6 of the IOC Assembly regarding the deployment of Profiling floats in the High Seas within the framework of the Argo Programme, 29 July 2008.

[129]   Peter Ehlers, 'The Governance of the Global Ocean Observing System (GOOS)' in Holger P. Hestermeyer and others (eds) *Coexistence, Cooperation and Solidarity: Liber Amicorum Rüdiger Wolfrum*, vol. II (Brill 2012), 1429.

[130]   (1992) 1771 UNTS 165.

[131]   Aurora Mateos and Montserrat Gorina-Ysern, 'Climate Change and Guidelines for Argo Profiling Float Deployment on the High Seas' (2010) 14 *ASIL Insight* www.asil.org/insights/volume/14/issue/8/climate-change-and-guidelines-argo-profiling-float-deployment-high-seas (last accessed 30 May 2015).

LOSC.[132] For example, in the Arctic, the US Arctic Region Policy outlines the need for access to the seabed and subfloor to understand climate change, stating that '[a]ccurate prediction of future environmental and climate change on a regional basis, … requires obtaining, analyzing, and disseminating accurate data from the entire Arctic region, including both paleoclimatic data and observational data'.[133] However, access predictability to the seabed and subfloor of the Arctic Ocean is an issue due to the slow progress of the process of confirming sovereign rights over natural resources in the extended continental shelf under the LOSC.[134]

### 3.4 Scientific Research Installations and Equipment

The same regime that governs the conduct of MSR also applies to the deployment and use of any observing installations or equipment within a given maritime zone, albeit in this case the activity is subject to additional requirements, relating, for example, to safety and navigation.[135] Thus, as the ARGOS float example demonstrates, if freely floating scientific equipment is deployed in one maritime zone and drifts into another the rules applicable to that equipment may change.[136] The rules on installations, structures and equipment also bring within the scope of the LOSC certain aspects of atmospheric research that may not otherwise be covered by marine instruments. For example, while the definition of 'marine geoengineering' in the London Protocol is not likely to cover all solar radiation management (SRM) research,[137] some activities, such as marine cloud brightening or atmospheric sulphate injection, will be covered by the LOSC to the extent that they employ marine-based research structures, platforms, installations or delivery by vessels.[138]

## 4. RESPONSIBILITY AND LIABILITY

If a MSR activity does result in harm to the marine environment, issues regarding legal responsibility and liability arise. In addition to the general rules on state responsibility

---

[132] Betsy Baker, 'Common Precepts of MSR Access in the Arctic' in Susanne Wasum-Rainer and others, *Arctic Science, International Law and Climate Change: Legal Aspects of Marine Science in the Ocean* (Springer 2012).

[133] United States National Security Presidential Directive and Homeland Security Presidential Directive NSPD 66/HSPD 25 'Arctic Region Policy' (2009) 48 *International Legal Materials* 274, E.4.

[134] Baker, above n 132.

[135] LOSC, Art. 258.

[136] Treves, above n 121, para. 20. See also James Kraska, Guillermo Ortuno Crespo and David W. Johnston, 'Bio-logging of marine migratory species in the law of the sea' (2015) 51 *Marine Policy* 394.

[137] See Karen N. Scott, 'Geoengineering and the marine environment', Chapter 21 in this volume.

[138] See Catherine Redgwell, 'Geoengineering the Climate: Technological Solutions to Mitigation – Failure or Continuing Carbon Addiction?' (2011) 2 *Carbon and Climate Law Review* 184–5.

regarding the breach of an international obligation by a state *vis-à-vis* other states,[139] the LOSC provides a specific basis for responsibility and liability where a wrongful act or omission occurs in respect of MSR.[140] States and international organizations are responsible and liable under Article 263(3) for damage caused by pollution of the marine environment as a result of MSR undertaken by them or on their behalf.[141] This rule links to the general provision on responsibility and liability for environmental damage in Article 235 of Part XII that entails, inter alia, a requirement to ensure that compensation or other relief is made available for damage caused.[142]

In some circumstances these provisions may be of limited use in ensuring legal accountability for specific damage arising from research activities to naturally variable, complex marine ecosystems. This is particularly so in the case of novel, often one-off, in situ experiments, for which scientific uncertainty is bound, by definition, to exist, given the very object and purpose of carrying out the research is to reduce scientific uncertainty. In such circumstances, the sticky wicket of establishing legal responsibility and liability for specific pollution damage incurred from marine research activities in accordance with Article 263(3) (and indeed in most environmental cases) concerns the requirement to prove to relevant evidentiary standards,[143] a causal link between a state's wrongful act and a loss or injury.[144] In such situations the precautionary principle, which applies in circumstances of scientific uncertainty in which it is difficult to prove cause-effect relationships, may operate to lower the standard of proof required to prove a claim of damage to the marine environment from polluting research activities.[145] An alternate approach would be to ease the burden of proving causation through some

---

[139]   See ILC Articles on State Responsibility, *Report to the United Nations General Assembly*, UN Doc A/56/10 (2001).

[140]   LOSC, Art. 263. See Wegelein, above n 9, 343–53.

[141]   LOSC, Art. 263(3).

[142]   LOSC, Art. 235.

[143]   Regarding the standard of proof applied by international courts and tribunals see Separate Opinion of Vice-President Wolfrum, *The M/V 'Saiga' Case (Saint Vincent and the Grenadines v. Guinea)* ITLOS Case No. 2 (1999); Separate Opinion of Judge Greenwood, *Case Concerning Pulp Mills on the River Uruguay (Argentina v. Uruguay)* [2007] ICJ Rep 21, paras 25–6. See also James Harrison, 'International Courts and Tribunals in the Settlement of Environmental Disputes and the Development of International Environmental Law' (2013) 25 *Journal of Environmental Law* 501.

[144]   Roda Verheyen, *Climate Change Damage and International Law: Prevention, Duties and State Responsibility* (Brill Academic Publishers 2004) 249.

[145]   Caroline E. Foster, *Science and the Precautionary Principle in International Courts and Tribunals: Expert Evidence, Burden of Proof and Finality* (Cambridge University Press 2011) 273; Miriam Haritz, *An Inconvenient Deliberation: The Precautionary Principle's Contribution to the Uncertainties Surrounding Climate Change Liability* (Kluwer Law International 2011) 306–309; Simon Marr, 'The Southern Bluefin Tuna Cases: The Precautionary Approach and Conservation and Management of Fish Resources' (2000) 11 *European Journal of International Law* 815, 822–3.

bespoke negotiated responsibility or liability scheme for marine environmental damage.[146] The possibility of devising alternative modes of legal accountability for damage to the marine environment is in fact expressly contemplated within the Convention. Article 304 stipulates that the 'provisions of [the] Convention regarding responsibility and liability for damage are without prejudice to ... the development of further rules regarding responsibility and liability under international law'.[147]

## 5. SETTLEMENT OF DISPUTES

Regarding the settlement of disputes related to MSR,[148] the LOSC recognizes the compulsory jurisdiction of an international court or tribunal pursuant to the general rules laid down in Articles 296 and 297, but subject to certain limitations and exceptions.[149] A specific limitation to the application of the compulsory settlement procedures exists in respect of the conduct of MSR in the EEZ and on the continental shelf. Disputes relating to allegations by a researching state that the coastal state has not lawfully exercised its rights or discretion under Articles 246 and 253 regarding a research project within these areas under national jurisdiction are excluded from the compulsory settlement mechanisms, although they may be submitted to conciliation at the request of any party subject to certain conditions.[150]

The interpretation and application of the LOSC provisions on MSR do not yet appear to have been the focus of an international dispute. However, marine 'research' more generally has been a contentious issue between states giving rise to international adjudication.[151] Given this precedent one can only speculate as to whether controversial MSR, such as perturbation experiments involving marine geoengineering, might also trigger inter-state litigation aimed at the protection of the marine environment in the future.[152]

---

[146] Verheyen, above n 144, 362–3. See generally Jutta Brunnée, 'International Legal Accountability through the Lens of the Law of State Responsibility' (2005) 36 *Netherlands Yearbook of International Law* 21.

[147] See also LOSC, Art. 235(3).

[148] Robin R. Churchill and A.V. Lowe, *The Law of the Sea, 3rd edn* (Manchester University Press 1999) 447–8 point out that marine scientific can also give rise to litigation in municipal courts. Regarding potential conflicts with the protection of the marine environment, see, eg, *Qikiqtani Inuit Association v. Canada (Minister of Natural Resources)* 2010 NUCJ 12 in which a Canadian court granted a temporary injunction to prevent seismic testing by the German RV *Polarstern* on the grounds that could potentially impact marine wildlife in the area. See also Hannah Hoag, 'Inuit concerns stall seismic testing' *Nature News* (12 August 2010) http://www.nature.com/news/2010/100812/full/news.2010.403.html (last accessed 4 June 2015).

[149] LOSC, Art. 264.

[150] LOSC, Art. 297(2).

[151] Eg, *Whaling in the Antarctic Case*; *Southern Bluefin Tuna Cases*.

[152] See generally Meinhard Doelle, 'Climate Geoengineering and Dispute Settlement under UNCLOS and the UNFCCC: Stormy Seas Ahead?' in Randal S. Abate (ed.) *Climate Change Impacts on Ocean and Coastal Law: U.S. and International Perspectives* (Oxford University Press 2015).

Within the context of other kinds of disputes relating to the interpretation and application of the law of the sea such as contested territorial claims, MSR can become a casualty of inter-state disagreements. This also has implications for the protection of the marine environment and its resources. For example, in the disputed areas of the South China Sea it is reported that claimant states have demonstrated reticence towards initiating collaborative research programmes, even though these are generally regarded as 'non-sensitive cooperative activities to be promoted'[153] and are necessary to conserve marine ecosystems and biodiversity in the region.[154] In legal terms, the LOSC is clear that scientific cooperation in the disputed territory would be legally irrelevant to any claim to maritime zones or their resources.[155] Beyond this, the promotion and cooperation in marine science could in fact contribute to the peaceful settlement of disputes, whereby multilateral research conducted collaboratively by claimant and non-claimant states could serve as a balm and 'confidence-building measure that would bring players from different countries together to address common concerns and thus learn to communicate and work with one another'.[156]

## 6. CONCLUSIONS AND QUESTIONS FOR FURTHER STUDY

The legal regimes in the LOSC for MSR in Part XIII and for the protection and preservation of the marine environment in Part XII are not static, and each influences the progressive development of the other. Furthermore, both are crosscutting issues in the Convention that frequently interact with the regimes for other ocean uses and different maritime zones. This chapter has examined the legal regime for MSR and its progressive development with a view to understanding its relationship to the regime for the protection and preservation of the marine environment.

In many respects, the rules and principles that regulate MSR and environmental protection are mutually reinforcing. The availability of scientific information is a prerequisite for effective environmental regulation. This is reflected in the normative structure of the LOSC, which requires that states promote, facilitate and cooperate in MSR. Specifically with regard to environmental protection, states are required to cooperate for the purpose of studies, research programmes and exchange of information and data about marine pollution and based on this information are required to develop appropriate scientific criteria for such regulations. A contextual reading of the relationship between Parts XII and XIII suggests that, in law, one regime does not stand above the other. Taking into account the particular circumstances, states can justify certain restrictive measures aimed at preventing damage to the marine environment, even if

---

[153]   Vu Hai Dang, *Marine Protected Areas Network in the South China Sea: Charting a Course for Future Cooperation* (Brill 2014) 248.

[154]   Edgardo D. Gomez, 'MSR in the South China Sea and Environmental Security' (2001) 32 *Ocean Development & International Law* 205; Dang, above n 153, 248.

[155]   LOSC, Art. 241.

[156]   Gomez, above n 154.

their actions have the effect of limiting the conduct of MSR, but only where such restrictions are necessary and reasonable.[157]

Wegelein suggests that because scientific knowledge is necessary for effective environmental regulation and management 'a distinction should be made between such research, which is necessary to provide a solid knowledge basis for informed management decisions… and such research, that is not directly related to environmental protection'.[158] However, it may not always be practicable to characterize the purpose of a proposed research project ex ante, and there is an element of the unknown in determining how potentially risky scientific research should be appropriately regulated. This is because research, by its very nature, is an investigative activity aimed at increasing new knowledge, and thus involves scientific uncertainty and is continually evolving. Regulation of MSR can produce secondary risks whereby restrictions on research activities can limit understanding of the marine environment and the impacts that human activities are having on the oceans. MSR can be restricted subject to a principle of 'not-unreasonable interference' with such activities.[159]

It is underscored, however, that MSR can have adverse effects on the marine environment. For example, extended scientific technical capability for data collection and in situ experimentation in the oceans gives us a much more comprehensive picture of the ocean system. However, these new oceanographic research methods and equipment may have direct adverse impacts on the marine environment. Therefore, environmental regulation of MSR activities can be justified in certain circumstances. An important development is the specification of best practices for the conduct of MSR for specific matters in accordance with the general principles in Article 240(b) and (d).[160] Another form of 'best practice' relates to the promotion of transparency relating to the planning and conduct of MSR by maximizing the benefits to the whole of society[161] and minimizing environmental damage by preventing redundant study.[162] It is noteworthy in this respect that the LOSC contains several provisions on scientific information sharing and the open publication and dissemination of research results, data and information. Full implementation of these provisions accords with the principle of mutual benefit, which qualifies the obligation of states in Article 242 to promote and cooperate in MSR. Moreover, the LOSC contains rules that make states responsible and liable for damage caused to the marine environment as a result of MSR undertaken by them or on their behalf. Further evolution of these rules on legal responsibility and liability may be necessary to ensure accountability and reparation for damage to the marine environment as a result of MSR. Another area for further enquiry relates to MSR that likely does not entail any direct or immediate physical harm to the environment, but which may justify additional regulatory control and oversight in the

---

[157]   See further regarding LOSC, Arts 194(4) and 240(d), this chapter, above.

[158]   Wegelein, above n 9, 76.

[159]   Graham, above n 35, 8. See also Hubert, above n 13, 337–8.

[160]   See OSPAR Code of Conduct for Responsible Marine Research.

[161]   Regarding transparency in international environmental law see generally Jutta Brunnée and Ellen Hey, 'Transparency and International Environmental Institutions' in Andrea Bianchi and Anne Peters (eds) *Transparency in International Law* (Cambridge University Press 2013).

[162]   See OSPAR Code of Conduct for Responsible Marine Research, paras 17 and 21–3. See also Ocean Fertilization Assessment Framework, para. 3.6.1.

face of high uncertainties and societal concerns associated with the modern 'techno-sciences'.[163] Further research regarding how the legal regime for MSR in Part XIII of the LOSC operates in this new era of 'post-normal' science is necessary.[164]

---

[163] Funtowicz and Ravetz, above n 16, 253.
[164] See above n 16 and n 17. Cf Oksana Udovyk and Michael Gilek, 'Participation and Post-normal Science in Practice? Reality Check for Hazardous Chemicals Management in the European Maritime Environment' (2014) 63 *Futures* 15.

# PART V

# REGIONAL APPROACHES TO THE PROTECTION OF THE MARINE ENVIRONMENT

# 16. Forty years of the UNEP Regional Seas Programme: from past to future

*Nilufer Oral*

## 1. INTRODUCTION

In 2014 the United Nations Environment Programme (UNEP) Regional Seas Programme (UNEP RSP) celebrated its fortieth anniversary. Since 1974, when the main threats to the marine environment were identified as land-based and vessel-source pollution, much has changed. While these traditional sources of pollution of the marine environment continue as risks, other environmental threats have become far more numerous and complex. Loss of marine biodiversity and habitats, threats to vulnerable marine ecosystems such as coral reefs, threats to the high seas, and threats from climate change are among the challenges the international community must now address collectively.

The UNEP RSP was established in 1974 to serve as the mechanism for promoting cooperation among States sharing a common 'regional' marine space. Initially its orientation focused on pollution prevention. However, as new international environmental challenges emerged and scientific knowledge grew, a surge in the number of international environmental instruments being adopted made the UNEP Regional Seas Programme the natural mechanism to promote regional implementation of these new instruments.

Over the years, UNEP, which was created as the principal international environmental protection body, has been successful in developing a large body of multilateral environmental agreements (MEAs). However, the challenge has been to implement these MEAs at the national level. Optimally, the UNEP RSP should serve as a robust mechanism for incorporating these obligations, as well as the international principles of environmental law and mechanisms as they relate to the marine environment and for promoting their regional and national implementation. The question is whether it has effectively done so?

This chapter examines the development of the UNEP RSP. It begins with a discussion of its development and overall structure and then provides a comparative assessment of the different Regional Seas Agreements (RSAs) that make up the Programme. The chapter provides a critical assessment of both the past successes of the UNEP RSP and of its future.

## 2. DEVELOPMENT OF THE CONCEPT OF 'REGIONAL SEAS' AND THE UNEP REGIONAL SEAS PROGRAMME

### 2.1 Law of the Sea and Regional Seas

The idea that seas with multiple coastal states could be governed or managed regionally emerged in the 1970s. Lewis Alexander was one of the first international legal scholars to undertake defining the role of marine regionalism for the new oceans law framework that was being developed at the Third Law of the Sea Conference (UNCLOS III), and particularly its application to semi-enclosed seas.[1] The concept was quite novel at the time and there was uncertainty as to how marine regionalism could be applied. Alexander posited that a special regional regime for regional or semi-enclosed seas could be based on two different categories. The first category would be exclusionary. In other words, littoral states would exclude outsiders from certain types of activities within the sea, such as military vessels, scientific vessels, potential polluters such as oil tankers and LNG carriers, or simply impose their own pollution standards.[2] The second category would be developmental in nature; that is, the coastal states bordering a semi-enclosed sea would 'join together to invest in improving the environment and the use of the seas resources'.[3] This could include the adoption of restrictive legislation such as fisheries conservation or pollution control measures, pollution control facilities or measures relating to oceanographic data acquisitions.[4]

Other scholars subsequently adopted Professor Alexander's definition and categorization.[5] The question of whether regional seas should have a special regime was

---

[1]  Lewis M. Alexander, 'Regionalism and the Law of the Sea: the Case of Semi-enclosed Seas' (1974) 2 *Ocean Development and International Law* 151. Alexander defined a semi-enclosed sea as one that had an area of at least 50,000 nautical miles, and that was a 'primary' sea, rather than an arm of a larger semi-enclosed body of water. At least fifty per cent of its circumference had to be occupied by land and the width of the connector between the sea and the open ocean could not represent more than twenty per cent of the sea's total volume. According to his definition there were twenty-five semi-enclosed seas of the world. See also, Lewis Alexander, 'Special Circumstances: Semi-enclosed Seas' in J.K. Gamble and G. Pontecorvo (eds), *Law of the Sea Institute Eighth Annual Conference* (1973) 201; Lewis M. Alexander, 'Regional Arrangements in the Oceans' (1977) 71 *American Journal of International Law* 84; Adelberto Vallega, 'The Regional Scale of Ocean Management and Marine Region Building' (1994) 24 *Ocean and Coastal Management* 17; Adelberto Vallega, 'The Regional Approach to the Ocean, the Ocean Regions, and Ocean Regionalisation – a Post-modern Dilemma' (2002) 45 *Ocean and Coastal Management* 721.

[2]  Alexander, 'Regionalism and the Law of the Sea' above n 1, 159.

[3]  Ibid 159–61.

[4]  Ibid.

[5]  Boleslaw Adam Boczek, 'Global and Regional Approaches to the Protection and Preservation of the Marine Environment' (1984) 16 *Case Western Reserve Journal of International Law* 39; Boleslaw Adam Bozcek, 'The Baltic Sea: a Study in Marine Regionalism' (1980) 23 *German Yearbook of International Law* 196; Malgosia Fitzmaurice, *International Legal Problems of the Environmental Protection of the Baltic Sea* (Kluwer Law International, 1992) M. Eduarda Gonçalves, 'Concepts of Marine Region and the New Law of the Sea' (1979) 3 *Marine Policy* 255.

debated during the Second Committee meetings of UNCLOS III, where several states raised the special concerns of enclosed and semi-enclosed seas in relation to protection of the marine environment and management of resources[6] and promoted the need for a special regime for enclosed and semi-enclosed seas.[7] While there was objection by some states to creating a separate category of seas under the new convention being negotiated,[8] ultimately Part IX on enclosed and semi-enclosed seas became part of the 1982 Law of the Sea Convention[9] (LOSC). The ultimate creation of this new category of 'regional' seas was a result of the recognition by the international community that certain seas, because they occupy a smaller marine space or because of their limited access to the world's oceans, when bordered by multiple coastal states, faced special concerns.

Although the LOSC did not provide a definition of a 'marine region', the Convention did include a separate section on 'global and regional cooperation'.[10] In addition, Part IX of the LOSC, on enclosed and semi-enclosed seas, specifically focused on cooperation for the protection of the marine environment by coastal states bordering enclosed and semi-enclosed seas in Article 123, which exhorts such states to cooperate with each other directly or through an *appropriate regional organization* (emphasis added). The areas of cooperation include coordination in: the management, conservation, exploration and exploitation of the living resources of the sea; the implementation of their rights and duties with respect to the protection and preservation of the marine environment; and in their scientific research policies and programmes. In addition, states are to invite other interested states or international organizations to cooperate with them. The UNEP RSP was established to play the role of such an international organization.

---

[6] For example, Iraq proposed to include the management, preservation, exploration and exploitation of marine living resources in semi-enclosed and enclosed seas beyond the territorial sea as issues which were to be agreed upon by the coastal States by regional arrangements *taking into account the activities of international organizations concerned in these fields*. The Iraqi proposal provided for the *joint management* among riparian states and that rules and regulations were to be based upon internationally agreed standards. U.N.Doc. A/Conf.62/C.2/ L.71 and Add.1 and Add.2 (1974), III *Official Records of the Third United Nations Conference on the Law of the Sea* 236.

[7] UN Doc. A/CONF.62/C.2/SR 38, Second Committee, 38th Meeting (1974) II *Official Records of the Third United Nations Conference on the Law of the Sea* 273 (*Official Records*).

[8] France objected to the concept of enclosed and semi-enclosed seas stating that these were not part of a 'traditional concept of international law', being of a purely geographical notion. The French delegate argued that creating special rules for these seas would risk establishing a *mare clausum*. Second Committee, 38th Meeting (1974) II *Official Records* 276.

[9] Adopted 10 December 1982, entered into force 16 November 1994, 1833 UNTS 3 (LOSC).

[10] Part XII, Section 2. For an in-depth analysis of the development of regionalism in the law of the sea, see: Erik Franckx, 'Regional Marine Environment Protection Regimes in the Context of UNCLOS' (1998) 13 *International Journal of Marine and Coastal Law* 307.

## 2.2  The Evolution of the UNEP Regional Seas Programme

Around the time that Lewis Alexander was developing the idea of a regional seas approach, the first global summit on the environment was held in Stockholm. One of the important outcomes of the historic 1972 United Nations Conference on the Human Environment (Stockholm Conference) was the establishment of the United Nations Environmental Programme (UNEP) as a subsidiary organ of the United Nations,[11] with a mandate to promote international cooperation in the field of environmental protection.[12] With specific reference to the marine environment, Principle 24 of the Stockholm Declaration,[13] called for multilateral cooperation to 'control, prevent, reduce and eliminate adverse environmental effects resulting from activities conducted in all spheres', including the oceans. This provided the basis for the framework of cooperation in regional governance of marine protection of regional seas under the UNEP RSP, which was subsequently established in 1974.[14]

## 2.3  UNEP Regional Seas after Stockholm

The 1992 United Nations Conference on the Environment and Development (Earth Summit) followed the landmark 1972 Stockholm Conference. The Earth Summit, held in Rio de Janeiro, adopted the Rio Declaration and Principles and the comprehensive Agenda 21 for Sustainable Development,[15] which was intended to provide a blueprint for environmental management at the global level for the twenty-first century. Chapter 17 of Agenda 21 was devoted entirely to oceans and the marine environment. Chapter 17 recognized the need for new approaches to marine and coastal management at all levels, including the regional level, that were integrated, precautionary and anticipatory

---

   [11]   UNEP was established under Art. 22 of the United Nations Charter. As a subsidiary organ of the UN and not a specialized agency of the United Nations under Art. 57 of the Charter, UNEP lacks autonomous status and a separate budget. Rather, its funding options are limited to voluntary contributions. See, Said Mahmoudi, 'The United Nations Environment Programme (UNEP): an Assessment' (1995) 5 *Asian Yearbook of International Law* 175.
   [12]   UNEP's mandate also includes the progressive development of environmental law. See Alexander Timochenko, 'UNEP Initiatives to Promote Compliance with Multilateral Environment Agreements' in Alexandre Kiss, Dinah Shelton and Kanami Ishibashi (eds) *Economic Globalization and Compliance with International Environmental Agreements* (Kluwer Law International, 2003) 125, 126.
   [13]   UN Doc. 48/14, 16 June 1972, 11 *International Law Materials* 1416 (1972). UN General Assembly Resolution 2997 (XXVII) of 15 December 1972, on the institutional and financial arrangements for international environmental cooperation, 12 *International Law Materials* 433 (1973). See, Patricia Birnie, 'The Development of International Environmental Law' (1977) 3 *British Journal of International Studies* 169.
   [14]   General Assembly Res. 2997, 27 U.N. GAOR Supp. (No. 30) at 30, UN Doc. A/8730 (1972); Peter Schroder, 'UNEP's Regional Seas Programme and the UNCED Future: Apres Rio' (1992) 18 *Ocean and Coastal Management* 101; Mark Allen Gray, 'The United Nations Environmental Programme: an Assessment' (1990) 20 *Environmental Law* 291.
   [15]   See, Report of the UN Conference on Environment and Development, UN Doc. A/CONF.151/26/Rev.1. The Rio Declaration and Agenda 21 are reproduced in (1992) 31 *International Legal Materials* 874.

and that were to be reflected in a separate programme for 'strengthening international, including regional cooperation and coordination'.[16] More specifically in relation to the UNEP RSP, states were called upon to consider, inter alia, 'strengthening, and extending where necessary,… the Regional Seas Programmes of UNEP'.[17]

Ten years later the 2002 Johannesburg Plan of Implementation (JPOI) of the World Summit on Sustainable Development[18] sought to consolidate the environmental developments of the past decade into a global plan of implementation, which included the sustainable development of the oceans and marine environment with specific mention of strengthening the UNEP RSP.[19] In 2012, forty years after the Stockholm Conference and twenty years after the first Rio summit, the Rio+20 Summit adopted as its final outcome a document entitled 'The Future We Want',[20] which included a commitment by governments to strengthening the role of UNEP as the leading global environmental authority.[21] Furthermore, governments committed to strengthening UNEP by providing it with 'secure, stable, adequate and increased financial resources'.[22] This begs the question as to how this will be reflected within the UNEP RSP.

### 2.4   UNEP's Vision and Strategy for the Regional Seas

UNEP's approach to the marine and coastal environment is clustered around the Regional Seas Programme, which focuses on six key issues: coastal area management, ecosystem and biodiversity, land-based activities, marine litter, sea-based pollution and small islands.[23] In addition, the RSP has created the Large Marine Ecosystems Programme (LMEs) as a sub-group of regional seas.[24]

One of the challenges UNEP has faced has been to adapt to and incorporate new and emerging issues, such as climate change, new principles, such as the precautionary principle, and mechanisms to promote compliance into its RSP. In order to make the RSP more responsive to developments and needs in the global environmental governance framework, the UNEP RSP has adopted a series of global strategic directions encompassing four-year periods. For example, the RSP Global Strategic Directions for 2013–16 consists of six strategic directions including: effective application of the

---

[16]   Agenda 21, para. 17.1.

[17]   Ibid, para. 17.119.

[18]   Johannesburg Plan of Implementation (JPOI), available at www.un.org/esa/sustdev/documents/WSSD_POI_PD/English/WSSD_PlanImpl.pdf (last accessed 30 May 2015).

[19]   JPOI, sect IV.

[20]   Available at www.uncsd2012.org/content/documents/727The%20Future%20We%20Want%2019%20June%201230pm.pdf (last accessed 30 May 2015).

[21]   'The Future We Want', para. 88.

[22]   Ibid.

[23]   See, www.unep.org/regionalseas/issues/default.asp (last accessed 30 May 2015).

[24]   K. Sherman and G. Hempel (eds), *The UNEP Large Marine Ecosystem Report: A perspective on changing conditions in LMEs of the world's Regional Seas* (UNEP Regional Seas Report and Studies No. 182, 2008). For discussion see, David Vousden, 'Large marine ecosystems and associated new approaches to regional, transboundary and "high seas" management', Chapter 18 in this volume.

ecosystem approach (SD1); contributing to the implementation of the *Manila Declaration* of the Global Programme of Action for the Protection of the Marine Environment from Land-based Activities (SD2); strengthening national and regional capacities for coastal and marine governance to improve coordination with other systems, such as LMEs and fisheries organizations (SD3); improving global knowledge and trends on the status of the marine environment that would contribute to the World Oceans Assessment (SD5); provision of tools, such as assessment of ecosystem services, to assist in decoupling economic development from environmental pressures (SD4); and strengthening collaboration mechanisms to address common regional objectives, partnerships and coordinated regional implementation of relevant MEAs as well as global and regional initiatives by United Nations Agencies (SD6).

A recent interim report by the UNEP RSP for the 2013–16 Strategic Directions lists different activities such as regional workshops, studies, reports and thematic projects as the modalities to be used to achieve the strategic directions.[25] What remains unclear is whether these strategic directions are in practice being effectively implemented in each of the RSPs under UNEPs auspices. For example, the strategic directions for 2008–12 consisted of nine global strategic directions that included, inter alia, enhanced sustainability and effectiveness of the RSP through increased country ownership by incorporation of the regional legal framework into national legislation, promoting compliance and enforcement mechanisms, involving civil society and the private sector, and building capacity (SD1). It is unclear, however, whether and if so in what manner UNEP assessed the implementation and outcome of this important global strategic direction at the end of 2012.

The other strategic directions for the 2008–12 period included: contribute to the implementation of the Beijing Declaration of the Global Programme of Action for the Protection of the Marine Environment from Land-based Activities (SD2); strengthen regional cooperation with the IMO for preparedness and response to oil pollution from maritime accidents (SD3); contribute to the implementation of the 2010 Biodiversity Targets including the establishments of a network of coastal and marine protected areas and planning of proper coastal and watershed use by 2012 (SD4); emphasize the need to implement the ecosystem approach in integrated marine and coastal management (IMCM) (SD5); assess impact of climate change on the marine and coastal environment taking into account environmental, social and economic factors and impacts on tourism, fisheries, human health, biodiversity, coastal erosion and small island ecosystems including promoting cooperation in the development of regional climate change adaptation strategies (SD6); intensify regional activities for the implementation of the Jakarta Mandate of the 1992 Convention on Biological Diversity (SD7); recognize the need for economic valuation of marine and coastal ecoservices for policy and decision-making (SD8); and, lastly, to facilitate the mainstreaming of the RSP

---

[25]    See, *Progress in the Implementation of the Regional Seas Strategic Directions 2013-2016*, 16th Global Meeting of the Regional Seas Conventions and Action Plans, available at www.unep.org/regionalseas/globalmeetings/151-16%20meeting/Progress%20Implementation%202013-2016.pdf (last accessed 30 May 2015).

activities with broader development activities including poverty reduction in developing countries (SD9).[26]

There is little overlap or sense of continuity, however, between the global strategic directions for the period 2008–12 and 2013–16 other than for land-based pollution and reference to the ecosystem approach. This begs the question as to whether UNEP is satisfied with the outcome of the global strategic directions for 2008–12.[27] For example, how has UNEP RSP contributed to the 2010 Biodiversity targets in each of its regional seas? How many new marine protected areas and networks were established by 2012 in the 18 RSPs? There would appear to be a need for more defined indicators to measure results achieved and for the adoption of clearly defined benchmarks rather than what appear to be more aspirational goals merely supported by small workshops, thematic studies and reports. This is to be distinguished from the indicators used to measure individual RSPs, many of which, such as the Black Sea RSP and Baltic Sea RSP, rely on periodic 'state of the environment' reports. Here the issue is what indictors should be used to assess the overall level of success of the overarching UNEP RSP Strategic Directions.[28] In this respect, an in-depth review examining indicators for the UNEP RSP, completed in 2013, noted the efforts to create a set of common Strategic Directions but also pointed to the 'differing levels of implementation of regional Action Plans' which the report observes '… have so far not been systematically centrally monitored to indicate the level of achievement of the implementation of Action Plans in different regions'.[29] In particular, the report focused on the use of ecosystem based indicators.

# 3. UNEP REGIONAL SEAS PROGRAMME STRUCTURE

## 3.1 The Programmes

The UNEP RSP consists of a total of eighteen individual regional seas programmes that fall under its auspices.[30] As identified in Table 16.1, there are three different classes of regional seas programmes: (1) the partner/independent programmes (Antarctic, Arctic, Baltic Sea, Caspian Sea and North-East Atlantic); (2) UNEP administered

---

[26] *Global Strategic Directions for the Regional Seas Programme 2008–2012: Enhancing The Role Of The Regional Seas Conventions And Action Plans*, UNEP Doc. UNEP(DEPI)/ RS.9/6, 31 October 2007.

[27] A draft scoping study of the Regional Seas Programme has been undertaken. See, Raphaël Billé, Lucien Chabason, Petra Drankier, Erik J. Molenaar and Julien Rochette, *Governance Paper* (Draft White Paper) UNEP Doc. UNEP(DEPI) APSM 1/WP.3 (15–17 July 2014), available at www.unep.org/regionalseas/globalmeetings/Abidjan_meeting_july_2014/ Governance%20Paper-uploaded.pdf (last accessed 30 May 2015).

[28] David Johnson, Angela Benn and Adelaide Ferreira, *Review of ecosystem-based indicators and indices on the state of the Regional Seas, Final Report* (UNEP 2013), paras 4.1, 4.2.

[29] Ibid, para. 2.14.

[30] Detailed information on the UNEP Regional Seas Programme is available at www.unep.org/regionalseas (last accessed 30 May 2015).

*Table 16.1   Regional Seas Agreements*

| UNEP Administered | Non-UNEP Administered | Independent Programme |
|---|---|---|
| Caribbean Region[a] | Black Sea[b] | Baltic Sea[c] |
| East Asian Seas (COBSEA)[d] | North-East Pacific[e] | North-East Atlantic Region[f] |
| Eastern Africa Region[g] | Red Sea and Gulf of Aden[h] | Caspian[i] |
| Mediterranean Region[j] | ROPME[k] | Arctic Region[l] |
| North-West Pacific Region (NOWPAP)[o] | South Asian Seas[m] | Antarctic Region[n] |
| Western Africa Region[p] | South-East Pacific Region[q] | |
| | Pacific Region[r] | |

*Notes:*

[a] Convention for the Protection and Development of the Marine Environment of the Wider Caribbean Region, opened for signature 24 March 1983, entered into force 11 October 1986, 1506 UNTS 157 (Cartagena Convention).

[b] Protection of the Black Sea Against Pollution (and Protocols), opened for signature 21 April 1994, entered into force 15 January 1994, 32 *International Legal Material*s 1101 (Bucharest Convention).

[c] Convention for the Protection of the Marine Environment of the Baltic Sea, opened for signature 22 March 1974, entered into force 3 May1980, as replaced with the Convention for the Protection of the Marine Environment of the Baltic Sea, opened for signature 9 April 1992, entered into force 17 January 2000, 1507 UNTS 167 (Helsinki Convention).

[d] There is no Convention for this regional sea. The coastal states adopted the Action Plan for the Protection and Development of the Marine and Coastal Areas of the East Asian Region, as revised in 1994. More recently the countries adopted a New Strategic Direction for COBSEA [Coordinating Body on the Seas of East Asia] (2008–2012). See www.cobsea.org (last accessed 30 May 2015).

[e] The Convention for Cooperation in the Protection and Sustainable Development of the Marine and Coastal Environment of the Northeast Pacific, opened for signature18 February 2002, not in force, available at http://www.unep.org/regionalseas/programmes/nonunep/nepacific/instruments/nep_convention.pdf (Antigua Convention) (last accessed 30 May 2015).

[f] The Convention for the Protection of the Marine Environment of the North-East Atlantic, opened for signature 22 September 1992, entered into force 25 March 1998, 2354 UNTS 70 (OSPAR Convention).

[g] Convention for the Protection, Management and Development of the Marine and Coastal Environment of the Eastern African Region, opened for signature 21 June 1985, entered into force 30 May 1996, as amended by the Nairobi Convention for the Protection, Management and Development of the Marine and Coastal Environment of the Eastern African Region, adopted 31 March 2010, available at http://www.unep.org/NairobiConvention/The_Convention/index.asp (Nairobi Convention) (last accessed 30 May 2015).

[h] Regional Convention for the Conservation of the Red Sea and Gulf of Aden Environment, opened for signature 14 February 1982, entered into force 20 August 1985, available at http://www.unep.ch/regional seas/main/persga/redconv.html (Jeddah Convention) (last accessed 30 May 2015).

[i] Framework Convention for the Protection of the Marine Environment of the Caspian Sea, signed 4 November 2003, entered into force 12 August 2006, available at http://www.tehranconvention.org/ (Tehran Convention) (last accessed 30 May 2015)

[j] See footnotes 35–41.

[k] Kuwait Regional Convention for Cooperation on the Protection of the Marine Environment from Pollution, opened for signature 24 April 1978, entered into force 1 July 1979 available at http://www2.unitar.org/cwm/publications/cbl/synergy/pdf/cat3/UNEP_regional_seas/convention_kuwait/convention.pdf (Kuwait Convention) (last accessed 30 May 2015).

[l] There is no convention for the Arctic region; however, in 1991, Canada, Denmark (including Greenland and Faroe Islands), Finland, Iceland, Norway, Russian Federation, Sweden and the United States, adopted the Arctic Environmental Protection Strategy (AEPS). In 1996, following the adoption of the Declaration

on Establishment of The Arctic Council (The Ottawa Declaration) 19 September 1996, the eight Arctic States established the Arctic Council. For information, see www.arctic-council.org (last accessed 30 May 2015).
[m] There is no Convention. In 1994 the People's Republic of China, the Republic of Korea, Japan and the Russian Federation adopted the Action Plan for the Protection, Management and Development of the Marine and Coastal Environment of the Northwest Pacific Region, adopted September 1994, available at http://www.nowpap.org/ (last accessed 30 May 2015).
[n] There is no regional Convention. The South Asian Sea Action Plan (SASAP) was adopted 24 March 1995, entered into force February 1997. For information see, http://www.unep.org/regionalseas/programmes/nonunep/southasian/ (last accessed 30 May 2015).
[o] The Antarctic Treaty, opened for signature 1 December 1959, entered into force 23 June 1961, 4 UNTS 71; Protocol on Environmental Protection to the Antarctic Treaty (Madrid Protocol) opened for signature 4 October 1991, entered into force 14 January 1998, 402 UNTS 1.
[p] Abidjan Convention for Co-operation in the Protection and Development of the Marine and Coastal Environment of the West and Central African Region, opened for signature 23 March 1981, entered into force 5 August 1984, available at http://abidjanconvention.org/ (last accessed 30 May 2015).
[q] Convention for the Protection of the Marine Environment and Coastal Areas of the South-East Pacific, opened for signature 12 November 1981, entered into force 19 May 1986) 1648 UNTS 3 (Lima Convention).
[r] Convention for the Protection of Natural Resources and Environment of the South Pacific Region, adopted 24 November 1986, entered into force 22 August 1990, available at http://www.sprep.org/legal/the-convention (Noumea Convention) (last accessed 30 May 2015).

*Source:* Adapted from Nilufer Oral, in Marta Chantal Ribeiro (ed.), *30 Years after the Signature of the United Nations Convention on the Law of the Sea: the Protection of the Environment and the Future of the Law of the Sea* (Coimbra Editora, 2014).

programmes (Caribbean Region, East Asian Seas, Eastern Africa Region, Mediterranean Region, North-West Pacific Region, Western Africa Region); and (3) Non-UNEP administered programmes (Black Sea Region, North-East Pacific Region, Red Sea and Gulf of Aden, the Regional Organization for the Protection of the Marine Environment (ROPME), South Asian Seas, South-East Pacific Region, Pacific Region).

The traditional approach for establishing a RSP begins with a 'transboundary diagnostic analysis' (TDA)[31] of the state of environmental degradation of the sea. A strategic action plan (SAP) is then adopted based on the findings of the TDA.[32] The SAP outlines the environmental problems and actions necessary to address the issues identified by the TDA. Each SAP contains various chapters on environmental assessment, environmental management, environmental legislation (eg, umbrella convention and implementing protocols), institutional arrangements, and financial arrangements. SAPs are signed by the representatives of the member states thereby constituting legal commitments. A key element of the each RSP is the programme of work (PW), which focuses on the implementation of the regional sea SAP. This is then followed by the negotiation and adoption of a framework convention and implementing protocols.

---

[31] Wang defines TDA as 'a scientific and technical assessment of the environment of an international ocean area. TDA identifies, quantifies, analyzes, and assesses the water-related environmental issues and problems, their causes and impacts in the environmental, socioeconomic, legal, political, and institutional context at the national, regional, and global levels. It normally also identifies and prioritizes solutions to the problems as well as the root causes of the problems'. Hanling Wang, 'An Evaluation of the Modular Approach to the Assessment and Management of Large Marine Ecosystems' (2004) 35 *Ocean Development & International Law* 267, 269.

[32] Ibid, 270.

However, as in the case of the Black Sea RSP, the framework convention was adopted in 1994 before the 1996 Black Sea TDA and SAP were completed.[33]

An overview of the legal framework for each of the thirteen RSPs directly related to UNEP reveals an uneven landscape of legal instruments that have been adopted and implemented ranging from the eight binding instruments that have been adopted for the Mediterranean region to no binding instruments as in the case of the East Asian RSP. In addition, there are substantive differences among the different legal instruments relating to the nature of the obligations and the principles and approaches of international environmental law that are adopted.

For example, the Mediterranean RSP, in addition to being the first of the programmes, is also among the most advanced in terms of the level of legal instruments that have been adopted and are in effect. In addition to the Mediterranean Action Plans and the Barcelona Convention[34] that was revised in 1995 to reflect developments in international environmental law following the Earth Summit, a number of important protocols have been adopted. These are: the Dumping Protocol,[35] the Emergency Response Protocol,[36] the Land-based Sources of Pollution Protocol,[37] the Specially Protected Areas and Biodiversity Protocol (SPAMI Protocol),[38] the Offshore

---

[33]   See, Nilufer Oral, *Regional Cooperation and Protection of the Marine Environment Under International Law: the Black Sea* (Martinus Nijhoff, 2013) 83–4.

[34]   Convention for the Protection of the Mediterranean Sea against Pollution (Barcelona Convention), adopted 16 February 1976, entered into force 12 February 1978, (1976) 15 *International Legal Materials* 285 (1976); as amended and renamed as the Convention for the Protection of the Marine Environment and the Coastal Region of the Mediterranean, adopted 10 June 1995, entered into force 9 July 2004, Doc. UNEP(OCA)/MED IG. 6/7 (BC Amendments), available   at   http://www.unepmap.org/index.php?module=content2&catid=001001004   (last accessed 30 May 2015).

[35]   Protocol for the Prevention of Pollution in the Mediterranean Sea by Dumping from Ships and Aircraft (Dumping Protocol), adopted 16 February 1976, entered into force 12 February 1978, 1102 UNTS 92. The Dumping Protocol was amended and recorded as Protocol for the Prevention and Elimination of Pollution in the Mediterranean Sea by Dumping from Ships and Aircraft or Incineration at Sea, adopted 10 June 1995, not yet in force, UNEP Doc. UNEP(OCA)/MED IG. 6/7, available at http://www.unepmap.org/index.php?module=content2& catid=001001001 (last accessed 30 May 2015).

[36]   Protocol Concerning Cooperation in Preventing Pollution from Ships and, in Cases of Emergency, Combating Pollution of the Mediterranean Sea (Emergency Response Protocol), adopted 25 January 2002, entered into force 17 March 2004, available at http://www. unepmap.org/index.php?module=content2&catid=001001001 (last accessed 30 May 2015). This Protocol replaced the Protocol Concerning Cooperation in Combating Pollution of the Mediterranean Sea by Oil and other Harmful Substances in Cases of Emergency, adopted 16 February 1976, entered into force 12 February 1978, 1102 UNTS 122.

[37]   Protocol for the Protection of the Mediterranean Sea against Pollution from Land-Based Sources and Activities (Land-based Sources Protocol), adopted 7 March 1996, entered into force 11 May 2008. This Protocol replaced the Protocol for the Protection of the Mediterranean Sea against Pollution from Land-Based Sources, adopted on 17 May 1980, entered into force 17 June 1983. For texts see, http://www.unepmap.org/index.php?module=content2&catid=001001001 (last accessed 30 May 2015).

[38]   Protocol Concerning Specially Protected Areas and Biological Diversity in the Mediterranean, (SPAMI Protocol), adopted 10 June 1995, entered into force 12 December 1999, 2102

Protocol,[39] the Hazardous Wastes Protocol,[40] and the ICZM Protocol.[41] In addition, in 2008 the Mediterranean RSP established the first compliance mechanism[42] for a UNEP RSP that includes a Compliance Committee.

By contrast, for example, the East Asian RSP, which like the Mediterranean RSP is directly administered by UNEP, has no umbrella convention or implementing protocols. The only instrument adopted by the Parties is the 1983 Action Plan[43] which was revised in 1994.[44] In addition, the Coordinating Body of the Seas of East Asia (COBSEA) adopted a New Strategic Direction for 2008–12.[45]

Other RSPs which do not have framework conventions or implementing protocols and which rely only on action plans are the South Asian RSP and the North-West Pacific RSP.

## 3.2  Institutional Structure

The UNEP Regional Seas Programme, also referred to as the regional sea conventions and actions plans (RSCAP), is a subsidiary body of the United Nations General

---

UNTS 203. Annexes to the SPAMI Protocol were adopted on 24 November 1996. This Protocol replaced the Protocol concerning Mediterranean Specially Protected Areas, adopted on 3 April 1982, entered into force 23 March 1986. For texts see, http://www.unepmap.org/index. php?module=content2&catid=001001001 (last accessed 30 May 2015).

[39]  Protocol for the Protection of the Mediterranean Sea against Pollution Resulting from Exploration and Exploitation of the Continental Shelf and the Seabed and its Subsoil (Offshore Protocol), adopted 14 October 1994, entered into force 24 March 2011, available at http:// www.unepmap.org/index.php?module=content2&catid=001001001 (last accessed 30 May 2015).

[40]  Protocol for the Prevention of Pollution of the Mediterranean by Transboundary Movements of Hazardous Wastes and Their Disposal (Hazardous Wastes Protocol), adopted 1 October 1996, entered into force 19 January 2008. UNEP Register of International Treaties and Other Agreements in the Field of the Environment (2005), 622; also available at http:// www.unepmap.org/index.php?module=content2&catid=001001001 (last accessed 30 May 2015).

[41]  Protocol on Integrated Coastal Zone Management in the Mediterranean (ICZM Protocol), adopted 21 January 2008, entered into force 24 March 2011, available at http://www. unepmap.org/index.php?module=content2&catid=001001001 (last accessed 30 May 2015). See also, *Adoption of the Action Plan for the implementation of the ICZM Protocol for the Mediterranean (2012-2019)*, Dec. UNEP(DEPI)/MED IG 20/8, 21 January 2012, available at http://www.pap-thecoastcentre.org/razno/Decision%202%20-%20ICZM%20Action%20Plan.pdf (last accessed 30 May 2015); Julien Rochette and Raphaël Billé, 'ICZM Protocols to the Regional Seas Conventions: What? Why? How?' (2012) 36 *Marine Policy* 377.

[42]  *Report of the 15th Meeting of the Contracting Parties to the Convention for the Protection of the Marine Environment and the Coastal Region of the Mediterranean and its Protocols*, Almeria, Spain, 15–18 January 2008, UNEP(DEPI)/MED IG.17/1018 January 2008, 5.

[43]  Action Plan for the Protection and Development of the Marine and Coastal Areas of the East Asian Region (1983), available at www.cobsea.org/documents/action_plan/ActionPlan 1983.pdf (last accessed 30 May 2015).

[44]  Action Plan for the Protection and Sustainable Development of the Marine and Coastal Areas of the East Asian Region (1994), available at www.cobsea.org/documents/action_plan/ ActionPlan1994.pdf (last accessed 30 May 2015).

[45]  See, www.cobsea.org/aboutcobsea/newtrategicdirection.html (last accessed 30 May 2015).

Assembly and not an autonomous specialized agency such as the International Maritime Organization.[46] UNEP is governed by a Governing Council, which as of 2013 enjoys universal membership.[47] The strengths and weaknesses of UNEP as the principal body in the United Nations system responsible for environmental protection have long been debated, including whether UNEP should be made into a specialized agency or even into a world environmental organization.[48] However, the decision taken at the Rio+20 Summit was to maintain its status as a subsidiary body but strengthen it. Only time will tell what impact this 'strengthening' of UNEP will have on the UNEP RSP. However, one indication can be gleaned from the outcome of the historic first Environment Assembly meeting of UNEP held in Nairobi 26–27 June 2014. The final outcome document adopted by the Ministers makes no explicit reference to strengthening the RSP, but merely makes reference to ensuring 'full implementation of multilateral agreements and other international and regional commitments in an effective and coordinated manner'.[49] Rather than looking to highlight components of UNEP such as the UNEP RSP, the final document and resolution focus on thematic areas, such as marine plastic litter and ecosystem-based adaptation, which is unfortunate given that strengthening the UNEP RSP would facilitate achievement of these thematic objectives in a more holistic and integrated manner.

The institutional structure of the various individual RSPs usually consists of a permanent secretariat or Regional Coordinating Unit (RCU), which is responsible for carrying out the activities in the programme of work (PW). In some RSPs the contracting parties have established Regional Activity Centers (RACs) to support the RSP Secretariat or RCU in carrying out components of the RSP action plan. For example, the Regional Activity Center for Specially Protected Areas (RAC-SPA) in the Mediterranean RSP is a key component in the implementation of the SPAMI Protocol.[50] Other RSPs, such as that for the Black Sea, have specialized advisory groups established by the member states to provide the Black Sea Commission with expertise and advice in support of the implementation of the Black Sea SAP.[51]

---

[46]   See generally, José Alvarez, *International Organizations As Law-Makers* (Oxford University Press 2005) and Geoffrey Palmer, 'New Ways to Make International Environmental Law' (1992) 86 *American Journal of International Law* 259, 260–64.

[47]   One of the outcomes of Rio+20 was to expand the UNEP Governing Council to include all United Nations member States. See, *The First Universal Session of the UNEP Governing Council/Global Ministerial Environment Forum*, 22 February 2013, Nairobi, Doc. UNEP GC.27/17.

[48]   See, Maria Ivanova, 'Institutional Design and UNEP Reform: Historical Insights on Form, Function and Financing' (2012) 88 *International Affairs* 565; Robert Faulkner, *The Handbook of Global and Environmental Policy* (Wiley-Blackwell 2013).

[49]   Ministerial outcome document of the first session of the United Nations Environment Assembly of the United Nations Environmental Programme, www.unep.org/pdf/Compilation_of_decisions_and_resolutions_unea_2014_unedited_advanced_copy.pdf (last accessed 30 May 2015).

[50]   SPAMI Protocol, above n 38.

[51]   See, www.blacksea-commission.org/_advisorygroups.asp (last accessed 30 May 2015).

### 3.3 Financing

The financing available for each RSP varies. There is no single or permanent source of financing provided by UNEP. Financing is provided by annual contributions by the member states of a RSP and through grants, project financing, subsidies, private sector, loans and other modalities. According to UNEP, long-term sustainable financing comes from three sources: domestic public sector, polluter and user-pay schemes, and/or international grants.[52] Financing is necessary for operational costs, which include funding the permanent secretariat or RCU, implementing the PW for the implementation of the SAP, and for the national implementation of the regional seas conventions and action plans (RSCAP).

Financing the secretariat is one of the principal costs for RSPs. This includes paying for staff salaries, housing, bills, and use of expert consultants.[53] This requires long-term sustainable financing. However, one of the problems identified by UNEP for most RSPs has been financial inconsistencies resulting from irregular member payments, non-payments or budget deficits.[54] Member state payments constitute one of the core sources of financing the RSP in addition to other external sources. However, given the varied levels of economic capacity of the different member states in the various RSPs, it is not surprising that member state payments have proven to be problematic in certain cases.

Other sources of funding come from grants for specific projects, loans and subsidies. The Global Environmental Facility (GEF) also provides financial support to developing countries. For example, one of its largest projects was the Black Sea – Danube River nutrient reduction project, which included operational financing of the Black Sea RSP Secretariat for a number of years.[55] Other international financial institutions, such as the World Bank or regional development banks such as the Asian Development Bank or African Development Bank are also important sources of funding for RSPs.

## 4. THEMATIC ACTIVITIES

### 4.1 Land-based Sources of Pollution and Activities

As was highlighted in Chapter 17 of Agenda 21,[56] the protection of the marine environment from land-based sources of pollution and activities was one of the key

---

[52] Financing the implementation of regional seas conventions and action plans: A guide for national action UNEP Regional seas Report and Studies No. 180 (2006), 1 www.unep.org/pdf/GPA/Financing_the_Implementation_of_Regional_Seas_Conventions_and_Action_Plans.pdf (last accessed 30 May 2015).

[53] According to a UNEP study conducted for the period between 2000–04, 50–80% of total budget went towards staff costs. See, ibid, 2.

[54] Ibid.

[55] The Black Sea Ecosystem Recovery Project (BSERP), GEF/C.15/Inf. 6, *World Bank Strategic Partnership for Nutrient Reduction in the Danube River Basin and Black Sea*, 11 Apr. 2000.

[56] Agenda 21, above n 15.

issues to be addressed by the UNEP RSP. Chapter 17 also recognized the role of regional and sub-regional action in addressing land-based sources of pollution, and specifically urged states to both assess the effectiveness of existing regional agreements and promote the development of new regional agreements, where appropriate.[57]

Out of the thirteen UNEP RSPs, eight have adopted separate protocols for regulating land-based sources or activities of pollution. Most of these are what are viewed as 'first generation' protocols; that is the first group of protocols adopted are based on the traditional coastal or shoreline approach. By contrast, the 'second generation' instruments, adopted to replace the former, as in the case in the Mediterranean and Black Sea RSPs, provide for a more holistic approach based on integrated marine and coastal zone management, and extend their scope of application to a broader river basin-wide approach.[58] The remaining first generation of 'shoreline' protocols do not cover inland activities within the drainage area discharging into the sea but remain limited to the narrower shoreline areas. Furthermore, the first generation protocols refer only to sources of pollution and not activities.[59]

In addition, the regional seas protocols on land-based pollution that do exist have adopted different principles and levels of obligation. For example, the 1999 Protocol Concerning Pollution From Land-Based Sources and Activities to the Convention for the Protection and Development of the Marine Environment of the Wider Caribbean Region (WCLBS)[60] imposes a general obligation on the parties to take the necessary measures to 'prevent, reduce and control' land-based sources of marine pollution. By contrast, the revised Mediterranean Protocol on Land-based Sources of Pollution imposes an obligation on the Parties to

> take all appropriate measures to prevent, abate, combat and eliminate to the fullest possible extent pollution of the Mediterranean Sea Area caused by discharges from rivers, coastal establishments or outfalls, or emanating from any other land-based sources and activities within their territories, giving priority to the phasing out of inputs of substances that are toxic, persistent and liable to bioaccumulate.[61]

## 4.2   Biodiversity and Protected Areas

The adoption of the Convention on Biological Diversity (CBD)[62] in 1992, and subsequent decisions of the states parties, in particular the Jakarta Mandate on the Conservation and Sustainable Use of Marine and Coastal Biological Diversity[63] and the

---

[57]   Ibid., paras 17.24, 17.25(b) and (c).

[58]   Sergei Vinogradov 'Marine Pollution via Transboundary Watercourses – An Interface of the "Shoreline" and "River-Basin" Regimes in the Wider Black Sea Region' (2007) 22 *International Journal of Marine and Coastal Law* 585, 591.

[59]   Ibid.

[60]   Adopted 9 October 1999, entered into force 13 August 2010, UNEP Register of International Treaties and Other Agreements in the Field of the Environment (2005) 677.

[61]   Land-based Sources of Pollution Protocol, above n 37 Art. 1.

[62]   Adopted 5 June 1992, entered into force 29 December 1993, 1760 UNTS 79 (CBD).

[63]   Decision CBD COP II/10 – Conservation and sustainable use of marine and coastal biological diversity (1995).

more recent Aichi Biodiversity Targets,[64] which call for the conservation of a minimum ten per cent of all coastal and marine areas, should be a key part of all RSPs.

Among the thirteen regional seas programmes directly affiliated with UNEP, seven have adopted a separate protocol for protection of marine biodiversity: the Wider Caribbean Region;[65] the Mediterranean;[66] Eastern Africa;[67] the Red Sea and the Gulf of Aden;[68] the Black Sea;[69] the South East Pacific;[70] and the Regional Organization for the Protection of the Marine Environment (ROPME).[71] Each of these protocols requires the parties to either individually or cooperatively establish protected areas to protect fragile and vulnerable ecosystems. For example, between 2010 and 2013, in the Wider Caribbean region 18 marine protected areas were listed.[72] The Mediterranean region has listed 33 marine protected areas under its protocol.[73]

The earliest of these protocols is the Protocol Concerning Protected Areas and Wild Fauna and Flora in the Eastern African Region.[74] Adopted before the CBD, it makes no reference to 'biodiversity' although it does include a provision on the protection of genetic diversity. Specifically, the Protocol establishes a duty on member states to take the necessary measures to protect rare or fragile ecosystems as well as rare, depleted, threatened or endangered species of wild fauna and flora and their habitats in the Eastern African region.[75] In addition, the parties are required to take measures to protect migratory species that are listed in Annex IV to the Protocol,[76] and to protect

---

[64] UNEP/CBD/COP/10/27, Strategic Plan For Biodiversity 2011-2020 and The Aichi Biodiversity Targets.

[65] Protocol to the Cartagena Convention Concerning Specially Protected Areas and Wildlife in the Wider Caribbean Region (SPAW Protocol), adopted 18 January 1990, entered into force 17 June 2000, 2180 UNTS 25974.

[66] SPAMI Protocol, above n 38.

[67] Protocol Concerning Protected Areas and Wild Fauna and Flora in the Eastern African Region, adopted 21 June 1985, entered into effect 30 May 1996, UNEP Register of International Treaties (1997) 318; Also available at www.unep.org/NairobiConvention/The_Convention/ Protocols/Protocol_Protected_Areas.asp (last accessed 30 May 2015).

[68] Protocol Concerning the Conservation of Biological Diversity and the Establishment of Networks of Protected Areas in the Red Sea and Gulf of Aden (RSGA Protocol), adopted 12 December 2005, not yet in force, available at http://www.persga.org/Documents/Doc_62_ 20090211123942.pdf (last accessed 30 May 2015).

[69] Black Sea Biodiversity and Landscape Protocol (Black Sea Protocol), adopted 14 June 2002, entered into force 20 June 2011, available at www.blacksea-commission.org/_convention-protocols-biodiversity.asp (last accessed 30 May 2015).

[70] Protocol for the Conservation and Management of Protected Marine and Coastal Areas of the South-East Pacific, adopted 21 September 1989, entered into force 1994, available at http://www2.unitar.org/cwm/publications/cbl/synergy/pdf/cat3/UNEP_regional_seas/convention_ lima/protocol_conservation.pdf (last accessed 30 May 2015).

[71] The ROPME Protocol has not yet been signed by the member states (Communication from Secretariat).

[72] See, www.car-spaw-rac.org/?Presentation-of-the-18-PAs (last accessed 30 May 2015).

[73] See, http://rac-spa.org/spami (last accessed 30 May 2015).

[74] Above n 67.

[75] Ibid, Art. 2.

[76] Ibid, Art. 6; Annex IV lists species of mammals and reptiles.

against the introduction of harmful invasive species.[77] However, this Protocol is one of the first generation protocols that pre-dates the CBD, UNCED and Agenda 21. Consequently it does not explicitly include protection of biodiversity or the principles and approaches adopted at UNCED such as precautionary principle, integrated management of marine coastal areas and the use of impact assessments. As such the Protocol is outdated and in need of amendment to ensure that the East African RSP is implementing current international standards and obligations. Admittedly, adopting amendments to legal instruments can take time. Nevertheless, considering that the Protocol went into effect nearly twenty years ago this should provide an incentive to UNEP to promote the updating of instruments to incorporate recent developments.

The Convention for the Protection and Development of the Marine Environment of the Wider Caribbean Region (Cartagena Convention) includes a provision on 'Specially Protected Areas' that requires the contracting parties to 'individually or jointly, take all appropriate measures to protect and preserve rare or fragile ecosystems, as well as habitat or depleted, threatened or endangered species'.[78] It also includes a preventive obligation to prevent species from becoming threatened or endangered. The 1990 Protocol Concerning Specially Protected Areas and Wildlife to the Cartagena Convention (SPAW Protocol),[79] was adopted as the regional instrument for implementing these provisions. The SPAW Protocol establishes the regional and cooperative legal framework for the protection of special areas and endangered species of flora and fauna. While the SPAW Protocol pre-dates the CBD its provisions are considered to be advanced and innovative,[80] and they have served as the model for subsequent regional seas protocols. The SPAW Protocol also includes a requirement for the parties to cooperate in the enforcement of measures adopted.[81] There are clear benefits to be derived from cooperative enforcement measures, such as strengthened enforcement through joint or coordinated monitoring, exchange of information and ensuring a harmonized approach, such as providing for similar levels of sanctions in each of the territories of the parties.

The Specially Protected Areas of Mediterranean Interest Protocol to the Barcelona Convention (SPAMI Protocol) provides for the establishment of a List of Specially Protected Areas of Mediterranean Interest (SPAMI List).[82] The SPAMI Protocol closely resembles the SPAW Protocol, although it was drafted subsequent to the adoption of the CBD and for this reason makes reference to it. The SPAMI Protocol is a hybrid of

---

[77]   Ibid, Art. 7.

[78]   Convention for the Protection and Development of the Marine Environment of the Wider Caribbean Region, opened for signature 24 March 1983, entered into force 11 October 1986, 1506 UNTS 157 (Cartagena Convention), Art. 10.

[79]   Above n 65.

[80]   On the innovative aspects of the SPAW Protocol see, Barbara Lausche, 'Wider Caribbean Region – A Pivotal Time to Strengthen Regional Instruments for Biodiversity Conservation' (2008) 23 *International Journal of Marine and Coastal Law* 499. A Memorandum of Cooperation (MOC) between the Secretariat of the Cartagena Convention and the SPAW Protocol and the Secretariat of CBD was concluded in 1997. The text of the MOC is available at www.cep.unep.org/cartagena-convention (last accessed 30 May 2015).

[81]   SPAW Protocol, above n 65, Art. 3.

[82]   SPAMI Protocol, above n 38, Art. 47.

the SPAW Protocol and the CBD. One innovation of the SPAMI Protocol is that it includes provisions for the establishment of transboundary protected areas[83] and marine protected areas in the high seas areas of the Mediterranean Sea.[84] To date twenty-one SPAMIs and one 'high seas' SPAMI, the Pelagos sanctuary, have been established.[85] The area covered by the Sanctuary includes some 87,500 km² of the northwestern Mediterranean including areas beyond national jurisdiction of any coastal state. The crowded geography of the Mediterranean Sea has created political and legal challenges to establishing maritime zones such as exclusive economic zones. The Pelagos Sanctuary stands as an exemplary cooperative undertaking to protect the marine environment through the use of high seas marine protected areas.

One important institutional creation of the SPAMI Protocol that is not part of the SPAW Protocol is the establishment of a Regional Activity Center for Specially Protected Areas (RAC-SPA), which is headquartered in Tunis. The SPAMI RAC-SPA has been actively promoting and working with the Mediterranean countries and stakeholders to promote the implementation of the SPAMI Protocol as well as to provide assistance in identifying, establishing, and managing marine protected areas.

In 2005, in order to preserve the rich biodiversity, including coral reefs, of the Red Sea and Gulf of Aden, the Parties to the Jeddah Convention[86] adopted the Protocol Concerning the Conservation of Biological Diversity and the Establishment of Networks of Protected Areas in the Red Sea and Gulf of Aden.[87] The Red Sea and Gulf of Aden Protocol includes detailed provisions on using environmental impact assessments,[88] the integrated coastal management approach[89] and also on access to genetic resources.[90] A network of twelve marine protected areas has been established in the region.[91]

The Black Sea Biodiversity and Landscape Protocol was adopted in 2002 and entered into effect in 2011.[92] The Black Sea Protocol adopts a similar approach to the SPAW and SPAMI Protocols with some notable differences. The Black Sea Protocol

---

[83] SPAMI Protocol Art. 5. The text of Art. 5 is virtually identical to Art. 9 of the SPAW Protocol.

[84] See, Tullio Scovazzi, 'Marine Protected Areas on the High Seas: Some Legal and Policy Considerations' (2004) 19 *International Journal of Marine and Coastal Law* 1, 11–13.

[85] On 25 November 1999 France, Italy and Monaco signed the Agreement on the Creation in the Mediterranean Sea of a Sanctuary for Marine Mammals (Pelagos Sanctuary Agreement). It came into effect 21 February 2002. See, Giuseppe Notarbartolo di Sciara and others, 'The Pelagos Sanctuary for Mediterranean Marine Mammals' (2008) 18 *Aquatic Conservation: Marine and Freshwater Ecosystems* 367; Tullio Scovazzi, 'The Mediterranean Marine Mammals Sanctuary' (2001) 16 *International Journal of Marine and Coastal Law* 132.

[86] Regional Convention for the Conservation of the Red Sea and Gulf of Aden Environment, opened for signature 14 February 1982, entered into force 20 August 1985, available at http://www.unep.ch/regionalseas/main/persga/redconv.html (Jeddah Convention) (last accessed 1 June 2015).

[87] RSGA Protocol, above n 68.

[88] RSGA Protocol, Art. 15.

[89] RSGA Protocol, Art. 14.

[90] RSGA Protocol, Art. 18.

[91] See, www.persga.org/inner.php?id=109 (last accessed 30 May 2015).

[92] Black Sea Protocol, above n 69.

requires the parties to develop a legal instrument of 'integrated coastal zone manage-ment' as part of their duty to 'encourage' intersectoral interaction at the regional and national levels.[93] In addition, the Black Sea Protocol requires each party to adopt rules and regulations on the liability for damage caused to the biological and landscape diversity caused by natural or juridical persons. Each party must ensure that its laws 'facilitate' legal action and the obtaining of 'prompt and adequate compensation or other relief' for damages caused by human activities or pollution.

The Protocol also mandates that the parties 'cooperate in developing and harmoniz-ing their laws, regulations and procedures relating to liability, assessment of and compensation for damage caused by human activities and/or pollution … in order to ensure the highest degree of deterrence and protection for the biological and landscape diversity of the Black Sea as a whole.'[94] Interestingly, this is the only one of the protocols to address the important issue of liability and compensation for environ-mental damage. However, it does not include any reference to the establishment of a 'network of protected areas', which is included in the SPAW, SPAMI and Red Sea and Gulf of Aden Protocols. Rather, the Strategic Action Plan that was adopted by the Black Sea states before the Protocol went into effect, provided for the development of Black Sea marine protected areas.[95] According to the Protocol, a new Strategic Action Plan was to be adopted by the parties by 2014, three years after the Protocol went into effect.[96]

### 4.3 Dumping at Sea

Dumping activities at sea are regulated, at the global level, through the IMO and the 1972 Convention on the Prevention of Marine Pollution by Dumping of Wastes and Other Matter[97] (London Convention) and its 1996 Protocol.[98] One of the functions of the UNEP RSP is to promote the implementation of these (and other) IMO instruments relevant to the protection of the marine environment at the regional level. However, only three of the thirteen RSPs (excluding the five partner programmes) have adopted protocols regulating dumping activities at sea: the Mediterranean,[99] the Black Sea[100] and the Pacific region.[101]

---

93   Black Sea Protocol, Art. 7. The language in Art. 7 may not, at first glance, appear to create such a duty but upon close reading the parties appear to be required to adopt an ICZM instrument. Specifically Art. 7 stipulates, 'The Contracting Parties shall encourage introduction of intersectoral interaction on regional and national levels through the introduction of the principles and development of legal instrument of integrated coastal zone management seeking the ways for sustainable use of natural resources and promotion of environmentally friendly human activities in the coastal zone'.

94   Black Sea Protocol, Art. 11(1)–(4).

95   Nilufer Oral, above n 33.

96   Black Sea Protocol, Art. 4(6).

97   Adopted 29 December 1972, entered into force 30 August 1975, 1046 UNTS 138.

98   1996 Protocol to the 1972 London on the Prevention of Marine Pollution by the Dumping of Wastes and Other Matter, adopted 7 November 1996, entered into force 24 March

## 4.4 Oil Spill Prevention, Preparedness and Response

Another area of importance recognized by the UNEP RSP and related also to the implementation of IMO instruments concerns emergency preparedness and response to oil spills at sea.[102] In reviewing the existing legal structure of the thirteen UNEP RSPs, with the exception of the Asian Sea region, the South-East Asia and North-West Pacific, the remaining nine have adopted emergency response protocols. However, only the Mediterranean[103] and Wider Caribbean Sea,[104] North-West Pacific Region (NOWPAP)[105] Marine Environmental Emergency Preparedness and Response Regional Activity Centre (MERRAC) regions have established emergency response centers. In the regions encompassing West, Central and South Africa, and Latin America and the Caribbean, the IMO and the International Petroleum Industry Environmental Conservation Association (IPIECA),[106] though its Global Initiative and in partnership with UNEP, have been working to strengthen cooperation on prevention, preparedness and response to oil spills.

---

2006, (1997) 36 *International Legal Materials* 1; See also, Philomene Verlaan, 'Geo-engineering, the Law of the Sea, and Climate Change' (2009) 4 *Carbon and Climate Law Review* 446, 453.

[99] Above n 35.

[100] Protocol on the Protection of the Black Sea Marine Environment Against Pollution by Dumping, adopted 21 April 1992, entered into force 14 April 1994, available at http://www.blacksea-commission.org/_convention-protocols.asp#Dumping (last accessed 30 May 2015).

[101] Protocol for the Prevention of Pollution of the South Pacific Region by Dumping, adopted 25 November 1986, entered into force 22 August 2005, available at http://www2.unitar.org/cwm/publications/cbl/synergy/pdf/cat3/UNEP_regional_seas/convention_noumea/protocol_prev_pollut.pdf (last accessed 30 May 2015).

[102] See, for example, 1990 International Convention on Oil Pollution, Preparedness, Response and Co-Operation, adopted 30 November 1990, entered into force 13 May 1995, (1991) 18 *Law of the Sea Bulletin* 37 (OPRC).

[103] Mediterranean Emergency Response Protocol, above n 36. The Regional Marine Pollution Emergency Response Centre for the Mediterranean Sea (REMPEC) assists the Mediterranean coastal States in ratifying, transposing, implementing and enforcing international maritime conventions related to the prevention of, preparedness for and response to marine pollution from ships. http://www.rempec.org (last accessed 30 May 2015).

[104] The Regional Marine Pollution Emergency Information and Training Center for the Wider Caribbean (REMPEITC-Caribe) is a Regional Activity Center (RAC) for the Protocol Concerning the Cooperation in Combating Oil Spills in the Wider Caribbean Region (Oil Spills Protocol); adopted 24 March 1983, entered into force 11 October 1986. See http://cep.unep.org/racrempeitc (last accessed 30 May 2015).

[105] The North-West Pacific Region Programme does not have an emergency response protocol but UNEP and the International Maritime Organization (IMO) have together established an emergency response center to develop effective regional cooperative measures in response to marine pollution incidents including oil and hazardous and noxious substance (HNS) spills. See http://www.nowpap.org/ (last accessed 30 May 2015).

[106] The IPIECA was established in 1974, following the creation of UNEP, by the oil and gas industry. See, www.ipieca.org/ (last accessed 30 May 2015).

## 4.5   Offshore Activities

Regulation at the regional level for offshore activities is even weaker. At a time when there are growing offshore activities for oil and gas in a number of regions such as the Mediterranean, Black Sea, Wider Caribbean Region, East Asian seas, and East Africa, the need for strong regional measures for protection of the marine environment is even greater. However, only the Red Sea and the Gulf of Aden,[107] ROPME[108] and the Mediterranean[109] RSPs have adopted regional protocols for offshore activities.

## 4.6   Climate Change

Since the 1992 Earth Summit, climate change has emerged as perhaps the single greatest cross-cutting threat to the environment, including oceans and coastal areas. Ocean acidification and its adverse impact on marine life and ecosystems,[110] loss of coastal areas to sea-level rise, and threats to small island states are among the principal threats facing the marine environment and people whose livelihood is dependent on the sea and coastal areas. There is clearly an urgent need to incorporate climate change considerations into the RSPs, particularly for developing countries that are especially vulnerable and will have greater difficulties in meeting the growing challenges and costs of adaptation to climate change. UNEP has been addressing climate change issues through various modalities, including the development of strategies and programmes, and partnerships with international organizations and agencies.[111] The question is, however, to what extent is climate change being incorporated into the Regional Seas Programmes?

The ICZM Protocol for the Mediterranean RSP[112] is the only legally binding instrument to specifically make reference to climate change.[113] The 2007 Black Sea –Transboundary Diagnostic Analysis included, for the first time, information on climate

---

[107]   Protocol Concerning the Regional Cooperation in Combating Pollution by Oil and other Harmful Substances in Cases of Emergency, adopted 20 February 1982, entered into force 20 August 1985, available at www.persga.org/Documents/Doc_62_20090211122726.pdf (last accessed 30 May 2015).

[108]   Protocol Concerning Regional Cooperation in Combatting Pollution by Oil and other Harmful Substances in Cases of Emergency, adopted 24 April 1978 and entered into force 1 July 1979, available at http://ropme.org/uploads/protocols/emergency_protocol.pdf (last accessed 30 May 2015).

[109]   The Offshore Protocol, above n 39.

[110]   For discussion see, Tim Stephens, 'Ocean acidification', Chapter 20 in this volume.

[111]   For example, the Ecosystem-based Adaptation Programme is designed to assist 'vulnerable communities adapt to climate change through good ecosystem management practices and their integration into global, regional, national and local climate change strategies and action plans'. See, www.unep.org/pdf/UNEP_CC_STRATEGY_web.pdf (last accessed 30 May 2015). See also 'Blue Carbon, The Role of Healthy Oceans in Binding Carbon' www.grida.no/files/publications/blue-carbon/BlueCarbon_screen.pdf (last accessed 30 May 2015).

[112]   Above n 41.

[113]   Specifically, Art. 5 of the ICZM Protocol in listing its objectives includes to 'prevent and/or reduce the effects of natural hazards and in particular of climate change, which can be induced by natural or human activities'.

change in relation to the Black Sea.[114] The South Asian Seas region has marginally included climate change in its action plan for monitoring the effects of climate and sea level change on the marine and coastal environment.[115] The East Asian RSP, which does not have any legal instrument,[116] has addressed climate change in a fragmented manner in, for example, the 2009 the Manila Declaration[117] and the 2011 post-tsunami Guide on Spatial Planning in the Coastal Zones of the East Asian Seas Region.[118] The North-West Pacific RSP which is also lacking in legal instruments, addressed climate change in its Medium-Term Strategy for 2012–17.[119] The Strategy focus includes developing national and regional adaptation strategies. The Red Sea and Gulf of Aden RSP is developing a programme on adaptation to climate change.[120]

The South Pacific RSP with its small island states is an area especially vulnerable to the adverse impacts of climate change and, not surprisingly, climate change is at the top of its four strategic priorities in its SAP 2011–15, the goal of which is for all members, by 2015, to 'have strengthened capacity to respond to climate change through policy improvement, implementation of practical adaptation measures, enhancing ecosystem resilience to the impacts of climate change, and implementing initiatives aimed at achieving low-carbon development.'[121] In addition, there are programmes such as the National Adaptation Plans of Action (NAPAs) that operate in conjunction with the UNFCCC support for the least developed countries (LDC).

[114]   Global Environmental Facility/ Black Sea Environmental Programme, Black Sea *Transboundary Diagnostic Analysis*, 1 May 2007, available at http://www.blacksea-commission.org/_tda2008-document5.asp (last accessed 30 May 2015).

[115]   *Action Plan for the Protection and Management of the Marine and Coastal Environment of the South Asian Seas*, adopted 24 March 1994, entered into force February 1997, para. 9.9, available at http://www.sacep.org/pdf/SAS%20Action%20Plan.pdf (last accessed 30 May 2015).

[116]   The East Asian Regional Seas Programme is implemented through the UNDP-GEF sponsored Partnerships in the Environmental Management for the Seas of East Asia (PEMSEA) and the Coordinating Body of the South Seas of East Asia (COBSEA).

[117]   *Manila Declaration on Strengthening the Implementation of the Integrated Coastal Management for Sustainable Development and Climate Change Adaptation in the Seas of East Asia Region*, Third Ministerial Forum, Manila, 26 November 2009, available at http://www.pemsea.org/publications/manila-declaration (last accessed 30 May 2015).

[118]   COBSEA, *Guide on Spatial Planning in the Coastal Zones of the East Asian Seas Region: Integrating Emerging Issues and Modern Management Approaches (2011)*, available at www.cobsea.org/documents/COBSEA%20Spatial%20Planning%20Regional%20Resource%20Document.pdf (last accessed 30 May 2015).

[119]   UNEP/NOWPAP IG. 16/10/1Rev.1 NOWPAP, *Medium Term Strategy, 2012-2017*, para. 46, available at www.nowpap.org/data/NOWPAP%20MTS%202012-2017.pdf (last accessed 30 May 2015).

[120]   See, www.persga.org/inner.php?id=217 (last accessed 30 May 2015).

[121]   See, www.sprep.org/Climate-Change/climate-change-overview (last accessed 30 May 2015).

*Table 16.2  Thirteen Regional Seas Protocols*

| Regional Sea | Land based | Dumping | Emergency response | Biodiversity (Protected areas) | Transport of hazardous substances | Offshore activities | ICZM | EIA | Compliance mechanism | UNEP administered |
|---|---|---|---|---|---|---|---|---|---|---|
| Mediterranean Sea | Y | Y | Y | Y | Y | Y | Y | N | Y | Y |
| Wider Caribbean | Revised | Revised | Revised | Revised | N | N | N | N | N | Y |
| Asian Sea | Y | N | N | Y | N | N | N | N | N | Y |
| Eastern Africa | Y | N | Y | Y [flora and fauna] | N | N | N | N | N | Y |
| North-West Pacific | N | N | N | N | N | N | N | N | N | Y |
| West Africa | N | N | Y | N | N | N | Draft | N | N | Y |
| Black Sea | Y | Y | Y | Y | N | N | N | N | N | N |
| North-East Pacific | Revised | N | N | N | N | N | N | N | N | N |
| Red Sea and Gulf of Aden | Y | N | Y | Y | N | N | N | N | N | N |
| ROPME | Y | N | Y | Y | Y | Y | N | N | N | N |
| South-East Asia | N | N | N | N | N | N | N | N | N | N |
| South-East Pacific | Y | N (Protocol on protection against radioactive pollution) | Y | Y [protected areas] | | N | N | N | N | |
| Pacific Region | N | Y | Y | N | N | N | N | N | N | N |

*Source:*Adapted from Nilufer Oral, in Marta Chantal Ribeiro (ed.), *30 years after the signature of the United Nations Convention on the Law of the Sea: the protection of the environment and the future of the Law of the Sea* (Coimbra Editora, 2014).

# 5.   ASSESSMENT FOR THE FUTURE OF THE UNEP REGIONAL SEAS PROGRAMME

An examination of the existing UNEP RSPs, excluding the independent programmes, reveals a somewhat uneven landscape of governance structures. For example, there are RSPs that have not yet adopted a framework convention. Furthermore, in those RSPs that have adopted legal instruments, as Table 16.2 demonstrates, there is little consistency in both the activities regulated and in the substantive content. For example, land based pollution is one of the principal activities that RSPs are to address. However, not all RSPs have adopted protocols on the issue and among the protocols that have been adopted there are significant differences in the legal frameworks, including in the principles and approaches adopted. While land based pollution has been addressed in a number of action plans, it is difficult to understand why the legal governance framework among the UNEP RSPs should be so varied. This is the situation in all the thematic areas such as marine biodiversity, shipping related activities and climate change. This difference is notable given that UNEP has specifically identified that one of the major objectives of the UNEP RSP is to be the principal platform for implementing global conventions, multilateral agreements, global programmes and initiatives at the regional level.[122] Moreover, close examination also reveals significant time lags between adoption of specific protocols and their entry into force. For example, the Mediterranean Offshore Protocol, adopted in 1994, only entered into force in 2011. Similarly, the Land-based Protocol for the Wider Caribbean, adopted in 1999, did not go into effect until 2011.

UNEP has attempted to address the challenges of adapting to new developments and emerging issues by adopting medium-term global strategies for the regional seas.[123] However, there seems to be little connection between these strategies and the objective of developing a comprehensive and effective regional legal governance framework that is implemented regionally and nationally for each of the RSPs. Furthermore, these strategies are aspirational and rely on workshops, studies and projects, which, while important in themselves, may not be adequate to strengthen the overall governance framework for implementation of international and regional commitments.

Climate change stands out as one of the most pressing challenges confronting the international community. The oceans and coastal areas are especially vulnerable to the adverse impacts of climate change. However, the existing governance structure of the RSPs reveals an uneven landscape and gaps in addressing climate change.

Nevertheless, the regional approach remains an important modality in ensuring the transfer of international obligations, principles and approaches to the national level through regional mechanisms, in promoting cooperation among coastal states sharing a common interest in a marine space, in ensuring greater collaboration and harmonization among these states in implementing different instruments, and in actively promoting

---

[122]   UNEP, *Regional Seas Conventions and Action Plans: a framework for regional coordination and cooperation to protect shared marine and coastal resources*, available at www.unep. org/ecosystemmanagement/Portals/7/Documents/factsheets/RSCAPs%20FactSheet%20web.pdf (last accessed 30 May 2015).

[123]   Ibid.

implementation. In relation to this last point, there is, however, a glaring gap in the UNEP RSP when it comes to the promotion of compliance. Only the Mediterranean RSP has formally adopted a compliance mechanism and created a compliance committee, whereas this should be a standard practice for all the UNEP RSPs.[124]

Despite its shortcomings, the UNEP RSP is important and has been a positive influence. However, its future viability and credibility requires that the legal foundation as structured around the legal instruments be standardized, operationalized and implemented.

---

[124] The OSPAR Convention also includes a provision on 'compliance' which requires the OSPAR Commission to assess compliance of the individual Parties with the Convention and decisions and recommendations adopted based on periodic reports, and to take the necessary steps to bring about *full* compliance: Art. 23. For an overview of the OSPAR compliance mechanism see, Rainer Lagoni, 'Monitoring Compliance and Enforcement of Compliance Through the OSPAR Commission' in Peter Ehlers and others (eds), *Marine Issues: From a Scientific, Political and Legal Perspective* (Martinus Nijhoff, 2002) 155.

# 17. Protecting polar environments: coherency in regulating Arctic shipping

*Tore Henriksen*

## 1. INTRODUCTION

Climate change is affecting the Arctic. The sea ice of the Arctic Ocean is retreating and thinning.[1] The Arctic Ocean is projected to be ice free in September by the middle of this century. This will affect the ecosystems, species and biodiversity of Arctic Ocean.[2] The retreat of the sea ice is opening the region to new and expanded human activities exposing the Arctic marine environment to extra pressure.[3] Fishing, petroleum activities, marine scientific research and shipping (including transport, tourism and naval activities) will all affect the marine environment.

The theme of this chapter is Arctic shipping and international regulation of this activity. Shipping is the activity most likely to increase over the next few years. Indeed, the prospect of trans-Arctic sailing routes reducing the distance between Europe and Asia by up to 40 per cent has led to enormous attention on Arctic shipping.[4]

Arctic marine ecosystems differ from other ecosystems.[5] They are covered by sea ice the whole or part of the year and subjected to seasonal extremes including lack of light, ice and low temperatures. Together with the environmental conditions of the ocean and the exchange of waters with the Atlantic and Pacific Oceans, these factors constitute key structuring elements of the ecosystems. The lack of light restricts the primary production during wintertime and the most productive areas are found in the adjacent seas. The consequence is extensive seasonal migrations of marine mammals and birds

---

[1]  B. Kirtman et al., "Near-term Climate Change: Projections and Predictability" in T.F. Stocker et al. (eds) *The Physical Science Basis. Contribution of Working Group I to the Fifth Assessment Report of the Intergovernmental Panel on Climate Change* (Cambridge University Press: Cambridge) 2013, 995.

[2]  P. Boyd et al., Chapter 6 'Oceans systems', 16, 38, and H.-O. Pörtner et al. Chapter 28 'Polar regions', 25, 26 in V.R. Barros et al. (eds), Climate *Change: Impacts, Adaptation, and Vulnerability.* Contribution of Working Group II to the *Fifth Assessment Report of the Intergovernmental Panel on Climate Change*, available at http://www.ipcc.ch/report/ar5/wg2/ (last accessed 30 May 2015).

[3]  Ibid.

[4]  Arctic Council, 'The Arctic Marine Shipping Assessment 2009 Report (April 2009), 44, 102 (AMSA Report 2009), available at www.pame.is/index.php/projects/arctic-marine-shipping/amsa (last accessed 30 May 2015).

[5]  Arctic Monitoring and Assessment Programme (AMAP), 'Identification of Arctic marine areas of heightened ecological and cultural significance: Arctic Marine Shipping Assessment (AMSA) IIc', (AMAP/CAFF/SDWG, Oslo 2013); Conservation of Arctic Flora and Fauna (CAFF), 'Arctic Biodiversity Assessment Status and Trends in Arctic Biodiversity: Synthesis' (Arctic Council, 2013).

into the Arctic Ocean. These factors also determine the vulnerability of Arctic ecosystems. The short feeding season, if disrupted, could result in some animals not getting enough food to cover the energy needed for their long migrations and for breeding.[6] Arctic species are dependent on feathers or fur to insulate against the cold, and can quickly die from exposure if that defence is compromised. These characteristics also serve to make Arctic species more vulnerable to oil spills and other disturbances.

Climate change poses probably the most serious threat to Arctic biodiversity.[7] The effects of climate change work in conjunction with other effects of human activities. Increased Arctic shipping will affect the risk of pollution from operational discharges and from accidents, noise and introduction of invasive species.[8] What distinguishes shipping in Arctic waters from other areas is the higher risk of environmental damage. The risk is affected by the vulnerability of the marine environment and by the conditions under which shipping is conducted. Pollution may have a greater impact on the Arctic environment, which may take longer to restore. Sea ice, icing, low temperatures, remoteness from ports and search and rescue, darkness, rapidly changing weather conditions, lack of experience of ships' crews, and lack of charting are some of the factors that affects the probability of incidents with resultant pollution.[9] These risks are affected by the limited oil-spill preparedness capacity.

Coastal states have a role under the UN Convention on the Law of the Sea Convention[10] (LOSC) in the protection of the marine environment within their EEZs and territorial sea. The Arctic coastal states have special competence to regulate navigation in ice-covered areas.[11] SOLAS 74[12] and MARPOL 73/78,[13] and other instruments adopted through the International Maritime Organization (IMO), are applicable to Arctic shipping. The need for specially crafted rules and standards to mitigate the distinctive hazards has been accepted. To that end, the IMO has hosted negotiations on an International Code for Ships Operating in Polar Waters (Polar Code). The Polar Code will include legally binding requirements on construction, design and equipment (CDEM) and on operational discharges of vessels navigating in Arctic and Antarctic waters.

---

    [6]   H.R. Skjoldal et al., 2009, *Arctic Marine Shipping Assessment (AMSA) Background Research Report on Potential Environmental Impacts from Shipping in the Arctic. Draft Version*, July 2009, available at http://www.pame.is/images/03_Projects/AMSA/AMSA_Background_ Research_Docs/Environmental_Impacts/6-1-Environmental-Impacts-from-Current-and-Future. pdf (last accessed 30 May 2015).
    [7]   CAFF, *Arctic Biodiversity Assessment: Report for Policy Makers* (CAFF, 2013).
    [8]   AMSA Report 2009, above n 4, 136–52.
    [9]   Ibid, 138.
    [10]   United Nations Convention on the Law of the Sea, adopted 10 December 1982, entered into force 16 November 1994, 1833 UNTS 3, Arts 21(1) (f) and 56(1)(b)(iii).
    [11]   LOSC, Art. 234.
    [12]   International Convention for the Safety of Life at Sea (SOLAS), adopted 1 November 1974, entered into force 25 May 1980, 1184 UNTS 278.
    [13]   International Convention for the Prevention of Pollution from Ships, as modified by the Protocol of 1978 relating thereto (MARPOL 73/78), adopted 2 November 1973 and 17 February 1978, entered into force 2 October 1983, 1340 UNTS 62.

The objective of this chapter is first to investigate the Polar Code and then assess its possible effect on the role of Arctic coastal states in the protection of the marine environment. Section 2 examines how the Polar Code addresses the hazards of Arctic shipping. This includes an investigation of if and how the hazards identified have been mitigated. Section 3 examines the impact of the Polar Code on the environmental jurisdiction of the Arctic coastal states, or those states with maritime zones in the Arctic Ocean. Canada and Russia currently regulate shipping on the basis of the extended jurisdiction conferred on Arctic coastal states by virtue of Article 234 of the LOSC. The other Arctic coastal states have thus far not invoked the Article 234 jurisdiction. Vessels exercising the rights of navigation in the territorial sea and the EEZs in Arctic waters are therefore seemingly subjected to different requirements and to varying levels of coastal state involvement. The question thus arises as to how to ensure coherency between the Polar Code and the regulations adopted by the Arctic coastal states. May the other states adopt legislation to apply the Polar Code requirements to navigation through their maritime zones? Will the Polar Code limit the jurisdiction of Canada and Russia under Article 234 of the LOSC? First, the questions regarding the Polar Code will be investigated, followed by the questions on the relationship between the Polar Code and Arctic coastal states before conclusions are drawn.

## 2. THE POLAR CODE

### 2.1 The Background to the Polar Code

The 2009 Arctic Marine Shipping Assessment (AMSA) commissioned by the Arctic Council, a 'high level inter-governmental forum to provide a means for promoting cooperation, coordination and interaction among the Arctic States',[14] included extensive analysis of the status, prospects and challenges of Arctic shipping.[15] The report concluded with a series of recommendations including that the Arctic States should support the efforts of the IMO to make the Arctic shipping guidelines mandatory.[16] The Arctic Council has approved these recommendations[17] and work on their implementation has started.[18] This work may result in proposals to the IMO for the adoption of measures under MARPOL or other conventions. Other results already include the

---

[14] Declaration on the Establishment of the Arctic Council, Ottawa 19 September 1996, (1996) Volume 35, Issue 6 – November 1996 *International Legal Materials* 1386.

[15] AMSA Report 2009, above n 4.

[16] Ibid, 6–7.

[17] Tromsø Declaration, on the occasion of the Sixth Ministerial Meeting of the Arctic Council, 29 April, 2009, Tromsø, Norway, available at http://www.arctic-council.org/index.php/en/document-archive/category/5-declarations (last accessed 31 May 2015).

[18] Arctic Council, *Status of Implementation of the AMSA 2009 Report Recommendation, May 2013* (AMSA Progress Report), available at http://www.pame.is/index.php/projects/arctic-marine-shipping/amsa (last accessed 31 May 2015).

adoption of regional agreements on search and rescue[19] and on oil pollution preparedness and response.[20]

The mandate of the IMO includes maritime safety and protection of the marine environment.[21] The Maritime Safety Committee (MSC) and the Marine Environmental Protection Committee (MEPC) are responsible for fulfilling these objectives and have treaty body functions under the SOLAS 74 and MARPOL 73/78 respectively.[22] Several IMO conventions are relevant for the protection of the marine environment, including SOLAS 74, MARPOL 73/78, Ballast Water Management Convention,[23] STCW Convention[24] and the Anti-fouling Convention.[25] These conventions are applicable to navigation in Arctic waters and some include special Arctic regulations.[26] In the aftermath of the *Exxon Valdez* disaster, however, there were further proposals for adopting specific CDEM rules and standards for vessels operating in ice-covered waters.[27] This resulted in the adoption of the Arctic Shipping Guidelines,[28] later succeeded by the Polar Shipping Guidelines.[29]

Following the adoption of the Polar Shipping Guidelines the MSC on the initiative of, inter alia, Denmark, Norway and the United States, with the endorsement of the

---

[19]   The Agreement on Cooperation in Aeronautical and Maritime Search and Rescue in the Arctic, adopted 21 April 2011, available at http://www.arctic-council.org/index.php/en/document-archive/category/20-main-documents-from-nuuk# (last accessed 31 May 2015).

[20]   Agreement on Cooperation on Marine Oil Pollution, Preparedness and Response in the Arctic, adopted 15 May available http://www.arctic-council.org/index.php/en/document-archive/category/425-main-documents-from-kiruna-ministerial-meeting (last accessed 31 May 2015).

[21]   Convention on the International Maritime Organization, adopted 6 March 1948, entered into force 17 March 1958, 289 UNTS 48, as amended, Art. 1(a).

[22]   Ibid, Arts 27–31 (MSC) and Arts 37–41 (MEPC).

[23]   International Convention for the Control and Management of Ships' Ballast Water and Sediments, adopted 16 February 2004 (not in force), BWM/CONF/36, available in Meeting Documents of IMODOCS at http://docs.imo.org (last accessed 31 May 2015).

[24]   International Convention on Standards of Training, Certification and Watchkeeping for Seafarers, adopted 1 December 1978, entered into force 28 April 1984, 1361 UNTS I-23001. Its annex has been amended, Adoption of Amendments to the Annex to the International Convention on Standards of Training, Certification and Watchkeeping for Seafarers (STCW), 1978 STCW/CONF.2/DC/1, 24 June 2010, available in Meeting Documents of IMODOCS at http://docs.imo.org (last accessed 31 May 2015).

[25]   International Convention on the Control of Harmful Anti-fouling Systems on Ships, adopted 5 October 2001, entered into force 17 September 2008, AFS/CONF/26, 18 October 2001, available in Meeting Documents of IMODOCS at http://docs.imo.org (last accessed 31 May 2015).

[26]   Heike Deggim, 'Ensuring Safe, Secure and Reliable Shipping in the Arctic Ocean' in P.A. Berkman and A.N. Vylegzhanin (eds), *Environmental Security in the Arctic Ocean* (Springer, 2013) 241, 243–4.

[27]   Øystein Jensen, 'Arctic Shipping Guidelines: Towards a Legal Regime for Navigation Safety and Environmental Protection?' (2008) 44(2) *Polar Record* 107, 108.

[28]   Guidelines for Ships Operating in Arctic Ice-Covered Waters, MEPC/Circ.399 23 December 2002.

[29]   Guidelines for Ships Operating in Polar Waters, Resolution A.1024(26), adopted on 2 December 2009 (Polar Shipping Guidelines).

MEPC, agreed to develop the guidelines into a mandatory Polar Code.[30] A subcommittee under the MSC was charged with the task.[31] A draft was submitted to the MSC and MEPC for approval and adoption in early 2014. The MSC approved the maritime safety part of the Polar Code in principle at its meeting in May 2014 and adopted this at its meeting in late 2014.[32] However, the MEPC was not able to approve the pollution prevention part of the Polar Code at its meeting in March 2014. It therefore established a correspondence group tasked with finalizing the relevant parts of the Polar Code, which was approved in late 2014.[33] The MEPC will adopt the relevant parts of the Polar Code at its meeting in May 2015.[34] The analysis in this chapter is based on the texts adopted by the MSC[35] and approved by the MEPC.[36]

## 2.2   The Structure of the Polar Code

In addition to the preamble and the Introduction, the Polar Code includes two main parts: Part I on maritime safety and Part II on pollution prevention.[37] Each part consists of mandatory and recommendatory sections.[38] Together with the mandatory sections, the Introduction is made legally binding through a new chapter XIV to SOLAS 74[39] and through amendments to the relevant annexes of MARPOL 74/78.[40] The two committees have coordinated the drafting of the preamble and introduction, which are

---

[30]   Report of the Maritime Safety Committee on Its Eighty-Sixth Session, para. 23.32, MSC 86/26. MEPC concurred with the proposal, Report of the Marine Environment Protection Committee on its Fifty-Ninth Session, para. 20.9, MEPC 59/24.

[31]   The subcommittees have been restructured and the responsibility for the Polar Code is located in the subcommittee on Ship Design and Construction, which is a merger of three subcommittees.

[32]   Report of the Maritime Safety Committee on Its Ninety-Fourth Session, item 3.61, MSC 94/21.

[33]   Report of the Marine Environmental Protection Committee at its Sixty-Seventh Session, item 9.44, MEPC 67/20.

[34]   IMO: Shipping in polar waters. Developments of an international code for ships operating in polar waters (Polar Code), available at www.imo.org/MediaCentre/HotTopics/polar/Pages/default.aspx.

[35]   Report of the Maritime Safety Committee on Its Ninety-Fourth Session, Annex 6 Resolution MSC.385(94) – International Code For Ships Operating In Polar Waters (Polar Code), MSC 94/21/Add.1.

[36]   Report of the Marine Environmental Protection Committee at its Sixty-Seventh Session, Annex 10 Preamble, Introduction and Part II of the Draft International Code for Ships Operating in Polar Waters, MEPC 67/20.

[37]   Polar Code, above n 35, Introduction, Section 4.

[38]   Polar Code, above n 35 and 36, Part I-A Safety measures and part I-B Additional Guidance regarding the provisions and Part I-A; Part II-A Pollution Prevention Measures and Part II-B Information and additional guidance to Part II-A.

[39]   Report of the Maritime Safety Committee on Its Ninety-Fourth Session, Annex 7 Resolution MSC.386(94) – Amendments to the International Convention for the Safety of Life at Sea (SOLAS), 1974, As Amended (New Chapter XIV), MSC 94/21/Add.1.

[40]   Report of the Marine Pollution Prevention Committee on its Sixty-Seventh Session, Annex 11 Draft amendments to MARPOL Annexes I, II, IV and V, MEPC 67/20.

common to both substantive parts of the Polar Code.[41] Chapter XIV to SOLAS 74 will enter into force on 1 January 2017.[42]

The Polar Code will be applicable to vessels operating in polar waters.[43] Polar waters include both the Arctic and Antarctic waters, with Arctic waters being defined as covering the same geographical area as provided for in the Arctic Shipping Guidelines.[44] The Polar Code will be applicable to vessels certified under SOLAS 74 (safety part) and MARPOL 73/78 (pollution prevention part).[45] However, the Polar Code is not applicable to state owned or operated vessels, smaller vessels, leisure boats and fishing boats. Smaller vessels and fishing vessels may be included at a later stage.[46]

The Polar Code is characterized by its two main approaches: it is both risk- and goal-based.[47] Its overall goal is to provide for maritime safety and the protection of the environment by addressing risks in polar waters, which are not adequately addressed by other IMO instruments.[48] It lists various types of hazards, which affect the risks of polar shipping, or the probability of occurrence and the seriousness of consequences, including sea ice, icing, low temperatures, darkness, weather conditions, remoteness from infrastructure (inadequate functioning of navigation and communication systems, navigational aids), lack of data (charts), lack of crew experience and the sensitivity of the environment.[49] These risks are to be mitigated through requirements relating to CDEM and to the operation of vessels as provided for in Part I-A and relating to preventing operational discharges as provided for in Part II-A. The relationship between the safety measures and protection of the environment is expressly recognized and it is accepted that these measures will reduce the likelihood of accidents.[50]

### 2.2.1   Safety measures

Part I-A includes chapters on structural requirements for operating in ice-covered areas, including the machinery to operate in low temperatures, adequate fire protection and life-saving appliances, navigational and communication equipment as well as requirements for manning and training of the crew.[51] Only some of the safety measures will be commented on in this chapter.

Three categories of vessels are introduced: defined according to their ability to navigate through or in ice-covered areas. While vessels in category A must be able to

---

[41]   Report of Report of the Maritime Safety Committee on Its Ninety-Fourth Session, item 3.25-3.27, MSC 94/21 and Report of the Marine Environmental Protection Committee at its Sixty-Seventh Session, item 9.36–9.39, MEPC 67/20.

[42]   Report of Report of the Maritime Safety Committee on Its Ninety-Fourth Session, item 3.65, MSC 94/21.

[43]   SOLAS amendments, above n 39, Chapter XIV, Reg. 2.1, cf. Reg. 1.4; MARPOL amendments, above n 40 Annex I Regulation 47, Annex II Regulation 22, Annex IV Regulation 18 and Annex V Regulation 14.

[44]   SOLAS Chapter XIV, above n 39, Reg. 1.3 and Polar Shipping Guidelines, sect. G–3.3.

[45]   Above n 43.

[46]   DE, Report to the Maritime Safety Committee, paras 10.7 and 10.10, DE 56/25.

[47]   Polar Code, above n 35, Preamble, para. 6 and Part I-A sect. 1.1.

[48]   Polar Code, above n 35, Introduction, sect. 1.

[49]   Polar Code, above n 35, Introduction, sect. 3.

[50]   Polar Code, above n 35, preamble, para. 5.

[51]   Polar Code, above n 35, Part I-A, chaps 3–12.

operate at least in medium first-year ice, category B vessels must be constructed to operate in thin first-year ice while category C vessels are designed to operate in open waters where the sea ice concentration is less than 1/10.[52] First-year ice has a thickness between 0.3 – 3.0 m.[53] The Polar Code includes demands on the construction or ice strengthening, stability and machinery for vessels to qualify for the categories.[54] A vessel in category C may navigate in sea ice with a thickness of less than 30cm without being ice strengthened.[55] Particular requirements are applicable to vessels intended to operate under low temperatures.[56] Their systems and equipment are to be fully functional at very low temperatures, including survival systems and equipment.[57] There are also requirements relating to the choice of construction materials, machinery, fire safety systems and navigational equipment to ensure the functionality of vessels at low temperatures.[58] Vessels must be manned by adequately qualified, trained and experienced personnel,[59] and further requirements that are more specific will be provided in the STCW Convention, which is to be amended.[60] Notably, the Polar Code does not include any requirement for an ice navigator as is provided for in the Polar Shipping Guidelines.[61]

The consequence of this risk-based approach is the adoption of requirements identifying specific operational limitations as to when, how, where and under which conditions vessels may navigate in polar waters. These limitations are to be stipulated in the Polar Ship Certificate, which all relevant vessels are required to carry.[62] Further, Part I-A includes requirements on the operation of vessels through the use of a Polar Water Operational Manual (PWOM). The PWOM shall set out procedures for reducing risks by ensuring that the vessel operates within these limitations or capabilities and has procedures for dealing with situations where it is confronting conditions exceeding its capabilities.[63] Vessels are required to use voyage-planning taking into account the hazards encountered through the planned route.[64] These hazards could include limited information on the hydrology, available information on extent and type of sea ice, and distance to search and rescue capabilities.

Since the risks of navigating within polar waters vary depending on spatial, temporal and climatic conditions, the goal-based approach, which allows for the adoption of

---

[52]   Polar Code, above n 35, Introduction, sects 2.1–2.3.
[53]   Polar Code, above n 35, Introduction, sect. 2.4 cfr Sect. 2.4.
[54]   Polar Code, above n 35, Part I-A, sects 3.3, 4.2.1.2 and 6.6.3.
[55]   Polar Code, above n 35, Part I-A, sect. 3.3.2.4.
[56]   It is defined as areas where the mean daily low temperature is below minus 10 degrees Celsius, Part I-A, sect. 1.2.8ter.
[57]   Polar Code, above n 35, I-A, sect. 1.4.
[58]   Polar Code, above n 35, Part I-A sect. 3.2.1 and 3.3.1.
[59]   Polar Code, above n 35, Part I-A, sect. 12.1.
[60]   Sub-Committee on Human Element, Training and Watchkeeping, Report to the Maritime Safety Committee, HTW 1/21, para. 11.
[61]   Polar Shipping Guidelines, sects 14.1.2 and 14.2.
[62]   Polar Code, above n 35, Part I-A, sect. 1.3. A model Polar Ship Certificate is found in Appendix 1.
[63]   Polar Code, above n 35, Part I-A, sect. 2.3.
[64]   Polar Code, above n 35, Part I-A, sect. 11.3.

flexible regulations to meet changing circumstances, seems particularly appropriate.[65] Indeed, the goal-based approach is increasingly being introduced into IMO instruments, in particular, SOLAS 74.[66] The goal-based standards consist of norms, which operate at different levels: the goals setting the high-level objectives; the functional requirements including the criteria to be met to fulfil the goals; and the regulations that set out the detailed requirements for meeting the functional requirements and the goals. Part I-A of the Polar Code is structured based on this approach.[67] Depending on the level of detail of the regulations, the addressees of the Polar Code – flag states – are provided a certain degree of discretion in regulating Arctic shipping. However, as discussed in section 2.2.2 below, the goal-based approach is not used in Part II-A.[68]

The use of the goal-based approach can be illustrated by the chapter on ship structure. It sets out construction requirements for vessels to operate in areas with sea ice and low temperatures. The goal is for the material and scantling of the structure to retain its integrity when responding to the environmental loads and conditions. Under the functional requirement, ice-strengthened vessels shall be designed to resist loads that are anticipated under the foreseen ice conditions. The detail regulation requires the flag States to approve the scantling of category A and B vessels and ice strengthened category C vessels on the basis of 'standards acceptable' to the IMO or other standards offering an 'equivalent level of safety'.[69] Thus, the Polar Code does not include any separate (prescriptive) regulations for ice strengthening of vessels. Instead, the Polar Class standards, as developed by the International Association of Classification Societies, are made applicable by reference.[70] Vessels are not required to be classified under the Polar Class standards. Other ice classifications may be used and vessels may have alternative design and arrangements including for the structure and machinery if these provide an equivalent level of safety.[71]

### 2.2.2   Environmental protection or pollution prevention?

The themes to be covered by the environmental protection chapter were set out quite broadly when the negotiations on the Code started.[72] It was proposed that the negotiations should apply a problem-oriented approach to assess what extra measures were necessary to meet the particular environmental and climatic conditions of polar

---

[65]   Polar Code, above n 35, Introduction, sect. 3.2.

[66]   Generic Guidelines for Developing IMO Goal-Based Standards, MSC.1/Circ.1394; Goal-based construction standards for new ships, available at www.imo.org/OurWork/Safety/SafetyTopics/Documents/1394.pdf (last accessed 1 June 2015).

[67]   Polar Code, above n 35, Part I-A, sect. 1.1.

[68]   Report of the Marine Environment Protection Committee on Its Sixty-Sixth Session, MEPC 66/21, para. 11.27.

[69]   Polar Code, above n 35, Part I-A, Chapter 2, sect. 3.3.2.

[70]   The standards 'acceptable' to IMO refers to the IASC Unified Requirements for Polar Ships. The footnotes to the regulations for category A and B vessels in sect. 3.3.2 indicate which Polar Classes are consistent with Category A and B vessels.

[71]   SOLAS Chapter XIV, above n 39, reg. 4.

[72]   Report of the Marine Environment Protection Committee on its sixtieth session, paras 21.5–21.11, MEPC 60/22, with reference to 'Any other Business: Environmental aspects of polar shipping', submitted by Norway, MEPC 60/21/1.

waters.[73] Environmental NGOs participated actively in the negotiating process and submitted extensive proposals for regulating shipping activities.[74]

The need for stricter regulations of operational discharges under the annexes of MARPOL 73/78 was highlighted. This included possible further restrictions on operational discharges of oil and oily mixtures under MARPOL Annex I. There were also arguments for additional requirements on treatment and discharge of sewage under MARPOL Annex IV as the polar conditions allow for slower decomposition. In particular, the operational discharges from cruise vessels, which account for a substantial portion of Arctic shipping activities, were a major source of concern. Discharges form these vessels include grey water (wastewater) which is not regulated under MARPOL 73/78. Stricter regulations on discharges of garbage such as food waste and animal carcasses (Annex V) were to be considered for the same reason as sewage. Another theme for consideration was emission of black carbon (soot and particles) originating from the combustion of fossil fuels by vessels. By reducing the reflecting effect of snow and sea ice, the black carbon contributes to the acceleration of ice melt.[75]

One of the major threats to the Arctic environment from shipping is accidental oil spills.[76] The risk is greatly enhanced by inadequate emergency preparedness capability and techniques and by the vulnerability of the environment. This triggered proposals, particularly advocated by the environmental NGOs, for banning the transport and use of heavy fuel oil. A similar ban is in place for the Antarctica.[77] In addition, the increased risk of introduction of invasive species to Arctic waters and between the Pacific and the Atlantic called for mitigating measures. The AMSA report further identified navigation in areas of heightened ecological significance, or in migratory areas of marine mammals, together with noise, as additional sources of risks to the marine environment.[78] However, these hazards were not addressed during the negotiations of the environmental chapter.

The negotiations on this part of the Polar Code were probably the most contentious. Part II-A consists of five chapters which correspond to the annexes to MARPOL 73/78. The first chapter will include a ban on the discharge of any oil and oily mixtures from any ship sailing in Arctic waters, providing it with a de facto special area status under Annex I.[79] A ban on transport and use of heavy grade fuel oil has not been included; the MEPC concluding that it was premature to adopt such regulations.[80] Nevertheless, a project under the Arctic Council on implementing the AMSA recommendations is

---

[73]  Ibid.

[74]  See eg, Development of a Mandatory Code for Ships Operating in Polar Waters: Wider environmental provisions for the Polar Code (FOEI, IFAW, WWF, Pacific Environment and CSC), DE 54/13/9; and Friends of the Earth International (FOEI), World Wide Fund For Nature (WWF), International Fund for Animal Welfare (IFAW) and Pacific Environment, SDC 1/3/15.

[75]  AMSA Report 2009, 140.

[76]  Ibid, 135.

[77]  MARPOL, Annex I, reg. 43.

[78]  AMSA Report 2009, 152–3.

[79]  Polar Code, above n 36, Part II-A, sect. 1.1.

[80]  Report of the sixty-fifth meeting of the Marine Environmental Protection Committee, paras 11.52–11.53, MEPC 65/22.

investigating ways of mitigating the risks, which may lead to proposals for new IMO regulations.[81] Until then vessels operating in Arctic waters are encouraged not to carry or to use heavy grade fuel oil.[82] A ban on discharges of noxious liquid substances and stricter distance regulations for discharge of sewage and garbage are also included.[83]

The proposals to regulate discharges of grey water, prevention of loss of containers with packaged dangerous goods in Arctic waters and of discharges of black carbon have not been considered for inclusion in the Polar Code.[84] The reason is probably that these issues have relevance beyond the Arctic waters and thus are not considered appropriate to include.

Part II-A primarily concerns operational discharges of pollutants.[85] It does not include requirements to prevent the introduction of alien species to Arctic waters. Such obligations may be derived from the Ballast Water Management Convention and the Anti-fouling Convention.[86] The intention has been to ensure that adequate measures are taken under these instruments.[87] Guidance on the application of these instruments in Arctic waters is provided in Part II-B.[88]

Ships routeing would be an adequate measure to prevent ship strikes of marine mammals and to avoid navigation through areas of heightened ecological significance. Such measures are not included in the Polar Code. The requirement to use voyage planning under Part I-A may, however, prevent vessels from navigating through such areas, or ensure that they take extra care when doing so.[89]

## 2.3 Assessment

The risks of Arctic shipping are addressed through the different chapters of the Polar Code. The safety measures provide for a general obligation to operate to reduce the level of risk to a minimum. It is difficult to assess whether the risks are adequately addressed, particularly given the format of the regulations. On the one hand, flag states have certain discretion in fulfilling the goals and functional requirements set out in Part I-A on safety measures. On the other hand, Part II-A on pollution prevention sets out their obligations quite clearly. However, the assessment provided here is rather about the hazards that were not addressed, particularly given the intention to adopt a 'holistic approach in reducing identified risks'.[90] Failure to address these hazards is, however, not surprising given the lack of any systematic approach to regulatory needs. The focus

---

[81]  See AMSA Progress Report and information available at http://pame.is/index.php/projects/arctic-marine-shipping/amsa (last accessed 1 June 2015).

[82]  Polar Code, above n 36, Part II-B, sec 1.

[83]  Ibid, Part II-Part II-A, sects 2.1.1, 4.2 and 5.2.

[84]  Report to the Maritime Safety Committee, para. 12.13, DE 55/22.

[85]  Ibid.

[86]  Development of a Mandatory Code for Ships Operating in Polar Waters. Environmental aspects of the Code (Norway) DE 60/21/1.

[87]  Report of the Marine Environment Protection Committee on its Sixty-third Session, para. 11.18, MEPC 63/23.

[88]  Polar Code, above n 36, Part II-B, sect. 4.

[89]  Polar Code, above n 35, Part I-A, sect. 11.3.6 and 11.3.8.

[90]  Polar Code, above n 35, Preamble, para. 7.

on safety measures is a natural consequence of charging a MSC sub-committee with leading the process. The lack of a clear mandate and instructions to the MEPC may have been a contributing factor. In addition, controversial proposals or proposals with implications for shipping beyond the Arctic have been avoided.

When establishing regulations based on geographical criteria there may be a need for coordination between different legal instruments and institutions. This is particularly important as the Polar Code will require amendments to SOLAS 74 and MARPOL 73/78. A draft chapter on working conditions was removed because this is not regulated through IMO instruments. The requirement of adequately trained crew is regulated through the STCW Convention. This is also the case of the prevention of introduction of invasive species from vessels, which are regulated through separate conventions. The question is to what degree the hazards of Arctic shipping will be mitigated through these instruments? The inclusion of recommendations on some of these issues may assist, but the extent to which the hazards of Arctic shipping are taken into consideration through other IMO instruments or instruments outside IMO will depend on initiatives taken by the Arctic coastal states.

## 3. ARCTIC COASTAL STATE SHIPPING REGULATIONS

### 3.1 General

The following section examines the impacts of the Polar Code on the (environmental) jurisdiction of the Arctic coastal states. With the exception of Greenland, the coastal states have all have declared a 12 nautical miles (nm) territorial sea.[91] The outer limits of the territorial sea of Greenland are three nm from the baselines.[92] In addition, all have established a 200 nm EEZ. Norway has established 200 nm fisheries zones off Svalbard and Jan Mayen.[93] In terms of navigation, these 200 nm zones covering most of the Norwegian Arctic waters are equivalent to the high seas.

The five Arctic coastal states have chosen two different approaches to their regulatory role. The USA, Denmark/Greenland and Norway have not adopted any specific Arctic shipping legislation. They rely on the 'normal' environmental jurisdiction provided by the law of the sea. Canada and the Russian Federation have adopted specific legislation for Arctic shipping, based on Article 234 of the LOSC. In

---

[91]  LOSC, Art. 3. This includes the USA which is not a contracting party to the LOSC; see the Summary of national claims provided by the UN, available at http://www.un.org/Depts/los/ LEGISLATIONANDTREATIES/PDFFILES/table_summary_of_claims.pdf (last accessed 31 May 2015).

[92]  Order No. 191 of 27 May 1963 on the Delimitation of the Territorial Sea of Greenland available at http://www.un.org/Depts/los/LEGISLATIONANDTREATIES/PDFFILES/DNK_ 1963_Order.pdf (last accessed 31 May 2015).

[93]  The fisheries zones are established under Regulations of 3 June 1977 No 6 (Svalbard) and Regulations of 23 May 1980 No. 4 (Jan Mayen) on the basis of the Act of 17 December 1976 No. 91 relating to the Economic Zone of Norway, available in English translation at http://www.un.org/depts/los/LEGISLATIONANDTREATIES/PDFFILES/NOR_1976_Act.pdf (last accessed 31 May 2015).

discussing the question on how the Polar Code may affect coastal state environmental jurisdiction, a distinction must thus be made between the normal and the extended coastal state environmental jurisdiction.

### 3.1.1   'Normal' coastal state environmental jurisdiction

The coastal state enjoys exclusive jurisdiction within the 12 nm territorial sea.[94] This jurisdiction includes the competence to adopt legislation for the preservation of the environment.[95] This includes regulation of operational discharges from vessels as well as rules and standards on their construction, design, equipment and manning and the navigation of the vessels. The coastal state is not competent to adopt regulations on construction, design, equipment and manning (CDEM) unless these regulations are implementing '… generally accepted international rules and standards' (GAIRS).[96] The jurisdiction of the coastal state over navigation within the adjacent EEZ is restricted to the protection and preservation of the marine environment.[97] The coastal state may take legislative measures to prevent pollution from vessels. However, these measures must conform to GAIRS.[98] The coastal state is not competent to adopt any unilateral measures relating to operational discharges, CDEM or the navigation of vessels. In practice, the coastal state is competent to adopt legislation implementing the regulations of MARPOL 73/78 and SOLAS 74 and other IMO and ILO instruments.[99]

### 3.1.2   Extended environmental jurisdiction

The Arctic coastal states are competent under Article 234 of the LOSC to adopt and enforce legislation to prevent pollution from vessels operating in ice-covered areas within the limits of their EEZ. There are no requirements that this legislation conform to the generally accepted international rules or standards or that it is approved by the competent international organization.[100] The Arctic coastal states thus have an extended environmental jurisdiction. This extended environmental jurisdiction may be exercised '… within the limits of the EEZ'. This includes the territorial sea and straits used for international navigation.[101] This extended jurisdiction is, however, conditioned: it is only applicable to 'ice-covered areas' where the presence of sea ice in combination with severe climatic conditions create obstacles or exceptional hazards to navigation

---

[94]   LOSC, Art. 2.
[95]   Ibid, Art. 21(1)(f).
[96]   Ibid, Art. 22(2).
[97]   Ibid, Art. 56(1)(b)(iii).
[98]   Ibid, Art. 211(5).
[99]   Erik Jaap Molenaar, *Coastal State Jurisdiction over Vessel-Source* Pollution (Kluwer Law International, 1998) 136; Henrik Ringbom, *The EU Maritime Safety Policy and International Law* (Martinus Nijhoff, 2008) 393; 'Article 21 – Laws and Regulations of the Coastal State Relating to Innocent Passage (II)' 2 in Center for Oceans Law and Policy, University of Virginia, *Commentary on the Law of the Sea Convention* (Martinus Nijhoff Publishers, 2013) Martinus Nijhoff Online, 25 August 2014 DOI:10.1163/ej.LAOS_9780792324713_184-203.
[100]   See eg, LOSC, Art. 211(5) and (6).
[101]   'Article 234 – Ice-Covered Areas (IV)' 2, in *Commentary on the Law of the Sea Convention* above n 99, Martinus Nijhoff Online, 17 September 2014 DOI:10.1163/ej.LAOS_9780792307648_392–398, paras 234.5(d), 397.

and where pollution of the marine environment in these areas could cause '... major harm or irreversible disturbance to the ecological balance ...' The ice-coverage condition is the most controversial. Extended jurisdiction is not applicable to just any ice-covered areas. In addition to creating obstacle or hazards to navigation, the ice must be present and cover the sea area for '... most of the year'. While no definition of 'most of the year' is provided, even a basic literal reading of the words indicates that it must at least exceed six months to qualify.[102]

The coastal states enjoy some degree of discretion in adopting measures under Article 234 although they are prevented from using this jurisdiction to promote their pure national interests. The measures adopted must promote the objective of pollution prevention, be non-discriminatory, be based on 'the best scientific evidence available' and have 'due regard' for navigation and protection of the environment. In other words, the Arctic coastal states are required to ensure that the measures adopted are necessary and reasonable.[103]

## 3.2 The Polar Code and Arctic Coastal State Environmental Jurisdiction

### 3.2.1 The Polar Code as an enabling factor?

The maritime safety and marine environmental protection legislation of the USA, Denmark in respect of Greenland, and Norway[104] is of general application. Norway has adopted a few regulations for the coastal waters of Svalbard under this legislation.[105] Denmark has adopted maritime safety and marine environmental protection regulations[106] for the Greenland maritime zones under its national legislation.[107]

---

[102]   Molenaar, above n 99, 420.

[103]   Kristin Bartenstein, 'The "Arctic Exception" in the Law of the Sea Convention: A Contribution to Safer Navigation in the Northwest Passage?' (2011) [42/1] *Ocean Development & International Law*, 22, 41; Molenaar, above n 99, 420.

[104]   Act of 16 February 2007 No. 09 relating to Ship Safety and Security, available in an English translation at http://www.sjofartsdir.no/PageFiles/3272/Ship%20Safety%20and%20 Security%20Act%20No.%209%20of%2016%20February%202007.pdf (last accessed 31 May 2015); Act of 17 April 2009 No. 19 on Harbour and Fairways, available in Norwegian at http://lovdata.no/dokument/SF/forskrift/2010-12-17-1607; Act of 17 April 2009 No. 19 on Harbour and Fairways, available in Norwegian at http://lovdata.no/dokument/SF/forskrift/2010-12-17-1607 (last accessed 31 May 2015).

[105]   Regulation of 30 December 2009 No. 1846 on Harbours and Fairways of Svalbard, available in Norwegian at http://lovdata.no/dokument/SF/forskrift/2009-12-30-1846 (last accessed 31 May 2015).

[106]   Royal Decree No. 71 of 29 January 2013 on the entry into force for Greenland of acts amending the Act on Safety at Sea, available in English translation at http://www.dma.dk/ SiteCollectionDocuments/Legislation/Acts/2013/Anordning-71-29012013-om%20ikrafttr%C3% A6den%20for%20Gr%C3%B8nland%20af%20love%20om%20%C3%A6ndringer%20af%20lov %20om%20sikkerhed%20til%20s%C3%B8s-.pdf (last accessed 31 May 2015); Anordning nr 1035 af 22. Oktober 2004 om ikrafttræden for Grønland af lov om beskyttelse af havmiljøet (Royal Decree No. 1035, 22 October 2004, on the Marine Act coming into force for Greenland).

[107]   Consolidated Act No. 72 of 17 January 2014 on Safety at Sea (Bekendtgørelse af lov nr. 72 af 17/01/2014 om sikkerhed til søs), available in English translation at www.dma.dk/Site CollectionDocuments/Legislation/Acts/2014/LBK-72-17012014-safety%20at%20sea.pdf (last accessed 31 May 2015) and Consolidated Act No. 963 of 3 July 2013 on the Protection of

The legislation of all three states provides for implementing the CDEM regulations of SOLAS 74 and MARPOL 73/78. These regulations are primarily applied to foreign-flagged vessels when calling at their ports. The US has adopted a separate set of regulations for inspection of vessels in its ports.[108] The Norwegian Port State Control Regulation[109] (including Svalbard) implements the Paris MoU on Port State Control[110] and the EU Port State Directive.[111] The Greenland maritime safety regulation provides the legal basis for port state control including detention of and banning the visit of vessels to Greenlandic ports.[112] Similarly, all three states have adopted legislation implementing the regulations of the MARPOL 73/78 annexes on operational discharges and emissions.[113] Both the Greenland marine protection regulation and the Norwegian legislation are applicable to foreign-flagged vessels operating in the territorial sea and the EEZ.[114] Norway has adopted a regulation providing the legal basis to enforce violations of these operational discharge regulations within its territorial sea and EEZ.[115] Violations of the Greenland marine protection regulation are

---

the Marine Environment (Bekendtgørelse af lov nr 963 af 03/07/2013 om beskyttelse av havmiljøet, available in Danish at https://www.retsinformation.dk/Forms/r0710.aspx?id= 145889#Not1 (last accessed 31 May 2015).

[108]   46 USC Chapter 33 (general) and Chapter 37 (oil tankers).

[109]   Regulation of 30 December 2010 No. 19849 concerning the control of foreign ships and mobile offshore units in Norwegian Ports, etc. (Port State Regulation), available in an English translation at http://www.sjofartsdir.no/en/legislation/regulations/control-of-foreign-ships-and-mobile-offshore-units-in-norwegian-ports-etc-port-state-control-regulations/ (last accessed 31 May 2015).

[110]   Paris Memorandum on Port State Control, available at https://www.parismou.org/about-us/memorandum (last accessed 31 May 2015).

[111]   Directive 2009/16/EC of the European Parliament and of the Council of 23 April 2009 on Port State Control, OJ L 131, p. 57. The EU legislation on maritime transport is relevant for the European Economic Area Agreement to which Norway is a party, see Agreement on the European Economic Area (EEA Agreement), Arts 47–52 and Annex XIII/V, (1994) *Official Journal of the European Community*, L1, 3. The EEA Agreement Art. 102 provides for the procedures for including new EU legislation into the EEA Agreement.

[112]   Above n 105, Part 5.

[113]   USA, 33 USC § 1907 (a). The US has not accepted Annex IV on sewage. The discharges of sewage by foreign vessels within the territorial sea are regulated in the Federal Water Pollution Control Act, 33 USC § 1322 (b)(1). Norway: Ship Safety and Security Act, Sect. 31 and Regulation of 30 May 2012 No. 488 on Environmental Safety for Vessels and Mobile Offshore Units, available at http://www.sjofartsdir.no/en/legislation/regulations/environmental-safety-for-ships-and-mobile-offshore-units1/ (last accessed 31 May 2015); Denmark: Anordning nr 1035 af 22. Oktober 2004 om ikrafttræden for Grønland af lov om beskyttelse af havmiljøet (Royal Decree No. 1035, 22 October 2004, on the Marine Act coming into force for Greenland, sects 8-9 (Annex I, oil), sects 10-13 (Annex II: noxious liquid substances in bulk), sects 14-15 (Annex III: Harmful substances in package form), sect. 16 (Annex IV: sewage) and sect. 17 (Annex V: Garbage)).

[114]   Royal Decree No. 1035, 22 October 2004, on the Marine Act coming into force for Greenland, sect. 3.

[115]   Regulations of 2 July 2007 No. 850 on investigation, stopping and boarding of foreign ships in the event of suspicion of an environmental violation, http://www.sjofartsdir.no/en/legislation/regulations/investigation-stopping-and-boarding-of-foreign-ships-in-the-event-of-suspicion-of-an-environmental-violation/ (last accessed 31 May 2015).

enforceable within the EEZ.[116] The regulations of MARPOL annexes I and II are applicable to foreign-flagged vessels navigating in the US internal waters and territorial sea. The regulations of annex V are also applicable to these vessels while in its EEZ.[117] In the US enforcement is primarily undertaken in port.

Denmark has amended its Safety at Sea Act to provide the legal basis for establishing enhanced safety requirements for vessels navigating in the maritime zones of Greenland.[118] The new legislation is primary aimed at regulating foreign-flagged passenger vessels but may be applied to other shipping activities and includes a wide set of measures. The purpose is to provide the legal basis for implementation of the Polar Code.[119] The amendment provides Denmark with the necessary legal basis to implement the extended environmental jurisdiction under Article 234 of the LOSC.

The environmental jurisdiction of the three coastal states, particularly within the EEZ, is dependent on the existence of relevant GAIRS.[120] In order for these states to apply the CDEM regulations of the Polar Code in the territorial seas and EEZs and its operational discharge regulations within their EEZs, these regulations necessarily have to qualify as GAIRS. In addition, these regulations must serve environmental protection objectives. The maritime safety and environmental objectives of the Polar Code are interlinked.[121] Its construction, design, equipment and manning requirements will reduce probabilities of accidents and thus protect the environment. Norway is excluded from applying possible GAIRS within its mainland maritime zones, which lie beyond the Arctic waters.

The meaning of the concept GAIRS has not been clearly set out in the LOSC. A study undertaken by the International Law Association (ILA) primarily focused on the meaning of 'generally accepted international'.[122] The concept is read as a requirement that the rules and standards have been widely applied by a large number of relevant states through their practice.[123] It is a standard less strict than that for the establishment of a rule of customary international law. The regulations of Polar Code may very well qualify as generally accepted under these criteria.

---

[116]   Above n 113, sect. 28ff.

[117]   33 USC §1902(a) (2) and (3). The provision uses the concept of navigable waters which includes internal waters and the territorial sea, 33 USC § 1901 (a)(7).

[118]   Act No. 618 of 12 June 2013 amending the Merchant Shipping Act and various other acts, sect. 3 (page 40), available in English. Translation at http://www.dma.dk/SiteCollection Documents/Legislation/Acts/2013/L-618-12062013-%C3%A6ndring%20af%20s%C3%B8loven %20og%20forskelige%20andre%20love.pdf (last accessed 31 May 2015).

[119]   Lovforslag L 154 (Folketinget 2012–2013) Forslag til Lov om ændring af søloven og forskellige andre love, 27–8, 31–2, available in Danish at www.folketingstidende.dk/RIpdf/ samling/20121/lovforslag/L154/20121_L154_som_fremsat.pdf (last accessed 31 May 2015).

[120]   'Article 211 – Pollution from Vessels (IV)', 2 in *Commentary on the Law of the Sea Convention* above n 99, Martinus Nijhoff Online. 09 September 2014 DOI:10.1163/ej.LAOS_ 9780792307648_176–206, paras 211.15(i), 204.

[121]   Polar Code, above n 35, sec 1, cfr preamble para. 5.

[122]   International Law Association, Committee on Coastal State Jurisdiction relating to Marine Pollution: Final Report, in *Report of the Sixty-Ninth Conference*, London 2000, 443–500 (ILA Report 2000).

[123]   Ibid., Conclusion No. 2, 475.

In addition, to qualify as 'rules or standards' regulations must have a certain level of precision.[124] Ambiguous regulations or regulations providing flag states with a broad margin of appreciation can hardly qualify as GAIRS. Particularly where the norms may be interpreted and applied differently as between coastal states this would run counter to the purpose of the GAIRS requirement, which is to ensure uniform application of international shipping regulations.[125]

The question is whether the regulations of the Polar Code qualify as rules or standards.[126] The regulations under Part II-A on discharge of oil and other operational discharges are clearly described.[127] They may become GAIRS and be proscribed and enforced by the Arctic coastal states in their EEZ. It is more doubtful whether the CDEM regulations of Part I-A qualify. Flag states may approve alternative arrangements and design for the structure, machinery, electrical installations, fire safety and life-saving appliances, which meet the relevant functional requirements.[128] Other equivalent standards of ice classification than the Polar Class may be approved.[129] In these cases, there are no specific rules or standards to proscribe, much less enforce. Other regulations on stability and subdivision also include conditions of a discretionary nature.[130]

To conclude, the Polar Code does not enable Arctic coastal states to apply the 'normal' environmental jurisdiction to prevent other types of risks of Arctic shipping than the operational discharges. They realistically may ensure the seaworthiness of vessels navigating through their Arctic waters in their capacity as port states. However, the control of ships in port states may be confined to controlling the Polar Ship Certificate and the other required documents.[131] Where the design and arrangement of the vessel is different from the regulations of the Polar Code this must be recorded in the Polar Ship Certificate.[132] Nevertheless, if the port states are to undertake further investigations to establish the equivalence of the design with the Polar Code requirements, they will need detailed insight into these alternatives and may be required to undertake a more detail physical inspection than is normal.[133]

---

[124]   Bernard Oxman, 'The duty to respect generally accepted international standards' (1991) 24 *New York University Journal of International Law and Politics* 109, 148.

[125]   ILA Report 2000, sect. 479.

[126]   Oxman, above n 124, 148.

[127]   Polar Code, above n 36, Part II-A, chaps 1, 2, 4 and 5.

[128]   Polar Code, above n 35, Part I-A, Chapter 1, sect. 1.1.2; SOLAS Chapter XIV above n 39, Reg. 4.

[129]   Polar Code, above n 35, Part I-A, sect. 3.3.2.

[130]   Ibid, Part I-A, sect. 4.3.

[131]   Ibid, Part I-A, sects 1.3 and 2.3.

[132]   SOLAS Chapter XIV, above n 39, Reg. 4.4.

[133]   Guidelines for the Approval of Alternatives and Equivalents as provided for in various IMO Instruments, MSC.1/Circ.1455, paras 3.8 and 7.5.

### 3.2.2 The Polar Code as a restrictive factor?

Both Canada[134] and Russia[135] claim sovereignty over parts of their Arctic waters based on historical title. These claims are contested by the US and other states.[136] Russia and Canada also base their regulation of international shipping on Article 234 of the LOSC.[137]

The Russian Northern Sea Route (NSR) legislation was amended in 2012.[138] The NSR Area covers the maritime area between Novaya Zemlya and the Bering Strait.[139] It includes the internal waters, the territorial sea and the EEZ. The NSR Administration is established to regulate access to and manage the traffic within the NSR Area.[140] The navigational rules include provisions on CDEM rules and standards, environmental protection and navigational standards.

---

[134]  The outer limits of the territorial sea and the EEZ in the Canadian Arctic are established on the basis of the straight baseline system established in force from 1986: see, eg, Territorial Sea Geographical Coordinates (Area 7) Order, SOR/85-872, available at http://laws-lois.justice.gc.ca/eng/acts/o-2.4/ (last accessed 31 May 2015). The question is whether these baselines may be established based on historical title or the criteria under the LOSC for straight baselines.

[135]  Some of the Russian Arctic straits have been enclosed by baselines as they '... historically have belonged...' to the Russian Federation: Federal Act on Internal Maritime Waters, Territorial Sea and Contiguous Zone of the Russian Federation, 17 July 1998, Arts 2 (4) and 11–13, available in English translation at www.un.org/Depts/los/LEGISLATIONAND TREATIES/PDFFILES/RUS 1998 Act TS.pdf (last accessed 31 May 2015).

[136]  Ted L. McDorman, *Salt Water Neighbors. International Ocean Law Relations between the United States and Canada* (Oxford University Press 2009), 236–7, 240 and 241–4; Clive Symmons, *Historic waters in the law of the sea: a modern re-appraisal* (Martinus Nijhoff Publishers, 2008), 1–3.

[137]  See 'Development of a Mandatory Code for Ships operating in Polar Waters. Procedure of Accounting for National Regulations', submitted by the Russian Federation, DE 55/12/23 1 February 2011. The Canadian viewpoints are described in D.M. McRae and D.J. Goundrey, 'Environmental Jurisdiction in Arctic Waters: The Extent of Article 234' (1982) 16(2) *University of British Columbia Law Review* 198, 209, and 'Safety of Navigation. Comments on document MSC 88/11', submitted by Canada, MSC88/11/3, 5 October 2010. See also, Rosemary Rayfuse, 'Coastal State Jurisdiction and the Polar Code: A Test Case for Arctic Oceans Governance?' in T. Stephens and D. VanderZwaag (eds), *Polar Oceans Governance in an Era of Environmental Change* 235 (Edward Elgar, 2014).

[138]  Federal Law of 28 July 2012 (N-132-FZ) on Amendments to Certain Legislative Acts of the Russian Federation concerning State Regulation of Merchant Shipping on the Water Area of the Northern Sea Route, Art 3. The English translation is available at the webpages of the Northern Sea Route Administration, http://www.nsra.ru/en/razresheniya/ (last accessed 31 May 2015).

[139]  Merchant Shipping Code of the Russian Federation, Art. 5.1(1) as amended by Federal Law of 28 July 2012 (N-132-FZ) on Amendments to Certain Legislative Acts of the Russian Federation concerning State Regulation of Merchant Shipping on the Water Area of the Northern Sea Route, Art. 3(3).

[140]  Merchant Shipping Code, Art. 5.1(2) and (3) as supplemented by Rules of Navigation on the Water Area of the Northern Sea Route, approved by the order of the Ministry of Transport of Russia, 17 January 2013 No. 7, sect. II, paras 2–20. An English translation is available at the webpages of the Northern Sea Route Administration http://www.nsra.ru/en/pravila_plavaniya/ (last accessed 31 May 2015).

The environmental jurisdiction of Canada over foreign-flagged vessels navigating the Northwest Passage is regulated under the Arctic Waters Pollution Prevention Act (AWPPA)[141] and the Shipping Act.[142] Both are applicable to shipping in the EEZ, territorial sea and internal waters.[143] The AWPPA provides for CDEM rules and standards, regulation of operational discharges and for navigational standards.[144]

The question is, will the the Polar Code restrict the extended environmental jurisdiction enjoyed by Canada and Russia? Article 234 does not include any reference to GAIRS or to any requirement of approval by the IMO for the coastal states to exercise the jurisdiction. In principle, Canada and Russia may adopt regulations that are different and/or stricter than the Polar Code if otherwise in compliance with the conditions of the provision. The adoption and entry into force of these instruments may be interpreted as acquiescence by these coastal states to restrictions on their jurisdiction.[145] Russia and Canada have argued for the inclusion of clauses to ensure the precedence of the LOSC.[146] The draft chapter XIV of SOLAS includes such a savings clause.[147] And Canada has argued for including similar clauses in the relevant annexes of MARPOL 73/78.[148] Clearly, the intention is that the Polar Code and the amendments of the relevant conventions will not limit the extended jurisdiction of the coastal states in ice-covered areas as such.

In addition, climate change may affect the extended environmental jurisdiction. The melting of the sea ice has led to questions on its future.[149] The jurisdiction is dependent on the presence of sea ice, which 'creates obstructions or extreme hazards' and is present in the areas in question for most of the year. The sea ice will continue to shrink and, in the future, the Arctic Ocean is projected to be almost ice free in September. Areas under Russian and Canadian jurisdiction will remain ice-covered but to varying

---

[141]   Arctic Water Pollution Prevention Act, RSC, 1985, c. A-12, available at http://laws.justice.gc.ca/eng/acts/a-12/ (last accessed 31 May 2015).

[142]   Canadian Shipping Act, SC, 2001, c. 26, available at http://laws.justice.gc.ca/eng/C-10.15/index.html (last accessed 31 May 2015).

[143]   Canadian Shipping Act, sect. 8; AWPPA, sect. 3(1). See, eg, sect. 2 where Canadian Arctic waters are defined to include '… the internal waters of Canada and the waters of the territorial sea of Canada and the exclusive economic zone of Canada, within the area enclosed by the 60th parallel of north latitude, the 141st meridian of west longitude and the outer limit of the exclusive economic zone …'

[144]   Arctic Waters Pollution Prevention Act, RS, 1985, c. A-12, Preamble, available at http://laws.justice.gc.ca/en/A-12/index.html (last accessed 31 May 2015).

[145]   Malcolm N. Shaw, *International Law*, (6th edn, Cambridge University Press, 2008) 87.

[146]   Development of a Mandatory Code for Ships Operating in Polar Waters: Procedure of Accounting for National Regulations, paras 4 and 5, DE/55/12/23; Report to the Maritime Committee, Statement of Canada, Annex 10, SDC 1/26.

[147]   SOLAS Chapter XIV, above n 39, Reg. 2(5).

[148]   Report of the Marine Environment Protection Committee on its Sixty-Sixth Session, para. 11.47, MEPC 66/21.

[149]   S. Lalonde, 'The Arctic Exception and the IMO's PSSA Mechanism: Assessing their Value as Sources of Protection for the Northwest Passage' (2013) 28 *The International Journal of Marine and Coastal Law* 401, 411; Erik Franckx, 'Should the Law Governing Maritime Areas in the Arctic Adapt to Changing Climatic Circumstances?' in T. Koivurova et al. (eds), *Climate Governance in the Arctic, Environment & Policy*, 119, 133, DOI 10.1007/978-1-4020-9542-9 6, C (Springer Science & Business Media BV, 2009).

extents and thicknesses for substantial periods of the year in foreseeable future.[150] The Polar Code may in fact provide the context within which to interpret the sea ice condition.[151] Both its thickness and concentration affect the hazard of navigating in sea ice.[152] Vessels operating in areas of thin first-year ice (30 to 70 cm) and in thicker ice where the concentration is above 1/10 are required to be ice-strengthened.[153] Thus, a more detailed and nuanced understanding of 'ice covered areas' would appear to be provided by the Code.

Even if the Polar Code does not, per se, limit the extended jurisdiction of the Arctic coastal states, it may have implications for its application. The measures are to have due regard for navigation and protection of the environment and are to be based on the best available scientific evidence. These conditions are particularly relevant when the Arctic coastal state adopts measures that are different from or stricter than those of the Polar Code. As an example, Canada has adopted a general ban on depositing any kind of waste into its Arctic waters.[154] Consequently, Canada is required to document the scientific basis for banning the discharge of grey water, which is not included in Part II-A of the Polar Code. Under Part I-A of the Polar Code the flag state may chose alternative CDEM rules and standards that provide equivalent levels of safety. The Arctic coastal states may establish more specific CDEM rules and standards, which has been done by both Russia and Canada. They have established conditions for navigation, which include the ice-class of the vessel, the time of the year of the planned voyage, the areas for the voyage, and the prevailing ice conditions.[155] Vessels can be instructed to use icebreaker assistance.[156] Those that are not ice strengthened are banned from sailing in these waters during parts of the year.[157] Vessels with higher ice strengthening

---

[150]  M. Collins et al., 'Long-term Climate Change: Projections, Commitments and Irreversibility' in T.F. Stocker et al. (eds) *Climate Change 2013: The Physical Science Basis. Contribution of Working Group I to the Fifth Assessment Report of the Intergovernmental Panel on Climate Change*, (Cambridge University Press, 2013), 1032.

[151]  Vienna Convention on Law of the Treaties, adopted 23 May 1969, entered into force 27 January 1980, 1155 UNTS 331, Art. 31(3)(c). See, Rosemary Rayfuse, 'Melting Moments: The Future of Polar Oceans Governance in a Warming World' (2007) 16(2) *Review of European Community & International Environmental Law* 196, 210.

[152]  Polar Code, Introduction, sect. 3.1.1.

[153]  Polar Code, Part I-A, sect. 3.3.2.2, cf. Introduction, sects 2.2, 2.4 and 2.7.

[154]  AWPPA, sects 2 and 4.

[155]  Russia: NSR Navigational Rules, sect. II, para. 10 and Annex 2. Canada: AWPPA, sects 11 and 12 as implemented in the Arctic Shipping Pollution Prevention Regulations CRC, c. 353, (available at http://laws-lois.justice.gc.ca/eng/regulations/C.R.C.,_c._353/index.html (last accessed 31 May 2015)) and Shipping Safety Control Zones Order, CRC, c. 356, (available at http://laws.justice.gc.ca/eng/C.R.C.-c.356/index.html (last accessed 31 May 2015)). The Canadian zone/date system is supplemented by Arctic Ice Regime Shipping System (AIRSS) Standards Arctic, see, eg, Shipping Pollution Prevention Regulations, sect. 6(3), to provide for more adaptability to changes in ice coverage. Further information is available at https://www.tc.gc.ca/eng/marinesafety/tp-tp12259-foreword-2870.htm#n2 (last accessed 31 May 2015).

[156]  Arctic Shipping Pollution Prevention Regulations, sect. 6(4) and (5).

[157]  NSR Navigational Rules, Annex 2, Criteria for the admission of ships to the Northern Sea Route in compliance with category of their ice strengthening, sect. 1, for ships without ice strengthening and with the category of ice strengthening Ice1–Ice3 during the navigation from July to November 15.

may operate for a longer period of the year and without icebreaker assistance, depending on their ice class and the prevailing ice conditions.[158] Canada has also set special regulations for vessels carrying oil.[159]

These regulations are consistent with the risk-based approach of the Polar Code under which vessels are to operate within their operational limitations.[160] However, they de facto restrict the rights of navigation as parts of the territorial sea and the EEZ are closed to some types of vessels for longer periods. In addition, some vessels are required to use icebreaker assistance to navigate through these waters. Such regulations do not conflict with the due regard requirement if they are based on a careful balance between navigational and environmental protection considerations. When sea ice conditions in an area create obstacles or hazards to particular types of vessels the environmental protection interests prevail. Perhaps most controversial is the determination of equivalence where vessels have an ice classification other than one recognized by the Arctic coastal state. The consequence may be that the ice class requirements are stricter for navigating in particular ice covered areas than the alternative design approved by the flag state. In any event, such requirement must be based on the best scientific evidence available. The Polar Class developed through the IASC may provide a basis for deciding on this equivalence. The MSC are developing guidelines for determining limitations for operation in ice, which may assist in harmonizing the requirements of the Polar Code and coastal States.[161]

### 3.3   Assessment

The Arctic coastal states should have an important role in regulating shipping in the region. The hazards of navigating in Arctic waters as referred to above necessitate an active coastal state. The Polar Code provides the flag state with considerable latitude in its implementation. It is necessary that the regulations are flexible when intended to regulate shipping within a region of varied and changing hazards. These norms are not enforceable by coastal states under the normal environmental jurisdiction. It is only the operational discharge regulations that are precise enough to be included in the normal coastal state environmental jurisdiction. The normal environmental jurisdiction does not provide for an active coastal state. The ability of Norway, Denmark/Greenland and USA to ensure the Arctic seaworthiness of vessels will primarily be through their capacity as port states. It may, however, be an impossible task to go beyond controlling the formal requirements. They will not have available information to assess whether the sailing conditions of the waters of the planned voyage are within the operational limits of the vessel.

---

[158]   NSR Navigational Rules, Annex 2, sect. 2, for ships with category of ice strengthening Arc4–Arc9 during the period of navigation from July to November, and sect. 3, for ships with category of ice strengthening Arc4–Arc9 during the period of navigation from January to June and in December). Sect. 4 includes rules for icebreakers.

[159]   Arctic Shipping Pollution Prevention Regulations, sect. 6.

[160]   Polar Code, Part I-A, sects 1.34bis and 1.5 and Chap 2.

[161]   Report of the Maritime Safety Committee on its Ninety-Fourth Session, Items 3.28–3.29.

Therefore, the extended environmental jurisdiction will remain an important and relevant part of the regulatory framework for Arctic shipping. Much of the focus has been on the state practice and on what have been considered violations of the freedom of navigation.[162] With the introduction of the Polar Code, there will be an increased and more nuanced focus on how this jurisdiction is to be exercised. The Polar Code may also provide a frame of reference for the exercise of the extended jurisdiction, with any deviations requiring particular justification.

## 4. CONCLUSIONS

The Polar Code addresses the different risks of Arctic shipping. Particularly important are its safety measures and its emphasis on ensuring that individual vessels operate within their limitations and capabilities. The inclusion of stricter regulations on operational discharges are helpful in protecting the Arctic marine environment. A ban on transport and use of heavy oil fuel will not be included. This is characteristic of the IMO where achieving consensus is essential. In addition, the desire to have the Polar Code adopted in a timely manner and the necessity of coordination in the adoption of mitigating measures under other IMO instruments, seem to have limited the scope of the Polar Code.

The IMO has a mandate to develop international rules and standards applicable within the legal framework of the LOSC. During the negotiations, no particular attention was paid to how the Polar Code is to be implemented within this framework. As usual, the main addressees of the IMO instruments are the flag states. In addition, Canada and Russia were successful in protecting their extended jurisdiction from any interference. The regulatory framework for Arctic shipping thus still appears to be somewhat fragmented: the Polar Code is directed at the flag states and does not necessarily address all hazards, whereas the Arctic coastal states are involved to differing degrees and Arctic regional cooperation is focused only on establishing important infrastructure such as for search and rescue and oil spill preparedness. The further development of the regulatory framework, in particular through the IMO, will depend on the involvement of and initiatives taken by the Arctic coastal states. This may include proposals for ships routeing measures or other regulations relating to navigation under SOLAS 74, special areas or emission control area status under MARPOL annexes, or combinations of such measures through the Particular Sensitive Sea Area scheme.[163] In addition, the hazards of Arctic shipping may also become relevant considerations in the development and application of further regulations, including those aimed at preventing and mitigating effects of climate change.

It is important that the Arctic coastal states continue to enjoy extended jurisdiction in ice-covered areas, in particular to ensure that vessels are seaworthy under the challenging Arctic conditions. The interests of the coastal states may not be identical

---

[162] See, eg, Letter of 19 March 2010 from the US Embassy in Ottawa to the Canadian Marine Safety Directorate, available at http://www.state.gov/documents/organization/179286.pdf (last accessed 31 May 2015).

[163] For discussion see, Henrik Ringbom, 'Vessel-source pollution', Chapter 5 in this volume.

and their interests may conflict with the interests of flag states, as, for example, on the level of environmental protection, where Canada has sought to prohibit discharges of garbage whereas Russia has opposed a ban on transport and use of heavy grade fuel oil.[164] Nevertheless, the work of the Arctic Council on mapping the Arctic marine environment may contribute to both a common understanding of regulatory needs and to future amendments to the Polar Code and other IMO instruments. The existence of the Polar Code, together with increased shipping activities in the Arctic, will bring more attention to the region and to the regulations adopted by the coastal states. The Arctic coastal states will thus need to pay increased attention to the justification and the scientific bases for their exercise of jurisdiction to ensure the continued legitimacy of their regulatory regimes. In this sense, the Polar Code may provide for a certain level of coherency in Arctic shipping regulation.

---

[164]   Report of the Marine Environment Protection Committee on its Sixty-fifth Session, para. 21.9, MEPV 65/22; Report of the Marine Environment Protection Committee on Its Sixtieth Session, para. 21.9, MEPC 60/22.

# 18. Large marine ecosystems and associated new approaches to regional, transboundary and 'high seas' management

*David Vousden*

## 1. INTRODUCTION

The world's oceans are currently facing a number of serious challenges to their integrity and sustainability as a result of a variety of anthropogenic impacts. Pollution is one obvious threat, both land-based in origin (eg, agricultural run-off, liquid waste discharges) and from offshore sources (eg, shipping, mining, oil and gas exploration). Over-exploitation of living marine resources is another major threat, particularly in areas where there is no legal control or enforcement. Such direct impacts are also exacerbated by the effects of climate change. These include species range shifts and changes in species composition (including the introduction of exotic and invasive species), changes in water column stratification, de-oxygenation and acidification of oceanic waters.[1] As a result of these alterations in the ocean environment and its associated living resources, human interactions with the marine environment are also having to adapt in the face of inevitable management implications for harvesting of 'shifting biomass', especially across jurisdictional boundaries, as well as alterations in fisheries distribution requiring associated changes in fleet structure and operations.[2] All of this represents significant challenges for ocean governance and the management of marine ecosystem sustainability, especially in those parts of the ocean that are beyond the jurisdiction and control of national governments or international treaties.[3]

Historically, where there have been active management processes in place, the coasts and oceans of the world have been managed on the basis of national political ownership, with clear boundaries having been established by legal definitions, such as

---

[1]    Intergovernmental Panel on Climate Change, 'Ocean Systems' in *Climate Change 2014: Impacts, Adaptation, and Vulnerability. Part. A: Global and Sectoral Aspects. Contribution of Working Group II to the Fifth Assessment Report of the Intergovernmental Panel on Climate Change* (Cambridge University Press, 2014) 3; and IPCC, 'The Ocean' in *Climate Change 2014: Impacts, Adaptation, and Vulnerability. Part. B: Global and Sectoral Aspects. Contribution of Working Group II to the Fifth Assessment Report of the Intergovernmental Panel on Climate Change* (Cambridge University Press, 2014) 55. On the problem of ocean acidification see Tim Stephens, 'Ocean acidification', Chapter 20 in this volume.

[2]    U.R. Sumaila, W. Cheung, V. Lam, D. Pauly and S. Herrick, 'Climate change impacts on the biophysics and economics of world fisheries' (2011) 1 *Nature Climate Change* 449 DOI: 10.1038/NCCCLIMATE1301.

[3]    See, eg, R. Rayfuse, 'Climate Change and the Law of the Sea' in R. Rayfuse and S. Scott, *International Law in the Era of Climate Change* (Edward Elgar, 2012) 147.

distance from shore, and by negotiated agreements with neighbours. As ocean and coastal governance has evolved, the ecosystem-based management approach is now commonly being embraced and adopted as a more appropriate replacement to these traditional, geopolitically focused management strategies.[4] The concept of Large Marine Ecosystems (LMEs) has emerged as a mechanism for the promotion of an ecosystem-based approach to oceans management. This approach is now being promoted through a number of regional initiatives, strongly supported by the United Nations and its agencies and partners, particularly the World Bank and the Global Environment Facility's International Waters Portfolio.

However, this new approach to oceans management brings with it new challenges. The management of resources and impacts within LMEs represents a particularly interesting case for marine environmental law. This is due to their transboundary nature and the need to find workable and pragmatic mechanisms for management within an ecosystem which may include not only territorial waters and exclusive economic zones (EEZs) but also areas beyond national jurisdiction (ABNJ), and to deal with the challenging situation presented by extended continental shelf agreements and awards.[5] More than ever before, there is a need for cross-sectoral and integrated dialogue and understanding within the management process at both the national level and within the regional context.[6] Furthermore, the complexities of trying to develop effective working mechanisms for the management of high seas areas that fall within the LME and which are adjacent to EEZs (through regional cooperation and agreement) have become a matter of urgency.[7] The concept of the 'tragedy of the commons'[8] comes back to haunt such efforts with the realization that any such management of resources and geographical areas outside national jurisdiction can only be through formal consensus and agreement.

---

[4]   See, eg, N.L. Christensen, A. Bartuska, J.H. Brown, S. Carpenter, C. D'Antonio, R. Francis, J.F. Franklin, J.A. MacMahon, R.F. Noss, D.J. Parsons, C.H. Peterson, M.G. Turner, and R.G. Moodmansee, 'The report of the Ecological Society of America Committee on the scientific basis for ecosystem management' (1996) 6 *Ecological Applications* 665. See also, K.L. McLeod, J. Lubchenco, S.R. Palumbi, and A.A. Rosenberg (2005) *Scientific Consensus Statement on Marine Ecosystem-Based Management*, signed by 221 academic scientists and policy experts with relevant expertise and published by the Communication Partnership for Science and the Sea, available at http://www.compassonline.org/science/EBM_CMSP/ EBMconsensus (last accessed 1 June 2015).

[5]   T. Schoolmeester and E. Baker (eds) 'Continental Shelf: The Last Maritime Zone' (UNEP/GRID-Arendal, 2009). On the extended continental shelf issues see Joanna Mossop, 'Reconciling activities on the extended continental shelf with protection of the marine environment', Chapter 8 in this volume.

[6]   D. Vousden and J. Stapley 'Evolving new governance approaches for the Agulhas and Somali Current Large Marine Ecosystems through Dynamic Management Strategies and partnerships' (2013) 7 *Environmental Development* 32.

[7]   D. Vousden, 'Improving Governance of Marine Areas beyond National Jurisdiction: Development of Management Options' *Proceedings of the 5th Global Conference on Oceans, Coasts and Islands* (UNESCO, 2010).

[8]   Garrett Hardin, 'The tragedy of the commons' (1968) 162 (3859) *Science* 1243.

The United Nations Convention on the Law of the Sea[9] (LOSC) provides a general framework for the management of ABNJ. However, this is insufficient in the absence of agreement from those parties whose interests lie in either the direct exploitation of such areas or in the freedom to undertake potentially harmful activities in ABNJ which would otherwise be prohibited in areas under national jurisdiction. Thus, effective management at the ecosystem level can only be fully realized within the context of two possible approaches. The first approach involves a more specific and stringent elaboration and actual enforcement of the concepts embraced by the LOSC through the negotiation of a new implementing agreement.[10] However, such agreement would need to achieve global consensus on a scale that could take years or even decades to negotiate and could still prove to be too dilute to be of any real management value. Alternately, effective ecosystem management might be achieved through the development of workable partnerships and alliances among governments, regional bodies, maritime industry and other ocean stakeholders that can arrive at a fully integrated and shared management approach leading to self-regulation.[11] These two approaches need not be mutually exclusive, and could be both complementary and parallel.[12] These approaches are discussed and explored further in this chapter within the context of tried and existing approaches as well as new developments and proposals.

## 2. LARGE MARINE ECOSYSTEMS AND THE SERVICES THEY PROVIDE

The concept of large marine ecosystems (LME) emerged from an American Association for the Advancement of Science Symposium in the mid-1980s which focused on the variability and management of large marine ecosystems.[13] Kenneth Sherman of the United States (US) National Oceanic and Atmospheric Administration's (NOAA) National Marine Fisheries Service and Lewis Alexander of the University of Rhode Island pioneered the concept of LMEs, which recognizes that large areas of the oceans function as ecosystems, and that pollution from air, land, and water, along with overexploitation of living resources, as well as natural factors, influence the varying productivity of these ecosystems. LMEs have since been defined as 'regional oceans of ecological continuity extending from the top of a river basin to the end of the adjacent

---

[9] Adopted 10 December 1982, entered into force 16 November 1994, 1833 UNTS 3 (LOSC).

[10] See, eg, High Seas Alliance, 'The Need for a New Implementing Agreement Under UNCLOS on Marine Biodiversity of the High Seas' available at http://highseasalliance.org/sites/highseasalliance.org/files/Need-for-IA.pdf (last accessed 1 June 2015). On the ongoing negotiations see also, Dire Tladi, 'Conservation and sustainable use of marine biodiversity in areas beyond national jurisdiction: towards an implementing agreement', Chapter 12 in this volume.

[11] D. Vousden and J. Stapley, above n 6.

[12] J. Ardron, K. Gjerde, S. Pullen and V. Tilot, 'Marine spatial planning in the high seas' (2008) 32 *Marine Policy* 832.

[13] J. Brenner and S. Arismendez, 'Large Marine Ecosystems' in Mark McGinley (ed.) (2009) *Encyclopedia of the Earth*, available at http://www.eoearth.org/view/artilce/154169 (last accessed 1 June 2015).

continental shelf and beyond to the seaward boundaries of coastal current systems'.[14] They constitute relatively large regions, 64 in total, of 200,000 km² or greater, the natural borders of which are based on four unique ecological criteria: bathymetry, hydrography, productivity, and trophically related populations.[15]

The world depends on the sustainability of, and reliable access to, the goods and services derived from LMEs. However, as with the oceans in general, LMEs and their resources are under threat from over-exploitation and/or inadequate management strategies that do not provide any support for sustainability of these goods and services.[16] A new approach has been developed through the Global Environment Facility and its various Implementing Agencies that aims to resolve this threat and to assist LME-bordering countries to develop more effective management approaches that can protect and sustain their valuable and renewal resources.[17] Nevertheless, the challenges are great. More than 40 per cent of the world's population (more than 2.8 billion people) live within 100 kilometres of the coast.[18] The 64 LMEs support 95 per cent of mean annual marine fisheries yields,[19] and more than 200 million people around the world are directly dependent on fisheries for their food security, while the annual goods and services from coasts and oceans are valued at US $12.6 million.[20]

Tourism is now the largest business sector of the world economy, accounting for 10 per cent of global GDP, one in twelve jobs globally, and 35 per cent of the world's export services.[21] Data indicates that international tourist arrivals increased by 4 per cent in 2012 and generated some US$ 1.3 trillion in export earnings with a forecasted increase in growth of 3 to 4 per cent by the end of 2013.[22] Coastal tourism is one of the fastest growing sectors of this global tourism and provides employment for many

---

[14]   K. Sherman, and G. Hempel, 'Perspectives on Regional Seas and the Large Marine Ecosystem Approach' in K. Sherman and G. Hempel (eds) *The UNEP Large Marine Ecosystems Report: A perspective on changing conditions in LMEs of the world's Regional Seas*, UNEP Regional Seas Report and Studies No. 182 (UNEP, 2008).

[15]   K. Sherman, 'Sustainability, biomass yields, and health of coastal ecosystems: An ecological perspective' (1994) 112 *Marine Ecology Progress Series* 277.

[16]   J. Lubchenco, 'Large Marine Ecosystems: The Leading Edge of Science, Management and Policy' in Kenneth Sherman and Sara Adams (eds), *Stress, Sustainability, and Development of Large Marine Ecosystems During Climate Changes: Policy and Implementation*, (United Nations Development Programme, 2013). See, also, A.M. Duda, 'GEF support for the Global Movement toward the Improved Assessment and Management of Large Marine Ecosystems' in K. Sherman, M.C. Aquarone and S. Adams (eds) *Sustaining the World's Large Marine Ecosystems* (IUCN, 2009).

[17]   D. Vousden, L.E.P. Scott, T.G. Bornman, N. Ngoile, J. Stapley and J.R.E.S. Lutjeharms, 'Establishing a basis for ecosystem management in the Western Indian Ocean' (2008) 104 *African Journal of Science* 417.

[18]   IOC/UNESCO, IMO, FAO, UNDP. (2011). A Blueprint for Ocean and Coastal Sustainability. Paris: IOC/UNESCO.

[19]   Sherman, Aquarone and Adams, above n 16.

[20]   Duda, above n 16.

[21]   M. Honey and D. Krantz, 'Global Trends in Coastal Tourism', Centre on Ecotourism and Sustainable Development for Marine Program (World Wildlife Fund, 2007).

[22]   United Nations World Tourism Organization, (2013) 11 'World Tourism Barometer'.

people and generates local incomes. For example, reef-based tourism generates over $1.2 billion annually in the Florida Keys (of the United States) alone.[23]

In 2009, offshore oil fields accounted for 32 per cent of worldwide crude oil production which is expected to rise to 34 per cent by 2025 (equivalent to 23 million barrels per day). Meanwhile, maritime transport is the backbone of international trade and a key engine driving globalization. Around 80 per cent of global trade by volume and over 70 per cent by value is carried by sea and is handled by ports worldwide; these shares are even higher in the case of most developing countries.[24] Following the global economic and financial crisis of 2008, the world fleet continued to expand until, by January 2012, it had increased by over 37 per cent in just four years.

Fifty five per cent of atmospheric carbon captured by living organisms is captured by marine organisms. Of this, between 50 to 71 per cent is captured by the ocean's vegetated habitats including mangroves, salt marshes, sea grasses and seaweed, so-called blue forests, which cover less than 0.5 per cent of the seabed.[25]

One relatively new area of exploitation of marine goods and services is that of mineral extraction taking place on the ocean floor. Polymetallic nodules have been attracting the interest of the mining community for some decades but have presented retrieval problems previously due to the depths involved. With the advent of new technologies, remotely operated vehicles (ROVs) can be used to sample likely areas and deposits, while extraction can be achieved either through a 'continuous bucket' line or a through a hydraulic suction system. Hydrothermal vents are currently attracting a lot of interest in view of their sulphide deposits which can contain valuable metals including gold, silver, cobalt, manganese and copper. However, the potential and actual damage to these unique ecosystems and the life-forms they support is of serious concern.[26]

The fundamental conclusion to be drawn from these observations is that the oceans are vitally important to the global economy as well as to the welfare and livelihoods of the millions of humans that depend on them for food security and as a source of income. Yet it is often the potential and real value of these goods and services and the poor management and control over their extraction or exploitation which can pose the greatest threat to their long-term sustainability and the overall well-being of LMEs. Better ecosystem-based management approaches within LMEs and by the relevant countries is a necessity in order to avoid these threats and to realize sustainable use and development of such goods and services.

---

[23]   UNEP, *Marine and coastal ecosystems and human well-being: A synthesis report based on the findings of the Millennium Ecosystem Assessment* (UNEP 2006).

[24]   United Nations Conference on Trade and Development, 'Review of Maritime Transport' (UNCTAD, 2012).

[25]   C. Nellmann, E. Corcoran, C.M. Duarte, L. Valdés, C. De Young, L. Fonseca, G. Grimsditch (eds), *Blue Carbon. A Rapid Response Assessment* (UNEP Grid-Arendal, 2009).

[26]   A.M. Post, *Deep Sea Mining and the Law of the Sea* (Brill, 1983) 358. See also Michael Lodge, 'Protecting the marine environment of the deep seabed', Chapter 7 in this volume.

## 3. THE PROBLEM OF LME MANAGEMENT – REVISITING THE TRAGEDY OF THE COMMONS

Some decades ago, Garret Hardin created the construct of the 'Tragedy of the Commons'.[27] This was essentially an economic theory by which individuals, acting alone and according to their own self-interest, will behave contrary to the long-term benefit of a larger stakeholder group by depleting a common resource to their own individual advantage. A good example of this is the over-fishing of the Grand Banks off Newfoundland.[28] The living resources on the Grand Banks made Canada one of the world's leading fishing economies and provided a stable livelihood not only for Canadians but for fishing countries all around the world that exploited these stocks. As a result of what can be described as a 'free-for-all' with little control, individual fishers and fishing nations drastically over-fished these stocks for the purpose of making a quick profit and with no consideration for the long-term sustainability of the fishery. As a consequence, the great shoals of cod that were closely associated with the Grand Banks had all but disappeared by the end of the twentieth century. The consequent widespread effects of this resource collapse on livelihoods both within and beyond the fishing communities (eg, unemployment benefit payments, housing costs and price collapse, costs of re-training, food supplies, etc.) created an economic depression which was felt across Canada.

Traditionally, the management of marine resources, including impacts from the adjacent watershed and coastal areas, has been conducted on a single-sector basis rather than through the evolution of the more multi-sectoral, integrated strategies that are necessary when taking an ecosystem-based, transboundary management approach. These sectoral approaches are destined for failure if they do not recognize and interact with the full panoply of national and regional economic and social interests and priorities. Indeed, many leading experts on high seas and ocean governance are now convinced that, in view of the escalating threats to our oceans from the growing impacts of climate change and other anthropogenic sources, there is now an urgent need for a transformation to a more suitable legal regime which is more cross-sectoral and integrated in its management approaches and strategies.[29]

For many years there has been a conflict of interest among maintaining biodiversity, sustaining the levels of resource exploitation, and ensuring continuous and lucrative employment and livelihoods. Yet, on the surface, this conflict of interest is not a rational one. Common sense would dictate that preserving sustainable employment levels and resource exploitation (for example in terms of catch per unit effort and maximum sustainable yields from fisheries) must surely be directly and positively related to maintaining biodiversity levels and to maintaining ecosystem goods and services through effective conservation of the status of these ecosystems and their

---

[27]   Hardin, above n 8.

[28]   C. Clover, *The End of the Line: How Overfishing Is Changing the World and What We Eat* (Ebury Press, 2005).

[29]   R. Rayfuse and R. Warner, 'Securing a sustainable future for the oceans beyond national jurisdiction: The legal basis for an integrated cross-sectoral regime for high seas governance for the 21st century' (2008) 23 *The International Journal of Marine and Coastal Law* 399.

resources. The problem is essentially one of simple mathematics and balancing two sides of an equation. There is a direct link between exploitation (taking out of the ecosystem) and ecosystem sustainability (maintaining the status quo of that same ecosystem to ensure its long-term sustainability). In any one marine ecosystem there will be one optimal level of exploitation that matches the demand. This can be related to both renewable resources, such as fish and tourism, and non-renewable resources such as oil and gas.

With respect to fish, for example, in principle, it is not in the fisherman's interest to over-exploit because this will: (a) threaten his/her continued food source and/or income; (b) likely increase the daily effort needed to achieve the same catch size; and (c) be a wasted effort if there is no market or demand (although this latter point is rarely applicable to community-level fisheries where subsistence and daily food requirements are the main 'demand'). Thus, in practice, it is in the interest of the fisher to exploit the resource to the maximum achievable level. However, while the concept of the tragedy of the commons clearly relates to the management challenges in areas beyond national jurisdiction, it can also be applicable within areas under national jurisdiction where an absence of effective management or enforcement of legislation creates an almost free and common access situation for those inclined to take it. In this fisheries exploitation situation the process is driven foremost by demand and then by opportunity. As coastal communities and inner cities grow, so inevitably does the demand for access to food supplies. A particular fishery may have been sustainable at one point and management practices within those parameters may have been effective in achieving sustainability. However, the constantly increasing demand now presents an opportunity to the fisher which is still effective in terms of effort versus cost. Even if there are fewer fish and catching them takes more effort, the rewards may warrant this in terms of food security and even the market prices that people are willing to pay. In this situation, the tragedy of the commons can relate more to continuous and relentless population growth placing ever-increasing demands on finite resources, both in the sense of non-renewable as well as unsustainable renewal.

Like fish, tourism is, on the surface, a renewable resource; particularly in the context of growing populations which should mean more tourists. However, tourism depends on people's expectations and demands. A pristine beach, a healthy coral reef, good recreational fisheries, and clean water are, among others, all requirements of high-quality tourism. If the quality of these requirements declines due to over-exploitation, pollution, and over-fishing it does not necessarily mean the demise of the tourism industry. The focus can switch from high-end, high-quality tourism, which is generally less intrusive and more sustainable, to a greater number of tourists paying less and therefore with lower expectations. The demand persists albeit from a different market and the potential income can remain the same. However, the overall level of exploitation and impact increases.[30] Sustainable, low impact tourism therefore becomes non-renewable as the ecosystem deteriorates, pollution levels rise and sensitive coastal habitats are destroyed, yet the exploitation remains profitable. Again, in the absence of

---

[30]   R.N. Batta, *Tourism and the Environment. A Quest for Sustainability* (Indus Publishing, 2000).

any effective management through planning laws, moratoria on numbers, and other mechanisms, tourism becomes yet another tragedy of the freedom of the commons.

Non-renewable resources such as oil and gas are, in effect, also part of the ecosystem. They are ecosystem goods and services that can be extracted but which are finite and irreplaceable in the context of human generations. As demonstrated over the years by the oil industry, the extraction process can have very negative effects on the marine environment.[31] Energy extraction and mining in the oceans inevitably have consequences in terms of both direct impact and pollution.[32] Consider, too, the shipping industry which moves thousands of ships around the world on a daily basis. Within national waters, strict laws on discharges may apply. The LOSC provides for a right of innocent passage through the territorial sea, but illegal discharge is not considered 'innocent' for these purposes.[33] However, the resources necessary to prevent and enforce national marine pollution laws are considerable and can be expected to be well beyond the means of many countries.[34] Cost and effort implications therefore encourage and reward the opportunistic law-breaker. It can then be in the economic interest of less ethical companies, which may deem potential legal challenges and subsequent penalties to be unlikely or insignificant, to reduce their efforts and costs in relation to pollution prevention and other impacts on the ecosystem to the level at which they can best evade national or international rules and scrutiny.

This could be considered, in some respects, to be an unfortunate ethical and moral extrapolation of the biological Darwinian concept of 'survival of the fittest'. In this case, the 'fittest' being those who can manage to exploit as much as possible to meet a demand and to out-compete their fellow exploiters either through the adoption of more efficient methods, contempt for and evasion of limits and rules, or deliberately operating in poorly regulated or regulation-free areas. These 'fittest' are then more likely to survive within the economic climate in which they operate. In some cases the risk of being caught and penalized can be outweighed by the benefits of breaching the law,[35] making such indifference to regulations and contempt for the 'law' all the more attractive. The costs of treating ship's discharges (ballast water, sewage, etc.) may be significant enough that the act of discharging underway and with little or no treatment represents a very small risk when weighed against the likelihood of exposure and subsequent penalty.

These issues related to control of access and regulation of exploitation and impact become more complicated within the transboundary and high seas scenario that lies at the heart of the LME management approach.

---

[31]    US National Research Council, *Oil in the Sea III: Inputs, Fates, and Effects* (National Academies Press, 2003).

[32]    B. Soyer, 'Compensation for Pollution Damage Resulting from Exploration for and Exploitation of Seabed Mineral Resources' in B. Soyer and A. Tettenborn (eds), *Pollution at Sea: Law and Liability* (Informa Law, 2012) 59.

[33]    LOSC, Art. 19.

[34]    See Henrik Ringbom, 'Vessel-source pollution', Chapter 5 in this volume.

[35]    S. Beder, 'Charging the earth: The promotion of price-based measures for pollution control' (1996) 16 *Ecological Economics* 51.

## 4.  LME GOVERNANCE CHALLENGES IN THE CONTEXT OF TRANSBOUNDARY MANAGEMENT AND ABNJ

If the management of human activities and impacts within a given LME is to be effective, it will necessitate transboundary interactions between those states exploiting the goods and services of the LME and the development and adoption of effective 'international' transboundary governance mechanisms for that LME. However, similar ethical, moral and, indeed, legal dilemmas exist within such a transboundary governance scenario as have been discussed above and in relation to the tragedy of the commons. A classic area for contention within a marine transboundary management system is the exploitation of fish stocks. In the transboundary context, adjacent states may exploit the same species or transboundary fish stock. The stock may migrate between waters under the national jurisdiction of the relevant states for a number of reasons (eg, following a food source; reacting to physical changes such as temperature; as part of a natural life-cycle where the species may breed, feed and/or mature in different geographical locations). Clearly this can have implications for the fisheries of each country. If one state catches immature fish before they have the opportunity to grow and migrate for breeding, this may deplete the potential catch for the adjacent state. Similarly, if the adjacent state catches the breeding stock before they have time to breed then there will be fewer recruits to return to the feeding grounds in the neighbouring state.

It is obvious that the situation may become more complicated, still, when a species in question is a straddling stock or a highly migratory one which moves between, or occurs in both, the EEZ of one or more states as well as the high seas. In this scenario, even the most equitable and beneficent of agreements for management of the stock at the transboundary level can be rapidly undermined either by fishermen from one of the states exploiting the stock beyond the EEZ or by distant water fleets from foreign countries over-exploiting the stock in the adjacent high seas ABNJ, thereby preventing sustainable recruitment into the EEZ.

Some 64 per cent of the world's oceans lie beyond the national jurisdiction of coastal states. ABNJ may also fall within the management boundaries of a Large Marine Ecosystem. Because of their high seas nature and their 'commons' status in terms of access and exploitation, this then presents very real management issues for the countries whose waters also fall within the LME and who attempt to manage activities within the LME boundaries. Under the LOSC,[36] responsibility for ensuring the long-term sustainability of living marine resources within the EEZ lies with coastal states. On the high seas, all states have a duty to cooperate with each other in adopting measures to manage and conserve living resources.[37] These obligations are further articulated in the 1995 Fish Stocks Agreement,[38] which provides the legal regime for

---

[36]   LOSC, Art. 62.
[37]   LOSC, Arts 116–20.
[38]   Agreement for the Implementation of the Provisions of the United Nations Convention on the Law of the Sea of 10 December 1982 relating to the Conservation and Management of Straddling Fish Stocks and Highly Migratory Fish Stocks, 1995, 2167 UNTS 3 (Fish Stocks Agreement or FSA).

the conservation and management of straddling and highly migratory fish stocks, including regarding the establishment of regional fisheries management organizations and agreements (RFMO/As) as the primary vehicle for cooperation between states.

In addition, the LOSC requires all states to protect and preserve the marine environment, including rare or fragile ecosystems and the habitat of endangered species, and to take measures to prevent, reduce and control pollution of the oceans.[39] However, the obligations expressed in the LOSC, are considered by many to be inadequate to protect marine biodiversity in ABNJ. Discussions are currently underway on the possibility of negotiating an Implementing Agreement on the conservation and sustainable use of marine biodiversity in areas beyond national jurisdiction.[40] However, the negotiations will inevitably face resistance from states with vested interests in the continuing exploitation of resources, both living and non-living, from biodiversity-rich and vulnerable areas of the high seas such as seamounts and hydrothermal vents.[41]

Because ABNJ are an integral part of the marine environment, it also follows that any effective, coherent ecosystem approach to marine environmental management and protection must include some form of management actions for ABNJ. It must also include a mechanism to manage these areas. There is a broad consensus now within the ocean governance community in support of the designation and management of a representative system of MPAs at regional and global scales including in ABNJ. Yet to date, barring one or two notable exceptions, very few MPAs have been declared in

---

[39]   LOSC, Art. 19.

[40]   The issues are well canvassed in a special section of (2014) 49 *Marine Policy* 81–194 on 'Advancing Governance of Areas beyond National Jurisdiction'. Articles include: K. Töpfer, L. Tubiana, S. Unger and J. Rochette, 'Charting pragmatic courses for global ocean governance', 85; M. Visbeck, U. Kronfeld-Goharani, B. Neumann, W. Rickels, J. Schmidt, E. van Doorn, N. Matz-Lück, A. Proelss, 'A Sustainable development goal for the ocean and coasts: Global ocean challenges benefit from regional initiatives supporting globally coordinated solutions', 87; E. Druel and K. Gjerde, 'Sustaining marine life beyond boundaries: Options for an implementing agreement for marine biodiversity beyond national jurisdiction under the United Nations Convention on the Law of the Sea', 90; J. Ardron, R. Rayfuse, K. Gjerde and R. Warner, ' The sustainable use and conservation of biodiversity in ABNJ: What can be achieved using existing international agreements?', 98; J. Rochette, S. Unger, D. Herr, D. Johnson, T. Nakamura, T. Packeiser, A. Proelss, M. Visbeck, A. Wright and D. Cebrian, 'The regional approach to conservation and sustainable use of marine biodiversity in areas beyond national jurisdiction', 109; K. Houghton, 'Identifying new pathways for ocean governance: The role of legal principles in areas beyond national jurisdiction', 118; N.C. Ban, S.M. Maxwell, D.C. Dunn, A.J. Hobday, N.J. Bax, J. Ardron, K.M. Gjerde, E.T. Game, R. Devillers, D.M. Kaplan, P.K. Dunstan, P.N. Halpin and R.L. Pressey, 'Better integration of sectoral planning and management approaches for the interlinked ecology of the open oceans', 127. See, also, Dire Tladi, 'Conservation and sustainable use of marine biodiversity in areas beyond national jurisdiction: towards an implementing agreement', Chapter 12 in this volume.

[41]   See, eg, G. Wright, J. Rochette, S. Unger, K. Gjerde and J. Ardron, 'The scores at half time: An update on the international discussions on the governance of marine biodiversity in areas beyond national jurisdiction', Institute for Sustainable Development and International Relations (IDDRI) Issue Brief, No 2 (IDDRI, 2014).

ABNJ,[42] primarily because of the management challenges within high seas areas and the difficulty of agreeing on who has responsibility and jurisdiction. In 2012 the IUCN World Conservation Congress called on states, individually and as members, to strengthen regional cooperation in ABNJ, defining as a matter of urgency special protection measures for seamounts, as well as designation and effective management of MPAs and benthic protected areas.[43]

In the southern oceans, the legal and procedural mechanisms required to designate MPAs and Marine Reserves have long been established. The southern ocean marine environment is governed by the Convention on the Conservation of Antarctic Marine Living Resources (CCAMLR)[44] and the Antarctic Treaty,[45] collectively referred to as the Antarctic Treaty System. Between these two bodies lies a relatively unique governance mechanism that can establish high seas MPA. Both CCAMLR and the Antarctic Treaty's Committee for Environmental Protection (CEP) have committed to the establishment of a representative network of MPAs as a priority.[46] Yet, despite this already agreed and established mechanism that would allow the Convention contracting parties to undertake fairly simple designation of such high seas management areas, the parties have consistently failed to agree and to deliver on this commitment.

The case of the North East Atlantic is more positive and, to some extent, ground-breaking. After several years of discussion, in 2009 the North East Atlantic Fisheries Commission (NEAFC) and the Commission for the Protection of the Marine Environment of the North-East Atlantic (OSPAR) established the world's first high seas MPAs. The OSPAR Convention[47] allows for the establishment of MPAs across the OSPAR maritime area, including in areas beyond national jurisdiction. To make these effective however, it was necessary to secure the agreement of the contracting parties to OSPAR as well as other stakeholders in the ABNJ, particularly those with a mandate for involvement in certain sectors such as mining, shipping and fishing.[48] To that end, OSPAR has worked towards strengthening mutual exchange and cooperation with the various relevant international bodies responsible for the management of specific human activities in ABNJ. It was agreed that OSPAR's role would be to inform such stakeholders as NEAFC on the best available knowledge regarding vulnerable eco-systems so that NEAFC could then act responsibly through its membership. In 2008

---

[42] B.C. O'Leary, R.L. Brown, D.E. Johnson, H. von Nordheim, J. Ardron, T. Packeiser and C.M. Roberts, 'The first network of marine protected areas (MPAs) in the high seas: The process, the challenges and where next' *Marine Policy* 36 (2012) 598–605.

[43] S.M. Garcia, H. Cohen, D. Freestone, C. Martinez, N. Oral, A. Rogers, P.A. Verlaan and D. Vousden, *An Ecosystem Approach to Management of Seamounts in the Southern Indian Ocean* (IUCN, 2013).

[44] Adopted 20 May 1980, entered into force 7 April 1982, 1329 UNTS 47.

[45] Adopted 1 December 1959, entered into force 23 June 1961, 402 UNTS 71.

[46] CCAMLR-XXIII, Report of the Twenty-Third Meeting of the Commission, (2004) para. 4.13 and CEP-IX, Report of the Ninth Meeting of the Committee for Environmental Protection (2006) paras 94 to 101.

[47] Convention for the Protection of the Marine Environment of the North-East Atlantic (the 'OSPAR Convention'), adopted 22 September 1992, entered into force 25 March 1998, 2354 UNTS 67.

[48] S. Christiansen, *Marine Protected Areas in areas beyond national jurisdiction: Proposed High Seas MPAs in the North East Atlantic by WWF 1998–2006* (WWF, 2007).

OSPAR and NEAFC finalized a Memorandum of Understanding (MOU) for cooperation, reaching agreement on the roles of their respective bodies and acknowledging their mutual interest and intent to cooperate in conserving marine living resources, including those located in ABNJ, and to further cooperate regarding marine spatial planning and area management. In 2009, NEAFC, following advice from OSPAR, closed specific areas within both it and OSPAR's region of competency to bottom fisheries with a view to protecting vulnerable marine areas in ABNJ. Fishing vessels flagged to NEAFC contracting parties were thus prohibited from fishing in these areas with bottom-impacting fishing gear.[49]

One final noteworthy 'jurisdictional' and management challenge to LMEs relates to the extended continental shelf (ECS) claims. Article 76 of the LOSC allows coastal states to claim an ECS beyond the normal 200 nm continental shelf limit and out to a maximum of 350 nm where certain criteria are met. To date more than 51 submissions have been filed with the Commission on the Limits of the Continental Shelf by states claiming ECS areas.[50] When finalized, these claims will bring more than 25 million square kilometres of seabed area under national jurisdiction. The water column above, however, will remain high seas and part of ABNJ, thereby posing an interesting management conundrum. Under UNCLOS, foreign vessels will be able exercise activities within the water column as long as they do not impact on the seabed or any living sedentary marine resources. The monitoring and enforcement implications for the country which has been awarded jurisdiction over the seabed underlying the 'high seas' will be complex and the subject of much negotiation.[51]

## 5.  LME MANAGEMENT AND OCEAN GOVERNANCE – DEFINING THE ROOT CAUSES OF THE PROBLEMS

Over and above these basic issues and threats related to use and abuse of LME goods and services there are other considerable constraints and hurdles to the effective governance and management of these ocean ecosystems. One such problem is, once again, a function of the 'operating in isolation' nature of human interactions (or the lack thereof), often commonly referred to as the 'silo' effect. Generally, there is a limited understanding of biogeochemical, physical and socioeconomic functions at the greater ecosystem level which is exacerbated when trying to consider these as interactive and connected functions and services. Science tends to maintain clear demarcations between the various scientific skill-sets and specializations.

---

[49]   For discussion see, eg, N. Lütz-Mack and J. Fuchs, 'The impact of OSPAR on protected area management beyond national jurisdiction: Effective regional cooperation or a network of paper parks?' (2104) 49 *Marine Policy* 155 and D. Freestone, D. Johnson, J. Ardron and K.K. Morrison, 'Can existing institutions protect biodiversity in areas beyond national jurisdiction? Experiences from two on-going processes' (2104) 49 *Marine Policy* 167.

[50]   Submissions are available on the website of the Commission on the Limits of the Continental Shelf: http://www.un.org/depts/los/clcs_new/clcs_home.htm (last accessed 1 June 2015).

[51]   For discussion see, Joanna Mossop, 'Reconciling activities on the extended continental shelf with protection of the marine environment' Chapter 8 in this volume.

This disconnect becomes even more marked when considering the natural and the social sciences. It is a relatively unusual event to find a physical oceanographer, a fish stock assessment specialist and a community welfare person discussing coastal fisheries and livelihoods issues together unless other parties have specifically made arrangements to create such cross-sectoral interaction. This lack of interaction leads to one of the more serious constraints associated with all types of ocean governance, that of the science-management-policy disconnect. Well-focused and targeted science concerning a particular large ecosystem may never see light beyond scientific publications or government shelves and storage facilities. There may be valid explanations and reasons for this. Managers and decision-makers want advice and need guidance on which to base management issues but scientists are reluctant to provide this without very strong evidence and support and often have little experience or, indeed, willingness to interact at the management or policy level. The decision-makers cannot wait for scientific certainty and may have to operate on limited knowledge and make decisions based on a 'best-guess' approach. However, the managers and decision-makers may also be equally responsible for operating in isolation. Governmental environment departments and fisheries divisions may, for example, make 'internal' decisions with no reference to each other or to related marine and maritime sectors such as tourism, shipping, energy and mining, let alone to other important national priorities such as health, education, social welfare or national fiscal constraints.[52] If the 'silo effect' represents a failure at the national level, this is only compounded by the 'isolationism' of decision-making and management at the regional and international level where the effective management of LMEs needs to reside.

Thus, while the economic and societal value of the world's LMEs is enormous in terms of revenues and in terms of food security and livelihoods, and while governments, industry and communities alike depend on these goods and services and their sustainable management, LMEs are all too frequently still managed within a single-sector 'silo' approach that allows for very little in the way of interaction between the various service providers, users and actors and processes having potential impacts on the LME. Knowledge is not shared effectively and thus management cannot be adaptive or contemporary.[53] The problem can be summarized sequentially through a number of constraints:

- Poor understanding and/or sharing of knowledge of ecosystem functions and interactions at the scientific and socioeconomic level;
- Ineffective and/or untimely translation of knowledge into governance in the context of recognizing trends and acting on those trends;
- Inadequate or absent management interaction and decision at both the national and regional (LME) level; and

---

[52]  See, eg, Report of the 12th Global Meeting of the Regional Seas Conventions and Action Plans, Bergen, Norway, 20–22 September 2010, UNEP Doc. (DEPI)/RS.12/8.
[53]  See, A. Rajabifard, A. Binns and I. Williamson, 'Administering the marine environment – the Spatial Dimension' (2005) 50 (2) *Spatial Science* 69. See, also, J. Ardron, R. Rayfuse, K. Grejde and R. Warner, 'The sustainable use and conservation of biodiversity in ABNJ: What can be achieved using existing international agreements?' (2014) 49 *Marine Policy* 98.

● Inability of management mechanisms to take action in the face of limited or absent advice and justification.

## 6. LME MANAGEMENT – ADDRESSING THE CHALLENGES

Effective management of LMEs depends not only on our knowledge of the ecosystem and its current status, but also on understanding directional trends in ecosystem change, and on how the management interventions have positive or negative effects on change over time.

Globally, a standard approach to developing management strategies within LMEs has been tried, tested and adopted through the Global Environment Facility (GEF) and its various Implementing Agencies.[54] The Global Environment Facility is a partnership for international cooperation where 183 countries work together with international institutions, civil society organizations and the private sector, to address global environmental issues.[55] This standard approach requires an initial baseline study first of the LME in question to gain a foundational understanding of the ecosystem as a whole in relation to physical, chemical and biological parameters and functions; the social and economic factors and constraints that link into the ecosystem's goods and services and depend on them; wherever possible an assessment of the value of the goods and services that are supported by the LME; and a review of existing institutional and administrative arrangements for management and governance. The baseline survey focuses not only on national status but on the transboundary nature of the goods, services, and threats to the sustainability of the ecosystem, and attempts to define the root causes of those threats. Standard LME parlance refers to this process as a Transboundary Diagnostic Analysis (TDA). This TDA then forms the basis of a regional Strategic Action Programme (SAP) on which the relevant states formally agree and through which they will act in unison to manage the goods and services and mitigate the threats and impacts within the overall regional LME system boundary.

Management of human impacts on LMEs (and the consequent threats to ecosystem goods and services and dependent communities) needs to be a dynamic process which depends on:

● a firm understanding of the biogeochemical processes that are functioning within the LME(s);
● how those processes support and affect the ecosystem good and services;
● how communities depend on those goods and services and interact with the ecosystem;
● a monitoring process that can measure changes in ecosystem goods and services and underlying biogeochemical processes (against an established baseline) as well as helping to define the linkages and relationship(s) between (human) impacts and changes;

---

[54]   See, eg, http://iwlearn.net/manuals/tda-sap-methodology (last accessed 1 June 2015).
[55]   D. Freestone, *The World Bank and Sustainable Development* (Brill, 2013).

- a reliable means of translating the results of the measurements and the related changes into appropriate management options and policy decisions or reforms;
- a rigorous mechanism to translate policy and management information needs into effective and rapid research activities.[56]

In order to be effective, therefore, a SAP needs to include a number of common elements.

## 6.1  Ocean Observations and Monitoring of Indicators

In the context of the ocean and coastal element of LMEs, the first requirement of any effective SAP is the need for a comprehensive system of ocean observation and monitoring of key indicators, including social and economic parameters. Clearly it would be prohibitively expensive and time-consuming to try to measure every physical, chemical and biological ocean-atmosphere parameter, let alone the social and economic status or the efficacy of policy and governance of an ocean ecosystem. The more common practice that has thus been adopted is to agree on specific indicators of health and well-being within the ecosystem-based management approach. All of the LME projects supported by GEF focus on the monitoring five specific modular areas: productivity; fish and fisheries; ecosystem health and pollution; socioeconomics; and governance. Within these modules, relevant states select the higher priority 'indicators' which are then balanced against national and regional capacity in order to measure such parameters on a sufficiently frequent and sustainable basis so as to ensure continuity of measurement and the likelihood of recognizing any significant changes that may have occurred.

## 6.2  Translating Results of Observations and Monitoring into Adaptive Management and Governance

Translating the results of observation and monitoring programs into adaptive management governance can be rather more complex than it first appears. This is because there has to be either: (a) clear confidence limits (in the scientific and statistical sense) in support of any conclusions, or (b) a fairly rigorous process of review and consensus/ agreement on the strength and reliability of any trends or directional changes that imply action should be taken. This process also requires a more comprehensive peer-review approach than has traditionally been the case in order to ensure that conclusions and subsequent proposed actions are not too narrowly focused but, rather, allow for input and guidance from other sectors.[57] This needs to be balanced against implications and priorities from other important stakeholders and spheres of interest and responsibility. What may appear to be an 'obvious' and logical proposed management reaction to a discovery that climate change is having a specific effect may need to be reconciled with the potentially negative implications that the particular management approach might have on other sectors such as tourism, fisheries or even education and health,

---

[56]  Vousden and Stapely, above n 6.
[57]  Ibid.

particularly in the face of budgetary ramifications. It is equally important that this process be seen as a progressive 'feedback' process whereby managers and decision-makers can identify and reflect their priority needs back to the scientific and technical level in order to focus research and studies on the core concerns related to a specific issue while simultaneously strengthening conclusions so as to lead to more, and more justifiable and appropriate, decision-making.

### 6.3 Capacity Building for Effective Governance

Capacity building can be defined as an objective and a consequent set of actions that focus on understanding and mitigating or removing obstacles that constrain or prevent individual people, groups, governments, organizations or businesses (in effect, the entire community) from realizing their goals while enhancing the abilities that will allow them to achieve measurable and sustainable results in the achievement of those goals. Most commonly, it is used in relation to overcoming developmental and managerial/governance constraints. Within this context, capacity building for ocean governance addresses much more than just training of scientists, managers, socio-economists, and so on. It also provides the means to strengthen the broader understanding of the ecosystem approach and effective management and governance at many levels from communities, schools and the work-place right through to policy-makers, company executives and heads-of-state. Moreover, capacity building embraces considerations of institutional capacity, such as physical and human resource ability, to carry out certain activities related to management and governance. Relevant questions to be explored and answered in this context include, for example: is there appropriate and calibrated measuring equipment? Does the country or region need more surveillance and enforcement personnel or vehicles? Is their appropriate software and expertise available to undertake modelling of data for fisheries or climate change? Are there available resources, funds or external supports that can be used to resolve these short-comings, and, perhaps the most fundamental consideration relating to capacity building, can this all be made sustainable?[58]

### 6.4 Dynamic Management as an Alternative for LME and Ocean Governance

Given the special characteristic of LMEs, both physical and legal, their governance requires a dynamic approach to management.[59] Traditional approaches of laborious and long-term scientific studies, although delivering a high level of confidence in the results and conclusions, are often criticized by management and policy-makers as being too slow and cautious. This has led to the adoption of the precautionary principle[60] to management which, although promoting a more prudent and discretionary attitude to activities, can tend to promote delays in activity which can stall progress and

---

[58]   Capacity Building for Sustainable Development: An overview of UNEP environmental capacity development initiatives. 2002 UNEP. ISBN: 92-807-2266-2.

[59]   Ibid.

[60]   J. Burger, 'Differing perspectives on the use of scientific evidence and the precautionary principle' (2003) 75 *Pure and Applied Chemistry* 2543.

development, frequently to the detriment of local communities and national interests. That is not to say that the precautionary principle is itself inappropriate. On the contrary, it is an essential first step in any management decision-making process. The precautionary principle, in its simplest iteration, promotes the strategy that wherever there may be a possibility that actions may be harmful, the standard and adopted position must be to either proceed with caution or even to agree to prohibit such actions until the actors can prove that their actions will be harmless. The difficulty with this extreme interpretation of the principles is that it tends to leave management at something of an impasse until a way forward can be found that is acceptable to all stakeholders.

Table 18.1 identifies the various implications of the different management approaches. A more dynamic management approach proposes a comprehensive review process for all existing data and conclusions that can then be 'weighted' on the basis of the strength and justification of their conclusions and balanced against the implications of taking various management options.

This more 'dynamic' management approach is now recognized as needed within ocean governance in the LMEs in order to progressively adapt to changing trends within a comprehensive and multi-sectoral environment.[61] Such an approach is also sometimes referred to as the 'weight-of-evidence' approach.

## 6.5 Reviewing the Weight of Evidence

The 'weight-of-evidence' approach promotes the early building and development of scientific arguments which, although not necessarily supported by per cent or higher confidence limits, can be considered to be strong enough to be indicative of a trend. Such a methodology is already well-established in various scientific fields, including medicine and law.[62] This approach is now being considered and adopted within environmental and fisheries management fields as a proactive step to implement the objectives of the precautionary principle. However, in most cases a formal system for review of trend indications and for making recommendations has yet to be developed and adopted within the ecosystem management and ocean governance scenarios.

In the specific case of LME management and ocean governance, in order to reach agreement on a reliable trend arising from a review of the weight of evidence, the conclusions must first be accepted by a comprehensive group of scientific peers, including social scientists and economists, who consider the evidence reliable enough and the trend identified as being strong enough to guide management decisions. The conclusions must then be presented in such a way that decision-makers can, as they deem necessary, act immediately and justifiably, while accepting that the science may need 'fine-tuning' and the confidence will need strengthening as a priority. It is

---

[61]  D. Vousden, 'Identifying and Responding to Climate Change in the Western Indian Ocean Region through Adaptive Management and Governance Strategies', Panel Presentation to the Regional Conference on Climate Change Adaptation in the Coastal Areas of the Western Indian Ocean, Grand Baie, Mauritius, 21–23 March 2011.

[62]  S. Krimsky, 'The weight of scientific evidence in policy and law' (2005) 95(S1) *American Journal of Public Health* Supplement 1.

*Table 18.1   Implications of various management approaches based on different data sources and levels of confidence*

| Basis for decision-making | Implications for scientists and knowledge specialists | Implications for managers and policy-makers |
| --- | --- | --- |
| *The 'confidence-based' approach* Based on the standard scientific requirements to be able to prove 95% or higher statistical 'confidence' in the results achieved | Scientists are highly confident in their conclusions and predictions and the end-results are very reliable. However, the process usually requires detailed and repetitive studies over a long time period (frequently years) | Managers and policy-makers cannot risk waiting for these 'high-confidence' conclusions and have to act faster to protect the interests of their 'stakeholders' (primarily the community at large) |
| *The precautionary approach* Where there is a possibility that actions may be harmful, the default position is to prohibit such actions until the actors can prove otherwise | Scientists are understandable nervous about 'sticking their necks out' and provide advice/guidance based on anything less than very high confidence limits (95% +) | Managers are uncomfortable at basing their country's management plans/strategies on what they often feel is a 'wait and see' and 'better safe than sorry' attitude, frequently based on limited supportive scientific evidence Policy-makers do not feel fully justified in making policy decisions which may threaten or impact on other social or economic priorities unless they have reliable 'justification' (clear advice from scientists) to support their decisions |
| *The dynamic management approach* Moves immediately forward from the Precautionary approach to agree on a weight-of-evidence that scientists and their peers feel comfortable in agreeing defines a clear indication or trend – and which can give managers and policy-makers sufficient confidence upon which to act acceptable confidence limits | Raises the profile and importance of science generally in the policy-making and management process. Encourage more support and funding in order to achieve more reliable results through a 'fast-track' process of priorities funding. Provide guidance to the scientific community on which areas of research are priority and most likely, therefore, to receive funding | Takes decision-making beyond the 'precautionary' approach (which has traditionally left policy-makers feeling vulnerable and indecisive) Provide senior government leaders at the economic/finance level and management level (as well other funding sources) with clearer guidance on where to prioritize activities and funding for both immediate management needs and further research |

*Source:*   Author.

important to deliver the conclusions of such a weight-of-evidence review process to decision-makers as a set of options that consider various scenarios related to cost, efficacy of resolution, and impacts on other sectors, including social welfare and local and national economy. This 'alternative scenario' approach then allows the decision-makers to do their job based on the best possible advice and information that addresses as many concerns and sectoral implications as possible.

Figure 18.1 shows a basic flow-chart of the various processes that would support a Dynamic Management Strategy. This starts with scientific research and knowledge capture, data analysis and conclusions. Where such conclusions can be supported by 95 per cent or more confidence limits then a traditional scientific paper would be drafted and presented for peer review and for publications. Where the end-results fall below the 95 per cent confidence limits but there is still felt to be some evidence supporting a hypothesis, then the research or study can be developed as a 'Trends' paper and sent to an appropriate review body. This body would have access to a roster of peer reviewers and would circulate the document to an appropriate broad selection of reviewers beyond just the primary focus of the study, with a specific view to seeking input at the social and economic level as well as from related fields of science.

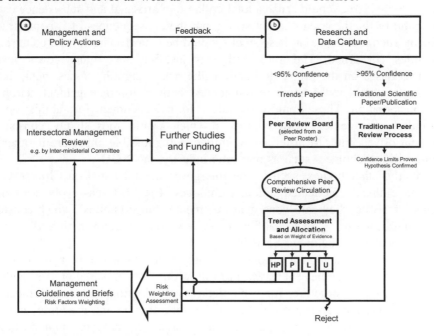

*Figure 18.1   Flow chart for a Dynamic Management Strategy*

The peer review group would then be able to allocate a level of confidence in the proposed trend based on the weight of evidence given in the paper by its authors. This weight of evidence could also include examples of similar research and studies that have identified similar trends. It would be the primary responsibility of the author(s) of the 'Trends' paper to try to identify such supportive work although the peer reviewers may also draw attention to such work where they are aware of it. Levels of confidence in the trend would then be assigned to a set of categories which could be allocated a statistical margin. An example could be:

- Highly Probable (H): This could cover the area just below the 95 per cent; confidence interval and down to 80 per cent;
- Probable (P): Between 65 and 80 per cent;
- Likely (L): Between 50 and 65 per cent;
- Unlikely (U): 50 per cent chance of certainty or less;

The 'Unlikely' category would, at this stage, be rejected from further consideration. The 'Likely' category would not necessarily trigger any further management response and would ordinarily be referred for further studies. However, both of the higher categories (Probable and Highly Probable) should also be considered through a 'weighting' assessment to ascertain the potential risks and the potential consequences of inaction, and allocate further prioritization based on such an assessment and possible consequences. For example, a set of scientific findings might decide that there is a 'Likely' trend showing that land-based run-off is directly impacting on crustacean fisheries which, if true, could cause a total collapse in artisanal and subsistence catches. The probability for the 'trend' is not strong but the consequences of it being true and there being such a collapse in these stocks would be catastrophic for the countries and communities concerned. Therefore, action is justified at a much lower level of confidence. Based on the probability and on the risk 'weighting' assessment, the peer review group would make some recommended options for management actions and policy consideration. These could constitute a formal document for submission to an inter-sectoral management review process which would most likely consist of a government-driven Inter-Ministerial committee with possible input from other non-governmental stakeholders such as maritime industry and NGOs.

Importantly, other bodies, such as the Intergovernmental Panel on Climate Change (IPCC), have already pioneered similar techniques. The IPCC has evolved a two-fold mechanism for what they call 'consistent treatment of uncertainties', which considers a level of confidence using five qualifiers (very low, low, medium, high and very high) and then allocates a Likelihood Scale.[63]

Finally, a set of management actions and policy decisions would be agreed by such a group which would then be sent forward to follow due governmental process within the national government structure, for example, formal adoption and management practices, possible Cabinet discussion of new policy for adoption and gazetting, and so on. Meanwhile, an intersectoral management body would also make recommendations for further studies, and, where appropriate, further funding, to strengthen the confidence in identified trends and support further research and data capture. The actions taken at the

---

[63]   M.D. Mastrandrea, C.B. Field, T.F. Stocker, O. Edenhofer, K.L. Ebi, D.J. Frame, H. Held, E. Kriegler, K.J. Mach, P.R. Matschoss, G.-K. Plattner, G.W. Yohe and F.W. Zwiers, 'Guidance Note for Lead Authors of the IPCC Fifth Assessment Report on Consistent Treatment of Uncertainties' (Intergovernmental Panel on Climate Change, 2010), available online: http://www.ipcc.ch/pdf/supporting-material/uncertainty-guidance-note.pdf (last accessed 1 June 2015).

management and policy level would be monitored and evaluated over time to also provide further guidance and fine-tuning on necessary research and studies.

## 6.6   Need for Accurate and Sustainable Data Input and Skill-sets for Interpretation

Even with the understanding that specific priority indicators will be measured, collecting reliable and sufficiently frequent data sets upon which to base management decisions is a very labour-intensive and costly process. Furthermore, being able to interpret the data and to model and predict potential trends and changes is a complex process requiring much experience in data input and interpretation. An effective monitoring, interpretation, management and decision-making process requires many skills and many different activities. As a result, partnerships for management are becoming more common within the context of ocean governance of LMEs.

In the western Indian Ocean, the Agulhas and Somali Current Large Marine Ecosystems (ASCLME) Project (Funded by the Global Environment Facility and implemented by the United Nations Development Programme) has been evolving such partnerships as a natural development, within the ecosystem monitoring and data analysis process, through a series of both formal and informal alliances and partnership agreements with regional and global institutions which share similar objectives and aims. The various partners have agreed to allocate funding and capacity to support the implementation of the SAP.

Such cooperative alliances are necessary, even at the national and regional level, in order to deliver effective monitoring, analysis, guidelines/policy-decisions and management. They become even more important within the context of areas beyond national jurisdiction. LMEs, by definition, almost always include ABNJ. Any management process for LMEs must therefore find a mechanism for equitable agreement and collaboration between all stakeholders in these high seas areas. One of the aims of the ASCLME Project and the SAP which it has negotiated between the participating states is to develop a management partnership which can effectively coordinate and oversee activities within the ABNJ that fall within the LME without alienating maritime industry or resource users in these areas. This is also one of the aims of a Southern Indian Ocean Initiative which is being proposed as a potential management mechanism for some of the seamounts that fall along the boundary of the ASCLME project in high seas areas, and which has been captured in a road map[64] that outlines the way forward and a list of deliverables towards achieving sustainable use and conservation of biodiversity in the Southern Indian Ocean.

The Benguela Current Commission takes a different approach to management and implementation of its adopted SAP. The Benguela Current LME is transboundary to the waters of Angola, Namibia and South Africa on the Atlantic southern coasts of Africa. The Commission was established in January 2007 as a single overarching entity to manage the activities that impact on or threaten the LME. A Benguela Current

---

[64]   The 'road map' is set out in Garcia et al., above n 43.

Convention was then signed by the Ministers of the three countries in March 2013.[65] This Convention commits the countries to:

1.  Prevent and eliminate pollution and take steps to protect the marine ecosystem against any adverse impacts;
2.  Undertake environmental impact assessments for activities that might have negative impacts on the marine and coastal environment;
3.  Collect, share and exchange data;
4.  Where possible, reverse and prevent habitat alteration and destruction;
5.  Protect vulnerable species and biological integrity; and
6.  Improve human capacity and infrastructure.

The highest policy and decision-making body of the Benguela Current Commission is the Ministerial Conference, which meets annually. The Ministerial Conference is advised by a number of subordinate committees which, in turn, depend on Regional Working Groups to provide them with the science and knowledge to make recommendations.[66]

In the Atlantic Ocean, the Sargasso Sea Alliance (SSA) was also created in 2010.[67] This Alliance is a partnership led by the Government of Bermuda, in collaboration with scientists, international marine conservation groups and private donors, who all share a vision of protecting the unique and vulnerable ocean ecosystem of the Sargasso Sea. The SSA aims to mobilize support from a wide variety of national and international organizations and governments to ensure legal protection for this critical ecosystem and to provide insights for the establishment of other MPAs on the high seas.[68] The Sargasso Sea has been described as an ocean within an ocean; a 'sea' without shores that covers nearly five million square kilometres. The Gulf Stream and North Atlantic Drift form the western and northern boundaries, the Canary Current forms the eastern boundary, and the North Equatorial Current and Antilles Current form the southern boundary. Bermuda is the only land mass within the Sargasso Sea. The SSA has three key objectives: to build an international partnership that will secure recognition of the ecological significance of the Sargasso Sea and the threats that it faces; to use existing regional, sectoral and international organizations to secure a range of protective measures for all or parts of the Sargasso Sea to address key threats; and to use the process as an example of what can and cannot be delivered through existing institutions in areas beyond national jurisdiction.

The SSA has the challenge of trying to operate and cooperate within a high seas framework alone, a constraint that has dominated discussions relating to the LOSC for some decades. The necessary linkages between sectors are difficult to make and

---

65  http://www.thegef.org/gef/news/benguela-current-convention (last accessed 1 June 2015).

66  Information on the Commission is available on its website, http://www.benguelacc.org (last accessed 1 June 2015).

67  Information on the Alliance is available on its website, http://www.sargassoalliance.org (last accessed 1 June 2015).

68  See, http://www.bios.edu/research/partnerships/sargasso-sea-alliance/ (last accessed 1 June 2015).

multi-sectoral protection is likely to involve a long drawn out process.[69] In March 2014, representatives from a number of stakeholder governments and territories signed the 'Hamilton Declaration on Collaboration for the Conservation of the Sargasso Sea'. The Hamilton Declaration is the result of a two year negotiation among interested governments that are either located in the broader Sargasso Sea area, have an interest in species within it or more generally in high seas conservation. It is historic in that it is the first non-binding instrument designed to provide a framework for inter-governmental collaboration to promote measures, through existing international organizations, to minimize the adverse effects of human activities in an ecosystem that is primarily in areas beyond national jurisdiction.[70] The long-term aim is to establish a commission for the management of the Sargasso Sea. In essence, therefore, the SSA is pursing the same objective for cross-sectoral stakeholder management and governance as the ASCLME Project but under rather different circumstances and with a formal commitment to a commission rather than a collaboration of existing mandates.

The International Commission for the Conservation of Atlantic Tunas (ICCAT) is an inter-governmental regional fisheries management organization responsible for the conservation of tunas and tuna-like species in the Atlantic Ocean and its adjacent seas. The conservation area addressed by this Commission covers the entire Atlantic Ocean and thus includes the SSA study area. The SSA attends various scientific meetings related to ICCAT, in particular its Sub-Committee on Ecosystems. The Sub-Committee has recommended continued cooperation with the SSA to develop a scientific collaboration plan and the Sub-Committee has further recognized that such cooperation provides a useful foundation for a case study relating to the implementation of the ecosystem-based fisheries management approach within the ICCAT region.[71]

On the other side of the world, the Partnerships in Environmental Management for the Seas of East Asia (PEMSEA) is a partnership arrangement involving various stakeholders of the seas of East Asia, including national and local governments, civil society, the private sector, research and education institutions, communities, international agencies, regional programmes, financial institutions and donors.[72] It is also the regional coordinating mechanism for the implementation of the Sustainable Development Strategy for the Seas of East Asia (SDS-SEA). This is a package of applicable principles, relevant existing regional and international action programmes, agreements and instruments, as well as implementing approaches, for achieving the sustainable development of the seas of East Asia. PEMSEA is governed by a regional partnership mechanism, the East Asian Seas Partnership Council, composed of Country Partners from the region as well as Non-Country Partners from different sectors. The

---

[69]   D. Freestone, 'Working to protect the "Golden Floating Rain Forest of the Atlantic Ocean"' (2014) 44 (1/2) *Environmental Policy and Law* 151. See, also, D. Freestone and K.K. Morrison, 'The Sargasso Sea Alliance: seeking to protect the Sargasso Sea' (2012) 27(3) *International Journal of Marine and Coastal Law*, 647 and D. Freestone and K.K. Morrison, 'The Sargasso Sea. The signing of the Hamilton Declaration on Collaboration for the Conservation of the Sargasso Sea: A new paradigm for high seas conservation? (2014) 29(2) *International Journal of Marine and Coastal Law*, 345.

[70]   Freestone and Morrison, ibid.

[71]   See, http://www.sargassoalliance.org (last accessed 1 June 2015).

[72]   See, http://www.pemsea.org/ (last accessed 1 June 2015).

objective of PEMSEA is to gather the stakeholders to work together and act dynamically and in a coordinated manner, within the SDS-SEA and the Sustainable Development of Coastal Areas framework, to:

● strengthen consensus among partners on approaches and strategies for addressing the identified threats to the environment and sustainable development of the Seas of East Asia;
● build confidence among partners through collaborative projects and programmes;
● achieve synergies and linkages in implementing the SDS-SEA among partners; and
● reduce in-country and regional disparities in capacities for sustainable coastal and ocean development and management.

Implementation of the SDS-SEA is the primary objectives of PEMSEA, in supporting governments and stakeholder partners to achieve their shared vision and mission. Execution of the Strategy by the various PEMSEA stakeholders[73] provides a more formal and legally binding partnership arrangement for the states of the East Asian Seas than currently exists within either the Sargasso Sea Alliance or the proposed partnership-based strategies of the western Indian Ocean. As such it is more in line with the Commission approach adopted by the Benguela Current countries. However, like BCC (and unlike the SSA or the Western Indian Ocean Strategic Action Programme) it does not address those ABNJ that fall within the LME area, despite being conscious of the challenges related to management of the East Asian seas in the context of adjacent ABNJ.

## 7.   CONCLUSION

The movement towards effective ocean governance focuses, at present, on the ecosystem-based management approach through the recognition of Large Marine Ecosystems as clearly definable areas within the world's oceans that are not limited by geopolitical boundaries. Although this is certainly a step forward in terms of logic, it presents new challenges for states and for all stakeholders in marine resources. The transboundary nature of LMEs has created a new and growing demand not only for cross-border collaboration between countries but also for the development of partnerships between government, private sector and other stakeholders that can also address regulatory management of areas beyond national jurisdiction that also fall within the boundaries of an LME.

In areas under national jurisdiction, adaptive management of LMEs is a challenging exercise in terms of identifying the capacity and resources for monitoring, for recognizing change and then for reacting to such change through management decisions and policy realignment. Nevertheless, mechanisms are being developed to assist this process through a more realistic approach to the review and analysis of data

---

[73]   See, http://www.pemsea.org/executing-strategy (last accessed 1 June 2015).

and the recognition that one of the primary objectives of such data collection and analysis is to support effective management processes and decisions.

In areas beyond national jurisdiction, there has been less of an incentive to develop such management mechanisms. While this is partly a result of a lack of direct 'ownership', it is also, perhaps, more pragmatically, a result of the absence of any right to control the resources that lie beyond national jurisdiction. In the absence of such a right, why would any state expend effort or resources to try to manage the vast areas and the resources involved?

In his famous paper on the tragedy of the commons, Hardin effectively denounced freedom and the lack of strict regulation on the basis that it inevitably allows self-interest to flourish and win. In the absence of any legally enforced control, he concluded that the tragedy of the commons was inevitable. However, new and innovative measures to broker partnerships and alliances for better management of areas beyond national jurisdiction are beginning to at least demonstrate a willingness for all stakeholders to collaborate.

Some of the logical steps forward would now seem to be:

- immediate development and implementation of collaborative agreements for managing the world's oceans, which include all stakeholders on equal terms and which aim to arrive at management decisions that will be implemented, either through global legal agreements and/or through self-regulatory commitments;
- stronger emphasis and financial support at the regional level to develop and implement ocean and coastal management at the level of LMEs (which is a far more logical and efficient management theatre than the old geopolitical jurisdictions, although not without its legal challenges);
- urgent priority given to more effective national, regional and global monitoring of the oceans, especially now when change is happening faster that we can even begin to understand and grasp the existing baseline situation;
- more importance given to understanding ocean-atmosphere interactions and raising the level of awareness of how these interactive areas of our planet drive the entire biogeochemical planetary system; and
- an overall order-of-magnitude increase in emphasis on capacity development for ocean governance in all of its forms and levels, from basic science and community engagement, through resource management, to policy-level understanding, and with a strong focus on the less-developed countries, many of which lie within hugely important marine ecosystems and many of which stand to feel the impacts of change (eg, from climate variability) far sooner and far more seriously.

In conclusion, it is apparent that the existing and previous archetypal management mechanisms for oceans and coast, based on national legislation or on somewhat 'wishful' compliance within formal convention agreements, are no longer adequate and, indeed, probably never were. A new order or regime is necessary that recognizes the interactive, transboundary nature of our oceans both within and beyond national jurisdictions. Stakeholders in the oceans and their resources, whether they be governments, private-sector interests, or the person in the street, need to collaborate and agree on management and regulatory processes that can be pragmatically followed and realistically observed and administered. As our planet becomes ever more populated and demands on resources and the urgent need for food security become paramount, the ocean's large marine ecosystems and the sustainability of their goods and services as renewable resources must be given a greater, if not the greatest priority, management-wise, for the welfare of the planet at the global and local scale, as well as for the long-term survival of mankind.

# 19. Towards a regional regime for the establishment of a network of marine protected areas in the South China Sea

*Hai Dang Vu*

## 1. INTRODUCTION

The South China Sea (SCS) is a body of water in the Pacific Ocean located between the Strait of Malacca and the Strait of Taiwan.[1] Considered one of the largest semi-enclosed seas in the world,[2] it is surrounded by China (including Taiwan), the Philippines, Brunei, Indonesia, Singapore, Malaysia, Thailand, Cambodia and Vietnam.[3] The primary activities involved in the exploitation of the SCS include fisheries, mariculture, oil and gas production, shipping and tourism.[4]

The SCS is recognized worldwide for its biodiversity richness, with the presence in the region of around 12 per cent of the world's mangrove forests, 34 per cent of the world coral reefs and hundreds of millions of hectares of coastal wetlands.[5] It is also an important fishing ground for countries in the region, with an estimated stock of 1027 species of fish, 91 species of shrimps and 73 cephalopods.[6] However, the marine environment of the SCS is under serious threat as a result of the rapid economic development and high population growth which the region has been experiencing over the last few decades. The greatest threats to the region are habitat loss and degradation, unsustainable exploitation of marine living resources and pollution of the aquatic environment.[7] According to estimates, as much as 70 per cent of the region's mangroves, 80 per cent of its coral reefs and up to 50 per cent of its seagrass beds have

---

[1]   US Energy Information Administration, *South China Sea* (EIA, 2013) 1 <http://www.eia.doe.gov> (last accessed 1 June 2015).

[2]   Liana Talaue-McManus, *Transboundary Diagnostic Analysis for the South China Sea*, EAS/RCU Technical Report Series No. 14 (Bangkok: UNEP, 2000) 1.

[3]   Hereafter referred to as SCS States.

[4]   Kenneth Sherman and Gotthilf Hempel (eds), *The UNEP Large Marine Ecosystem Report: A Perspective on Changing Conditions in LMEs of the World of Regional Seas*, UNEP Regional Seas Report and Studies No. 182 (Nairobi: UNEP, 2009) 255.

[5]   For detail, see UNEP, *Mangroves in the South China Sea*, UNEP/GEF/SCS Technical Publication No.1 (Bangkok: UNEP, 2004) 2; UNEP, *Coral Reefs in the South China Sea*, UNEP/GEF/SCS Technical Publications No. 2 (Bangkok: UNEP, 2004) 2; and UNEP, *Wetlands Bordering the South China Sea*, UNEP/GEF/SCS Technical Publication No. 4 (Kingston: UNEP, 2004) 4.

[6]   Pakjuta Khemakorn, *Sustainable Management of Pelagic Fisheries in the South China Sea Region* (New York: the United Nations, 2006) 19.

[7]   Talaue-McManus, above n 2.

been lost or severely degraded due to, among other things, the conversion of coastal land, destructive fishing practices and pollution.[8]

Urgent measures are needed for the protection and conservation of habitats and the marine living resources of the SCS. One of the most effective tools to protect the coastal and marine environment, which can be used to 'save' the SCS, is marine protected areas (MPA). The Conference of the Parties (COP) of the Convention on Biological Diversity (CBD), of which all SCS States are parties, has called for the establishment of comprehensive, effectively managed and ecologically representative national and regional marine protected areas networks that cover at least 10 per cent of the coastal and marine areas in the world by 2020.[9] As the coverage rate of MPAs in the SCS is far lower than 10 per cent,[10] SCS States need to make much greater efforts in designating MPAs to even come close to achieving the CBD's objective.

The most important obstacle to regional cooperation in the protection of the marine environment and resources of the SCS is the existence of very complicated territorial and maritime disputes, including the disputed claims relating to the Paracels, the Spratlys and to China's nine-dotted line.[11] This complexity is exacerbated by the fact that there are areas of overlapping claims between States where even the disputed status is contested by at least one party.[12] Needless to say, given their complexity and geopolitical sensitivity, these disputes will not be resolved in any foreseeable future. In the absence of their resolution, then, the objective of this chapter is to analyze the possible development of a regional regime for the establishment of a network of MPAs in the SCS. To achieve this objective, the chapter first reviews the current status of regional cooperation relating to MPAs in the SCS. It then suggests concrete components of a potential regional regime for MPAs in the SCS.

---

[8]   For details see Sherman and Hempel (eds), above n 4, 304; UNEP, *Strategic Action Programme for the South China Sea*, (Bangkok: UNEP, 2008) 3 (UNEP, SAP); and C. Wilkinson et al., *South China Sea*, GIWA Regional Assessment 54, (Kalmar: University of Kalmar, 2005) 149. Currently, the biggest damage to the coral reefs in the SCS comes from the ongoing massive land reclamation works undertaken by China which lead to the permanent physical changes of many features in the Spratlys. These activities were estimated to cause a loss of about 108.9 million dollars every year to SCS countries. See Edwin Espejo, "Philippines counts the cost of China build-up in disputed sea" (24 April 2015) *Asian Correspondent* <http://asiancorrespondent.com/132378/philippines-counts-the-cost-of-china-build-up-in-disputed-sea/> (last accessed 2 July 2015).

[9]   *Strategic Plan for Biodiversity 2011–2020*, Decision X/2, 10th Meeting of the COP to the CBD, Nagoya, Japan, 18–29 October 2010.

[10]   It is estimated that the coverage of MPAs in the SCS Large Marine Ecosystem and the Gulf of Thailand Large Marine Ecosystem, two sub-regions of the SCS, are 0.31% and 0.8%, see Sherman and Hempel (eds), supra note 4 at 255 and 297.

[11]   Hai Dang Vu, 'Towards A Regional MPA Network in the South China Sea: General Perspectives and Specific Challenges' (2012) 26 *Ocean Yearbook* 291 at 307. For details relating to the disputes in the South China Sea, see, eg, Ralf Emmers, *Geopolitics and Maritime Territorial Disputes in East Asia* (New York: Routledge, 2010) and Gillian Triggs, *Maritime Boundary Disputes in the South China Sea: International Legal Issues*, University of Sydney Law School Legal Studies Research Paper No. 09/37 (May 2009).

[12]   Hai Dang Vu, 'A Bilateral Network of Marine Protected Areas between Vietnam and China: An Alternative to the Chinese Unilateral Fishing Ban in the South China Sea?' (2013) 44(2) *Ocean Development and International Law* 145, 158.

# 2. THE STATUS OF REGIONAL COOPERATION RELATING TO MPAs IN THE SCS

This first section reviews the status of regional cooperation relating to MPAs in the SCS. Concretely, it lists regional mechanisms that could play a role in the establishment of MPAs and a network of MPAs in the SCS. It reviews the adopted commitments relating to MPAs and networks of MPAs and cooperative initiatives that have been undertaken to establish networks of MPAs under these mechanisms. A detailed analysis is also provided of the Project on 'Reversing the Environmental Degradation Trend in the South China Sea and Gulf of Thailand' (SCS Project), the most important cooperative process in support of the establishment of a regional network of MPAs in the SCS to date.

## 2.1 Relevant Regional Mechanisms

MPAs and networks of MPAs have been and could be the basis for cooperation under various regional mechanisms having a competence, either functional or territorial, concerning the protection of the marine environment and resources in the SCS. Regional mechanisms having the mandate in the protection of the marine environment and resources are not the only relevant mechanisms. Those with a mandate in other areas, such as conflict prevention and economic development, are also relevant.

In terms of institutions responsible for the protection of the marine environment in the East Asian Seas region, the Coordinating Body for the Seas of East Asia (COBSEA)[13] and the Partnerships in Environmental Management for the Seas of East Asia (PEMSEA) play a role.[14] Indeed, commitments relating to MPAs have been made and projects relating to MPAs have been implemented under the framework of both organizations. Regional agreements concluded to implement the Convention on Migratory Species of Wild Animals (CMS) also have a role to play[15] through, for example the Memorandum of Understanding on the Conservation and Management of Marine

---

[13] COBSEA was established to be responsible for the implementation of one of UNEP's 13 Regional Seas Programmes: the Action Plan for the Protection and Sustainable Development of the Seas of East Asia; see UNEP Regional Seas, *Action Plan for the Protection and Sustainable Development of the Marine and Coastal Areas of the East Asian Region*, Annex IV, Doc. COBSEA (OCA)/EAS IG5/6 (1994) (East Asian Seas Action Plan).

[14] Originally an initiative focused on developing integrated coastal management and marine pollution management demonstration sites, PEMSEA was institutionalized in 2003 to implement the Sustainable Development Strategy for the East Asian Seas (SDS-EAS). The SDS-EAS, attached to the Putrajaya Declaration of Regional Cooperation for the Sustainable Development of the Seas of East Asia (Putrajaya Declaration), 2003, is a package of principles, objectives and implementation approaches for achieving sustainable development of the seas of East Asia; see *Putrajaya Declaration*, East Asian Seas Congress 2003, Putrajaya, Malaysia, 12 December 2003 (PEMSEA) <http://www.pemsea.org/publications/putrajaya-declaration-regional-cooperation-sustainable-development-seas-east-asia> (Putrajaya Declaration) (last accessed 1 June 2015).

[15] Adopted in 1979 to protect migratory species through their range, the CMS encourages the conclusion of regional agreements for the protection of species between States located in their migratory range; see Convention on the Conservation of Migratory Species of Wild Animals, 23 June 1979, 1651 UNTS 333, Arts IV.3 and 4 (CMS).

Turtles and their Habitats of the Indian Ocean and Southeast Asia (IOSEA Marine Turtles-MOU),[16] and the Memorandum of Understanding on the Conservation and Management of Dugongs and their Habitats throughout their Range (MOU-Dugong).[17] These MOUs comprise, in their Conservation and Management Plans, commitments to conserve and rehabilitate habitats of marine turtles and dugongs and MPA-related planned activities such as identification, designation, removal and mitigation of threats to and rehabilitation of critical areas for these species.[18]

Organizations established to promote regional cooperation in marine fisheries with a territorial relevance to the SCS are also relevant in this context. The Southeast Asia Fisheries Development Center (SEAFDEC)[19] carries out studies on marine species and habitats in the region, which could provide scientific support for the establishment of MPAs in the SCS.[20] The Asia-Pacific Fisheries Commission (APFIC)[21] acts as a regional consultative forum and information broker to increase knowledge of fisheries and aquaculture.[22] Both could play a supportive role in the establishment of MPAs in disseminating scientific knowledge and information and enhancing the awareness of States in the region about MPAs. Similarly, the Intergovernmental Oceanographic Commission's Sub-Commission for the Western Pacific (IOC-WESTPAC), established

---

[16]    Concluded in 2001, the IOSEA-Marine Turtles MOU's objective is to protect marine turtles. This MOU covers the waters and coastal States of the Indian Ocean, Southeast Asia, extending eastwards to the Torres Strait. Currently, six SCS States have signed the IOSEA-Marine Turtles MOU (Cambodia, Indonesia, Malaysia, Philippines, Thailand and Vietnam); see *IOSEA-Marine Turtles MOU*, 23 June 2001 <http://www.ioseaturtles.org/> (IOSEA-Marine Turtles MOU) (last accessed 1 June 2015).

[17]    Concluded in 2007 in Abu Dhabi, United Arab Emirates, the MOU-Dugong aims to protect dugongs, which are found in the coastal and island waters from East Africa to Vanuatu, between latitudes 27° North and South of Equator. So far, 21 States have signed the MOU-Dugong, two of which are SCS States (Philippines and Thailand); see *The MOU-Dugong*, adopted at the 3rd Meeting on Dugong Conservation and Management, Abu Dhabi, 28–31October 2007 (CMS) <http://www.cms.int/> (last accessed 1 June 2015).

[18]    See *Conservation and Management Plan*, annexed to the IOSEA-Marine Turtles, see *IOSEA-Marine Turtles MOU*, above n 16, Annex and Dugong Conservation and Management Plan, associated to the *Dugong MOU*, ibid.

[19]    The SEAFDEC is a regional organization established in 1967 to promote fisheries development in Southeast Asia. Members of the Center are Myanmar, Cambodia, Indonesia, Japan, Laos, Malaysia, Philippines, Singapore, Thailand and Vietnam. As the area of competence of SEAFDEC is marine and inland fisheries and all SCS states, except China, are Members, its territorial competence includes, a fortiori, part of the SCS; see *Agreement Establishing the SEAFDEC*, 30 January 1968, 651 UNTS 20.

[20]    For instance, SEAFDEC has done studies relating to aquatic species of international concern such as sea turtles, sharks, sea cucumbers and cetaceans; see, for example, SEAFDEC, *Annual Report 2010* (Bangkok: SEAFDEC, 2011) 24.

[21]    APFIC is a FAO Regional Fishery Body established in 1948. The geographical area of competence of APFIC covers FAO Statistical Area 04 for inland and aquaculture, the Yellow Sea and its adjacent waters, the SCS and its adjacent waters and the Bay of Bengal for marine fisheries. The membership of APFIC is currently 21 Members, including Cambodia, China, Indonesia, Malaysia, Philippines, Thailand, and Vietnam; see *APFIC Agreement*, 9 November 1948 (APFIC) <http://www.apfic.org/the-apfic-agreement.html> (last accessed 8 June 2015).

[22]    *About APFIC* (APFIC) <http://www.apfic.org/about.html> (last accessed 8 June 2015).

in 1989, is in charge of international oceanographic research programmes, training and technical assistance and sharing of information and knowledge.[23] Research undertaken under IOC-WESTPAC could provide useful scientific information and knowledge to support the establishment of MPAs and networks of MPAs in the region.

Mechanisms established to prevent conflict and promote confidence-building measures and cooperative activities in the SCS include the Declaration on the Conduct of Parties in the South China Sea (DOC)[24] and the Workshops in Managing Potential Conflicts in the South China Sea (SCS Workshops).[25] Both mechanisms consider marine environmental protection an important confidence-building measure and co-operative activity that relevant States can implement while waiting to resolve territorial disputes in the SCS.[26] Thus, the DOC and SCS Workshops could provide a venue for SCS States to implement cooperative and confidence-building activities to support and facilitate the establishment of MPAs in the SCS. Beyond these, the Asia Pacific Economic Forum (APEC)[27] and the Association of Southeast Asian Nations (ASEAN) both have a mandate relating to the protection of the marine environment.[28] APEC,

---

[23]   See *WESTPAC Terms of Reference*, adopted at the 1st Intergovernmental Session of the IOC Sub-Commission for the Western Pacific, Hangzhou, China, 5–9 February, 1990, Annex IV. Its territorial scope covers approximately the North Western part of the Pacific Ocean with 20 Member States including China, Indonesia, Malaysia, Philippines, Singapore, Thailand and Vietnam; see *Report of the 1st Session of the IOC Regional Committee for the Western Pacific*, Tokyo, Japan, 21–24 February 1979, 7.

[24]   The DOC was signed between China and ASEAN States in 2002 to help avoid conflict and promote cooperation in the SCS; see *DOC*, Phnom Penh, 4 November 2002 (ASEAN) <http://www.asean.org/asean/external-relations/china/item/declaration-on-the-conduct-of-parties-in-the-south-china-sea> (last accessed 8 June 2015).

[25]   The SCS Workshops are a series of informal workshops organized by Indonesia since 1990 with the participation of all the five claimants in the Paracel and Spratly Islands dispute and other ASEAN countries. The purpose of the workshops is to develop confidence-building measures in the SCS and to promote cooperation activities between littoral States; see Yann-Huei Song, 'Managing the Potential Conflicts in South China Sea: Taiwan's Perspectives', *East Asian Institute Paper N.14* (Singapore: World Scientific Publishing and Singapore University Press, 1999) 20.

[26]   Parties to the DOC commit to implement confidence-building measures and cooperative activities, in particular in the area of marine environmental protection and a number of projects relating to the protection of the marine environment of the SCS have been implemented under the SCS Workshops.

[27]   APEC is an intergovernmental forum established in 1989 to promote economic development between 21 Asia-Pacific economies, including Brunei, China, Hong Kong, Indonesia, Malaysia, Philippines, Singapore, Chinese Taipei/Taiwan, Thailand, and Vietnam, see *Statement of the 1989 APEC Ministerial Meeting* and *Chairman Summary Statement of the 1989 APEC Ministerial Meeting*, Canberra, Australia, 6–7 November 1989.

[28]   ASEAN is a regional organization in Southeast Asia established in 1967 to build a comprehensive regional cooperation between Southeast Asian States to achieve peace, stability and development. ASEAN currently comprises 10 Members: Brunei Darussalam, Cambodia, Indonesia, Laos, Malaysia, Myanmar, Philippines, Singapore, Thailand and Vietnam; see ASEAN Declaration, 8 August 1967 (ASEAN) <http://www.asean.org/asean/about-asean/overview> (last accessed 8 June 2015).

under its ocean-related agenda,[29] has made various commitments relevant to MPAs[30] and has implemented a number of projects which could support the establishment of MPAs and networks of MPAs in the region.[31] ASEAN has established a regime of ASEAN Heritage Parks[32] and made commitments relating to MPAs under its 1985 Agreement on the Conservation of Nature and Natural Resources,[33] as well as under its measures adopted in the sector of fisheries cooperation.[34] ASEAN has also close cooperation with China in the area of environmental cooperation.[35]

Finally, a number of sub-regional and bilateral arrangements are also relevant, such as the Turtles Islands Heritage Protected Area, the Gulf of Tonkin Fisheries Agreement, the Cooperative Mechanism on the Safety of Navigation and Protection of the Marine Environment in the Straits of Malacca and Singapore and the Pan-Tonkin Gulf Economic Forum.[36] Sub-regional networks of MPAs have been or could be established under these mechanisms.

---

[29]   *Ocean and Fisheries* (APEC) <http://www.apec.org/Groups/SOM-Steering-Committee-on-Economic-and-Technical-Cooperation/Working-Groups/Ocean-and-Fisheries.aspx> (last accessed 1 June 2015).

[30]   See, eg, *Paracas Action Agenda*, 3rd Ocean-Related APEC Ministerial Meeting, Paracas, Peru, 11–12 October 2010.

[31]   Eg, the Project 'Marine Ecosystem Identification and Mapping in the Asia-Pacific Region', which ended in 2008, aimed to provide agreed science-based criteria to be used in the identification of marine ecosystems, a set of variables to monitor and assess changes and the creation of maps of marine ecosystems in the APEC region; see *Marine Ecosystem Identification and Mapping in the Asia-Pacific Region*, Project No.MRCWG 03/2007 (APEC) <https://aimp2.apec.org/sites/PDB/Lists/Proposals/DispForm.aspx?ID=784> (last accessed 8 June 2015).

[32]   *ASEAN Declaration on Heritage Parks*, 18 December 2003 (ASEAN) <http://www.asean.org/news/item/asean-declaration-on-heritage-parks> (last accessed 8 June 2015).

[33]   For details, see *Agreement on the Conservation of Nature and Natural Resources*, 9 July 1985, Art 13 (ASEAN) <http://environment.asean.org/agreement-on-the-conservation-of-nature-and-natural-resources/> (last accessed 8 June 2015). The Agreement has not yet entered into force.

[34]   See for example, 'Food Security and Sustainable Fisheries Plan 2020', adopted at the *ASEAN-SEAFDEC Conference on Sustainable Fisheries for Food Security towards 2020 Fish for the People 2020: Adaptation to a Changing Environment*, 13–17 June 2011, Bangkok, Thailand (Food Security and Sustainable Fisheries Plan 2020).

[35]   See *China-ASEAN Strategy on Environmental Protection Cooperation 2009–2015* (China-ASEAN Environmental Cooperation Center, 2009) <http://www.chinaaseanenv.org/english/events/271416.shtml> (last accessed 1 June 2015).

[36]   For details about these arrangements, see 'Memorandum of Agreement between the Government of the Republic of the Philippines and the Government of Malaysia on the Establishment of the Turtle Islands Heritage Protected Area, May 19th 1996' (2002) 1(2) *Journal of International Wildlife Law & Policy* 157; Agreement between the People's Republic of China and the Socialist Republic of Vietnam on Cooperation in Fisheries in the Gulf of Tonkin, 25 December 2000 (National Boundary Committee-Ministry of Foreign Affairs of Vietnam) <http://123.30.50.199/sites/vi/hiepdinhhoptacngheca-gid-a84f2f41-nd-e6a9f6ac.aspx> (last accessed 6 June 2015); Sam Bateman, 'Regime Building in the Malacca and Singapore: Two Steps Forwards, One Step Back' (2009) 4:2 *The Economics of Peace and Security Journal* 45; and Daisoke Hosokawa, 'Pan-Beibu Gulf Economic Cooperation: China's New Initiative in Cooperation with ASEAN' (July 2009) 60:2 *Osaka Kaidai Sonku* 67.

Though many regional institutions and arrangements could contribute to the establishment of MPAs and a network of MPAs in the SCS, the level of importance of their contribution varies. Some mechanisms, like COBSEA, PEMSEA, ASEAN and regional agreements concluded for the implementation of the CMS, can play a more important role by pushing for regional agreement relating to MPAs under their framework and engaging in systematic and comprehensive efforts to support the establishment of MPAs and networks of MPAs in the region. Other mechanisms, such as SEAFDEC, APFIC, IOC-WESTPAC, DOC, SCS Workshops and APEC may, due to their mandate, be expected to play a more supportive role. To that end, they can serve as fora in which representatives from SCS States can exchange and make declarations about MPAs or networks of MPAs in the SCS. They can also engage in activities to enhance the awareness and the capacity of regional States in respect of MPAs and networks of MPAs, as well as to facilitate inter-State cooperation.

## 2.2   Relevant Regional Commitments and Cooperative Initiatives

### 2.2.1   Regional commitments relating MPAs and networks of MPAs
In terms of regional commitments, no treaty has yet been concluded under any of the above-mentioned regional mechanisms. Instead, provisions on MPAs and networks of MPAs are found mostly in soft-law instruments, including agreements, declarations, MOUs, resolutions as well as plans and programmes of action. This seems to be in accordance with the traditional 'ASEAN way' to build multilateral regimes in the region.[37]

The content of these regional commitments varies. They may be as general as commitments for the conservation of habitats,[38] sustainable use of marine resources,[39] implementation of integrated coastal management,[40] and regional cooperation to protect the marine environment.[41] They may also call directly for the establishment of MPAs,[42] fisheries *refugia*,[43] transboundary MPAs[44] and networks of MPAs.[45] Some commitments are very specific, such as identifying important areas, agreeing on selection criteria and setting in place nomination procedures. In addition, commitments under different regional mechanisms seem to complement each other in enhancing prospects for the establishment of MPAs and networks of MPAs.

---

[37]   Vu, above n 11, 314.
[38]   Such as those under the IOSEA-Marine Turtles and Dugong MOUs.
[39]   Putrajaya Declaration, above n 14, 53.
[40]   'Manila Declaration on Strengthening the Implementation of Integrated Coastal Management for Sustainable Development and Climate Change Adaptation in the Seas of East Asia Region', *The 3rd Ministerial Forum East Asian Seas Congress 2009*, Manila, Philippines, 26 November 2009, para. 9(h).
[41]   Putrajaya Declaration, above n 14, 53.
[42]   *Paracas Action Agenda*, above n 30, para. 1.2.
[43]   Food Security and Sustainable Fisheries Plan 2020, above n 34.
[44]   Putrajaya Declaration, above n 14, 56.
[45]   East Asian Seas Action Plan, above n 13, 5.

### 2.2.2 Cooperative initiatives to establish regional networks of MPAs

Two concrete initiatives have been developed to establish networks of MPAs with a territorial relevance to the SCS: the ASEAN Heritage Parks and the IOSEA Network of Sites of Importance for Marine Turtles.

*2.2.2.1 ASEAN Heritage Parks*    The regime of ASEAN Heritage Parks is established by the ASEAN Declaration on Heritage Parks, 2003.[46] ASEAN Heritage Parks are defined as 'protected areas of high conservation importance, preserving in total a complete spectrum of representative ecosystems of the ASEAN region'. The objectives for their recognition are to enhance the awareness, management and conservation of ASEAN natural heritage through a regional network of representative protected areas and to generate greater collaboration between ASEAN members in preserving their shared natural heritage.[47] To be qualified as an ASEAN Heritage Park, a protected area must meet a number of ecological and legal criteria and be transboundary, unique, and of high ethno-biological significance for endangered or precious biodiversity.[48]

To nominate a site to the List of ASEAN Heritage Parks, an ASEAN Member must submit complete information on the nominated national protected area to the ASEAN Center for Biodiversity.[49] The ASEAN Center for Biodiversity compiles all the information and documents and submits them to the ASEAN Working Group on Nature Conservation and Biodiversity for terrestrial parks or to the ASEAN Working Group on Coastal and Marine Environment for marine parks. These Working Groups then make recommendations for consideration by the ASEAN Senior Officers on the Environment and the ASEAN Secretariat. The ASEAN Senior Officers consider the recommendations and seek the listing approval of the ASEAN Environment Ministers. The management of the ASEAN Heritage Parks is taken in charge by the ASEAN Working Group on Nature Conservation and Biodiversity.[50] So far, a total of 33 protected areas have been included in the list of ASEAN Heritage Parks, some of which are located in coastal and marine areas.[51]

Among the regional mechanisms, ASEAN seems to have achieved the most progress with the establishment of the List of ASEAN Heritage Parks. However, apart from the fact that China, a major player in the SCS, is not a Member of this organization, the regime of ASEAN Heritage Parks itself has many limits. First, as long as the ASEAN Agreement on the Conservation of Nature and Natural Resources has not yet entered into force,[52] there is no regionally agreed definition of protected area or what measures an ASEAN Member could apply to manage and protect its protected areas. Second,

---

[46]    ASEAN Declaration on Heritage Parks, above n 32.

[47]    ASEAN Center for Biodiversity, The ASEAN Heritage Parks: A Journey to the Natural Wonders of Southeast Asia (Laguna: ASEAN Center for Biodiversity, 2010) 1.

[48]    Ibid, 3.

[49]    *ASEAN Center for Biodiversity* <http://chm.aseanbiodiversity.org/index.php?option=com_wrapper&view=wrapper&Itemid=110&current=110> (last accessed 1 June 2015).

[50]    ASEAN Center for Biodiversity, above n 47, 4.

[51]    For detail, see *ASEAN Heritage Park* (ASEAN Center for Biodiversity) <http://chm.aseanbiodiversity.org/index.php?option=com_wrapper&view=wrapper&Itemid=110&current=110> (last accessed 1 June 2015).

[52]    Above n 33.

many elements for the management of ASEAN Heritage Parks are still missing, such as a disqualification procedure for those parks which do not fulfill the conditions to remain on the List, a regional monitoring system, and regional measures to support the conservation of these parks.

*2.2.2.2   The IOSEA Network of Sites of Importance for Marine Turtles*   The   IOSEA Network of Sites of Importance for Marine Turtles was established by a resolution of the IOSEA Marine Turtles MOU's Signatory States at its sixth meeting in 2012.[53] The overall goal of the network is to 'promote the long-term conservation of sites of regional value for benefit of marine turtles and their habitat'.[54]

To nominate a site to become part of the Network, the IOSEA Focal Point of Signatory State who has territorial jurisdiction over the site must submit potential sites to the Secretariat at least six months before the Meeting of Signatory States. The nominated sites will then be reviewed by the IOSEA Advisory Committee which makes recommendations to the Meeting of Signatory States for inclusion or rejection. Each Meeting of the Signatory States will have on its agenda the consideration of any new candidate site.[55] A suite of provisional criteria to evaluate the possibility of including an individual site as part of the network was also adopted,[56] which will be reviewed by the Advisory Committee and validated by experiences gained through the nomination of sites in practice.[57]

As to the activities for the implementation of the network, the underlying principle is that the network should not impose any new binding financial commitments or new legal obligations on Signatory States. To this end three scenarios are envisaged based on the availability of future funding: limited or no new funding, moderate new funding and substantial new funding. For each scenario, a different list of activities to be implemented is provided to support the network.[58]

Up to the end of 2014, nine sites have been proposed to be included into the IOSEA Network of Sites of Importance for Marine Turtles but none is located in the SCS.[59]

---

[53]   Resolution to Establish the IOSEA Network of Sites of Importance for Marine Turtles in the Indian Ocean-South-East Asia Region, adopted by the IOSEA-Marine Turtles Signatory States at their 6th Meeting 23–27 January 2012, Bangkok, Thailand.

[54]   Guidance for the Establishment of a Network of Sites of Importance for Marine Turtles in the Indian Ocean-South-East Asia Region, adopted by the IOSEA-Marine Turtles Signatory States at their 6th Meeting 23–27 January 2012, Bangkok, Thailand, 2.

[55]   Ibid, 4.

[56]   For details of these provisional criteria, see *Provisional Criteria for the Evaluation of Sites Nominated for Inclusion in the Network of Sites of Importance for Marine Turtles in the Indian Ocean-South-East Asia Region*, Working Paper #2 (22 September 2011), the 6th Meeting of IOSEA-Marine Turtles Signatory States 23–27 January 2012, Bangkok, Thailand.

[57]   See *Guidance for the Establishment of a Network of Sites of Importance for Marine Turtles in the Indian Ocean-South-East Asia Region*, above n 54, 11 and *Resolution to Establish the IOSEA Network of Sites of Importance for Marine Turtles in the Indian Ocean-South-East Asia Region*, above n 53, para. 2.

[58]   *Guidance for the Establishment of a Network of Sites of Importance for Marine Turtles in the Indian Ocean-South-East Asia Region,* above n 54, 5.

[59]   For details, see IOSEAN-Marine Turtles <http://www.ioseaturtles.org/iosea_meeting. php?id=17> (last accessed 1 June 2015).

Arguably, a network of MPAs is emerging under the framework of the IOSEA-Marine Turtles MOU. However, this network will not be comprehensive for two reasons. First, it will be a 'single-species' network, aimed only at the protection of marine turtles. Second, though it might lead to the establishment of MPAs in the SCS, this marine region is not its specific focus as an ecological unit for protection.

## 2.3   The SCS Project

The SCS Project was a six-year project funded by the GEF and implemented by UNEP between 2002 and 2008. The project was developed under the framework of COBSEA with the involvement of seven SCS States: China, the Philippines, Indonesia, Malaysia, Thailand, Cambodia and Vietnam. Its main objective was to create a regional environment in which all stakeholders, at all levels, could cooperate to address environmental issues of the SCS.[60]

The most important output of the SCS Project was the adoption of a Strategic Action Programme for the SCS (SAP), which proposed future cooperative activities to address the priority concerns and issues identified in the SCS.[61] Six areas of action were proposed: mangroves, coral reefs, seagrass, coastal wetlands,[62] management of fish habitat and fish stocks, and management of land-based pollution loadings.[63] An institutional framework was also envisioned for the implementation of the SAP with, at the head, a Ministerial Memorandum of Understanding and, at the lower level, a Regional Strategic Action Programme as well as bilateral and sub-regional Agreements and national-action plans.[64]

In addition to the SAP, the SCS Project also produced a number of specific outputs relating to MPAs and networks of MPAs. This section reviews those outputs and the initiatives undertaken to implement the SAP.

### 2.3.1   Specific MPAs-related outputs of the SCS Project
Specific MPA-related outputs of the SCS Project include the establishment of regionally prioritized lists of sites of management intervention, the establishment of a network of demonstration sites, the determination of targets for management and conservation of habitats and the development of first steps towards a regional network of *refugia*.

---

[60]   *South China Sea Project UNEP Final Project* (14 December 2001) paras 17 and 18 (GEF) <http://www.thegef.org/gef/project_detail?projID=885> (last accessed 1 June 2015).

[61]   Ibid, para. 7.

[62]   Under the SCS Project, activities in the wetland sub-component are focused on five specific types of wetlands: intertidal flats, estuaries, lagoons, peat swamps and non-peat swamps, see UNEP, *Coastal Wetlands in the South China Sea*, UNEP/GEF/SCS Technical Publications No.4 (Bangkok: UNEP, 2004) 2.

[63]   UNEP, SAP, above n 8.

[64]   Ibid, 64.

*2.3.1.1 Establishment of regionally prioritized lists of sites for management intervention* Under the SCS Project, regionally prioritized coral reef, mangrove, seagrass and wetland sites for management intervention were determined based on defined criteria[65] and a procedure for ranking.[66] The result of the activity was the listing of 26 mangrove, 43 coral reef, 26 seagrass and 40 wetland sites as prioritized for management intervention.[67] For each site, analyses must be done to review its environmental threats, management intervention that can be initiated to address the issue as well as the cost-benefit of each potential intervention.[68]

This listing of habitat sites as prioritized for management intervention in the SCS could be very useful for any potential exercise to establish MPAs and a network of MPAs in the region. Not only could it constitute the basis for determining in which areas MPAs need to be established, but it could also be used to indicate, in case of a network of MPAs, which areas should be designated as MPAs as a matter of priority.

*2.3.1.2 Establishment of a network of demonstration sites* Another activity carried out under the SCS Project was the establishment of demonstration sites for monitoring, restoration and public awareness. A total of 22 demonstration sites were chosen from the above-mentioned prioritized list, among which the most highly ranked received funding from the GEF to implement demonstration activities.[69] Key achievements of this activity were, inter alia, the establishment of an effective mechanism for local coordination of planning and management of environment and resources, capacity building for long-term management of coastal resources and environment, and encouragement of transboundary management of resources and environment.[70]

An additional important success was the establishment and operation of a regional social network to ensure information and experience exchange. This was achieved through the organization of a number of meetings between people having vested

---

[65]　For detail about these criteria; see Report of 1st Meeting of the Regional Scientific and Technical Committee for the UNEP/GEF South China Sea Project, Pattaya, Thailand, 14–16 March 2002, Doc.UNEP/GEF/SCS/RSTC.1/3, 5 and Annex 4.

[66]　Report of the 2nd Meeting of the Project Steering Committee for the UNEP/GEF South China Sea Project, Hanoi, Viet Nam, 16–18 December 2002, Doc.UNEP/GEF/SCS/PSC.2/3, 12.

[67]　John Pernetta, Terminal Report February 2002 to December 2008 of the Project Director to the United Nations Environment Programme, the Global Environment Facility and the Project Steering Committee for The UNEP/GEF Project entitled: 'Reversing Environmental Degradation Trends in the South China Sea and Gulf Of Thailand', Project No. GF/2730-02-4340 (25 February 2009), 19.

[68]　Report of 2nd Meeting of the Regional Scientific and Technical Committee for the UNEP/GEF South China Sea Project, Nha Trang, Vietnam, 11–13 December 2002, Doc. UNEP/GEF/SCS/RSTC.2/3.

[69]　Report of 3rd Meeting of the Project Steering Committee for the UNEP/GEF South China Sea Project, Manila, Philippines, 25–27 February 2004, Doc. UNEP/GEF/SCS/PSC.3/3, Annex 4. Demonstration activities included the creation of inter-sectoral management boards, preparation of management and business plans, economic valuation of resources, enhancement of public awareness, close liaison and involvement of local communities and stakeholders in interventions, see Report of 8th Meeting of the Regional Scientific and Technical Committee for the UNEP/GEF South China Sea Project, Trat Province, Thailand, 11–14 December 2007, 17.

[70]　Pernetta, Terminal Report, above n 67, 29.

interests in the SCS Project. Those meetings provided opportunities for people engaged in demonstration sites and in other project activities to share experiences and learn from each other.[71]

This example of the establishment of a network of demonstration sites provides a powerful precedent for the establishment of MPAs in the SCS by providing a management framework and useful learning experiences in how to deal with conservation issues.

*2.3.1.3   Determination of targets for the management and conservation of habitats*   A number of targets proposed by SAP for the management of mangroves, coral reefs, seagrass and wetlands in the SCS were a direct commitment relating to MPAs or could, at least, lead to the establishment of MPAs. Concretely, one of the targets set for future mangrove management was to have 4.49 per cent of the total mangrove area transferred to National Park and Protected Areas status. The specific target for coral reef management was, by 2015, at least 70 per cent of the existing area of coral reefs in the 82 target coral sites to be put under an appropriate form of sustainable management. Specific targets for management and conservation of seagrass to be achieved by 2012 were to bring 21 managed areas of seagrass under sustainable management, to amend management plans of seven existing MPAs with significant areas of seagrass habitat and to adopt seven new MPAs focusing on seagrass habitats identified in the prioritized listings. As for wetlands, the specific targets for management were, by 2012, to set up or update management plans in a number of specific wetland sites and to increase protection in at least seven wetland areas.[72] Unfortunately, as no arrangement has been adopted for the monitoring of the implementation of SAP, there is no way of knowing whether these targets have been reached.

*2.3.1.4   Developments of first steps towards a regional system of fisheries refugia*   The development of a system of fisheries *refugia*[73] was considered as the primary activity

---

[71]   Ibid, 12 and 28.

[72]   UNEP, SAP, above n 8.

[73]   Fisheries *refugia* was defined in the context of the Project as 'spatially and geographically defined, coastal or marine areas in which specific management measures are applied to sustain important species (fisheries resources) during critical stages of their life cycle, for their sustainable use', see UNEP, SAP, above n 8, Information Box 1. The Working Group on Fisheries of the South China Sea Project also noted the difference between the concept of fisheries refugia and MPAs. Criteria of selection of MPAs typically relate to the achievement of objectives of biodiversity conservation or political gain and MPAs are widely understood by stakeholders as no-take areas. Meanwhile, *refugia* are selected based on the critical linkage between the sites and the life-cycle of fishes and promote sustainable exploitation rather than prohibition of fishing. However, it recognized MPAs can be used for the protection of fisheries and consequently qualified as *refugia* if they are selected based on the critical linkage between areas and species and are not no-take zones, see Christopher Paterson and John Pernetta, Marine Protected Areas and the Concept of Fisheries Refugia Developed by the Regional Working Group on Fisheries, on behalf of the Regional Working Group on Fisheries (South China Sea Project, 21 May 2006) <http://www.unepscs.org/index.php?option=com_remository&Itemid= 132&func=fileinfo&id=519> (last accessed 1 June 2015).

under the fisheries component of the SCS Project.[74] Many outputs of the Project which could facilitate the establishment of a regional system of refugia in the SCS have been achieved. For example, intergovernmental guidelines for the establishment of fisheries refugia were approved and have become part of the ASEAN-SEAFDEC Regional Guidelines for Responsible Fisheries in Southeast Asia.[75] A total of 52 known spawning and nursery areas were identified, of which a number are under development or potential development as refugia.[76]

In the SAP, two specific targets were set to be achieved for the fisheries component by 2012: to develop a regional system of a minimum of 20 fisheries *refugia* for the management of priority transboundary fish stocks and endangered species and to prepare and implement fisheries management systems in the identified *refugia* based on, and consistent with the ASEAN-SEAFDEC Guidelines for Responsible Fisheries in South East Asia.[77] These first-step achievements provided an important support, in particular scientific support, for potential cooperative initiatives in fisheries management and establishing MPAs in the future.

### 2.3.2   Initiatives for the implementation of SAP

A number of mechanisms for the implementation of the SAP have been developed, two of which could open the window for future cooperation to protect the marine environment and resources in the region, namely a SAP Implementation Project and a Fisheries *Refugia* Project. Regarding the SAP Implementation Project, a 'Zero Order Draft of the Main Text of the UNEP/GEF Project to Implement the Strategic Action Programme for the South China Sea' was agreed within the framework of the SCS Project in 2008.[78] The text proposed that the COBSEA Secretariat would serve as the GEF Regional Executing Agency within which a South China Sea Strategic Action Programme Implementation Unit would be established to oversee the implementation of the SAP and the day-to-day management of activities under the project.[79] A Project Identification Form was developed by COBSEA Secretariat for the implementation of the Strategic Action Programme.[80] At the latest COBSEA meeting in 2013, it was

---

[74]   Helen T. Yap and Josh Brann, Reversing Environmental Degradation Trends in the South China Sea and Gulf of Thailand: Terminal Evaluation at 24 (GEF, 22 May 2009) <http://www.gefonline.org/projectDetailsSQL.cfm?projID=885> (last accessed 1 June 2015).

[75]   SEAFDEC, Supplementary Guidelines on Co-management Using Group User Rights, Fishery Statistics, Indicators and Fisheries Refugia (Bangkok: SEAFDEC, 2006).

[76]   Pernetta, Terminal Report, above n 67, 22.

[77]   UNEP, SAP, above n 8, 39. Apart from the Guidelines mentioned in n 75 above, there are another four Regional Guidelines for Responsible Fisheries in Southeast Asia, see (SEAFDEC) <http://repository.seafdec.org.ph/handle/10862/741> (last accessed 8 June 2015).

[78]   *Report of 10th Meeting of the Regional Scientific and Technical Committee for the UNEP/GEF South China Sea Project*, Pattaya, Thailand, 17–19 December 2008, Doc. UNEP/GEF/SCS/RSTC.10/3, Annex 5.

[79]   Ibid.

[80]   *Report of the 20th Intergovernmental Meeting of the Coordinating Body on the Seas of East Asia*, 2–5 November 2009, Ha Long City, Vietnam, Doc. UNEP/DEPI/COBSEA IGM 20/15 (2009), Agenda Item 4.

informed that the Project Identification Form was waiting for country endorsement before submitting to GEF.[81]

With respect to the Fisheries *Refugia* Project, it was decided that the fisheries component would be elaborated in a separate GEF project proposal.[82] A Project Identification Form for a GEF project, entitled 'Establishment and Operation of a Regional System of Fisheries *Refugia* in the South China Sea and Gulf of Thailand' was developed and approved by GEF in 2013.[83] The objective of the project is to operate and expand a network of fisheries *refugia* in the region for the improved management of fisheries and critical habitat linkages. Components of the project include the identification and management of fisheries and critical habitat linkages in the South China Sea and Gulf of Thailand, improving the management of critical habitats for fish stocks of transboundary significance and information management and dissemination. Its participants are Cambodia, Indonesia, Philippines, Thailand, Malaysia, Vietnam and SEAFDEC. The project is scheduled to be implemented over four years with a total budget of about 15 million USD.[84]

The SCS Project, although being a time-limited effort, has made many important contributions to the establishment of a network of MPAs in the SCS. The project was able to establish a list of regionally prioritized SCS habitat sites that require management intervention, which could serve as a basis to determine components of a potential network of MPAs in the SCS in the future. Demonstration activities, such as the creation of inter-sectoral management boards, preparation of management and business plans and economic valuation of the resources implemented in those sites, could also provide experiences in managing MPAs in participating States. Many activities supporting the development of a regional network of fisheries *refugia* were also implemented. Most importantly, the Project was able to serve as a basis for further cooperation for the protection of the marine environment and of sustainable fisheries in the SCS.

---

[81]    Report of the 21st meeting of the Coordinating Body on the Seas of East Asia, 26 March 2013, Bangkok, Thailand, Doc. UNEP/DEPI/COBSEA IGM 21/(6), 5.

[82]    Pernetta, Terminal Report, above n 67, para. 12.2.

[83]    *Report of the 8th Meeting of the Regional Scientific and Technical Committee for the UNEP/GEF South China Sea Project, above n* 69, paras 12.2, 25.

[84]    Establishment and Operation of a Regional System of Fisheries Refugia in the South China Sea and Gulf of Thailand Project Identification Form (5 April 2013), online: GEF online <http://www.thegef.org/gef/sites/thegef.org/files/gef_prj_docs/GEFProjectDocuments/International%20Waters/Regional%20-%20(5401)%20-%20Establishment%20and%20Operation%20of%20a%20Regional%20System%20o/4-6-13%20-%20PIF%20and%20PPG%20doc.pdf> (last accessed 1 June 2015).

# 3. SUGGESTED COMPONENTS FOR A REGIONAL REGIME FOR MPAs IN THE SCS

According to regime theory,[85] and based on relevant experiences from other regional seas like the Northeast Atlantic, the Baltic and the Mediterranean with regards to cooperation relating to MPAs,[86] it is suggested that the building of a regional regime for MPAs could greatly facilitate the cooperation between States for the development of a transboundary network of MPAs. Thus, this section suggests a number of concrete components for a potential regional regime for MPAs in the SCS with necessary adaptations taking into account the region's geopolitical realities. These components include: a regional framework agreement for MPAs; an institutional arrangement for regional cooperation on MPAs; a database of MPAs in the SCS; a list of MPAs of SCS importance; a regional monitoring program for existing MPAs; a specialized compliance mechanism; and a monitoring mechanism. As the detailed analysis of these different components has already been undertaken in other works by the author,[87] a summary of the results of the analysis follows.

As a first matter it is clear that the regional framework agreement for MPAs in the SCS region should be a soft-law text such as a declaration or an MOU dealing with more comprehensive topic such as protection of marine environment or protection of marine biodiversity with an Annex dealing with MPAs. The potential regional framework agreement for the protection of the marine environment in the SCS under the Project to Implement SAP could be a suitable venue. The content of the agreement could feature non-prejudice clauses,[88] an agreed definition of MPAs,[89] requirements relating to their establishment and management, protective measures to be applied in the area, and clear terms on cooperative duties at the regional level. Finally, to deal with the SCS disputes, the scope of territorial application of the proposed agreement should be limited to coastal and near-shore areas.

---

[85] See Stephen D. Krasner (ed.), *International Regimes* (Ithaca: Cornell University Press, 1983).

[86] All these three regions have adopted specific regional instruments relating to MPAs and developed regional arrangements, including institutional arrangements to support the establishment of a regional network of MPAs. For more details about the establishment of MPAs and networks of MPAs in these marine regions, see the OSPAR Commission <http://www.ospar.org/> (last accessed 1 June 2015); the Helsinki Commission <http://www.helcom.fi/> (last accessed 1 June 2015) and the Mediterranean Action Plan (MAP) <http://www.unepmap.org/> (last accessed 1 June 2015).

[87] Hai Dang Vu, *Towards Marine Protected Areas Network in the South China Sea: Charting a Course for Regional Cooperation* (Leiden: Martinus Nijhoff Publishers, 2014) 252–7. See also Hai Dang Vu, 'Towards a Network of Marine Protected Areas in the South China Sea: Options to Move Forwards' (2014) 28 *Ocean Yearbook* 235–43.

[88] They are clauses to safeguard States' rights and claims relating to the law of the sea to be established, which may, otherwise, arise when an MPA is designated.

[89] It should be noted that it would be better for the regional agreement to broadly incorporate in its definition all existing area-based tools prescribed under relevant international treaties, regional agreements and in national laws that reflect, to any degree, an MPA. This inclusive approach would avoid the complication of having too many alternative MPA regimes.

Second, the institutional arrangement for regional cooperation on MPAs should comprise at least two organs. The first organ should be a decision-making body to supervise the implementation of the regional agreement relating to MPAs. It should operate under the form of a regular Meeting of the Member States of which decisions should be adopted on the basis of unanimity. The second organ should be an operational unit to assist Member States in implementing the regional framework instrument.

The institutional arrangement for cooperation on MPAs in the SCS could be developed at two regional levels and nested within three possible mechanisms: at the SCS-wide level and under the emerging regional framework for cooperation in the management of the marine environment of the SCS of the SAP Implementation Project; or at the East Asian Seas-level under COBSEA or PEMSEA.

Third, the inventory of natural sites of conservation interest should be established from information gathered through regional prioritized lists of sites for management intervention under the SCS Project.[90] These inventories should be prepared at the national level pursuant to regionally agreed guidelines and formats. They should contain information useful for the conservation and monitoring of each site such as name, location and area of the site, reasons for inventorying it, threats, conservation status and agency in charge; and be reviewed and updated regularly.

Fourth, the list of MPAs of SCS importance should be established to cover habitats representative of the SCS ecosystem and areas critical for preserving the ecological processes of the marine region along with procedures for accepting of an MPA onto the list, the review of its status and its removal from the list. In accordance with the regional framework agreement, the list should contain initially only MPAs established from the outer edge of the contiguous zone landward and not MPAs established in an area subject to overlapping claims but where the disputed status is disputed by at least one claimant.

Fifth, the Regional Monitoring Program for MPAs should be created to monitor the effectiveness of established MPAs. The programme could be a separate initiative or part of a larger programme to monitor the marine environment of the region in its most important aspects (such as biodiversity conservation, pollution prevention and climate change control and adaptation). The first important task for a regional monitoring program for MPAs should be to agree at the regional level on a set of performance indicators to measure the extent to which established MPAs meet their conservation targets.

Finally, the specialized regional compliance mechanism should be a body with the limited mandate to promote compliance with regional requirements in regard to the list of MPAs of SCS importance. This body should have the responsibility to regularly review an MPA of SCS Importance to help determining whether it still fulfills all agreed requirements to be on the List. In case of non-compliance with these requirements, it should also provide advice, recommendations, assistance and help to the relevant State to redress the situation.

The power to decide whether an area fulfills the requirements to stay on the List of MPAs of SCS Importance should not belong to the body in charge of ensuring

---

90   See above section 2.3.1 Specific MPAs-Related Outputs of the SCS Project.

compliance but rather to the Meetings of Member States based on the information provided by the former. However, this body should have the ability to evaluate efforts of a State in redressing the situation. This evaluation could serve as the basis for the Meetings of Member States to decide to remove an MPA from the list of MPA of SCS importance where necessary.

These above elements are the most important components of a regional regime for MPAs in the SCS. The process of establishing such a complete regime could be a long and difficult road. Nevertheless, SCS States should move forwards step-by-step by aiming towards the long term, focusing efforts on easy tasks first and avoiding having too many expectations.

# 4. CONCLUSION

This chapter has reviewed the current status of the regional cooperation for MPAs and a network of MPAs in the SCS and has suggested a number of concrete components for a potential regional regime to establish a network of MPAs in this regional sea. As this endeavour requires a high level of integration between regional States, the development of a regional regime for MPAs might appear too ambitious for the time-being considering the complexity of the interstate disputes and the current nature of regional cooperation in the protection of the marine environment in the SCS. However, based on experience from other regions, the development of a regional regime is certainly an approach that SCS States should seriously consider to safeguard the invaluable marine environment and resources of the SCS. One practical way to make it feasible is to start with simple and ad hoc cooperative projects which have a limited effect in protecting the SCS as a whole but which might contribute to the enhancement of mutual trust between SCS States and regional cooperation in marine environmental protection. This would surely strengthen, in the long-term, chances for more integrative initiatives such as the development of a regional regime for MPAs.

# PART VI

# CLIMATE CHANGE AND THE MARINE ENVIRONMENT

# 20. Ocean acidification

*Tim Stephens**

## 1. INTRODUCTION

The oceans are vitally important to the regulation of the Earth's climate. They achieve this in several ways. They absorb heat from the atmosphere, and this has significantly slowed global warming caused by increased concentrations of greenhouse gases in the atmosphere.[1] The oceans have also put a brake on global warming by being a store of 'blue carbon'; taking up around a third of all carbon released from human activities.[2] But while this has been beneficial for the climate it has had profound impacts on the world's oceans as it has caused ocean acidification. This is the progressive change in the chemistry of the world's oceans as they draw down carbon dioxide ($CO_2$) from the atmosphere. It is now widely recognized that ocean acidification is changing ocean productivity, with enormous implications for ocean ecosystems and the societies and economies dependent upon them.[3] This threat has been acknowledged at the highest levels, with ocean acidification being the subject of a special report by the United Nations Secretary-General on Oceans and the Law of the Sea in 2013.[4] Ocean acidification has been acknowledged by the United Nations General Assembly as an 'alarming' phenomenon, to which all States should make significant efforts to tackle.[5]

Ocean acidification and climate change are linked. Carbon dioxide is the major greenhouse gas by volume, and it is also the main driver of ocean acidification. This means that controlling global warming by reducing concentrations of $CO_2$ in the atmosphere will also address ocean acidification. In the 2009 Copenhagen Accord[6] the international community agreed that 'the increase in global temperature should be below 2°C' in order to meet the objective of the United Nations Framework Convention on Climate Change (UNFCCC) to avoid 'dangerous anthropogenic interference with

\* The author acknowledges the valuable research collaboration with Rachel Baird and Meredith Simons that inspired sections of this chapter, subject to the usual disclaimer that any errors or omissions are those of the author alone. This chapter was written while the author was a Visiting Fellow at the Centre for International and Public Law at the Australian National University College of Law in 2013.

[1] Geoffrey K. Vallis, *Climate and the Oceans* (Princeton University Press, 2012) Chapter 7.

[2] David Archer, *The Global Carbon Cycle* (Princeton University Press, 2010) 116.

[3] J.T. Mathis et al., 'Ocean Acidification Risk Assessment for Alaska's Fishery Sector' (2014) *Progress in Oceanography*, advance online publication, DOI: 10.1016/j.pocean. 2014.07.001.

[4] United Nations Secretary-General, *Oceans and the Law of the Sea: Report of the Secretary General to the General Assembly*, UN Doc A/68/71 (8 April 2013).

[5] Resolution 69/245, UN Doc A/RES/69/245 (1 December 2014).

[6] Decision 2/CP.15, UN Doc FCCC/CP/2009/11/Add.1 (30 March 2010).

the climate'.[7] But while the international community has set a temperature guardrail, no such limit has been adopted for ocean acidification. Moreover it is not known if the atmospheric $CO_2$ concentration that the 2°C temperature limit involves (around 450 ppm $CO_{2e}$) would avoid dangerous ocean acidification.

This chapter examines how ocean acidification is addressed in international law, and what the future may hold in store for the regulation of one of the most pressing threats to the marine environment. It is seen that the phenomenon is currently not directly controlled by any treaty regime, and is indirectly regulated by an uncoordinated assortment of environmental treaties and soft-law instruments. The precautionary principle, and the desirability of setting clear sustainability goals for the oceans, suggests the need for the international community to set a single upper limit for the atmospheric concentration of $CO_2$ to match both climate change and ocean acidification mitigation goals, as both environmental problems are symptoms of the same cause – human interference with the global carbon cycle.

## 2.   OCEAN ACIDIFICATION: PROCESS AND IMPACTS

### 2.1   The Chemical Process

Ocean acidification is a relatively straightforward chemical process, at least by comparison with climate change. When $CO_2$ dissolves in water, it reacts with $H_2O$ to form carbonic acid ($H_2CO_3$), which dissociates to form hydrogen carbonate ions ($HCO_3^-$, also called 'bicarbonate') and hydrogen ions ($H^+$). Hydrogen ions combine with carbonate ions ($CO_3^{2-}$) in the water to form further hydrogen carbonate ions. This means that there is less carbonate available for calcifying organisms such as corals and shellfish to build their structures. In addition, ocean acidification causes the erosion of existing calcium carbonate life forms. While over long time scales ocean acidification will gradually reduce through natural buffers, it is occurring at an unprecedented rate and faster than most natural systems can adapt.

The chemical reactions behind ocean acidification are readily observed and described in the laboratory environment. Where the complexity lies is in the diversity of effects of ocean acidification in real-world conditions. There is seasonal and regional variation in the rate of ocean acidification; it is occurring faster in colder than in warmer waters. There is also considerable variability in its ecological impacts as it affects some species and marine environments more seriously than others. Moreover, there are biophysical and biogeochemical processes at work that affect the overall process of ocean $CO_2$ uptake, including down-welling to deeper waters, up-welling to shallower waters, and out-gassing; a process which is known as the 'solubility pump'. The solubility pump is affected by warming seas caused by climate change, as $CO_2$ is less soluble in warmer seas,[8] and this means that climate change is reducing the capacity of the oceans to absorb $CO_2$.

---

[7]   Opened for signature 9 May 1992, entered into force 21 March 1994, 1771 UNTS 165.

[8]   H.D. Matthews and K. Caldeira, 'Stabilizing Climate Requires Near-Zero Emissions' (2008) 35 *Geophysical Research Letters* L04705.

The 'carbonation' of the world's oceans through ocean acidification is leading to unprecedented alterations to their chemistry.[9] While the oceans are inherently slightly alkaline (with a pre-Industrial Revolution pH of around 8.1), oceanic pH is declining rapidly. There has been a 0.1 unit decline in pH (which equates to a 30 per cent increase in acidity, as the pH scale is logarithmic) over the last century,[10] and the oceans have a lower pH today than they have had in the previous 500,000 years.[11] The pH level of the oceans is projected to decline by 0.2–0.3 units below the pre-industrial level by 2100.[12] If $CO_2$ emissions are not reduced, then the magnitude of the change to the geochemistry of the world's oceans will be unprecedented in at least the last 300 million years of Earth's history.[13]

## 2.2  Impacts on Marine Organisms and Ecosystems

Ocean acidification is a more recently identified environmental impact from $CO_2$ emissions than global warming. This means that far less is known about its effects. However, the available evidence indicates that ocean acidification will have serious and lasting impacts on a number of marine organisms and will radically alter biophysical processes in the oceanic environment.[14]

A great many marine organisms and animals, including corals, form structures from calcium carbonate in the ocean. This is only possible where there is a sufficient concentration of carbonate in seawater. Many calcifying organisms are already feeling the impacts of declining seawater pH, and carbonate levels could fall below those needed to sustain coral reef accretion by 2050.[15] There is some evidence that some calcifying species such as the *Emiliania huxleyi* plankton, which is at the base of the ocean food chain, may respond through adaptive evolution to the changing carbon chemistry of the oceans,[16] while others, such as corals, and Antarctic krill *Euphausia superba*, are highly vulnerable and may not survive.[17] One recent study on Antarctic

---

[9]   Jean-Pierre Gattuso and Lina Hansson, 'Ocean Acidification: Background and History' in Jean-Pierre Gattuso and Lina Hansson (eds), *Ocean Acidification* (Oxford University Press, 2011) 1.

[10]   T. Friedrich et al., 'Detecting Regional Anthropogenic Trends in Ocean Acidification Against Natural Variability' (2012) 2 *Nature Climate Change* 167.

[11]   Ove Hoegh-Guldberg et al., 'Coral Reefs under Rapid Climate Change and Ocean Acidification' (2007) 318 *Science* 1737.

[12]   W.R. Howard et al., 'Ocean Acidification. Marine climate change impacts and adaptation report card for Australia' (CSIRO, Australia, 2012).

[13]   Bärbel Hönisch et al., 'The Geological Record of Ocean Acidification' (2012) 335 *Science* 1058, 1062. See also C. Turley, J.M. Roberts and J.M. Guinotte, 'Corals in Deep-Water: Will the Unseen Hand of Ocean Acidification Destroy Cold-Water Ecosystems?' (2007) 26 *Coral Reefs* 445.

[14]   J.-P. Gattuso et al., 'Contrasting Futures for Ocean and Society from Different Anthropogenic $CO_2$ Emissions Scenarios' (2015) 349 *Science* 45.

[15]   Hoegh-Guldberg, above n 11.

[16]   Kai T. Lohbeck, Ulf Riebesell and Thorsten B.H. Reusche, 'Adaptive Evolution of a Key Phytoplankton to Ocean Acidification' (2012) 5 *Nature Geoscience* 346.

[17]   Christopher Doropoulos et al., 'Ocean Acidification Reduces Coral Recruitment by Disrupting Intimate Larval-Algal Settlement Interactions' (2012) 15 *Ecology Letters* 338.

krill, which examined the susceptibility of krill eggs to ocean acidification, concluded that the entire Southern Ocean krill population may collapse by 2300, with dire consequences for the entire Antarctic ecosystem.[18] Another recent assessment of corals concluded that if emissions continue unchecked, then no oceans will be able support coral reef growth by the end of this century.[19]

Increases in $CO_2$ concentrations not only affect calcifying organisms, but can also have other impacts. For instance, increased water temperatures and increased $CO_2$ can reduce the aerobic capacity of some fish.[20] In larger waterbreathing animals, acidosis (increased acidity in body fluids) decreases cellular energy use and lowers respiratory activity.[21]

### 2.3   Impacts on Societies and Economies

A disruption of the oceanic food chain as a result of ocean acidification would have major flow on social and economic impacts, as many fisheries may become extinct or fisheries populations decline so that they become commercially unviable to exploit.[22] There are other potential economic impacts including lost tourism revenue in places such as the Great Barrier Reef, and risks of shoreline erosion as coastal coral reefs are damaged or destroyed.[23] In recognition of the broad-ranging and connected impacts of climate change and ocean acidification, in 2009 the United States Environmental Protection Agency reached an 'Endangerment Finding' under Section 202(a) of the *Clean Air Act* (US),[24] noting that '[c]limate change and ocean acidification will likely impair a wide range of planktonic and other marine calcifiers such as corals'.[25] However, this is an isolated example of national policy interest in ocean acidification. Unlike climate change impacts, which have attracted regulatory attention following an assessment of its significant economic impacts,[26] there has been no comprehensive

---

[18]   S. Kawaguchi et al., 'Risk Maps for Antarctic Krill under Projected Southern Ocean Acidification' (2013) 3 *Nature Climate Change* 843.

[19]   K.L. Rickie, J.C. Orr, K. Schneider and K. Caldeira, 'Risks to Coral Reefs from Ocean Carbonate Chemistry Changes in Recent Earth System Model Projections' (2013) 8 *Environmental Research Letters* 034003.

[20]   P.L. Munday et al., 'Interacting Effects of Elevated Temperature and Ocean Acidification on the Aerobic Performance of Coral Reef Fishes' (2009) 388 *Marine Ecology-Progress Series* 235.

[21]   H.O. Pörtner, M. Langenbuch and A. Reipschläger, 'Biological Impact of Elevated Ocean $CO_2$ Concentrations: Lessons from Animal Physiology and Earth History' (2004) 60 *Journal of Oceanography* 705.

[22]   See further R. Allan and A. Bergin, 'Ocean Acidification: An emerging Australian Environmental Security Challenge' (2009) 1 *Australian Journal of Maritime and Ocean Affairs* 49. See also S.R. Cooley and S.C. Doney, 'Anticipating Ocean Acidification's Economic Consequences for Commercial Fisheries' (2009) 4 *Environmental Research Letters* 024007.

[23]   Gattuso and Hansson, above n 9, 14. See also UN Secretary General, above n 4, 10–11.

[24]   Endangerment and Cause or Contribute Findings for Greenhouse Gases under Section 202(a) of the Clean Air Act, (2009) 74 *Federal Register* 66496.

[25]   Ibid, 66534.

[26]   See, eg, Ross Garnaut, *The Garnaut Climate Change Review* (Cambridge University Press, 2008).

assessment of the economic impacts of ocean acidification. There is an urgent need for such an assessment, and it is now possible to undertake at least preliminary investigations given the substantial increase in scientific knowledge in recent years.

## 2.4 Policy Responses: Mitigating and Adapting to Ocean Acidification

The policy response to ocean acidification requires addressing the biophysical carbon cycle that links the atmosphere and oceans, which is being perturbed by human activities, and which has flow-on impacts for human societies and economies (see Figure 20.1, below).

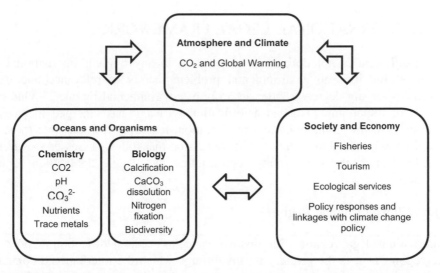

*Souce:* Adapted from Jean Pierre Gattuso and Lina Hansson, 'Ocean Acidification: Background and History' in Jean Pierre Gattuso and Lina Hansson (eds), *Ocean Acidification* (Oxford University Press, Oxford, 2011) 1, 17.

*Figure 20.1  Linkages between climate change, ocean acidification, and social and economic activities*

Ocean acidification is occurring rapidly and in circumstances where there is significant uncertainty as to how serious its marine environmental impacts will be. Unlike climate change, where a host of adaptation strategies are possible,[27] ocean acidification presents fewer opportunities for ecosystems and societies to become acclimatized. Highly controversial proposals have been advanced to 'geoengineer' the climate to address its worst effects (such as by managing solar radiation by injecting large volumes of sulphur dioxide in the stratosphere).[28] But ocean acidification presents even

---

[27] See Jonathan Verschuuren (ed.), *Research Handbook on Climate Adaptation Law* (Edward Elgar, 2013).

[28] Karen N. Scott, 'International Law in the Anthropocene: Responding to the Geoengineering Challenge' (2013) 34 *Michigan Journal of International Law* 309, 320. See also Clive Hamilton, *Earth Masters: Playing God with the Climate* (Allen and Unwin, 2013), Chapter 3.

more limited options for a geoengineering response. There is no technological 'quick fix' to ocean acidification; more than 13 billion tonnes of limestone would need to be deposited in the oceans each year to address the absorption of current $CO_2$ emissions.[29] This makes the ocean acidification problem a clear instance where the preventive and precautionary principles should be applied, and where the only prudent policy response is to reduce and ultimately eliminate greenhouse gas emissions from human activities. As Rau et al. have noted, 'short of stabilizing if not reducing atmospheric $CO_2$ there may ultimately be no perfect or even satisfactory conservation options for the ocean, either globally or regionally'.[30]

## 3.   THE INTERNATIONAL LEGAL FRAMEWORK

Ocean acidification is not defined or referred to in any binding international legal instrument.[31] But it is an environmental problem that is of relevance and can be addressed (to varying degrees) under an array of environmental regimes.[32] One of the challenges of responding to ocean acidification is that it has emerged in an era of environmental regime complexity and proliferation, rendering it impossible to be fully addressed by any standalone treaty.[33] The discussion that follows assesses the strengths and weaknesses of the main treaty regimes that have some application to ocean acidification.

### 3.1   The Climate Change Regime

The international legal regime with most relevance to ocean acidification is the climate change regime, as it is the primary means through which the international community is seeking to control emissions of the major greenhouse gases, including $CO_2$. However, as currently structured, the climate regime is concerned exclusively with regulating global warming. It therefore ignores ocean acidification and even encourages the use of the oceans as a carbon sink to address climate change, even though this would worsen ocean acidification. This is not surprising given that at the time the

---

[29]   See, however, Harvey who argues that adding vast quantities of limestone powder to the oceans could help mitigate both climate change and ocean acidification: L. Harvey, 'Mitigating the Atmospheric $CO_2$ Increase and Ocean Acidification by Adding Limestone Powder to Upwelling Regions' (2008) *Journal of Geophysical Research* 113.

[30]   Greg H. Rau, Elizabeth L. McLeod and Ove Hoegh-Guldberg, 'The Need for New Ocean Conservation Strategies in a High-Carbon Dioxide World' (2012) 2 *Nature Climate Change* 720, 723.

[31]   UN Secretary-General, above n 4, 12.

[32]   Rachel Baird, Meredith Simons and Tim Stephens, 'Ocean Acidification: A Litmus Test for International Law' (2009) 4 *Carbon and Climate Law Review* 459.

[33]   On regime complexity in international environmental law generally see Margaret A. Young, *Trading Fish, Saving Fish: The Interaction Between Regimes in International Law* (Cambridge University Press, Cambridge, 2011). See also Daniel Drezner, 'The Power and Peril of International Regime Complexity' (2009) 7 *Perspectives on Politics* 65.

UNFCCC and Kyoto Protocol[34] were negotiated in the 1990s, ocean acidification had not been examined in depth in the scientific literature, and therefore had little visibility to policy-makers.

Article 2 of the UNFCCC expresses the objective of the climate regime which is to stabilize greenhouse gas concentrations in the atmosphere at a level that would prevent dangerous anthropogenic interference with the climate system. The UNFCCC defines the 'climate system' to mean the totality of the atmosphere, hydrosphere, biosphere and geosphere and their interactions.[35] However, it is doubtful whether there is any requirement under the UNFCCC to address ocean acidification. This conclusion is supported by several key provisions of the convention. Article 1(2) of the UNFCCC defines 'climate change' as the change of climate attributed to human activity that alters the composition of the global atmosphere, a definition that does not embrace chemical changes to the oceans. Moreover, Article 1(1) states that the 'adverse effects' of climate change are those involving alterations in the physical environment or biota resulting from climate change which have significant deleterious effects on composition, resilience or productivity of natural and managed ecosystems. As a consequence, the core obligation of the UNFCCC, set out in Article 3, to protect the climate system and limit its adverse effects, does not include any obligation to prevent ocean acidification.

The UNFCCC has an obvious and understandable atmospheric rather than oceanic focus. This is reinforced in the Kyoto Protocol, which sets targets for reducing or limiting emissions on the basis of their impacts upon the atmosphere, rather than the oceans. The Kyoto Protocol groups together the major greenhouse gases or groups of gases [$CO_2$, methane ($CH_4$), nitrous oxide ($N_2O$), hydrofluorocarbons (HFCs), per-fluorocarbons (PFCs) and sulphur hexafluoride ($SF_6$)] when determining global and national emissions budgets, with no distinction drawn between them. This makes sense from a climate change perspective as the Kyoto Protocol is concerned with addressing heat-trapping gases. If a state chooses to prioritize the control of emissions of a more potent greenhouse gas (such as $CH_4$) over a less potent greenhouse gas (such as $CO_2$) this is perfectly consistent with the climate regime. The Kyoto Protocol therefore establishes no quantified obligation to reduce emissions of $CO_2$, the main gas causing ocean acidification, and instead allows states to meet their commitments by limiting their $CO_2$ *equivalent* emissions of greenhouse gases.[36] Indeed parties to the Kyoto Protocol could even *increase* $CO_2$ emissions, so long as there is a corresponding reduction in other greenhouse gases.

There are other aspects of the climate regime that are in tension with efforts to control ocean acidification. Article 1 of the UNFCCC defines a 'reservoir' to be a component of the climate system where a greenhouse gas or a precursor of a greenhouse gas is stored, and defines a 'sink' to be any process, activity or mechanism which removes a greenhouse gas, an aerosol or a precursor of a greenhouse gas from the atmosphere. Under Article 4(1)(d) parties are required to promote sustainable management and to cooperate in the conservation and enhancement of sinks and

---

[34] Kyoto Protocol to the United Nations Framework Convention on Climate Change, opened for signature 11 December 1997, entered into force 16 February 2005. 2303 UNTS 148.

[35] UNFCCC, Art. 1(3).

[36] Kyoto Protocol, Art. 3(1).

reservoirs of all greenhouse gases, including oceans. This means that the UNFCCC can be interpreted as encouraging states to use natural sinks, including the oceans, to store greater quantities of carbon even if this would exacerbate acidification.[37] In summary, the oceans as a store of 'blue carbon' are seen by the UNFCCC as part of the solution to climate change, rather than as a natural system requiring protection from changes to the carbon cycle.

The situation has not improved since the conclusion of the UNFCCC in 1992. With the exception of the issue of sea level rise, successive conferences and meetings of the parties and subsidiary bodies of the UNFCCC and the Kyoto Protocol have devoted little attention to ocean acidification or oceans issues generally. Galland et al. note that '[d]espite its significant role in climate regulation and vulnerability to climate change, the ocean is often relegated to footnotes and afterthoughts in the development of climate policy'.[38] They suggest that oceanic threshold data could be used, in a similar way to thresholds of climate sensitivity to greenhouse gases, to design and support emission reduction targets for $CO_2$ that consider both ocean warming and ocean acidification, which are having a combined impact upon many marine organisms and ecosystems.[39]

## 3.2   Other Atmospheric Pollution Regimes

Ocean acidification is not the first acidification problem to be confronted by international law. Some of the earliest developments in international environmental law came in response to 'acid rain' which, like ocean acidification, also has its root cause in atmospheric pollution, albeit primarily from sulphur dioxide ($SO_2$) rather than $CO_2$. Acid rain was identified as a by-product of $SO_2$ emissions from industry early in the twentieth century, and was the subject of the celebrated *Trail Smelter Case*[40] between the United States and Canada, in which it was found that Canada was under an international legal obligation to control emissions from a metals smelter in British Columbia to prevent damage to farming land in the United States.

Acid rain was the 'poster child' environmental issue in many Northern industrialized states from the 1960s, as it visibly stripped landscapes of their vegetation, and caused damage to limestone buildings of major cultural significance. Concerns about acid rain led to concerted national and international efforts to control its causes. In North America and Europe, at least, such efforts have been largely successful. The 1979 Convention on Long-Range Transboundary Air Pollution (LRTAP),[41] negotiated within the United Nations Economic Commission for Europe (UNECE), is a framework

---

[37]   Active, water-column, $CO_2$ sequestration has attracted attention within other regulatory regimes, including those dealing with marine pollution. See below, and Karen N. Scott, 'Geoengineering and the marine environment', Chapter 21 in this volume.

[38]   Grantly Galland, Ellycia Harrould-Kolieb, and Dorothée Herr, 'The Ocean and Climate Change Policy' (2012) 12 *Climate Policy* 764, 765.

[39]   Ibid, 767.

[40]   *Trail Smelter Case (Canada/United States of America)*, initial decision, 16 April 1938, final decision, 11 March 1941, 3 RIAA (1941).

[41]   Opened for signature 13 November 1979, entered in force 16 March 1983, 1302 UNTS 218.

convention that is supplemented by eight detailed protocols that establish strict targets for reducing acid rain. Over the thirty years the regime has been in force it has been adjusted to adopt contemporary principles of environmental management, including the precautionary principle. The Convention now has 51 parties, and the UNECE is seeking to extend the application of the regime across the geographical reach of the UNECE region, which includes not only North America and Western Europe, but also Eastern Europe, South East Europe, the Caucasus, and Central Asia.

The most recent development in the LRTAP regime has been the adoption of the 1999 Protocol to Abate Acidification, Eutrophication and Ground-Level Ozone.[42] The Protocol establishes emissions ceilings from 2010 for four types of pollutant: sulphur, nitrous oxides (NOx), Volatile Organic Compounds (VOCs) and ammonia, and seeks to cut emissions of these substances very significantly. For example, sulphur emissions are to be reduced by over 60 per cent from 1990 levels. The regime not only sets headline targets but, crucially, matches these with limits for particular sources of emissions, for example from industrial plants and processes and from transport. In 2012 the Protocol was further extended, with amendments to include national emission reduction commitments for 2020 and onwards.[43]

The LRTAP regime provides an important precedent for a possible international legal response to ocean acidification, because it incorporates a precautionary, science-based approach to the acid rain problem. Significantly, Article 2 of the 1999 Protocol provides that one of the objectives of the regime is to ensure that a 'critical load of acidity' is not exceeded, including in marine environments. There is no reason in principle why a similar regulatory approach could not be taken in respect of ocean acidification. However the impediments to doing so are economic, political and legal. The economic hurdle is that $CO_2$ emissions are produced from a wider array of activities than $SO_2$ emissions, and are therefore not able to be constrained at low cost through technical standards and new technologies, such as $SO_2$ 'scrubbers', or flue-gas desulfurization. Politically, $CO_2$ is more challenging than $SO_2$ abatement because of the economic costs, and can only be dealt with globally rather than in respect of regional air sheds. The legal difficulty in addressing ocean acidification, in a similar targets and timetables approach as $SO_2$, is that there is already a regime for controlling $CO_2$ which, as we have seen, currently has no application to ocean acidification as a problem.

### 3.3 Marine Pollution Control Regimes

Although there is an extensive body of law that has brought some aspects of marine pollution under control, it currently has very limited application to ocean acidification.

---

[42] Opened for signature 30 November 1999, entered into force 17 May 2005, UN Doc EB.AIR/1999.

[43] See the consolidated text at http://www.unece.org/fileadmin/DAM/env/lrtap/full%20text/ Informal_document_no_17_No23_Consolidated_text_checked_DB_10Dec2012_-_YT_-_10.12. 2012.pdf (accessed 2 June 2015).

The 1982 United Nations Convention on the Law (LOSC) of the Sea,[44] establishes general obligations on all parties to reduce marine pollution from any source,[45] and to ensure that one type of pollution is not transformed into another,[46] an obligation of obvious relevance in the context of ocean acidification. Under the umbrella of the LOSC, a framework convention, a raft of treaties and soft-law instruments have been adopted to address marine pollution from vessel, terrestrial, and atmospheric sources.[47] The success of these regimes is largely determined by the source they target; while dumping of wastes at sea and vessel-source oil and other pollution has been controlled very effectively since the 1970s, land-based and atmospheric pollution of the marine environment have largely escaped regulation, at least at a global scale. This is despite the fact that around 80 per cent of pollution that enters the marine environment comes from land-based discharges and atmospheric sources.[48]

### 3.3.1   Vessel-source pollution and ocean dumping regimes

The aim of the 1972 London Convention[49] is to prevent pollution of the oceans by the dumping of materials that could endanger human health or harm the marine environment. The London Convention is to be replaced by the more stringent 1996 London Protocol,[50] but given the limited ratification of the latter it continues to apply to those states that have not yet joined the later instrument. Under the 1996 London Protocol, dumping at sea of any substance is prohibited, unless it can be shown not to damage the marine environment. The treaty gives effect to the precautionary principle, by requiring parties to apply

> a precautionary approach to environmental protection from dumping ... whereby appropriate preventive measures are taken when there is reason to believe that wastes ... are likely to cause harm even when there is no conclusive evidence to prove a causal relation between inputs and their effects.[51]

The chief relevance of the London ocean dumping regime for ocean acidification is that it limits the intentional placement of $CO_2$ in the marine environment. Hence, any plans to store $CO_2$ in geological formations under the seabed, on the seabed, at sufficient depths such that the high pressures will act to condense $CO_2$, or in the water column will need to comply with the terms of the regime. In line with the 1996 London

---

[44]   Opened for signature 10 December 1982, entered into force 16 November 1994, 1833 UNTS 397.

[45]   LOSC, Pt XII.

[46]   LOSC, Art. 195.

[47]   See, generally, Donald R. Rothwell and Tim Stephens, *The International Law of the Sea* (Hart, 2010) Chapter 15.

[48]   Ibid, 339.

[49]   Convention on the Prevention of Marine Pollution by Dumping of Wastes and Other Matter, Opened for Signature 29 December 1972, entered into force 30 August 1975, 1046 UNTS 120.

[50]   Protocol to the Convention on the Prevention of Marine Pollution by Dumping of Wastes and Other Matter, Opened for signature 8 November 1996, entered into force 24 March 2006, 36 *International Legal Materials* 1.

[51]   1996 London Protocol, Art. 3(1).

Protocol's precautionary approach, several measures have been adopted to regulate the active use of the water column as a carbon sink. At the first meeting of the parties in 2006, amendments to the 1996 London Protocol were agreed which permitted the storage of $CO_2$ under, but not on or above, the seabed.[52] Sub-seabed carbon sequestration involves the placement of $CO_2$ streams in undersea geological formations, a technology that has been endorsed by the parties to the Protocol as a way of mitigating climate change and ocean acidification. But there are risks associated with $CO_2$ sequestration, including the chance that $CO_2$ will leak into the water column and exacerbate ocean acidification. To reduce these risks in 2012 the IMO adopted detailed Specific Guidelines for the Assessment of Carbon Dioxide for Disposal into Sub-Seabed Geological Formations.[53]

In relation to the water column, the parties to the London Dumping regime have taken a more precautionary approach. In 2008 the parties agreed to a moratorium on ocean fertilization, except for legitimate scientific research.[54] Ocean fertilization describes a collection of processes under which carbon sequestration by the oceans can be enhanced, such as through the dumping of iron, phosphorous or nitrogen compounds to promote the growth of phytoplankton which absorb $CO_2$. The process is defined in the 2008 resolution as 'any activity undertaken by humans with the principal intention of stimulating primary productivity in the oceans, not including conventional aquaculture, or mariculture, or the creation of artificial reefs'.[55] While some ocean fertilization technologies are expected to have limited acidification effects, at least one process could potentially exacerbate ocean acidification, namely schemes to enhance the upwelling of deep seawater artificially through the use of large tubes placed in the water column.[56] While upwelling occurs naturally, proponents for schemes to increase the upwelling effect argue that it will mitigate climate change by bringing more nutrient rich waters to the surface zones, which acts as a natural fertilizer, promoting phytoplankton growth without the use of additives. However the side effect of this technology, if adopted widely, will be higher rates of ocean acidification, as colder waters absorb much greater volumes of $CO_2$ than warmer waters.[57] In 2010 the parties adopted an 'Assessment Framework for Scientific Research Involving Ocean Fertilization'[58] which guides parties in assessing proposals for ocean fertilization research, and includes detailed environmental assessment rules. And in 2013 the parties to the London Protocol agreed on a new Article 6bis, which provides that parties shall not allow the placement of matter into the sea from vessels, aircraft, platforms or other man-made structures at sea for marine geoengineering purposes unless the activity is authorized under a permit.[59]

---

[52]   IMO Doc. LC-LP.1/Circ.5, 27 November 2006.
[53]   IMO Doc. LC 34/15, Annex 8, 2 November 2012.
[54]   Resolution LC-LP.1, 31 October 2008.
[55]   Ibid.
[56]   Phillip Williamson and Carol Turley, 'Ocean Acidification in a Geoengineering Context' (2012) 370 *Philosophical Transactions of the Royal Society A* 1974.
[57]   R.A. Feely et al., 'Evidence for Upwelling of Corrosive "Acidified" Water onto the Continental Shelf' (2008) 320 (No 5882) *Science* 1490.
[58]   Resolution LC-LP.2, 14 October 2010.
[59]   Resolution LP.4(8), 18 October 2013.

The other, related, regime dealing with marine pollution is built around the 1973 International Convention for the Prevention of Pollution from Ships as Modified by the Protocol of 1978 Relating Thereto (MARPOL).[60] MARPOL seeks 'to achieve the complete elimination of intentional pollution of the marine environment by oil and other harmful substances and the minimisation of accidental discharge of such substances.'[61] MARPOL combines a relatively short convention text with six compendious Annexes dealing, among other things, with prevention of pollution from oil, sewage, garbage and other substances, and also air pollution, including $CO_2$ emissions.

Annex VI addresses the 'Prevention of Air Pollution from Ships', and entered to force in May 2005. Unlike Annex I, which deals with oil pollution, Annex VI is not mandatory. However it has been fairly widely supported, with 75 contracting parties as at August 2014, accounting for almost 95 per cent of world merchant tonnage. Annex VI was added to MARPOL by a specific protocol in 1997, and initially only set limits on the sulphur and nitrous oxides (SOx and NOx) that may be emitted from ship exhausts. It also prohibited the deliberate discharge of ozone-depleting substances, many of which also have warming properties as greenhouse gases. The Annex VI emissions standards have become stricter over time. And in a very significant move, in 2011 the IMO adopted new mandatory technical and operational energy efficiency measures to reduce $CO_2$ and other greenhouse gas emissions from ships. These measures entered into force on 1 January 2013. This was a major development in terms of climate change mitigation policy, as it was the first time that there had been agreement to curb emissions, globally, across an entire transport sector. Shipping emissions account for around 2.7 per cent of global $CO_2$ emissions, and prior to the 2011 amendments being adopted, it was projected that $CO_2$ emissions from shipping would increase by up to 300 per cent by 2050.[62]

However, although the amendments to Annex VI are important, they will have a relatively small impact in controlling climate change and ocean acidification. Although shipping emissions are substantial, they are small by comparison with the main sources of $CO_2$, which are land-based fossil fuel consumption to generate electricity, and land-use change such as deforestation.

### 3.3.2 Global programme of action

The law of the sea can deal with ocean acidification only in a limited way, by controlling the intentional disposal of $CO_2$ into the oceans. However, this is always likely to be a fairly minor cause of the ocean acidification problem, which is primarily being driven by the natural uptake of $CO_2$ from the atmosphere as $CO_2$ concentrations increase.

The oceanic uptake of $CO_2$ can be conceptualized as either an atmospheric or terrestrial source pollution problem. We have seen that there is a well-developed collection of regimes applicable to atmospheric pollution at both regional and global

---

[60]   Opened for signature 17 February 1978, entered into force 2 October 1983, 1340 UNTS 62.

[61]   MARPOL, Preamble, 4th Recital.

[62]   *Oceans and the Law of the Sea: Report of the Secretary-General,* UN Doc A/64/66/Add.1 (25 November 2009), 349.

scales, although none of these currently address the impact of $CO_2$ pollution on the oceans. Nor are there any current frameworks for dealing with $CO_2$ pollution as a form of marine pollution originating from land-based activities. In this respect $CO_2$ is not different from many other land-based marine pollution problems that are very poorly regulated.

There is only one instrument of global application to land-based marine pollution – the Global Programme of Action for the Protection of the Marine Environment from Land-Based Activities (GPA).[63] The GPA is a non-binding plan of action adopted in 1995 by 108 states and the European Community. It provides guidance to national and regional authorities in developing and implementing plans to prevent, reduce, control and to eliminate the degradation of the marine environment from all land-based activities. Although the GPA is not binding, it does have the virtue of expressing specific targets for pollution reduction for nine source categories: sewage; persistent organic pollutants; radioactive substances; heavy metals; oils; nutrients; sediments; litter and physical alterations and destruction of habitats.

However, $CO_2$ emissions are not captured by any of the GPA pollution categories. VanderZwaag and Powers have noted that, as a consequence, there is considerable uncertainty as to whether the GPA has any real application to the marine environmental impacts of climate change.[64] In an opening paragraph, the GPA includes a general reference to the UNFCCC as one of several treaties that are relevant for the protection and preservation of the marine environment, but in the body of the text climate change is not identified as an area for attention by governments.

### 3.4  Biodiversity Conservation Regimes

#### 3.4.1  Convention on Biological Diversity

Ocean acidification carries major implications for biological diversity in the oceans, and this has been recognized in several decisions adopted by the Conference of the Parties to the 1992 Convention on Biological Diversity (CBD).[65] In 2008, at the ninth meeting of the Conference of the Parties, the parties noted the moratorium on ocean fertilization activities adopted under the auspices of the IMO, and urged all CBD parties to comply with it.[66] In a separate decision, the Conference of the Parties requested that all available scientific information on ocean acidification, including its effects on marine biodiversity, be compiled and synthesized and made available for

---

[63]  Global Programme of Action for the Protection of the Marine Environment from Land-based Activities, UNEP(OCA)/LBA/ IG.2/7, 1995. See further http://www.gpa.unep.org/ (last accessed 2 June 2015).

[64]  David VanderZwaag and Ann Powers, 'The Protection of the Marine Environment from Land-Based Pollution and Activities: Gauging the Tides of Global and Regional Governance', (2008) 23 *International Journal of Marine and Coastal Law* 423, at 439.

[65]  Opened for signature 5 June 1992, entered into force 29 December 1993, 1760 UNTS 79.

[66]  COP IX/16 Biodiversity and Climate Change, UNEP/CBD/COP/DEC/IX/16, 9 October 2008.

future Conferences of the Parties and meetings of the Subsidiary Body on Scientific, Technical and Technological Advice.[67]

This knowledge has been fed into several more recent initiatives within the CBD. In 2010, the 10th Conference of the Parties, adopted a strategic plan for biodiversity.[68] The plan is significant because it is the first time an effort has been made to set a specific target for addressing ocean acidification. In Target 10 the parties committed to a climate change and ocean acidification goal: '[b]y 2015, the multiple anthropogenic pressures on coral reefs, and other vulnerable ecosystems impacted by climate change or ocean acidification are minimized, so as to maintain their integrity and functioning.' More recently, in Decision XI/17, adopted in 2012, the Conference of the Parties adopted a list of Ecologically or Biologically Significant Marine Areas (ESBAs) which included the 'Western South Pacific high aragonite saturation state zone'. This area, located in the western south Pacific, in the South Equatorial Current, has the highest recorded saturation rates of aragonite and it may be the last marine area to drop below key pH thresholds. For this reason, the area was described as having 'special biological and ecological value' as a marine ecosystem 'where the impact from ocean acidification will be slowest and from which recovery may potentially be the quickest'.[69]

In sum, the focus of the CBD in relation to ocean acidification has primarily been upon the impacts of changing ocean chemistry upon coral reef ecosystems. The parties to the CBD have sought to improve planning, management and research to minimize the impacts of ocean acidification on the ocean environment. However, the CBD regime has not sought to go further than this by, for example, identifying an acceptable ocean pH threshold which should not be exceeded, and it defers to the UNFCCC for the adoption of measures to curb $CO_2$ emissions to address climate change and ocean acidification.

### 3.4.2   Regional biodiversity regimes

Within several regional biodiversity regimes ocean acidification has also been a subject of growing concern. The following discussion highlights two regional regimes applying to polar waters where attention has been given to the ocean acidification problem. This reflects the reality that these colder marine areas are feeling the impacts of ocean acidification much earlier than other regions.

In May 2013, the Arctic Council, which comprises the eight states with territorial north of the Arctic Circle, adopted a major new declaration on Arctic affairs, the *Kiruna Declaration*.[70] That declaration was adopted against the background of several major expert reports released prior to, and at the same time as, the 2013 Arctic Council

---

[67]   COP IX/20 Marine and Coastal Biodiversity, UNEP/CBD/COP/DEC/IX/20, 9 October 2008.

[68]   Cop X/2 The Strategic Plan for Biodiversity 2011-2020 and the Aichi Biodiversity Targets, UNEP/CBD/COP/DEC/X/2, 29 October 2010.

[69]   COP XI/17 Marine and Coastal Biodiversity: Ecologically or Biologically Significant Marine Areas, UNEP/CBD/COP/DEC/XI/17, 5 December 2012, Table 1.

[70]   See http://www.uarctic.org/Arctic-Council_Kiruna_declaration_2013_9UVgQ.pdf.file (last accessed 2 June 2015).

Meeting, including the *Arctic Ocean Acidification Assessment*[71] and the broader *Arctic Ocean Review*.[72] The *Kiruna Declaration* includes relatively strong language on ocean acidification, stating that the Arctic Council members:

> **Welcome** the Arctic Ocean Acidification assessment, **approve** its recommendations, **note** with concern the potential impacts of acidification on marine life and people that are dependent on healthy marine ecosystems, **recognize** that carbon dioxide emission reductions are the only effective way to mitigate ocean acidification, and **request** the Arctic States to continue to take action on mitigation and adaptation and to monitor and assess the state of Arctic Ocean acidification.

The *Arctic Ocean Acidification Assessment* included three recommendations to the Arctic Council, namely that it: (1) urge member states, observer countries, and the global society to reduce the emission of carbon dioxide as a matter of urgency; (2) call for enhanced research and monitoring efforts that expand understanding of acidification processes and their effects on Arctic marine ecosystems and northern societies that depend on them; and (3) urge its member states to implement adaptation strategies that address all aspects of Arctic change, including ocean acidification, tailored to local and societal needs.

In the Southern Ocean, ocean acidification is beginning to be considered by the Commission for the Conservation of Antarctic Marine Living Resources, which was established by the 1980 Convention on the Conservation of Antarctic Marine Living Resources (CCAMLR).[73] CCAMLR is part of the broader Antarctic Treaty System (ATS), and was originally devised primarily to manage stocks of krill. However it also seeks to promote the sustainable management of a host of species in the Southern Ocean, and the Antarctic marine ecosystem more broadly. CCAMLR's overarching objective is 'the conservation of Antarctic marine living resources'[74] including 'fin fish, molluscs, crustaceans and all other species of living organisms'.[75] This objective and the specific reference to shell-forming organisms is significant from the perspective of ocean acidification given the particular susceptibility of molluscs and crustaceans to changing carbon chemistry.

---

[71] Arctic Monitoring and Assessment Programme, *Arctic Ocean Acidification Assessment: Summary for Policy-makers* (AMAP, Oslo, 2013).

[72] *Arctic Ocean Review: Final Report* (Protection of the Arctic Marine Environment (PAME) Secretariat, Akureyri, 2013). For a discussion of possible governance responses to climate change in the Arctic Ocean see Rosemary Rayfuse, 'Melting Moments: The Future of Polar Oceans Governance in a Warming World' (2007) 16 *Review of European Community and International Environmental Law* 196. See also David VanderZwaag and Tim Stephens (eds), *Polar Oceans Governance in an Era of Environmental Change* (Edward Elgar, Cheltenham, 2014).

[73] Opened for signature 20 May 1980, entered into force 7 April 1982, (1980) 19 *International Legal Materials* 841.

[74] CCAMLR, Art. 2(1).

[75] Ibid, Art. 1(2).

For several years ocean acidification has been discussed within the CCAMLR Scientific Committee,[76] which advises the Commission on the best available science on the state of the Antarctic marine ecosystem, however quite remarkably ocean acidification has not attracted significant attention within the Commission itself. Being part of the ATS, CCAMLR also has the benefit of advice from the Scientific Committee on Antarctic Research (SCAR), which provides independent scientific advice to Antarctic Treaty Consultative Meetings (ATCMs). SCAR recently published its 'Antarctic Climate Change and the Environment Report' which includes extensive discussion of ocean acidification in the Southern Ocean.[77] SCAR has an Action Group on Ocean Acidification, and also an Expert Group on Antarctic Climate Change and the Environment which prepares annual climate change updates to the ATCMs and to CCAMLR.

Despite the high level of awareness among the Antarctic science community, ocean acidification has not been considered in any significant way by the CCAMLR Commission. This is despite the growing evidence, synthesized by the CCAMLR Scientific Committee itself,[78] that increased $CO_2$ levels may have serious impacts upon stocks of krill, which are the basis of the Antarctic food chain.

## 4.   A UNFCCC PROTOCOL ON OCEAN ACIDIFICATION?

Ocean acidification exists in an international legal twilight zone and its causes and consequences are peripherally, or potentially, regulated by multiple regimes (see Table 20.1, below). However, there is not, and is not likely to be, an omnibus regime that addresses the underlying systemic causes of ocean acidification – the anthropogenic disturbance of the carbon cycle, which is having impacts upon several environmental spheres: the atmosphere, through climate change; the hydrosphere, through increasing rates of evaporation and precipitation, and ocean acidification; and the biosphere, as species and ecosystems are affected by climate change and ocean acidification.

Designing an appropriate regime to respond to ocean acidification and the disturbance of the carbon cycle more generally seems a Sisyphean task. Earth scientists describe the current geological epoch not by its conventional stratigraphic title, the Holocene, but instead as the 'Anthropocene'[79] in reference to the extent of human influence upon the global environment. Human activities have changed the composition of the atmosphere, introduced ineradicable chemical and nuclear contaminants, set in motion the melting of the cryosphere, altered the chemistry of the oceans, fragmented

---

[76]   See, eg, *Report of the Thirty-First Meeting of the Scientific Committee for the Conservation of Antarctic Marine Living Resources* (2012), 182–3 (examining ocean acidification impacts on krill biology).

[77]   John Turner et al., 'Antarctic Climate Change and the Environment: An Update' (2014) 50 *Polar Record* 237.

[78]   S. Kawaguchi et al., 'Impacts of Ocean Acidification on Antarctic Krill Biology: Preliminary Results and Future Research Directions' CCAMLR WG-EMM-12/32 (2012).

[79]   Jan Zalasiewicz et al., 'The Anthropocene: A New Epoch of Geological Time' (2011) 369 *Philosophical Transactions of the Royal Society A* 835.

*Table 20.1   Cross section of key treaty regimes of potential relevance for regulating ocean acidification*

| REGIME | SCOPE OF APPLICATION |
| --- | --- |
| Climate Regime | Addresses atmospheric carbon, but is not a constitution for global carbon cycle and does not apply directly to ocean acidification |
| UN Convention on Law of the Sea | Contains general obligations to protect marine environment from pollution (Art. 1(4)), from any source (Art. 194(1)) |
| MARPOL | Regulates vessel source marine pollution, including air pollution from ships (Annex VI amendments impose limits on $CO_2$ emissions from vessels) |
| London Protocol | Regulates dumping of pollutants at sea, allows undersea storage of $CO_2$ and places moratorium on ocean fertilization |
| Global Programme of Action (soft-law instrument) | Seeks to control terrestrial (including atmospheric) source marine pollution, but $CO_2$ not referred to |
| Conv. on Long Range Trans. Air Pollution | $SO_2$ and acid rain. Not applicable to $CO_2$ |
| Convention on the Conservation of Antarctic Marine Living Resources | Cold waters fishery regime (Scientific Committee, consideration but no Conservation Measures adopted in response to ocean acidification) |

*Source:*   Author.

major water basins, damaged or destroyed many biodiverse habitats, and driven the Holocene extinction event. Virtually every component of the Earth's environment, including the lithosphere – the rocky outer layer of the Earth – has felt the influence of *homo sapiens*.

If the scale of the changes to the Earth's subsurface, surface and atmosphere seems too great to fathom, then the idea that international law is capable of moderating human influence on the global environment also appears beyond imagining. The growing field of 'Earth Systems Science' has helped to integrate scientific investigation of Earth systems and their interaction, and where 'planetary boundaries' of habitability may lie.[80] Some scholars within the social sciences have begun to consider how global governance mechanisms and institutions can address the anthropogenic planetary transformations that are the hallmark of the Anthropocene. For instance, researchers within the 'Earth Systems Governance Project' have advanced arguments for a step-change in global environmental governance akin to the 'Charter moment' that marked the establishment of the United Nations system of collective security following the Second World War.[81]

---

[80]   Roger M. Gifford et al., *To Live Within Earth's Limits: An Australian Plan to Develop a Science of the Whole Earth System* (Australian Academy of Science, 2010).

[81]   F. Biermann et al., 'Navigating the Anthropocene: Improving Earth System Governance' (2012) 335 *Science* 1306; F. Biermann et al., 'Transforming Governance and Institutions for Global Sustainability: Key Insights from the Earth System Governance Project' (2012) 4 *Current Opinion in Environmental Sustainability* 51.

Whether this is achievable remains doubtful given that it would require the almost complete transformation of a dense body of existing norms and institutions. What is certainly achievable, however, are several concrete measures that would improve the visibility of the ocean acidification problem in international environmental law.

The first, and more urgent priority, is to improve the level of scientific knowledge of the ocean acidification challenge at global, regional, national and local scales. In a similar manner to climate change research, which has examined atmospheric sensitivity to certain concentrations of greenhouse gases, this research needs to identify oceanic sensitivity to atmospheric concentrations of $CO_2$, the rate of ocean acidification, and its impacts upon species and ecosystems. In a promising development, the Inter-governmental Panel on Climate Change in its Fifth Assessment Report for the first time considered ocean acidification in some detail.[82] However, ocean-specific studies of similar scale and stature are required, and this is beginning to be recognized through processes such as the United Nations World Ocean Assessment.[83]

Second, there needs to be comprehensive assessments of the effects of ocean acidification on national economies, and in respect of vulnerable economic sectors (such as fisheries, and tourism).[84] Such assessments could be built upon existing work carried out in respect of climate change, as there has already been extensive consideration given to the economic costs of climate change to a number of marine sectors and industries, including fisheries.[85]

The third step, only possible on the basis of sound scientific and economic analysis, is global agreement upon an acceptable pH threshold or range. Such agreement could take varying forms. It could for instance be expressed in a Resolution or Declaration on Ocean Acidification adopted by the United Nations General Assembly. Another soft-law approach could be to follow the practice in the climate change context, and agree upon an instrument akin to the Copenhagen Accord, which includes a temperature target. In this respect, the Accord notes the 'scientific view that the increase in global temperature should be kept below 2 degrees Celsius'.

Fourth, amendments will be needed to the UNFCCC and the Kyoto Protocol to recalibrate several aspects of the climate regime. As Gattuso et al. observe in their comprehensive assessment of the compounding climate and acidification threats to the oceans, 'any new global agreement that does not minimize the impacts on the oceans will be incomplete and inadequate.'[86] Key changes needed are the removal of incentives to utilize the oceans as carbon sinks, and, crucially, to place higher priority upon reducing emissions of $CO_2$ over other greenhouse gases. Ideally, the climate regime should include a mechanism for including an appropriate atmospheric $CO_2$ benchmark that addresses both climate change and ocean acidification goals. Neither the UNFCCC nor the Kyoto Protocol currently include a temperature target, let alone an atmospheric

---

[82]   IPCC, *Climate Change 2013: Impacts, Adaptation and Vulnerability. Contribution of Working Group II to the Fifth Assessment Report of the Intergovernmental Panel on Climate Change* (Cambridge University Press Cambridge 2013) Vol I, Chapter 6 'Ocean Systems'.

[83]   See http://www.worldoceanassessment.org/ (last accessed 2 June 2015).

[84]   See, eg, Mathis et al., above n 3.

[85]   See, eg, Edward A. Allison et al., 'Vulnerability of National Economies to the Impacts of Climate Change on Fisheries' (2009) 10 *Fish and Fisheries* 173.

[86]   Gattuso et al., above n 14, 52.

$CO_2$ concentration target. However, the LRTAP and MARPOL regimes indicate the feasibility of including evidence-based environmental thresholds and targets, and a similar approach could conceivably be adopted in the climate change regime context. There is a significant opportunity for this to occur in the present context because of the ongoing discussions towards an agreement that would replace or supplement the climate regime by 2015.

Given that it is the main forum in which $CO_2$ emissions reductions are being discussed, the climate regime remains the most relevant mechanism by which the cause of ocean acidification can be addressed. It is not possible (or desirable) to de-link ocean acidification from climate change in the global policy response, and for this reason proposals for ocean acidification to be addressed by a single, standalone, instrument, for instance through a protocol to the LOSC, are misplaced.[87] While the climate regime is the main arena in which ocean acidification can be addressed, it is clearly not the only treaty regime of relevance and an effective and integrated legal and policy response will require interventions across the broad patchwork of environmental regimes discussed in this chapter.

## 5. CONCLUSION

Throughout its history, international environmental law has developed in a mostly reactive way to address specific environmental problems, and in many areas this has yielded positive results (such as the successful control of vessel-sourced oil pollution of the marine environment). However, ocean acidification exemplifies the challenge of global environmental governance in the Anthropocene, as it involves interference with a global environmental system – the carbon cycle. It is not an environmental issue such as nuclear waste, heavy metal pollution, acid rain, and many other discrete by-products of industrial development, that are solvable by limited and technical interventions that have been the hallmark of domestic and international environmental law-making since the 1970s. Instead it demands a broader, 'Earth Systems', approach, that needs to be delivered across multiple, intersecting, environmental regimes.[88]

This chapter has surveyed the range of international environmental regimes that have some application to the ocean acidification problem, highlighting treaty systems that are currently hindering an effective response, and those where there are significant opportunities for further amendment and development to deal with the 'other $CO_2$ problem'. For all the weaknesses of the climate regime, and despite the dangers of adding a new and complex type of environmental change to the crowded agenda before climate negotiators, it remains the 'main game'. This is because it is the central arena in which the global community is discussing $CO_2$ emissions abatement of the scale

---

[87] See, eg, Verónica González, 'An Alternative Approach for Addressing $CO_2$-Driven Ocean Acidification' (2012) 12 *Sustainable Development Law and Policy* 45; Rakhyun E. Kim, 'Is a New Multilateral Environmental Agreement on Ocean Acidification Necessary?' (2012) 12 *Review of European Community and International Environmental Law* 258.

[88] See generally Frank Biermann, *Earth System Governance: World Politics in the Anthropocene* (MIT Press, 2014).

necessary to have the required impact upon oceanic pH levels. However, there is also significant opportunity for developments within other environmental regimes to add momentum to the climate negotiations, by enabling further scientific research, and, as has been seen in the context of both the CBD and the Arctic Council, by being conduits for clear statements of the need to reduce $CO_2$ emissions as a matter of urgency.

# 21. Geoengineering and the marine environment

*Karen N. Scott*

## 1. INTRODUCTION

Climate change arguably constitutes the greatest long-term threat to the health of our oceans. The IPCC Fifth Assessment Report on Climate Change (Working Group I) concludes that it is virtually certain that the upper ocean (above 700 m) has warmed between 1971 and 2010, and that it is likely that this trend began in the 1870s.[1] Moreover, the Report also indicates that climate change has likely impacted upon ocean salinity levels and has led to changes in water circulation and ocean biochemistry, notably, decreasing the pH level of the oceans.[2] It is estimated that ocean acidity has increased by thirty per cent since the beginning of the Industrial Revolution[3] and it is predicted that ocean acidity could increase by 150 per cent by 2050.[4] Global mean sea level has risen by 0.19 m between 1901 and 2010[5] and the extent of Arctic Ocean ice-coverage reached an all-time minimum in September 2012.[6] A warmer and increasingly acidic ocean is likely to significantly impact ecosystems and vulnerable species. Coral bleaching is probably the most visible impact of a warmer ocean[7] but climate change has already been associated with variations in the distribution and abundance of fish[8] and phytoplankton.[9] Ocean acidification presents a significant risk

---

[1]  M. Rhein et al., 'Observations: Ocean' in T.F. Stocker (ed.) et al., *Climate Change 2013: The Physical Science Basis. Contribution of Working Group I to the Fifth Assessment Report of the Intergovernmental Panel on Climate Change* (Cambridge University Press 2013) 257 (hereinafter, IPCC 5th Assessment Report). See also John M. Lyman, Simon A. Good, Victor V. Gouretski et al., 'Robust warming of the global upper ocean' (2010) 465 *Nature* 334.

[2]  IPCC 5th Assessment Report, ibid, 257–9.

[3]  Secretariat of the Convention on Biological Diversity, *Scientific Synthesis of the Impacts of Ocean Acidification on Marine Biodiversity* (Technical Series No. 46) (Montreal: Secretariat of the Convention on Biological Diversity, 2009), 9.

[4]  Ibid.

[5]  IPCC 5th Assessment Report, above n 1, 258.

[6]  J. Cohen, J. Jones, J.C. Furtado and E. Tziperman, 'Warm Arctic, cold continents: A common pattern related to Arctic sea ice melt, snow advance and extreme winter weather' (2013) 26 *Oceanography* http://dx.doi.org/10.5670/oceanog.2013.70. See also V.N. Livina and T.M. Lenton, 'A recent tipping point in the Arctic sea-ice cover: abrupt and persistent increase in the seasonal cycle since 2007' (2013) 7 *The Cryosphere* 275.

[7]  Barbara E. Brown, 'Coral bleaching: causes and consequences' (1997) 16 (Suppl.) *Coral Reefs* S129.

[8]  M.J. Salinger, 'A brief introduction to the issue of climate and marine fisheries' (2013) 119 *Climatic Change* 23.

[9]  Séverine Alvain, Corinne Le Quéré, Laurent Bopp et al., 'Rapid climatic driven shifts of diatoms at high latitudes' (2013) 132 *Remote Sensing of Environment* 195.

to calcifying marine organisms as well as coral and coastal defences[10] and is a particular threat to the Arctic Ocean ecosystem.[11]

However, increasingly, the oceans are being characterized as a potential solution to, rather than simply a victim of, climate change. Constituting the largest natural reservoir of carbon dioxide,[12] $CO_2$ is naturally transferred from the surface of the ocean to deep water by means of ocean circulation through the biological and solubility pumps.[13] Scientists and engineers have postulated that if either or both of these pumps could be enhanced, in order to draw down greater quantities of $CO_2$ into the deep ocean, this would operate as an effective climate change mitigation measure. The deliberate, large scale manipulation of environmental systems for the purpose of climate change mitigation, of which the enhancement of the oceans' biological and solubility pumps represent an example par excellence, is commonly termed geoengineering.[14] By no means confined to the oceans – geoengineering strategies have been proposed to manipulate the biosphere, the atmosphere and even solar radiation levels in outer space[15] – it is nevertheless within the marine environment that geoengineering research is most advanced. As such, it is unsurprising that legal and policy initiatives associated with marine geoengineering are also relatively advanced and, in the case of one strategy – ocean fertilization – a nascent regulatory regime is emerging.

This chapter will critically assess marine geoengineering as a novel and controversial use of the marine environment from the perspective of the law of the sea. It will begin with an assessment of the first and thus far, only, regulatory framework specifically designed to manage a subset of geoengineering activities, ocean fertilization: the 2013 amendments to the 1996 Protocol[16] to the 1972 London (Dumping) Convention.[17] The chapter will explore the extent to which the new framework developed in these amendments provides an appropriate and robust response to the environmental and ethical challenges posed by ocean fertilization activities. In light of the fact that the 2013 amendments are not yet in force and will, once they enter into force, bind only a relatively few states in respect of a very narrow range of geoengineering activities, this

---

[10]   Scott C. Doney et al., 'Ocean acidification: a critical emerging problem for the oceans' (2009) 22 *Oceanography* 16, 18. See also, Tim Stephens, 'Ocean acidification', Chapter 20 in this volume.

[11]   C.P.D. Brussard, A.A.M. Noordeloos, H. Witte et al., 'Arctic microbial community dynamics influenced by elevated $CO_2$ levels' (2013) 10 *Biogeosciences* 719.

[12]   Secretariat of the Convention on Biological Diversity, *Scientific Synthesis of the Impacts of Ocean Fertilization on marine Biodiversity*, above n 3, 9.

[13]   Ibid.

[14]   David W. Keith, 'Geoengineering the climate: history and prospect' (2000) 25 *Annual Review of Energy and the Environment* 245, 247.

[15]   For an introduction to geoengineering strategies generally see Naomi E. Vaughan and Timothy M. Lenton, 'A review of climate geoengineering proposals' (2011) 109 *Climatic Change* 745.

[16]   1996 Protocol to the 1972 London Dumping Convention, (adopted 8 November 1996, entered into force 24 March 2006) (1997) 36 *International Legal Materials* 7 (London Protocol). The 2013 amendments have not yet entered into force.

[17]   1972 Convention on the Prevention of Marine Pollution by Dumping of Wastes and other Matter (adopted 29 December 1972, entered into force 30 August 1975) (1972) 11 *International Legal Materials* 1358 (London Convention).

chapter will then go on to examine the broader rights and responsibilities incumbent on states under the 1982 United Nations Convention on the Law of the Sea (LOSC)[18] and the dumping regime with respect to marine geoengineering activities more generally. In particular, this chapter will explore the extent to which global obligations to protect the marine environment and to control scientific research provide appropriate tools for managing the risks posed by geoengineering. Finally, the chapter will conclude with some thoughts on the risks of developing a regulatory regime for geoengineering under the law of the sea in isolation from a broader ethical debate over the relationship between geoengineering, emissions reductions and climate change mitigation more generally.

## 2. GEOENGINEERING THE MARINE ENVIRONMENT

The transition of geoengineering from the fringes to the mainstream of scientific and, increasingly, policy debate arguably began with the publication of an article by Nobel laureate Paul J. Crutzen in 2006 in which he advocated the injection of sulphur into the stratosphere in order to reflect sunlight and thus cool the planet.[19] However, the manipulation of weather and climate for anthropogenic purposes has a much longer history[20] and 'geoengineering' as a term of art was first coined in 1977.[21] Nevertheless, the revival of geoengineering-related research over the last few years owes much to an increasing loss of faith among states, scientists and policy-makers in the climate change regime. Despite the agreement of 195 states to stabilize 'greenhouse gas concentrations in the atmosphere at a level that would prevent dangerous anthropogenic interference with the climate system' under Article 2 of the 1992 United Nations Convention on Climate Change (UNFCCC),[22] and the specific targets accepted by most developed states under the 1997 Kyoto Protocol,[23] greenhouse gas emissions actually *increased* by 40 per cent between 1992 and 2008.[24] In May 2013, atmospheric concentrations of

---

[18]   1982 United Nations Convention on the Law of the Sea (1982) (adopted 10 December 1982, entered into force 16 November 1994) 1833 UNTS 3 (LOSC).

[19]   P.J. Crutzen, 'Albedo enhancement by stratospheric sulfur injections: a contribution to resolve a policy dilemma?' (2006) 77 *Climatic Change* 211.

[20]   See James Rodger Fleming, *Fixing the Sky. The Checkered History of Weather and Climate Control* (Columbia University Press 2010) and David W. Keith, 'Geoengineering the climate: history and prospect' (2000) 25 *Annual Review of Energy and the Environment* 245.

[21]   Cesare Marchetti, 'On geoengineering and the $CO_2$ problem' (1977) 1 *Climatic Change* 59.

[22]   1992 UN Framework Convention on Climate Change (entered in force 21 March 1994) (1992) 31 *International Legal Materials* (1992) 851.

[23]   1997 Protocol to the Framework Convention on Climate Change (Kyoto Protocol) (entered into force 18 June 2001) (1998) 37 *International Legal Materials* 22.

[24]   Ian Allison et al., *The Copenhagen Diagnosis* (The University of New South Wales Climate Change Research Centre 2009), 7.

$CO_2$ officially reached 400 parts per million (ppm),[25] an increase from approximately 280 ppm at the onset of the Industrial Revolution,[26] and are now higher than at any point in the last 3 to 5 million years.[27] Moreover, the IPCC Fifth Assessment Report (Working Group I) has recently concluded that '[a] large fraction of anthropogenic climate change resulting from $CO_2$ emissions is irreversible on a multi-century to millennial time scale, except in the case of a large net removal of $CO_2$ from the atmosphere over a sustained period'.[28] It is consequently unsurprising, perhaps even inevitable, that 'Plan B' – in the form of geoengineering – is now the subject of tentative but serious consideration by scientists, commentators, governments[29] and international organizations. Even the IPCC Fifth Assessment Report (Working Group I) acknowledged the existence of geoengineering proposals although the authors expressed scepticism as to their long-term effectiveness owing to a lack of evidence.[30]

Divided into two categories, geoengineering technologies are designed either to remove $CO_2$ from the atmosphere or to manage solar radiation. Techniques aimed at the removal of $CO_2$ from the atmosphere (CDR) primarily focus on enhancing or expanding mechanisms that naturally perform this function. Examples include afforestation or reforestation,[31] soil-carbon

---

[25] 'Global carbon dioxide in atmosphere passes milestone level' *The Guardian*, 10 May 2013.

[26] Michael R. Raupach et al., 'Global and regional drivers of accelerating $CO_2$ emissions' (2007) 104 *Proceedings of the National Academy of Sciences* 10288, 10288.

[27] Ian Allison et al., above n 24, 9.

[28] IPCC Fifth Assessment Report, Working Group I, Summary for Policy Makers, 20.

[29] See for example reports issued in the UK: Living with Environmental Change (LWEC) Geoengineering Report: *A forward look for UK research on climate impacts of geoengineering* (by Chris Jones, Phil Williamson, Jim Hayward et al.) (2013) for the Department of Energy and Climate Change; The Royal Society (UK), *Geoengineering the climate. Science, governance and uncertainty* (Royal Society Policy Document 10/09/2009); the Fourth Report of Session 2008–09 of the House of Commons, Innovation, Universities, Science and Skills Committee, *Engineering: turning ideas into reality, Volume 1* (HC 50-1); *Government Response to the Committee's Fourth Report* (House of Commons Innovation, Universities, Science and Skills Committee, *Engineering: turning ideas into reality: Government Response to the Committee's Fourth Report* (Fifth Special Report of Session 2008–09, HC 759); House of Commons Science and Technology Committee, *The Regulation of Geoengineering* (Fifth Report of Session 2009–10) (HC 221); *Government Response to the House of Commons Science and Technology Committee 5th Report of Session 2009–10: The Regulation of Geoengineering* Cm 7936. See also reports issued in the US: Kelsi Bracmort, Richard K. Lattanzio and Emily Barbour, *Geoengineering: Governance and Technology Policy* (Congressional Research Service Report for Congress, R41371, 2010); Chairman Bart Gordon, Committee on Science and Technology, US House of Representatives, *Engineering the Climate: Research Needs and Strategies for International Coordination Report* (111 Congress, Second Session, October 2010).

[30] IPCC Fifth Assessment Report, Working Group I, Summary for Policy Makers, 21.

[31] See Josep G. Canadell and Michael R. Raupach, 'Managing forests for climate change mitigation' (2008) 320 *Science* 1456; Leonard Ornstein, Igor Aleinov and David Rind, 'Irrigated afforestation of the Sahara and Australian Outback to end global warming' (2009) 97 *Climatic Change* 409; Kenneth R. Richards and Carrie Stokes, 'A review of forest carbon sequestration cost strategies: a dozen years of research' (2004) 63 *Climatic Change* 1; Brent Sohngen, 'Forestry Carbon Sequestration' in Bjørn Lomborg, *Smart Solutions to Climate Change.*

sequestration,[32] the use of $CO_2$ absorbing algae on building surfaces[33] and even the capture and storage of atmospheric $CO_2$ by artificial 'trees'.[34] By contrast, solar radiation management (SRM) techniques are not designed to reduce atmospheric concentrations of $CO_2$. Rather, they attempt to offset the temperature increases associated with climate change through reflecting sunlight back into space or deflecting it from the Earth altogether. Techniques range from the benign but likely ineffective urban albedo enhancement[35] to the rather more ambitious whitening of marine clouds[36] or the stratosphere in order to reflect solar radiation back into space.[37] The most radical ideas seek to deflect rather than reflect solar radiation through the placement of strategic mirrors or sunshades between the earth and the sun or in orbit around the earth.[38]

---

*Comparing Costs and Benefits* (CUP 2010) 114; Massimo Tavoni, Brent Sohngen and Valentina Bosetti, 'Forestry and the carbon market response to stabilize climate' (2007) 35 *Energy Policy* 5346.

[32] See Raj K. Shrestha and Rattan Lal, 'Ecosystem carbon budgeting and soil carbon sequestration in reclaimed mine soil' (2006) 32 *Environment International* 781.

[33] Eduardo Jacob-Lobes, Carols Henrique Gimenes Scoparo and Telma Teixeira Franco, 'Rates of $CO_2$ removal by *Aphanothece microscopic Nägeli* in tubular photobioreactors' (2008) 47 *Chemical Engineering and Processing* 1365.

[34] K.S. Lackner, 'Capture of carbon dioxide from ambient air' (2009) 176 *The European Physical Journal, Special Topics* 93.

[35] Hashem Akbari, Surabi Menon and Arthur Rosenfeld, 'Global cooling: increasing world-wide urban albedos to offset $CO_2$' (2009) 94 *Climatic Change* 275, 277 and Robert M. Hamwey, 'Active amplification of the terrestrial albedo to mitigate climate change: an exploratory study' (2007) 12 *Mitigation and Adaptation Strategies for Global Change* 419.

[36] John Latham et al., 'Global temperature stabilization via controlled albedo enhancement of low-level maritime clouds' (2008) 366 *Philosophical Transactions of the Royal Society A* 3969; Stephen Salter, Graham Sortino and John Latham, 'Sea-going hardware for the cloud albedo method of reversing global warming' (2008) 366 *Philosophical Transactions of the Royal Society A* 3989.

[37] P.J. Crutzen, above n 19; Robert E. Dickinson, 'Climate engineering: a review of aerosol approaches to changing the global energy balance' (1996) 33 *Climatic Change* 279; Yu A. Izrael, 'Field experiment on studying solar radiation passing through aerosol layers' (2009) 34 *Russian Meterology and Hydrology* 265; Philip J. Rasch et al., 'An overview of geoengineering of climate using stratospheric sulphate aerosols' (2008) 366 *Philosophical Transactions of the Royal Society A* 4007; Alan Robock, Luke Oman and Georgiy L. Stenchikov, 'Regional climate responses to geoengineering with tropical and Arctic $SO_2$ injections' (2008) 113 *Journal of Geophysical Research* D16101; A.F. Tuck et al., 'On geoengineering with sulphate aerosols in the tropical upper troposphere and lower stratosphere' (2008) 90 *Climatic Change* 315.

[38] See Roger Angel, 'Feasibility of cooling the earth with a cloud of small spacecraft near the inner Legrange point (L1)' (2006) 103(46) *Proceedings of the National Academy of Sciences* 17184; James Early, 'Space-based solar shield to offset greenhouse effect' (1989) 42 *Journal of the British Planetary Society* 567; Takanobu Kosugi, 'Role of sunshades in space as a climate control option' (2010) 67 *Acta Astronautica* 241; D.J. Lunt et al., '"Sunshade World": a fully coupled CGM evaluation of the climatic impacts of geoengineering' (2008) 35 *Geophysical Research Letters* L12710; C.R. McInnes, 'Space-based geoengineering: challenges and requirements' (2010) 224(3) *Proceedings of the Institute of Mechanical Engineers, Part C: Journal of Mechanical Engineering Science* 571; Jerome Pearson, John Oldson and Eugene Levin, 'Earth rings for planetary environment control' (2006) 58 *Acta Astronautica* 44.

Ocean-based geoengineering has thus far largely focused on CDR rather than SRM, although at least one proposal purports to enhance the ocean's surface albedo through the creation of reflective microbubbles in the sea.[39] The technique which has benefited from the most significant attention to date seeks to enhance the ocean's biological pump and increase the draw-down of $CO_2$ from surface waters to the ocean's depths. This strategy exploits the fact that particular regions, most notably the Southern Ocean and the Equatorial Pacific, are relatively unproductive in biological terms owing to the low availability of nutrients such as iron, nitrogen or phosphate.[40] In 1990 scientist John Martin postulated that iron dust artificially added to these regions would stimulate biological productivity, creating algal blooms, which would draw down $CO_2$ from the ocean's surface into its depths where it would be sequestered for hundreds if not thousands of years.[41] The results from both natural[42] and artificially induced fertilization confirm that plankton biomass responds to the addition of iron, and that surface levels of $CO_2$ are temporarily reduced.[43] However, the extent to which $CO_2$ has actually been drawn down and sequestered within the deep ocean as a result of the thirteen official ocean fertilization experiments to date is variable.[44] More generally, it is unclear how large the fertilized area needs to be in order to draw down a meaningful quantity of $CO_2$[45] and it is uncertain as to how long the sequestration of $CO_2$ lasts for, compromising its potential effectiveness as a climate change mitigation measure.[46] Potential unintended impacts of ocean fertilization include the introduction of toxic

---

[39]   Russell Seitz, 'Bright water: hydrosols, water conservation and climate change' (2011) 105 *Climatic Change* 365.

[40]   H.J.W. de Baar and P.W. Boyd, 'The Role of Iron in Plankton Ecology and Carbon Dioxide Transfer of the Global Oceans' in Roger B. Hansen et al. (eds) *The Changing Ocean Carbon Cycle: A Midterm Synthesis of the Joint Global Ocean Flux Study* (CUP 2000) 61, 107; Robert A. Duce and Neil W. Tindale, 'Atmospheric transport of iron and its deposition in the ocean' (1991) 36 *Limnology and Oceanography* 1715.

[41]   John H. Martin, 'Glacial-interglacial $CO_2$ change: the iron hypothesis' (1990) 5 *Paleoceanography* 1. See also, Nicolas Cassar et al., 'The Southern Ocean biological response to Aeolian iron deposition,' (2007) 317 *Science* 1067 and P.W. Boyd, J. Jickells, C.S. Law et al., 'Mesoscale iron enrichment experiments 1993–2005: synthesis and future directions' (2007) 315 *Science* 612.

[42]   George A. Wolf, David S.M. Billett, Brian J. Bett et al., 'The effects of natural iron fertilization on deep-sea ecology: the Crozet Plateau, Southern Indian Ocean' (2010) 6(6) *Public Library of Science One* e29697.

[43]   Philip Williamson, Douglas W.R. Wallace, Cliff Law et al., 'Ocean fertilization for geoengineering: a review of effectiveness, environmental impacts and emerging governance' (2012) 90 *Process Safety and Environmental Protection* 475, 477.

[44]   Ibid. See also CBD, *Scientific Synthesis of the Impacts of Ocean Fertilization on Marine Biodiversity,* above n 3.

[45]   K. Buesseler et al., 'The effects of iron fertilization on carbon sequestration in the Southern Ocean' (2004) 304 *Science* 417.

[46]   S. Blain, 'Effect of natural iron fertilization on carbon sequestration in the Southern Ocean' (2007) 446 *Nature* 1070; P. Boyd et al., 'A mesocale phytoplankton bloom in the polar Southern Ocean stimulated by iron fertilization' (2000) 407 *Nature* 695; K. Caldeira and P. Duffy, 'The role of the Southern Ocean in uptake and storage of anthropogenic carbon dioxide' (2000) 287 *Science* 620; Patrick Martin et al., 'Iron fertilization enhanced net community production but not downward particle flux during the Southern Ocean iron fertilization experiment LOHAFEX'

algae,[47] disruption of the ecosystem food chain,[48] oxygen depletion, ocean acidification[49] and the release of gases such as methane and nitrous oxide.[50] Iron is by no means the only nutrient suggested by proponents of ocean fertilization. Other options include the artificial addition of volcanic ash,[51] phosphate[52] and urea[53] to the oceans and the utilization of vertical pipes to pump deep water nutrients to the surface.[54]

Marine-based geoengineering proposals are not however, confined to ocean fertilization. Less well-publicized proposals include the disposal of baled crop residues in the deep ocean[55] and so-called macroalgal afforestation: the creation of macroalgal forests (comprising kelp and other seaweeds) which store $CO_2$ and can be utilized in the production of biofuels.[56] Other proposals focus on enhancing the solubility as opposed to the biological ocean pump, which also transports $CO_2$ from the surface to the depths of the ocean, and seek to strengthen down-welling currents through the modification of sea-ice – technologically and economically unfeasible[57] or increasing ocean alkalinity through the addition of limestone powder or soda ash.[58] Known as 'weathering', this latter technique is not only designed to increase the ocean's capacity to store atmospheric $CO_2$ but it also aims to reduce the effects of the 'other' climate change

---

(2013) 27 *Global Biogeochemical Cycles* 1; Victor Smetacek et al., 'Deep carbon export from a Southern Ocean iron-fertilized diatom bloom' (2012) 487 *Nature* 313.

[47]   Q. Schiermeier, 'The oresmen' (2003) 421 *Nature* 109, 110.

[48]   A. Strong, 'Ocean fertilization: time to move on' (2009) 461 *Nature* 347.

[49]   Phillip Williamson, Douglas W.R. Wallace, Cliff Law et al., above n 43, 480–8. See also H. Damon Matthews et al., 'Sensitivity of ocean acidification to geoengineered climate stabilization' (2009) 36 *Geophysical Research Letters* L10706 DOI: 10.1029/2009/GL037488.

[50]   J. Furhman and D. Capone, 'Possible biogeochemical consequences of ocean fertilization' (1991) 36 *Limnology & Oceanography* 1951; M. Lawrence, 'Side-effects of ocean iron fertilization' (2002) 297 *Science* 1993.

[51]   Svend Duggen, P. Croot, Ulrike Schacht et al., 'Subduction zone volcanic ash can fertilize the surface ocean and stimulate phytoplankton growth: evidence from biogeochemical experiments and satellite data,' (2007) 34 *Geophysical Research Letters*, L01612.

[52]   Richard S. Lampitt, E.P. Achterberg, T.E. Anderson et al., 'Ocean fertilization: a potential means of geoengineering?' (2008) 366 *Philosophical Transactions of the Royal Society A* 3, 919, 3, 923.

[53]   Julia Mayo-Ramsay, 'Environmental, legal and social implications of ocean urea fertilization: Sulu Sea example' (2010) 34 *Marine Policy* 831.

[54]   See J. Lovelock and C Rapley, 'Ocean pipes could help the earth to cure itself' (2007) 449 *Nature* 403; A. Yool et al., 'Low efficiency of nutrient translocation for enhancing oceanic uptake of carbon dioxide' (2009) 114 *Journal of Geophysical Research* 114.

[55]   S. Strand and G. Benford, 'Ocean sequestration of crop residue carbon: recycling fossil fuel carbon back to deep sediments' (2009) 43 *Environmental Science and Technology* 1001.

[56]   Antione de Ramon N'Yeurt, David P. Chynoweth, Mark E. Capron et al., 'Negative carbon via ocean afforestation' (2012) 90 *Process Safety and Environmental Protection* 467.

[57]   S. Zhou and P. Flynn, 'Geoengineering downwelling ocean currents: a cost assessment' (2005) 71 *Climatic Change* 203.

[58]   L.D.D. Harvey, 'Mitigating the atmospheric $CO_2$ increase and ocean acidification by adding limestone powder to upwelling regions' (2008) 113 *Journal of Geophysical Research* C04028; Haroon S. Kheshgi, 'Sequestering atmospheric carbon dioxide by increasing ocean alkalinity' (1995) 20 *Energy* 915.

problem: ocean acidification.[59] Finally, it is worth noting that at least one SRM geoengineering strategy – marine cloud brightening – involves the release of salt from vessels or other ocean-going craft[60] and consequently, may have implications for others using the oceans for purposes such as navigation, fishing, research and minerals exploitation.

## 3.   THE EMERGING REGULATORY FRAMEWORK FOR OCEAN FERTILIZATION: THE 2013 AMENDMENTS TO THE 1996 PROTOCOL TO THE 1972 LONDON CONVENTION

The first and thus far only, international instrument to directly regulate marine – or indeed any form of – geoengineering for climate mitigation purposes is the 1996 Protocol to the 1972 London (Dumping) Convention. In October 2013, at the eighth meeting of the parties, the 45 states party to the Protocol adopted wide-ranging amendments to the Protocol providing a basis for the regulation of ocean fertilization in particular and, potentially, marine geoengineering more generally.[61]

Geoengineering for the purposes of the amended Protocol is defined as 'a deliberate intervention in the marine environment to manipulate natural processes, including to counteract anthropogenic climate change and/ or its impacts, and that has the potential to result in deleterious effects, especially where those effects may be widespread, long lasting or severe.'[62] Perhaps the most notable feature of this definition is that it is broad and not confined to activities that involve the abandonment, disposal or placement of matter in the oceans. As will be discussed below, the amended Protocol currently limits its regulatory application to marine geoengineering that comprises placement in the oceans and this is consistent with the essential mandate of the dumping regime. However, the definition of marine geoengineering itself is deliberately designed to be expansive and undoubtedly provides scope for regulating a much broader range of geoengineering activities in the future. Integral to the definition of geoengineering is the notion of harm. However, the threshold of that harm is relatively low, the effects of geoengineering must merely be deleterious, and although the definition particularly notes the risk that effects may be 'widespread, long-lasting or severe' this is by no means a pre-requisite for categorizing the activity in question as 'marine geoengineering' for the purposes of the Protocol. A final feature worthy of note is that any activity which constitutes a 'deliberate intervention in the marine environment to manipulate natural processes' is classified as geoengineering irrespective of the purpose of that manipulation, although the objective of climate change mitigation is highlighted in the definition. Consequently, artificial fertilization for the purposes of scientific research –

---

[59]   Jennie C. Stephens and David W. Keith, 'Assessing geochemical carbon management' (2008) 90 *Climatic Change* 217, 228.

[60]   See the references cited in note 36, above.

[61]   Resolution LP.4(8) *on the Amendment to the London Protocol to Regulate the Placement of Matter for Ocean Fertilization and other Marine Geoengineering Activities* (18 October 2013).

[62]   Art 1(5)*bis* of the amended Protocol (amendment not yet in force).

outside of the field of climate change – or to enhance the productivity of fish stocks is categorized as geoengineering and, depending on the form of that activity, is subject to the regulatory regime established by the Protocol. The decoupling of geoengineering from the aims and objectives of engineers is sensible and should preclude would-be climate manipulators attempting to evade the regime under a smokescreen of an alternative and ostensibly permitted purpose.[63]

The regulatory framework for geoengineering is developed under a new article in the Protocol, Article 6*bis*, which stipulates that Contracting Parties 'shall not allow the placement of matter into the sea from vessels, aircraft, platforms, or other man-made structures at sea for marine geo-engineering activities listed in Annex 4, unless the listing provides that the activity or the sub-category of an activity may be authorized under a permit'.[64] Article 6*bis* goes on to stipulate that Parties must adopt administrative or legislative measures relating to the issue of permits, and may only issue permits for geoengineering purposes where the activity has undergone an assessment 'which has determined that pollution of the marine environment from the proposed activity is, as far as practicable, prevented or reduced to a minimum'.[65] The regulatory framework is consequently presently confined to geoengineering activities that require the placement of matter in the marine environment such as iron or other nutrients (in the case of iron fertilization), weathering techniques (involving the introduction of alkaline substances) or baled crops. Arguably, strategies involving the deployment of ocean pipes comprising the 'placement of matter into the sea' are similarly covered by Article 6*bis*. It is less certain that the placement of reflective material *onto* as opposed to *into* the sea is encompassed by Article 6*bis* although a teleological or purposive interpretation of this provision would support its inclusion in the marine geoengineering regulatory regime. However, the creation of microbubbles through 'the expansion of air saturated water through vortex nozzles'[66] is likely to be excluded from the remit of Article 6*bis* – since 'matter' is effectively not 'placed' into the sea. Furthermore, the regime does not cover schemes such as marine cloud brightening which utilize the oceans as a tool from which to effect geoengineering but which do not involve the placement of matter therein. Moreover, it is worth noting that geoengineering as defined is limited to 'deliberate' interventions in the marine environment and consequently, Article 6*bis* does not apply to soluble iron released from vessels as part of their normal operation.[67] Finally, consistent with the parameters of the dumping regime, the application of Article 6*bis* does not extend to matter placed into the sea from land-based facilities.

---

[63] Such as increasing fish biomass, the ostensible purpose of activities undertaken by the Ocean Nourishment Corporation. See Rosemary Rayfuse, 'Drowning our sorrows to secure a carbon free future? Some international legal considerations relating to sequestering carbon by fertilising the oceans' 31 (2008) *UNSW Law Journal* 919, 921–2.

[64] Art 6*bis* (1) of the amended Protocol (amendment not yet in force).

[65] Art 6*bis* (2) of the amended Protocol (amendment not yet in force).

[66] Russell Seitz, above n 39, 366.

[67] The notion of utilizing the release of soluble iron from vessels as part of their normal operations has recently been explored. See Akinori Ito, 'Global modelling study of potentially bioavailable iron input from shipboard aerosol sources to the ocean' (2013) 27 *Global Biogeochemical Cycles* 1.

Emulating the reverse listing approach adopted in respect of dumping by the Protocol, Article 6*bis* institutes a presumption that marine geoengineering is generally *not* permitted subject to limited exceptions agreed upon by the parties and listed in Annex 4. The 2013 amendments insert a new Annex 4 into the Protocol and, at this stage, only ocean fertilization 'constituting legitimate scientific research' is listed as an activity which may be authorized by a permit.[68] Ocean fertilization is defined as 'any activity undertaken by humans with the principal intention of stimulating primary productivity in the oceans'.[69] As noted above, this definition is consequently broad enough to encompass fertilization designed to stimulate biological productivity for food production purposes although the regime does exclude fertilization for 'conventional aquaculture, or mariculture, or the creation of artificial reefs.'[70] Both Article 6*bis* and Annex 4 make the issue of a permit in respect of listed geoengineering activities – currently only ocean fertilization for scientific purposes – subject to compliance with a Risk Assessment Framework as set out in Annex 5 of the Protocol.

The Risk Assessment Framework was originally adopted in 2010 by virtue of a non-binding resolution[71] and amended in 2013 when incorporated into the Protocol. Pursuant to this framework, an initial assessment must be undertaken in order to determine whether the proposed activity falls within the scope of Annex 4, i.e. whether it constitutes ocean fertilization for legitimate scientific research. Parties must then undertake a full environmental assessment of the proposed activity, including consideration of the site of the proposed experiment, the likely environmental impact of the experiment and the risks (both known and unknown) associated with it. Where experiments are authorized, the framework requires parties to put in place procedures to permit monitoring and, where appropriate, facilitate adaptive management in respect of the experiment. Significantly, the framework requires parties to act with caution, and stipulates that where adverse effects are predicted, projects should be abandoned.[72] The amendments to the Framework adopted in 2013 principally broaden its scope in order to render it applicable to any geoengineering activity listed in Annex 4 and make a number of minor amendments to its text.

The speed – at least by international standards – with which the states party to the 1996 Protocol acted in order to develop a pre-emptive and highly precautionary regulatory regime for marine geoengineering is commendable. It was also necessary given the relatively high degree of commercial interest in fertilization projects, and the fact that one relatively large-scale unauthorized iron fertilization incident had already taken place, off the coast of Canada, in 2012.[73] Nevertheless, it is important to sound a note of caution, particularly with respect to the global reach of this regime.

---

[68]   Annex 4.1, 1996 Protocol as amended (amendment and Annex not yet in force).
[69]   Annex 4.1.1, 1996 Protocol as amended (amendment and Annex not yet in force).
[70]   Ibid.
[71]   Resolution LC.LP.2 (2010) *on the Assessment Framework for Scientific Research Involving Ocean Fertilization.*
[72]   Ibid.
[73]   In July 2012 the Haida Salmon Restoration Corporation deliberately dumped 100 metric tonnes of iron sulphate into the ocean off the coast of western Canada. The scheme, which dumped five times more iron into the ocean than any of the previous thirteen iron fertilization experiments carried out to date, was ostensibly designed to both increase local salmon

First, notwithstanding the broad definition of geoengineering provided for under the amended Protocol, its regulatory mandate is currently confined to activities that involve placement of matter in the sea from vessels, aircraft and offshore platforms. It is not comprehensive and, given the parameters and essential objects and purposes of the Protocol, it is open to question as to whether marine geoengineering that does not involve the placement of matter in the sea should be regulated under this regime. Second, the amendments require acceptance by two-thirds of the states party to the Protocol in order to enter into force and are fairly obviously not binding prior to their entry into force. Third, once the amendments do enter into force they will bind only those state parties that have accepted them and do not create obligations for states party only to the 1972 London Convention or the 1982 LOSC. The general provisions of application to marine geoengineering under the LOSC will be discussed below, but it is worth noting that the obligations of parties under Articles 210 and 216 of the Convention to adopt laws to prevent, reduce and control dumping which are no less effective 'than the global rules and standards' are generally interpreted as incorporating the standards set out in the 1972 Convention rather than the 1996 Protocol.[74] The LOSC itself provides for no internal mechanism to determine if, and at what point, those standards are replaced by those set out in the Protocol, but given that the Protocol has been ratified by less than half the number of states currently party to the 1972 Convention it would be premature to suggest such an interpretation is imminent. Moreover, the obligations as set out in both Articles 210 and 216 appear to be explicitly confined to dumping at sea (which is defined by the LOSC in terms very similar to the 1972 Convention and 1996 Protocol[75]) rather than 'placement' and, even if these provisions are eventually interpreted to incorporate the 1996 Protocol standards on dumping, it is far from clear that they can be extended to incorporate the Protocol's standards on placement, under which the regulation of geoengineering takes place.

Consequently, in the short to medium term the majority of states will not in fact be subject to the marine geoengineering regime as developed under the 1996 Protocol but rather, will be bound by the rather more flexible – or at least open-textured – obligations to protect the marine environment, to regulate marine scientific research and to have due regard for other users under the law of the sea more generally. It is to these principles and obligations this chapter now turns.

---

populations and to sequester carbon dioxide. See Jeff Tollefson, 'Ocean-fertilization project off Canada sparks furore' (2012) 490 *Nature* 458. The scheme was not authorized by the Canadian government. See the Statement by the Delegation of Canada on the Issue of the Ocean Fertilization Incident off the West Coast of Canada in July 2012 reproduced in the *Report of the Thirty-Fourth Consultative Meeting and the Seventh Meeting of the Contracting Parties* (LC 34/15, 23 November 2012), Annex 3.

74   R.R. Churchill and A.V. Lowe, *The Law of the Sea* (3rd edn), (Manchester University Press 1999) 369.

75   LOSC, Art. 1(5).

## 4.  THE LAW OF THE SEA AND MARINE GEOENGINEERING

Notwithstanding that the 2013 amendments to the 1996 Protocol are yet to enter into force and are not, in any case, designed to be comprehensive, marine geoengineering is not taking place within a legal vacuum. Rather, like all other operators in the oceans, marine geoengineers must have due regard to the rights and obligations of coastal states and other users of the oceans, and must comply with standards relating to environmental protection and the conduct of scientific research as set out under the law of the sea. The 1982 LOSC establishes what has been described as a 'constitution for the oceans'[76] and strives to attain a balance between the various interests of multiple actors including states, scientists, entrepreneurs and the international community as a collective. This essential framework is augmented by numerous global and regional instruments, which develop complex regulatory regimes in respect of particular issues such as environmental protection or the safety of shipping as well as customary or other principles of international law which constrain or guide state activity in order to achieve particular aims such as environmental protection, participation in decision-making or holding states and other actors responsible for harm.

The principle providing the foundation for the law of the sea is the freedom of the high seas, now codified in Article 87 of the 1982 LOSC. Six freedoms are specified in Article 87 including the freedom of marine scientific research, which has the most direct relevance to marine geoengineering at this stage. However, any activity which is not prohibited and which does not compromise the reservation of the high seas for peaceful purposes[77] can benefit from the status as a high seas freedom[78] and consequently, marine geoengineering for any purpose arguably constitutes a freedom of the high seas. Nevertheless, those freedoms are by no means absolute. High seas users must have due regard for the interests of other states[79] and this principle has direct application to activities that involve the placement of objects – such as ocean pipes – into the sea, which may hinder navigation or where those activities seek to change the local ecology of a region impacting on fish stocks, and thus hindering the freedom to fish. Moreover, states exercising high seas freedoms must similarly have due regard to their obligations under the LOSC with respect to the protection of the environment, the management of activities in the Area and the regulation of scientific research.[80] These obligations – particularly those designed to protect the environment – arguably limit the freedom to carry out large-scale marine geoengineering activities on the high seas.

With respect to geoengineering activities taking place in coastal waters, coastal states benefit from exclusive jurisdiction over marine scientific research within their territorial seas and exclusive economic zones (EEZ) and can consequently control the extent and

---

[76]  Tommy T.B. Koh, 'A Constitution for the Oceans' (Statement by President Koh at the final session of the Conference at Montego Bay, 6 and 11 December 1982) reprinted in United Nations, *The Law of the Sea: United Nations Convention on the Law of the Sea* (1983) E.83.V5.

[77]  LOSC, Art. 88.

[78]  LOSC, Art. 87 uses the term 'inter alia' before listing the six high seas freedoms indicating that those six cannot be considered exclusive. See R.R. Churchill and A.V. Lowe, above n 74, 206.

[79]  LOSC, Art. 87(2).

[80]  Ibid.

nature of any marine geoengineering research they choose to carry out or authorize.[81] Nevertheless, coastal states are similarly obliged to have due regard to the rights and duties of other states, particularly with respect to the freedom of navigation, and must also act consistently with their obligations under the Convention in relation to marine scientific research and environmental protection.[82] The exploitation of the territorial sea/EEZ for climate-related geoengineering purposes similarly falls within the exclusive jurisdiction of coastal states[83] and activities, such as the creation of macroalgal forests, must also respect the rights of other users and the more general provisions of the 1982 LOSC.

The 1982 LOSC establishes, in essence, a permissive framework for marine geoengineering but controls the nature and extent of geoengineering activities through the application of the principle of due regard, which is nevertheless contextual and subject to interpretation by individual states and, more importantly, under rules relating to environmental protection and the control of scientific research.

### 4.1 Marine Geoengineering and the Protection of the Environment

The protection and preservation of the marine environment is a fundamental aim and objective of the 1982 LOSC[84] and Article 192 creates a general obligation to this effect in Part XII of the Convention.[85] Article 193 acknowledges the sovereign right of states to exploit their natural resources, which arguably includes the capacity of the ocean to sequester $CO_2$, but subjects that right to their duty to protect and preserve the marine environment. These obligations are naturally subject to interpretation by individual states but it would not be unreasonable to conclude that geoengineering activities which lead to increased ocean acidification compromising ecosystem function or which precipitate toxic algal blooms are inconsistent with a state's obligation to protect and preserve the marine environment. Moreover, particular obligations are imposed on states to protect rare or fragile ecosystems especially where they provide habitat for depleted, threatened or endangered species.[86]

In assessing the environmental risks posed by marine geoengineering, states must apply a precautionary approach and explicitly consider the myriad of uncertainties and knowledge gaps associated with the impact of manipulating the ocean carbon cycle. Although not identified as a specific principle within the 1982 LOSC, the precautionary approach has evolved within both treaty law and custom to provide a fundamental component of the decision-making process in the context of activities likely to have a significant detrimental impact on the marine environment. Judicial support for this position can now be found at the highest level[87] and in its 2011 advisory opinion on the

---

[81]   LOSC, Arts 56(b)(ii), 245 and 246.

[82]   LOSC, Art. 56(2).

[83]   LOSC, Art. 56(1)(a).

[84]   LOSC, Preamble.

[85]   LOSC Art. 192 stipulates that 'States have the obligation to protect and preserve the marine environment'.

[86]   LOSC, Art. 194(5).

[87]   See for example the 2010 decision of the International Court of Justice in the *Pulp Mills on the River Uruguay* Case (Argentina v. Uruguay) [2010] ICJ Rep 14 where the Court

*Responsibilities of States Sponsoring Persons and Activities in the Area,*[88] the Seabed Disputes Chamber of the International Tribunal for the Law of the Sea (ITLOS) observed:

> [t]hat the precautionary approach has been incorporated into a growing number of international treaties and other instruments, many of which reflect the formulation of Principle 15 of the Rio Declaration. In the view of the Chamber, this has initiated a trend towards making this approach part of customary international law. This trend is clearly reinforced by the inclusion of the precautionary approach in the Regulations and in the 'standard clause' contained in Annex 4, section 5.1 of the Sulphides Regulations. So does the following statement in paragraph 164 of the ICJ judgment in *Pulp Mills on the River Uruguay* that 'a precautionary approach may be relevant in the interpretation and application of the provisions of the Statute' (ie the environmental bilateral treaty whose interpretation was the main bone of contention between the parties). This statement may be read in light of article 31(3)(c) of the Vienna Convention, according to which the interpretation of a treaty should take into account not only the context but 'any relevant rules of international law applicable in the relations between the parties'.[89]

In applying a precautionary approach to decision-making associated with marine geoengineering activities states must carry out an environmental impact assessment (EIA) in order to identify and respond to potential risks.[90] A basic – and qualified – EIA obligation is set out in Article 206 of the 1982 LOSC in respect of activities likely to cause pollution, but the process of EIA has developed significantly beyond those basic requirements within other treaties of application to the marine environment such as the 1991 Environmental Protocol to the 1959 Antarctic Treaty[91] and, in the context of ocean fertilization, by the 1996 London Protocol.[92] More generally the obligation to conduct an EIA in respect of activities with the potential for significant harmful changes to the marine environment has been endorsed as a principle of general international law to be applied in both a transboundary and a commons context by the ICJ[93] and the ITLOS Seabed Disputes Chamber respectively.[94] The substantive content of both the precautionary approach and the process of EIA is not established for the purposes of the 1982 LOSC and consequently there is significant scope for interpretation and indeed disagreement over the extent and the nature of the obligation imposed on states and, importantly, whether the identification of serious risks imposes an

---

concluded that the precautionary approach may be relevant in the interpretation of the statute in dispute between Argentina and Uruguay relying implicitly on Article 31(3)(c) of the 1969 Vienna Convention on the Law of Treaties (at para. 164).

[88]    *Responsibilities and Obligations of States Sponsoring Persons and Entities with Respect to Activities in the Area (Advisory Opinion)* [2011] ITLOS Rep 10, para. 135.

[89]    Ibid.

[90]    See R. Warner, 'Environmental assessment in marine areas beyond national jurisdiction' Chapter 14 in this volume.

[91]    1991 Protocol on Environmental Protection to the Antarctic Treaty (adopted on 4 October 1991, entered into force 14 January 1998) 30 *International Legal Materials* 1461.

[92]    See the Risk Assessment Framework adopted in Resolution LC.LP.2 (2010) *on the Assessment Framework for Scientific Research Involving Ocean Fertilization*, which will be formally incorporated into the Protocol in Annex 5 once the 2013 amendments enter into force.

[93]    *Pulp Mills on the River Uruguay,* above n 87, para. 204.

[94]    ITLOS, *Advisory Opinion,* above n 88, paras 145 and 148.

obligation to refrain from the activity altogether. Moreover, unless a specific obligation can be found to reverse the burden of proof – such as in the case of the 1996 London Protocol or the 1991 Environmental Protocol to the Antarctic Treaty – it cannot be presumed when applying the principle more generally that the burden of proving that an activity such as marine geoengineering is safe lies with the proponent of that activity. Finally, it must be conceded that applying the precautionary approach with or without an EIA is particularly complex in respect of geoengineering. An assessment of such activities cannot take place in isolation of the broader context of climate change and the environmental risks associated with inaction or action that is otherwise ineffective to the marine environment.[95]

To the extent that marine geoengineering can be categorized as 'pollution of the marine environment' as defined by Article 1(4) of the 1982 LOSC, Article 194 of the Convention imposes an obligation on states to take 'all measures to prevent, reduce and control pollution of the marine environment from *any* source'. More specifically – and of particular relevance to geoengineering – Article 196 of the LOSC requires parties to 'take all measures necessary to prevent, reduce and control pollution of the marine environment resulting from the use of technologies under their jurisdiction or control'. Whilst geoengineering is designed to manipulate the ocean carbon cycle through interference with either the biological or the solubility pump, and undoubtedly creates a risk of significant environmental harm as a result of such interference, not all geoengineering strategies can be categorized as 'pollution of the marine environment'. The definition of marine pollution under the LOSC comprises 'the introduction by man, directly or indirectly, of substances or energy into the marine environment, including estuaries, which results or is likely to result in such deleterious effects as harm to living resources and marine life, hazards to human health, hindrance to marine activities, including fishing and other legitimate uses of the sea, impairment of quality for use of sea water and reduction of amenities'.[96] Ocean fertilization arguably falls within this definition where the fertilizer – such as iron, volcanic ash or urea – is 'introduced' into the marine environment through artificial means, but is likely to be excluded if the nutrients are already located within the ocean, albeit in the deep ocean, and pumped to the surface by means of ocean pipes. Weathering techniques are similarly likely to be encompassed by the definition of pollution but techniques such as macroalgal afforestation and marine cloud brightening are fairly obviously excluded. The extent of the obligation to prevent pollution under the 1982 LOSC is, as in the case of the more general obligation to protect and preserve the marine environment, subject to the discretion of individual states and, consequently, open to variable interpretation. Where, however, marine geoengineering can be classified as a specific form of pollution that is subject to more detailed regulation by the LOSC, it may be subject to much tighter control. At this stage, geoengineering that involves the disposal, abandonment of matter in the oceans such as ocean fertilization or weathering techniques is the

---

[95] For a discussion of geoengineering and the precautionary principle more generally see: Kevin Elliot, 'Geoengineering and the Precautionary Principle' (2010) 24 *International Journal of Applied Philosophy* 237; Elizabeth Tedsen and Gesa Homann, 'Implementing the Precautionary Principle for climate engineering' (2013) 7 *Carbon and Climate Law Review* 90.

[96] LOSC, Art. 1(4).

most likely candidate for such tighter controls, under Articles 210/ 216 of the 1982 LOSC and the dumping regime.

States party to the 1982 LOSC are required to adopt laws and regulations to prevent, reduce and control pollution by dumping in the marine environment and those laws and regulations must be no less effective than 'the global rules and standards'.[97] Dumping is defined under the Convention as the 'deliberate disposal of wastes or other matter from vessels, aircraft, platforms or other man-made structures at sea'[98] excluding the disposal of waste incidental to shipping or offshore operations[99] and the placement of matter for a purpose other than the mere disposal thereof, provided that such placement is not contrary to the aims of the Convention.[100] As noted above, the global rules and standards specified in Article 210 of the 1982 LOSC are generally interpreted to refer to the standards set out in the 1972 London (Dumping) Convention. The 1972 Convention comprises one part of the dumping regime and is in the process of being supplanted by a Protocol, adopted in 1996, which updates and significantly tightens controls on what may be dumped and under what conditions at sea.

Dumping is defined under both the 1972 Convention and 1996 Protocol in almost identical terms as Article 1(5) of the 1982 LOSC.[101] Ocean fertilization and weathering techniques clearly constitute the introduction of matter into the sea but it is open to debate whether that matter is 'disposed of' given that its introduction into the marine environment is designed to serve a purpose: to create an algal bloom or to increase ocean alkalinity. Moreover, both instruments exclude 'placement of matter for a purpose other than the mere disposal thereof, provided that such placement is not contrary to the aims' of the Convention and Protocol. The amalgamation of both the components of the definition of dumping has created significant discussion among states and commentators as to whether the dumping regime has in fact a mandate to control geoengineering technologies which, whilst involving introducing matter into the marine environment, do not fit the classic definition of dumping.[102] Despite these juridical concerns, in 2008 the parties to the 1972 Convention/1996 Protocol pragmatically adopted a non-binding resolution within which they agreed that the dumping regime should regulate ocean fertilization[103] and, in recent developments described above, have adopted amendments to the Protocol which develops this mandate. The 2008 resolution also asserted that ocean fertilization for purposes other than scientific

---

97   LOSC, Art. 210(1) and (6).

98   LOSC, Art. 1(5)(a).

99   LOSC, Art. 1(5)(b)(i).

100   LOSC, Art. 1(50(b)(ii).

101   See London Convention, Art. III(1)(a)(i); London Protocol, Art. 1.4.1.1.

102   See for example David Freestone and Rosemary Rayfuse, 'Ocean iron fertilization and international law' (2008) 364 *Marine Ecology Progress Series* 227; Rosemary Rayfuse, Mark G. Lawrence and Kristina M. Gjerde, 'Ocean fertilisation and climate change: the need to regulate emerging high seas uses' (2008) 23 *International Journal of Marine and Coastal Law* 297; Philomène Verlaan, 'Geo-engineering, the law of the sea, and climate change' (2009) 4 *Carbon and Climate Law Review* 446; Karen N. Scott, 'Regulating ocean fertilization under international law: the risks' (2013) 7 *Carbon and Climate Law Review* 108.

103   Resolution LC.LP.1 (2008) *on the Regulation of Ocean Fertilization.*

research is regarded as contrary to the aims and objectives of the dumping regime. This resolution is however, non-binding, and it is therefore necessary to examine the application of the current binding rules to geoengineering under the dumping regime.

The 1972 Convention prohibits the dumping of matter listed in Annex I and permits Annex II matter to be dumped subject to a special permit. Matter listed in neither Annex I nor Annex II may be dumped in the oceans with a general permit. The matter associated with ocean fertilization or weathering techniques – such as iron dust, phosphate, urea or limestone powder is not currently listed in either Annex I or Annex II and, as such, may potentially be dumped subject to a general permit. It is nevertheless worth noting that matter 'which, though of a non-toxic nature, may become harmful due to the quantities in which they are dumped, or which are liable to seriously reduce amenities' is listed in Annex II. Although the harm threshold specified here is unlikely to be met in respect of individual geoengineering research activities, a large-scale deployment of ocean fertilizer or the cumulative impacts of multiple smaller deployment activities may well meet the criteria. Even in such a case, however, the dumping of matter is not precluded, it is simply made subject to the requirements associated with the issue of a special permit. Nevertheless, although not formally binding, national agencies examining applications for permits to dump fertilizers or weathering agents for non-scientific purposes, should arguably consider the moratorium adopted in resolution LC.LP.1 (2008) in their decision-making processes.[104] Where applications relate to legitimate ocean fertilization for scientific research purposes, the detailed Risk Assessment Framework set out in Resolution LC.LP.2 (2010)[105] discussed above in the context of the 2013 Protocol amendments, whilst not mandatory, should also similarly be considered as part of the national decision-making process.

The 45 states parties to the 1996 Protocol are subject to a less flexible regime than that permitted under the 1972 Convention/1982 LOSC notwithstanding that the amendments designed to regulate geoengineering more generally have yet to enter into force. In contrast to the 1972 Convention, the 1996 Protocol adopts a reverse listing approach to dumping and permits only matter listed in Annex I to be dumped subject to a special permit and relatively stringent conditions.[106] Ocean fertilizers and weathering tools are not explicitly listed in Annex I although provision is made for the issue of permits in respect of 'inert, inorganic, geological material'. It is unlikely that iron, phosphate, urea and limestone could be considered inert as their very purpose is to stimulate a reaction in the ocean environment such as the creation of a phytoplankton bloom or the alteration of the chemistry of seawater. Consequently, fertilizers and weathering agents cannot be dumped into the marine environment unless they can be categorized as 'placement of matter for a purpose other than mere disposal thereof, provided that such placement is not contrary to the aims' of the Protocol.[107] Ironically, the adoption of the 2013 amendments to the Protocol, which seek to regulate

---

[104]  Ibid.
[105]  Resolution LC.LP.2 (2010) *on the Assessment Framework for Scientific Research Involving Ocean Fertilization.*
[106]  London Protocol, Art. 4.1.1.
[107]  London Protocol, Art. 4.2.2.

geoengineering and, more specifically, ocean fertilization, as 'placement' as opposed to 'dumping' activities strengthen the argument that relies on this exception. However, the qualification to this exception – that the placement must not be contrary to the aims of the Protocol – operates as a significant constraint on geoengineering 'placement' activities. Resolution LC.LP.1 (2008) states clearly that all ocean fertilization activities that do not constitute legitimate scientific research (and arguably, which do not conform to the Risk Assessment Framework adopted in Resolution LC.LP.2 (2010)) should be considered contrary to the aims of the Protocol. Although non-binding, this Resolution provides an important tool for interpreting the placement exception under the Protocol in the interim period pending entry into force of the 2013 geoengineering amendments.

In the absence of a designated regulatory regime for geoengineering, environmental obligations under the law of the sea, and international environmental law more generally,[108] provide important controls on geoengineering activities that create a significant risk to the marine environment. The London Convention/Protocol non-binding moratorium on ocean fertilization not constituting scientific research together with the similarly non-binding moratorium[109] on geoengineering more generally adopted by the parties to the 1992 Convention on Biological Diversity[110] constitue a signficant moral if not legal constraint on decision-makers considering authorization of marine geoengineering activities. However, until the 2013 amendments to 1996 Protocol enter into force it is individual states that act as interpreters and arbiters of the right to exploit, and the obligation to protect, the marine environment. Given the risks associated with geoengineering and the threat to the ocean environment from climate change it is likely that states will adopt quite different interpretations as to where the balance between those rights and obligations lies.

## 4.2   Marine Geoengineering and the Control of Scientific Research

Most geoengineering activities taking place within the marine environment currently constitute research rather than actual climate change mitigation.[111] As noted above, marine scientific research constitutes a high seas freedom[112] and whilst research activities are subject to the exclusive jurisdiction of coastal states in waters under their jurisdiction,[113] those states are normally expected to consent to requests to carry out

---

[108]   See Karen N. Scott, 'International law in the anthropocene: responding to the geo-engineering challenge' (2013) 34 *Michigan Journal of International Law* 309.

[109]   See CBD Decision IX/16 (2008) *Biodiversity and Climate Change* at C.4; CBD Decision X/33 (2010) *Biodiversity and Climate Change*, para. 8(w); CBD Decision XI/20 (2012) *Climate Related Geoengineering*.

[110]   1992 Convention on Biological Diversity, (entered into force 29 December 1993) (1992) 31 *International Legal Materials* 818 (CBD).

[111]   The exception is the 2012 fertilization which took place off the coast of Western Canada and, according to the Haida Salmon Restoration Corporation was deliberately intended to increase local salmon production and to sequester $CO_2$. See the text and reference in note 73, above.

[112]   LOSC, Arts 87(1)(f), 239.

[113]   LOSC, Arts 56(1)(b)(ii), 245 and 246.

research in their EEZ, particularly where that research is intended to 'increase scientific knowledge of the marine environment for the benefit of all mankind'.[114] However, consent may be withheld where the research involves the introduction of harmful substances into the marine environment[115] and this exception would undoubtedly cover fertilization or weathering based activities. Moreover, marine scientific research irrespective of location must be carried out in accordance with Parts XII and XIII of the LOSC and, in particular, with the principles set out in Article 240 of the Convention. Specifically, states must comply with principles related to the publication and dissemination of information connected to proposed major projects and the promotion of transfer of data, information and knowledge to developing states,[116] ensure that all activities undertaken in the Area[117] – including geoengineering – are for the benefit of mankind[118] and, most importantly, comply with the environmental safeguards discussed above as set out in Part XII of the LOSC.

Beyond the 1982 LOSC marine scientific researchers may well have to comply with additional obligations imposed by other global and regional regimes. In the context of geoengineering, the Risk Assessment Framework developed under the 1972 Convention/1996 Protocol provides the most comprehensive set of controls on marine scientific research to date. Its remit is currently limited to ocean fertilization and its obligations are voluntary rather than mandatory at this stage but once the 2013 amendments to the 1996 Protocol enter into force it will be both binding and of application to marine geoengineering projects more generally for those states party to the Protocol. The other instrument worth noting in the context of scientific research is the 1991 Environmental Protocol to the 1959 Antarctic Treaty, which imposes probably the most stringent controls on scientific research to date. Of limited geographical application – to the area south of 60° South Latitude[119] – the Protocol nevertheless establishes a comprehensive system of environmental impact assessment of application to all activities – including scientific activities[120] – and stringent controls designed to prevent pollution and to protect wildlife, especially vulnerable ecosystems and habitats.[121] However, notwithstanding the geographical proximity of a number of the ocean

---

[114] LOSC, Art. 246(3).
[115] LOSC, Art. 245(5)(b).
[116] LOSC, Art. 245.
[117] The Area is defined as 'the seabed and ocean floor and subsoil thereof, beyond the limits of national jurisdiction' (LOSC, Article 1(1)(1)) and is subject to the regime established under Part XI of the LOSC and its Part XI Implementation Agreement:1994 Agreement Relating to the Implementation of Part XI of the United Nations Convention on the Law of the Sea of 10 December 1982 (adopted on 28 July 1994, entered into force 28 July 1996) 1836 UNTS 42.
[118] LOSC, Art. 140.
[119] 1991 Environmental Protocol, Art. 3(1). It should be noted that the Protocol does acknowledge and seek to protect the Antarctic environment and dependent and associated ecosystems (Art. 2).
[120] 1991 Environmental Protocol, Art. 8 and Annex I.
[121] Ibid, Art 3 and Annexes II, IV and V.

fertilization experiments the parties to the Antarctic Treaty/Environmental Protocol have thus far taken little interest in Southern Ocean geoengineering.[122]

Globally the controls on marine scientific research beyond those related to environmental protection are relatively light. There are however, very real ethical questions about whether such research should be encouraged and, more broadly, how geoengineering is managed in relation to research and activities designed to mitigate climate change by other means such as emissions reductions and adaptation. However, these are issues which arguably cannot be debated within the context of the law of the sea and require a broader, global forum.

## 5.  GEOENGINEERING AND THE RESOLUTION OF DISPUTES

The scope for disagreement among the states party to the 1982 LOSC – and even the 1972 London Convention/1996 Protocol – over the interpretation of rights and obligations under the law of the sea as they relate to geoengineering is manifest. In contrast to most other multilateral environmental agreements, the 1982 LOSC benefits from a system of compulsory dispute resolution, and it is notable that a number of disputes between parties in the past have focused on environmental issues.[123] Parties to the Convention are subject to a general obligation to settle disputes peacefully[124] by any means they so choose but if they are unable to reach a settlement they are subject to compulsory dispute resolution procedures under Article 281 of the 1982 LOSC. Disputes may be resolved by the ITLOS, the International Court of Justice, an Annex VII Tribunal or, potentially an Annex VIII Tribunal, depending on the choice made by the disputing parties.[125] Although the Annex VII Tribunal is the default dispute resolution institution in the event that the parties cannot agree or have made no choice as to their preferred option,[126] the thus far under-used Annex VIII Tribunal has particular appeal for geoengineering-related disputes as its mandate specially refers to disputes relating to scientific research, environmental protection and pollution by dumping.[127] In contrast to the other institutions Annex VIII Tribunals comprise expert adjudicators rather than lawyers.[128] Furthermore, provision is also made for the

---

[122]   On the regulation of ocean fertilization and the Antarctic Treaty see Karen N. Scott, 'Scientific Rhetoric and Antarctic Security' in Alan D. Hemmings, Donald R. Rothwell and Karen N. Scott (eds), *Antarctic Security in the Twenty-First Century: Legal and Policy Perspectives* (Routledge 2012) 284, 297–9.

[123]   For example, *MOX Plant (Ireland v United Kingdom)* (Provisional Measures) (ITLOS), (2002) 41 *International Legal Materials* 405; *Land Reclamation by Singapore In and Around the Straits of Johor (Malaysia v Singapore)* (Provisional Measures) [2003] ITLOS Rep 10 (ITLOS); *Responsibilities and Obligations of States Sponsoring Persons and Entities with Respect to Activities in the Area (Advisory Opinion)* [2011] ITLOS Rep 10 (Seabed Disputes Chamber, ITLOS).

[124]   LOSC, Arts 279 and 280.

[125]   LOSC, Art. 287.

[126]   LOSC, Art. 287(5).

[127]   LOSC, Annex VIII, Art. 1.

[128]   LOSC, Annex VIII, Art. 2.

settlement of disputes under the 1996 Protocol to the 1972 London Convention, and disputes may be referred to the Arbitral Procedure set out in Annex 3 of the Protocol or parties may use one of the procedures provided for in Article 287 of the 1982 LOSC.[129] Although perhaps premature to discuss geoengineering in the context of dispute resolution given the early stage of scientific research, there are clear advantages in utilizing adjudicatory means to begin to develop substantive interpretations of key obligations such as precaution, due regard and pollution prevention and control.

## 6. CONCLUDING REMARKS

Despite representing a novel – some might suggest even aberrant – form of oceans exploitation, marine geoengineering is to a limited extent manageable using principles and concepts well known to the law of the sea in order to protect the environment, control scientific research and manage the delicate balance between the interests of coastal states, user states and the international community more generally. Nevertheless, the relatively open-textured and flexible nature of many of these principles undeniably supports a multiplicity of, and even significant divergence in, interpretation of obligations, leading potentially to different regional or even individual approaches to whether and under what circumstances marine geoengineering is permitted. The nascent regime for geoengineering which involves the placement of matter in the oceans evolving under the 1996 Protocol to the 1972 London Convention represents an important step in establishing clear, global and binding standards with respect to at least some forms of marine geoengineering, and the option of compulsory dispute resolution under the 1982 LOSC provides at least a theoretical prospect of clarifying the substantive content of certain environmental principles and concepts.

The greatest challenge facing us with respect to marine geoengineering however, lies beyond the law of the sea. Managing ocean fertilization to minimize its risk to the marine environment is all very well but, just as importantly, we need to regulate other geoengineering strategies – whether based in the hydrosphere, biosphere, atmosphere or even outer-space – in order to manage their interactions and their collective and cumulative impacts. This is a task arguably not particularly well suited to the 1996 London Protocol or even the 1982 LOSC, and, at the very least, law of the sea institutions need to begin to actively coordinate and cooperate with other regimes and institutions such as the 1992 CBD and 1992 UNFCCC in their approach to geoengineering.[130] Even more importantly, we need to consider geoengineering regulation in the context of climate change mitigation more generally and specifically, in light of our obligations – extant and future – to reduce emissions.

---

[129]  London Protocol, Art. 16.

[130]  On the issue of institutional cooperation and coordination in the context of geoengineering see Karen N. Scott, 'Transboundary Environmental Governance and Emerging Environmental Threats: Geo-engineering in the Marine Environment' in Simon Marsden and Robin Warner (eds), *Transboundary Environmental Governance in Inland, Coastal and Marine Areas: Asia an Australian Perspectives* (Ashgate Publishing 2012) 223.

The impetus to begin developing a regulatory framework for marine geoengineering is understandable and, on a pragmatic level should be supported. But it threatens to side-step these important ethical questions. Furthermore, it risks providing implicit legal and indeed moral support for geoengineering as a climate change mitigation measure before the ethics of geoengineering have had a chance to be addressed in the round at the global level. The very fact that geoengineering research is taking place and that institutions such as the 1996 Protocol are developing tools to manage its risks inevitably has consequences for how the debate on climate change and geoengineering is framed. The legal and policy responses to these very real challenges however, lie beyond the law of the sea and are arguably best addressed within the realm of the climate change regime.[131]

---

[131]   See Karen N. Scott above n 108, 353–6.

# Index